UNEXPECTED STATE

INDIANA SERIES IN MIDDLE EAST STUDIES
Mark Tessler, *editor*

UNEXPECTED STATE
*British Politics and
the Creation of Israel*

Carly Beckerman

Indiana University Press

This book is a publication of

Indiana University Press
Office of Scholarly Publishing
Herman B Wells Library 350
1320 East 10th Street
Bloomington, Indiana 47405 USA

iupress.indiana.edu

© 2020 by Carly Beckerman

All rights reserved
No part of this book may be reproduced or utilized in any form or by any means, electronic or mechanical, including photocopying and recording, or by any information storage and retrieval system, without permission in writing from the publisher. The paper used in this publication meets the minimum requirements of the American National Standard for Information Sciences—Permanence of Paper for Printed Library Materials, ANSI Z39.48–1992.

Manufactured in the United States of America

Cataloging information is available from the Library of Congress.
ISBN 978-0-253-04640-6 (hardback)
ISBN 978-0-253-04641-3 (paperback)
ISBN 978-0-253-04643-7 (ebook)

1 2 3 4 5   25 24 23 22 21 20

For Ursus

Contents

	Acknowledgments	ix
	Introduction	1
1	A Usable Past	8
2	The Balfour Zeitgeist, 1917–1928	34
3	The Passfield Reversal, 1929–1935	61
4	The MacDonald Betrayal, 1936–1939	101
5	From War to Withdrawal, 1940–1948	142
	The Last Word	185
	Bibliography	191
	Index	205

Acknowledgments

During my time researching and writing this book, I have benefited from the help of many individuals whose support deserves acknowledgment. First and foremost, I would like to thank Asaf Siniver for his ideas and insight and for challenging me to develop as a researcher. I would also like to thank Clive Jones, Anoush Ehteshami, Emma Murphy, and John Williams for their unwavering support.

I must also express appreciation to the Truman Presidential Library for providing a grant that allowed me to conduct research at the library's archive in Missouri. In addition, thank-yous are owed to Lena Moral-Waldmeier for her research assistance and to the kind and helpful archivists at the National Archives in Kew, the Parliamentary Archives, London School of Economics Archives, Cadbury Archives, Durham Archives, United States National Archives, Truman Presidential Archives, and the United Nations Archives.

I would also like to say thank you to James Boys for his help in those early years, to my parents, Carol and Jon, for their boundless enthusiasm, and to my friends, Eleanor Turney, Beth Kahn, and Emily Thomas, for keeping me laughing (mostly at myself).

Finally, I would like to thank Andy Shuttleworth for his support and encouragement in difficult moments. I could not have finished this without him.

UNEXPECTED STATE

Introduction

The Balfour Declaration is a document that, despite having been written in 1917, still stirs staunch pride or vehement disgust, depending on who you ask. It was a brief but momentous memo, ostensibly from (but not written by) British foreign secretary Arthur James Balfour. Although delivered to Baron Lionel Walter Rothschild and published in *The Times*, Balfour's note was, realistically, addressed to Jews around the world as it pledged Britain's support for a Jewish national home in Palestine. Since British forces invaded the Holy Land a month after the letter was issued and only vacated Palestine in 1948 as Israel formally declared its existence, Balfour's declaration has achieved a somewhat contradictory symbolic status—as a sign of Britain's laudable achievement in, and devastating culpability for, the subsequent triumph of Zionism.

Former British prime minister David Cameron described this historic document as "the moment when the State of Israel went from a dream to a plan," but it is generally considered throughout the Arab world to be Britain's "original sin."[1] Supporting one viewpoint over the other depends on personal political preferences, but neither perspective is rooted in fact. The idea that Balfour signed a letter commencing the intentional and purposeful march toward Israeli statehood—in a territory that, at the time, was part of an Islamic empire and contained relatively few Jews—has become alarmingly unquestionable. Challenging this dichotomous history of British sentiment/animosity is always a precarious endeavor, but that is precisely what this book intends to do. *Unexpected State* aims, for the first time, to explain the *how* and the *why* behind Britain's policies for Palestine. It argues that domestic politics in Westminster played a vital and inadvertent role in British patronage of and then leniency toward Zionism, allowing the British Empire to foster a Jewish national home and suppress Arab rebellion. Therefore, this book argues that the "muddling through" of everyday British politics was instrumental in conceiving and gestating a Jewish state.

By investigating how British governments endured moments of crisis with the representatives of Zionism, and how they dealt with indecision over the future of Palestine, it is possible to uncover a relatively clear pattern. The tumult of Westminster politics and Whitehall bureaucracy harnessed the idea of a Jewish presence in Palestine as a convenient political football—an issue to be analogized with and used pointedly to address other more pressing concerns, such as Bolshevism in the 1920s, Muslim riots in India in the early 1930s, and appeasement shortly before the start of World War II. The result was a stumbling, ad hoc policy journey toward Israel's birth that never followed any centralized plan. Rather, for the British Empire of 1917, conditions culminating in Israeli independence were distinctly unlikely and unexpected.

Why such a situation occurred, however, is not exactly a straightforward inquiry, and the answer is relevant to a much wider discourse than merely the annals of obscure historical analysis. An ongoing search for peace in the Middle East cannot ignore how contemporary perceptions of the conflict are intimately bound to the parties' understanding of their shared history. There are, naturally, multiple versions of this history, but, although the importance of Britain's tenure in Palestine is hardly challenged, curiously few scholars have asked how British policy toward Palestine was made. This refers particularly to high policy decided by the cabinet in Westminster rather than the day-to-day activities of administering the territory, which was conducted chiefly through the bureaucracy of the Colonial Office.

What emerges within the relevant literature, instead, is a consistent recourse to stubborn, unsubstantiated myths about British intentions and motivations—misconceptions that, in turn, fuel other attitudes that are distinctly unhelpful, such as the idea of an all-powerful Zionist lobby or the championing of Palestinian victimhood. This is explained extensively in chapter 1, but the "myths" on trial here are broadly those that highlight British politicians' personal feelings toward Jews or Arabs, as though these prejudices *must* have had a substantial impact on Britain's imperial planning. The main problem with this thinking is that it is too easy to describe any number of contextual factors that may have influenced the direction of British policy. However, the evidence that bias drove or determined Britain's relationship with Zionism and Palestine is frequently lacking. As the decision makers themselves are long dead and understandably unavailable for cross-examination, how then is it possible to determine, with any accuracy, what thought processes occupied their minds during the interwar period?

Bearing in mind this question, it is important to stress that some valid boundaries must be placed on the themes and issues explored in this type of investigation. Therefore, this book uses an innovative politics-first approach to illustrate four critical junctures of Britain's policy making between the beginning of its occupation of Palestine in December 1917 and its withdrawal in May 1948. The following chapters argue that, contrary to the established literature on Mandate Palestine, British high policy reflected a stark lack of viable alternatives that left little room for consideration of personal biases, allegiances, or sentimental attachments to either Zionism or Arab nationalism during the tense moments when choices had to be made. This approach reveals how decisions about the future of Palestine were frequently more concerned with fighting narrow domestic or broader international political battles than preventing or dealing with a burgeoning conflict in a tiny strip of land on the Mediterranean.

As many previous books have focused chiefly on day-to-day interactions in Palestine, they have relied heavily on the original documentation of the Palestine administration and the high commissioner as well as his dealings with the Colonial Office in London and the diaries and memoirs of prominent Zionist leaders such as Chaim Weizmann and David Ben-Gurion. This has meant that scholarly discussions about British policy decisions have been conducted almost exclusively through the prism of external parties' opinions about what was going on in London at the time. As this book concentrates specifically on British policy decisions, the focus has been placed on British archives as well as relevant collections held in the United States that are useful for examining the postwar Mandate period.

The Politics-First Approach

British policies generated many of the "demographic, economic, military, and organizational" conditions that were essential for Israel to achieve its statehood,[2] so a thorough investigation into the reasoning and motivations that informed British policy making helps clarify a major moment in world history. Toward this end, this book deals primarily with the dynamics of choice in British policy making. It asks, given the range of available options, *how* and *why* did British governments make their final decisions? What factors *did* and *did not* influence those choices? Answering these questions is not simply a matter of combing the archives. Indeed, a great deal of the scholarship related to British Palestine has struggled in this regard because it ignores principles of political psychology.[3] Without an appreciation for how the political brain operates, it is very difficult to discern causes from contexts.

Therefore, this book is based on a fundamental premise derived from political psychology—that the primary and immediate consideration of decision makers in government is their own political survival, making every other concern secondary.[4] Therefore, policy makers faced with a crisis and a range of potential options will automatically discard any courses of action that threaten their political careers, deciding what to do based only on the possibilities that are leftover.[5] Crucially, it does not matter how beneficial any of the discarded alternatives would have been for the economy, or the military, or the country as a whole—that benefit could not compensate for the political risk felt by politicians.[6] This amounts to a "politics-first" way of understanding how leaders make choices, and it helps provide a much better understanding of policies that seem to have been irrational or counterproductive.[7]

In applying this lens to Britain's Palestine policy at four key junctures during the Palestine Mandate, it is possible to demonstrate why the cabinet decided to pursue action that worsened the burgeoning conflict between Palestine's two communities, sometimes in a manner that seemed entirely contrary to British interests, and how these policy decisions were often concluded without direct reference to the desires of either Zionists or Palestinian Arabs. This analysis provides an invaluable contribution, revealing how the development of policy in Palestine was based primarily on the need to satisfy British domestic political concerns. This was not because Palestine was unimportant but, rather, because Palestine policy frequently overlapped with multiple issues more crucial to the political survival of individual governments.

Therefore, this book highlights precisely how, while actual decisions varied during the British Mandate, Palestine policy making was driven by mechanisms that significantly narrowed the scope of options available to politicians as they tried to deal with successive crises. This means that although colorful, interesting, and engaging, the personal quirks, biases, and beliefs of decision makers had little demonstrable impact. There simply was no room, no space, for these feelings, because successive governments during this period faced a series of overly precarious political circumstances in general. This created a dynamic of "muddling through" that is detailed and evidenced in later chapters, demonstrating how the political climate prevented any kind of British grand strategy for the future birth of a Jewish state.

A Note on the Research

An execution of this politics-first approach is achieved by assessing a series of key events using archival documents, attempting to trace how decisions developed. This book is concerned with four specific junctures: (1) the decision to reaffirm the Jewish national home in the Churchill White Paper of 1922; (2) the reversal of the Passfield White Paper in 1931; (3) the decision to issue the MacDonald White Paper in 1939; and (4) the decision to withdraw from Palestine made in 1947. These particular moments have not been selected from a wider pool of options; they represent four distinct periods of policy making during British rule over Palestine. Each period is defined by a problem in Palestine—a violent riot or protest—that was serious enough to demand a policy decision from the British cabinet in Westminster rather than the Palestine administration in Jerusalem or simply the Colonial Office. The disturbances always preceded two commissions of inquiry followed by a statement of policy, which remained in place until the next violent outbreak necessitated another reassessment. These four predicaments represent the only instances when the central British government became directly involved in shaping Palestine's burgeoning conflict, and these decisions had the long-term consequences that make their study vital to understanding formative stages in the Israeli-Palestinian conflict.

This book does not, however, provide a separate analysis of the decision-making behind the original Balfour Declaration in 1917 (see chap. 1). This is because the subject has already been covered in great depth and also because an extremely vague wartime promise of dubious sincerity, which was released initially as a private letter rather than as a white paper, does not necessarily constitute imperial policy. Rather, the affirmation of the Balfour Declaration is the real starting point for British policy making toward Palestine and the declaration itself is a natural component of analyzing the Churchill White Paper of 1922.

These insights are based on extensive primary research. As well as the substantial collections held at the National Archives in Kew (referred to in notes as TNA), others used are the Cadbury Archives in Birmingham, the Parliamentary Archives in Westminster, the London School of Economics Archives, the Cambridge Archive Centre, the University of Durham special collections, the Truman Presidential Library in Missouri, the United Nations Archives in New York, and the US National Archives in Maryland. This material includes a variety of source types, including government documents, reports, and memoranda as well as personal diaries, memoirs, correspondence, speeches, press conferences, and debates. As the research is focused specifically on decision makers in Westminster rather than Jerusalem, Israeli archives have been deliberately avoided. This is because books that offer commentary on the psychology of British actions in Mandate Palestine have never made this subject their chief concern, and so the distanced interpretations of prominent Zionists, whose material is held in those archives, have already informed existing but flawed understandings of British intentions and motivations (see chap. 1).

Structure of the Book

After introducing the aims and scope of this book, chapter 1 explains how histories of the Israeli-Palestinian conflict are never neutral or benign, highlighting how important it is to correct inaccuracies in our preconceptions about the Mandate period.

Then, in chapter 2, this book's initial historical analysis concerns the Churchill White Paper of 1922 and why the British government decided to affirm the policy of a Jewish national home that was first articulated in the Balfour Declaration in 1917. This was despite violent Arab protests and Palestine's questionable military or strategic value. Two commissions of inquiry concluded that the government's policy, a draft Mandate based on the Balfour Declaration, was the source of Palestine's unrest. Why then, was the policy reaffirmed? This time period represented a Balfour Zeitgeist, in which the policy's confirmation in 1922 meant it remained unquestioned until a large-scale riot erupted in Palestine in 1929.

The second investigation deals with policy formulated following this later outbreak of violence. Chapter 3 details the government's attempts to acknowledge and manage the underlying problems between Palestine's Arab majority and Zionist minority. After another two commissions of inquiry, the government released a white paper named for the colonial secretary Lord Passfield, which attempted to limit Jewish immigration and land purchase in Palestine. This white paper constituted an understandable response to the conclusions offered by two independent investigations, but it was reversed only three months later. Why did this U-turn occur? The reversal meant that significant tensions in Palestine continued to be ignored, and from the early 1930s built to an Arab Revolt in Palestine, from 1936 to 1939.

Chapter 4 covers the next part of this study, which is centered on the British reaction to this larger rebellion. Again, two commissions of inquiry advised the government that basic Mandatory policy positions were fomenting Palestine's unrest. The first commission recommended partition, and the second advised against that plan. In 1939, the government issued the MacDonald White Paper, which promised Palestine its independence within ten years and set a cap on Jewish immigration for five years, after which any further immigration required Arab approval. This appeared to be a radical departure from the Balfour Zeitgeist, and from the pressures that caused a reversal of the Passfield White Paper, but why did it happen? The MacDonald White Paper stood as official British policy throughout World War II and into the postwar period, which witnessed an intense Jewish insurgency and burgeoning civil war in Palestine.

The fourth and final evaluation then, discussed in chapter 5, deals with British withdrawal from Palestine. After the war, there were two final commissions of inquiry: one conducted in concert with the United States and another by a UN Special Committee. The first recommended a binational state, whereas a majority opinion of the UN commission advocated partition. The British government, however, decided on neither of these courses and instead initiated a withdrawal plan in late 1947. After more than thirty years committed to the territory out of political and perceived strategic necessity, why did the British government make this final decision?

Together, these sections represent the building blocks of a more comprehensive understanding of British policy making toward Palestine during the Mandate and how it revolved around periods of violence. By teasing out precisely which issues and concerns drove British leaders during and after Palestine's riots and rebellions, it is possible to identify patterns of behavior. While some established literature has offered incomplete explanations of British behavior during this time, none have approached the subject in a systematic fashion or offered conclusions within a political psychology framework designed specifically for this task. This is exactly what this book is intended to address, as it seeks to uncover the root causes of British policy toward Palestine, from 1917 to 1948, and to demonstrate how British politicians' self-serving mind-sets and incoherent actions created the necessary conditions for an otherwise unexpected state.

Notes

1. "David Cameron's Speech to the Knesset in Israel," gov.uk, 12 March 2014, https://www.gov.uk/government/speeches/david-camerons-speech-to-the-knesset-in-israel (accessed June 1, 2015); Sharif Nashashibi, "Balfour: Britain's Original Sin," Al Jazeera, 4 November 2014, http://www.aljazeera.com/indepth/opinion/2014/11/balfour-britain-original-sin-201411472940231416.html (accessed June 1, 2015).

2. Walid Khalidi, "The Palestine Problem: An Overview," *Journal of Palestine Studies* 21, no. 1 (1991): 5–16, 7; Walid Khalidi, "A Palestinian Perspective on the Arab-Israeli Conflict," *Journal of Palestine Studies* 14, no. 4 (1985): 35–48.

3. Charles Ronald Middleton, *The Administration of British Foreign Policy 1782–1846* (Durham, NC: Duke University Press, 1977); Matthew Hughes, *Allenby and British Strategy in the Middle East* (London: Frank Cass, 1999); Bruce Westrate, *The Arab Bureau: British Policy in the Middle East 1916–1920* (University Park: Pennsylvania State University Press, 1992); Richard Grayson, *Austen Chamberlain and the Commitment to Europe: British Foreign Policy 1924–29* (London: Frank Cass, 1997); John Darwin, *Britain, Egypt and the Middle East: Imperial Policy in the Aftermath of War 1918–1922* (London: Macmillan, 1981); Paul Doerr, *British Foreign Policy 1919–1939* (Manchester: Manchester University Press, 1998); Philip Reynolds, *British Foreign Policy in the Inter-War Years* (London: Longmans, Green, 1954); Matthew Hughes, *British Foreign Secretaries in an Uncertain World, 1919–1939* (Oxon: Routledge, 2006); Isaiah Friedman, *British Pan-Arab Policy, 1915–1922* (New Brunswick, NJ: Transaction, 2010).

4. Alex Mintz and Nehemia Geva, eds., "The Poliheuristic Theory of Foreign Policy Decisionmaking," in *Decisionmaking on War and Peace: The Cognitive-Rational Debate* (Boulder, CO: Lynne Rienner, 1997), 81–102; Alex Mintz, ed., "Integrating Cognitive and Rational Theories of Foreign Policy Decision Making: A Poliheuristic Perspective," in *Integrating Cognitive and Rational Theories of Foreign Policy Decision Making* (New York: Palgrave Macmillan, 2002), 1–10.

5. Ibid.

6. Ibid.

7. Alex Mintz, "How Do Leaders Make Decisions? A Poliheuristic Perspective," *Journal of Conflict Resolution* 48, no. 1 (2004): 3–13.

1 A Usable Past

History Is Not Neutral

All histories of the Israeli-Palestinian conflict are contentious, not just because they cover sensitive issues but because they have become weaponized in the service of contemporary political aims. These historical narratives are not "true" in the neutral sense but, instead, provide a version of the past that helps define a community and hold it together. Historians are intrinsically aware that these stories are biased, selective, and tailored to the community's needs, creating "a usable past."[1] Unfortunately, this perpetual reinforcement of different versions of the same history tends to promote conflict. The dueling stories perpetuate a sense of danger, victimhood, and blame while justifying a continuation of hostilities and rationalizing the use of illegal or unethical tactics.[2] An awareness of this unhelpful cycle burdens historians with a moral obligation to dissect those versions of the past that promote conflict and preclude compromise.[3]

Although neither Israeli nor Palestinian public opinion is monolithic, it is accurate to describe a dominant narrative valuable to each nation. Consequently, it is possible to grasp how a lack of scholarship investigating British intents and motives during the Mandate period has helped fuel myths of Israeli (or, in this instance, pre-state Zionist) power versus Palestinian Arab helplessness—ideas that reinforce the larger, conflict-promoting narratives.

Since the state's creation in 1948, Israel's traditional historical narrative has been constructed as a celebration of triumph against overwhelming odds. The events preceding Israel's independence were, naturally, interpreted in light of this heroic image. Stories of Britain's Mandate in Palestine were dominated by somewhat contradictory claims of Zionist influence in the halls of Westminster and accusations of British negligence and betrayal. The construction of a colossal enemy was also necessary to paint the Israel Defense Forces as a moral military. Although Zionist militias fought British and then Arab troops after World War II, their status as the forerunner to Israel's Defense Forces was based on the idea of reluctance, the result of internal and external aggression forcing war upon the proto-Israeli community.

Israel's traditional narrative, for example, blames Arab leaders for the Palestinian refugee crisis, for commanding villagers to flee and then refusing to accept partition or coexistence. This moment of "birth" left Israel surrounded by purported enemies and subject to Palestinian terrorism, despite an alleged willingness to pursue peace if only their adversaries would do the same. This romantic image, of David facing Goliath, has also been adopted by Israel's supporters around the globe. In the United States, for example, features of the unrevised, unfiltered Zionist histories are repeated through news broadcasting, school textbooks, church teachings, and general discourse.[4] Although it seems absurd in many respects, the old myth that Palestine was "a land without a people for a people without a land" still persists under these conditions.[5]

Understandably, early histories of the Mandate followed a similar ethos. These books were chiefly about the struggles and successes of Zionist, eastern European elites. Interestingly, these histories seem to have gone hand in hand with the years of Labor Party dominance in Israel—celebrating the values of socialism and democracy. Examples include Koestler's *Promise and Fulfilment* and Kimche's *Both Sides of the Hill*.[6] Ultimately, these works portrayed Zionism as a national liberation ideology. Within this context, the complexities of British politics and individual politicians' roles, motives, and frustrations when dealing with the question of Palestine were largely immaterial. History had simply become "proof of the legitimacy, morality, and exclusivity of the Jewish people's right to the country, to the entire country."[7] Although the Israeli narrative has subsequently been punctured by a revisionist movement that gained momentum in the 1980s, Britain's role in the history has remained relatively constant.

Mostly looking inward, scholars such as Benny Morris, Ilan Pappe, Tom Segev, and Avi Shlaim built on the earlier work of Simha Flapan and other critical writers to interrupt the accepted doctrine. Ostensibly, they focused on atrocities, falsehoods, general aggression, Israel's culpability for the Palestinian refugee crisis, and Israeli belligerence that sabotaged tentative opportunities for peace. Ultimately, however, Israel's "new" history did not shed its Zionist roots and represented an additional rather than a replacement paradigm, and the scholarship attracted a great deal of domestic criticism. Shabtai Teveth and Efraim Karsh were particularly vitriolic, with Karsh accusing the revisionists of falsifying evidence. As the dominant Israeli narrative had operated "invisibly and involuntarily," research that challenged this widely accepted version of events felt subversive and aggressive.[8]

This is why it is crucial to note that the revisionist process did not occur in a disinterested vacuum. Collective memory had helped form an Israeli identity in the initial years of state formation, but the traditional narrative began to break down as the state became more secure. A groundbreaking triumph for the right-wing Likud Party in Israel's 1977 elections caused further disintegration. This was because an inflammatory rivalry between electoral campaigns in the next election, in 1981, included intense "history wars." A heated debate ensued about the nature of Likud leader Menachem Begin's role in resisting British imperialism versus the alleged corruption among Labor Party members who had enjoyed decades of uninterrupted power.[9] By contesting Israeli history between them, the two major political blocks exposed the traditional narrative's arbitrary character and provided the catalyst for a new period of critical social thinking.[10] Dealing with the controversies of 1948 seemed pertinent under these political conditions, but a revised history of British policy during the Mandate has never felt urgent or necessary, in the same way, for Israeli politics. Interestingly, the same is true for Palestinian or Arab narratives, leading to curious agreement on points of history involving Britain that have somewhat escaped scholarly attention.

In contrast to the dominant Israeli history, Arab and Palestinian perspectives have never presented a singular narrative. Like the Israeli version, they veer between celebrating perceived victories and lamenting the weaknesses imposed by an outside power. Although they tend to agree on basic principles, a great deal of the narrative has always been internally disputed.[11] Wider Arab and Palestinian narratives are joined in blaming Great Britain and the United States for establishing a Jewish state in the predominantly Arab Middle East and united in condemning the expulsion of Palestinian Arabs to create a Jewish state. All versions of the Arab narrative reject Israel's assertion that Palestinian villagers took voluntary flight in 1948, but details of the history change from state to state, between classes (populist vs. elite), and depending on how critical they are of civilian as opposed to military leaders, among many other details.[12] Wider Arab historiography, for example, has celebrated Egyptian, Syrian, and Jordanian fighters in the war of 1948 but simultaneously portrays the Palestinians as weak and ineffectual.[13]

In the specifically Palestinian context, collective memory celebrates figures such as Izz ad-Din al-Qassam, a Syrian-born Islamic preacher and fighter who was killed in a firefight with British Mandate police in 1935. Al-Qassam's death is remembered as a key moment that sparked the general strike and uprising beginning in 1936; his memory was used during the First Intifada, which began in 1987, to rally Palestinians as "people of martyrs, grandsons of al-Qassam," and, of course, al-Qassam also lends his name to the military brigades of Hamas today.[14] However, the memory of al-Qassam and the celebration of many subsequent Palestinian martyrs exist in parallel with a more dominant narrative of collective helplessness. This is embodied in the memory of Deir Yassin. Although a massacre took place at this village, there was also a pitched battle in which Palestinian fighters resisted a stronger Israeli force for eight hours, a factor conveniently thrown aside in favor of the powerlessness motif.[15] As Saleh Abdel Jawad notes, "[. . .] Palestine was seen as a weak, unprepared society overwhelmed by a stronger and more organized force [. . .]" and even Palestinians tend to favor explanations of the Nakba that blame external factors, like British deceit and Arab disunity.[16]

A good example of this enduring attachment to the idea of Palestinian helplessness is Al Jazeera's 2008 documentary *Al-Nakba* in which an entire hour-long episode is devoted to the Palestinian Arab uprising of 1936–1939, in which not a single victory—military or otherwise—is mentioned. As "[r]esistance is fundamental to the new Palestinian narrative," it seems incongruous that Palestinian resistance to the British in the 1930s is still portrayed solely in terms of victimization.[17] Even in a British-made fictional television show such as *The Promise*, Palestinian Arabs lack agency and are helpless in the face of both British troops and Zionist paramilitary fighters. Palestinian helplessness, then, is a paradigm that is also paradoxically repeated and reconstructed by outside observers wishing to support the community and further its interests, even when that narrative is unnecessarily self-defeatist.

There are, of course, exceptions to the widespread characterization of Palestinians as helpless and/or victimized. Rashid Khalidi's work provides a pertinent example of "new" Palestinian history. He details the shortcomings of Palestinian Arab leadership during the Mandatory period, blaming catastrophes in both the 1930s and the 1940s on its failure "to agree on appropriate strategies, to mobilize and organize the populace effectively, to create an accepted and recognized representative national quasi-state forum [. . .], and to break decisively with the structures of colonial control."[18]

Likewise, overall approaches to studying the Mandate have shifted to recognize how the Arab community in Palestine was sidelined in overly Zionist-oriented histories of the era. The "new" historians ostensibly challenged the traditional Israeli narrative, but their intellectual freedom to do so was largely hampered by a preexisting Zionist-centric attitude that left the Palestinians as observers rather than participants in their own history.[19] Works that redress this imbalance include Hadawi's *Palestine: Loss of a Heritage*, his *Bitter Harvest*, and Walid Khalidi's *From Haven to Conquest*.[20] As these newer histories were based largely on oral testimonies—since many archives remain closed in Israel—"it was the voices of the dispossessed who were now to be heard [. . .]."[21]

In terms of the Mandate, these "new narratives asserted a benign rather than conspiratorially hostile Britain."[22] However, this characterization appears to have been chiefly a reaction against the Israeli narrative of Britain's compliance and then betrayal. Recasting the empire from a lead role to a background player has not altered the victimization narrative. Therefore, although scholars such as Nicholas Roberts and Zeina Ghandour[23] have leveled criticism at Mandate history texts for ignoring or misrepresenting the less powerful side, this argument appears to be made from inside the narrative of Palestinian passivity and helplessness, not in an attempt to disrupt it. The result is a set of historical interpretations that disagree on a great number of points related to the other's true intentions and actions but largely agree on the role Britain played in their shared experiences—creating a powerful Israel and a helpless Palestinian community. These ideas have endured without much questioning over whether that characterization of Britain is accurate.

Further complicating these histories, external parties often adopt the most rigid version of each community's rendition of events. This is often the case with otherwise unconnected observers who also feel a stake in the conflict—whether for religious or political reasons—and then "pick a side" and repeat the traditional, dominant narrative with greater fervor than many Israelis or Palestinians. This has left a great deal of Britain's role during the Mandate period curiously pristine in comparison to the debates about 1948 and after. This bias regarding the Mandate was noted in the 1990s, when Kenneth Stein "described a field in which 'advocacy of a political viewpoint may supersede nuances of terminology, the causation of events, or the mechanisms of change in the conflict's evolution.'"[24] Likewise, Zachary Lockman saw academics working "within a 'Zionist or Arab/Palestinian nationalist historical narrative'" that limited their analyses.[25] The Mandate is, in effect, a forgotten ancestor to contemporary narratives that are constantly reinforced to validate nationhood for both Israelis and Palestinians, albeit in different ways. Why and how British policy helped create this situation is a vital component of interrupting the narrative cycle.

Neglected Origins

Although the effects of British decision-making have been widely researched, reasons behind Britain's Palestine policy have been left largely unexplored. How did the British government make decisions regarding Palestine? What were the motives, intentions, and goals behind them? Answering these questions is necessary because, notwithstanding some notable exceptions, the vast majority of studies of the Israeli-Palestinian conflict settle for only a cursory overview of this period.[26] Works on the Mandate tend to use British policy decisions as plot devices, focusing only on each new white paper's effect on relations between Jews and Arabs in Palestine. British decision-making toward Palestine has provided the focus of very few scholarly investigations to date.

Although the work of historians such as William Roger Louis and Michael J. Cohen, for example, have explored in great detail the domestic and international political constraints on Palestine policy, their work has focused exclusively on the later Mandate and withdrawal.[27] This means that no study has been dedicated to British policy making during the entire Mandate and certainly none that tries to bring in political psychology. In addition, this book intends to address one prevalent trend within the literature.

As previous histories have centered on the role of the Colonial Office and the Palestine high commissioner (focused as they have been on day-to-day administration of the Mandate within Palestine), they have relied on certain assumptions, some stubborn myths, and frequent oversimplification to explain dynamics within the real corridors of British power. There has been an almost automatic recourse to highlighting British politicians' personal feelings toward Zionism or Arab nationalism. Epitomizing this is a comment offered by Shlomo Ben-Ami: "Frequently driven by pro-Zionist sentiments, and notwithstanding the apprehension of many in the mandatory administration at the ruthless drive of the Zionists, an apprehension sometimes fed by a strong anti-Semitic bias as much as it was driven by a genuine sympathy for the dispossessed Arab fellahin, or by a romantic, Lawrence of Arabia brand of admiration for the Arab 'wild man,' the policy makers in London and the high commissioners on the ground were essentially the protectors of the Zionist enterprise."[28]

Although these attitudes may have been prevalent, they did not necessarily direct policy in Westminster, and connecting the two uncritically is partly the result of source choice. Investigating principally the Zionist Archives in Jerusalem and the papers of officials serving in Palestine has created a history of British intents and purposes based on the supposition of parties far from the action, whose uninformed fears and frustrations naturally bled into their interpretations of cabinet policy making. This has resulted in the survival of largely unfounded "explanations"—such as simple ideas of Zionist and Arab pressure on the British government—in what are otherwise academically rigorous studies. Examining the British Mandate from only Jerusalem's perspective provides an incomplete version of events that does not help clarify the inner workings of Westminster during the Mandate years.

Other, more specific myths have also been allowed to endure for similar reasons. By providing a survey analysis of British Palestine policy through a review of the current literature, it is possible to discern a dominant Mandate narrative and highlight its neglected dimensions that are addressed in later chapters. This chapter charts some of the most common themes found in the established scholarship: Zionism and Arab nationalism in the British imagination; riots and rebellion in the interwar period; lobbying and influence; and the Mandate and the international community.

Zionism and Arab Nationalism in the British Imagination

A major recurring theme in British Mandate historiography is the importance placed on ideas of Zionism and Arab nationalism in the British imagination, an emphasis with its roots in studies of Britain's three infamous wartime promises. Between 1915 and 1917, the British government entered into three separate pledges that involved the future of Palestine: the Hussein-McMahon correspondence, the Sykes-Picot Agreement, and the Balfour Declaration. As this book argues that later British decisions were not driven by ideology, it is necessary to admit that these foundation pledges did involve a degree of sentiment combined with practical concerns. However, the importance of ideology has been vastly overstated; these initial promises provide an important foundation for understanding the Mandate as a whole, but they are not sufficient devices for understanding British behavior in the thirty years that followed. As a great deal of studies have focused on this topic and they often contradict each other, the following overview is intended to demonstrate a combination of the factors that drove British policy making under the curious and distinct political atmosphere created by a world war.

First, the Hussein-McMahon correspondence produced Britain's initial Palestine pledge, to Hashemite ruler Sharif Hussein of Mecca and his sons Ali, Abdullah, Faisal, and Zeid. Despite Hussein's exalted position within the Ottoman Empire as guardian of the holy cities, he suffered a tense relationship with Constantinople.[29] Consequently, Hussein's son Abdullah (future king of Jordan) penned an official approach to the British oriental secretary in Cairo, Sir Ronald Storrs, in July 1915.[30] Abdullah's letter ostensibly opened formal negotiations between "the Arabs," represented by Sharif Hussein, and Great Britain, represented not by Storrs but by his superior, the district commissioner to Cairo Sir Henry McMahon. What followed was a series of dispatches between July 1915 and March 1916—the Hussein-McMahon correspondence. These communiqués outlined a deal in which the sharif agreed to lead a revolt against Ottoman forces in the Middle East, and, in return, Britain would aid the creation of an independent Arab state.[31] While Hussein did indeed lead the Great Arab Revolt in June 1916, it was the letters of negotiation rather than his military action that proved politically and historically significant. The correspondence became highly controversial due to a sustained debate over what, exactly, Britain had pledged to the Arabs, whether it included Palestine, and how this affected the legitimacy of later promises to the French and, ultimately, to the Zionists.

The principal issue was one of wording. Abdullah's opening letter proposed an Arab state encompassing most of the Middle East.[32] In response, McMahon specifically excluded "portions of Syria lying to the west of the districts of Damascus, Homs, Hama and Aleppo," claiming this was necessary because "the interests of our ally, France, are involved in them both."[33] These exclusions were based on vague instructions from Foreign Secretary Sir Edward Grey, but a problem later arose from McMahon's use of the word *district*, or *vilayet* in the Arabic version sent to Hussein. Damascus, Homs, Hama, and Aleppo were cities, and so the concept of their districts was open to interpretation.[34] As Palestine had existed without boundaries for nearly five hundred years under Ottoman control, it was difficult to ascertain whether, according to McMahon's exclusions, Palestine was inside or outside the area promised to an Arab state.[35] This first promise has been made famous in the West largely by David Lean's 1962 film, *Lawrence of Arabia*. In the story, British generals and politicians are presented as a combination of enthusiastic Orientalists and evil imperialists, which is echoed in Ben-Ami's comment above. A great deal of research has been conducted into British intentions in this case, but opinion is divided.[36] The same is true regarding interpretations of the second promise, made to France.

The Sykes-Picot Agreement was the result of negotiations between the attaché to the imperial war cabinet, Sir Mark Sykes, and French diplomat François Georges-Picot conducted during the latter stages of McMahon's correspondence with Hussein. These Anglo-Franco talks produced an explicit division of the Middle East into British and French spheres of influence, resulting in a debate questioning whether the Sykes-Picot Agreement contradicted promises made to Hussein. The problems associated with McMahon's wording have been discussed already, so the question of imperial duplicity hinges on why Britain entered into a second pledge. The agreement with France allowed Britain the political freedom to pursue an offensive through Ottoman territory without fearing that its principal ally would become hostile, either during or after the war. French ambassador Paul Cambon, for example, had complained during the initial Hussein-McMahon correspondence that there was "too much talk in Cairo" and that this was discourteous to France, which "regarded Syria as a dependency."[37]

War Secretary Lord Horatio Herbert Kitchener also recognized the potential diplomatic storm arising from McMahon's correspondence with Hussein, posing the question to Sykes a month later: "May you not be straining your relations with France very gravely if you assume you have come to an agreement with them and take action in Syria?"[38] The resulting negotiations were an exercise in preventive diplomacy. Rather than a rejection of the previous promise, this new agreement facilitated the Hussein-McMahon agreement because "without the British offensive there could have been no Arab revolt; and without the Sykes-Picot Agreement there would have been no British offensive."[39] The motive was to prevent a misunderstanding in which French politicians believed they were being double-crossed. Then, as Sir Mark Sykes calmly noted, "All we have to do is not to mix ourselves up with religious squabbles."[40]

Although the later establishment of a British Mandate in Palestine often leads commentators to assume that Sykes and Picot allotted the entire area to Britain, their agreement actually shared Ottoman Palestine between several authorities. A brown area on the map prepared during the negotiations indicated that most of Palestine west of the Jordan River would be under international administration, and this was dependent upon consultation with Britain and France's mutual ally Russia, as well as with the sharif. Within the blue area allotted to France, Britain

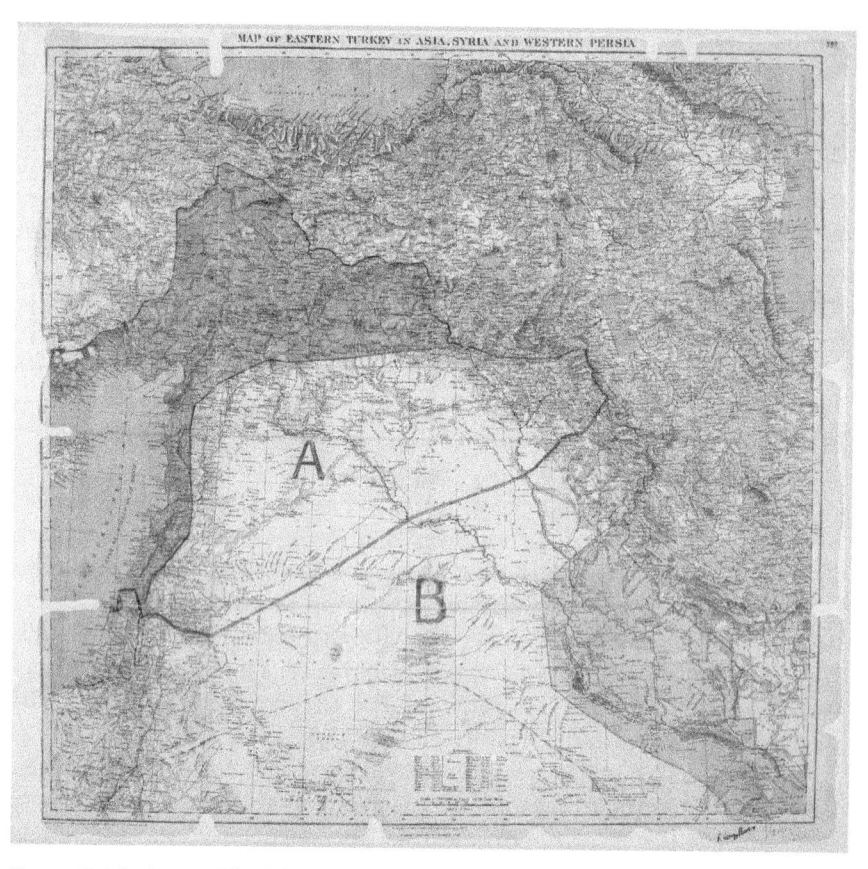

Fig. 1.1. Original map of the Sykes-Picot Agreement in 1916. Area A was intended to be France's sphere of influence, and Area B was allocated to Britain to form the basis of an Arab state. © The National Archives.

reserved the ports of Haifa and Acre with the right to build a railway linking them to Baghdad, in its own red area. The northern tip of Palestine above Lake Tiberius was to be part of France's annexed Syrian territory, whereas Palestine's regions west of the Jordan River and south of Gaza were part of the Arab state under British protection, leaving the now-Israeli city of Beersheba, for example, as unequivocally Arab owned.[41] (See fig. 1.1.) The spirit if not the letter of this Sykes-Picot Agreement did come to fruition during postwar talks, but again this was partly due to Britain's third promise, made to the Zionist movement.

On 2 November 1917, British foreign secretary Arthur James Balfour lent his signature to a short letter addressed to Zionism's high-profile patron, Baron Lionel Walter Rothschild. In fewer than 150 words, the message conveyed, for the first time in Jewish history, the support of a great power to the cause of a Jewish homeland in Palestine: "His Majesty's Government view with favour the establishment in Palestine of a national home for the Jewish people, and will use their best endeavours to facilitate the achievement of this object, it being clearly understood that nothing shall be done which may prejudice the civil and religious rights of existing non-Jewish communities in Palestine, or the rights and political status enjoyed by Jews in any other country."[42] The Balfour Declaration was a key juncture in the history of Britain's involvement with Palestine; it laid the foundations—however unsteady they proved to be—for the British Mandate and a pro-Jewish Palestine policy that would continue until the brink of World War II. These initial British interests in Palestine evolved from two considerations: securing military lines of communication, and—after the Sykes-Picot Agreement—preventing a French Palestine.

British politicians sought the means during wartime to limit long-term German threats to the empire.[43] This was because "the acquisition by Germany—through her control of Turkey—of political and military control in Palestine and Mesopotamia would imperil the communication [. . .] through the Suez Canal, and would directly threaten the security of Egypt and India."[44] Although the Sykes-Picot Agreement had concluded with an international Holy Land, neither party was satisfied. If the War Office wanted to secure communication between Great Britain and the East, they would first need to block residual but insistent French claims to Palestine (which were bolstered by France's history of protecting Catholicism in the region).[45] In bullish style, Prime Minister David Lloyd George intended to use British forces advancing on Gaza to present the French with a fait accompli—British occupation of Palestine would constitute a strong claim to ownership.[46] They did not, therefore, need Zionism in the traditional military sense. This forceful strategy, however, risked a direct political confrontation with a much-needed ally. To avoid this eventuality, the ubiquitous Sir Mark Sykes pursued Zionism—a "just cause" with interests in Palestine—to provide the legitimacy for what were fundamentally strategic claims.[47] As a result, Sykes began to introduce Zionist interests in his negotiations with Picot.[48]

It was not until the first British invasion of Palestine was in motion, however, that Sykes contacted the two men who would figure most prominently in British-Zionist diplomacy. In January 1917, he met with the secretary general of the World Zionist Organization, Nahum Sokolow, and president of the British Zionist Organization, Chaim Weizmann, and the two leaders made it clear to Sykes that they favored British rule in Palestine. The following month Sykes introduced Sokolow to Picot, and the amicable meeting resulted in the opening of a Zionist mission in Paris. Thus, by the spring of 1917, the Zionist agenda was reassuringly recognized by the Triple Entente. This, combined with an underlying anti-Semitic belief in the power and pro-German tendencies of world Jewry, led to the final British agreement to the Balfour Declaration.[49]

When the war cabinet approved the letter—drafted in negotiations between the Foreign Office, Sykes, and several Zionists—on 31 October 1917, the action passed because they believed "the vast majority of Jews in Russia and America, as, indeed, as over the world, now appeared to be favorable to Zionism. If we could make a declaration favourable to such an ideal, we should be able to carry on extremely useful propaganda both in Russia and America."[50] This conviction provided the final motivation—targeting American and Bolshevik Jews for propaganda—in approving the Balfour Declaration. It was merely the final step on a longer journey through military communication requirements and the need to keep France out of Palestine.

If, however, the Hussein-McMahon correspondence is seen as a promise motivated by Orientalist fascination with the bedouins, or if the Balfour Declaration is viewed as a morally intentioned return of the Jews to their homeland that was brought about by the lobbying skill of Weizmann and Sokolow, then the result is an impression of British decision-making based on sentiment and ideology. This implies that politicians were free to make decisions regarding the future of Palestine unhindered by political constraints. Ben-Ami's quote exemplifies this misunderstanding, but it pervades the literature on Mandate Palestine in more subtle and nuanced ways that result in misleading views of British policy. This is discussed in greater detail below and forms the basis for the historical intervention contributed by this book.

Riots and Rebellion in the Interwar Period

During the interwar period, there were three main outbreaks of violence that each resulted in a statement or change of British policy toward Palestine. Mandate histories tend to use this convenient chronology as a plot device to move the reader through a discussion of Jews' and Arabs' relations during the time period. As British motives during these instances are not the primary focus of other studies, cabinet policy making in Westminster is largely assumed to follow the same wartime influences that led to the Balfour Declaration, and, crucially, no deeper investigation is attempted.

The first violent outbreak was characterized by the Nebi Musa riots of April 1920 and the Jaffa riots of May 1921. The Nebi Musa procession is traditionally a celebration of Moses and also a rally against the Crusades, and this Muslim holiday attracted an influx of revelers to Jerusalem's Old City every year. In 1920, the traditional procession clashed with members of a Zionist group called Beitar, which had decided to stage its own demonstration, and the situation escalated into a riot.[51] Nine deaths, hundreds of injuries, and the sheer scale of destruction demanded a commission of inquiry. It was led by Major General P. C. Palin.

This was the first British attempt to redress Jewish-Arab tensions in Palestine, but its findings were highly critical of Zionists, positing that they, "by their impatience, indiscretion and attempts to force the hands of the Administration, are largely responsible for the present crisis."[52] The Palin Commission, however, was never published, and, just as Palestine's military occupation transformed into a civilian administration, another riot began on 1 May 1921. These disturbances continued for two more days in Jaffa and spread to the surrounding region leading to attacks on Jewish agricultural settlements.[53] Again, the violence necessitated an official inquiry—the Haycraft Commission—which repeated many of Palin's concerns and recommended a clarification in policy to prevent further violence. The result in Westminster was the Churchill White Paper, published in June 1922. On 24 July 1922, the League of Nations then officially awarded Britain's Mandate to govern Palestine.[54] The British government, therefore, possessed ample evidence that the policy of supporting a Jewish national home in Palestine was creating violent tension but chose nevertheless to pursue it.

Although the allotment of blame for these early outbreaks of violence varies between scholarly interpretations—Tom Segev for example, chooses to highlight incidents of horrific violence perpetrated against Jerusalem's Jewish families,[55] whereas Haim Gerber focuses on the clash between Muslims and Zionist political demonstrators[56]—there has been no investigation of why Britain responded with the Churchill White Paper in 1922. The traditional Mandate narrative always includes some discussion of this white paper, but scholars' differing opinions about its contents (discussed more below) have informed their analyses of British deliberations without making this the focus of their research. In actuality, the exact sequence of events that led up to the Churchill White Paper form an important foundation in understanding how the British government developed policy during the rest of the Mandate.

For High Commissioner Sir Herbert Samuel, the problems created by the Mandate were too great and he left Palestine bitter and disillusioned in 1925. His successor, Sir Herbert Plumer, oversaw a period of relative calm in Palestine—possibly because a recession in Poland meant Jewish immigration declined during his tenure.[57] In fact, this calm remains one of the enigmas of British rule since tensions failed to either dissipate or erupt. Believing Palestine's tranquility was permanent, Plumer dismantled several armed units.[58] Leaving with a successful record in 1928, Plumer informed his replacement, Sir John Chancellor, that "the main security problems deserving attention were in Transjordan, not in Palestine."[59] A wave of unprecedented violence swept the country only a few months later.

The disturbances of 1929 were sparked by a long series of events connected with the Western or "Wailing" Wall in Jerusalem—beginning on the Jewish holiday of Yom Kippur in 1928 and culminating in a Zionist demonstration on 15 August 1929 and a Muslim protest the following day.[60] Rumors that Jews were killing Muslims spread to other cities and some whole Jewish families were killed in their homes. The reaction from Westminster constituted another two commissions of inquiry. Although these investigations did not blame the Jewish community for all Arab woes in Palestine, they did admit that immigration into a flooded labor market was impractical (one problem being that the end of Ottoman conscription had left many more able-bodied young men in the area than in previous generations). Since the Balfour Declaration and the Mandate instructed that Jewish immigration should not prejudice the position of any other group in Palestine, and both commissions demonstrated the potential harm created by adding to the labor market at that time, the Mandatory power had a "duty to reduce, or, if necessary, to suspend" immigration until unemployment had eased.[61] This was not an issue of fairness but of peacekeeping and riot prevention. Whitehall prepared a new statement of policy—the Passfield White Paper.

This new white paper built on the foundations of Churchill's earlier policy, but it made establishing the Jewish national home through force of numbers significantly less likely. The Passfield White Paper, however, lasted less than four months. In February 1931, Prime Minister James Ramsay MacDonald wrote to Chaim Weizmann and essentially reversed the immigration restrictions included in the Passfield White Paper.[62] This so-called Black Letter has led to an impression that the documents prepared by Sir Walter Shaw, Sir John Hope-Simpson, and finally the Colonial Office under Lord Passfield are immaterial to the study of British Palestine. This is because, to date, there are very few analyses of why the white paper was reversed (discussed more below).

The third, and most violent, episode of Arab-Jewish clashes in the interwar period began in mid-April 1936. As little action had been taken after MacDonald's letter, the situation in Palestine continued to fester. Smaller disturbances became more commonplace, but they achieved no political recognition and were repelled through the use of force alone; one example was the October-November demonstrations of 1933 when Westminster was assured that Palestine's government could handle any future breaches of the peace.[63] This confidence was called into question during the Arab Revolt of 1936–1939, which erupted in two distinct phases: the first was championed by urban elites involved with the Higher Arab Committee and focused mainly on political protest and a general strike. The British civil administration dealt with this mainly through concessions and diplomacy, negotiating via—among others—Abdullah of Transjordan and Iraq's foreign minister Nuri Pasha, utilizing their connections to calm protestors and prepare for yet another inquiry. This report ignited a second stage in the revolt.[64]

Led by Lord Robert Peel, the Royal Commission was asked to examine wide issues of British obligations to Arabs and Jews. Although the commission was sent ostensibly to "study," their report betrayed an underlying conviction that the real problem was opposition to the Mandate; it was unworkable, and every solution except partition would provide only illusory and temporary relief.[65] They decided that the troubles of 1936 reflected "the same underlying causes as those which brought about the 'disturbances' of 1920, 1921, and 1933 [. . .]. All the other factors were complementary or subsidiary, aggravating the two causes or helping to determine the time at which the disturbances broke out."[66] These "other factors" were trends, such as developing Arab independence in Iraq, Transjordan, Egypt, Syria, and Lebanon; high Jewish immigration and Jewish pressure on Palestine due to the Nazi regime in Germany; Jewish ability to appeal directly to His Majesty's Government by means denied to the Arabs; distrust in British promises following the Hussein-McMahon correspondence; and provocative Jewish nationalism and modernism.[67]

Consequently, the final report recommended an end to the Mandate and a two-state solution.[68] This report marked a real departure from all investigations and statements of policy that preceded it, and reactions from the interested parties ranged from cautious Zionist endorsement to vitriolic Arab condemnation (apart from Abdullah) and split British opinion.[69] The plan's widespread rejection was based either on the moral refusal of Britain's right to give Arab land to Jews or on the grounds that it betrayed the Balfour Declaration, appeased Arab violence, or damaged Anglo-Arab relations.[70]

In Palestine, the publication of Peel's recommendations in July 1937 provoked the second phase of the Arab revolt—a violent but initially successful peasant rebellion that British forces met with a ruthless crackdown. The British cabinet headed by Prime Minister Neville Chamberlain then appointed a further commission in December 1937 to gather the technical details needed to implement partition. Traditional scholarship attests that these investigators were strongly encouraged to deliver a negative opinion.[71] Indeed, the Woodhead Commission reported that they were "unable to recommend boundaries which will afford a reasonable prospect of the eventual establishment of self-supporting Arab and Jewish states."[72] To a question of two states, therefore, the answer was a resounding *No*.

Although scholarship focused on this rebellion has since highlighted how some tactics utilized in Britain's counterinsurgency campaign would be unacceptable or illegal by contemporary standards, scholars tend to assume that British methods implicitly satisfied norms of conduct in the mid-1930s. Scholars such as Yehoshua Porath, Michael J. Cohen, and Simon Anglim, for example, echo the insistent British denials of these atrocities. Porath asserts that "reaction to the strike and the revolt remained almost to the end rather reserved."[73] Whereas

Cohen accepts that "all kinds of charges were levelled" at British troops, he labels these as merely "rumor and propaganda."[74] Likewise, Anglim dismisses allegations as "the insurgents using various methods to try to influence public opinion in the wider world."[75] These assessments accept official government accounts while downplaying the testimony of Palestinian Arabs as well as British police, soldiers, and diplomats. They contrast sharply with the works by historians such as Jacob Norris, Matthew Hughes, and Tom Segev that describe a casual brutality involved in British methods that were employed against the Arab Revolt.[76] These more critical scholars, however, may dilute the impact of revealing British forces' abuses in Palestine by not distinguishing between crimes with differing levels of severity, a subject discussed in greater depth in chapter 4.

There has also been little contemporary inclination to address elements of the 1930s revolt that do not fit contemporary needs. Both Israeli and Palestinian narratives emphasize continuity with the past before 1948 as a source of legitimacy, and this means that the rebellion in Mandate Palestine has been reconstructed as a moment of protonational unity.[77] Unfortunately, this requirement for a usable past means the revolt has assumed a quasi-scared character; it is a powerful symbol, and, perhaps as a result, has been largely excused from academic scrutiny.[78] Zionist history tends to downplay the revolt in 1936–1939, referring to it as a series of riots or as *HaMeora'ot*, the "events," "happenings," or "disturbances."[79] Palestinian guerrillas' surprising successes against the forces of a mighty empire have, as a result, been squeezed out of the popular memory.[80] The movement is remembered as a flawed endeavor that simply imploded, which is an unfair characterization and one that obscures British forces' brutal and in some cases illegal tactics used to crush the revolt. This has left issues such as class divisions, intracommunal violence, and execution of traitors underexplored. This lack of examination also inadvertently reinforces the idea of Palestinian helplessness with a conveniently linear time line from the 1930s to the 1940s and beyond.[81]

After its resounding rejection by all parties concerned, the idea of partition was formally dropped in November 1938, and, instead, the government invited Jewish and Arab representatives to a conference in London.[82] Colonial Secretary Malcolm MacDonald authorized the drafting of a new policy in conjunction with the Foreign Office under Lord Halifax. Although its terms were rejected in meetings with both Zionist and Arab delegates, the resulting MacDonald White Paper, of 1939, outlined a commitment to independence in Palestine within ten years and essentially halted the Jewish national home.[83] In the interim, immigration during the following five years would allow Jewish numbers in Palestine to reach approximately one-third of the population—economic capacity permitting. Numerically, this translated into an additional seventy-five thousand legal Jewish immigrants in total.[84] The policy represented a complete reversal of the spirit of Britain's earlier commitment to the Balfour Declaration. Rather than a stand-alone incident, however, it was part of the larger pattern of policy making throughout the period of British rule.

In Palestine, the new policy embittered Jews who compared the MacDonald White Paper to the Nuremberg Laws. Jewish paramilitary organizations, the Irgun (a right-wing group founded in 1937 by Revisionist Zionists) and its radicalized splinter group, the Stern Gang, attacked British installations, blew up phone booths and post offices, attacked Arab civilians in markets and coffeehouses, and committed a total of 130 murders in the few short months between Britain's new policy and the outbreak of World War II.[85] The Jewish Agency's paramilitary wing, the Haganah, agreed to support Britain's war effort. They fought the white paper by facilitating illegal immigration, but the Irgun continued violent attacks throughout the war.[86] British troops continued to fight what they termed *Jewish terrorism*, but when evidence of the Holocaust was discovered, widespread horror and outrage turned Palestine policy from a purely British concern into an international crisis. These outbreaks of violence form the spine of a dominant Mandate narrative, but various interpretations of how they led to British policy making are often characterized by overly simple explanations of lobbying and influence.

Lobbying and Influence

The idea that pro- or anti-Zionist feelings drove Palestine policy is one that reappears frequently in the Mandate literature alongside other tenuous explanations for British policy choices that do not withstand even a small degree of scrutiny. The most common instances of this relate to the formulation of the Churchill White Paper in 1922 and the reversal of the Passfield White Paper in 1931.

The most memorable aspect of the Churchill White Paper policy was that, in theory and for the first time, this document tied Jewish immigration to Palestine's economic capacity "to ensure that the immigrants should not be a burden upon the people of Palestine as a whole, and that they should not deprive any section of the present population of their employment."[87] How scholars have explained this development depends on whether they have perceived it as a change or a continuation of policy. Avi Shlaim, for example, views the Churchill White Paper as the beginning of Britain's withdrawal from Zionism.[88] Likewise, Benny Morris cites the reason for the Churchill White Paper as a change of personality in Downing Street from pro-Zionist Liberal Lloyd George to the ambivalent Conservative Andrew Bonar Law, leading to more balanced language in Britain's dealings with Zionism.[89] The problem with this analysis is that Lloyd George resigned on 22 October 1922, months after the white paper was written and published.[90] Conversely, Gudrun Kramer and James Renton posit that Britain allied itself with Zionism to justify its occupation to the other Great Powers (especially France) at the Supreme Council of the Paris Peace Conference in San Remo.[91] Acting supposedly under the Wilsonian principles of nonannexation and national self-determination, Britain had chosen to justify its rule over Palestine by presenting itself as the protector of Zionism.[92] This is echoed in John McTague's work, which notes that by appointing the first high commissioner to Palestine as Sir Herbert Samuel, a Jew and a Zionist, the British prime minister appeared determined to promote the Balfour Declaration regardless of internal advice to the contrary.[93] In this respect, the white paper was an instrument of governance, imposing a minor limitation that was necessary to maintain the commitment to Zionism.

This seemingly unshakable commitment did, of course, face its first test in the Passfield White Paper of 1930 despite its swift reversal in 1931. Scholars tend to assume that the activities of Zionist lobbyists, such as Chaim Weizmann, placed the British government under immense pressure to recant the Passfield policy and that this was the sole reason for its reversal. Shlomo Ben-Ami, for example, notes that "before it could even come into effect, Passfield's white paper was for all practical purposes abrogated by Chaim Weizmann's skillful lobbying."[94] Similarly, Benny Morris writes, "By early 1931 well-applied Zionist pressure in the press and lobbying by Weizmann in London bore fruit."[95] The same reasoning is found in Yehoshua Porath's work, citing "Zionist pressure" in the reversal of policy, in Ilan Pappe's *A History of Modern Palestine*, Neil Caplan's *Contested Histories*, and many others.[96] Such explanations of British behavior are, however, overwhelmingly anecdotal; little attention has been paid to the evidence, which is rarely supplied. Pederson, for example, notes that "[h]istorians usually and rightly credit Weizmann's remonstrance and effective lobbying for that *volte-face*" and cites Norman Rose's *The Gentile Zionists* to illustrate this point.[97] It is particularly interesting that Rose is credited with this idea as it appears nowhere in his book. Instead, Rose offers an account that highlights parliamentary political infighting and at no point credits Weizmann with a victory.[98]

Rather than Rose's work, which is based heavily on research at the Weizmann Archives, this myth is actually most likely the result of Chaim Weizmann's own account in his autobiography, *Trial and Error*.[99] In what Christopher Sykes agrees is a highly biased account of the negotiations with British politicians, Weizmann paints the British attitude as incompetent and colored by anti-Semitism.[100] Accounts of the white paper's reversal are rarely granted more than a sentence or two in histories of the Mandate or Anglo-Zionist relations, and there seems to have been a widespread acceptance of these largely unfounded assumptions. The idea that Chaim Weizmann successfully lobbied the British government stems from his own personal interpretation of events but is one that has been repeated often without citation or further academic investigation.[101]

A small number of scholars have attempted to provide a more nuanced explanation for this reversal decision, but most analyses remain unsatisfactory. One argument points to a Whitechapel by-election as the reason for Labour's apparent collapse under pressure.[102] Crucially, however, the by-election took place on 3 December 1930, two months before MacDonald wrote to Weizmann. James Hall, the Labour candidate in Whitechapel, won this election after securing support from the British chapter of the international Zionist organization, Poalei Zion. This was despite the Liberal Party candidate actually being Jewish and the fact that every other candidate publicly denounced the white paper.[103] Although Hall did not actively defend the new policy, his election pamphlets and documentation did repeat the official government interpretation of Passfield's white paper, that it was both a continuation of the Mandate and the Churchill White Paper of 1922.[104] It is incongruous, therefore, to explain the government's reversal decision by implying that it was a preventive measure directed toward this by-election; neither the timing, months before MacDonald's letter to Weizmann, nor the campaign, in which the Labour candidate won by tacitly supporting the white paper and still securing Zionist support, demonstrate a plausible causal relationship. This by-election, however, was certainly important in retrospect, and, in relation to the government's correspondence with Chaim Weizmann, this is discussed in greater detail in chapter 3.

Another opinion about this incident points to a letter to *The Times* written by preeminent lawyers Lord Hailsham and Sir John Simon. Taking what amounted to a pro-Zionist stance, the letter demanded an opinion from The Hague on whether limiting Jewish immigration violated the official Mandate for Palestine.[105] The scholarly argument, therefore, cites Prime Minister MacDonald's desire to avoid such scrutiny as the reason for reversing Passfield's white paper.[106] The problem with this reasoning, however, is that Hailsham and Simon specifically focused on criticizing two specific paragraphs of the white paper, neither of which were mentioned in MacDonald's letter to Weizmann. If Hailsham and Simon's criticisms were crucial, then why were their arguments absent from the final reversal? No evidence has been presented to demonstrate that MacDonald viewed interference from The Hague as a credible threat, and, indeed, these accusations leveled at the white paper met only sarcasm and scorn at the Colonial Office (see chap. 3). On its own, the Hailsham and Simon letter provides only a half-formed explanation. The letter was important, but for a different reason: Hailsham and Simon were preeminent lawyers, but, more importantly, they were both also former and future cabinet ministers from the Conservative and Liberal Parties, respectively. Their letter to *The Times* is evidence of a larger campaign to destabilize an already weak Labour government. Unfortunately, this domestic political angle has largely been ignored.

Although both Norman Rose and Gudrun Kramer mention the importance of political infighting within Westminster, their studies are not dedicated to the full reasoning behind Passfield's reversal.[107] Rose, for example, notes that "MacDonald must have been extremely sensitive" to rumors of Zionist activism against his government around the world but chose not to investigate this idea further.[108] Coupled with this collection of unexplored assumptions about the reversal of the Passfield White Paper is a general apathy to the event. Major works such as Gelvin's *One Hundred Years of War* fail to even mention the Passfield White Paper, and other scholars, such as Michael J. Cohen, deliberately avoid it and proceed in the Mandate narrative directly from 1928 to 1936.[109] Asking why the Passfield White Paper was reversed is crucial for understanding how and why British policy evolved during the entire Mandate. The lack of scholarly attention received by this incident is also indicative of how British politicking has been overlooked in the relevant works of history. Comparatively, the final theme has been covered in more detail by Mandate scholars, but again it lacks integration into the broader perspective of how British policy was crafted throughout the period.

The Mandate and the International Community

As the British Mandate for Palestine was a trusteeship of the League of Nations, policy toward it always had to consider the international community. External involvement in Palestine politics, however, was particularly prominent in only two distinct time periods of Britain's thirty-year administration: when (following the Arab Revolt) negotiations led to the MacDonald White Paper of 1939, and when (after World War II) US president Harry Truman involved American politics in Palestine policy.

Although British policy making during the Arab Revolt has received far more attention than earlier incidences, the targeted focus of such studies limits their usefulness. Michael J. Cohen's excellent analysis of the later Mandate, for example, highlights the domestic political constraints placed on the British government in the late 1930s but betrays such a study's truncated scope by implying that earlier decisions were not equally the result of Realpolitik. Cohen writes, "The white paper was the result of diminishing options in the Arab Middle East on the eve of war,"[110] but it also "reflected a dramatic change from prior British policy in the area, in particular from the British attitude towards the Zionists, which previously had been at worst bureaucratically neutral and at best openly sympathetic."[111] In contrast, chapter 3 argues that the deliberations leading up to the MacDonald White Paper were conducted in exactly the same fashion as policy in the 1920s and early 1930s—representing the beginning of Britain's ultimate withdrawal from "the Holy Land."

World War II then created two significant developments with regard to British policy in Palestine. All previous Palestine policy had been relatively secretive—from patronage for Zionism in the 1920s to Arab self-determination in 1939. A new postwar internationalism, however, coupled with the public outcry for Europe's Holocaust survivors meant that the United States and members of the fledgling United Nations (UN) pressured Britain for a real moral, rather than purely strategic, policy in Palestine.[112] The British Mandate hosted two final investigative commissions that demonstrated this new context. First, the Anglo-American Committee of 1946 attempted and failed to repair a rift between British and American administrations on the subject of Palestine. Second, when Britain referred the problem to the UN in 1947, the UN Special Committee on Palestine (UNSCOP) conducted its own investigation.

The US president, Harry Truman, had publicly called for the admission of one hundred thousand Jewish refugees into Palestine, but the prospect presented a peacekeeping nightmare for British authorities. The Anglo-American report then reiterated this demand and concluded that the best solution was a single binational state in which "Palestine shall be neither a Jewish state nor an Arab state."[113] The report, therefore, simply suggested reconciling what throughout the 1920s and 1930s had remained irreconcilable. Unable to solve the conflict, unaided by any practical American suggestions, and under financial and political pressure created by the plummeting postwar economy, the British cabinet approved referring the issue to the UN.[114] The final UNSCOP report constituted both a majority and a minority opinion; whereas the minority suggested a federal state with a permanent but autonomous Jewish minority, the majority preferred partition.[115] If the solution was partition, however, this presented a further question of its enforcement. In keeping with all previous negotiations, the Arabs of Palestine rejected both partition and the minority federal plan, but the UN General Assembly voted for partition on 29 November 1947. Rather than accept the responsibility, the British government decided to withdraw.

This final Palestine policy decision has been characterized in the literature in several ways. Traditional Zionist history asserts that referral to the UN was either a ploy designed to push Palestine's Jews back into British arms once the UN failed to offer a solution or a punishment to allow the invasion of Arab armies who would eradicate the Jewish homeland. Conversely, Arab historiography has viewed British withdrawal as a plot to aid the creation of a single (Jewish) state in Palestine.[116] Alternatively, either the decision has been presented as tactical, meaning Prime Minister Attlee and Foreign Secretary Bevin identified the UN vote as a perfect opportunity to rid the empire of costly Palestine, or British forces were withdrawn out of economic necessity and war wariness.[117] However, investigations of the Westminster bubble during this critical time period are frequently sidelined in favor of discussing Zionist terrorist activities after the war—implying that the bombing of the King David Hotel in Jerusalem in June 1946 or the hanging of two kidnapped sergeants in 1947 provided the final impetus to leave.[118] The commissions are mentioned only to highlight what appeared to be Britain's ineptitude in dealing with the postwar crisis in Palestine.

This apparent "dithering" has led scholars such as Benny Morris and James L. Gelvin to describe referral to the UN as dumping the Palestine issue onto another party.[119] This is not only an unfair characterization of Ernest Bevin's attempts to reach an Arab-Jewish agreement through negotiations but also an oversimplified analysis of British decision-making during this turbulent era. This perception is also part of the literature's constant conflation of Britain's referral to the UN in February 1947 with the decision to withdraw made in September 1947. Confusing the time line obscures any helpful understanding of the British psychology behind policy making at the end of the Mandate and misrepresents the primary motivations driving key members of government. Rather than being merely plot devices or the backdrop to a Zionist insurgency, the final commissions of the Mandate demonstrate Britain's need to achieve a delicate and precarious balance of diplomatic interests. This is discussed in detail in chapter 5.

Thinking Outside the Story

Britain's Palestine policy evolved from staunch support for the Jewish national home after the Balfour Declaration of 1917 to plans for an independent Arab Palestine in 1939 that had to be reassessed following World War II. This gradual reversal of policy coincided with a series of riots and rebellions in Palestine between Arabs and Jews in the 1920s, 1930s, and 1940s and Britain's inability to devise a workable solution to this ongoing tension. The Mandate years witnessed periods of violence, and these are generally used as plot devices in the established literature, highlighting how the British reaction to these crises worsened the burgeoning conflict. These periods of violence and four major themes constitute the dominant Mandate narrative, but it remains incomplete.

Notes

1. Daniel Bar-Tal and Gavriel Salomon, "Israeli-Jewish Narratives of the Israeli-Palestinian Conflict," in *Israeli and Palestinian Narratives of Conflict: History's Double Helix*, ed. Robert I. Rotberg (Bloomington: Indiana University Press, 2006), 19–46, 23; Nurit Peled-Elhanan, *Palestine in Israeli School Books: Ideology and Propaganda in Education* (London: I. B. Tauris, 2012), 4.

2. Bar-Tal and Salomon, "Israeli-Jewish Narratives of the Israeli-Palestinian Conflict," 24–25.

3. Mordechai Bar-On, "Conflicting Narratives or Narratives of a Conflict?" in *Israeli and Palestinian Narratives of Conflict: History's Double Helix*, ed. Robert I. Rotberg (Bloomington: Indiana University Press, 2006), 152–153.

4. Marcy Jane Knopf-Newman, *The Politics of Teaching Palestine to Americans: Pedagogical Strategies* (New York: Palgrave Macmillan, 2011), 9.

5. Knopf-Newman, *Politics of Teaching Palestine to Americans*, 3.

6. Arthur Koestler, *Promise and Fulfilment: Palestine 1917–1949* (London: Macmillan, 1949); Jon Kimche, *Both Sides of the Hill: Britain and the Palestine War* (London: Secker and Warburg, 1960).

7. Zeev Sternhell, *The Founding Myths of Israel: Nationalism, Socialism and the Making of the Jewish State* (Princeton, NJ: Princeton University Press, 1998), 334.

8. Michael Feige, "Introduction: Rethinking Israeli Memory and Identity," *Israel Studies* 7, no. 2 (2002): v–xiv, vii–viii, 8.

9. Ibid.

10. Ibid.

11. Saleh Abdel Jawad, "The Arab and Palestinian Narratives of the 1948 War," in *Israeli and Palestinian Narratives of Conflict: History's Double Helix*, ed. Robert I. Rotberg (Bloomington: Indiana University Press, 2006), 72–114, 74.

12. Jawad, "Arab and Palestinian Narratives of the 1948 War," 75–79.

13. Robert I. Rotberg, ed., "Building Legitimacy through Narrative," in *Israeli and Palestinian Narratives of Conflict: History's Double Helix* (Bloomington: Indiana University Press, 2006), 1–18, 8.

14. Ted Swedenburg, *Memories of Revolt: The 1936–1939 Rebellion and the Palestinian National Past* (Fayetteville: University of Arkansas Press, 2003), 1–2.

15. Jawad, "Arab and Palestinian Narratives of the 1948 War," 89.

16. Bar-On, "Conflicting Narratives or Narratives of a Conflict?" 146; Jawad, "Arab and Palestinian Narratives of the 1948 War," 88.

17. Rotberg, "Building Legitimacy through Narrative," 11.

18. Rashid Khalidi, *The Iron Cage: The Story of the Palestinian Struggle for Statehood* (Oxford: OneWorld, 2007), 105.

19. Nicholas E. Roberts, "Re-Remembering the Mandate: Historiographical Debates and Revisionist History in the Study of British Palestine," *History Compass* 9, no. 3 (2011): 215–230, 219–220.

20. Sami Hadawi, *Palestine: Loss of a Heritage* (San Antonio, TX: Naylor Company, 1963); Sami Hadawi, *Bitter Harvest: A Modern History of Palestine* (Buckhurst Hill: Scorpion Publishing Ltd, 1990); Walid Khalidi, *From Haven to Conquest: Readings in Zionism and the Palestine Problem until 1948* (Washington DC: Institute for Palestine Studies, 1987); Emma Murphy, unpublished manuscript.

21. Murphy, 8.

22. Ibid., 11.

23. Roberts, "Re-Remembering the Mandate"; Zeina B. Ghandour, *A Discourse on Domination in Mandate Palestine* (Oxon: Routledge, 2010).

24. Roberts, "Re-Remembering the Mandate," 215.

25. Ibid.

26. Ilan Pappe, *A History of Modern Palestine: One Land, Two Peoples* (Cambridge: Cambridge University Press, 2006); Avi Shlaim, *Israel and Palestine: Reappraisals, Revisions, Refutations* (London: Verso, 2009); Avi Shlaim, *The Iron Wall: Israel and the Arab World* (London: Penguin Books, 2001); Martin Van Creveld, *The Land of Blood and Honey: The Rise of Modern Israel* (New York: St. Martin's, 2010); Colin Schindler, *A History of Modern Israel* (Cambridge: Cambridge University Press, 2008); Ian Bickerton, *The Israeli-Palestinian Conflict: A History* (London: Reaktion Books, 2009); Gregory Harms, *The Palestine-Israel Conflict: A Basic Introduction* (London: Pluto Books, 2008).

27. Michael J. Cohen, "British Strategy and the Palestine Question 1936–1939," *Journal of Contemporary History* 7, nos. 3–4 (1972): 157–183; Michael J. Cohen, "Secret Diplomacy and Rebellion in Palestine, 1936–1939," *International Journal of Middle East Studies* 8, no. 3 (1977): 379–404; Michael J. Cohen, *Palestine: Retreat from the Mandate—The Making of British Policy, 1936–45* (London: Paul Elek, 1978); Michael J. Cohen, *Palestine to Israel: From Mandate to Independence* (Oxon: Routledge, 1988); William Roger Louis, *The British Empire in the Middle East 1945–51* (Oxford: Clarendon, 1984); William Roger Louis, ed. *The End of the Palestine Mandate* (London: I. B. Tauris, 1986).

28. Shlomo Ben-Ami, *Scars of War, Wounds of Peace: The Israeli-Arab Tragedy* (London: Weidenfeld and Nicolson, 2005), 9.

29. Jonathan Schneer, *The Balfour Declaration: The Origins of the Arab-Israeli Conflict* (London: Bloomsbury, 2010), 28–29.

30. Elie Kedourie, *In the Anglo-Arab Labyrinth: The McMahon-Husayn Correspondence and Its Interpretations, 1914–1939* (Cambridge: Cambridge University Press, 1976), 4.

31. The European empires did not, paradoxically, mean "independence" as though the new Arab state would be sovereign and free from colonial rule. As seen in the Sykes-Picot Agreement, "France and Great Britain are prepared to recognise and protect an independent Arab state" and, in that area, they "shall be allowed to establish such direct or indirect administration or control as they desire and as they may think fit to arrange with the Arab State or Confederation of Arab States." British and French Governments, "The Sykes-Picot Agreement (May 15–16, 1916)," in *The Israeli-Arab Reader*, ed. Walter Laquere and Barry Rubin (New York: Penguin, 2008), 15.

32. Cmd. 5957, 1939, "From Sherif Hussein to Sir Henry McMahon, 14 July 1915," *Miscellaneous No. 3, Correspondence between Sir Henry McMahon G.C.M.G., G.C.V.O., K.C.I.E., C.S.I. His Majesty's High Commissioner at Cairo and the Sherif Hussein of Mecca.*

33. Cmd. 5957, 24 October 1915, 14 December 1915.

34. C. Ernest Dawn, "Elie Kedourie, in the Anglo-Arab Labyrinth," *International Journal of Middle East Studies* 9, no. 1 (1978): 128–130, 128.

35. Noam Levin, Ruth Kark, and Emir Galilee, "Maps and the Settlement of Southern Palestine, 1799–1948: An Historical/GIS analysis," *Journal of Historical Geography* 36, no. 1 (2010): 1–18, 3.

36. Isaiah Friedman, "The McMahon-Hussein Correspondence and the Question of Palestine," *Journal of Contemporary History* 5, no. 2 (1970): 83–122; Kedourie, *In the Anglo-Arab Labyrinth*; Marian Kent, "Asiatic Turkey, 1914–1916," in *British Foreign Policy under Sir Edward Grey*, ed. F. H. Hinsley (Cambridge: Cambridge University Press, 1977); Charles D. Smith, "The Invention of a Tradition: The Question of Arab Acceptance of the Zionist Right to Palestine during World War I," *Journal of Palestine Studies* 22, no. 2 (1993): 48–61; Leonard Stein, *The Balfour Declaration* (London: Valentine Mitchell, 1961); Arnold Toynbee, "The McMahon-Hussein Correspondence: Comments and a Reply," *Journal of Contemporary History* 5, no. 4 (1970): 185–201; Mayir Vereté, "The Balfour Declaration and Its Makers," *Middle Eastern Studies* 6, no. 1 (1970): 48–74.

37. FO 371/2486/34982, 20 October 1915, McMahon to Grey dis. no. 131, secret, the National Archives, Kew (hereafter TNA).; CAB 24/1, 16 December 1915, "Evidence of Lieutenant Colonel Sir Mark Sykes, Bart., M.P., on the Arab Question," TNA.

38. CAB 24/1, 16 December 1915, "Evidence of Lieutenant Colonel Sir Mark Sykes."

39. FO 608/107, n.d., Peace Conference, "French Claims to Syria" memorandum by Sir Arthur Hirtzel, TNA, 2256.

40. CAB 24/1, 16 December 1915, "Evidence of Lieutenant Colonel Sir Mark Sykes."
41. British and French Governments, "The Sykes-Picot Agreement (May 15–16, 1916)," in *The Israeli-Arab Reader*, ed. Walter Laquere and Barry Rubin (New York: Penguin, 2008), 15.
42. British foreign minister Arthur Balfour, "The Balfour Declaration," *The Israeli-Arab Reader*, ed. Walter Laqueur and Barry Rubin (New York: Penguin, 2008), 16.
43. James Renton, "Flawed Foundations: The Balfour Declaration and the Palestine Mandate," in *Britain, Palestine and Empire: The Mandate Years*, ed. Rory Miller (Farnham, UK: Ashgate, 2010), 15–37, 18.
44. CAB 21/77, n.d., Committee of the Imperial War Cabinet on Territorial Desiderata in the Terms of Peace, 1917, TNA.
45. CAB 21/77, Committee of the Imperial War Cabinet on Territorial Desiderata.
46. Vereté, "Balfour Declaration and Its Makers."
47. Geoffrey Lewis, *Balfour and Weizmann: The Zionist, The Zealot and the Emergence of Israel* (London: Continuum, 2009), 110.
48. Isaiah Friedman, *The Question of Palestine 1914–1918* (New York: Schocken Books, 1973), 116.
49. Mark Levene, "The Balfour Declaration: A Case of Mistaken Identity," *English Historical Review* 107, no. 422 (1992): 54–77, 58.
50. CAB 23/4, 31 October 1917, War Cabinet Minutes, TNA.
51. Haim Gerber, *Remembering and Imagining Palestine: Identity and Nationalism from the Crusades to the Present* (Basingstoke, UK: Palgrave Macmillan, 2008), 94; Pappe, *History of Modern Palestine*, 83, 93.
52. Gerber, *Remembering and Imagining Palestine*, 70.
53. Cmd. 1540, 1921, *Palestine. Disturbances in May, 1921. Reports of the Commission of Inquiry with Correspondence Relating Thereto*, 17.
54. Naomi Shepherd, *Ploughing Sand: British Rule in Palestine, 1917–1948* (London: John Murray, 1999), 82.
55. Tom Segev, *One Palestine, Complete: Jews and Arabs under the British Mandate* (London: Abacus, 2000), 140–141.
56. Gerber, *Remembering and Imagining Palestine*, 93.
57. Segev, *One Palestine, Complete*, 289.
58. Ibid., 290.
59. Evyatar Freisel, "Through a Peculiar Lens: Zionism and Palestine in British Diaries, 1927–31," *Middle Eastern Studies* 29, no. 3 (1993): 419–444, 422.
60. Cmd. 3530, 1930, *Report of the Commission on the Palestine Disturbances of August, 1929*, 164.
61. Cmd. 3692, 1930, *Statement of Policy by His Majesty's Government in the United Kingdom*.
62. Renton, "Flawed Foundations," 36.
63. Yitzhak Gil-Har, "British Intelligence and the Role of Jewish Informers in Palestine," *Middle Eastern Studies* 39, no. 1 (2010): 117–149, 120.
64. Avi Shlaim, *The Politics of Partition: King Abdullah, the Zionists, and Palestine 1921–1951* (Oxford: Oxford University Press, 1998), 52.
65. Penny Sinanoglou, "The Peel Commission and Partition, 1936–1938," in *Britain, Palestine and Empire: The Mandate Years*, ed. Rory Miller (Farnham, UK: Ashgate, 2010), 119–140, 140.
66. Cmd. 5479, 1937, *Palestine Royal Commission Report*, 510–511.
67. Cmd. 5479, *Palestine Royal Commission Report*, 512.

68. Ibid., 534.

69. T. G. Fraser, "A Crisis of Leadership: Weizmann and the Zionist Reaction to the Peel Commission's Proposals, 1937–38," *Journal of Contemporary History* 23, no. 4 (1988): 657–680, 671; Christopher Marlowe, *Seat of Pilate: An Account of the Palestine Mandate* (London: Cresset, 1959), 150.

70. Rory Miller, ed., "Introduction," in *Britain, Palestine and Empire: The Mandate Years* (Farnham, UK: Ashgate, 2010), 1–14, 7.

71. Aaron Klieman, "The Divisiveness of Palestine: Foreign Office versus Colonial Office on the Issue of Partition, 1937," *Historical Journal* 22, no. 2 (1979): 423–441, 441.

72. Cmd. 5854, 1937–1938, *Palestine Partition Commission Report*, 14.

73. Porath, *Emergence of the Palestinian Arab National Movement, 1929–1939*, 195.

74. Michael J. Cohen, "Sir Arthur Wauchope, the Army, and the Rebellion in Palestine, 1936," *Middle Eastern Studies* 9, no. 1 (1973): 19–34, 22.

75. Simon Anglim, "Orde Wingate and the Special Night Squads: A Feasible Policy for Counter-terrorism?" *Contemporary Security Policy* 28, no. 1 (2007): 28–41, 29.

76. Jacob Norris, "Repression and Rebellion: Britain's Response to the Arab Revolt in Palestine of 1936–39," *Journal of Imperial and Commonwealth History* 36, no. 1 (2008): 25–45; Matthew Hughes, "From Law and Order to Pacification: Britain's Suppression of the Arab Revolt in Palestine, 1936–1939" *Journal of Palestine Studies* 39, no. 2 (2010): 6–22; Segev, *One Palestine, Complete*.

77. Swedenburg, *Memories of Revolt*, 19.

78. Ibid., 21.

79. Ibid., 13.

80. Ibid., 14.

81. Ibid., 21.

82. Shlaim, *Politics of Partition*, 61.

83. Cmd. 6019, 1938–1939, *Palestine. Statement of Policy*.

84. Cmd. 6019, *Palestine. Statement of Policy*.

85. Segev, *One Palestine, Complete*, 441.

86. Ibid.

87. Cmd. 1700, 1922, *Palestine. Correspondence with the Palestine Arab Delegation and the Zionist Organization*.

88. Shlaim, *Iron Wall*, 10.

89. Benny Morris, *Righteous Victims: A History of the Zionist-Arab Conflict, 1881–1999* (London: John Murray, 2000), 103.

90. Yehoshua Porath, *The Emergence of the Palestinian-Arab National Movement 1918–1929* (London: Frank Cass, 1984), 166.

91. Gudrun Kramer, *A History of Palestine: From the Ottoman Conquest to the Founding of the State of Israel* (Princeton, NJ: Princeton University Press, 2008), 162; Renton, "Flawed Foundations."

92. Renton, "Flawed Foundations," 18.

93. John J. McTague, "The British Military Administration in Palestine 1917–1920," *Journal of Palestine Studies* 7, no. 3 (1978): 55–76, 71.

94. Ben-Ami, *Scars of War, Wounds of Peace*, 9.

95. Morris, *Righteous Victims*, 117.

96. Porath, *Emergence of the Palestinian-Arab National Movement 1918–1929*, 136; Pappe, *History of Modern Palestine*, 93; Neil Caplan, *The Israel-Palestine Conflict: Contested Histories*

(Chichester, UK: Wiley-Blackwell, 2010), 80; Weldon C. Matthews, *Confronting an Empire, Constructing a Nation* (London: I. B. Tauris, 1988), 83; Segev, *One Palestine, Complete*; Roza El-Eini, *Mandated Landscape: British Imperial Rule in Palestine 1929–1945* (New York: Routledge, 2006); Renton, "Flawed Foundations."

97. Susan Pederson, "The Impact of League Oversight on British Policy in Palestine," in *Britain, Palestine and Empire: The Mandate Years*, ed. Rory Miller (Farnham, UK: Ashgate, 2010), 39–66, 52.

98. Norman Rose, *The Gentile Zionists* (London: Frank Cass, 1973), chap. 1.

99. Chaim Weizmann, *Trial and Error: The Autobiography of Chaim Weizmann* (London: Hamish Hamilton, 1949).

100. Christopher Sykes, *Cross Roads to Israel* (London: Collins, 1965), 116; Weizmann, *Trial and Error*, 413.

101. Notable exceptions include Marlowe, *Seat of Pilate*, 124; Rose, *Gentile Zionists*, chap. 1; Kramer, *History of Palestine*, 235.

102. Gabriel Sheffer, "British Colonial Policy-Making towards Palestine (1929–1939)," *Middle Eastern Studies* 14, no. 3 (1978): 307–322.

103. Joseph Gorny, *The British Labour Movement and Zionism 1917–1948* (London: Routledge, 1983).

104. PREM 30/69/366, November 1930, James Hall Election Pamphlet, TNA.

105. Lord Hailsham and John Simon, "British Policy in Palestine," *The Times*, 4 November 1930, 15.

106. Gabriel Sheffer, "Intentions and Results of British Policy in Palestine: Passfield's White Paper," *Middle Eastern Studies* 9, no. 1 (1973): 43–60.

107. Rose, *Gentile Zionists*, chap. 1; Kramer, *History of Palestine*, 235.

108. Rose, *Gentile Zionists*, 17.

109. Cohen, *Palestine to Israel*.

110. Cohen, *Palestine: Retreat from the Mandate*, 87.

111. Ibid.

112. Kermit Roosevelt, "The Partition of Palestine: A Lesson in Pressure Politics," *Middle Eastern Journal* 2, no. 1 (1948): 1–16, 11.

113. Cmd. 6808, 1945–1946, *Report of the Anglo-American Committee of Enquiry Regarding the Problems of European Jewry and Palestine*.

114. Ellen J. Ravndal, "Exit Britain: British Withdrawal from the Palestine Mandate in the Early Cold War 1947–1948," *Diplomacy and Statecraft* 21, no. 3 (2010): 416–433, 419.

115. "United Nations Special Committee on Palestine Report to the General Assembly, Volume 1," Lake Success, New York, 1947, chap. 6, pt. I, 1.

116. Avi Shlaim, "Britain and the Arab-Israeli War of 1948," *Journal of Palestine Studies* 16, no. 4 (1987): 50–76, 51.

117. Mark Tessler, *A History of the Israeli-Palestinian Conflict* (Bloomington: Indiana University Press, 2009), 261; Kate Utting, "The Strategic Information Campaign: Lessons from the British Experience in Palestine 1945–1948," *Contemporary Security Policy* 28, no. 1 (2007): 48–62, 56; Pappe, *History of Modern Palestine*, 120–121.

118. Elizabeth Monroe, *Britain's Moment in the Middle East 1914–1956* (London: Methuen, 1965), 165–166.

119. Benny Morris, *The Birth of the Palestinian Refugee Problem Revisited* (Cambridge, Cambridge University Press, 2004), 12; James L. Gelvin, *The Israel-Palestine Conflict: One Hundred Years of War* (Cambridge: Cambridge University Press, 2005), 124.

2 The Balfour Zeitgeist, 1917–1928

The Balfour Declaration of 1917 became the first in a chain of events committing the British government to a Jewish national home in Palestine. Extended in the draft Mandate for Palestine and confirmed in the Churchill White Paper of 1922, this national home policy continued almost unquestioned until the Palestine riots of 1929 prompted a reassessment. This period, therefore, represented a "Balfour Zeitgeist," but it was a phase of British foreign policy that was not without frustration and confusion regarding its implementation. Rather than drawing a linear time line from 1917 onward, it is vital to recognize that the 1922 decision to confirm the principles of the declaration was highly uncertain. When examining the situation British politicians found themselves in, it also appears that their chosen course of action was somewhat irrational. Between the declaration and its affirmation, two British commissions of inquiry uncovered fundamental and irresolvable flaws in the national home policy, meaning that any rational analysis of its costs versus its benefits would not have recommended continuing.

In order to provide a cogent explanation of this decision, it is necessary to tease out the particular motivations and constraints of Britain's key decision makers at the time. This chapter, therefore, uses the politics-first framework to demonstrate how and why the British government decided to affirm the policy in 1922. It argues that in the first instance, the government rejected alternatives that were too risky politically. This can be seen particularly in the areas of governmental prestige, tussles surrounding bureaucratic politics, the cabinet's considerations of postwar economic decline, and the dangers posed by interparty rivalry. Once any overly politically risky plans had been dropped, the government merely double-checked that remaining policy options satisfied Britain's strategic objectives. Finally, this chapter highlights how the national home policy remained untouched by both Conservative and Labour governments in the 1920s due to a perception of "sunk costs," that is, too many commitments had already been made for anyone to attempt a U-turn. Rather than a Palestine policy based on national interests or one developed specifically for people and problems in the territory under consideration, this chapter reveals a Palestine policy based primarily on the need to satisfy unrelated political concerns.

What Were the Options?

State leaders are expected to judge any potential new policies based on a rational calculation of costs versus benefits.[1] Therefore, in order to explain the British decision to affirm the national home policy in 1922, it is first necessary to acknowledge that several factors make this decision seem irrational. A simple assessment of information available to politicians at the time would have supported ending the national home policy. This is evident from the reports submitted in 1920 and 1921 by two commissions of inquiry. Following the Nebi Musa riots of April 1920, the Palin Commission pinpointed fundamental flaws in the policy of supporting a Jewish national home, and, following the Jaffa riots of May 1921, the Haycraft Commission independently reiterated many of the same concerns.

The first major riots under British rule occurred roughly two-and-a-half years after the Balfour Declaration was first issued, but the Palin Commission found it was "undoubtedly the starting point of the whole trouble."[2] The Arabs of Palestine were struggling to reconcile an Anglo-French Declaration of self-determination with the promise of a Jewish home in Palestine, "giving rise to a sense of betrayal and intense anxiety for their future."[3] The announcement of a Jewish Zionist, Sir Herbert Samuel, as Palestine's first high commissioner was thought to exacerbate the situation.[4] General Edmund Allenby in command in Palestine believed "that appointment of a Jew as first Governor will be highly dangerous."[5] He anticipated that "when news arrives of appointment of Mr. Samuel general movement against Zionism will result, and that we must be prepared for outrages against Jews, murders, raids on Jewish villages, and raids into our territory from East."[6] In contrast, many British and French politicians were concerned about the actions of Zionists rather than Arabs. To reassure the French prime minister, Colonial Secretary Winston Churchill "expatiated on the virtues and experience of Sir Herbert Samuel, and pointed out how evenly he was holding the balance between Arabs and Jews and how effectively he was restraining his own people, as perhaps only a Jewish administrator could."[7]

Although the Palin report pointed toward "provocative" Zionist behavior as an immediate cause of the riots, it highlighted the real doubts underlying Arab animosity; "at the bottom of all is a deep-seated fear of the Jew, both as a possible ruler and as an economic competitor."[8] These anxieties became a familiar theme in all riots during the British Mandate. Also, in blaming Zionists for the disturbances, the commission report could not avoid implicating British support for Zionism in the violence. It asserted that "the Administration was considerably hampered in its policy by the direct interference of the Home Authorities," a thinly veiled criticism of policy emanating from the Foreign Office.[9] Major General Palin and his fellow commissioners warned the British government "[t]hat the situation at present obtaining in Palestine is exceedingly dangerous" and "a very firm hand" was necessary to "hold the scales as between all parties with rigid equality" to avert "a serious catastrophe."[10] However, as Samuel took charge of Palestine from the military administration before the Palin report was complete, he issued a general amnesty and declared the matter closed. On 15 July 1920, and before he had read it, Samuel telegraphed the Foreign Office to advise against publishing the Palin Commission "irrespective of contents."[11] The dangers, fears, and tensions highlighted in the report might have been inconsequential if another riot on a worse scale had not erupted the following year in Jaffa. These disturbances were also the subject of an investigation, headed by the chief justice of Palestine, Sir Thomas Haycraft.

Although the Haycraft Commission did not question the national home as a viable policy, its report reiterated the fundamental tensions between Arabs and Zionists in Palestine. The immediate cause of the Jaffa riots was a clash between Jewish labor demonstrators: Achdut HaAvoda, the powerful majority organization that possessed a permit to conduct a rally, and Miflagat Poalim Sozialistim, an inflammatory and banned group that did not.[12] The labor dispute finished relatively quickly, but police found Arabs smashing windows in Menshieh and "a general hunting of the Jews began."[13] It was recognized immediately that the underlying cause was Arab hostility toward the Jewish national home, and, on 14 May, Samuel announced a temporary prohibition on immigrants landing at the port of Jaffa and began preparations for another commission of inquiry.[14] Haycraft posited that "the Bolshevik demonstration was the spark that set alight the explosive discontent of the Arabs, and precipitated an outbreak which developed into an Arab-Jewish feud."[15] Although appalled by the violence, Haycraft and his fellow commissioners believed that Arab antipathy in Jaffa resulted in part from a perceived Jewish arrogance, since newly arrived young men and women tended to stroll the streets arm in arm in "easy attire," holding up traffic and singing songs. This did not fit with conservative Arab ideas of decorum. Haycraft detected, therefore, "no inherent anti-Semitism in the country, racial or religious."[16]

The report concluded that "the fundamental cause of the Jaffa riots and the subsequent acts of violence was a feeling among the Arabs of discontent with, and hostility to, the Jews, due to political and economic causes, and connected with Jewish immigration."[17] Politically, the main fear was "that the Jews when they had sufficiently increased in numbers would become so highly organised and so well armed as to be able to overcome the Arabs, and rule over and oppress them."[18] Economically, the influx of skilled Jewish laborers and artisans was seen as a threat to Arab livelihoods.[19] The Haycraft Commission provided the British government with another accurate illustration of Arab-Jewish tension in Palestine, but it could not offer a solution without extending beyond its remit and questioning the overarching policy: "Much, we feel might be done to allay the existing hostility between the races if responsible persons on both sides could agree to discuss the questions arising between them in a reasonable spirit, on the basis that the Arabs should accept implicitly the declared policy of the government on the subject of the Jewish national home, and that the Zionist leaders should abandon and repudiate all pretensions that go beyond it."[20] Without suggesting a political change, the commission had no practical advice to offer.

In light of the tensions highlighted by these commission reports, the government in London was presented with three options: continue supporting the creation of a Jewish national home in Palestine—imposing it with the threat or use of force; limiting the national home policy in a manner acceptable to its critics; or repudiating the policy altogether. The general staff articulated these options in practical terms: "(a.) An alteration of policy as regards Jewish immigration; (b.) An increase in the British garrison; or (c.) The acceptance of serious danger to the Jewish population."[21] The cabinet agreed their courses were to "withdraw from their Declaration, refer the Mandate back to the League of Nations, set up an Arab National government and slow down or stop the immigration of Jews: or they could carry out the present policy with greater vigour and encourage the arming of the Jews."[22] Far from a simple continuation of the Balfour Declaration policy, the entire question of Britain retaining Palestine was under review. In June 1921, the new Middle East Department of the Colonial Office advised "it is idle to consider what steps should now be taken [. . .] until we have made up our minds whether we wish to retain the Mandates."[23] As colonial secretary, Winston Churchill found the situation highly troubling, writing how "[b]oth Arabs and Jews are armed and arming, ready to spring at each other's throats."[24]

By August, it was obvious to the cabinet that "peace was impossible on the lines of the Balfour Declaration."[25] The situation required some form of action, not least to protect the British officials administering Palestine. Governor of Jerusalem Sir Ronald Storrs wrote in his diary at the time, "[W]e remain, all of us, in unstable equilibrium until, after two years and a half, somebody can be found to take any decision."[26] However, deliberations leading to an affirmation of the national home policy in 1922 at no point included consideration of either Zionist or Arab interests in Palestine. Concerns about prestige, difficulties created by bureaucratic turf wars, the political ramifications of postwar economic decline, and interparty rivalry truncated the list of solutions to Britain's woes in Palestine, not because they were bad ideas but because they were too risky for the politicians involved.

Concerning International Prestige

The threat to dignity, or the need for prestige, is an inherently dangerous topic for individual politicians and whole governments.[27] In the context of British policy making in the early 1920s, threats to prestige were about Britain's stature within the international community. Although British policy on the Jewish national home was officially made in Westminster, it acquired an international element first as a wartime promise approved by the Triple Entente, then in the draft Mandate assigned to Britain by the principal Allied powers in 1920 (Britain, France, Italy, and Japan with a US representative present), and, finally, in negotiations with the League of Nations and the United States for their definitive approval.[28] These complicating factors meant that, due to concerns for international prestige, the British government could not reverse their commitment to the national home policy.

Palestine's retention by the British Empire was not a foregone conclusion but became more likely after World War I ended. Ultimately, for Britain, the problem of Palestine's trusteeship was less an issue of imperial expansionism and more about avoiding unwelcome intrusions. British military, strategic, and energy interests in Egypt, Arabia, and Mesopotamia made the prospect of a rival power in Palestine immediately following a world war decidedly unattractive. British prime minister Lloyd George and French prime minister Georges Clemenceau agreed in secret that Britain would annex Palestine and oil-rich Mosul in Mesopotamia in exchange for an exclusively French Syria and share of the Mosul oil.[29] Through this bargaining and a pledge of good faith toward the published Balfour Declaration, which facilitated League of Nations approval, the principle of a British Palestine became diplomatically entrenched very early—before British officials had time to appreciate the potential difficulties this entailed.

A further complication was the Treaty of Sèvres with Turkey, signed in August 1920. Article 95 of the Turkish peace treaty reinforced the draft Mandate in committing Britain to supporting a Jewish national home in Palestine.[30] Since the document carried signatures from Britain and the Dominions (including India), France, Italy, Japan, Armenia, Belgium, Greece, Poland, Portugal, Romania, Serbia, Czechoslovakia, and Turkey, the scale of international agreement essentially prevented repudiation of the national home without creating a legal quagmire.[31] The Balfour Declaration had rapidly become the entire public basis of a British Palestine, and the length of negotiations with the French and other powers made it less and less likely that the national home could be reversed without substantial international humiliation, if the necessary agreements from league members could be achieved at all.[32] Churchill noted that the French were feeling the same about Syria and Lebanon as British politicians were about Palestine and Mesopotamia: "utterly sick of pouring out money and men."[33] Both powers, however, had bargained for the new territories through a larger international framework that was nearly impossible to reverse.

By June 1921, the power of this international body to inflict humiliation on the British Empire became readily apparent. There was a "serious risk" that when the Council of the League of Nations next met to vote on the final mandates, they would be rejected on the basis of Italian and American objections.[34] Italy was raising the concerns of the Vatican regarding guardianship of Christian holy places in Palestine, and the US State Department, despite its position outside the league, formally objected to their exclusion from the consultation process.[35] In light of this diplomatic deadlock and the problems Britain was already facing in Palestine, the option to withdraw from the territory altogether was considered.[36] On a diplomatic level, the British government considered taking the opportunity to reject the terms of the national home policy while the entire Mandate was in question by "publicly confessing that they [the terms] are insecurely based and rebuilding them on a firmer foundation."[37] Unfortunately for the policy's opponents, however, the council of the league agreed to postpone a final vote from 1921 to July 1922 rather than create a situation in which all prior negotiations were void. This meant that after June 1921, any modifications to the Mandate would have required separate approval from the Great Powers within the prohibitively short period of one year.[38] American support for the draft Mandate was forthcoming on 3 May 1922—in a joint resolution by the US Congress—but this meant Britain was merely further entrenched in the national home policy.[39]

Between this public American declaration of support and the final league vote on 22 July 1922, the Churchill White Paper was published. It not only confirmed the national home policy but also specifically cited the diplomatic ties preventing its alteration: the "Declaration, reaffirmed by the Conference of the Principle Allied Powers at San Remo and again in the Treaty of Sèvres, is not susceptible of change."[40] By incorporating the language of the Balfour Declaration into the Mandate and Treaty of Sèvres, Britain had officially recognized a legal obligation to serve two masters. Governor of Jerusalem Sir Ronald Storrs, for example, referred to the highly unsteady first civilian administration in Palestine as "making a bicycle and riding it at the same time."[41] Ultimately, the legal and diplomatic quagmire associated with reversing the Balfour Declaration meant this option presented far too great a risk to Britain's international standing, for which the government would be held responsible. This situation was reinforced by the difficulties inherent in bureaucratic turf wars over Britain's newly acquired territories in the Middle East.

Turf Wars in Whitehall

This time period also witnessed a turf war erupt between the Foreign and Colonial Offices over the Middle East, the product of earlier and lingering tensions between the Foreign and War Offices as well as the Foreign Office and 10 Downing Street. This created an atmosphere within government that increased the political pain expected from any potential abandonment of the Jewish national home policy.

Immediately after World War I, responsibility for Palestine was divided between two cabinet offices. The War Office administered the Occupied Enemy Territories Administration (OETA) in Palestine following the invasion in December 1917. The organization acted under a chief administrator taking his orders from the commander-in-chief (General Allenby) through the general officer commanding.[42] While the War Office was responsible for executing policy, it acted on instructions from the Foreign Office, which received intelligence on the OETA directly from a chief political officer stationed in Palestine.[43] Colonel Meinertzhagen was the last to serve in this awkward position and wrote, "[S]uch work is tantamount to that of a spy on Allenby's staff."[44] When the military administration gave way to the civilian high commissioner Sir Herbert Samuel in July 1920, Samuel also began his tenure under direction from the Foreign Office.[45] This monopoly on Palestine policy, however, was challenged directly by the formation of a new Middle East Department in the Colonial Office. Lord Curzon was foreign secretary at the time, and his specific expertise was Eastern affairs. This, coupled with simmering rivalry between Lord Curzon and Prime Minister David Lloyd George in the search for a postwar peace settlement in Europe, made the Middle East even more important to the "essence" of the Foreign Office at this time and contributed to a propensity to fight for the Middle East as its "turf."[46]

Between the resignation of Arthur James Balfour as foreign secretary in 1919 and Lloyd George's downfall in October 1922, there was tension between the Foreign Office and the Office of the prime minister over European peace negotiations. Lord Curzon inherited a weakened Foreign Office, partly as a result of wartime conditions but also due to Balfour's apparent tendency to concede control over Foreign Policy relatively easily.[47] Rather than using the traditional Foreign Office channels, Lloyd George dominated postwar foreign affairs through presidential-style summit diplomacy, keeping close control of the agenda and minutes, and leading War Secretary Winston Churchill to complain that the record bore little resemblance to his memory of discussions.[48] The lack of information coming out of the Paris Peace talks, for example, was a matter of great contention at the Foreign Office. They complained that "we rarely receive, except occasionally through private channels on which it is not often easy to take prompt action, any official intimation of the decisions reached by the Councils of four or five."[49] This personal and semisecret style of diplomacy caused a certain amount of antagonism within the British government at large, leading Conservative statesman Andrew Bonar Law to promise specifically in his 1922 election address that all future international conferences would be handled by the Foreign Office and not by him personally.[50] This came too late, however, to have any effect on relations between the Foreign and Colonial Offices over Palestine policy.

Between December 1920 and the Churchill White Paper of 1922, there was a turf war between the Foreign and Colonial Offices over control of the Middle

East. As early as February 1918, Lord Curzon had suggested a new department for Middle East affairs, but he had always intended it to be an entirely independent new ministry or part of the Foreign Office.[51] Although the initial universal desire was for an entirely new ministry, it was prohibitively costly.[52] Players with a stake in foreign affairs subsequently lined up in support behind either a new department in the Foreign Office under Lord Curzon or one in the Colonial Office under the next colonial secretary, Winston Churchill. India Secretary Sir Edwin Montagu removed his ministry from consideration because "India expected her Secretary of State to mind her own affairs, [and] it was derogatory to her dignity to be treated as a part-time job."[53] What ensued was an argument regarding expertise. Curzon wrote to the cabinet that "Mr. Churchill prefers the Colonial Office, but I think must be very imperfectly acquainted with the views or interests of the States of the Middle East, if he thinks that such a transference [. . .] would lead to an immediate solution of the difficulties by which we are confronted."[54] Rather than highlight problems of correct administration, Curzon tried to paint Palestine as a diplomatic issue, irremovably connected to "the jealous and complex interests of foreign Powers arising out of their ecclesiastical pretensions, their commercial interests, and their acute rivalry," reiterating claims to the region as part of Foreign Office "turf."[55] If the new department for the Middle East was not installed in the Foreign Office, Curzon concluded, "it would merely mean that the work would have to be done twice over, and that there would be general confusion."[56]

However, on 31 December 1920, the new department was, by a majority vote, assigned to the Colonial Office.[57] This appears chiefly to have been the result of bullying from Churchill. A revolt had broken out in the Iraqi region of Mosul in May, and Churchill issued the cabinet an ultimatum requiring either withdrawal to Basra and ignoring the chaos in the rest of Iraq—"a grave political blunder"—or giving the Colonial Office a new department for the Middle East with the political authority needed to restore order in the two mandates of Palestine and Mesopotamia.[58]

This meant, however, that true to Lord Curzon's predictions, since the Foreign Office could not realistically stop being a player in the Middle East, the two departments vied for control during the diplomatic wrangling described above and the parliamentary infighting demonstrated below. As is liable to happen in turf wars, this created a situation inimical to decisive change.[59] Even after the final division of responsibilities was in place, Churchill continued to agitate for complete control within the Colonial Office: "The more I study the Middle Eastern problem," he wrote to Lloyd George, "the more convinced I am that it is impossible to deal with it unless the conduct of British affairs in the whole of the Arabian peninsula is vested in the Middle Eastern Department [. . .]. I must have control of everything in the ringed fence."[60] Churchill was convinced that the split had produced nothing but "paralysis and confusion of action."[61] This was because "Feisal or Abdullah, whether in Mesopotamia or Mecca; King Hussein at Mecca; Bin Saud at Nejd; Bin Rashid al Hail' the Sheikh of Kuwait; and King Samuel at Jerusalem are all inextricably interwoven, and no conceivable policy can have any chance which does not pull all the strings affecting them."[62]

The issue was not differing opinions between departments on the moral or practical value of the Jewish national home—the Palin and Haycraft Commissions both demonstrated the grave problems inherent in the Balfour Declaration. Instead, the bureaucratic turf struggles of the Foreign and Colonial Offices meant there were too many cooks peering over the roiling Palestine broth. The prospect of further frustration and disagreement simply predisposed those ministries to ignore large or sweeping potential solutions.

Cuts and Commitments

The economy may seem more like an objective part of assessing the national interest than a strictly political issue, but, in times of hardship, perceptions of the economy become deeply political. The postwar coalition under Lloyd George was faced with the major task of reconstruction. As a prolonged economic crisis hit Britain by 1920–1921, the government was under pressure to spend less abroad and more at home. One of the most expensive elements of Britain's empire was the number of troops needed to maintain it. This meant that postwar economic decline strongly impacted deliberations about the Jewish national home in Palestine. Imposing the threat or use of force on it—that is, stationing troops in sufficient numbers to protect a very small Jewish minority from the Arab majority—presented far too much risk to the politicians who would be held responsible for that spending.

In December 1918, the coalition manifesto emphasized economic development, cutting the war debt and making "the inevitable reductions in our military and naval establishments with the least possible suffering to individuals and to the best advantage of industry and trade."[63] However, the severe contraction of markets during the war (including the loss of Britain's largest trading partner, Germany) meant Britain slid quickly into its first globalized economic crisis. An industrial recession struck in May 1920, and Britain was facing a high unemployment problem by the end of the year. More than two million were out of work in December 1921, and the average unemployment rate stayed over 10 percent for several years, higher than anything recorded before the war.[64] These economic problems also brought large-scale industrial action. A "triple alliance" of workers from the mining, railway, and transport industries provided continual unrest.[65] As well as the demonstrations, marches, and occasional violence of British workers, the government was also trying to deal with complaints from big business and institutions such as the Bank of England, all clamoring for cuts.[66] However, a complicating factor was Britain's victory in 1918, placing it at the center of imperial authority and a communal responsibility for world governance as part of the Supreme Allied Council and then the League of Nations. This meant a continual commitment to deploy troops in border regions of Germany as well as vast and diverse new sections of the empire in Africa, which conflicted with the election priority of reduced military spending.

In terms of the Middle East, this conflict between maintaining an empire and satisfying the domestic need for economies was embodied by Winston Churchill's time at the War and Colonial Offices. Churchill pushed the new Middle East Department "towards a curtailment of our responsibilities and our expenditure."[67] Before the new department was assigned to the Colonial Office, Churchill complained bitterly about the waste created by the War Office, which followed instructions from the Foreign Office in the Middle East.[68] He charged that the result was villages "inhabited by a few hundred half naked native families, usually starving," being occupied by "garrisons on a scale which in India would maintain order in wealthy provinces of millions of people" and that this waste would continue "as long as the department calling the tune has no responsibility for paying the piper."[69] Churchill was only prepared to invest in fertile territories, such as East and West Africa, where development could contribute rapidly to British coffers.[70] For the Middle East, he recommended placing responsibility for maintaining order on the air force; this would be much cheaper than army garrisons or cavalry because it required only a few airstrips with no earthbound lines of communication or animals.[71]

This focus on spending cuts meant considerations of cost came before the safety of Britain's Zionist subjects in Palestine. Chief of the imperial general staff Henry Wilson called the cabinet's attention to the weakness of British garrisons in the Middle East in May 1920. This was due to the delay in a peace settlement with Turkey, the inability to enforce its terms, French problems with Turks and Arabs in Cilicia—"disasters which have obliged the French government to reinforce that theatre up to 48 battalions (reinforcements which are not sufficient to avoid still further disasters)"—and "the very unsettled interior condition of both Palestine and Egypt."[72] The general staff feared the boundaries of economy would leave them unable to fulfill imperial policy. They pointed to a "real danger" and how the government's pro-Zionist stance was "likely to increase our difficulties with the Arabs, and there are already indications that military action may be necessary, both to maintain the frontier and concurrently to preserve peace internally."[73]

These warnings were issued one month after the Nebi Musa riots in Palestine, but Churchill made no reference to either the army's advice or the violent outburst in Jerusalem in policy discussions regarding the Middle East or Palestine specifically. The issue of cost became important even before the draft Mandate was complete. Lloyd George believed "that the raising of money for the development of Palestine is a most important matter and that the government should do all it reasonably can to facilitate this."[74] As a result, Foreign Secretary Curzon was advised to "have a talk with the representatives of the Zionist Organization and find out whether it is possible to meet some of their views without modifying the principles upon which the Mandate it based."[75] This was because the bulk of financing for development of the Jewish national home was expected to come from Zionist fund-raising, easing the future burden on the British Treasury.

On 26 January 1921, Churchill called for the further reduction of troops in Palestine, which the general staff advised were too low in number and invited rebellion.[76] The Jaffa riots broke out three months later. Nevertheless, despite assuming responsibility for Palestine first in the War Office and then in the Colonial Office, the only relevant issue to Churchill remained spending cuts. A means to this end was a series of Middle East conferences where various regional leaders and officials could be summoned to "effect economies in the Middle East."[77] This was a source of frustration to Zionist supporters who wanted active British involvement in building the national home. Colonel Meinertzhagen, for example—a professed Zionist advocate who worked in both the OETA and the Middle East Department—declared, "Winston does not care two pins, and does not want to be bothered about it. He is reconciled to a policy of drift. He is too wrapped up in home politics."[78]

Even the people seconded to Cairo for the conferences demonstrated Churchill's priorities. Rather than Arabists or policy experts, the guests from London were chief of the air staff Sir Hugh Trenchard, director of military operations Major General Radcliffe, J. B. Crosland from the Finance Department of the War Office, and Sir George Barstow of the Treasury.[79] The word *Zionism* was left off the conference agenda; that it was discussed at all is only implied by two minutes: "Policy in Palestine under the Mandate" and "Special Subjects."[80] Churchill did travel to Palestine and consulted with both Arabs and Jews, but he merely urged them to get along for the benefit of all.[81] Once back in Parliament, he even dismissed their complaints with derision: "The Arabs believe that in the next few years they are going to be swamped by scores of thousands of immigrants from Central Europe, who will push them off the land, eat up the scanty substance of the country and eventually gain absolute control of its institutions and destinies. As a matter of fact, these fears are illusory."[82]

This was not a political discussion that could result in reduced expenditure. Instead, the colonial secretary focused his Palestine discussions on Transjordan.[83] In order to save money, the sharifian Prince Abdullah would administer Transjordan with British advisers and a small contingent of troops, refrain from attacking French Syria, and prevent cross-border raids; in return, the British would cut Zionism off at the Jordan River, thereby sparing them the soldiers and administrators needed to extend it.[84] This also allowed Churchill to plausibly claim that he was honoring the Hussein-McMahon correspondence.

The Jaffa riots themselves did not alter Churchill's position on this issue of cost. General Walter Norris Congreve submitted a memo to the Colonial Office in June 1921 entitled "Situation in Palestine"; it said Palestine was in "increasing danger" that would require "heavy expenditure" and meet "bitter resentment" from Zionists "for not protecting them better."[85] "I do not think," Congreve concluded, "things are going to get better in this part of the world, but rather worse."[86] Churchill circulated this memo to the cabinet but only to highlight how he disagreed with it. This was one month after the Jaffa riots, but neither the unrest nor advice from local officials appeared in policy discussions on cuts.[87]

Indeed, despite troop reductions, Churchill still saw Palestine as too expensive. When a danger arose in the summer of 1921 that the League of Nations would refuse Britain her mandates, Churchill suggested complete withdrawal on the basis that "His Majesty's Government have spent over one hundred million pounds in Palestine and Mesopotamia since the armistice."[88] Churchill even suggested to Lloyd George, believing he would agree, that Britain should offer "to hand over to the charge of the U.S. either or both of the Middle Eastern Mandates we now hold, if they should desire to assume them."[89] The colonial secretary advocated this course of action in cabinet where, to everyone's surprise, Balfour supported the idea, noting that it "ought to be very seriously examined."[90] Cutting costs in Palestine became one of the colonial secretary's favorite topics: "But whatever may be done about it," Churchill wrote, "the fact remains that Palestine simply cannot afford to pay for troops on the War Office scale."[91]

Instead, the colonial secretary recommended getting rid of British troops altogether and relying instead on police, Indian troops, "and lastly upon arming the Jewish colonies for their own protection."[92] Churchill's enterprise in economy was so comprehensive that even the infamous Geddes Committee on National Expenditure, which called for huge sweeping cuts across Whitehall's already nervous departments, confessed that while it found "very heavy expenditure" in Palestine, Egypt, and Constantinople, there was little more Palestine could afford to give up.[93] Geddes recognized the problem characterized by "the maintenance of internal order in a comparatively small country, and [how] the difficulties which have arisen are due to the attitude of the Arab population toward the Zionist policy adopted by the Government."[94] While many secretaries of state called the Geddes "axe" irresponsible, it perfectly complemented Churchill's own thinking within the Colonial Office.

As war and then colonial secretary, Winston Churchill's singular drive to reduce spending reflected the political situation faced by the entire coalition government. The expense associated with troops meant Palestine could not receive the necessary reinforcements to protect the Zionist experiment from violence. In a time of widespread industrial action, high unemployment, and general economic downturn, the political cost was too high and this option was simply too risky. In this sense, considerations of the economy were closely connected to problems associated with interparty politics.

Conservative Complaints

One of the most important aspects of Britain's early Palestine policy was its relationship with interparty politics. Criticisms coming mainly from the Conservative Party were highly problematic. The "coupon" election of December 1918 left the Liberal David Lloyd George as prime minister at the head of a majority Conservative coalition. Dissension with his leadership grew steadily, and virulent parliamentary criticism of the government's Palestine policy meant the coalition was unable to continue the national home as it stood in the Balfour Declaration and draft Mandate (which included a commitment to put it into effect).[95] Some element of the policy, therefore, absolutely had to change.

The coupon election of December 1918 was a means of extending Lloyd George's prime ministerial tenure. After he ousted the fellow Liberal Herbert Henry Asquith, in 1916, Lloyd George relied heavily on Conservative support. The *coupon*, a derogatory term employed by Asquith, was a letter of endorsement signed by the prime minister and the Conservative leader Bonar Law, recognizing its recipient as the official coalition candidate in his constituency.[96] Owing to the immediate postwar popularity of the prime minister and the significant expansion of voting rights in 1918, the coupon was a powerful tool. The majority of recipients were Conservatives (364 as opposed to 159 Liberals), which reflected the reality of the Liberal Party as a spent force.[97] As the postwar political climate was marked by a significant swing to the right—the main issues were the fate of Germany and the kaiser, with many calling for his trial and execution along with the expulsion of Germans from Britain—the atmosphere among the electorate favored a Conservative victory. Liberal leader Asquith lost his seat to an "uncouponed" Conservative, and the Conservative Party even swept the vote in the traditional Liberal stronghold of Manchester.[98] This climate placed a great deal of right-wing pressure on Lloyd George at the head of his coalition cabinet.

After violence erupted in Palestine in 1920 and 1921, the government's handling of Zionism became one of several key issues for which to criticize Lloyd George. Although there had been a substantial amount of backbench support for the Balfour Declaration in 1917, this had merely reflected a need for wartime coalition solidarity that was hardly necessary by 1920.[99] The idea of costs versus benefits was a recurring political theme, and Conservative MPs Sir Frederick Hall, Sir Harry Brittain, and Sir Henry Page-Croft raised the issue in July 1920 and again in December that "an enormous amount of money has been expended in this direction for which we are not getting any return."[100] Opposition to the national home then began in earnest in March 1921 (with Sir Joynson-Hicks calling for publication of the Palin Commission) and continued in the House of Lords following the Jaffa riots.[101]

Complaints included the unlimited nature of Zionist immigration and how this led to Bolshevik infiltration, with the Conservative MP Joynson-Hicks highlighting how advice to "be very careful about introducing the right class of immigrants, and about not introducing too many at a time" had been "totally disregarded."[102] The issue of native rights was also brought up in both Houses in defense of Palestinian Arabs. Conservative peer Lord Lamington, for example, defended British control of Palestine while criticizing the Zionist element: "[W]hilst it might be quite possible to give to a child a spoonful of jam containing a lot of noxious medicines, the child would not be pleased with the jam in that condition. That is practically an analogy in regard to this Mandate as held by us."[103]

The main interparty dispute, however, remained costs. On 8 June, Joynson-Hicks had raised the point that "[b]efore we occupied this little country there was harmony, and the Turks only kept 400 regular troops in Palestine. We appear now to require at least 8,000, for whom this country has to pay."[104] This was a prevalent theme; Sir Esmond Harmsworth added, "The Jews are a very wealthy class, and should pay for their own national home if they want it [. . .]. As representing a portion of the British taxpayers, I do protest most strongly that any money of theirs should be thrown away in Palestine."[105] In response, Colonial Secretary Churchill advised, "While the situation still fills us with a certain amount of anxiety [. . .] I believe it is one that we shall be able to shape [. . .] within the limits of the expense I have mentioned."[106] Later that month, he advised the cabinet to withdraw from Palestine.[107] This was because the Liberal Churchill and the rest of the coalition were beginning to feel a great deal of pressure on the Palestine issue. The criticisms they faced were potent because they reflected political issues masquerading as practical concerns, and these fell largely under the Conservative banner of "Anti-Waste."

The coalition government tried to downplay interparty differences, so many policy debates raged in the press instead.[108] An overwhelming majority of the 1918-enfranchised population (79.1%) had never voted before and were clamoring for information about politics. This enhanced the role of newspapers, especially with regard to foreign affairs, for which the press was one of very few public sources of information.[109] Consequently, the press outlets that were highly critical of the Lloyd George government were also quite powerful. This was demonstrated by the Anti-Waste League, a campaign led by Conservative peer and press baron Lord Rothermere and championed in the House by his son, the above-mentioned MP Esmond Harmsworth. Using an ax as its symbol to represent spending cuts, it was credited with winning two by-elections in Conservative seats.[110] One sign that Lloyd George felt under pressure from this movement was the formation of the Committee on National Expenditure under the chairmanship of Conservative politician and businessman Sir Eric Campbell Geddes, which, as expected, called for major spending reductions across most departments.[111] Rothermere's brother, Lord Northcliffe, was also using his papers *The Times*, the *Daily Mail*, and the *Daily Mirror* to criticize Palestine based on its cost as well as the idea that handing Muslim holy sites to Jews would inflame India. Northcliffe's death in 1922 meant these papers passed to Rothermere and they too became direct proponents of Anti-Waste.

In the same period, previously supportive Lord Beaverbrook also abandoned Lloyd George and used his *Daily Express* and *Sunday Express* to propagate the myth of a Jewish conspiracy and to claim British politicians were being manipulated by Chaim Weizmann and other "mystery men"; also included in this press revolt were *The Spectator* and the *Morning Post*, which questioned the loyalty of Jewish Liberal politicians such as Palestine high commissioner Sir Herbert Samuel and India secretary Sir Edwin Montagu.[112] This was particularly unsound since Montagu had been one of few politicians adamantly opposed to the Balfour Declaration in 1917, arguing that it placed the status of Jews around the world in jeopardy.[113] However, it would be a mistake to view these anti-Semitic attacks outside their political context. Montagu was a target principally because he opposed the Anti-Waste League and Geddes's spending cuts.[114] The sheer virulence of such press attacks made many members of the coalition cabinet nervous. In an exchange with Samuel in February 1922, Churchill fought with Samuel over the responsibility to fund the Palestine gendarmerie. Due to the "growing movement of hostility, against Zionist policy in Palestine" Churchill as colonial secretary struggled to afford the new expense politically rather than financially.[115]

Opposition to the national home continued to grow, and there was a major debate in the Commons on 9 March 1922.[116] Churchill requested extra funds for salaries and expenses (including the gendarmerie) in the Middle East and was careful to stress that Palestine had been quiet and immigration was more closely monitored, since "[w]e cannot have a country inundated by Bolshevist riffraff."[117] He was met again with accusations of cost versus benefit in Palestine. Unionist MP Sir J. D. Rees asked "whether the Palestine Mandate is absolutely irrevocable, because the advantages to us I for one cannot see, and it seems to me a deplorable thing that we should be keeping down the Arabs in their own country at a large expense to our own country."[118] The Conservative MP Frederick Macquistan added, "[T]o the question of Palestine, I must say that that is a great mystery to the average Briton, especially if he is unemployed and sees good money going for the benefit of people who he always thought knew far more about money than he did."[119] The same points were being raised time and again. This discussion, however, was only the precursor to a more controversial debate in the House of Lords in June.

Lord Islington introduced a motion against the Palestine Mandate on the basis that the national home policy broke promises made to the Arabs and "unless it is very materially modified, it will lead to very serious consequences. It is literally inviting subsequent catastrophe."[120] To the government's chagrin, Islington's motion carried by 60 votes to 29.[121] This had symbolic more than legal importance and was followed by a Commons debate less than two weeks later. Joynson-Hicks called for a motion to decrease the colonial secretary's salary as a procedural ploy to introduce a vote on Palestine, on the basis that the Mandate had never been referred to the House for approval.[122] It had the opposite outcome to the one Joynson-Hicks intended. Churchill secured a vote of confidence 292 to 35.[123] Crucially, one vital document had been published on 1 July 1922, between the two debates, and this was the Churchill White Paper.[124]

In publishing the white paper with records of communication between the colonial secretary and Arab as well as Zionist leaders, the government was addressing domestic political challenges rather than the tangible problems of governing Palestine under a dual obligation. The Churchill White Paper answered accusations that Britain was depriving Palestine's Arabs of their own home: "Unauthorized statements have been made to the effect that the purpose in view is to create a wholly Jewish Palestine. [. . .] His Majesty's Government regard any such expectation as impracticable and have no such aim in view."[125] To demonstrate this, the white paper formally linked immigration to the Palestine economy, following the example set by Samuel immediately after the Jaffa riots.[126] It also addressed the charge of broken promises: "The whole of Palestine west of the Jordan was [. . .] excluded from Sir Henry McMahon's pledge."[127] Answering allegations that the national home would inflame Indian opinion, the white paper highlighted how "the present administration has transferred to a Supreme Council elected by the Moslem community of Palestine the entire control of Moslem Religious endowments (Waqfs), and of the Moslem religious Courts."[128] Against lingering claims of Bolshevist infiltration—as described in the Haycraft Commission—the document stressed that "[i]t is necessary also to ensure that persons who are politically undesirable be excluded from Palestine."[129] Lord Islington had declared in June that the national home policy could not continue unaltered, and he was correct. Under the pressure of interparty politics played out in Parliament and in the press (see fig. 2.1), the coalition was forced to reevaluate a national home policy based solely on the Balfour Declaration.

Fig. 2.1. A parody election poster, published in *The Star* on 15 November 1922, making fun of Britain's asinine coalition politics. © David Low / Solo Syndication.

Satisfying the War Office

After the government rejected potential policies that came with insufferable political risk, only one alternative remained. The British government could neither entirely support nor repudiate the national home, leaving only the possibility of continuing but imposing limitations designed to address the policy's administrative weaknesses and political critics. The government literally had no other choice. All that was left was to double-check that this last available course of action was acceptable more broadly across British national interests.[130] In the case of postwar Palestine, decision makers were preoccupied with a single requirement, that the ongoing presence in Palestine would be strategically sound. Palestine was debatable as a military asset, but any policy had to satisfy British military and strategic interests in the region as a whole. Rather than maximizing benefits, this was about preventing costs.

During and after World War I, the British cabinet frequently considered the prospect of another similar conflict. Safeguarding routes to India, including lines of communication through Egypt and the Suez Canal, was paramount. These lines of communication became even more important after the war because Britain's empire had grown in Asia and Africa as well as the Middle East. These new holdings included former German territories (Tanganyika, South-West Africa, New Guinea, and Samoa); Turkish territories (Palestine, Transjordan, and Mesopotamia including Mosul); and the requirement to station British troops in Persia and in Constantinople to defend the Dardanelles Straits. There was also a need to increase troop numbers in Egypt to combat the rise of a powerful national movement in 1919 and in India to protect borders from the emerging Soviet Union as well as to battle insurgency.[131] However, the importance of Palestine in this geopolitical worldview was a matter of opinion.

In June 1918, Lloyd George asserted that "if we were to be thrown back as an Empire upon our old traditional policy of utilising the command of the sea in order to cut off our enemies from all the sources of supply and from all possible means of expansion, north, east, south, and west, Palestine would be invaluable."[132] It "secured the defence of Egypt" and losing Palestine "would not only involve the interruption of a main artery of our imperial communications, but would react upon our whole situation in the East, and even in India."[133] Immediately postwar, in December 1918, the army agreed with maintaining Palestine as a buffer state, but only "so long as it can be created without disturbing Mohammedan sentiment."[134]

As British policy of a Jewish national home did indeed inflame Arab and Muslim opinion, the army and key members of the cabinet began to express doubts regarding its military value. By November 1920, chief of the imperial general staff advised the cabinet that Palestine "has no strategical interest for the

British Army" but it "constitutes a serious potential drain on its resources."[135] Winston Churchill retained the post of war secretary at this time, and he agreed: "So far as the security of the Empire is concerned, we are the weaker, rather than the stronger, by the occupation of Palestine."[136] His successor at the War Office, Sir Worthington Laming Worthington-Evans, espoused the opposing view, that uprisings in Egypt and Mosul increased Palestine's importance, and the debate continued in Parliament into 1923.[137] Even those such as Churchill, who openly questioned Palestine's strategic value in private, publicly supported the "buffer state" line of reasoning. It provided a simple and convenient explanation for British entanglement in Palestine. Both sides of this debate, however, understood that Palestine could not be allowed to fall to a rival power. The tiny country was not necessarily crucial to British strategic defense of the empire, but a foreign obstruction there could be devastating.[138]

Therefore, as long as Palestine remained in friendly hands, the military planners were placated. The only politically viable option was to continue with the national home policy by imposing limitations on it. This alternative left Palestine in British possession, which was acceptable to its imperial strategists.

In Too Deep?

The years 1920–1922 were crucial in bringing about the confirmation of the national home policy in the Churchill White Paper, but the Balfour Zeitgeist continued throughout most of the 1920s despite a rapid turnover of British governments during this time. This continuing commitment was the result of sunk costs. The recognized phenomenon of sunk costs refers to an escalation of commitment that is not rational (because governments weighing the expected costs versus benefits associated with any course of action should not take into account resources that have already been spent).[139] On a personal level, this behavior is common. It would include activities such as continuing in a deeply unfulfilling career simply because of the time and money already spent on it. On a governmental level, just this kind of "irrational" process occurred under a new Conservative administration in 1923, under a Labour government in 1924, and again in 1926 under Conservative direction.

Four months after the Churchill White Paper was published, Prime Minister Lloyd George suffered a political mutiny that led to a general election in November 1922. For those Conservative backbenchers who had vigorously campaigned against the Middle East mandates, it was an opportunity to exert influence in favor of withdrawal. However, as the Anti-Waste League and parliamentary condemnations of the coalition government's Middle East policies had largely been directed politically at Lloyd George, the issue did not maintain its potency once he had left Downing Street. Press baron Lord Beaverbrook told the Conservative

Leader Bonar Law he would be using his newspapers to pressure Conservative candidates, urging the tax-paying public to ask who was in favor of leaving Palestine and Mesopotamia. The World Zionist Organization monitored this "bag and baggage" campaign carefully, but they found that a mere twenty-six candidates supported it (and, out of those, only seventeen were elected).[140]

Bonar Law privately wrote to Foreign Secretary Curzon referring to the Palestine Mandate and saying, "you know how keen I am to get rid of it," but at an election address in London, he declared he would "not be stampeded on the issue by Beaverbrook and Rothermere."[141] During the campaign, prominent Conservative politicians Leopold Amery and Austen and Neville Chamberlain expressed a desire to continue the national home pledge, as did former war secretary Worthington-Evans, former Chancellor Sir Robert Horne, and twenty-seven Conservative MPs.[142] Despite the fear and intimidation that anti-Zionist Conservatives in the Anti-Waste League had previously inspired, Lloyd George's departure left them largely neutralized.

However, the Conservative victory in 1922 led many Arab politicians to believe the policy would be overturned.[143] The immediate result was the return—after unsuccessful negotiations with the Colonial Office under Winston Churchill—of an Arab Delegation to London in January 1923.[144] Although the new colonial secretary, the duke of Devonshire, received them and insisted there would be no departure from the white paper policy, the cabinet fully expected a new lobbying campaign.[145] In February 1923, the Middle East Department submitted a memo to the cabinet explaining to the new government how "[w]e are, in fact, committed to the Zionist policy before the whole world in the clearest and most unequivocal fashion" and stressing how repudiation of the Balfour Declaration meant returning the Mandate to the League of Nations and evacuating Palestine immediately.[146] On 27 March, Lord Islington revived the opposing argument by introducing a motion in the House of Lords to change Palestine's constitution on the basis that Arabs had boycotted the vote.[147] The motion failed, but when Conservative prime minister Bonar Law resigned in May 1923 and was succeeded by Stanley Baldwin, the new prime minister dealt with the Palestine uncertainty by calling for another committee to report on policy.[148]

This committee, however, was a political exercise and not a comprehensive review of policy. Members were under pressure from supporters of the Palestine Arab Delegation—whose memorandum to the British government secured the signatures of more than one hundred Conservative MPs including 40 percent of backbenchers—but this anti-Zionism posed no political danger to any member of the committee, which consisted of secretaries of state and ministers previously associated with both sides of the Palestine argument.[149] These included Devonshire, Curzon, Amery, Worthington-Evans, and Joynson-Hicks.[150] Despite the wide swath of views this group had expressed as individuals at an earlier date, they heard evidence only from High Commissioner Sir Herbert Samuel.[151] Predictably, no member seriously considered reversing the national home policy because it possessed "a cumulative weight from which it is well-nigh impossible for any government to extricate itself without a substantial sacrifice of consistency and self-respect, if not of honour. Those of us who have disliked the policy are not prepared to make that sacrifice."[152] They decided it was no longer pertinent to discuss the original promise made in 1917: "There are some of our number who think that that Declaration was both unnecessary and unwise, and who hold that our subsequent troubles have sprung in the main from its adoption. But that was nearly six years ago. We cannot ignore the fact that ever since it has been the accepted policy of His Majesty's Government."[153] The cabinet accepted these conclusions, marking an official Conservative commitment to the national home. This, crucially, depoliticized the issue for the 1920s.

When a Labour government was elected in 1924, the national home was reviewed again. Like the Liberal Churchill and Conservative Devonshire before him, Labour colonial secretary Thomas agreed there was no option but to continue: "My own view is that we have no alternative but to adhere to the policy of carrying out the terms of the Balfour Declaration as interpreted by our predecessors. I do not underrate the difficulties, but I am satisfied that the difficulties of any alternative course would be even greater" and the cabinet agreed.[154] Similarly, when Conservative Stanley Baldwin became prime minister again later that year, Palestine policy remained unchanged. Sunk costs meant the British government, regardless of party platform, could find no benefit in altering the commitment to a Jewish national home in Palestine.

Indeed, a period of tranquility in Palestine—actually caused by a Polish recession and a substantial reduction in Jewish immigration and settlement—meant British officials viewed the white paper policy as a success.[155] The effective depoliticization of the national home coupled with the absence of riots meant Palestine became less and less important as the decade progressed. In 1927, only 3,034 new Jewish immigrants were recorded in Palestine and 5,071 left.[156] All was quiet, and so Samuel's successor as high commissioner, Lord Plumer, saw little need for the inflated troop and police numbers stationed in Palestine since 1921, and with Colonial Secretary Amery's approval, began to disband them.[157] When riots and widespread violence erupted in Jerusalem in 1928–1929, the illusion and the Balfour Zeitgeist came to an end.

Unresolved Tensions

The Balfour Zeitgeist was a phase of British policy marked by a commitment to the Jewish national home in Palestine. There was no period of linear policy that continued from 1917 until Palestine's major riots in 1929. Rather, there was a crucial episode of decision-making in 1920–1922 when the policy was questioned and then confirmed, albeit with limitations, in the Churchill White Paper. Considering the findings of two commissions of inquiry following the 1920 Nebi Musa riots and the 1921 Jaffa riots, the decision to confirm Britain's commitment to the national home in 1922 seemed unsupportable. Instead, a politics-first approach demonstrates how and why the British government came to its decision to affirm the national home.

In the first instance, Britain's government rejected options that were highly politically risky. Taking prestige and bureaucratic politics into account meant the opportunity to repudiate the national home was untenable. The state of the postwar economy meant the option to impose the national home with the threat or use of force was also inflammatory and had to be dropped. Finally, interparty rivalry left the government unable to continue the national home as it stood in the Balfour Declaration and draft Mandate. Consequently, only one alternative was left available. This option was then checked against the War Office's requirements for strategic planning in the region. Due to the perception of "sunk costs," this policy was then continued throughout most of the 1920s under governments representing all shades of the mainstream political spectrum. What this meant in the 1920s, however, was that the Jewish-Arab tensions in Palestine remained unresolved, as did their propensity to affect, and be impacted by, British domestic politics.

Notes

1. Graham Allison, *Essence of Decision: Explaining the Cuban Missile Crisis* (Boston: Little, Brown, 1971), 30.
2. WO 32/9614, 1920, "Jerusalem Riots: Courts of Enquiry," TNA.
3. WO 32/9614, "Jerusalem Riots: Courts of Enquiry."
4. Bernard Wasserstein, "Herbert Samuel and the Palestine Problem," *English Historical Review* 91, no. 361 (1976): 753–775, 755.
5. LG/F/12/3/32, 6 May 1920, Allenby to Lloyd George, Parliamentary Archives.
6. LG/F/12/3/32, 6 May 1920, Allenby to Lloyd George.
7. LG/F/9/2/54, 11 January 1921, Notes on Churchill's Conversations in Paris, Parliamentary Archives; LG/F/9/2/54, 12 January 1921, Churchill to Lloyd George, Parliamentary Archives.
8. WO 32/9614, "Jerusalem Riots: Courts of Enquiry."
9. Ibid.
10. Ibid.
11. Ibid.
12. Cmd. 1540, 1921, "Palestine. Disturbances in May, 1921." *Reports of the Commission of Inquiry with Correspondence Relating Thereto*, 21.
13. Cmd. 1540, "Palestine. Disturbances in May, 1921," 25.

14. Ibid., 35.
15. Ibid., 43.
16. Ibid., 53–54.
17. Ibid.
18. Ibid.
19. Ibid.
20. Ibid.
21. CAB 24/126, 8 July 1921, "The Military Aspect of the Present Situation in Palestine," TNA.
22. CAB 23/26, 18 August 1921, Cabinet Minutes, TNA.
23. CAB 24/125, 8 June 1921, "Palestine and Mesopotamia Mandates. Circulated by the Secretary of State for the Colonies," TNA.
24. CAB 24/127, 4 August 1921, "The Financial Position. Memorandum by the Secretary of State for India," TNA.
25. CAB 23/26, 18 August 1921, Cabinet Minutes.
26. Ronald Storrs, *Orientations* (London: Nicholson and Watson, 1937), 388. The work of Sir Ronald Storrs reflects a particularly patriarchal attitude to Jews and Arabs in Palestine that is reflected in his largely discredited accounts of life and intercommunal conflict within the territory itself. His diary, however, is a useful indicator of one imperial British perspective of these interactions.
27. Storrs, *Orientations*.
28. CAB 24/159, 17 February 1923, "Palestine. Memorandum by the Secretary of State for the Colonies," TNA.
29. Cedric James Lowe and M. L. Dockrill, *The Mirage of Power: British Foreign Policy, Volume II, 1914–1922* (Cambridge: Routledge, 1972), 359.
30. CAB 24/125, 2 June 1921, "League of Nations. 'A' Mandates. Note by the Secretary," TNA.
31. CAB 24/159, 17 February 1923, "Palestine."
32. FO 608/98/588, 1919, "British Delegation, Correspondence and Papers Relating to Middle East (Political): Peace Congress and Palestine," TNA.
33. LG/F/9/2/54, 11–12 January 1921, "Notes on Churchill's Conversations in Paris," Churchill to Lloyd George, Parliamentary Archives.
34. CAB 24/125, 8 June 1921, "Palestine and Mesopotamia Mandates."
35. CAB 24/126, 29 June 1921, "The Recent Meeting of the Council of the League of Nations. Note by Mr. Fisher," TNA; CAB 24/136, 16 May 1922, "League of Nations. Palestine Mandate. Note by the Acting Secretary," TNA.
36. CAB 24/125, 8 June 1921, "Palestine and Mesopotamia Mandates."
37. Ibid.
38. CAB 24/126, 29 June 1921, "Note by Mr. Fisher."
39. CAB 24/159, 17 February 1923, "Palestine."
40. Cmd. 1700, 1922, *Palestine. Correspondence with the Palestine Arab Delegation and the Zionist Organisation.*
41. Storrs, *Orientations*, 458.
42. WO 32/9614, "Jerusalem Riots: Courts of Enquiry."
43. WO 32/9614, "Jerusalem Riots: Courts of Enquiry."

44. Richard Meinertzhagen, *Middle East Diary 1917–1956* (London: Cresset, 1959), 88. Much like the work of Sir Ronald Storrs, Colonel Meinertzhagen's diary is replete with biased and inflated accounts of his interactions with Zionists, but it is useful for illustrating his opinions about British politics.

45. CAB 24/159, 17 February 1923, "Palestine."

46. Valerie Hudson, *Foreign Policy Analysis: Classic and Contemporary Theory* (Lanham, MD: Rowman and Littlefield, 2007).

47. Gaynor Johnson, "Curzon, Lloyd George and the Control of British Foreign Policy, 1919–22: A Reassessment," *Diplomacy and Statecraft* 11, no. 3 (2000): 49–71, 50.

48. Kenneth O'Morgan, *Consensus and Disunity: The Lloyd George Government 1918–1922* (Oxford: Clarendon, 1979), 111; Lowe and Dockrill, *Mirage of Power*, 336.

49. FO 608/98/8365, 1919, "British Delegation, Correspondence and Papers Relating to Middle East (Political): Peace Congress and Palestine," TNA.

50. Frederick Walter Scott Craig, ed., *British General Election Manifestos 1900–1974* (London: Macmillan, 1975), 36.

51. CAB 24/4, 20 February 1918, "Report of the Egyptian Administration Committee," TNA.

52. CAB 24/106, 20 May 1920, "Mesopotamia. Note by the Secretary of State for War Covering Four Memoranda," TNA.

53. CAB 24/107, 2 June 1920, "Mesopotamia and Middle East: Question of Future Control," TNA.

54. CAB 24/107, 8 June 1920, "Future Administration of the Middle East," TNA.

55. CAB 24/107, 8 June 1920, "Future Administration of the Middle East."

56. Ibid.; CAB 24/110, 16 August 1920, "A Middle Eastern Department," TNA.

57. CAB 23/23, 31 December 1920, Cabinet Minutes, TNA.

58. CAB 23/23, 31 December 1920, Cabinet Minutes.

59. David Kozak, "The Bureaucratic Politics Approach: The Evolution of the Paradigm," in *Bureaucratic Politics and National Security: Theory and Practice*, ed. David Kozak and James Keagle (Boulder: L Reinner, 1988), 3–15; Hudson, *Foreign Policy Analysis*.

60. LG/F/9/2/54, 12 January 1921, Churchill to Lloyd George, Parliamentary Archives.

61. LG/F/9/2/54, 12 January 1921, Churchill to Lloyd George.

62. Ibid.

63. Craig, *British General Election Manifestos*, 29–30.

64. Stephen Constantine, *The Making of British Colonial Development Policy, 1914–1940* (Cambridge: Routledge, 1984), 89.

65. Leopold Amery, *My Political Life: Volume 2, War and Peace 1914–1929* (London: Hutchinson, 1953), 205.

66. Constantine, *Making of British Colonial Development Policy*, 90.

67. CAB 24/106, 20 May 1920, "Mesopotamia."

68. Ibid.

69. Ibid.

70. Ibid.

71. Ibid.

72. Ibid.

73. Ibid.

74. LG/F/13/1/29, 28 October 1920, Lloyd George to R. H. Campbell, Parliamentary Archives.
75. LG/F/13/1/29, 28 October 1920, Lloyd George to R. H. Campbell.
76. CAB 24/118, 26 January 1921, "Proposed Reduction in the Garrison in Palestine. Memorandum by the Secretary of State for War," TNA.
77. CAB 24/122, April 1921, "Report on Middle East Conference Held in Cairo and Jerusalem, March 12–30, 1921," TNA.
78. Meinertzhagen, *Middle East Diary*, 112.
79. CAB 24/122, April 1921, "Middle East Conference Held in Cairo and Jerusalem."
80. CAB 24/126, 1921, "Report of the Cairo Conference," TNA.
81. CAB 24/122, April 1921, "Middle East Conference Held in Cairo and Jerusalem."
82. House of Commons Debates, 14 June 1921, series 5, vol. 143, cols. 285–286.
83. House of Commons Debates, 14 June 1921, cols. 285–286.
84. CAB 24/126, "Report of the Cairo Conference."
85. CAB 24/125, 9 June 1921, "The Situation in Palestine. Memorandum by the Secretary of State for the Colonies," TNA.
86. CAB 24/125, 9 June 1921, "Situation in Palestine."
87. CAB 24/131, November 1921, "Palestine. Memorandum by the Secretary of State for the Colonies," TNA.
88. CAB 24/125, 8 June 1921, "Palestine and Mesopotamia Mandates."
89. LG/F/9/3/51, 9 June 1921, Churchill to Lloyd George, Parliamentary Archives.
90. LG/F/25/1/39, 14 June 1921, Hankey to Lloyd George, Parliamentary Archives.
91. LG/F/9/3/86, 3 September 1921, Churchill to Lloyd George, Parliamentary Archives.
92. LG/F/9/3/86, 3 September 1921, Churchill to Lloyd George.
93. Cmd. 1589, 1922, *Committee on National Expenditure. Third Report of Committee on National Expenditure.*
94. Cmd. 1589, Committee on National Expenditure.
95. Cmd. 1785, 1923, *League of Nations. Mandate for Palestine, Together with a Note by the Secretary-General Relating to Its Application to the Territory Known as Trans-Jordan, under the Provisions of Article 25.*
96. Trevor Wilson, "The Coupon and the British General Election of 1918," *Journal of Modern History* 36, no. 1 (1964): 28–42.
97. Wilson, "Coupon and the British General Election," 36–37.
98. Ibid., 40–41.
99. Harry Defries, *Conservative Party Attitudes to Jews, 1900–1950* (London: Frank Cass, 2001), 99.
100. House of Commons Debates, 15 July 1920, series 5, vol. 131, col. 2595; House of Commons Debates, 2 December 1920, series 5, vol. 135, col. 1439.
101. House of Commons Debates, 3 March 1921, series 5, vol. 138, col. 2030; House of Lords Debates, 8 June 1921, series 5, vol. 45, cols. 470–479; House of Commons Debates, 14 June 1921, col. 265–334; House of Lords Debates, 15 June 1921, series 5, vol. 45, cols. 559–573.
102. House of Lords Debates, 8 June 1921, cols. 470–479.
103. House of Lords Debates, 15 June 1921, cols. 559–563.
104. House of Lords Debates, 8 June 1921, cols. 470–479.
105. House of Commons Debates, 14 June 1921, cols. 265–334.
106. Ibid.

107. Michael Makovsky, *Churchill's Promised Land: Zionism and Statecraft* (London: Yale University Press, 2007), 103.
108. O'Morgan, *Consensus and Disunity*, 169.
109. Michael Kinnear, *The Fall of Lloyd George: The Political Crisis of 1922* (London: Macmillan, 1973), 21–22.
110. Kinnear, *Fall of Lloyd George*, 24.
111. Cmd. 1581, 1922, *Committee on National Expenditure. First Interim Report of Committee on National Expenditure*; Cmd. 1582, 1922, *Committee on National Expenditure. Second Interim Report of Committee on National Expenditure*; Cmd. 1589, 1922, *Committee on National Expenditure. Third Report of Committee on National Expenditure*.
112. Defries, *Conservative Party Attitudes to Jews*, 109–110.
113. CAB 24/24, 23 August 1917, "The Anti-Semitism of the Present Government," TNA.
114. CAB 24/127, 4 August 1921, "Financial Position."
115. CAB 24/134, April–May 1922, "Cost of Palestine Gendarmerie," TNA.
116. House of Commons Debates, 9 March 1922, series 5, vol. 151, cols. 1535–1604.
117. House of Commons Debates, 9 March 1922, cols. 1535–1604.
118. Ibid.
119. Ibid.
120. House of Lords Debates, 21 June 1922, series 5, vol. 50, cols. 994–1033.
121. House of Lords Debates, 21 June 1922, cols. 994–1033.
122. House of Commons Debates, 4 July 1922, series 5, vol. 156, cols. 221–343.
123. House of Commons Debates, 4 July 1922, cols. 221–343.
124. Howard Grief, *The Legal Foundation and Border of Israel under International Law* (Jerusalem: Mazo, 2008).
125. Cmd. 1700, Palestine.
126. Ibid.
127. Ibid.
128. Ibid.
129. Ibid.
130. John Steinbruner, *The Cybernetic Theory of Decision: New Dimensions of Political Analysis* (Princeton, NJ: Princeton University Press, 2002); Charles Ostrom and Brian Job, "The President and the Political Use of Force," *American Political Science Review* 80, no. 2 (1986): 541–566; Xinsheng Lui, "The Poliheuristic Theory of Decision and the Cybernetic Theory of Decision: A Comparative Examination," in *Integrating Cognitive and Rational Theories of Foreign Policy Decision Making*, ed. Alex Mintz (New York: Palgrave Macmillan, 2002), 159–168.
131. O'Morgan, *Consensus and Disunity*, 117–118.
132. CAB 23/43, 11 June 1918, "Shorthand Notes of the Fifteenth Meeting of the Imperial War Cabinet, Held in London at 10, Downing Street, S.W., on Tuesday, June 11, 1918, at 12 noon," TNA.
133. CAB 23/44A, 21 June 1918, Note by the Secretary, TNA.
134. FO 609/99/1327, 1918, "Peace Conference: British Delegation, Correspondence and Papers," TNA.
135. CAB 24/132, 20 January 1922, "The Interim Report of the Committee on National Expenditure. Army Estimates," TNA.
136. CAB 24/117, 18 December 1920, "The Palestine Garrison. Memorandum by the Secretary of State for War," TNA.

137. CAB 24/129, 9 November 1921, "The Situation in the Near East. Memorandum by the Secretary of State for War," TNA.
138. FO 609/99/1327, "Peace Conference."
139. Jonathan Renshon and Stanley Renshon, "The Theory and Practice of Foreign Policy Decision Making," *Political Psychology* 29, no. 4 (2008): 509–536, 536.
140. CZA, Z4/1878 I, cited in Defries, *Conservative Party Attitudes to Jews*, 111–112.
141. *Jewish Chronicle*, 10 November 1922, 11, cited in Defries, *Conservative Party Attitudes to Jews*, 112.
142. CZA Z4/1878 I, cited in Defries, *Conservative Party Attitudes to Jews*, 113.
143. CAB 24/159, 17 February 1923, "Palestine."
144. Ibid.
145. Ibid.
146. Ibid.
147. House of Lords Debates, 27 March 1923, series 5, vol. 53, cols. 639–669.
148. CAB 23/46, 27 June 1923, Cabinet Minutes, TNA.
149. Defries, *Conservative Party Attitudes to Jews*, 111.
150. CAB 24/160, 27 June 1923, "Cabinet. Palestine Committee," TNA.
151. CAB 24/160, 27 June 1923, "Cabinet. Palestine Committee."
152. CAB 24/161, 27 July 1923, "Cabinet. Committee on Palestine. The Future of Palestine," TNA.
153. CAB 24/161, 27 July 1923, "Future of Palestine."
154. CAB 24/165, 19 February 1924, "Cabinet. Palestine. Memorandum by the Secretary of State for the Colonies," TNA; CAB 23/47, 21 February 1924, Cabinet Minutes, TNA.
155. Christopher Sykes, *Cross Roads to Israel* (London: Collins, 1965); CAB 24/140, 30 December 1922, "Situation in Palestine," TNA.
156. Sykes, *Cross Roads to Israel*, 111.
157. Ibid., 111–112.

3 The Passfield Reversal, 1929–1935

THE BALFOUR ZEITGEIST coincided with a period of calm in Palestine, during which British politicians were able to ignore lingering Jewish-Arab tensions, leading to rapid reductions in costly troops and police. However, a conflict over Jerusalem's "Wailing" Wall in 1928 roused the passions of both Jews and Arabs in Palestine, resulting in violence on a horrific scale the following year.[1]

In preparation for Yom Kippur in 1928, the Jewish beadle erected a screen at the Western Wall to separate male and female worshippers. This action was interpreted in the Muslim community as a sign of ownership, and since the Temple ruins were legally part of Muslim waqf property, British forces forcibly removed the screen to prevent rioting. This incident created an atmosphere of political tension that continued to simmer. On 15 August 1929, a group of young Jewish right-wing activists demonstrated at the Wall—followed by Muslims counterdemonstrating—and British efforts to mediate the approaching crisis failed, leading to a bloodbath only days later.[2] The following week Muslim activists streamed into Jerusalem armed with sticks and knives, and rumblings that Jews were killing Arabs inspired mass murder, looting, and destruction elsewhere in the country. Raymond Cafferata, for example, Hebron's British police superintendent, reported mob attacks on Jewish homes that led to murder and mutilation, but he possessed only a fraction of the force needed to restore the peace. Only the kindness of twenty-eight Arab households saved Jewish lives in Hebron, a fact that thoroughly shamed British administrators who prided themselves on maintaining order.[3] The British government responded with two commissions of inquiry that directly resulted in the Passfield White Paper of 1930. (See fig. 3.1.)

This document represented the first substantial attempt to limit the Jewish national home in Palestine, not indefinitely but to an extent designed to cool Arab hatreds and prevent rioting in the future. Nevertheless, this new policy was reversed. The volte-face was articulated in a letter sent from Prime Minister James Ramsay MacDonald to Chaim Weizmann in February 1931, giving rise to the belief that Zionist lobbying had successfully harnessed the British Empire's foreign policy.[4]

Demonstrating a more realistic and coherent explanation for the reversal decision requires examining the British government's political pressure points in more depth. The two commissions of inquiry highlighted dangerous levels of Jewish-Arab antagonism in Palestine as a direct result of Arab unemployment

Fig. 3.1. "Wails or Warwhoops?": a cartoon, published in the *Evening Standard* on 27 August 1929, insinuating that the widespread and deadly riots in Palestine were the result of Muslim fanaticism and Zionist arrogance. © David Low / Solo Syndication.

and landlessness, which was blamed locally on Jewish immigration and land purchase.[5] Therefore, the Passfield White Paper was an understandable and expected attempt to solve the problem by limiting Jewish immigration and land purchase in line with available advice. The decision to reverse it, however, appears almost inexplicable. The committee warnings and recommendations remained constant, so why reject a publicly acknowledged, targeted, and actionable policy?

Taking a politics-first approach creates more clarity, not only regarding the initial decision to issue the Passfield White Paper in 1930 but also regarding the subsequent decision to undermine it in 1931, until an Arab Revolt in the late 1930s prompted a reevaluation. During this period, politicians rejected politically risky options, particularly those that dangerously inflamed internal party politics and parliamentary politics. The government then decided among the remaining alternatives by focusing on preventing damage to the economy. Ultimately, however, the British government's handling of Palestine policy, between the MacDonald letter of 1931 and the beginning of the Arab Revolt in 1936, became crystallized. Following the political storm motivating Passfield's reversal, all identifiable options were politically impossible.

Rather than a Palestine policy based on a narrow interpretation of the role played by Zionist lobbying, this analysis reveals a Palestine policy based primarily on the need to maintain a modicum of unity within government and across parties, which was threatened by the strategic pro-Zionist activism of opposition leaders as well as more sincere Zionist sympathies of some Labour Party backbenchers.

A Narrow Range of Alternatives

Like affirming the Mandate in 1922, the decision to reverse the Passfield White Paper also defied the recommendations of those officials sent to investigate the underlying causes of unrest. Based on information available to politicians at the time, investing in Palestinian Arab agriculture or limiting Jewish immigration and land purchase in Palestine would have been predictable courses of action.[6] This was evident from the reports submitted in 1930 by two commissions of inquiry and, indeed, demonstrated by the issuing of the Passfield White Paper.

In the immediate aftermath of violence in Palestine, these two commissions of inquiry were charged with investigating the root of the problem and recommending a solution. The first was led by distinguished jurist Sir Walter Shaw and the second was composed of only one man, Sir John Hope-Simpson. Just as earlier commissions investigating violence had concluded in the early 1920s, all but one member of the team led by Sir Walter Shaw identified that "the difficulties inherent in the Balfour Declaration and in the Mandate for Palestine are factors of supreme importance in the consideration of the Palestine problem."[7]

Palestine had suffered a severe economic downturn during the mid-1920s, and, despite provisions of the Churchill White Paper of 1922 having stipulated that immigration should be based on economic capacity, this had largely been ignored.[8] The Shaw Commission found that both immigration and Jewish land purchase during the 1920s meant "a landless and discontented class is being created."[9] This was potentially a very dangerous development, and the commission decided that the only solution was a radical overhaul of agriculture and expansion of cultivation.[10] The report then recommended a scientific inquiry "into the prospects of introducing improved methods of cultivation in Palestine" so a new land policy could be based on science rather than politics.[11] The problem was considered acute enough that the Colonial Office temporarily halted Jewish immigration into Palestine under the Labour Schedule in May 1930, pending the scientific land report.[12] As Sir John Hope-Simpson was experienced in ethnic conflicts, having acted as the League of Nations' vice-chairman of the Refugee Settlement Commission in Greece, and (at the time) was considered neither demonstrably pro-Arab nor pro-Zionist, he was entrusted with the task.[13]

After two months of researching scientific reports written during the Mandate, as well as conducting interviews and traveling the country, Sir John

Hope-Simpson concluded that "there is at the present time and with the present methods of Arab cultivation no margin of land available for agricultural settlement by new immigrants, with the exception of such undeveloped land as the Jewish Agencies hold in reserve."[14] Many Jews and some British officials in Palestine regarded Arab unemployment and landlessness as a myth, but Hope-Simpson affirmed the growing problem—also manifest to a lesser degree in the Jewish community—after hearing testimony from employers who said they could meet their labor needs multiple times over. These misfortunes, Hope-Simpson noted, were then ascribed, "probably quite erroneously, to Jewish competition."[15] Like the Shaw Commission, Hope-Simpson saw the only solution as intensive development, and, to that end, "drastic action is necessary."[16] Hope-Simpson also included a huge host of small, practical suggestions from limiting the orange crop and encouraging the cultivation of other fruits, to reducing fees and taxes in line with the fall of the price of crops, and even ensuring schoolmasters received agricultural training.[17] Fundamentally, however, he found that "[t]here exists no easy method of carrying out the provisions of the Mandate. Development is the only way. Without development, there is not room for a single additional settler."[18] In light of these two commission reports, the cabinet committee on Palestine, led by Colonial Secretary Lord Passfield, was faced with the necessity of action.

The government in Westminster had several key options: do nothing, repudiate the national home, amend the Mandate, reinforce the national home, invest in Arab agriculture, or limit Jewish immigration and land purchase. Palestine's high commissioner, Sir John Chancellor, outlined these alternatives as (1) removing the privileged position of the Jews and allowing a measure of self-government or (2) installing enough military in Palestine to protect the Jews.[19] Conversely, Shaw Commission member MP Harry Snell defined the choice as either allaying "Arab anxiety by the easy device of restricting Jewish immigration, in which case you lay yourself open to a suspicion of evading the Mandate," or "you should rescue the Arab farmer from his situation of indebtedness."[20] Furthermore, Sir John Hope-Simpson himself stated the options as, "[u]nless Great Britain is prepared to surrender the Mandate (and I understand that the Dutch are willing to accept it), she will be compelled to undertake the expense of development. These are the two alternatives, and there is no avenue of escape."[21] Importantly, a politics-first approach comes to the same conclusion.

The option to do nothing was most likely discarded immediately because it would have resulted in a surge of political criticism accusing the government of evading fundamental responsibilities to keep the peace. Due to the issue of sunk costs, as discussed previously, the option to repudiate the national home was also discarded immediately. Unlike the machinations surrounding the development of the Churchill White Paper in 1922, no official seriously suggested returning the Mandate to the League of Nations. Amending the Mandate was also dismissed as an option very early; this would have required consent from the league and a great deal of time spent lobbying other members for their support while the situation remained unresolved. Passfield himself noted that "[t]he objections to a revision of the actual terms of the Mandate seem to me insuperable."[22] Reinforcing the national home meant pouring in funding for security, and, while the Palestine administration did increase security measures following the riots in 1929, this was an impractical long-term solution even before the Great Depression. All of these options failed to meet political requirements as they would have initiated intolerable domestic political criticism. Investing in development or limiting Jewish immigration and land purchase were the only politically viable options remaining.

In terms of parliamentary politics, Passfield understood that the general policy of the white paper would not be welcomed warmly, but he did not predict the outrage it would produce from Zionists and members of every party. This was because criticism directed at the white paper, such as Hailsham and Simon's letter to *The Times* outlined in chapter 1, was couched in the language of international law but created political rather than legal problems. The colonial secretary had warned Weizmann beforehand, giving him an overview of the Hope-Simpson report and the policy under consideration, and Passfield believed that Weizmann "took it very well indeed" while stressing that "there should be no numerical limitation on the ultimate number of Jews."[23]

Prime Minister MacDonald had even reiterated Britain's commitment to the Jewish national home and the dual obligation on 3 April 1930, and the text of this speech was included in the white paper; it was "an international obligation from which there can be no question of receding."[24] Taking into account Weizmann's reluctant but nevertheless apparent acquiescence, MacDonald's reiteration of Britain's commitment to the national home, and Passfield's regular communications with the prime minister during cabinet committee deliberations, there was no warning of the political storm that followed.[25] Believing the two options of restricting Jewish immigration and investing in Arab agriculture satisfied political requirements, the government allowed these alternatives to be weighed against the most important aspect of national interest at the time: the economy.

As the American stock market crash of 1929 was developing into an international financial crisis that heralded stagnation and unemployment for British voters, it is important to recognize that development in Palestine necessitated either a guaranteed loan or grant-in-aid from the Colonial Office.[26] When the cabinet committee on Palestine submitted their first report to the cabinet on 15 September 1930, it was a detailed plan for the development that Hope-Simpson had advised was urgently necessary. However, the cost of Hope-Simpson's plan was unknown until a further financial committee delivered the blow: "Sir John Hope-Simpson's scheme involved the expenditure of some £6,000,000, spread over ten years, the interest on which would have to be guaranteed by the Exchequer. This would probably necessitate a loan spread over twenty years, the service of which would require £400,000 a year. This sum, however, did not include the capital cost of the land."[27] These amounts were much higher than anything the cabinet committee had considered, and they were advised to reassess the situation in light of this new information.[28] The state of the economy was so dire that in late 1930 the Treasury reimposed its control over Palestine's finances and sent an investigator, Sir Simon O'Donnell, to rate the Palestine administration's efficiency and judge where economies could be made.[29] The committee prepared a new report following this financial information and concluded that "in present circumstances a proposal to spend many millions on land settlement of Jews and Arabs in Palestine would meet with serious opposition in Parliament and the country."[30]

Consequently, the committee returned to the cabinet on 24 September with new suggestions. They decided that Britain was under a moral if not legal obligation to recompense Arabs dispossessed by British policy in Palestine. They agreed that the Jews should be allowed, at their own expense, to continue developing the land they already owned and that this should suffice to permit Jewish settlement for the following five years.[31] Jewish immigration would be restricted to numbers suitable for those reserve lands or immigrants who could be absorbed comfortably into the industrial population.[32] Unfortunately, there is no full transcript of this meeting. The minutes merely record that after "considerable discussion" the cabinet agreed to approve the committee's draft policy including their new points, following the realization of the cost of Hope-Simpson's scheme.[33] The outcome was a compromise of some very limited development and compensation as well as limits on the rate of expansion of the Jewish national home. The draft policy was subject to many minor alterations and was published as the Passfield White Paper on 21 October 1930. Regarding the question of peace, Passfield's new policy articulated the belief that "so long as widespread suspicion exists, and it does exist, amongst the Arab population, that the economic depression, under which they undoubtedly suffer at present, is largely due to excessive Jewish immigration, and so long as some grounds exist upon which this suspicion may be plausibly represented to be well founded, there can be little hope of any improvement in the mutual relations of the two races."[34] This prompted condemnation from both Conservative and Liberal Party leaders, which both Passfield and MacDonald failed to predict.[35]

By February 1931, the white paper had been undermined so severely as to constitute reversal. This was done in a published letter from MacDonald to Weizmann offering an "authoritative interpretation" of the Passfield White Paper and British policy in Palestine.[36] Far from limiting land purchase or Jewish immigration, the MacDonald letter stressed that centralized control over land purchase would be "regulatory and not prohibitive" and that "His Majesty's Government did not imply a prohibition of acquisition of additional land by Jews," which, of course, was the entire point of Passfield's policy.[37] Regarding immigration, the letter asserted that "His Majesty's Government did not prescribe and do not contemplate any stoppage or prohibition of Jewish immigration in any of its categories,"[38] which, again, ran counter to both the Shaw and Hope-Simpson commission reports as well as the deliberations of the cabinet committee on Palestine and the approval they received from the cabinet as a whole.

As the final text of the letter "had been agreed upon between representatives of the Jewish Agency and [another] Committee appointed by the Cabinet on the 6th November 1930," Zionist leaders appeared to have exerted a great deal of influence on the decision, contributing to the belief in the power of lobbying.[39] However, the calculations behind the reversal of the Passfield White Paper were more nuanced. Weizmann did orchestrate a campaign by writing letters to prominent newspapers as well as the League of Nations' Permanent Mandates Commission (PMC). He encouraged his supporters and friends—of which he had many among the British elite—to do the same, but these efforts always constituted more of a public show of protest than an exercise in secret diplomacy.[40] Negotiations with Zionists from November 1930 until January 1931 began with the Foreign Office trying to convince Weizmann and his colleagues that the white paper was a sound legal policy and ended with a volte-face. In these short months between the publication of the white paper and the MacDonald letter, the government came under severe criticism internationally, but, most important, domestically from opposition Liberal and Conservative parties. The polarizing nature of Passfield's new policy meant that the range of alternatives for dealing with its aftermath was narrowed to only two options: to continue with the white paper, or to reverse it. During this time, the factors that were most pressing to Labour's survival in government were internal party politics and the closely related problem of parliamentary politics.[41] Detailing the risk associated with these issues demonstrates just how little room Labour politicians had to maneuver.[42]

Crumbling from Within

A key source of political instability in 1930–1931 was internal party politics. The minority Labour government held only a fragile grip on power, and a problem that presented high levels of risk to that power was disunity within the Labour Party itself.[43] Labour foreign policy was marked by a commitment to the League of Nations, the credibility and stature of which was, therefore, highly important.[44] As Labour's traditional stance toward Zionism was staunchly supportive, James Ramsay MacDonald's government also faced the added complication of rebellion by key Labour Party backbenchers. Both of these issues—attitude to the League and party sentiment for Zionism—became dangerously inflamed due to interparty rivalry, which is discussed in detail below. Labour's precarious unity combined with the government's numerical weakness meant that there was simply no feasible way to continue with the Passfield White Paper.

In terms of foreign policy, the Labour Party's focus on the League of Nations constituted support for a program of arms limitation, eradication of outstanding grievances, arbitration of international disputes, and collective security.[45] The point was to prevent further global conflicts and—although this goal proved impractical—Labour leaders viewed their time in office as a historic opportunity for peace.[46] This foreign policy, however, did not reflect the party's grassroots priorities; instead, it was the brainchild of Labour's intelligentsia, most notably Foreign Secretary Arthur Henderson (described by Lady Frances Davidson as "that prim old Methodist").[47] The policy was then sold to the rest of the party.[48] In addition, by the autumn of 1930, there was a general problem with "[d]iscontent and disillusionment" along the front bench. Lady Passfield remarked how the Labour leaders were "strangled by the multitudinous and complicated issues raised in government departments; and by the alarming gravity of two major problems—India's upheaval and the continuous and increasing unemployment."[49]

As such, the intellectual commitment to the league was a potentially weak point in the armor of Labour Party unity. Paradoxically, as the Palestine Mandate was granted and theoretically supervised by the Council of the League of Nations, it was also divisive for British Palestine policy to even appear in contravention of league authority. This Labour Party commitment to the league faced its first criticisms from the PMC—the body appointed to oversee all mandates—in the summer of 1930. To further complicate matters, when various politicians wrote their letters to *The Times* months later to protest against the Passfield White Paper, their criticisms were more poignant because they echoed accusations leveled by the PMC.

Following the Shaw Commission report, although Foreign Secretary Henderson assured the Council of the League of Nations that Britain had no intention of deviating from a policy based on the Balfour Declaration, the council requested that the PMC conduct a thorough examination of this new document.[50] Prime Minister MacDonald received a copy of the PMC's report on 28 July 1930 and said it "was not pleasant reading."[51] The report contained a very grave charge: "that the partial inaction of the Mandatory Power as regards its obligations to the Palestinian population both Arab and Jewish is the fundamental cause of the friction which eventually culminated in the serious disorder of August 1929."[52] Charging Britain with negligence, the PMC was discarding the Shaw Commission's evidence and conclusions as well as any new policy they inspired. In response, Colonial Office undersecretary Sir Drummond Shiels tried to reassure the council; he advised that "there is no new policy; there is no secret to be disclosed; and that the British government stands today where it did when it accepted the Mandate, and with the same policy."[53]

Months later, however, in the face of criticism following the publication of Passfield's new white paper, Shiels's statement, in hindsight, could easily have been interpreted as a lie told directly to the Council of the League of Nations. Tension built in October immediately following the white paper's publication. Allegations arose that it "crystallised" the Jewish national home.[54] This term had come directly from the report of the PMC: "The Policy of the Mandatory would not be fairly open to criticism unless it aimed at crystallising the Jewish national home at its present stage of development."[55] The PMC's opinion that Britain had been responsible for Jewish-Arab tensions, its preference for Zionist arguments over an official British investigation, and Shiels's apparent dishonesty with regard to policy all contributed to an atmosphere in which Britain's relationship with the League of Nations was mutually wary. This meant that the minority Labour government did not relish the thought of further censure from the league, a development that would risk creating rifts within a party already potentially divided ideologically on the Palestine issue.

The Labour Party had been officially pro-Zionist since two-and-a-half months before the Balfour Declaration by approving the War Aims Memorandum, which called for a Jewish return to Palestine.[56] Its main proponent was Sydney Webb, who became Lord Passfield and the future colonial secretary and reflected the party's general support for self-determination among national ethnic groups, including in India.[57] By 1930, the strongest Labour supporters of Zionism were Joseph Kenworthy in the House of Commons and Josiah Wedgewood in the Lords.[58] Kenworthy, for example, wrote to Weizmann immediately after the white paper's publication, assuring him he had the support of many non-Jewish MPs and would correct this "blunder."[59]

Kenworthy had a general commitment to pragmatism in ethnic conflicts and did not consider British conciliations in the face of violence to be good policy unless they actually solved the problem at hand. He released a book in 1931 called *India: A Warning* highlighting all of the problems with finding a constitutional solution in India; his attitude was not partisan but intended to warn fellow politicians that succumbing to the violence of one particular ethnic group would not solve fundamental obstacles to peace and stability.[60] As discussed further below, this sort of reasoning was also directly relevant to perceptions of Palestine.

In the House of Lords, Wedgwood had been a friend to Zionism since the 1920s, joining with both James Ramsay MacDonald and future chancellor Philip Snowden in organizing the Palestine Mandate Society, a pro-Zionist lobby group.[61] MacDonald had even visited Palestine in 1922 and subsequently argued that the Arab claim to self-determination was invalid because "Palestine and the

Jews can never be separated" and "the Arab population do not and cannot use or develop the resources of Palestine."[62] MacDonald, Passfield, and Snowden, therefore, had all been involved in promoting the Zionist movement with their like-minded colleagues before attaining high office. Once confronted with the Shaw and Hope-Simpson reports, however, they all approved a new policy based on limiting Jewish immigration to Palestine.[63] This preexisting sentiment juxtaposed against the Passfield White Paper of 1930 had the potential to create a split within the Labour Party that, if left uncorrected, posed a real danger to the government's longevity.

When the white paper was published on 21 October 1930, the criticism it attracted seemed to have an impact on MacDonald's thinking relatively quickly. On 6 November, the cabinet decided to create a new committee for Palestine policy.[64] Primarily, the new committee was tasked with legal clarification of Palestine policy in cooperation with an authority such as the Lord Advocate. It would also "get in touch with the representatives of the Zionists in the most politic and tactful manner possible in the circumstances and should make recommendations as to the attitude to be taken up by the government in view of the reception of the recently issued white paper."[65] MacDonald then met with Chaim Weizmann the same day, when he purportedly told the Zionist leader, "There is no white paper."[66] This unequivocal comment was most likely an off-the-record exclamation, and there is little other indication that the decision to reverse the white paper had been made by 6 November. Indeed, MacDonald had written to Weizmann the day after the document's publication to advise him that "a closer study of what is laid down in the statement of policy will show you that it is far better than you seem to imagine, and that whatever you may object to in it is a very reasonable price to pay if we can secure closer cooperation in Palestine."[67] In addition, the prime minister wrote again a week later to stress that their differences over the policy were minor and based on misunderstandings and phraseology.[68] Weizmann had understood this to mean "that some amending interpretation of the White Paper is being considered" and he telegrammed his American counterpart, Felix Warburg, to this effect immediately after meeting MacDonald.[69]

Bringing the Zionists into discussions in this manner undoubtedly began with the aim of making absolutely sure that the new policy was legal and sound. This is why the cabinet wanted "clarification" conducted in conjunction with the Lord Advocate and why the initial approach was kept secret—the announcement of Zionist participation in the new Palestine subcommittee remained classified until the parliamentary debate on 17 November.[70] Gestation of the reversal idea had only just begun, and the government would have been unlikely to proceed with a difficult Commons debate and an impassioned defense of the white paper had the decision to reverse it already been made.

Rather, the main issue remained correcting any appearance that Labour intended to undermine league authority. Assigning Foreign Secretary Arthur Henderson as chair of the new committee facilitated this aim.[71] This also served a second purpose of soothing internal politics, as Henderson was far more popular within the party than MacDonald, especially when the extent of backbench antipathy for the white paper became clear during the debate.[72] This parliamentary debate is discussed in more detail below, but Kenworthy, for example, publicly railed against his own party leadership and advised the House that "Colonial secretaries have come under the lash of my tongue in the past and others will do the same unless the Colonial Office policy is changed."[73]

This added Palestine to the lengthy list of issues already angering Labour backbenchers under MacDonald's leadership. The prime minister found himself at the mercy of "rumours of dissensions, intrigues and crises in the government ranks" and Conservative politician Austen Chamberlain believed this was "a case in which the proverb is true that there is no smoke without fire."[74] Under this strain, Conservatives believed "Ramsay is terribly overworked, shows some signs of fretfulness which attacks him in such conditions, and might be upset by an accident."[75] Before the Palestine issue could become such an "accident," reaching out to representatives of the Zionist movement to liaise with a new cabinet committee on Palestine was less a direct reaction to their demands and more of a safety measure intended to guard against party divisions over the League of Nations. Later in November, December, and January, these negotiations became a way of plastering over the fissures left by the Labour leadership's shifting commitment to Zionism.

As the prime minister would have recognized this rebellious streak among his own backbenches after the white paper's publication, why did the cabinet not anticipate a breaking of ranks beforehand? Although it is very difficult to explain why a particular threat did not occur to the relevant politicians, it is likely that the new policy's internal effect was considered manageable. The threat became dangerously exacerbated, however, by the vocal and unrelenting opposition raised by Conservative and Liberal leaders. Internal party politics was not necessarily enough on its own to constitute too much political danger, but it primed the situation, most likely lowering the threshold of what was considered acceptable risk. Once combined with parliamentary politics, the frustrations of internal disagreements meant the Passfield White Paper was stillborn.

Firing across the Aisles

The two issues of internal party politics and parliamentary politics are closely related in this case because the latter represented a skillful, if not entirely on purpose, manipulation of the former. The minority Labour government depended foremost on its own unity to maintain power, but it also relied heavily on Liberal Party support.[76] Following publication of the Passfield White Paper, this weakness was exploited effectively by the appearance of a Liberal-Conservative alliance. This rhetorical joining of forces heightened and prolonged the debate that was so divisive within Labour's own ranks. The approaching India Conference in mid-November 1930 exacerbated the white paper problem, and despite its critics across the aisle posing emotional and even fallacious arguments against Passfield's policy, a coherent and comprehensive governmental rebuttal proved unpersuasive. MacDonald was already in a precarious position, and India policy had proved dangerously disruptive the previous year. A parliamentary debate on the Passfield White Paper demonstrated these continuing divisions—which were confirmed by a diminished majority in the Whitechapel by-election—and these factors accumulated to ensure that discussions with Zionists (which initially aimed to provide legal clarification) resulted in a complete reversal of the offending policy. These features of parliamentary machinations combined with Labour's internal disunity, making any attempt to continue the Passfield White Paper all but impossible.

As well as unstable levels of support for foreign policy within his own party, MacDonald had to contend with the inherent difficulties of minority governance; he relied on varying degrees of cross-party support for foreign policy initiatives to prevent polarized parliamentary debates that risked splitting his own party.[77] In March 1930, for example, MacDonald wrote to Passfield to arrange some discussion on whether a new white paper on Palestine policy was urgently required, but stressing that "it could only be [. . .] with the general support of all parties in the House of Commons."[78] Likewise, the prime minister's son, Malcolm MacDonald, noted how it was always "important that the Liberals at any rate should support their proposals."[79]

Labour had inherited an empire in disarray. In addition, there was a looming global depression, stronger dominions, colonial nationalisms, and the rise of the United States as a world power. This all meant that imperial policy had become an exercise in calculated control through concession and compromise—a balance between firmness and conciliation. These issues also had the power to arouse great parliamentary passions within and across parties.[80] Conservative chairman Leopold Amery called this problem Labour's "paralysing ineptitude."[81] In this atmosphere, however, all party heads recognized the importance of some degree of cooperation in private negotiations.[82] As such, MacDonald had conferred with both Conservative leader Stanley Baldwin and Liberal de facto leader David Lloyd George in March 1930—specifically with regard to the Shaw Commission—to ask for "the guidance of your views on what should be done now."[83] Although no notes from this meeting exist, it was necessary because the consequences of trying to move ahead without cross-party support had proved nearly disastrous for India policy the previous year, in circumstances highly similar to the debate that followed the Passfield White Paper.

When Labour came to power in 1929, the existing legislation on India's internal government was the Montagu-Chelmsford Act of 1921, which was due for review.[84] To this end, a Statutory Commission chaired by Liberal MP Sir John Simon had been formed to investigate and recommend the next stages of constitutional development.[85] Differences of opinion regarding the degree and pace of this self-rule cut across parties.[86] India had growing provincial nationalisms, and Lord Irwin, a Conservative peer cooperating with the government, suggested giving Indian politicians a veneer of responsibility and protoindependence to produce a sedative effect.[87] Before the Simon Commission could present its report, however, the government issued the Irwin Declaration based on this principle on 31 October 1929.[88]

Whereas both Conservative and Liberal leaders had agreed to this Labour government policy adopted from Irwin, the problem was with the declaration itself.[89] Liberal Lord Reading, the former viceroy to India, criticized the wording as dangerously ambiguous and sacrificing long-term stability for short-term pacification.[90] Reading's stature commanded a great deal of authority, and his objections allowed Lloyd George and other Liberals to refuse consent for the declaration, stiffening the instinctive opposition of Peel, Austen Chamberlain, Churchill, and other Conservatives whom Baldwin was unable to restrain once it became known that the declaration had not received Simon Commission approval.[91] This meant Baldwin also had to withdraw his support since diehard Conservative opposition (mostly Churchill, who was looking for an issue with which to revive his career) placed the Conservative leader's own position in profound peril.[92]

The result was a major hardening against minority-Labour's India policy among both Conservatives and Liberals.[93] The cabinet issued a communiqué specifically stating what Irwin's ambiguity had attempted to conceal: that the declaration involved no change of policy. This sparked outrage in India, leading to the need for repressive measures by May 1930 and leaving bitter and substantial disagreements between parties in Westminster.[94] In the year following the Irwin Declaration, however, there was a subtle and tenuous shift within Parliament back toward a more bipartisan line. Labour stood firmly behind the declaration and, despite a flurry of Liberal uncertainty, was ultimately supported by Lloyd George with Conservatives acting as a check on hurried constitutional development.[95] India remained a crucial issue, however, and the cabinet was meeting twice a day in the summer of 1930 to discuss it.[96] The situation also stayed tenuous for MacDonald. Lady Passfield recorded in her diary during this time that "the Labour government is on the rocks and may any day be wrecked."[97]

This tense situation continued throughout 1930 when the government had to deal with the Imperial Conference and the India Round Table only to be blindsided politically by the subsidiary issue of Palestine. This convergence of similar crises left the prime minister "overwhelmed with work" and in a terribly exposed political position.[98] Cross-party cooperation was vital but shaky. Austen Chamberlain expressed an opinion, common among the prime minister's supporters and rivals, that "there is too much trouble ahead; Ramsay is not, I think, the man to deal with it."[99] The uneasy consensus on India policy built up the previous year was the product of luck rather than adroit political maneuvering on the part of the Labour government and, approaching the first of a series of India Round Table conferences in November 1930, was directly threatened by the fallout from Passfield's white paper.

While it would be overly simplistic to state that Palestine and India policy were decided in tandem, the period 1929–1930 marked one of the few occasions when India policy colored all of British politics.[100] In addition, the conflict in Palestine bore some of the hallmarks British politicians associated with India, such as ethnic conflict and "natives" agitating for political rights. Conservative Party chairman Leopold Amery remarked how the violence in Palestine would be "familiar to most Indian administrators."[101] This meant that attitudes to Palestine among the British political elite were, to some extent, informed by how they viewed the India problem, with which they were far more familiar. Who were the "natives" in Palestine, and which group required suppressing and which protecting? Neither Palestine's Jews nor its Arabs escaped the paternalistic racism emanating from the House of Commons that was associated with British imperialism more generally and the India question in particular in 1930.

In this context, any perception of weakness to imperial subjects around the world had to be considered very carefully. It would be a mistake, however, to consider that the two issues held equal weight in British politics: "little Palestine with its troubles—insignificant to the rest of the world," Lady Passfield wrote, "is likely to be forgotten in concern over the revolution which some say is going on in India. For the next six weeks, the P.M. and other Cabinet Ministers, having finished with the Dominions, will be absorbed in the Round Table Conferences to settle the fate of India—or rather the British in India."[102] Palestine was, paradoxically, both important (because it threatened to disrupt Labour's cross-party support for the India Round Table conference) and insignificant (as India was the chief and all-consuming concern). This meant that although the government's and certainly Passfield's early concern when formulating the new Palestine policy had been avoiding any appearance of capitulation to either outside lobbying or parliamentary pressure, the political storm created by its publication altered their priorities.[103]

At first, the dominant voice within the cabinet on this issue was that of the colonial secretary, who stressed the need to remain firm against any and all external parties. This meant ignoring both the borderline anti-Semitic complaints of

Palestine's high commissioner Sir John Chancellor and "the persistent bombardment by the Jews, in personal intercourse, in formal interviews, in newspaper propaganda, in insidious threats of ulterior action, notably electoral pressure at home and international public opinion abroad, and all the rest of it [. . .]."[104] Passfield seemed, for example, to take great pride in resisting Zionist lobbying to lift a ban on immigration under the Labour schedule imposed by Chancellor with cabinet approval: although "very strong pressure has been brought to bear upon His Majesty's Government to rescind the suspension without awaiting the Report of Sir John Hope-Simpson," he wrote, "[s]o far, all demands to rescind or modify the suspension have been resisted by His Majesty's Government."[105] This unwavering position was justified within the Colonial Office by the argument for a stable empire.

Crucially, this attitude of forbearance against the "Jewish hurricane," as Passfield referred to it, endured during the new policy's preparation in cabinet committees in the summer of 1930 and obviously did not prevent its publication on 21 October. Weizmann, for example, threatened to resign on 13 October but the white paper was still published two weeks later.[106] In contrast, the political danger following publication of the Passfield White Paper emanated chiefly from within the British political establishment and stemmed from many criticisms leveled at the white paper that represented more political strategy than principled objection.[107] Accusations directed by Liberal and Conservative leaders against the Labour government were not really about the text of the white paper or the policy it contained. Before outlining the attacks made by Conservative and Liberal party politicians, however, it is necessary to sketch a portrait of these opposition leaders' own precarious careers in 1930 to illustrate their motives.

Conservative leader Stanley Baldwin had barely survived the Irwin Declaration debacle by appeasing his vocal critics within the Conservative Party. When Baldwin spoke in Parliament on the India issue, for example, "there had been no word of approval from his own colleagues and as soon as Lloyd George got up Winston and Worthington-Evans on each side of him leant forward and punctuated every sentence with emphatic 'hear hears!'"[108] The Conservative leader was in danger of having to resign because "[i]f the matter had gone to division half his colleagues would have voted against him."[109] As a moderate who was facing diehard backbench opinion, especially with regard to India, the Conservative leader could ill afford to support any government policy that appeared to acquiesce in the face of demands even remotely similar to those of the India Congress. In the case of Palestine, Arabs were comparable to Indians—not because British politicians viewed Jews as nonindigenous but because they were Caucasian, European, and therefore perceived very differently in the interwar imperial mind-set. Approaching the India Round Table in 1930, Baldwin deliberately retreated from frontline politics and declined to serve on Britain's delegation to the conference.[110] He wrote to Lord Irwin on 16 October to say that in preparing for the conference, he "kept off, partly to keep [Lloyd George] off and partly because the political situation is far too tricky to allow me to be immersed in a Conference when every crook in the country is out for my scalp."[111]

In this environment, the Conservative Party chairman (and former colonial secretary) Leopold Amery was highly concerned with keeping Baldwin in his leadership position.[112] Amery was a known Zionist sympathizer who had been involved with securing Palestine's advantageous borders in 1920 but did not support the cause at the Arabs' expense—he simply did not believe that the Arabs were losing anything. This is evident in an article Amery wrote for *The Pioneer* in December 1929. He was, first and foremost, a British imperialist: "The terms of the Balfour Declaration make it plain that the creation of the Jewish national home did not imply the setting up of a Jewish nationalist state or the support, in favour of the Jews, of that essentially intolerant type of racial or linguistic nationalism which has devastated Europe by its conflicting claims for political domination. Equally it left no room, in Palestine at least, for the assertion of that type of nationalism by the Arabs."[113] His motivations may be clearer when considering Amery's recollections after a dinner party the previous year; Amery admitted "[. . .] our object is to have Palestine permanently within the ambit of our commonwealth of peoples."[114] Fundamentally, Amery's loyalty was to his country's status, to his party's position, and so, at that moment, to Baldwin. Between them, they also felt subject to the opposition of Conservatives who still favored joining in a coalition with the Liberal Party and were marginalized by David Lloyd George's removal in 1922. These dissenters had included Austen Chamberlain, making the former foreign secretary an important man to court.

The policy that joined many along the Liberal and Conservative benches was free trade within the empire, which was the particular cause of the press barons, Lord Beaverbrook and Lord Rothermere. These men also formed the United Empire Party to split the Conservative vote and pressure against India reform.[115] The press barons opposed Lloyd George when he was prime minister on the basis of an antiwaste campaign, but, by 1929, they were undermining Stanley Baldwin's leadership of the Conservative Party over India and the free trade issue, the latter of which was championed by David Lloyd George and aroused suspicions of collaboration between the three men. Baldwin, for example, asked his shadow cabinet, "What is your reading of the Beaverbrook-Rothermere game? And under which thimble is the pea, or in other words Ll.G.?"[116]

In a moment of frustration in dealing with this situation, Amery suggested the Baldwin-loyalists within the party should sign a letter to their leader saying, "All your old colleagues conscious of each other's senility desire to tell you that not one of them has any objection to any of the others being bumped off [. . .]."[117] While assassinating the diehard Conservatives was not an option, their various outrages were at least relatively predictable. Baldwin and Amery were determined to beat the press barons and the diehards at their own game: "I am fighting with beasts at Ephesus," Baldwin wrote, "and I hope to see their teeth drawn and their claws broken before the battle is over!"[118] On 23 October, one tactic for this war became apparent. The Conservative leadership penned a letter to *The Times* signed by Baldwin, Amery, and Chamberlain to protest against the Passfield White Paper.[119] Rather than being aimed solely at the Labour government's apparent anti-Zionism, however, the letter also targeted divisive factions within Conservative ranks. It was part Zionist sympathy and part political strategy.

The letter was first constructed in conjunction with Arthur Balfour's niece and Zionist campaigner Baffy Dugdale. Amery recounted how "Mrs Dugdale [...] came in very much concerned about the Palestine White Paper" and believed that the Conservative Party should "dissociate themselves as promptly as possible from the government in this matter."[120] Amery agreed and ushered Mrs. Dugdale in to see Stanley Baldwin, inviting her to begin "drafting something before she came back and lunched with us."[121] Mrs. Dugdale then took Baldwin's "general instructions as to the points to be brought out in a letter," which she drafted and then Amery revised and amended with Baldwin and Austen Chamberlain.[122] Weizmann credited his colleague Sir Lewis Namier with inspiring Mrs. Dugdale, but it was Leopold Amery who organized the Conservative opposition to the white paper.[123]

Amery even recruited Austen Chamberlain for this purpose. As well as being a known Zionist sympathizer, Chamberlain had opposed Baldwin over the Irwin Declaration and had no confidence in him as a leader, noting how, "to recall an old cartoon of 'Punch,' a manifesto in his hands becomes 'a wet blanket.'"[124] Chamberlain, however, did not relish the thought of a party run by the press barons and opposed attempts to force Baldwin's resignation on the grounds that it "would be hailed as a triumph for themselves by Rothermere and Beaverbrook" and "would lend itself to every form of misconception and be deeply wounding [...]."[125] Baldwin was not a passive observer in this political infighting, but he found it very draining and sympathized with James Ramsay MacDonald's similar situation, seeing the prime minister as "a good man and true, fighting for his life."[126] The same was not true for Baldwin's opinions of David Lloyd George: "no constitution can stand public life today when you get near seventy," Baldwin wrote, "unless you are made like L.l.G. with no bowels, no principles, no heart and no friends."[127] The Liberal leader was, incidentally, also under pressure from his own party. While Amery did not necessarily want a parliamentary debate on the Palestine white paper, "fearing that it would show divisions in our own ranks," it was members of David Lloyd George's Liberal Party who pushed for a date and organized it.[128]

It is important to note that Lloyd George had been a divisive figure for Liberal politics since 1916 when he ousted Prime Minister Asquith and then fronted a majority Conservative government against the wishes of many within his party. Until Lloyd George suffered a similar coup at the hands of his coalition partners in 1922, the former prime minister lent broad support to the Zionist enterprise. As noted previously, however, this was less the result of sentiment and ideology than the opportunities and constraints created by postwar diplomacy. Regardless, whenever the Palestine issue surfaced subsequently in debate, Lloyd George vociferously defended the Zionist movement—and thereby his own tenure as prime minister.

By 1930, his unofficial position as leader of the Liberal Party was also tenuous. Lloyd George had led a vote against the government in July 1930 and lost, simply because many Liberal MPs had defied the whip and sided with the government.[129] Sir John Simon, of the Simon Commission in India, was also close to challenging Lloyd George for the leadership of the Liberal Party, and the letter he sent with Conservative politician Lord Hailsham to *The Times*, protesting the Passfield White Paper, was a tacit challenge to the Liberal leader's authority.[130] Lloyd George was also bitterly frustrated with the Liberal Party's marginalized position and support for a Socialist party that was failing to live up to its radical reforming intentions.[131] As MacDonald refused to supply an arrangement that gave the dwindling Liberal Party any lifeline, Lloyd George attempted to exploit Conservative dissatisfaction with Baldwin to win back some of his former coalitionists and attract younger, more progressive Tories into his sphere.[132]

Baldwin recognized the tactic, noting that "the Goat has finally failed to get any real arrangements with Labour and rumour has it he is going to make another attempt on us."[133] Baldwin's assessment was that "[t]he Liberal Party is cracking badly and Labour is running about with its' tail between its' legs. Ramsay is tired and rattled. An election may come any day but I still feel they will see the New Year in [. . .]."[134] Lady Passfield recognized, however, that "all three parties are in a devil of a mess."[135] This was the political context in which the Passfield White Paper was published on 21 October 1930 and then debated in the House of Commons on 17 November. Both Baldwin (through Amery) and David Lloyd George had previous ties to Chaim Weizmann and Zionism, more generally, and this meant they were also well placed to use Zionist arguments to guard against internal criticism (in the case of Baldwin) or undermine a disappointing government usurping the Liberal Party's position in British politics.

As mentioned previously, the initial criticisms came in the form of two letters to *The Times* and these were followed by the crucial parliamentary debate. The first letter came from Baldwin, Amery, and Austen Chamberlain. It accused the Labour government of abandoning the Jewish national home policy, stating, "they have laid down a policy of so definitely negative a character that it appears to us to conflict [. . .] with the whole spirit of the Balfour Declaration and of the statements made by successive governments in the last 12 years."[136] The effect of this policy, the letter charged, was "to create a feeling of distrust in that British good faith which is the most precious asset of our foreign Imperial policy."[137] The letter was relatively brief, and as such made no reference to the Shaw or Hope-Simpson Commissions nor to any of the specific arguments utilized by the white paper.

Following this, on 4 November, two lawyers and former cabinet ministers, Lord Hailsham and Sir John Simon, wrote their letter to *The Times*, which purported to compare provisions of the white paper to the terms of the Mandate.[138] Hailsham was a Conservative, the former Lord Chancellor, and Simon, of the aforementioned Simon Commission in India, had served as a Liberal Home Secretary.[139] As a Conservative, Hailsham was predictably opposed to Labour, and the Irwin Declaration had seriously undermined Simon both politically and personally. Described by Lady Passfield as "[t]hat smooth faced, slim and ingratiating personage," Simon was not characterized as a politician who accepted such insults to his stature with ease; he and his wife were "admirable citizens; but they have far too much contempt for other people and are far too obstinate and dogmatic, too assured of their own enlightenment."[140]

Hailsham and Simon's letter accused the government's new Palestine policy of flouting Britain's international obligations as a member and trustee of the League of Nations.[141] Furthermore, it called for "the Council of the League of Nations to obtain from the Hague Court an advisory opinion on the questions involved."[142] As the Labour government's League of Nations policy was a potentially divisive issue and the report from the PMC had been damning in places, this was hardly an attractive proposal in Downing Street. As with the Irwin Declaration, however, such criticism of the Passfield White Paper was not concerned with the actual policy, but, instead, "[a]lleged ambiguities and unfriendliness," how it looked and sounded.[143] Following these letters to *The Times*, a debate in Parliament on 17 November shook the government's already unstable foundations.

Comprising targeted attacks from Liberal and Conservative MPs designed to embarrass the government rather than clarify points of policy, the debate was centered on issues like anti-Semitism and breaches of faith. The government's response, however, had been prepared in advance by the Colonial Office and so was directed against the substance of these complaints rather than their political motivations. This led to a situation in which "the facts" of the white paper were immaterial to its survival.

Speaking first, Lloyd George led the attack, accusing the government of anti-Semitism and hypocrisy, and he attempted to drive a wedge between the prime minister (who was present) and the colonial secretary (who was not), by questioning "whether the Prime Minister himself was fully consulted before this document was issued."[144] Chancellor's comments on this speech were as blunt as ever: "L.G.'s speech was typical—all sentiment and hot air."[145] Lloyd George also struck at the heart of Labour's commitment to the league, specifically highlighting how the PMC "was full of the most severe criticism of their administration" and "[t]heir answer was practically to tear up the Mandate."[146] During the debate, Amery echoed Lloyd George's sentiments, remarking that "no one wishes to acknowledge the parentage of this undesirable child. I do not suppose that the Prime Minister is prepared to elucidate this problem of disputed parentage."[147] MacDonald never answered these comments, but, of course, he had approved the policy—as had a cabinet committee, the full cabinet, and as far as Lord Passfield was concerned, Chaim Weizmann.[148]

It is important to note that this was routine parliamentary antagonism and was not necessarily unanimously designed to try and topple the government on this relatively minor issue. Amery wrote, for example, that "[i]t was important to push the Govt. hard but not to have a division which might either have finally confirmed the White Paper or alternatively defeated the Govt. and committed the Socialist Party to Passfield's anti-Zionist policy."[149] Nevertheless, the danger to Labour was cumulative.

In response to these attacks, it was Colonial Office undersecretary Shiels's assignment to speak in defense of the government, which in principle was not a difficult task. The prime minister had originally charged Henderson with the duty, but defending the government's policy so publicly would have placed him in an awkward position vis-à-vis the beginning of Anglo-Zionist talks.[150] Shiels highlighted that "[t]here seems to have been some obvious misunderstanding" of the Passfield White Paper, but he was merely being polite.[151] The vociferous nature of the opposition from Liberals and Conservatives in *The Times* had already been identified as both fallacious and underhanded. Palestine high commissioner Sir John Chancellor openly expressed this opinion, writing to O. G. R. Williams directly at the Colonial Office to say he was "greatly concerned about the letter which Baldwin, Chamberlain and Amery have written to the *Times*. If all parties would accept H.M.G.'s statement of policy, there would be some prospect of future peace in Palestine. If they are going to make it a party question, Palestine will become a running sore and a potential danger to the safety of the Empire, like Ireland."[152] In correspondence with Sir John Evelyn Shuckburgh in the Colonial Office's Middle East Department, Chancellor added, "I share your view as to the mischievous character of the Baldwin-Chamberlain-Amery letter. No doubt it was inspired by Amery."[153] After both letters had been published, the Colonial Office prepared a defense of the white paper, and their memoranda formed the basis of Shiels's defense.

At the Colonial Office, O. G. R. Williams was responsible for the full rebuttal to Hailsham and Simon's letter. Williams noted that the letter purported to compare the white paper with the official Mandate but mentioned only the Mandate's preamble, Article II, and Article VI, omitting any reference to protecting non-Jewish populations.[154] As well as misleadingly paraphrasing the white paper, Hailsham and Simon also ignored the findings of Hope-Simpson and created an impression of the new policy that was "quite untrue."[155] Williams did highlight, however, how Hailsham and Simon's reference to The Hague was purely political since "it would be so framed as to be exceedingly unfavourable and humiliating to His Majesty's Government [. . .] owing to the peculiar composition of the Hague Court."[156] This was the only part of the letter that was troubling, not because the issue really would necessitate referral to The Hague but because dealing with the threat exposed the government's financial motivations for cutting Jewish immigration rather than investing in development.[157]

Other than revealing this slightly mercenary policy-making procedure, the arguments opposed to the white paper prompted only incredulity at the Colonial Office. Passfield himself drafted a letter to *The Times*, stating "[i]t is reassuring to find from their letter published in your columns [. . .] that such high authorities as Lord Hailsham and Sir John Simon do not indicate anything in the Palestine White Paper inconsistent with the Balfour Declaration and the Mandate save in so far as they seek to draw from language used in paragraphs 15, 19 to 23 and 28 three inferences, not one of which is justified."[158] These inferences, Passfield added, "are made plausible only by an inaccurate representation of the contents of the paragraphs referred to, not one of which is quoted verbatim."[159] High Commissioner Chancellor echoed the absurdity of this situation, noting that "[t]he local Jewish criticisms of the statement of policy, for the most part, condemn it for things that it does not contain."[160]

In Parliament, Shiels reiterated polite versions of these sentiments and stressed his earlier opinion that the "White Paper makes no change whatever in the interpretation of the Mandate," but, rather, "[w]hat it does is to emphasize the necessity for a more exact application of the absorptive capacity principle."[161] Therefore, Shiels argued, "[i]t is obvious that the suggestion that this government is seeking to crystallise the Jewish national home in its present position is without a shadow of foundation."[162] Although the prime minister spoke very little during the debate, to this point he did add that "I have said again and again and I say now that the Mandate is to be carried out. But when we come to the condition of Palestine we must admit that the Mandate has to be carried out in such a way that civil disorder is not going to result from its operation."[163]

In this sentiment, the usually competitive Foreign and Colonial Offices were in agreement. Foreign Secretary Henderson had received the full text of Zionist objections to the white paper the week before the debate via the prime minister's pro-Zionist son, Malcolm MacDonald. The Eastern Department of the Foreign Office had then prepared a full rebuttal that raised almost identical points to the defense written by the Colonial Office without conferring between the two.[164] Both ministries agreed that there was "no intention to crystallise the status quo."[165] The Foreign Office noted how "it is clear that, so long as an acute unemployment problem exists in Palestine (whether of Jews or Arabs), it is the duty of the Mandatory, under Article 6 of the Mandate, to restrict immigration into Palestine (whether Jews or Arabs)."[166] The bureaucracy, therefore, was united on the Palestine issue. The disagreements over Passfield's white paper were between politicians.

During the parliamentary debate, it was Leopold Amery who brought up the subject of India. Amery declared that Palestine's 1929 riots were "an old-fashioned religious outbreak of the type with which the Indian administration is only too familiar."[167] He was trying to draw a comparison between "giving in" to Arabs in Palestine and acquiescing to Indian self-rule, hinting at the Irwin Declaration. "This is not the first White Paper of this kind that has appeared," Amery declared, and pointed to unrest throughout the world "because of the White Papers which are poured out from the Colonial Office and which we are afterwards told do not mean what they appear to say."[168] Amery's speech was aimed at a continued appeasement of the diehard, anti-Baldwin group within the Conservative Party. This is why the arguments against the white paper had little relation to the document's actual contents. Even Malcolm MacDonald admitted that "[t]he substance of the white paper is all right [. . .] its embroidery is all wrong."[169]

While the rank and file of the House of Commons indulged in emotional arguments for and against the new policy, party leaders were busy calculating. The outcome of the debate was not necessarily instrumental for Amery and Baldwin, merely their noted opposition to a white paper that appeared to reward Arab violence in Palestine with decreased Jewish immigration. No majority was necessary, and so the plethora of opinion expressed during the debate posed no fundamental problems for Conservative leaders other than the slight embarrassment Amery originally hoped to avoid.

As expected, condemnation and support were not unanimous among any party. Colonel Charles Howard-Bury, for example, was Conservative MP for Chelmsford and spoke in support of the government, which he believed had "acted very courageously and impartially in producing that White Paper."[170] Another Conservative MP, Sir George Jones, admonished the character of the debate, stating "that it would be a calamity if the Palestinian question were involved in party politics in this country."[171] The Liberal MP Sir Rhys Hopkin Morris defied his own leader by highlighting how "it would be a moment of very grave importance in the history of this country if it were recognised that international events of this kind are to be part of the ordinary battle of party conflict."[172] Labour MP Frederick Cocks also called attention to the political machinations underway, saying Lloyd George "had one eye on the Mount of Olives and the other on a part of the East End of London where a by-election is about to take place and where there is a population of very hard-working and able Zionists."[173]

Other Labour members lent support to the opposition. Daniel Hopkin, for example, raised the specter of anti-Semitism, asserting that "[a]ccording to this White Paper, if a Jew buys land he is wrong. If he is a farmer, he is wrong. It seems to me that to some people Trotsky is always a Jew but Einstein is always a German. Every time he is wrong."[174] To Hopkin, this made the white paper "the greatest mistake of any Minister since the time when we lost the American colonies."[175] Although both Liberal and Conservative parties were relatively untroubled by backbench dissent in this debate, Labour could ill afford such breaking of ranks. Amery understood this and gave his assessment of the debate as follows:

> My speech drew the PM who was thoroughly woolly; full of general gush about the Zionists but not really precise as to what the government meant to do [. . .] Walter Elliot wound up for us quite effectively, and then Alexander replied, a meagre ill formed speech which did not satisfy the House. Kenworthy rose full of indignation, was cut short but re-opened after the usual reading of bills, to ask questions which Alexander dodged by walking away leaving poor Shiels, sick and sorry, to make as good a defense as he could to a series of persistent questions as to whether the government stood by the White Paper or not. My summary of the debate was "From White Paper to white sheet."[176]

First Lord of the Admiralty, Lord Alexander, argued that the debate vindicated Labour, asserting that "the so-called case against the government as stated to-night had been a very damp squib."[177] Alexander challenged "any impartial Member of the House who has sat right through this debate and heard all the speeches, to summarise the arguments [. . .] and to say if he does not agree with me that, in the main, the debate has not shown that there is a strong feeling in this House on the part of a majority against the position of the government."[178] This is where Labour's problem arose, however. The government needed more than a majority on this single issue as it required its own unity as well as cross-party support for foreign policy in general. This situation left the prime minister "cross about Palestine" and particularly annoyed with the colonial secretary. Lady Passfield wrote how "the Shaw Commission and Hope-Simpson, with his report, both nominees of Sidney's, have been too pro-Arab; a White Paper (which the P.M. saw and approved) was 'tactless'—indeed he allowed Lloyd George in his virulent attack on the White Paper, to assert that the P.M. has not seen it—which was mean of MacDonald."[179] The beleaguered Shiels, late in the evening debate, was badgered into asserting that "[i]t is quite obvious, surely [. . .] that the White

Paper, as explained and amplified today, certainly stands."[180] This, however, was unlikely. The Labour government was fragile on foreign policy, had already been undermined by criticism from the League of Nations, was threatened over the potential loss of cross-party support on India, and was faced with the realization that a few key pro-Zionist Labour MPs also opposed the white paper.

The younger MacDonald noted how the main problem was that "[i]f you dispute Hope-Simpson then certainly disagree with White Paper; that is a fundamental controversy."[181] Like many British-Zionist sympathizers, however, he did not tend to speak out against the two investigative commissions but instead took offense principally because the white paper seemed to focus unnecessarily on criticizing the Jews. He wrote that the "[d]ocument is typical of Colonial Office accustomed to take paternal interest in self-helpless native race [. . .]. White Paper shows lamentable and disastrous imbalance."[182] Malcolm MacDonald vehemently defended Zionism during this period, writing that "[i]f such censures are to be written, how many pages might be written about Arab assassins!"[183] The young Labour politician's own legacy on Palestine, however, would prove even more unpopular and controversial during his tenure as colonial secretary in the late 1930s (see chap. 4).

In addition, supplementing this internal split and external antagonism was the very tangible Whitechapel by-election results of 3 December 1930, which showed a significantly reduced Labour majority. These different factors combined to deliver the death knell to Passfield's white paper, but it was a slow-burn decision that did not materialize until protracted talks between Zionists and the Palestine cabinet subcommittee disruptively spilled into the next calendar year.

Immediately after the debate, James Ramsay MacDonald was still clinging to the official interpretation of the white paper. He wrote to Dr. Myer Solis Cohen in Philadelphia: "I am in an awful state of pressure. You will have seen the repeated contentions of the government that, as a matter of fact, the White Paper is no upset of the Mandate. The position in Palestine has got very dangerous, and the responsibility has to be shared by both the Jews and the Arabs on the spot. We must get things a little quieter; otherwise, nothing but disaster is ahead."[184] Following the by-election, the government needed to end the white paper debate and soothe internal divisions exacerbated by Liberal and Conservative opposition.[185] This meant that the Anglo-Zionist discussions had to be closed as quickly as possible. The prime minister had ceded this issue to Foreign Secretary Arthur Henderson on 6 November to organize a cabinet subcommittee, which did include Lord Passfield, and confer with Chaim Weizmann and other Zionist leaders to "clarify" the white paper.[186] Although this clarification did result in an effective reversal of the white paper, this was certainly not the original intention. As noted above, the talks began as a legal exercise and a means of convincing the policy's Zionist critics that it did not violate the Mandate.

Henderson's notes for the negotiations demonstrate his confidence in the government's stance. "If 'the position' of the Arabs is 'positively changed for the worse,'" Henderson wrote, "the government must take steps to put things right."[187] Zionist criticisms, he decided, "lose a good deal of their force because they assume intentions on the part of His Majesty's Government which are contrary to the facts."[188] The foreign secretary was also annoyed by Zionist memoranda's prolific citations of Hailsham and Simon's letter to *The Times* without a single reference to Lord Passfield's rebuttal of 5 November.[189]

In addition, Henderson criticized Zionist negotiator Leonard Stein's selective and misleading quotes, how he represented the policy as more anti-Zionist than it really was by eliminating the government's references to working with the Jewish Agency.[190] The oft repeated accusation that the white paper blamed Arab unemployment solely on Jewish immigration, for example, was one instance "of incomplete quotation and misinterpretation of the white paper. Great stress was laid on this particular misinterpretation in the ingenious perversion of it contained in a letter to Lord Passfield from Dr Weizmann, which Dr Weizmann published in 'The Times.'"[191] That part of the white paper, Henderson noted, spelled out Arab suspicions but in no way endorsed them.[192] The foreign secretary believed another tactic was to minimize the problem of dispossessed Arab cultivators because Weizmann and his colleagues "for political reasons" had to go "as far as possible towards satisfying their more extreme supporters who sympathise with the revisionist policy of a Jewish state in their time."[193] Lady Passfield offered a simple explanation of Zionist opposition to the white paper despite all the government's assurances: "It was not the Statement of Policy but the facts revealed by Hope-Simpson's report that he was up against," she wrote, "it was these facts that were so damning. Weisman is in the difficult position of a Company Promoter, confronted with an adverse expert's report, damaging to his prospective enterprise."[194]

As it was not the British government's priority to establish a Jewish state, Henderson believed it was Britain's duty to issue the white paper.[195] It is important to preface these opinions, however, with the knowledge that Henderson entered into these Anglo-Zionist talks with an eye on the League of Nations where his top priority throughout the autumn of 1930 was German disarmament. The foreign secretary was wary of and slightly bitter about Zionism's international activities. "On the publication of the Shaw Report," he wrote, "there is reason to suppose that every effort was made by the Jews to influence the Permanent Mandates Commission unfavourably against His Majesty's Government."[196] Another member of the Foreign Office later scribbled an additional note: "though it must be admitted that there is no documentary or other proof."[197]

The Palestine subcommittee first met Zionist representatives on 17 November and the initiation of these talks was announced that day. It was hoped that the beginning of the subcommittee's discussions would provide some inoculation against criticisms anticipated at the debate, but Shiels was unconvinced: "I am rather doubtful about the electoral help we shall get," he wrote to Henderson, "as Amery, L.l.G. and Co. are heavily in with Weizmann [. . .]."[198] This first meeting had been postponed at Weizmann's request, but it was merely a procedural affair and the group adjourned after an hour to observe the debate in the Commons.[199] What followed was a series of face-to-face meetings and negotiations via correspondence until late January 1931. Throughout these talks, Chaim Weizmann alternated between confidence in his ability to secure a reversal of the white paper, and gloom and uncertainty regarding the direction of negotiations with Henderson's committee. Two days after the debate, for example, Weizmann informed Amery that "[a]lthough the government is retreating very slowly and with not too much grace, a retreat it is."[200] However, a few days later Weizmann wrote that, he wrote "I don't know exactly what will be the result of our present negotiations with the government—I am writing at a time when events are about to break [. . .]. I do not know how our negotiations will end. This is no easy matter."[201]

The first draft of what became the MacDonald letter was received by Weizmann on 29 November, and he remarked that the "impression here is unfavourable."[202] This first draft, labeled "the Henderson letter" at this stage, was very long and essentially constituted the full rebuttals already made by Passfield, Shiels, and the Colonial and Foreign Offices.[203] It did contain some of the key reversing phrases found in the final letter, but these were accompanied by extensive contextual caveats. While noting that the Passfield White Paper made land control "regulatory and not prohibitive," the first draft also included a section saying, "it does involve a power to veto transactions which are inconsistent with the tenor of the general scheme."[204] As well as assurances that there would be no stoppage of immigration in any category, the first draft included sprawling provisos asserting the government's right to restrict immigration in line with economic capacity.[205]

Weizmann considered that Passfield was poisoning the atmosphere against them, believing "the old man malignantly sabotages everything."[206] Lord Passfield's relationship with the Zionist negotiators was indeed extremely strained at times. Lady Passfield wrote that her husband partially admired Weizmann, stating the Zionist diplomat was "a disinterested idealist, a clever administrator, an accomplished intellectual—all rolled into one. But he is a champion manipulator—and uses arguments and devices, regardless of accuracy, straightforwardness or respect for confidence, or other honourable undertakings [. . .] 'A clever devil: I take my hat off to him.'"[207] Mostly there was frustration between them. Although "Sidney started with a great admiration for the Jew and a contempt for the Arab," Lady Passfield wrote, "he reports that all the officials, at home and in Palestine, find the Jews, even many accomplished and cultivated Jews—intolerable as negotiators and colleagues."[208]

From the Zionist delegation's perspective, the problem was that Henderson and two other committee members, Alexander and Shaw, had no prior dealings with their cause, creating long, drawn-out meetings in which the intricacies had to be explained and the busy Henderson in particular became very irritable.[209] In contrast, Weizmann wrote, "Passfield does know the thing, but he is so artful and shifty that you never know when you have got him to agree to something."[210] Looking at the meeting transcripts and Henderson's notes, it does seem that he was well versed in the problems of Palestine but simply refused to yield on the government's right to issue the white paper and his belief that the Zionist criticisms were unfounded. Henderson told Weizmann he was being "supersensitive," and quoted Shiels's parliamentary defense of the white paper during meetings.[211] The foreign secretary challenged Weizmann on every point, demonstrating how these talks were originally intended to persuade and intimidate rather than placate Weizmann and his fellow Zionists. "[O]ur whole object," Henderson stated, is "to clear up matters that are ambiguous, that have been misstated or misunderstood [. . .]. I want you and your colleagues to be quite clear in your mind that the fullest possible opportunity is given to you to state every possible objection your people have to this White Paper. You can expect nothing more."[212] The foreign secretary specifically wanted to avoid any action that looked like a withdrawal of the original white paper.[213]

By mid-December, Weizmann complained that "[t]he negotiations with the government drag on rather inconclusively."[214] A redraft of the Henderson letter reached Weizmann, but it included only minor changes following advice from a legal committee, and the alterations constituted technical changes to language in two paragraphs of a document more than twenty pages long.[215] There was still no agreement by the end of December.[216] Weizmann, however, had met with MacDonald on Christmas Eve and found that "the prime minister seems really anxious that our negotiations should end in a successful agreement."[217] Malcolm MacDonald records this meeting slightly differently, noting that nothing much was said about the subcommittee conference other than it needed to be complete before Weizmann could bring up other subjects like Palestine administration staff and the development scheme.[218]

The Palestine subcommittee was achieving very little, and Henderson was due to leave London for Geneva on 9 January.[219] In preparation for his absence, the foreign secretary authorized another redraft of the letter. This was written by the Lord Advocate and Malcolm MacDonald, both identified by Weizmann as friends of their cause, in conjunction with Leonard Stein, Louis Namier, Major Hind (another Zionist), and even Weizmann himself.[220] It was finished on 7 January in time to be circulated to the cabinet committee and to Henderson before he left for Geneva, resulting in a few further amendments and a fourth draft of the letter.[221] It was during these January meetings that the final letter took shape by cutting out all of the caveats and provisos concerning Britain's right to limit Jewish immigration and land purchase that Henderson had defended since the previous November. Further changes were agreed via written correspondence on 22 January 1931, but they were all superficial—all offending wording had already been removed from the British draft.[222] There was a final meeting between Zionists and the Palestine subcommittee on 30 January and suddenly they had complete agreement. The fifth draft of the letter was finalized during this session and was approved by the cabinet on 4 February 1931.[223] By this time, Weizmann admitted to Malcolm MacDonald: "I am afraid you are sick of the sight of my blue paper [. . .],"[224] which the Zionist leader almost always used for his flourishingly handwritten correspondence.

The reversal of the Passfield White Paper, therefore, did not occur until January 1931 and evolved slowly during that month. It is likely that as Henderson pressed on doggedly in discussions with Zionists, James Ramsay MacDonald worried more about the depressing statistics of the Whitechapel by-election and the negotiations' anticipated effect on upcoming parliamentary business. The India issue was due to resurface early in the new year.

On 23 January, the prime minister officially closed the first stage of the India Conference, which was due to continue within a few months. Indeed, Lady Passfield noted that Palestine could be tidied away, but "[d]uring the next year, whichever party is in power, it is India that will claim attention."[225] She called the closing speech "a gorgeous success" but stressed that India's constitutional development would remain an ongoing concern.[226] The same was true of Labour's internal divisions. The prime minister, for example, expressed how he was "getting very tired [. . .] of the number of letters I get from colleagues ending, for one reason or another, with a threat that they must resign. I think it is about time that I started playing the same sort of card."[227] It appears that the weight of holding the Labour Party together on an issue made more divisive by the arguments of Conservative and Liberal politicians, who were partially motivated by preserving their own leadership positions, was simply too tiresome. The minority Labour government found it less politically risky to concede to the terms of a letter drafted and amended by the prime minister's own son and a legal authority in the Lord Advocate than to continue to defend the Passfield White Paper against what both the Foreign Office and the Colonial Office agreed were unfounded accusations. Baldwin wrote that "[t]he government is decaying daily and I can't see how in any way they can hold on much longer [. . .]," and he was correct.[228] There may have been no official alliance between Baldwin, Amery, and Lloyd George, but the effect on MacDonald was the same.[229] In a bid to maintain Labour unity and avoid derailing India policy, the government was unable to continue with the Passfield White Paper.

A Failure to Act

Although the British government was faced with only a single main option of reversing the white paper, there were also two subsidiary alternatives: Labour's elite could reverse the Passfield White Paper and replace it with extensive development, as originally intended, or reverse the Passfield White Paper without extensive development. One of these options was far more attractive in terms of broad national interest, which, in 1930–1931, was focused on the economy.

The Economy Crashes

Unlike in the situation during the Balfour Zeitgeist, the economy for the Labour government during the Passfield debacle was an objective national problem rather than a debatable political one. Distinct from the embattled Lloyd George coalition, the minority Labour government was not facing a campaign like "Anti-Waste" because the press barons (Lords Beaverbrook and Rothermere) were thorns largely in Baldwin's side. Since the Passfield White Paper did not fall close to a general election, the economy was not overly politicized in this specific episode. Rather, over the period and subject in question, specifically October 1930–February 1931, the financial crisis following the collapse of the US stock market in 1929 was a constant, looming, material fact rather than a chiefly political problem in which the issue was a matter of perception.[230]

As a result of these real financial constraints, the option to reverse the Passfield White Paper was not dependent on a commitment to the development program of Sir John Hope-Simpson, already rejected once due to its high costs when the white paper was first published. The original cabinet committee on Palestine had determined that Britain was under a moral if not legal obligation to compensate Arabs disadvantaged by British policy, but the expenditure required was open to substantial manipulation because it depended entirely on how the number of dispossessed Arabs was calculated.[231]

During the parliamentary debate, MPs such as Lloyd George, Samuel, and Amery called for extensive development of Palestine along the lines originally proposed by Hope-Simpson.[232] Ultimately, however, extensive development failed to escape economic constraints for a second time, and the option to reverse the white paper without a large development program was far more attractive. Incidentally, these MPs raised no objections when the white paper's provisions relating to Jewish immigration and land purchase were rescinded but not replaced with the agricultural development that Hope-Simpson had identified as urgently necessary. Therefore, just as the Passfield White Paper began as a program to prevent violence in Palestine but was restrained by the economic situation, so too was its reversal, prompted by a need to maintain political power and limited in viability due to financial pressures.

After 1931

Even though Passfield's policy was reversed in this somewhat humiliating spectacle, he wrote to Henderson, "I think you were thoroughly justified in embarking on the discussions in the political emergency."[233] After 1931, the constraints that led to this course of action only grew, meaning that the British government's handling of Palestine policy between the MacDonald letter of 1931 and the beginning of the Arab Revolt in 1936 remained stagnant. Following the political storm created by the Passfield White Paper, and the reemergence of the economy as a political problem later in 1931, politicians could identify no potential policy that was both safe politically and good for the national interest.[234] The India problem continued within British politics, notwithstanding a tense settlement reached between Irwin and Gandhi in March 1931.[235] The Labour government then fell in August as the financial crisis reached new heights and the Conservative Party orchestrated a takeover, succeeding in splitting Labour in the process.[236] As the crisis deepened and London's financial sector called for cuts in government spending, continued tensions in Palestine failed to materialize on the new government's agenda.[237] Although the cabinet discussed individual issues, such as forming a Palestine trade preference, establishing a legislative council, and dealing with the rise in immigration following Hitler's ascension in Germany, the question of overall policy remained unaddressed.[238]

In 1932, the colonial secretary again placed the issue of Jewish immigration before the cabinet, and, rather than proposing a change of policy, he suggested that the determination of economic capacity be left entirely in the hands of the high commissioner stationed in Jerusalem. Another committee was formed to consider the question.[239] This adroitly removed Westminster from the immediate realm of responsibility and safely ignored the findings of the Hope-Simpson Commission.[240] In addition, the Colonial Office pressured the Palestine administration to develop a greater budget surplus, which meant spending less on development.[241] Although "[n]ew agricultural stations, demonstration plots, research, etc., were provided for," such schemes were tiny in comparison to the needs Hope-Simpson had identified.[242] Whereas the one-man commission had found thousands of Arab families either directly or indirectly dispossessed or made unemployed by British policy in Palestine, in February 1933 the colonial secretary asked that compensation be restricted to ex-tenants.[243] Tensions in Palestine continued to mount.

Unlike the period between the Jaffa riots in 1921 and those in 1929, the interlude between the Passfield White Paper and the next great outbreak, what became the Arab Revolt, was not calm at all. On 15 April 1931, the high commissioner "reported that in several areas, of which he gave details, the Zionists had bought property and were undertaking eviction proceedings against Arab families," which Weizmann was unable or unwilling to prevent.[244] Riots broke out in October 1933, the Palestine police opened fire, and Arab hostility resulted in frequent demonstrations through Jerusalem and Jaffa.[245] Sir Arthur Wauchope, the new high commissioner, even expressed concern over delays to his shipments of tear gas by 1934.[246] Wauchope expressed, however, that such demonstrations were not "serious as a threat to the State" until the "*fellaheen*" peasant farmers joined the riots.[247] "Should religious as well as political cries be raised," Wauchope warned, "a number of the *fellaheen*, many of whom are landless and many very poor, will join; [. . .] Our difficulties therefore are liable to be far more formidable in the future than they have been in the past."[248] The high commissioner then went on to list exactly the same political, religious, and economic grievances that the Shaw and Hope-Simpson reports highlighted following the 1929 riots.[249] By the late 1930s, violence in Palestine erupted on a hitherto unfathomable scale.

A Crystallized Policy

The "Passfield Reversal" was a period in Britain's policy making toward Palestine that marked the first stages of Britain's withdrawal from the Jewish national home policy. Following the riots of 1929, two commissions of inquiry highlighted the need to invest in Arab agriculture and limit Jewish immigration and land purchase, in line with economic capacity, in order to keep the peace. These investigations resulted in the Passfield White Paper that was subsequently reversed following Conservative and Liberal opposition and lengthy consultations with prominent Zionists. Unlike many previous works on the Mandate that have characterized this incident as little more than a triumph of Chaim Weizmann's diplomatic skills, this chapter highlights the role played by Conservatives' and Liberals' use of Zionist arguments for their own political ends.

Baldwin feared the Conservative diehards who equated Arabs of Palestine with Indians agitating for self-rule and vociferously opposed both. Lloyd George was acutely aware of the Liberal Party's rapidly declining status and sought to defend his own prime ministerial record, which witnessed both the Balfour Declaration and the official Mandate, and simply to grapple for position. MacDonald's government was placed in jeopardy by the divisive nature of this ongoing debate, and he sought to solidify the new policy's legal standing while placating key backbenchers by assigning Henderson to confer with the Zionists. Henderson was focused on Europe and disarmament, and concerns for the ongoing India conference and poor performance in the Whitechapel by-election combined to make the Passfield White Paper too risky. The threshold for risk seems to have been significantly lower than previous Palestine policy-making episodes, and this can be attributed to Labour's even more fragile hold on power than the atmosphere surrounding Lloyd George's coalition government of the early 1920s. Following February 1931, all policy options were accompanied by unacceptable levels of political risk, effectively crystallizing the British government's own Palestine policy until tensions erupted again in 1936.

Notes

1. Cmd. 3530, 1930, *Report of the Commission on the Palestine Disturbances of August 1929*, 155.
2. Gerber, *Remembering and Imagining Palestine*, 108.
3. Segev, *One Palestine, Complete*, 326.
4. Porath, *Emergence of the Palestinian-Arab National Movement 1918–1929*, 136; Pappe, *A History of Modern Palestine*, 93; Caplan, *Contested Histories*, 80; Matthews, *Confronting an Empire, Constructing a Nation*, 83; Segev, *One Palestine, Complete*. El-Eini, *Mandated Landscape*; Renton, "Flawed Foundations."
5. Cmd. 3530, *Commission on the Palestine Disturbances of August 1929*.
6. Allison, *Essence of Decision*; Paul MacDonald, "Useful Fiction or Miracle Maker: The Competing Epistemological Foundations of Rational Choice Theory," *American Political Science Review* 97, no. 4 (2003): 551–565.
7. Cmd. 3530, *Commission on the Palestine Disturbances of August 1929*, 150–163.
8. Ibid., 161.
9. Ibid., 162.
10. Ibid.
11. Ibid., 166.
12. Gorny, *British Labour Movement and Zionism*, 69.
13. CAB 24/212, 9 May 1930, "Palestine: Statement with Regard to British Policy," TNA, 4.
14. Cmd. 3686, 1930, *Report on Immigration, Land Settlement and Development or Hope-Simpson Report*, 141.
15. Cmd. 3686, *Immigration, Land Settlement and Development*, 135.
16. Gorny, *British Labour Movement and Zionism*, 142.
17. Ibid., 142–153.
18. Ibid., 153.
19. CO 733/183/77050, 17 January 1930, Chancellor to Passfield, TNA, cited in Gabriel Sheffer, "Intentions and Results of British Policy in Palestine: Passfield's White Paper," *Middle Eastern Studies* 9, no. 1 (1973): 43–60, 44.
20. House of Commons Debates, 17 November 1930, series 5, vol. 245, cols. 146–147.
21. CAB 24/215, 18 August 1930, Hope-Simpson to Passfield, TNA.
22. CAB 24/211, 27 March 1930, Memorandum by the Secretary of State for the Colonies, TNA.
23. PREM 1/102, 3 October 1930, Passfield to Ramsay MacDonald, TNA.
24. House of Commons Debates, 3 April 1930, series 5, vol. 237, cols. 1466–1467.
25. PREM 1/102, 12 August 1930, Passfield to Ramsay MacDonald, TNA.
26. PREM 1/102, 10 August 1930, "Cabinet Committee on Policy in Palestine. Memorandum on the Financial Situation of Palestine by Sir John Campbell, Financial Advisor to the Secretary of State," TNA, 29.
27. CAB 23/65, 19 September 1930, Cabinet Minutes, TNA, 2.
28. CAB 23/65, 19 September 1930, Cabinet Minutes, 3.

29. MAC 9/5/29, 18 November 1930, Passfield to Chancellor, reproduced by permission of Durham University Library; MAC 9/5/18, 5 January 1931, Shuckburgh to Selby, reproduced by permission of Durham University Library.
30. CAB 24/215, September 1930, "Cabinet Committee on Policy in Palestine Second Report," TNA, 2.
31. CAB 24/215, September 1930, "Cabinet Committee on Policy in Palestine Second Report," 3; CAB 23/65, 24 September 1930, Cabinet Minutes, TNA, 10.
32. CAB 23/65, 24 September 1930, Cabinet Minutes, 10.
33. Ibid.
34. Cmd. 3692, 1930, *Statement of Policy by His Majesty's Government in the United Kingdom*.
35. CO 733/183/2, October 1930, "Discussion of Amendments," TNA.
36. James Ramsay MacDonald, 14 February 1931, "The Palestine White Paper, an Interpretation, Prime Minister's Letter," *The Times*, 8.
37. James Ramsay MacDonald, 14 February 1931, "Palestine White Paper, an Interpretation."
38. Ibid.
39. CAB 23/66, 4 February 1931, Cabinet Minutes, TNA, 10.
40. Chaim Weizmann, *The Letters and Papers of Chaim Weizmann, Volume XV Series 3 October 1930–June 1933* (New Brunswick, NJ: Transaction Books, 1978).
41. Alex Mintz, "How Do Leaders Make Decisions? A Poliheuristic Perspective," *Journal of Conflict Resolution* 48, no. 1 (2004): 3–13.
42. Mintz, "How Do Leaders Make Decisions?"
43. Michael Hughes, *British Foreign Secretaries in an Uncertain World*, 82.
44. Henry Winkler, "The Emergence of Labour Party Foreign Policy," *The Journal of Modern History* 28, no. 3 (1956): 247–258, 247.
45. Winkler, "The Emergence of Labour Party Foreign Policy," 247.
46. Ibid.
47. Lady Davidson Papers; partly in *Davidson Memoirs*, 355, in Philip Williamson, ed. *Baldwin Papers: A Conservative Statesman, 1908–1947* (Cambridge: Cambridge University Press, 2004), 246.
48. Williamson, ed. *Baldwin Papers*, 254.
49. LSE/PASSFIELD/1/2/9, 1 July 1930, Diary of Beatrice Webb.
50. Pederson, "The Impact of League Oversight on British Policy in Palestine," 47.
51. CAB 23/64, 28 July 1930, Cabinet Minutes, TNA, 4.
52. CAB 24/214, 29 July 1930, "Palestine: Comments of His Majesty's Government on Report of Permanent Mandates Commission, Memorandum by the Secretary of State for the Colonies," TNA.
53. CAB 24/214, 29 July 1930, "Palestine: Comments of His Majesty's Government.
54. Stanley Baldwin, Austen Chamberlain, and Leopold Amery, 23 October 1930, "British Policy in Palestine, the White Paper, Conservative Leaders' Comments," *The Times*, 15.
55. PREM 1/102, 10 August 1930, "Cabinet Committee on Policy in Palestine. Memorandum by the Secretary of State for the Colonies," TNA, 8.
56. Labour Party and Trades Union Congress, *Memorandum on War Aims* (London: Inter-Allied Labour and Socialist Conference, 1917); Paul Keleman, "Zionism and the British Labour Party: 1917–39," *Social History* 21, no. 1 (1996): 71–87, 71–72.
57. Keleman, "Zionism and the British Labour Party" 71–72; Rose, *Gentile Zionists*, 70.

58. Paul Lamont Hanna, *British Policy in Palestine* (Washington: American Council on Public Affairs, 1942), 98.
59. Kenworthy to Weizmann, 21 October 1930, *Letters and Papers of Chaim Weizmann, Volume XV*, 2.
60. Joseph Kenworthy, *India: A Warning* (London: E. Matthews and Marrot, 1931).
61. Kenworthy to Weizmann, 21 October 1930, *Letters and Papers of Chaim Weizmann, Volume XV*, 2.
62. James Ramsay MacDonald, *A Socialist in Palestine* (London: Jewish Socialist Labour Confederation, 1922), 18, cited in Keleman, "Zionism and the British Labour Party," 73.
63. CAB 23/65, 24 September 1930, Cabinet Minutes.
64. CAB 23/65, 6 November 1930, Cabinet Minutes, TNA.
65. CAB 23/65, 6 November 1930, Cabinet Minutes.
66. Rose, *Gentile Zionists*, 20.
67. PREM 30/69/579, 22 October 1930, Ramsay MacDonald to Weizmann, TNA.
68. MacDonald to Weizmann, 31 October 1930, *Letters and Papers of Chaim Weizmann, Volume XV*, 33.
69. Weizmann to Malcolm MacDonald, 5 November 1930, *Letters and Papers of Chaim Weizmann, Volume XV*, 34; Weizmann to Warburg, 6 November 1930, *Letters and Papers of Chaim Weizmann, Volume XV*, 35.
70. Weizmann to Amery, 13 November 1930, *Letters and Papers of Chaim Weizmann, Volume XV*, 38.
71. CAB 23/65, 6 November 1930, Cabinet Minutes.
72. Andrew Thorpe, "Arthur Henderson and the British Political Crisis of 1931," *Historical Journal* 31, no. 1 (1988): 117–139, 119.
73. House of Commons Debates, 17 November 1930, cols. 203–204.
74. AC4/1/1-1358, 18 November 1930, Austen Chamberlain to Mary Carnegie, Cadbury Research Library: Special Collections, University of Birmingham.
75. AC4/1/1-1358, 18 November 1930, Austen Chamberlain to Mary Carnegie.
76. Gorny, *British Labour Movement and Zionism*, 80.
77. Ibid., 51.
78. CO 733/183/1, 19 March 1930, JRM to Passfield, TNA.
79. MAC 8/12/2, n.d., MacDonald Notes, reproduced by permission of Durham University Library.
80. Phillip Williamson, *National Crises and National Government* (Cambridge: Cambridge University Press, 1992), 79.
81. AMEL 1/5/3, n.d., draft article for *Home and Empire*, Churchill Archives Centre, the Papers of Leopold Amery.
82. Williamson, *National Crises and National Government*, 79.
83. PREM 1/102, 19 March 1930, Ramsay MacDonald to Baldwin, Lloyd George, Passfield and Henderson, TNA.
84. Stuart Ball, *Baldwin and the Conservative Party: The Crisis of 1929–1931* (London: Yale University Press, 1988), 109.
85. Williamson, *National Crises and National Government*, 90.
86. Ibid., 84–85.
87. Ibid., 86.
88. Ball, *Baldwin and the Conservative Party*, 109.

89. Williamson, *National Crises and National Government*, 86.
90. Ibid.
91. Ibid., 87.
92. Ball, *Baldwin and the Conservative Party*, 114.
93. Williamson, *National Crises and National Government*, 87.
94. MacDonald Diary, 10 November 1929, cited in Williamson, *National Crises and National Government*, 87-90.
95. Ball, *Baldwin and the Conservative Party*, 114.
96. LSE/PASSFIELD/1/2/9, 9 July 1930, Diary of Beatrice Webb.
97. LSE/PASSFIELD/1/2/9, 9 July 1930, Diary of Beatrice Webb.
98. PREM 30/69/676, 30 October 1930, NB to Stevenson, TNA.
99. AC4/1/1-1358, 18 November 1930, Austen Chamberlain to Mary Carnegie.
100. Sarvepalli Gopal, *The Viceroyalty of Lord Irwin 1926-1931* (Oxford: Clarendon, 1957), 113.
101. AMEL 1/5/12, 1 of 2, n.d., draft article, Churchill Archives Centre, the Papers of Leopold Amery.
102. LSE/PASSFIELD/1/2/9, 30 October 1930, Diary of Beatrice Webb.
103. PREM 1/102, 10 August 1930, "Cabinet Committee on Policy in Palestine. Memorandum by the Secretary of State for the Colonies," 4.
104. PREM 1/102, 10 August 1930, "Cabinet Committee on Policy in Palestine."
105. Ibid., 7.
106. Rose, *Gentile Zionists*, 16.
107. Ibid., 18.
108. Lytton to Irwin, 9-10 November 1929, Halifax Indian Papers Mss Eur c. 152/18/309, in Williamson, *Baldwin Papers*, 224.
109. Lytton to Irwin, 9-10 November 1929, Halifax Indian Papers in Williamson, *Baldwin Papers*, 224.
110. Baldwin to Joan Davidson, 2 November 1930, Lady Davidson papers partly in *Davidson Memoirs*, 354, M&B 578-9, in Williamson, *Baldwin Papers*, 243.
111. Halifax Indian Papers. Mss Eur c. 152/19/147, in Williamson, *Baldwin Papers*, 239.
112. LG/F/39/2/28, Blankenberg to Amery, 1 November 1920, Parliamentary Archives; Lady Davidson Papers, partly in *Davidson Memoirs*, Baldwin to Davidson, 13 November 1930, in Williamson, *Baldwin Papers*, 246.
113. AMEL 1/5/46, 1 of 2, December 1929, "The Future in Palestine" *The Pioneer*, Churchill Archives Centre, the Papers of Leopold Amery, 5-6.
114. AMEL, 1/5/46, 2 of 2, 26 July 1928, "My Recollections after Dinner Written the Same Night. Unchecked, Unauthorised and Largely Inaccurate." Josiah Wedgewood, Churchill Archives Centre, the Papers of Leopold Amery.
115. Williamson, *Baldwin Papers*, 225-232.
116. Amery Diaries, II, 59-60 (30 January 1930) in Williamson, *Baldwin Papers*, 226.
117. Baldwin to Davidson, 13 November 1930, Lady Davidson Papers, partly in *Davidson Memoirs*, 355, in Williamson, *Baldwin Papers*, 246.
118. Baldwin to Sir John Simon, 19 February 1930, Simon Papers 62/228, in Williamson, *Baldwin Papers*, 228.
119. Baldwin, Chamberlain, and Amery, 23 October 1930, "British Policy in Palestine," *The Times*, 15.

120. Leopold Amery, 22 October 1930, *The Empire at Bay: The Leo Amery Diaries 1929–1945* (London: Hutchinson, 1988), 85.
121. Amery, *Empire at Bay*, 85.
122. Ibid.
123. Weizmann to Amery, 23 October 1930, *Letters and Papers of Chaim Weizmann, Volume XV*, 1; Weizmann to Warburg, 24 October 1930, *Letters and Papers of Chaim Weizmann, Volume XV*, 8.
124. AC39/2/1-56, 9 October 1930, Austen Chamberlain to Neville Chamberlain, Cadbury Research Library: Special Collections, University of Birmingham.
125. AC39/2/1-56, 9 October 1930, Austen Chamberlain to Neville Chamberlain.
126. Gwynne to Louis Grieg, 11 November 1930, Gwynne Papers 20, in Williamson, *Baldwin Papers*, 245.
127. Baldwin to Salisbury, 19 January 1931, Hatfield House Archives 4M/139/45, in Williamson, *Baldwin Papers*, 250.
128. Amery, 6 November 1930, *Empire at Bay*, 88.
129. LSE/PASSFIELD/1/2/9, 11 July 1930, Diary of Beatrice Webb.
130. Robert Self, ed. Chamberlain to Hilda, 14 February 1931, *The Neville Chamberlain Diary Letters Volume 3* (Aldershot: Ashgate, 2000), 237.
131. John Campbell, *Lloyd George: A Goat in the Wilderness, 1922–1931* (Aldershot: Gregg Revivals, 1993), 253.
132. Campbell, *Lloyd George*, 253.
133. Baldwin to Davidson and Joan Davidson, 27 November 1930, Lady Davidson Papers partly in *Davidson Memoirs*, 355–6, M&B 579, in Williamson, *Baldwin Papers*, 246–247.
134. Baldwin to Davidson, 6 November 1930, Lady Davidson Papers partly in *Davidson Memoirs*, 354–5, M&B 579, in Williamson, *Baldwin Papers*, 244–245.
135. LSE/PASSFIELD/1/2/9, 11 July 1930, Diary of Beatrice Webb.
136. Baldwin, Chamberlain, and Amery, 23 October 1930, "British Policy in Palestine," *The Times*, 15.
137. Ibid.
138. Lord Hailsham and John Simon, 4 November 1930, "British Policy in Palestine," *The Times*, 15.
139. Defries, *Conservative Attitudes to Jews, 1900–1950*, 145.
140. LSE/PASSFIELD/1/2/9, 9 July 1930, Diary of Beatrice Webb; LSE/PASSFIELD/1/2/9, 29 March 1930, Diary of Beatrice Webb.
141. Lord Hailsham and John Simon, 4 November 1930, "British Policy in Palestine," *The Times*, 15.
142. Ibid.
143. CO 733/183/3, October–November 1930, "Notes on Jewish Criticisms of White Paper," TNA.
144. House of Commons Debates, 17 November 1930, cols. 80–81.
145. FO 800/282, 3 December 1930, Hope-Simpson to Campbell, TNA.
146. House of Commons Debates, 17 November 1930, cols. 81–82.
147. Ibid., cols. 114–115.
148. PREM 1/102, 3 October 1930, Passfield to Ramsay MacDonald, TNA.
149. AMEL 1/5/46, 2 of 2, 5 February 1951, Palestine Debate, 16 November 1930, Churchill Archives Centre, the Papers of Leopold Amery.

150. FO 800/282, 14 November 1930, Henderson to Cabinet, TNA.
151. House of Commons Debates, 17 November 1930, cols. 92–93.
152. CO 733/183/3, 22 October 1930, Chancellor to Williams, TNA.
153. PREM 1/103, 16 November 1930, Chancellor to Shuckburgh, TNA.
154. CO 733/182/8, 4 November 1930, Memorandum by Williams, TNA.
155. CO 733/182/8, 4 November 1930, Memorandum by Williams.
156. Ibid.
157. CO 733/183/3, 21 November 1930, "Memorandum on the Policy of His Majesty's Government as Set Out in the October White Paper," TNA.
158. CO 733/182/8, 5 November 1930, Draft Letter, Passfield to *The Times*, TNA.
159. CO 733/182/8, 5 November 1930, Draft Letter.
160. CO 733/183/3, 22 October 1930, Chancellor to Williams.
161. CO 733/183/3, October–November 1930, "Jewish Criticisms of White Paper."
162. House of Commons Debates, 17 November 1930, cols. 96–97.
163. Ibid., cols. 115–116.
164. FO 800/282, 14 November 1930, "Notes on Jewish Statement Communicated by Mr Malcolm Macdonald," TNA.
165. FO 800/282, 14 November 1930, "Notes on Jewish Statement."
166. Ibid.
167. House of Commons Debates, 17 November 1930, cols. 108–109.
168. Ibid., cols. 114–115.
169. MAC 9/4/41, n.d., MacDonald Notes, reproduced by permission of Durham University Library.
170. House of Commons Debates, 17 November 1930, cols. 139–140.
171. Ibid., cols. 163–164.
172. Ibid.
173. Ibid., cols. 164–165.
174. Ibid., cols. 186–187.
175. Ibid., cols. 138–139.
176. Amery, 17 November 1930, *Empire at Bay*, 90.
177. House of Commons Debates, 17 November 1930, cols. 196–197.
178. Ibid.
179. LSE/PASSFIELD/1/2/9, 14 December 1930, Diary of Beatrice Webb.
180. House of Commons Debates, 17 November 1930, cols. 210–211.
181. MAC 9/4/41, n.d., MacDonald Notes, reproduced by permission of Durham University Library.
182. MAC 9/4/43, n.d., MacDonald Notes, reproduced by permission of Durham University Library.
183. MAC 9/4/44, n.d., MacDonald Notes, reproduced by permission of Durham University Library.
184. PREM 30/69/676, 19 November 1930, JRM to Solis Cohen, TNA.
185. CAB 23/65, 11 November 1930, Cabinet Minutes, TNA, 6.
186. CAB 23/66, 4 February 1931, Cabinet Minutes.
187. FO 800/282, November 1930, "Detailed Comments on a Memorandum by Mr. Leonard Stein. The Palestine White Paper of October 1930," TNA.
188. FO 800/282, November 1930, "Comments on a Memorandum by Mr. Leonard Stein."

189. Ibid.
190. Ibid.
191. Ibid.
192. Ibid.
193. Ibid.
194. LSE/PASSFIELD/1/2/9, 30 October 1930, Diary of Beatrice Webb.
195. FO 800/282, November 1930, "Comments on a Memorandum by Mr. Leonard Stein."
196. Ibid.
197. Ibid.
198. FO 800/282, 15 November 1930, Shiels to Henderson, TNA.
199. Weizmann to Samuel, 26 November 1930, *Letters and Papers of Chaim Weizmann, Volume XV*, 49; MAC 9/3/80, 17 November 1930, Weizmann to Malcolm MacDonald, reproduced by permission of Durham University Library.
200. Weizmann to Amery, 19 November 1930, *Letters and Papers of Chaim Weizmann, Volume XV*, 44.
201. Weizmann to Wormser, 21 November 1930, *Letters and Papers of Chaim Weizmann, Volume XV*, 47; Weizmann to Beilinson, 27 November 1930, *Letters and Papers of Chaim Weizmann, Volume XV*, 51–53.
202. Weizmann to Henderson, 1 December 1930, *Letters and Papers of Chaim Weizmann, Volume XV*, 55; Weizmann to Jacobson, 4 December 1930, *Letters and Papers of Chaim Weizmann, Volume XV*, 56.
203. FO 800/282, 29 November 1930, Henderson to Weizmann, TNA.
204. FO 800/282, 29 November 1930, Henderson to Weizmann.
205. Ibid.
206. Weizmann to Sokolow, 7 December 1930, *Letters and Papers of Chaim Weizmann, Volume XV*, 57.
207. LSE/PASSFIELD/1/2/9, 30 October 1930, Diary of Beatrice Webb.
208. LSE/PASSFIELD/1/2/9, 30 October 1930, Diary of Beatrice Webb.
209. Weizmann to Warburg, 11 December 1930, *Letters and Papers of Chaim Weizmann, Volume XV*, 63–64.
210. Ibid.
211. FO 800/282, 18 November 1930, "Verbatim Notes Taken by Stenographer at 2nd Meeting of Members of the Cabinet with Jewish Representatives Held on Tuesday 18 November," TNA.
212. FO 800/282, 18 November 1930, "Verbatim Notes Taken by Stenographer at 2nd Meeting."
213. FO 800/282, 27 November, "Informal Minutes of Cabinet Policy in Palestine," TNA.
214. Weizmann to Bentwich, 17 December 1930, *Letters and Papers of Chaim Weizmann, Volume XV*, 69; Weizmann to Rothschild, 24 December 1930, *Letters and Papers of Chaim Weizmann, Volume XV*, 76.
215. FO 800/282, 17 December 1930, "Redraft of December 17 of Paragraphs 8 and 9 of Letter Sent by the Secretary of State for Foreign Affairs to Dr. Weizmann, Dated November 29, Regarding British Policy in Palestine, Embodying Amendments Agreed on by Drafting Committee at Meetings December 11 and by Legal Committee on December 17," TNA.
216. MAC 9/4/38, 31 December 1930, Weizmann to Malcolm MacDonald, reproduced by permission of Durham University Library.

217. Weizmann to Bentwich, 17 December 1930, *Letters and Papers of Chaim Weizmann, Volume XV*, 69; Weizmann to Rothschild, 24 December 1930, *Letters and Papers of Chaim Weizmann, Volume XV*, 76.

218. MAC 9/6/30, 24 December 1930, Interview between the Prime Minister, Dr. Weizmann and Mr. Namier at 9:30 a.m., reproduced by permission of Durham University Library.

219. MAC 9/8/2–9/8/58, 27 April 1931, Historical Summary of Discussions Leading Up to the Prime Minister's Letter of February 13th, 1931, to Dr. Weizmann, reproduced by permission of Durham University Library.

220. MAC 9/8/2–9/8/58, 27 April 1931, Historical Summary of Discussions.

221. Ibid.

222. MAC 9/5/36, 22 January 1931, "Proposed Corrections in Mr. Henderson's Draft Letter," reproduced by permission of Durham University Library.

223. Weizmann to Vera Weizmann, 30 January 1930, *Letters and Papers of Chaim Weizmann, Volume XV*, 95.

224. MAC 9/6/33, 8 February 1930, Weizmann to Malcolm MacDonald, reproduced by permission of Durham University Library.

225. LSE/PASSFIELD/1/2/9, 14 December 1930, Diary of Beatrice Webb.

226. LSE/PASSFIELD/1/2/9, 22 January 1931, Diary of Beatrice Webb.

227. PREM 30/69/676, 31 October 1930, Ramsay MacDonald to Lord Arnold, TNA.

228. Baldwin to Davidson and Joan Davidson, November 1930, Lady Davidson Papers, partly in *Davidson Memoirs*, in Williamson, *Baldwin Papers*, 247.

229. Gwynne Papers 20, Gwynne to Louis Grieg, 11 November 1930, in Williamson, *Baldwin Papers*, 245.

230. CAB 24/217, 9 December 1930, "Draft White Paper. Statement of the Principal Measures Taken by H.M. Government in Connection with Unemployment," TNA, 2.

231. CAB 24/215, 15 September 1930, "Cabinet Committee on Policy in Palestine Second Report," TNA, 3.

232. House of Commons Debates, 17 November 1930, cols. 85–210.

233. FO 800/282, 26 December 1930, Passfield to Henderson, TNA.

234. John D. Fair, "The Conservative Basis for the Formation of the National Government of 1931," *Journal of British Studies* 19, no. 2 (1980): 142–164, 150.

235. Gopal, *Viceroyalty of Lord Irwin*, 98.

236. Ibid.

237. Ibid.

238. CAB 23/70, 23 February 1932, Cabinet Minutes, TNA; CAB 23/71, 6 April 1932, Cabinet Minutes, TNA.

239. CAB 23/71, 6 April 1932, Cabinet Minutes, TNA, 12.

240. CAB 24/231, 28 June 1932, "Memorandum by the Secretary of State for India," TNA.

241. Roza El Eini, "Government Fiscal Policy in Mandatory Palestine in the 1930s," *Middle Eastern Studies* 33, no. 3 (1997): 570–596, 577.

242. El Eini, "Government Fiscal Policy," 581.

243. CAB 22/237, February 1933, "Memorandum by the Secretary of State for the Colonies," TNA; CAB 23/75, 8 February 1933, Cabinet Minutes, TNA, 9.

244. CAB 23/66, 15 April 1931, Cabinet Minutes, TNA, 19.

245. CAB 24/247, 18 December 1933, High Commissioner to Secretary of State for the Colonies, TNA.

246. CAB 23/78, 16 January 1934, Cabinet Minutes, TNA, 31.
247. CAB 22/237 February 1933, "Memorandum by the Secretary of State for the Colonies," TNA.
248. CAB 24/247, 18 December 1933, High Commissioner to Secretary of State for the Colonies, TNA.
249. CAB 22/237 February 1933, "Memorandum by the Secretary of State for the Colonies," TNA.

4 The MacDonald Betrayal, 1936–1939

THE ARAB REVOLT (1936–1939) preceded events that appeared to represent a major shift in British policy toward Palestine. Despite a commitment to the Jewish national home expressed in the Balfour Declaration, the official Mandate, the Churchill White Paper, and the "Black Letter" of 1931, the MacDonald White Paper of 1939 seemed to abrogate any further obligation to Zionism. Instead, this new policy committed Britain to an independent Palestine with a permanent Jewish minority. Considering the difficulties faced by previous British governments in attempting to withdraw from the Jewish national home, this new direction was highly controversial. Labeled "betrayal" and "appeasement," the MacDonald White Paper was in many ways a direct result of the violent uprising of the Arab Revolt.[1] Demonstrating why, however, is more complicated than a simple analogy with the Munich Agreement.

Unlike the Churchill White Paper and reversal of Passfield's white paper, this decision to end the Jewish national home would indeed have seemed rational in terms of Britain's national interest (i.e., through weighing costs vs. benefits for the state as a whole). Between the beginning of the Arab Revolt and the publication of the MacDonald White Paper, two commissions of inquiry resolutely presented the British government with the same fundamental and irresolvable flaws in the national home policy that had characterized all previous investigations, leading the government first to pursue partition of Palestine and then to decide in favor of a single-state solution. In the context of imminent war in Europe, this decision reflected the adoption of advice from two preeminent committees in order to end rebellion in the empire and refocus attention and resources closer to home. This, however, is an incomplete picture, not least because similar reasoning fails to explain previous British behavior toward Palestine. Looking at the relevant politicians' political problems lends an additional insight, a more nuanced understanding that demonstrates specifically which governmental concerns influenced the decision to abandon Zionism and why this sudden shift in policy actually represented far more continuity than change.

During this episode, the decision makers' key concerns centered around diplomatic needs, bureaucratic politics, and parliamentary politics. The government then chose among the only politically viable alternatives by trying to minimize the burden for Britain's strategic and economic imperatives. Rather than a sudden U-turn in Palestine policy as the result of appeasement, this chapter reveals a rebalancing of diplomatic interests in the Middle East necessitated by the Italian and German threats and made possible by a large Conservative majority in the House of Commons.

Searching for Solutions

In the time period under consideration, the British government was presented with a severe problem in the form of the Arab Revolt in Palestine, and their range of options for dealing with this situation was determined by the essentially contradictory reports of two commissions of inquiry: the Peel Commission in 1937 and the Woodhead Commission in 1938.

Each of these investigations identified the Arab Revolt as a severe intensification of previous, neglected disturbances. Unrest in the early 1930s had been a direct result of increased legal and illegal Jewish immigration into Palestine due to the rise of Hitler in Germany. This immigration had exceeded fifty thousand in 1933 and peaked at sixty-two thousand in 1935, doubling the Jewish population in a very short time period that coincided with severe drought and agricultural hardship in Palestine.[2] These levels of Jewish immigration did not threaten to reverse the Arabs' large demographic majority, but the new influx of German Jews was perceived as a dangerous precedent, the latest anxiety in a cumulative response to Zionism that inspired Palestine's Arabs to fear for their future. When the uprising began in April 1936, it evolved as a response to this increased Jewish presence, a series of reprisal murders between Jews and Arabs, parliamentary rejection of a Palestine Legislative Council, and refusal to grant three demands presented by the Arab Higher Committee: cessation of Jewish immigration, prohibition of land sales to Jews, and the creation of a national government.[3] The rebellion began in the form of a general strike accompanied by outbreaks of violence and sabotage directed at Jews, British officials, and fellow Arabs, and the British government's response entailed both repressive measures and authorization of the Palestine Royal (Peel) Commission to make recommendations for a political solution.

The answer, according to Lord Peel's commission, was decisive; the recommendation was the partition of Palestine, which far exceeded the committee's terms of reference.[4] While the committee was charged with finding both the causes of and the solutions to Palestine's problem, it was not technically empowered to undermine the Balfour Declaration. This original statement of intent and the official Mandate had accepted a British obligation to Zionism, but commissioners found that violence in Palestine during the 1920s and 1930s was consistently caused by an Arab desire for independence coupled with fear and hatred for the Jewish national home.[5] This had been exacerbated by the strides toward independence achieved by Iraq, Transjordan, Egypt, Syria, and Lebanon as well as the pressure of immigration from Germany, the perceived injustice of McMahon's correspondence with Sharif Hussein, and "the intensive character of Jewish nationalism."[6]

Finding that "[n]either Arab nor Jew has any sense of service to a single state,"[7] the commission report concluded that any measures taken to ease the situation "might reduce the inflammation and bring down the temperature, but they cannot cure the trouble."[8] This was because an "irrepressible conflict has arisen between two national communities within the narrow bounds of one small country."[9] Peel, therefore, viewed repression as the only other way to maintain peace in Palestine, which was an expensive and morally objectionable course, a "dark path" that would also exacerbate the problem.[10] "While neither race can justly rule all Palestine," the committee members decided, "we see no reason why, if it were practicable, each race should not rule part of it."[11]

At the time, this was considered not only the best plan but the only feasible solution. Peel's partition proposals, however, amounted to nothing more than a preliminary sketch, recommending a very small Jewish state in the north of Palestine, an Arab entity joined to Transjordan with an exchange of population between the two, and a British enclave from Jerusalem to the sea.[12] (See fig. 4.1.)

Designed to address what they viewed as "fundamentally a conflict of right with right," this partition principle was readily accepted by the Colonial Office and cabinet, tentatively approved by Zionist leaders, but totally rejected by Palestine's Higher Arab Committee.[13] Partition was based on an English idiom: "Half a loaf is better than no bread," but the idea of giving even a square inch of Arab land to Zionists was objectionable enough to ignite a second and more intense phase of the Palestine rebellion in the autumn of 1937.[14] District Commissioner Lewis Andrews was murdered and Arab rebels took control of large swaths of territory, government forces evacuated Beersheba and Jericho, and the rebels besieged Jaffa. For a few days in October 1938, the rebels even had de facto control of the Old City of Jerusalem.[15] These successes prompted a harsher British response.

By the interwar period, Britain had established its self-image as a humane empire, having avoided brutalities akin to the Belgian Congo, German Southwest Africa, or French Algeria, and many British officials prided themselves on their empire's focus on the rule of law.[16] This does not, however, mean tactics were humane by modern standards, simply that in the 1930s they were legal. Army manuals forbade stealing from or mistreating civilians but provided for shooting rioters, collective punishment, and "retribution."[17] The violence, property damage, and humiliation inflicted by British forces during this period of suppression were of a harrowing nature and threatened to destroy all relations between the Arabs and the civilian government in Palestine. By 1938, High Commissioner Sir Arthur Wauchope was barely managing to temper the actions of British armed

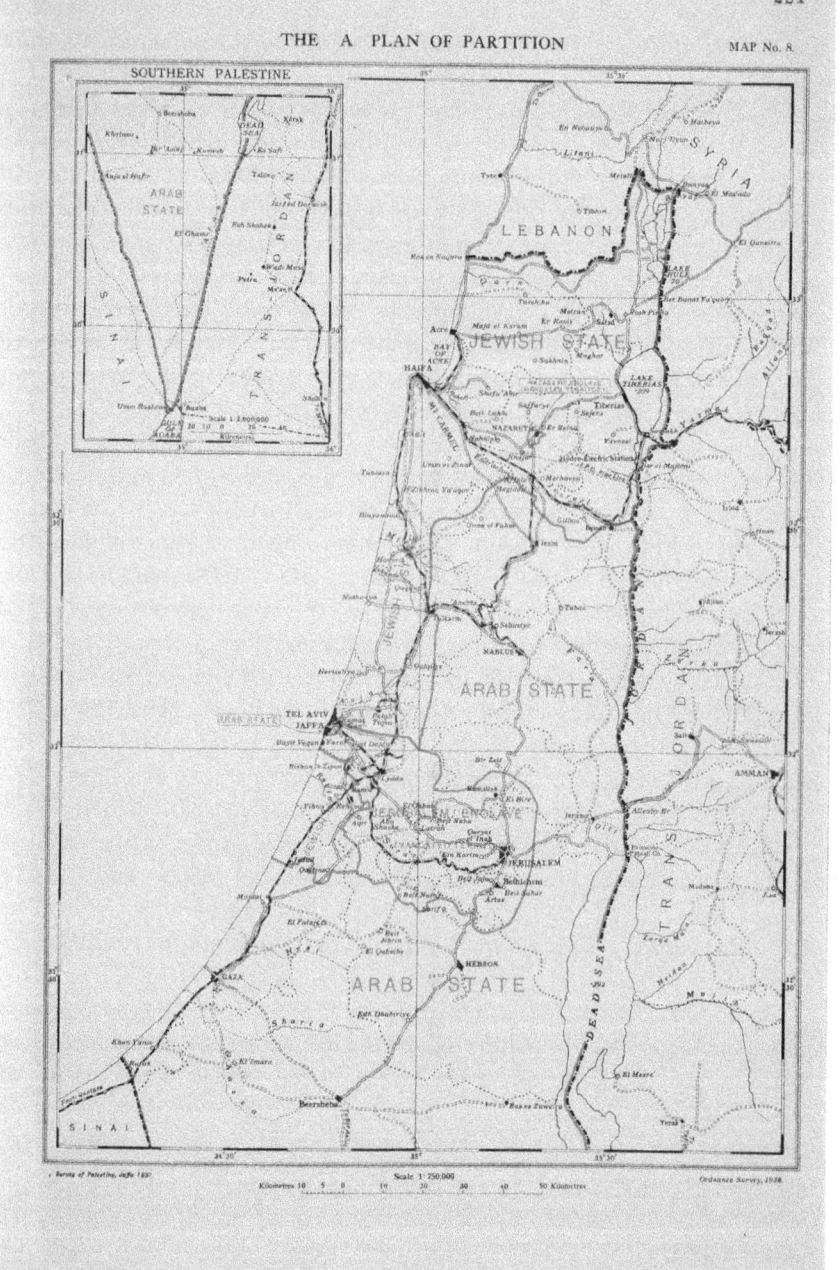

Fig. 4.1. Original map produced by the Peel Commission in 1937. The Jewish areas were intended to be independent, but the Arab areas would have become part of Transjordan. © The National Archives.

forces. When he looked for a political solution to the revolt and challenged army efforts to institute martial law, the Colonial Office replaced him with the more compliant Sir Harold MacMichael.[18] An even greater repressive effort was thought to be required, but the need for and purpose of a second investigating commission also gradually evolved in the cabinet during the autumn of 1937.

Chaired by Sir John Woodhead, the technical or partition commission was ostensibly charged with determining the best route toward implementing partition. Its verdict, however, undercut the principle. The Woodhead Commission returned three plans, A, B, and C, with varying borders, levels of subsequent British responsibility, and economic integration. This report concluded that any partition scheme that involved population transfer was doomed to failure due to the necessity of implementing such a scheme by force or leaving large minorities in each new state.[19] The commission was also unable to devise any boundary formulation that left Jewish areas defensible and Arab territory economically sound.[20] As Britain would need to conclude treaty agreements with both states, it was also likely to find itself in the impossible situation of having to defend the Jewish state from outside attack after incurring the expense of implementing partition.[21] One member of the commission, T. Reid, felt the need to add, "it may be said that one cannot make an omelette without breaking a few eggs, but it would not be easy to find an omelette in any possible scheme of partition."[22] (See fig. 4.2.)

Rather than ending on a negative note, however, the Woodhead Commission instead proposed partition with two very large British enclaves in the north and south that withheld fiscal autonomy from both Jews and Arabs, creating an economic federalism between the two with a British administration serving as the federal government.[23] This would have required a very high financial liability for the foreseeable future and would not have alleviated the rebellion already inflamed over the idea of Jewish statehood within Palestine.[24] Although the commission report specifically stated that Arab antagonism toward partition did not oblige them to return a verdict that no scheme was practicable, the report permitted no other conclusion.[25] It admitted than even economic federalism would not be satisfactory to either Arabs or Jews, and certainly not to the Treasury.[26] As a result, the cabinet officially rejected partition in November 1938.[27]

Following these two commissions, therefore, the British government was seemingly left with very few options. Peel had determined that partition was the only way forward, "at least a chance of ultimate peace," and Woodhead had demonstrated the impossibility of its implementation.[28] Although it took a relatively long time to realize in the context of what was otherwise a matter of urgency, the government was eventually faced with a stark choice between continuing to support the Jewish national home, thereby suppressing Arab protest indefinitely, and somehow surrendering the obligation to Zionism contained in the Mandate.

Fig. 4.2. "The Judgement of Solomon Chamberlain": a cartoon, published in the *Evening Standard* on 9 July 1937, hinting that the biblical king's wisdom was lost on British Palestine's battling communities. © David Low / Solo Syndication.

After concurrent bilateral negotiations in early 1939 at St. James's Palace, the MacDonald White Paper utilized Woodhead's arguments but not the commission's recommendations, declaring that "the establishment of self-supporting independent Arab and Jewish states within Palestine has been found to be impracticable."[29] Instead, the white paper committed Britain to Palestinian independence after a transitional period of ten years, allowing the Jewish population to increase to roughly 30 percent of Palestine's total inhabitants over five years—a plan permitting about seventy-five thousand immigrants, made up of ten thousand per year as well as twenty-five thousand refugees.[30] After that, further immigration would require Arab consent, meaning the Jewish national home (if not a Jewish state) was officially established.[31] As war approached in Europe, this white paper represented the most rational course, but the reasoning behind rejecting partition, as well as the priorities involved in choosing between Britain's two client-nations in Palestine, was more complex than a simple assessment of costs versus benefits. An understanding of the political constraints demonstrates how even this sudden change of policy in 1939 was entirely in keeping with British policy makers' logic toward the burgeoning Arab-Zionist conflict.

On the eve of World War II in 1939, the issues that were most important to British decision makers at this time centered on their diplomatic efforts abroad, bureaucratic infighting at home, and the dynamics of parliamentary politics. By analyzing how the government interpreted risk in the context of imminent war, it becomes clear that only one option was politically sound enough to be measured against the broader needs of national interest.[32]

Diplomatic Juggling

The most important issue on the British political agenda concerning Palestine in 1936–1939 was diplomacy. The second half of the 1930s witnessed a pervading threat of imminent war spread throughout the government. Diplomacy, therefore, became directly linked to regime survival. In this context, Britain's empire and spheres of influence were both its strongest asset (in the event of friendly, acquiescent mass mobilization and support) and a major source of vulnerability (should popular uprisings break out or formerly subject leaders alter their allegiances). Added to this concern was the necessity of securing, or rather avoiding offending, public opinion of other Great Powers such as the United States. Palestine, unhappily for the British government, combined these delicate facets of international diplomacy, pitting Arab leaders in the Middle East and Muslim opinion in India against Zionism, ostensibly the United States, and a traditionally pro-Zionist Council of the League of Nations.

In the late 1930s, the desire for Arab goodwill toward Britain was an overriding concern. No Arab leaders, least of all the Palestinians, applied direct pressure on the British government. Instead, Arab leaders jockeyed for regional prominence and position vis-à-vis Britain on the Palestine issue. There were no threats to break diplomatic ties, only a widespread underlying fear in Westminster of Italian and German infiltration of the Middle East or the catastrophic wartime loss of physical and communication routes through the Suez Canal to India. The perceived necessity of placating opinion in the Middle East far outweighed the importance of Zionist opinion, not least because the US State Department deliberately refrained from interfering and the League of Nations only became involved shortly before World War II was declared. In addressing the risks associated with each of these parties, the government found that it was unable to continue with the options of partition or indefinite repression under the Mandate due to uncertain relations with Arab leaders of the Middle East. In contrast, the political risks posed by Jewish and Zionist opinion (as well as the attitudes of the United States and the League of Nations) were perfectly tolerable at this juncture, allowing the option of acting against the national home to be considered further in terms of its impact on key aspects of the national interest.

Throughout this period, regional Arab leaders, rather than Palestinian politicians, were central to British decision-making, a phenomenon that arose initially due to the general strike in Palestine and was then seized upon by Foreign Secretary Anthony Eden, the Committee on Imperial Defence (CID), and eventually the Colonial Office. Involving regional leaders in the British Empire's Middle East policy was a new phenomenon in the 1930s. Although initially beneficial, this broader spectrum of actors became increasingly worrisome. The Peel Commission had been delayed by approximately three months while twenty thousand reinforcements restored order in Palestine and the strike came to a close, but only with the face-saving help of Ibn Saud of Arabia, King Ghazi of Iraq, and Emir Abdullah of Transjordan.[33] For the Arab states, their participation was a matter of prestige, but it was initiated against the backdrop of more grassroots agitation for the Arabs of Palestine. Even in the House of Commons, William Gallacher, the Communist MP for West Fife, pointedly defended their strike: "It is asked, why are not the Arabs satisfied with the improvements in wages and in this and that? There never was an invader at any time who did not justify his invasion on that very ground—'We have given you a mess of pottage, so what is all this nonsense about a birthright?' Have the Arabs a case? Yes, they have a case. They have had a rotten deal."[34] Rebellion was nothing surprising for imperial administrators, but the Peel Commission highlighted how the most striking feature of Palestine's revolt was the degree to which it "roused the feeling of the Arab world at large against Zionism and its defenders."[35] Although the support offered by Egypt, Transjordan, Saudi Arabia, and Yemen was "by no means a powerful, all-embracing popular sentiment" and was largely confined to opposition groups, the issue gradually intensified as the British inability to solve the immediate crisis dragged on for years.[36] At the cabinet level, it was Foreign Secretary Anthony Eden who repeatedly warned of the consequences of Middle Eastern opinion solidifying against Britain over Palestine.

As Palestine's Arabs viewed partition with the same moral and material objection that was directed against the more vague policy of building a Jewish national home, Eden initially argued against the Peel Commission's proposals, even though the cabinet had rapidly accepted partition on the recommendation of the colonial secretary, William Ormsby-Gore (whom, incidentally, Lady Passfield described as "small and Welsh in appearance").[37] Eden had been cautioning the cabinet regarding Palestine's wider implications since before Peel arrived in the country, and the new partition policy did little to assuage his concerns. Highlighting the military implications, Eden noted how "troubles in Palestine have been watched with the keenest anxiety in the neighbouring Arab and Moslem-countries."[38] More importantly, he explained that "Saudi Arabia, the Yemen and Iraq have now become of great importance to His Majesty's government from the point of view of imperial communications. The air route to India and Australasia must cross over either Iraqi or Saudi territories; between Cairo and the Protected States of the Persian Gulf, and it is not open to doubt that if Iraq and Saudi Arabia were to become hostile to British policy, they would be able seriously to interrupt Imperial communications with the East."[39] After Peel's partition proposals, part of this problem was population transfer and the negative political impact of its enforcement—the realization that "partition can now only be imposed by force."[40]

Considering the very small size of Peel's suggested Jewish state and the number of Jews needing to flee Germany, Eden pointed out to the cabinet that the Jewish state's urge to expand would be "well-nigh irresistible."[41] Then what would be Britain's responsibility? "If any stimulus were required to their rapidly growing nationalism," Eden argued, "it is hard to imagine any more effective method than the creation of a small dynamic State of hated foreign immigrants on the seaboard of the Arab countries with a perpetual urge to extend its influence inland."[42] Arabs would view the establishment of this entity as treachery, and, crucially, it would not solve the military problem. Britain would have to protect minorities in the new states, and so Eden questioned whether "we see any limit to the extent to which these troops are likely to be involved?"[43] Such intervention could have had disastrous diplomatic repercussions in Egypt, Iraq, Saudi Arabia, and Yemen.

In Egypt, the Suez Canal was vital, and Britain had already accepted many concessions on this point in negotiating an independence treaty with the Egyptians.[44] In addition, oil supplies from Iraq would be "seriously threatened."[45] There were also similar dangers in Saudi Arabia and Yemen that were intensified by the Italian invasion of Abyssinia in 1935 and Italian overtures toward the two kings. Yemeni protests against Britain's Palestine policy, for example, preceded an Italo-Yemeni Treaty.[46] Based on this interpretation of Middle East politics, Eden concluded that the only way to ensure peace with the Arabs was to provide "some assurance that the Jews will neither become a majority in Palestine, nor be given any Palestinian territory in full sovereignty."[47]

Similar arguments were forthcoming from the Committee on Imperial Defence (CID) and high-ranking British officials who dealt with the new Arab states. The CID, for example, consistently warned of Iraq, Saudi Arabia, Yemen, and Persia becoming "uncertain friends" after Palestine's political leaders rejected partition, "which would be a most serious embarrassment to us in the event of war with Germany."[48] The India secretary, Lord Zetland, also voiced concerns that "Moslem opinion in India was now becoming rather aggressive on the question of partition."[49] Although by 1938 the India threat had dissipated except for "occasional expressions of indignation in the press and speeches by minor Muslim politicians," this did not prevent it being used as an argument for Arab concessions in 1939.[50] Another official who provided somewhat frantic advice was Miles Lampson, British ambassador to Egypt.

Lampson advised Malcolm MacDonald—who had assumed the post of colonial secretary following Ormsby-Gore's frustrated resignation in 1938—that pro-Palestine agitation in Egypt was the political tool of opposition leader Nahas Pasha but that Egyptians knew they were dependent on Britain for their security and well-being.[51] Lampson told Macdonald that any policy pursued in Palestine was unlikely to render Arab loyalties a positive asset, but if they were turned against Britain they would provide a formidable tool in enemy hands.[52] This measured advice acquired an urgent tone very quickly, however, as Miles wrote to MacDonald to plead that "unless the Arabs get satisfaction over immigration we must face the fact that, if war comes, we shall have to take on the Arabs as well as the Italians and Germans."[53] Time, he considered, was of the essence, as "[t]he longer you delay that no doubt painful decision, the less value you will get from making it. If you leave it until the verge of European War you will get no value at all."[54] These arguments built over the course of the Arab Revolt to back the British government into what it perceived to be a diplomatic corner. (See fig. 4.3.)

The content, therefore, of the MacDonald White Paper emerged in phases. The government had adopted partition in 1937, but arguments against it from Eden, the CID, Lord Zetland, and others meant that its longevity as a policy was almost instantly in question. The Woodhead Commission was a response to this debate, and its conclusions were rumored to be negative toward partition months before the final report was published. Meanwhile, Ormsby-Gore's successor as colonial secretary, Malcolm MacDonald, quickly accepted the view that partition was impracticable due to wider Arab opinion. This was despite his own pro-Zionist background—MacDonald had already served at the Colonial Office and left in 1936 when he wrote to Chaim Weizmann: "I need not tell you how sorry I was to leave the Colonial Office, and so to give up the official connection with Palestine. But you know I shall always watch developments there with sympathy, and if I can be of any help at any time you only have to let me know."[55]

Following Woodhead's rejection of partition, however, MacDonald and the rest of the government released a command paper agreeing with its conclusions and calling for a conference to negotiate a political settlement between the two parties. MacDonald was well aware that no settlement was likely and that Britain would still have to impose a solution.[56] It was imperative, however, that the ultimate policy formulation be acceptable to regional Arab leaders and not necessarily to the Arabs of Palestine: "It is more important," MacDonald informed the cabinet, "that we should regain the full sympathy of these neighbouring governments than that we should secure the friendship of the Palestinian Arabs; they are the countries whose lukewarm support or actual hostility in case of war would have most unfortunate results."[57] This was despite the recognition that Arab states were unlikely to support Germany and Italy, having sided with Britain during the Munich crisis "with scarcely any mention of the embarrassing

The MacDonald Betrayal, 1936–1939 | 111

Fig. 4.3. "Palestine–London Shuttle Service": a cartoon, published in the *Evening Standard* on 22 July 1938, during the height of the Arab Revolt, poking fun at Britain's diplomatic conundrum. © David Low / Solo Syndication.

situation in Palestine."[58] Regardless, the colonial secretary continued to assert that "we cannot ignore the repeated warnings of our representatives in that part of the world, and the strength of feeling of the Arab public generally against our Palestine policy is making it more and more impossible for their rulers to maintain a pro-British attitude."[59]

This was how the government abandoned partition, but it was only through the course of discussions at St. James's Palace in January, February, and March 1939 that the intractable nature of Arab demands became clear. As a result, the cabinet went from agreeing to only harsh restrictions on Jewish immigration and land purchase to supporting an independent Palestine within ten years.[60] The Palestine delegation rejected these proposals on the basis that the interim period was too long. In contrast, although "the representatives of the neighbouring Arab States had taken this attitude in public, behind the scenes some of them had told us that they regarded our proposals as wise and reasonable."[61] In particular, Saudi delegate Fuad Bey Hamza said in private that "while their hearts were with the Palestinian Arabs, they had brought not only their hearts, but also their heads, to London."[62] Independence was important but as a principle rather than an immediate outcome. It had even "been suggested by the Arab representatives that a solution could be reached on the lines of the regime which had been in force for some years in Iraq, while arrangements for a constitutional Assembly were being worked out. A provisional government of Iraqi Ministers had been established, with British advisers; during this period, which lasted some four years, the Iraqi Ministers had been a facade, and the British advisers had been the real rulers of the country. Nuri Pasha was urging us to follow this precedent."[63]

As a result, MacDonald finally put to the cabinet what he had already discussed with both delegations: that they should announce an end to the Mandate and the establishment of an "independent" Palestinian state "with British advisers to run the show."[64] The figure of seventy-five thousand additional Jewish immigrants over five years was finalized—MacDonald had originally argued for more than three hundred thousand—and Prime Minister Neville Chamberlain admitted there was no better bargain they could strike for the Jews, though he felt they had been roughly treated.[65] "The plain fact," MacDonald told the cabinet, "was that the Jews had made no attempt to co-operate with the Arabs in the last twenty years, but they would now have to do so."[66] This was largely the attitude taken with Zionist leaders after Ormsby-Gore's departure.

Rather than adopting the rhetoric often heard in Parliament that portrayed Zionism as a special and enlightened movement, MacDonald's language implied equality with Palestine's Arabs and an air of disdain, trivializing the conflict as merely a battle of interests in which "each of them wants to be the master."[67] When Zionists threatened to boycott the St. James's Conference after British refusal to allow ten thousand refugees into Palestine, Chamberlain and MacDonald understood that "the Jews" simply were not in a position to withdraw.[68] The opinion of actual Zionists, therefore, was almost inconsequential. The fact that they did not have an impact on the British political calculations in this period of decision-making should come as no surprise, however, as they had never possessed that type of direct influence. Previously supportive elements in the House of Commons (discussed more below), the League of Nations, and the United States either shrank away from the issue or wielded too little influence to be of assistance.

The "betrayal" of the MacDonald White Paper was self-imposed, in believing Zionism had harnessed the foreign policy of the British Empire only to realize this was not the case. Although both Chamberlain and MacDonald still professed affection for Zionism, this had no impact on their deliberations. Upon the release of MacDonald's white paper, the colonial secretary drafted a letter that Chamberlain sent to Chaim Weizmann saying, "I greatly regret that this should be so, and that it should be necessary to apply some measure of disappointment to long and ardently cherished hopes. I have always recognised and admired your single-minded devotion."[69] In the end it was understood that, regardless of Palestine policy, in a war with Germany the Zionists had nowhere to turn but Britain.[70] No intervention on their behalf was forthcoming.

Opinions on Zionism coming from the United States and the League of Nations were not particularly important in this period of policy making. Although Ormsby-Gore had frequently warned of rampant American displeasure over the abandonment of partition, this, as the Foreign Office predicted, never materialized.[71] The US State Department made it clear to British ambassador Lindsey that they were receiving thousands of telegrams on the issue, but "that this was merely a personal message for our information," because "the United States Government did not wish to appear to be interfering in any way with the conduct of matters which were within the province of His Majesty's Government."[72] MacDonald did discuss the release of the white paper with US ambassador to Britain, Joseph P. Kennedy, "who had been in a somewhat gloomy mood" and had thought that "Jews, in his view, were unpopular in America, but he thought they might be able to work up a certain amount of anti-British agitation; the results of which would not, however, last for very long."[73] In terms of US opinion, the government received notification only of very low level pleas such as letters from a Presbyterian and a Methodist minister, resolutions by the Massachusetts cities of Worcester and Chelsea, and a request to continue the Mandate from a New Jersey senator, as well as many individual concerned citizens and even one telegram from the American Arab National League urging the opposite, for Britain not to be swayed by "Jewish clamor."[74]

These combined factors led Mr. Baggallay at the Foreign Office to "regard Middle Eastern opinion, which might be permanently and seriously hostile, as outweighing American opinion, which would probably be only temporarily incensed."[75] He concluded that "[o]ur interests here are far too important to be made the plaything of the Jews of America, however important they may be politically."[76] Eventually, the US State Department did issue a series of telegrams noting American rights to be consulted regarding changes in the Mandate, but the Foreign Office dismissed them as preelection posturing.[77] Likewise, the League of Nations never posed a political risk.

Cabinet ministers anticipated that the Permanent Mandates Commission would be split four to three on whether MacDonald's white paper was legal within the terms of the Mandate and that it would be referred to September's full meeting of the Council.[78] This was indeed the verdict, but, before the full Council of the League of Nations could render its judgment, war was declared.[79] Ultimately, the options to partition Palestine or continue the Mandate using indefinite repression were dropped due to the importance of Arab and Muslim opinion. In contrast, the option to act in contravention of previous obligations to the Jewish national home passed the political test due to a lack of effective opposition in Geneva, in Washington, or, as discussed below, in the House of Commons.

War Crimes and Public Relations

Complicating the need for international diplomacy were rumors circulating about the nature of Britain's counterinsurgency operations in Palestine. It would appear that the War Office, in particular, viewed the cessation of Arab rebellion as a key imperative in the face of potential war in Europe and was prepared to defy international and British norms of conduct in order to achieve that objective. This goal was pursued with such enthusiastic cruelty that it could have severely complicated the Foreign Office's diplomatic preparations for war.

Eventually reinforced by approximately twenty-five thousand men, British armed forces and later the police in Palestine fell under the commands of General Dill, Major General Wavell, and Lieutenant General R. Haining with divisions commanded by Major Generals R. O'Connor and B. Montgomery; these men credited themselves with suppressing the Arab Revolt by late 1939.[80] However, by highlighting how these men operated with respect to the three principles of conduct in warfare—discrimination, necessity, and proportionality—it becomes clear that some tactics were unsavory even to imperial Britain. Subsequent accusations of wanton violence attracted unwelcome attention, which undoubtedly made the seas of international opinion even more difficult to navigate.

The public commitment to discrimination was evident in British assertions that Palestinian Arab villagers should not be targeted unnecessarily through collective punishment (in the form of punitive searches and home demolitions). The War Office argued that all of their activities met the principle of necessity, and they justified the use of military courts and large numbers of death sentences on this basis as well. Proportionality specifically related to unnecessary suffering in the form of summary beatings, killings, or torture, and this was the subject on which British responses to criticism aroused suspicion rather than reassurance. Whereas British tactics in the first two categories were admitted and defended publicly—implying that they satisfied standards of the time—allegations that British forces systematically employed disproportionate violence were kept secret, were denied, and remained uninvestigated, implying that these activities would have failed the test of public opinion.

Combatants or Civilians?

Discrimination between soldiers and civilians was a principle applied in theory but not in practice during the Arab Revolt in Palestine. The 1907 Hague Convention had expressly stipulated differentiation between combatants and civilians, and Palestine's military leadership asserted that it was fully adhered to at all times.[81] In 1939, for example, to answer condemnations that ordinary Palestinian Arab villagers were being targeted unfairly by British troops, the War Office issued the following statement: "[U]nderlying all efforts to suppress this rebellion, one fact had always to be uppermost. Namely, the forces in Palestine were not dealing with an enemy of the Empire but with the rebellious activities of a section of a race who are themselves members of the British Community of Nations. Therefore, at all times, it has been necessary to ensure that every repressive action by the Military should be guided by the principles of minimum force, firmness, fairness and impartiality."[82]

This was careful rhetoric, but principled discrimination was made almost impossible by the military's almost universally inclusive definition of combatants. As there was great popular support for the revolt as well as widespread intimidation of civilians by those engaging in the uprising, there was hardly a single villager in all of Palestine that the British military considered a true civilian. General Haining largely refused the existence of noncombatants among Palestine's Arab population. Since Haining saw "no organised rebel army in the accepted sense, against which troops can act to the exclusion of the remaining peaceful citizens," High Commissioner MacMichael was able to assure the colonial secretary that "every practicable effort is made to spare innocent villagers."[83] However, he underlined "innocent" to emphasize that those being punished were, of course, considered guilty.[84] This cyclical attitude resulted in the moral and legal justification for collective punishment, most notably punitive searches and home demolitions.

Searches of rural villages were conducted with the aim of finding weapons caches. The assumption was that "[p]ractically every Arab village in the country is well stocked with lethal weapons."[85] This, however, was rarely the case, and British troops' oft frustrated hunt for large deposits of firearms led them to accuse villagers of deliberately concealing them elsewhere, another assumption that seemed to justify turning the searches into punitive exercises. Searching villages was "not a gentle business" because the police had often been targeted by rebels, and, in frustration, "they did retaliate."[86] Police and troops emptied and mixed a year's supply of grains, sugar, olive oil, and kerosene, ransacked houses, and destroyed furniture until nothing was left.[87] One Palestine police officer noted how "in the villages anything European is looked upon with suspicion, the only exception being Singer sewing machines and which are the first things the soldiers destroy when searching a house."[88] Deputy governor of the Jaffa District, Aubrey Lees believed that these searches also included "extensive robbery and looting," including of life savings.[89] This process became a sort of concessionary prize for brigades who failed to catch a particular group of rebels. "We nearly caught up with a band of the bad boys," Constable Burr wrote home to his parents, "but they slipped across the border, we would have gone after them but had our D.S.P. with us but he let us beat up a village where they had stayed the night."[90]

During these punitive searches, villagers were often concentrated in cages as an inducement to surrender hidden weapons. The best-known example of this occurred in the village of Halhul in May 1939.[91] A Scottish regiment called the Black Watch erected two wire cages, one in the shade containing food and water and the other positioned in the sun with less than a pint of water per day.[92] Those who betrayed the position of a rifle hoard could pass from the "bad" cage to the "good" cage, but there was no option for villagers who did not know where any rifles were hidden.[93] Between ten and fourteen villagers died, and the detainees were only freed after eight days when they gave up forty old Turkish rifles.[94] The district commissioner of Jerusalem, Edward Keith-Roach "was instructed that no civil inquest should be held," but the high commissioner decided the incident warranted compensation, which was paid "at the highest rate allowed by the law, [. . .] over three thousand pounds to the bereft families."[95] This was considered an unfortunate episode, but the method was not prohibited from further use. Likewise, home demolition was a tactic used throughout the revolt despite its dubious merit.

In June 1936, the port of Jaffa proved too difficult to police as chasing suspects through this part of town and the surrounding alleyways was tantamount to suicide. On the pretext of a public health order, the British administration decided to demolish large sections of the old city of Jaffa.[96] Later, when the Palestine administration enacted the Defence Orders in Council of 1937 to give the military and police greater powers, no alternative justification for demolition was required other than the belief that its inhabitants were aiding rebels.[97]

Such large operations were atypical, however, as demolition was largely saved for rural villages, some of which, such as Mi'ar in October 1938, were leveled completely, and again the tactic was punitive rather than purely strategic. "The procedure now when a soldier is killed," wrote Constable Burr, "is to blow up the nearest village and for this purpose deep sea mines are being supplied by the *Malaya*."[98] The use of sea mines and oversize explosive charges by royal engineers was intended to cause collateral damage. Lieutenant General Carr described one instance of this in the town of Qala, where several residents were suspected of participating in rail sabotage: "I saw to it that the [Royal Engineers] put in extra explosive to not only demolish the culprits' houses but also those adjoining it. In all I had eight houses obliterated."[99] Between 1936 and 1940, the authorities destroyed approximately two thousand houses, and British troops even forced some Arabs to demolish their own homes one brick at a time.[100]

These procedures hardly helped win the hearts and minds of Palestine's rural Arab population. On multiple occasions the Arab Women's Society appealed to Palestine's high commissioner on this basis: "The demolition of any house in a village is liable to estrange the whole village," they wrote, "[t]he destruction of the house-effects of a poor villager who, in all probability, might be innocent, would make an enemy of him."[101] It was obvious to the Women's Society that "[i]n many cases these villagers have been the target of revenge by both the Government and the armed men."[102] However, despite possessing doubtful strategic merit and the potential for bad public relations, these punitive searches and home demolitions were never denied. Instead, they were justified publicly by the principle of military necessity.

Justifying Tactics

British authorities in Palestine, as well as their counterparts in Westminster, publicly rationalized dangerous search methods and home demolitions through the principle of military necessity. This maxim was also used to warrant particularly harsh sentences imposed by Palestine's military courts. In terms of international norm violation, however, such public validation meant that although these tactics would be viewed as unnecessarily harsh today, they did seem to meet criteria for "humaneness" in war during the 1930s.

Searches were considered unfortunate but unavoidable. Labour MP Sir Herbert Morrison, for example, raised the dilemma of holding villages responsible for individual's crimes, noting how "this kind of thing is not particularly palatable to us," but concluding somewhat erroneously that the practice served as a deterrent to "murder and anarchy" that "must be put down."[103] Despite the compensation that had to be paid to dead villagers' families after some searches, High Commissioner MacMichael continued to justify methods used at Halhul, and another similar incident at the village of Beit Rima, on the basis that the areas were "notoriously 'bad' and both were known to contain large numbers of illegal arms."[104] MacMichael blamed the deaths at Halhul on "a combination of unfortunate circumstances which included abnormally hot weather" and the age of the men who died.[105] Taking a comparable attitude, General Haining insisted that police and troops were not ordered to destroy furniture and food stores: "Stringent orders are issued and every precaution taken to prevent looting or wanton destruction of property or food."[106] Damage was blamed on villagers leaving cupboards locked so they had to be broken in order to conduct the search.[107] Constable Kitson, however, remembered that "we did certainly mess villages up" and "[w]e didn't lose any sleep over these things."[108]

Similarly, High Commissioner MacMichael defended demolitions as necessary measures against those aiding and abetting rebels, and, by the summer of 1936, the legal powers to demolish had been expanded significantly.[109] In June, the colonial secretary announced to Parliament that "[h]ouses and buildings from which firearms have been discharged or bombs thrown, or any houses in villages in other areas where the inhabitants have committed or abetted acts of murder, violence or intimidation, the actual offender being unknown, may be appropriated by the Government and demolished without compensation."[110] This tactic was justified as "fully recognised and understood by the Palestinian Arabs" and their tribal, collectivized mentality, and was "necessary" because a crime had been committed but police had no definitive proof indicating by whom.[111] The British belief in the efficacy of these measures failed to grasp their radicalizing effect on ordinary Palestinian villagers. Collective punishment was deemed "the only method of impressing the peaceful but terrorised majority that failure to assist law and order may, in the long run, be more unpleasant than submitting to intimidation."[112] The same counterproductive thinking was applied to sentencing in military courts.

In the first stage of the revolt, discharging a weapon or throwing a bomb at British forces, regardless of the damage it caused, became an offense punishable by death, and damage to property or sabotage warranted life imprisonment.[113] These were not common sentences throughout the empire. A former India secretary raised concerns that "when if we shut up a single Bengalee terrorist there were questions about our interfering with the liberty of the subject, searching his house, and so on. What is the situation today?"[114] The Arab Revolt in Palestine was so dire, however, that "the very drastic regulations such as the death penalty for using arms" was viewed as a "regrettable necessity."[115] The military courts avoided civilian interferences, and laws of evidence were relaxed so that an officer could swear to testimony he heard from a witness if the witness was presumed dead, could not be found, or for reasons of his safety could not be produced in public.[116] Between 1937 and 1939, the number of Arab detainees in Palestine increased tenfold to some nine thousand prisoners, and more than one hundred of these were hanged.[117]

Although justified domestically by military necessity, the courts were ineffectual as a deterrent. District Commissioner Keith-Roach, who had to attend every execution in his capacity as sheriff, remarked how "[t]he irony of the whole process was that not a single execution made the slightest difference to public security, to Arab opinion, to Arab fears, to Arab respect for law, or to Arab action."[118] Keith-Roach was a minority opinion at the time, however, and these procedures were generally considered too merciful. Constable Burr noted how "[t]he military courts started off well but, as we expected are being too lenient and want too much evidence to convict them, so any Johnny Arab who is caught by us now in suspicious circumstances is shot out of hand."[119] Indeed, even the impartial commission led by Lord Peel—sent to Palestine in hope of solving the political problem—criticized the government for being too compassionate.[120] Likewise, the League of Nations' PMC rebuked British authorities for not instituting martial law when disturbances first commenced.[121] There appears to have been a widespread and international consensus, therefore, that counterinsurgency tactics in Palestine that were validated by the principle of military necessity did meet international standards of behavior in war. The same, however, was not true of British methods that were publicly denied.

Unnecessary Suffering

In 1930s Palestine, British forces and police undermined the proportionality principle in several key ways: summary beatings, shootings, unofficial destruction of houses, and torture for the purposes of interrogation. These activities were not permissible according to the international norms of the time, and this is evident in the Foreign, Colonial, and War Offices' responses to allegations of atrocities, which were fervently denied but never officially investigated.

First, testimonies of British troops and police highlight the widespread mistreatment of Palestinian Arabs, including those suspected of rebel activity and others presumed guilty by association. Detainees, for example, were used as human shields to guard against road and rail mining.[122] Private Bellows, of the Royal Hampshire Regiment admitted that this was "[r]ather a dirty trick, but we enjoyed it."[123] When a captive fell from the hood of a vehicle during this process, "if he was lucky he'd get away with a broken leg, but if he was unlucky the truck coming up behind would hit him. But nobody bothered to go and pick the bits up."[124] A soldier named Arthur Lane also recalled an incident when his regiment caught seven Arabs after a small firefight and assaulted the men until "this lad's eye was hanging down on his cheek. The whole eye had been knocked out and it was hanging down and there was blood dripping on his face."[125] Prisoners were struck with "rifle butts, bayonets, fists, boots, whatever."[126] Other mistreatment also included stripping captives naked and blasting them with a fire hose, an act justified by the assessment that these "dirty buggers" needed a bath.[127] Officers witnessed this treatment, which was "definitely done with their approval."[128] Humiliation and beatings also escalated to murders that were rarely investigated.

The killings largely occurred as reprisals. Major Bertrude Augustus Pond noted how "soldiers would see Arab *atrocities*, and there were some of their mates killed and on occasions, they, the troops, became bloody angry."[129] Pond knew of "one or two occasions" when this resulted in the shooting of prisoners, but he also believed these were isolated incidents, after which "the unit itself, however much they had been provoked, felt ashamed of what had happened in some regiments."[130] The Royal Ulster Rifles, for example, reportedly destroyed the village of Kafr Yasif, demolishing between 60 and 150 houses and killing between 9 and 25 of its inhabitants in retaliation for two British deaths.[131] Similar atrocities seem to have occurred at al-Bassa, where the Royal Ulsters allegedly huddled approximately fifty villagers under a bus, detonated explosives under the vehicle, and burned the village.[132] At Miksa, a number of murdered Arab villagers were initially blamed on militant Zionists but this was later exposed as the work of British police, a response to the death of a constable in the village.[133] Constable Burr also recounted how a military regiment seconded to the police captured twelve Arabs near the Mosque of Oman and promptly bayoneted them all to a wall: "that's the type of men we need out here," he wrote, "they are taught in the army that the spirit of the bayonet is to kill."[134]

There was only one successful prosecution against British forces or police for murders of this nature, but this single case demonstrated a clear line between what was and what was not publicly acceptable treatment of suspected rebels held in custody. In January 1939, four British constables were charged with murdering Mohammed el Haddad, a man arrested for possessing a revolver who then later reportedly tried to escape.[135] The incident had occurred in full view of Jaffa's German colony, and the publicity made it impossible to ignore. Haddad had been unarmed and handcuffed when the shooting occurred, at a distance of only a few yards, and on a back street in Jaffa that was a significant detour from the constables' route between police stations.[136] In addition, the fatal shot was fired after Haddad was already down.[137] All four men were convicted, but only Constable Wood, who had fired that fatal round, lost his appeal.[138] Despite convincing evidence that Haddad had been taken to a Jaffa alleyway with the intent to kill him, the only element of this very public crime that British officials treated as normatively problematic was the shot fired when Haddad was incapacitated. It is possible to infer, therefore, that killing an escaping prisoner was acceptable and met the threshold of necessity, even if the circumstances could, at best, have been avoided and, at worst, were very suspicious, whereas murdering an injured detainee did not meet these standards of "humaneness." In contrast, the use of torture for interrogation consistently failed to meet any standards of British and international codes of conduct in war.

Torture occurred in special interrogation centers established by colonial policing expert, Charles Tegart.[139] At these clandestine centers, "'selected' police officers were to be trained in the gentle art of 'third degree,' for use on Arabs until they 'spilled the beans.'"[140] This was not as secret a practice as the perpetrators intended. The Arab Ladies of Jerusalem complained about their practices of "whipping and beating with canes," and Edward Keith-Roach demanded that the center in his area of Jerusalem be closed.[141] Victims' testimonies were also translated by Miss Frances Newton and disseminated by the Arab Centre in London as pamphlets.[142] Prominent Palestinian notable Jamal al Husseini even wrote a letter to the League of Nations requesting an impartial commission to investigate accusations of summary shootings, rape, beatings, scorching with hot iron rods, forcing prisoners to stand under cold showers for hours, "applying immense pressure on the stomach and back until the victim faints from pain (after evacuating all contents of the stomach)," torture involving genitals, and removing fingernails.[143] The deputy governor of Jaffa, Aubrey Lees, also described similar tortures when writing to a friend in England, claiming he heard them from the victims.[144]

Numerous low-level reports were also produced by concerned officials serving in the region. One of the most damning came from Mr. Ogden at the British Consulate in Damascus, who apologetically drew the Foreign Office's attention to his realization that "third degree" was taking place in Palestine.[145] He dismissed Newton's translations as "exaggerated and mendacious" but wanted to stress that he had "heard from several independent sources that such methods are by no means unknown to police in Palestine."[146] He believed that Charles Tegart handpicked a "body of men, all British, who are sworn to secrecy. The victims are taken by night to a house outside Jerusalem [. . .]. Here the G-men, as I am told they are called, are permitted to inflict every form of torture they can think of."[147] This included hanging a man upside down and urinating on his mouth and nose.[148] "This sort of thing, if it is true," Ogden wrote, "ought to stop, and quickly. The publicity given to it is rapidly taking away the last shreds of our reputation as colonial administrators and will do us no end of harm if used by certain European countries which are not at present too friendly."[149] This was because no argument could be made that such activities fit the principle of military necessity.

Indeed, these were not simply British standards being violated; concerns were raised regarding Germany and Italy's use of such information and how this would influence world opinion.[150] Hitler had already called attention to "the poor Arabs" and told "Churchill, Eden, and other critics of appeasement that they should apply their 'prodigious knowledge' and 'infallible wisdom' to Palestine, where things had 'a damnably strong smell of violence and precious little of democracy.'"[151] A public statement had been issued when the four constables were charged with murdering Haddad, principally because "we should be more liable to criticism in German press and elsewhere to the effect that our previous denials of 'atrocity stories' had been based either on ignorance or on suppression of the truth, that it was now evident that these stories were true."[152]

International taunts meant that the War Office viewed allegations against British troops not as legitimate complaints but as "propaganda," dismissing Miss Newton as an "eccentric old lady" and peddler of "atrocity stories" while the Foreign Office tried to assure the Council of the League of Nations that "[t]here is no ground for the allegations regarding the conduct of the police and military forces."[153] The Colonial Office also tried to reassure the public that "[e]very allegation of irregular conduct is made the subject of immediate enquiry."[154] However, one line was crossed out of the Colonial Office statement, which read, "His majesty's Government are satisfied, after most careful enquiry, that they are entirely unfounded."[155] There was never any investigation into allegations of general brutality, and officials in Westminster merely forwarded any concerns contritely to the high commissioner in Palestine.

The colonial secretary, for example, urged MacMichael that "[t]here is the paramount consideration, with which I know you agree, that we must set our faces absolutely against any development of 'black and tan' methods in Palestine. The only way to stop such a development is to stamp it out at the very beginning"; he stressed that "[i]t is of the utmost importance that individuals amongst them should not be guilty of any action which would bring the Force and the Administration into disrepute."[156] The Foreign Office also forwarded complaints to MacMichael. The head of the Middle East Department wrote to him confessing he felt "rather apologetic" about "referring this matter to you for comment, but I should like to be put in a position to deny that there is any foundation whatever for this extraordinary allegation."[157]

For his part, MacMichael admitted that "he had little doubt that, in the stress of the present extremely tense conditions of Palestine, roughness had sometimes been used in dealing with persons thought to be responsible for the killing of British troops or officials," but he believed "that any suggestion of the use of terrorist methods or torture should be whole-heartedly repressed."[158] The only course of action taken was the high commissioner's promise that "he would mention the matter again to the General Officer Commanding, who is now in general charge of both troops and police, and ask him to do his best to ensure that no methods of this sort were employed."[159] The army, however, had almost a free hand in Palestine with no effective civilian oversight, making these polite requests somewhat futile.

During the first stage of the revolt in 1936, the civil administration had been able to curb military excesses, but High Commissioner Wauchope was removed, largely for interfering, and his successor, Sir Harold MacMichael, ceded power over the police and armed forces to the general officer commanding (GOC) during the second more violent stage of rebellion.[160] The GOC controlled Palestine through various area commanders, who were merely advised by their civilian counterparts, the district commissioners. MacMichael had been stripped of all authority by 1938.[161] In terms of singling out any blameworthy parties, the GOC's approval would, at the very least, have been necessary to maintain and dismantle interrogation centers, to which the high commissioner had presumably called General Haining's attention at least twice. This is why Matthew Hughes has called the brutality displayed in Palestine a systemic problem rather than a small collection of exceptional abuses.[162]

As the various GOCs held the power to order or prevent "irregular" methods and did not seem amenable to the latter, it is reasonable to presume that the War Office agreed with their tactics. Conversely, the Colonial and Foreign Offices wished to prevent politically explosive revelations from coming to light, and they implored the high commissioner to prevent excessive force, overlooking that he had no power to do so. In addition, soldiers and police could expect to escape prosecution as long as their crimes remained unobserved by large numbers of Western or foreign witnesses. The prosecution of four constables for the murder of Haddad seems to have been the only case of its kind brought to court during the revolt.[163] Otherwise, the response to accusations largely abdicated responsibility. The Foreign and Colonial Offices were content to believe War Office denials and failed to pursue the claims separately. In sharing his concerns about torture in Palestine, Mr. Ogden at the consulate in Damascus laid the blame appropriately. "[I]t is not the police who are to blame in Palestine, nor the army. They are thoroughly demoralized by the continued state of sub-war," he wrote. "In my opinion the blame lies with H.M.G. [His Majesty's Government] for having allowed such a situation to develop. It is pathetic that any British administration should be reduced to using such methods to retain control over a country."[164]

The fact that summary shootings, beatings, and torture defied international standards of behavior is evident in the British attempts to conceal such activities from the world at large. By continually denying claims made by Palestinian Arabs and British officials that cruel and unusual methods were being used in Palestine, but simultaneously allowing the practices to continue, British authorities must have believed they were helping in some way to suppress the rebellion. The irregular methods were presumably justified internally by the principle of necessity, but their lack of public airing implies that these tactics defied international codes of conduct, demonstrated by the broadcasting efforts of Germany and Italy as well as British attempts to reassure the Council of the League of Nations. Whereas British counterinsurgency tactics involving punitive searches and home demolitions were not problematic for public relations, indiscriminate killings and torture were. One member of the Palestine police aptly summarized the methods used to quash the Arab Revolt: "In order to fight terrorists," he said, "we became terrorists, more or less."[165] This was a situation made worse by, and which worsened, the crisis of pending war in Europe that colored policy making toward Palestine.

Reprising Turf Wars

In addition, yet another turf war between the Foreign Office and the Colonial Office over Palestine policy frustrated the government's will to act. Throughout 1937 and part of 1938, the two secretaries of state for these ministries—Colonial Secretary William Ormsby-Gore and Foreign Secretary Anthony Eden—entered into a cabinet-level power struggle ostensibly over the Peel Commission's partition proposals. This turf war came to an end only when both men resigned from the cabinet in 1938—Eden in February and Ormsby-Gore in May—and were replaced by Malcolm MacDonald and Lord Halifax (formerly Lord Irwin of the Irwin Declaration), respectively. Eden had found the Foreign Office a challenging posting, not least because of his relatively junior status among fellow cabinet secretaries. Writing later, Eden admitted,

> I was aware that my appointment was not welcome to all my elders in the Cabinet, where there was no lack of former Foreign Secretaries and other aspirants to the office. I knew that Baldwin's support would be fitful and lethargic. I had also seen the practice . . . of a multiplicity of Ministers taking a hand at redrafting a dispatch. On one of these occasions about a year later, I began to protest vigorously, when Baldwin passes me a note: "Don't be too indignant. I once saw Curzon burst into tears when the Cabinet was amending his dispatches." After the meeting, he told me I must remember that out of my twenty colleagues, there was probably not more than one who thought he should be Minister of Labour and nineteen who thought they should be Foreign Secretary.[166]

Eden faced a built-in tradition of turf wars that began again with William Ormsby-Gore over the Palestine question, though Ormsby-Gore supported him on other issues. The subsequent colonial secretary, Malcolm MacDonald, then adopted the Foreign Office view of partition, but the delay created by bureaucratic politics allowed the situation in Palestine to worsen considerably. This turf war raged between only the two cabinet secretaries themselves, hardly involving their staffs, and was fought as though they were arguing a heated debate over strategy versus compassion. This prompted the prime minister to intervene in a way that caused the severe delay. This process of bureaucratic infighting added more than a year to British deliberations, a procrastination that pushed the decision about Palestine until after the Munich Crisis and much closer to imminent war in Europe.

It is important to note that the turf war played out between Ormsby-Gore and Eden, heading up their respective ministries, as they each attempted to maximize their institution's agendas and goals.[167] The Colonial and Foreign Offices were traditional bureaucratic rivals, where chief players were often undersecretaries and heads of department, meaning that much of the game playing took place below cabinet level. However, the conflict between lower ranked officials and office staffs was not crucial in this instance. In 1937, the Colonial Office Middle Eastern Department was headed by O. T. R. Williams, one of four assistant undersecretaries of state, supervised by Sir Cosmo Parkinson and often Sir John Shuckburgh, who presented information to Ormsby-Gore.[168] The day-to-day running of Palestine fell within the Colonial Office remit, but Palestine's international diplomatic ties were handled by the Eastern Department of the Foreign Office.[169] George Rendel headed this department, which reported to Sir Lancelot Oliphant and upward to Anthony Eden.[170] Previous studies have detailed the antagonism between these ministry staffs,[171] but these dynamics were not overly relevant for policy making at this time. The key figures (in terms of how interdepartmental conflict had an impact on decisions) sat in the cabinet. This is where the delay was created. The foreign secretary had a much wider scope than the colonial secretary, and it was this scope—in considering the impact of Palestine policy across Britain's Middle East strategic interests—that gave him a legitimate role in the development of policy during the Arab Revolt. Repeatedly, however, the colonial secretary attempted to reinterpret the crisis as a small, isolated incident that should be dealt with equitably rather than strategically, an argument essentially against Foreign Office interference.

This may appear to be a cynical reading of the Colonial Office's attempt to do what was best for Palestine, but Ormsby-Gore's early evaluation of the rebellion demonstrates agreement with what became the Foreign Office argument, and it was only after Eden's involvement that Ormsby-Gore became hostile regarding any cabinet discussions on abandoning partition. When Peel's proposals were discussed and the colonial secretary advocated the partition plan, Ormsby-Gore wrote privately that "without a reasonable measure of assent on the part of the two peoples concerned, no scheme of partition involving the establishment of two independent States can be put into effect."[172] Ormsby-Gore had pinned his colors on partition in order to prevent the appearance of indecision or uncertainty following the publication of Peel's recommendations.[173] This meant that he could not accept Eden's arguments without tacitly surrendering responsibility on this issue to the Foreign Office.

Several months later, when international tension increased over Italy's joining with Germany in the Axis and leaving the league, as well as Japan's threat to the British position in Asia, the Foreign Office took a renewed interest in the Palestine problem and its ramifications across the region. This began a series of memoranda[174] in which the two secretaries of state jockeyed for position on the issue within the cabinet. Ormsby-Gore accused Eden of ignoring "fundamental realities of the Palestine problem," and the foreign secretary labeled Ormsby-Gore's assessment of regional Arab amity as "unfounded and misleading."[175] A direct result of Ormsby-Gore's defensive posture was the need for a second commission. Although the Colonial Office did not appoint Sir John Woodhead and his fellow commissioners until March 1938, their mission came under intense discussion between Ormsby-Gore and Eden in the cabinet. Was the commission merely a "technical" commission as Ormsby-Gore argued, tasked with implementing partition? Or, as Eden advocated, was it a "partition" commission, possessing the right to judge partition impracticable?[176] Ormsby-Gore managed to get the word *technical* inserted into the commission's terms of reference by securing the prime minister's private approval, a measure that Eden referred to as having "gone too far."[177]

In May 1937—before the Peel Commission had returned its report—Neville Chamberlain replaced Stanley Baldwin as prime minister; he acted with far more intervening authority than the beleaguered Baldwin had demonstrated. On 8 December 1937, Chamberlain mediated between the two men, asserting that while "evidence available to the world was as yet not sufficient to carry the conviction that partition was impracticable," and "if the Government were to make such an announcement it would be criticised for having surrendered to threats and force," the commission should not be debarred from concluding that "in their view no workable scheme could be produced."[178] This, Chamberlain asserted, "need not antagonise the Arab States! Neither need it exclude the possibility of a change of policy if the Commission showed partition to be unworkable."[179] The cabinet generally agreed that an announcement committing Britain to enforcing partition would create unrest in India while at the same time any "impression of vagueness" had proved just as fatal in the past.[180] This meant that the technical/partition commission, which became the Woodhead Commission, provided a convenient tool to help the government appear decisive when it was anything but. The final decision between the two arguments was delayed until some unknown date in the future. Woodhead was appointed three months later, traveled to Palestine in April, and presented the committee's findings in November 1938, nearly a year after Chamberlain had intervened within the cabinet.

As Eden resigned in February 1938 and Ormsby-Gore followed in May, the bureaucratic dynamic surrounding a search for peace in Palestine changed significantly. Although the traditionally pro-Zionist Malcolm MacDonald assumed Ormsby-Gore's post, he did not defend partition on the basis of an "equitable" solution. Instead, as MacDonald shared none of Ormsby-Gore's responsibility for the adoption of partition, he was able to approach the issue free from his predecessor's defense of Colonial Office turf. Although it is unlikely that MacDonald assumed his new post with a bureaucratic politics agenda in mind, his agreement with the Foreign Office and CID opinion that Arab support was threatened by Palestine policy actually won the bureaucratic battle for the Colonial Office. Without a policy to rail against, the Foreign Office possessed no legitimate reason to claim Palestine policy was within its remit. The documents that deal with Palestine policy formation following Eden and Ormsby-Gore's resignations are dominated by Malcolm MacDonald in discussions with Prime Minister Chamberlain; the new foreign secretary, Lord Halifax, is hardly mentioned. This relationship may have been the result of pressure on MacDonald to act quickly, which was very difficult before the Woodhead Commission returned its findings. MacDonald anticipated that the inquiry would return a verdict of no confidence in partition, but this was by no means certain.

The Woodhead Commission, far from receiving instructions simply to reject partition, found the task set to them exceedingly difficult. Woodhead noted "that if he had known how difficult this job was when it had been offered to him, he would have refused to undertake it!"[181] MacDonald pestered the committee continually for an early submission because he needed time to assess their policy recommendations and formulate ideas to take to the cabinet. The colonial secretary had heard rumors that the commission would repudiate partition and believed it would be better for the Arab insurrection for this news to emerge sooner rather than later.[182] MacDonald pleaded with Woodhead, "saying that he would appreciate that the European situation increased the desirability of our getting Palestine policy settled as early as possible."[183] Woodhead, however, refused to provide him with early data or even discuss the matter in private over dinner to avoid overt interference or the appearance of impropriety.[184] "If I came and dined with him and his colleagues for the purpose which I had in mind," the colonial secretary offered, "I would not try to influence their decision. If they liked, I would not open my mouth, except to put food into it, throughout the evening."[185] When the conclusions did eventually emerge in November 1938, they provided the perfect opportunity to retreat officially from the policy that appeared to endanger British strategic interests in the Middle East—a consideration that was only pertinent due to the looming threat of a second world war.

Ultimately, although staff at the respective ministries were indeed pitted against each other in terms of their opinions, it remained the relationship between William Ormsby-Gore and Anthony Eden that fueled a turf war between the Foreign Office and the Colonial Office in 1937–1938. This is evidenced by the profound change witnessed once these two men left the government and a final consensus emerged. There was a real fear of losing Arab support in the event of war, which was an opinion shared and reiterated by many more officials than Rendel, Oliphant, and Eden. Most important, the year's delay caused by bureaucratic infighting made it harder for the British government to support the Jewish national home. This was because Arab attitudes only hardened against repressive British counterinsurgency measures the longer they continued, and Arab leaders only became more indignant over the perceived lack of interest in Westminster. Added to this disruptive delay was a lack of probing parliamentary criticism, which meant repudiating the Jewish national home no longer posed much of a political risk.

Unusually United

It is important to discuss Parliament because the body had been highly influential in directing Britain's deliberations on Palestine in both 1922 and 1930. However, in 1939 a lack of effective parliamentary opposition rendered the Jewish national home politically inert, a situation that would have seemed impossible during the policy-making dynamics discussed in earlier chapters. This was due to two reasons: Prime Minister Chamberlain and Colonial Secretary MacDonald shared the opinion that British deterrence was not harmed by concessions in Palestine by 1939; in addition, a large Conservative majority in the House of Commons meant the government could risk losing support from a sizable number of Conservative MPs (i.e., those who equated Palestine's independence with appeasement). Amery, for example, wrote to Eden that "[t]he whole business is a replica on a small scale of the European situation."[186] Incidentally, although Ormsby-Gore had opposed Eden's attitude to Palestine, he had supported him in the cabinet on the crisis with Germany.[187]

First, the architects behind the MacDonald White Paper—MacDonald himself (who was a former Labour MP and the son of James Ramsay MacDonald) and Prime Minister Chamberlain—did not think that resolving the revolt in Palestine through diplomatic gestures endangered Britain's standing in the world. This meant that the policy they developed did not represent as much of a fundamental change as it appeared. Britain's empire had a history of rebellion, and the idea of repressive measures to restore "order" followed by concessions was not new. MacDonald had specifically questioned Sir Miles Lampson about the impact of abandoning partition. "Would not this be greeted as a sign of our decadence?" he asked, as "[t]he Germans and Italians would certainly urge this in all their propaganda."[188] At the Colonial Office, the veteran imperial administrator Shuckburgh had expressed similar concerns, that "there was a danger that terrorists would declare that they had won their first battle and must now carry on with the work of driving the Jews into the sea."[189] Lampson merely replied, however, that "[i]n a way the British were always giving way to this sort of pressure. They had done so in the cases of Ireland and India and even of Egypt [. . .] On the whole their credit was far greater after the event than before."[190] Pretending Britain had always remained firm in the face of local challenge was futile. Rather than associating the rejection of partition with Munich and appeasement, the colonial secretary and the prime minister came to view it as part of imperial governance. Ultimately, Britain could concede ground, but the empire attempted, if possible, to avoid the appearance of it.

This attitude was most apparent during interdepartmental discussions on Palestine in October 1938. MacDonald noted that "if concessions were to be made, it was essential to avoid the appearance of a surrender to terrorism; we must show the world that our decision has its roots in justice, not force; and thorough-going measures for the restoration of security must therefore precede and accompany the proposed declaration of policy."[191] This is why communications about Palestine with regional Arab leaders were conducted clandestinely. Chamberlain, for example, wrote to Egyptian prime minister Mahmoud Pasha in October 1938 to assure him they were seeking a solution beyond repression, but it was marked "secret."[192] The colonial secretary also argued that the key leader in the revolt, mufti of Jerusalem Haj Amin al Husseini, would have to be represented at bilateral talks because "no considerations of prestige should prevent us from coming to terms with the one man who can, on his side, guarantee peace. The vicious circle of rebellion—investigation—half settlement has got to be broken, and this is apparently the only way of breaking it."[193] When Palestine's new high commissioner, Sir Harold MacMichael, protested that "His Majesty's Government cannot treat with instigators of murder," Sir G. Bushe from the Colonial Office replied, "On the contrary, peace in Ireland was made by a treaty between Cabinet Ministers and 'murderers.'"[194] MacDonald agreed, and argued that rejecting partition in this manner would create some opposition in Parliament. However, this antipathy would be largely irrelevant because "His Majesty's Government is only committed to consulting Parliament before embarking on a new constructive policy."[195] The transparent secrecy involved in courting wider Arab opinion continued even when the government had to defend its policy to Parliament. When the House of Commons debated an end to partition in October 1938 and then voted on the white paper in May 1939, at no point did government representatives use the "Arab opinion" argument to justify Palestinian independence.

By the late 1930s, the national government (a Labour-Conservative alliance created by a Conservative takeover of Ramsay MacDonald's government in August 1931) was very secure. Still dominated by Conservatives since a general election in 1935, the government felt very little threat from parliamentary politics. There were only 8 Labour MPs and 33 Liberals versus 387 Conservatives.[196] There was, however, a proportion of Conservative MPs who opposed the Neville Chamberlain cabinet over the policy of appeasement. Those who resisted the Munich Agreement of 1938 saw parallels in the MacDonald White Paper's concessions to Palestinian Arabs. Consequently, they opposed the white paper, too, by an extension of principle. This vocal but unthreatening group materialized when MPs officially debated the white paper on 22–23 May 1939. The debates were centered on moral rather than strategic questions and were totally dominated by criticisms of the policy, with no backbench opinion being voiced in support of the government (a situation highly out of character with previous debates). The final vote vindicated the government's position—meaning that 268 MPs who voted in favor of the white paper had declined to defend it publicly. Opposition in these debates was mainly mounted by the very small number of Labour MPs and two vocal Conservative opponents of appeasement: Leopold Amery and Winston Churchill.

Criticizing the white paper on the basis of appeasement, Amery declared that "[i]t is preposterous to ask the House to shut its eyes, open its mouth and swallow this half-baked project."[197] The white paper only invited "more intransigence, more violence, more pressure from neighbouring States," and was "a direct invitation to the Arabs to continue to make trouble."[198] His multiple speeches were

Fig. 4.4. "November Fifth in Palestine": a cartoon, published on Guy Fawkes Night in the *Evening Standard* in 1938, making light of Palestine's explosive potential. © David Low / Solo Syndication.

long and heated, and Churchill stood up to agree, asking, "What will our potential enemies think? What will those who have been stirring up these Arab agitators think? Will they not be encouraged by our confession of recoil? Will they not be tempted to say: 'They're on the run again. This is another Munich.'"[199] These arguments were echoed across parties and in the House of Lords, by Lord Snell and the former high commissioner to Palestine, Herbert Samuel. To these men, neither partition nor the white paper presented an adequate solution.

Instead they advocated merely "perseverance." Churchill, for example, had criticized the government's lack of a decision in November 1937, accusing the cabinet of doing nothing except "palter and maunder and jibber on the Bench."[200] He had also openly opposed partition in an article for the *Jewish Chronicle* citing the pending war in Europe and an inevitability of armed conflict in Palestine as his reason.[201] Then, in the debate over the MacDonald White Paper in 1939, Churchill declared that he was bound to vote against the government's proposals: "I could not stand by and see solemn engagements into which Britain has entered before the world set aside for reasons of administrative convenience or—and it will be a vain hope—for the sake of a quiet life [...] I should feel personally embarrassed in the most acute manner if I lent myself, by silence or inaction, to what I must regard as an act of repudiation."[202] (See fig. 4.4.)

In the final vote, Churchill abstained—perhaps demonstrating that he, like all of the 268 MPs who voted "yes" reluctantly admitted that there was little other choice.[203] Amery, with 178 other MPs, voted against the white paper, but the government still won by a margin of 89. As predicted, the government could afford to lose votes and split the party on this single issue—it simply had a large enough majority. Therefore, although parliamentary politics and the sometimes hollow rhetoric of strident members of the House had proved influential in earlier events, by 1939 the unusually large Conservative majority in the House of Commons protected key decision makers from political fallout, allowing them to consider policy options that had previously been far too risky for British politicians.

Meeting National Needs

It was clear that British forces could not continue indefinitely with repression in Palestine, nor could British diplomats implement partition. This left only one option, which was to repudiate or end the British obligation toward building a Jewish national home. This sole course of action also had to satisfy a key aspect of British national interest in 1939. In the case of Palestine policy—as Britain approached World War II—one issue emerged as crucial for all members of government. This was the need to ensure military and strategic planning and readiness. The option of ending the Jewish national home was found to be unproblematic in this regard.

Preparing for War

As war approached, military or strategic needs were, naturally, highly salient. The war played a large role in determining which issues were politicized, but more tangible military considerations (plans of the chiefs of staff, for example) were critical enough that they had to be considered separately as well. Crucially, any option considered politically sound by the cabinet had to satisfy the needs of the army, navy, and air force. Palestine had to remain available and in a manner that did not draw troops away from vital areas of defense in the Middle East. The white paper met both of these conditions.

First, as Leopold Amery highlighted in the Commons, Palestine was crucial to the British military because it was "the Clapham Junction of all the air routes between this country, Africa and Asia."[204] It also occupied an important naval position following Italy's conquest of Abyssinia, what Amery called "new conditions in the Mediterranean," with the port at Haifa allowing a flow of oil supplies from Baghdad.[205] Palestine occupied a key position in the defense of Egypt and India for a dual reason. As well as the British military requiring use of Palestine, the armed forces could not afford any other power to take its place there and threaten these vital British holdings. This had been a consideration throughout the 1920s and 1930s, with fears that renouncing the Jewish national home would mean returning the Mandate to the league for reassignment. By creating a situation in which Britain would continue to act as trustee, for the interim period before independence and official treaty negotiations (which were supposed to secure an indefinite British military presence), the white paper removed this threat. It envisioned a ten-year transition period for Palestinian independence, to be followed by a full treaty, which was the same process that allowed Britain to grant Egypt "independence" while keeping control of the canal.[206] Although "the General Staff strongly criticised the absence from the White Paper of a more specific statement as to the strategical safeguards," the document kept Britain in Palestine unencumbered by an indefinite insurrection (that was, incidentally, being extended by regional Arab leaders such as Ibn Saud, who had been funding Palestine's rebellion).[207]

Troops deployed in Palestine were needed to defend the Suez Canal in the event of war. If Italy blocked the Red Sea entrance to the Canal, reinforcements from India would need to be transported to Egypt overland from the Persian Gulf, through Palestine.[208] This plan would have been severely complicated by the general strike. As the Peel partition plan was written during the first, less violent stage of the Arab Revolt, it was directed at this strategic need. Partition, when proposed, was not primarily an attempt to settle the Arab-Jewish problem philanthropically, but merely to solve the immediate political and monetary costs that weighed Britain down.[209]

Troops could not continue to be siphoned away from key strategic zones in the Middle East. Indeed, the cost of troops and hardware was of vital concern to the chiefs of staff, and the broad swath of territory Britain "protected" during the interwar period had already led to a reappraisal of military thinking on this topic. In October 1937, the chiefs of staff stressed the policy of "self-sufficiency" in the Middle East to avoid moving squadrons needed to protect vital areas such as the Suez Canal.[210] Defending the empire in a state of tension with limited resources had become a sensitive subject. The Arab Revolt in Palestine required reinforcements paid for by the Palestine administration in the region of £3.5 million (approximately £185 million today) but they had to be diverted from other tasks.[211]

Also, while partition might have seemed attractive initially as a means of securing the Mediterranean against Italian incursion following Italy's successful invasion of Abyssinia, this thinking was easily reversible as a second war between European powers crept ever closer.[212] If Britain needed to mobilize, then simultaneously creating two new states in the Middle East would have upset the status quo, incurred immediate expense, and commanded far too much attention considering the primacy of European affairs.[213] Regardless, partition was universally unacceptable and failed to restore the quiet in Palestine that military strategists needed. Although a great deal of force was applied to try and fix the situation, Britain lacked the manpower, funding, and public backing necessary to endure in Palestine without a proper political solution.[214]

By 1939, the violent element of the Arab Revolt had been largely eliminated and the white paper gave Britain more security vis-à-vis the other Arab leaders. Vitally, a placated and even an independent Palestine still meant a strong British military presence without an uncontrollable drain on resources, ensuring that the MacDonald White Paper satisfied the needs of military readiness and strategic planning.

The MacDonald Compromise

The MacDonald White Paper of 1939 is often considered to mark a major shift in British policy toward Palestine. The white paper stated Britain's objective was "the establishment within ten years of an independent Palestine State."[215] This was portrayed as a direct response to the violence in Palestine, highlighting the Arab fear of Jewish domination and how this "has produced consequences which are extremely grave for Jews and Arabs alike and for the peace and prosperity of Palestine."[216] Instead of seeking to expand the Jewish national home indefinitely by immigration, the cabinet chose to allow further immigration only if the Arabs were prepared to acquiesce. Theoretically, this proviso relieved British troops of the tangible burden of policing Palestine solely to protect the growing national home. It also guarded against the diplomatic furor with regional Arab leaders who were opposed to Zionism and purported to avoid assuming the moral burden of ceasing Jewish immigration—the Arabs would make that decision.

When examining the calculations behind this document in the context of Britain's previous policy formulations (the Churchill White Paper of 1922 and the MacDonald "Black" Letter in 1931), the decision in 1939 represents continuity as well as change. This is because the politicians' preferences, if not the final decision, followed a very similar pattern to earlier incidents. In every period, the British cabinet was presented with authoritative interpretations of tensions in Palestine that rested on Arab opposition to the policy of building a Jewish national home. Political constraints had, however, until the late 1930s, prevented the government following advice to vigorously implement, reduce, or end the policy.

Whereas the Chamberlain government did not interpret Palestine data any differently than its predecessors, it possessed the impetus of impending war and the strength of a large majority in the House necessary to carry out a "rational" policy. Interparty politics had played a large role in denying previous governments this luxury. Former India secretary Lord Winterton noted, for example, how "if during all the troubles that we had in India, the Hindu and Moslem disturbances, that if in speaking as Under-Secretary I had to deal with a state of affairs in which there was in this House either a Pro-Moslem or a Pro-Hindu bloc, it would have been impossible for me to discharge my duties, because the government of India could not have maintained order."[217]

Also, the new policy was only as finite as the conditions that made it necessary, and it was still MacDonald's hope that there would be an eventual return to the idea of partition in the future.[218] Political conditions might improve over time, or they might deteriorate. As such, the white paper also included a provision that after ten years, independence could be postponed.[219] This was not a disingenuous article of the document, merely a safeguard against an unknowable future condition of international relations. By repudiating the Jewish national home and instead supporting a Palestinian Arab bid for autonomy masquerading as independence, Britain gave up nothing of value to its present or future political or strategic interests in the Middle East, making it difficult to label the policy as appeasement.

Far from an analogy with the Munich Agreement of 1938—which was a foreign policy anomaly pursued to avoid war with another European power—MacDonald's white paper was merely the routine exercise of diplomacy within Britain's own empire. Negotiations at the London Conference represented a familiar practice of short-term conciliation.[220] While labeled "appeasement" by some of those MPs who opposed Munich, the comparison was an emotional reaction to an otherwise normal act of concession and compromise. MacDonald himself was resigned to what he considered to be a less than ideal policy: "I don't think I did make such a good job of Palestine; but the problem was insolvable on any short-term lines, and there was little else we could do in the circumstances and at the time that would have given us the essential minimum of trouble in the Near East now. In the end Jew and Arab alike will have gained from our policy."[221] He also pleaded publicly that "[w]e cannot treat a million Arabs in their own country as though they did not exist."[222] The decision was made in the context of a crisis, but it also reflected a rational weighing of costs versus benefits. Also, it is important to remember that Palestine remained but a sideshow to the European situation, and books and memoirs on those involved in British foreign policy during the critical time period of 1938–1939 rarely even list Palestine in the index.[223]

World War II then stalled further cabinet-level considerations of Palestine policy, despite a violent campaign orchestrated by the Jewish paramilitary organizations, the Irgun and the Stern Gang. When allied troops began to liberate concentration camps, however, the horror of the Holocaust meant Britain was again severely constrained by diplomacy. Rather than only regional Arab states, by 1945, the cabinet had to contend with a new superpower in strident support of the Jewish cause.

Notes

1. Arthur Koestler, *Promise and Fulfilment: Palestine 1917–1949* (London: Macmillan, 1949); Cohen, "Secret Diplomacy and Rebellion in Palestine, 1936–1939," 379.
2. Cohen, "Secret Diplomacy and Rebellion in Palestine," 380; W. F. Abboushi, "The Road to Rebellion, Palestine in the 1930s," *Journal of Palestine Studies* 6, no. 3 (1977): 23–46, 26–28.
3. Cohen, "Secret Diplomacy and Rebellion in Palestine," 379; Cmd. 5479, 1937, *Palestine Royal Commission Report*, 97.
4. CAB 24/264, 25 August 1936, Ormsby-Gore to Smuts, TNA.
5. Cmd. 5479, *Palestine Royal Commission Report*, 110–111.
6. Ibid., 111–112.
7. Ibid., 370.
8. Ibid., 368.
9. Ibid., 370.
10. Ibid., 371–372.
11. Ibid., 375.
12. Ibid., 377–389.
13. Ibid., 2.
14. Ibid., 394; Abboushi, "Road to Rebellion," 42.
15. Segev, *One Palestine, Complete*, 414.
16. Matthew Hughes, "The Banality of Brutality: British Armed Forces and the Repression of the Arab Revolt in Palestine, 1936–39," *English Historical Review* 124, no. 507 (2009): 313–354, 315.
17. Hughes, "Banality of Brutality," 316.
18. Ibid., 319.
19. Cmd. 5854, 1938, *Palestine Partition Commission Report*, 84.
20. Cmd. 5854, *Palestine Partition Commission Report*, 86.
21. Ibid., 87.
22. Ibid., 281.
23. Ibid., 14, 101.
24. Ibid., 14.
25. Ibid., 100.
26. Ibid., 244.
27. Cmd. 5893, 1938, *Palestine. Statement by His Majesty's Government in the United Kingdom*.
28. Cmd. 5479, *Palestine Royal Commission Report*, 376.
29. Cmd. 6019, 1939, *Palestine. Statement of Policy*.
30. Cmd. 6019, *Palestine. Statement of Policy*.
31. Ibid.
32. Ibid.
33. Cmd. 5479, *Palestine Royal Commission Report*, ix.
34. House of Commons Debates, 19 June 1936, series 5, vol. 313, cols. 1367–1369.
35. Cmd. 5479, *Palestine Royal Commission Report*, 105.
36. Porath, *Emergence of the Palestinian-Arab National Movement: 1929–1939*, 230.

37. Cmd. 5513, 1937, *Statement of Policy by His Majesty's Government in the United Kingdom*; CAB 24/270, 25 June 1937, "Report of Palestine Royal Commission: Memorandum by the Secretary of State for the Colonies," TNA; CAB 23/88, 5 July 1937, Cabinet Minutes, TNA; LSE/PASSFIELD/1/2/9, 7 March 1930, Diary of Beatrice Webb.
38. CAB 24/263, 20 June 1936, "Cabinet. Palestine: Memorandum by the Secretary of State for Foreign Affairs," TNA.
39. CAB 24/263, 20 June 1936, "Cabinet. Palestine."
40. CAB 24/273, 19 November 1937, "Cabinet. Palestine: Memorandum by the Secretary of State for Foreign Affairs," TNA.
41. CAB 24/273, 19 November 1937, "Cabinet. Palestine."
42. Ibid.
43. Ibid.
44. Ibid.
45. Ibid.
46. Ibid.
47. Ibid.
48. CAB 24/278, 14 September 1938, "Committee of Imperial Defence. Chiefs of Staff Sub Committee, Appreciation of the Situation in the Event of War Against Germany," TNA.
49. CAB 23/90A, 17 November 1937, Cabinet Minutes, TNA, 13.
50. CAB 24/277, 14 June 1938, "Quarterly Survey of the Political and Constitutional Position in British India for the Period from 1st February to 30th April, 1938," TNA; CAB 24/282, 18 January 1939, "Cabinet. Palestine. Memorandum by the Secretary of State for the Colonies," TNA.
51. PREM 1/352, 2 September 1938, Notes by MacDonald, TNA.
52. PREM 1/352, 2 September 1938, Notes by MacDonald.
53. CAB 24/281, 6 December 1938, Ambassador to Cairo to MacDonald, TNA.
54. CAB 24/281, 6 December 1938, Ambassador to Cairo.
55. MAC 9/9/10, 8 January 1936, MacDonald to Weizmann, reproduced by permission of Durham University Library.
56. CAB 23/98, 15 March 1939, "Cabinet Minutes and Appendix with Draft White Paper," TNA.
57. CAB 24/282, 18 January 1939, "Cabinet. Palestine. Memorandum."
58. Ibid.
59. Ibid.
60. CAB 24/283, 30 January 1939, "Cabinet. Committee on Palestine Report," TNA; CAB 23/97, 1 February 1939, Cabinet Minutes, TNA; CAB 23/97, 8 March 1939, Cabinet Minutes, TNA.
61. CAB 23/98, 22 March 1939, Cabinet Minutes, TNA.
62. CAB 23/97, 15 February 1939, Cabinet Minutes, TNA.
63. CAB 23/97, 22 February 1939, Cabinet Minutes, TNA.
64. CAB 23/97, 2 March 1939, Cabinet Minutes, TNA.
65. CAB 23/97, 8 March 1939, Cabinet Minutes.
66. Ibid.
67. CAB 24/282, 18 January 1939, "Cabinet. Palestine. Memorandum."
68. CAB 23/96, 14 December 1938, Cabinet Minutes, TNA, 14–15.
69. PREM 1/352, May 1939, "Palestine. Situation and Policy in Palestine," Chamberlain to Weizmann, TNA.

70. PREM 1/352, 23 February 1939, MacDonald to Chamberlain, TNA.
71. CAB 24/273, 3 December 1937, Cabinet. Policy in Palestine, TNA; FO 371/21873/E851, 14 February 1938, Notes, TNA.
72. FO 371/21881 E5999, 13 October 1938, Notes, TNA.
73. CAB 23/99, 10 May 1939, Cabinet Minutes, TNA.
74. CO 733/406/7, 1939, "American Opinion. Mandate over Palestine," TNA.
75. CO 733/386/13, 11 October 1938, "Palestine Discussions," TNA.
76. FO 371/21881 E5999, 14 October 1938, "Note by Baggallay on U.S. Public Opinion," TNA.
77. FO 371/21882 E6030, 17 October 1938, Notes, TNA.
78. CAB 23/100, 28 June 1939, Cabinet Minutes, TNA.
79. CAB 23/100, 19 July 1939, Cabinet Minutes, TNA.
80. Edward Keith-Roach, *Pasha of Jerusalem: Memoirs of a District Commissioner under the British Mandate* (London: Radcliffe, 1994), 193; Matthew Hughes, "From Law and Order to Pacification: Britain's Suppression of the Arab Revolt in Palestine, 1936–39," *Journal of Palestine Studies* 39, no. 2 (2010): 6–22, 6.
81. Larry May, "Killing Naked Soldiers: Distinguishing between Combatants and Noncombatants," *Ethics and International Affairs* 19, no. 3 (2005): 39–53, 40.
82. WO 191/88, 12 December 1939, Foreword by General Barker to "History of Disturbances in Palestine 1936–1939," TNA.
83. WO 32/4562, 12 January 1938, "Palestine, 1938—Allegations against British Troops," TNA.
84. CO 733/368/9, September 1938, High Commissioner to Colonial Secretary, TNA.
85. Burr Papers, 88/8/1, n.d., Letter to Mum and Dad, Imperial War Museum (IWM).
86. 10688, Reel 1/6, Interview with Reubin Haig Kitson.
87. Norris, "Repression and Rebellion," 33–34; CO 733/371/4, n.d., Lees to Unknown, TNA.
88. Burr Papers, 88/8/1, 9 September 1938, Letter to Mum and Dad, IWM.
89. CO 733/371/4, Lees to Unknown.
90. Burr Papers, 88/8/1, 19 December 1937, Letter to Mum and Dad, IWM.
91. Matthew Hughes, "The Practice and Theory of British Counterinsurgency: The Histories of the Atrocities at the Palestinian Villages of al-Bassa and Halhul, 1938–1939," *Small Wars and Insurgencies* 20, nos. 3–4 (2009): 528–550, 533.
92. Hughes, "Practice and Theory of British Counterinsurgency," 533.
93. Ibid.
94. Ibid., 534.
95. Ibid.
96. Porath, *Emergence of the Palestinian-Arab National Movement, 1929–1939*, 180.
97. Norris, "Repression and Rebellion," 33.
98. Burr Papers, 88/8/1, 9 September 1938, Letter to Mum and Dad.
99. Norris, "Repression and Rebellion," 33.
100. Ibid.; Hughes, "From Law and Order to Pacification," 11.
101. CO 733/368/9, 11 August 1938, Arab Women's Society to High Commissioner, TNA.
102. CO 733/368/9, 11 August 1938, Arab Women's Society.
103. House of Commons Debate, 19 June 1936, series 5, vol. 313, cols. 1384–1386.
104. WO 32/4562, 22 September 1939, High Commissioner to Colonial Secretary, "Draft Commentary," TNA.
105. WO 32/4562, 22 September 1939, High Commissioner to Colonial Secretary.
106. WO 32/4562, 12 January 1938, "Palestine, 1938."

107. Ibid.
108. 10688, Reel 1/6, Interview with Reubin Haig Kitson.
109. WO 32/4562, 22 September 1939, High Commissioner to Colonial Secretary.
110. House of Commons Debate, 19 June 1936, series 5, vol. 313, cols. 1316–1317.
111. WO 32/4562, 12 January 1938, "Palestine, 1938."
112. Ibid.
113. House of Commons Debate, 19 June 1936, series 5, vol. 313, cols. 1316–1317.
114. Ibid., cols. 1337–1340.
115. Ibid.
116. WO 191/89, April 1939, "Report on Military Control in Palestine 1938/9," TNA.
117. Norris, "Repression and Rebellion," 40; Porath, *Emergence of the Palestinian-Arab National Movement, 1929–1939*, 240.
118. Keith-Roach, *Pasha of Jerusalem*, 198.
119. Burr Papers, 88/8/1, 19 December 1937, Letter to Mum and Dad.
120. Charles Townshend, "The Defence of Palestine: Insurrection and Public Security, 1936–1939," *English Historical Review* 103, no. 409 (1988): 917–949, 919.
121. Ibid.
122. Keith-Roach, *Pasha of Jerusalem*, 196.
123. Norris, "Repression and Rebellion," 34.
124. 10295, Reel 2/22, Interview with Arthur Lane, IWM.
125. 10295, Reel 2/22, Interview with Arthur Lane.
126. Ibid.
127. Pond Papers, 78/27/1, n.d., Chapter VII, IWM.
128. 10295, Reel 3/22, Interview with Arthur Lane, IWM.
129. Pond Papers, 78/27/1, Chapter VII.
130. Ibid.
131. Norris, "Repression and Rebellion," 35–36.
132. Hughes, "Practice and Theory of British Counterinsurgency," 531–532.
133. CO 733/371/3, 10 August 1938, High Commissioner to Colonial Secretary, TNA.
134. Burr Papers, 88/8/1, n.d., Letter to Mum and Dad.
135. CO 733/371/4, 3 April 1939, Mrs. Lowick to Mr. Luke, TNA; CO 733/371/4, 26 November 1938, Most Secret, Attorney General to High Commissioner, TNA. Similar incidents also took place after World War II, when British soldiers used heavy-handed and illegal measures to target Jewish militia members. David Cesarani, *Major Farran's Hat* (Oxford: OneWorld, 2007).
136. CO 733/371/4, 25 March 1939, "Note of Interview Between Sir G. Bushe and Mr. Wood (Constable's Father)," TNA; CO 733/371/4, 26 November 1938, Most Secret, Attorney General to High Commissioner.
137. CO 733/371/4, 3 April 1939, Mrs. Lowick to Mr. Luke.
138. Ibid.
139. Norris, "Repression and Rebellion," 28.
140. Keith-Roach, *Pasha of Jerusalem*, 191.
141. CO 733/368/9, 5 February 1938, Arab Ladies of Jerusalem to High Commissioner, TNA; Keith-Roach, *Pasha of Jerusalem*, 191.
142. Rory Miller, "The Other Side of the Coin: Arab Propaganda and the Battle against Zionism in London," *Israel Affairs* 5, no. 4 (1999):198–228, 203.

143. WO 32/4562, 12 June 1939, Husseini to Permanent Mandates Commission, TNA.
144. CO 733/371/4, Lees to Unknown.
145. FO 371/21881, 8 September 1938, Ogden to Baggallay, TNA.
146. FO 371/21881, 8 September 1938, Ogden to Baggallay.
147. Ibid.
148. Ibid.
149. Ibid.
150. Miller, "Other Side of the Coin," 204.
151. Robert Lewis Melka, "Nazi Germany and the Palestine Question," *Middle Eastern Studies* 5, no. 3 (1969): 221–233, 226.
152. CO 371/4, 5 December 1938, Colonial Secretary to High Commissioner, TNA.
153. WO 32/4562, 1 December 1938, "Hostile Propaganda in Palestine. Its Origin, and Progress in 1938. Signed by General Haining," TNA.
154. CO 371/4, 5 December 1938, Colonial Secretary to High Commissioner.
155. CO 371/4, 2 December 1938, Colonial Secretary to High Commissioner, TNA.
156. CO 733/371/3, 19 September 1938, Colonial Secretary to High Commissioner, TNA.
157. FO 371/21881, 24 September 1938, Shuckburgh to MacMichael, TNA.
158. FO 371/21881, 27 September 1938, G. W. Furlonge to Baggallay, TNA.
159. FO 371/21881, 27 September 1938, G. W. Furlonge to Baggallay.
160. Cohen, "Sir Arthur Wauchope, the Army, and the Rebellion in Palestine, 1936," 19; WO 32/4178, December 1936, "Memorandum of Comments by the High Commissioner on General Dill's Report on Events in Palestine from the 15th September to the 30th October, 1936," TNA.
161. WO 191/89, April 1939, "Report on Military Control in Palestine 1938/9."
162. Hughes, "Practice and Theory of British Counterinsurgency," 537.
163. Hughes, "From Law and Order to Pacification," 8.
164. FO 371/21881, 8 September 1938, Ogden to Baggallay.
165. 10688, Reel 1/6, Interview with Reubin Haig Kitson.
166. Anthony R. Peters, *Anthony Eden at the Foreign Office, 1931–1938* (London: St. Martin's, 1986), 251.
167. Alex Mintz and Karl DeRouen, *Understanding Foreign Policy Decision-Making* (Cambridge: Cambridge University Press, 2010), 71.
168. Klieman, "Divisiveness of Palestine," 424.
169. Ibid., 425.
170. Ibid.
171. Ibid.; Aaron Klieman, "Bureaucratic Politics at Whitehall in the Partitioning of Palestine, 1937," in *Great Powers in the Middle East, 1919–1939*, ed. Uriel Dann (New York: Holmes and Meier, 1988), 128–154.
172. CAB 24/270, 25 June 1937, "Report of Palestine Royal Commission."
173. Ibid.
174. CAB 24/272, 9 November 1937, "Cabinet. Policy in Palestine: Memorandum by the Secretary of State for the Colonies," TNA; CAB 24/273, 19 November 1937, "Cabinet. Palestine"; CAB 24/273, 1 December 1937, "Cabinet. Policy in Palestine: Memorandum by the Secretary of State for the Colonies," TNA.
175. CAB 24/273, 19 November 1937, "Cabinet. Palestine"; CAB 24/273, 1 December 1937, "Cabinet. Policy in Palestine."

176. PREM 1/352, 13 December 1937, Eden to Ormsby-Gore, TNA.
177. PREM 1/352, 16 December 1937, Foreign Office Note, TNA, 228.
178. CAB 23/90A, 8 December 1937, Cabinet Minutes, TNA, 5–15.
179. CAB 23/90A, 8 December 1937, Cabinet Minutes, 5–15.
180. Ibid.
181. PREM 1/352, 14 September 1938, Notes by MacDonald, TNA.
182. PREM 1/352, 14 September 1938, Notes by MacDonald.
183. Ibid.
184. Ibid.
185. Ibid.
186. AMEL 1/5/46, 2 of 2, 11 October 1938, Amery to Eden, Churchill Archives Centre, the Papers of Leopold Amery.
187. Peters, *Anthony Eden at the Foreign Office*, 333.
188. PREM 1/352, 2 September 1938, Notes by MacDonald.
189. PREM 1/352, 7 September 1938, "Colonial Office Conference," TNA.
190. PREM 1/352, 2 September 1938, Notes by MacDonald.
191. CO 733/386/13, 7 October 1938, "Palestine Discussions," TNA.
192. PREM 1/352, 26 October 1938, Chamberlain to Pasha, TNA.
193. CO 733/386/13, 12 October 1938, "Palestine Discussions," TNA.
194. CO 733/386/13, 7 October 1938, "Palestine Discussions."
195. Ibid.
196. Defries, *Conservative Party Attitudes to Jews*, 153.
197. House of Commons Debates, 22 May 1939, series 5, vol. 347, cols. 2015–2016.
198. House of Commons Debates, 22 May 1939, cols. 2013–2014.
199. House of Commons Debates, 23 May 1939, series 5, vol. 347, cols. 2176–2177.
200. House of Commons Debates, 24 November 1937, series 5, vol. 329, cols. 2031–2032.
201. Defries, *Conservative Party Attitudes to Jews*, 160.
202. House of Commons Debates, 23 May 1939, cols. 2168–2169.
203. Defries, *Conservative Party Attitudes to Jews*, 170.
204. House of Commons Debates, 19 June 1936, series 5, vol. 313, cols. 1351–1352.
205. House of Commons Debates, 19 June 1936, cols. 1351–1352.
206. CAB 24/284, 24 February 1939, "Cabinet. Palestine, Minutes of Cabinet Committee," TNA.
207. CAB 23/99, 1 May 1939, Cabinet Minutes, TNA; FO 371/21878 E3791, 27 June 1938, Notes, TNA; FO 371/21878 E3793, 27 June 1938, Notes, TNA.
208. Marlowe, *Seat of Pilate*, 151.
209. Sheffer, "British Colonial Policy-Making towards Palestine," 318.
210. Cohen, "British Strategy and the Palestine Question," 182–183.
211. Cmd. 5479, *Palestine Royal Commission Report*, 106.
212. Cohen, "British Strategy and the Palestine Question," 157.
213. Sheffer, "British Colonial Policy-Making towards Palestine," 319.
214. Mahmoud Yazbak, "From Poverty to Revolt: Economic Factors in the Outbreak of the 1936 Rebellion in Palestine," *Middle Eastern Studies* 3, no. 3 (2000): 93–113, 95; Cmd. 5479, *Report of the Royal Commission*, 519.
215. Cmd. 6019, 1939, *Palestine. Statement of Policy*.
216. Cmd. 6019, *Palestine. Statement of Policy*.

217. House of Commons Debates, 19 June 1936, cols. 1337–1338.
218. CAB 24/282, 18 January 1939, "Cabinet. Palestine. Memorandum."
219. Cmd. 6019, 1939, *Palestine Statement of Policy*.
220. Sheffer, "British Colonial Policy-Making towards Palestine," 309.
221. MAC 2/5/95, n.d., Malcolm MacDonald's notes on his tenure at the Colonial Office before the war, reproduced by permission of Durham University Library.
222. CAB 24/282, 18 January 1939, "Cabinet. Palestine. Memorandum."
223. Peters, *Anthony Eden at the Foreign Office*.

5   From War to Withdrawal, 1940–1948

When Clement Attlee's Labour government was voted into power in July 1945, it was faced with a stark postwar reality. As well as problems such as financial ruin, occupation of Germany, the beginnings of a Cold War with the Soviet Union, and a reinvigorated independence movement in India, Palestine was one of many pressing issues dominating the political landscape in these initial postwar years. Palestine, however, had explosive potential. The MacDonald White Paper of 1939 had left a rift between British authorities and the Jewish Agency in Palestine. Paramilitary groups such as the Haganah, Irgun, and its offshoot, the Stern Gang, repeatedly attacked British forces, which were deporting thousands of illegal Jewish immigrants—Holocaust survivors—to camps in Cyprus. Tension and violence escalated, and explanations of British withdrawal from Palestine in May 1948 tend to cite war fatigue and the empire's measurably decreased economic capacity as key elements of this decision.[1] However, the actual discussions about leaving Palestine altogether were mostly related to political concerns—frustrated diplomacy and fear of the unknown ways in which this might damage Britain's already exhausted economy.

Like much of the empire's adventures in Palestine, the British decision to withdraw abruptly in 1948 does not appear to make a great deal of rational sense. After the war ended and Labour ascended to power, two commissions of inquiry in 1945–1946 and 1947 recommended an end to Britain's Palestine Mandate, but only in the form it had taken since the 1920s. Labour was in favor of this outcome, but the nature of Palestine's constitutional development placed Britain in a seemingly hopeless political quandary. The Anglo-American Committee of 1946 recommended a binational state for Arabs and Jews under British trusteeship, whereas a majority of the UN Special Committee on Palestine in 1947 advocated partition and independence. Between these two investigations, Foreign Secretary Ernest Bevin had attempted to secure agreement between Palestine's Jews and Arabs on either of these solutions as well as a plan for provincial autonomy. No proposals met with mutual agreement, however, leaving Britain between a Zionist position supported by the president of the United States and a set of Arab demands endorsed by leaders across the Middle East. This meant that between 1945 and late 1947, the British government found itself totally incapable of making a final policy decision.

A simple assessment of costs versus benefits cannot account for this inertia, as politicians should have been able to simply select the best of available options.[2] This is why understanding the government's political psychology is so important, because the principle that politicians put their own political survival before other considerations of the national interest helps us understand British paralysis over Palestine after the war. British decision makers rejected all of the policy alternatives that were too risky for them politically, and diplomacy appears to have been the most crucial setting in which these fears played out. Until September 1947, all available options came with devastating political consequences, leaving Palestine policy in a state of paralysis concealed by ongoing but unprofitable negotiations.

In 1947, however, an additional option was introduced that did meet the British government's political needs: as everyone awaited a vote over partition in the United Nations, there was suddenly an opportunity for Britain to wash its hands of Palestine without sacrificing its international relationships. This would only be viable if such a solution satisfied the broader needs of national economic and strategic interests. Rather than an empire fleeing from one of its previously vital strategic outposts, this analysis reveals a challenging and time-sensitive balancing of diplomatic interests between east and west and long-term strategic planning in the context of short-term economic pressure. The lack of politically viable options led to a lengthy delay in deciding Palestine policy, an end to which was only made possible by relinquishing any further Mandatory responsibility.

The Final Choice

At the annual Labour Party Conference in 1944, the party platform drafted by future chancellor Hugh Dalton was strongly pro-Zionist.[3] It advocated a Jewish state in Palestine with expanded borders and encouraged local Arabs to emigrate in exchange for compensation.[4] This position, dubbed "Zionism Plus," favored unlimited Jewish immigration into Palestine, specifically without consideration of economic capacity, and so rejected the MacDonald White Paper.[5] Upon election to government in July 1945, Ernest Bevin believed his own negotiating skills (developed through years as a union leader) could resolve the Palestine problem. Convinced that he could forge an agreement, Bevin boasted, "if I don't get a settlement, I'll eat my hat."[6] Attlee's government, however, soon realized the difficulties of their position regarding Palestine, finding themselves in similar constraints to those binding Neville Chamberlain's cabinet in 1939. An uprising in Palestine had the potential to create wider diplomatic problems, and the government's range of options was reflected in the polarized plans produced by two commissions of inquiry: the Anglo-American Committee and the UN Special Committee on Palestine. Although, by 1945, the alternatives presented by these investigations were already well known, it is important to realize that the commissions took place specifically in order to search for new options.

The first postwar investigation, the Anglo-American Committee, resurrected the option of a binational state with provincial autonomy. The Peel Commission had rejected this alternative in 1937 because it required Jewish and Arab cooperation, but the idea was reprised in 1945–1946. As an investigation, the Anglo-American Committee was a direct result of increased American awareness of the Jewish displaced persons (DPs) problem in Europe. In mid-1945, the horrors of the Holocaust were still unraveling, and President Truman seemed particularly affected by public servant Earl G. Harrison's report of the poor living conditions among DPs encamped in the American zone of occupied Germany.

Like the Jewish Agency—whose immigration quota under the 1939 white paper was nearing completion—Harrison called for the immediate admission of one hundred thousand Jewish DPs into Palestine.[7] Truman then echoed this demand on 31 August 1945, but Attlee's government had barely moved into their offices and found compliance with this request fraught with difficulties.[8] There was the potential for a second Arab uprising against British forces in Palestine that would compound the Jewish insurgency growing there since the MacDonald White Paper, and such large-scale immediate immigration would also have made Attlee's government appear callously indifferent to British-Arab obligations outlined in 1939. Faced with pressure from across the Atlantic, Bevin orchestrated a joint venture with the United States to persuade its representatives of the merits of the British way of thinking.[9] Appointed 13 November 1945, the committee did not report its findings until 20 April 1946.

Five months of investigation and negotiation yielded a unanimous report among the Anglo-American Committee members. This report relied very heavily on the extensive investigation conducted by the Peel Commission in 1937 but came to different conclusions. It made ten recommendations, of which the most important were immediate immigration of one hundred thousand Jewish DPs from Germany to Palestine and a new Palestinian constitution to establish a binational state in which the majority would not be able to dominate the minority.[10] The committee members also advised for a continuation of the Mandate pending a trusteeship agreement with the United Nations.[11] Although the committee recognized the problems associated with enacting such a proactive policy while "Palestine is an armed camp," they believed that withdrawal would only bring "prolonged bloodshed the end of which it is impossible to predict."[12]

To enforce a blending of Arab and Jewish nationalisms, the committee recommended "that, if this Report is adopted, it should be made clear beyond all doubt to both Jews and Arabs that any attempt from either side, by threats of violence, by terrorism, or by the organization or use of illegal armies to prevent its execution, will be resolutely suppressed."[13] The report did not specify who, exactly, would achieve this suppression. This is worth noting since Britain was already embroiled in such a conflict, and the committee found the realities of this quite disturbing, noting how they "became more and more aware of the tense atmosphere each day."[14] Faced with an unhappy situation, therefore, the committee had recommended a well-intentioned policy but one that seemed ignorant of the entire history of British-mandated Palestine as well as the aspirations of both Arab and Jewish communities. How to implement these recommendations, therefore, remained a difficult proposition. President Truman, for his part, reiterated his demand for the one hundred thousand immigration permits without reference to the constitutional development necessary to make this possible. Without an agreed framework for implementation, the joint committee was virtually useless.

As a result, Truman agreed to send two groups of advisers to Britain to negotiate a scheme for moving forward. The first was charged with discussing only the practicalities of admitting one hundred thousand Jews to Palestine. The second round of negotiations was led by Lord President of the Council Sir Herbert Morrison and US State Department official Henry F. Grady. This resulted in the Morrison-Grady plan of a binational state, with Arab and Jewish provinces and a separate Jerusalem and Negev under British rule.[15] This left a central government with final control of departments such as defense, customs and excise, the police, and the courts but with an elective legislature in the Jewish and Arab provinces whose bills required approval from the high commissioner.[16] In theory, Jewish DPs could immigrate into the Jewish province, and this meant the plan fulfilled recommendations made by the Anglo-American Committee. As the joint investigative commission had already rejected provincial autonomy, however, the link was somewhat tenuous.

Provincial autonomy also comprised only the beginning of a solution, as negotiations with Arabs and Jews would still be necessary for implementation. Unsurprisingly, President Truman rejected the plan due to the intolerable delay it would create for DPs seeking immigration visas. Regardless, provincial autonomy was presented to the British Parliament as a basis for negotiations.[17] As Conservative MP Oliver Stanley noted during the policy debate on 31 July 1946, however, this scheme was a year in the making and still lacked American support.[18] It was pointless discussing the Anglo-American Committee report, Stanley declared, as "that Report is dead, although, it is only fair to say, it has been buried with the very highest honours."[19] Provincial autonomy remained the official basis for negotiations, but representatives of the Jewish Agency refused to attend. Their most basic demand was some form of partition. In 1947, this was also recommended by the UN Special Committee on Palestine.

Partition had been rejected in 1938 after Sir John Woodhead's commission found it impracticable. The idea did, however, reemerge in the thinking of Winston Churchill's national wartime government. Churchill's cabinet had flirted with the idea of partition along the lines originally suggested by Peel—with Arab Palestine annexed to Transjordan—but they never made a decision and the issue was shelved following Lord Moyne's assassination by the Stern Gang in November 1944.[20] Churchill especially believed that implementing almost any policy initiative was impossible in the face of terrorist activities and would likely destabilize the Middle East.[21] After the war, partition reentered the realm of possibility again, albeit unofficially, because it formed the basic demands of Jewish Agency representatives involved in private negotiations with Ernest Bevin through 1946 and 1947. Then, after the Palestine issue was referred to the United Nations, the option to partition was forcibly reasserted.

Over four months, the UN Special Committee on Palestine investigated the Palestine problem and signed its report on 31 August 1947.[22] Made up of representatives from eleven countries (Australia, Canada, Czechoslovakia, Guatemala, Holland, India, Iran, Peru, Sweden, Uruguay, and Yugoslavia), its composition specifically avoided any members of the Security Council and reflected the geopolitical balance of power in the UN.[23] The Higher Arab Executive boycotted UNSCOP proceedings, but representatives from Egypt, Iraq, Lebanon, Saudi Arabia, Syria, and Transjordan agreed to participate.[24] The boycott, however, effectively meant that while the UNSCOP committee was swamped with memoranda, letters of appeal, reports, witness testimony, and evidence submitted by advocates of the Jewish, Zionist, and DP cause, there was little seen of the opposing argument unless it was included in British documentation. After nearly forty UNSCOP meetings, the Arab states and Pakistan did all testify on behalf of the Palestinian Arab cause, but the amount of paperwork—in comparison to documents advocating the Zionist cause—was miniscule. In August, UNSCOP asked to see British documents on various partition plans, but the committee had to be educated on the Palestine issue virtually from scratch.[25] Sir Henry Gurney and the British liaison MacGillivray gave testimony that was almost totally confined to basic facts and figures regarding population, taxation, immigration laws, average incomes and how the Palestine administration operated.[26] In this context, the committee report was returned remarkably quickly, albeit with two different conclusions.

The majority plan suggested partition into Jewish and Arab states with the city of Jerusalem under international supervision and all areas joined by an economic union.[27] This was deemed necessary because, just as Sir John Woodhead had reported in 1938, the Arab state would not, on its own, be economically viable.[28] The scheme then required Britain to continue the Mandate for an interim period that would allow the immigration of 150,000 Jews into Palestine.[29] Based to a large degree on Lord Peel's commission of 1937, the majority opinion agreed with Peel's earlier observations: "that the claims to Palestine of the Arabs and Jews, both possessing validity, are irreconcilable, and that among all of the solutions advanced, partition will provide the most realistic and practicable settlement."[30] The majority opinion intended to divide Palestine into two sovereign states with an internationalized City of Jerusalem under the following specifications: "The proposed Arab State will include Western Galilee, the hill country of Samaria and Judea with the exclusion of the City of Jerusalem, and the coastal plain from Isdud to the Egyptian frontier. The proposed Jewish State will include Eastern Galilee, the Esdraelon plain, most of the coastal plain, and the whole of the Beersheba sub-district, which includes the Negev."[31]

In contrast, the minority position advocated by India, Iran, and Yugoslavia called for an independent federal state after a transitional period entrusted to an appointee of the General Assembly's choosing.[32] The majority, however, believed this type of binational or cantonized state was unworkable because the constant oversight necessary to keep both populations in parity would be nearly impossible.[33] These proposals were then refined through ad hoc committee and plenary meetings and put to a vote in the General Assembly on 29 November 1947.

There were, therefore, three options available to British decision makers in the late 1940s. In the House of Commons, president of the board of trade, Sir Richard Stafford Cripps announced in August 1946 that "there are three possible alternatives for Palestine in the future—partition [. . .]; the present scheme, or something of that character; and, thirdly, the return to the status quo."[34] This meant that other than partition, which had already been removed from consideration in 1938 with the Woodhead Commission, the alternatives were to create a binational state along the lines suggested by the Anglo-American Committee (more precisely, with provincial autonomy as agreed in the Morrison-Grady proposals) or to continue with the Mandate unaltered, adhering to the last defined policy as articulated in the MacDonald White Paper of 1939. The presence of this "do nothing" option meant that conventional Palestinian independence still remained plausible. Partition was then officially reintroduced by the UNSCOP report.

There was, of course, a final alternative that has not been discussed above. The option to withdraw without committing British resources to any form of a solution was obviously within the range of possibilities because it became the final decision. When this opportunity entered the debate, however, it was dependent on the rejection of all other alternatives. It was only when faced with an overwhelming prospect—that the General Assembly could vote in favor of an impossible partition—that the opportunity to withdraw completely became politically feasible. This is explored in greater detail below.

Diplomacy and Delay

In the context of postwar deliberations on Palestine policy, there was only one key issue that dominated all discussions: diplomacy. Britain's devastatingly weakened postwar position gave diplomacy a new level of importance. The souring of certain political relationships was potentially destructive to the fragile economy, but the consequences were only vaguely predictable, and this degree of uncertainty only increased the general sense of risk. This sole key issue then surfaced in three different ways: in negotiations with the United States, with the Jewish Agency, and with the Arab states. An analysis of how the British government identified risk after World War II vis-à-vis these parties demonstrates how the politicians' political needs could not be satisfied by any other type of benefit for the national interest (i.e., such as to the economy or military). This left no feasible options until after the UNSCOP report was returned in 1947. When the single viable course of action (of withdrawing from Palestine) suddenly seemed possible, it also satisfied the major demands of national economic and strategic interest.[35]

Division with the United States

When President Truman called for one hundred thousand Jewish DPs to enter Palestine, he was declaring a new level of American interest in the Palestine problem. This was the result of widespread horror following the Holocaust and Earl Harrison's report detailing survivors' poor treatment within the American occupation zone in Germany.[36] Although initially driven by humanitarian concerns, the president's involvement in the Palestine question also acquired importance in his own domestic political sphere in a way that was in direct conflict with the home politics of Attlee's government. Due to the importance of US-UK relations following World War II, and President Truman's humanitarian and politically motivated support for Zionism, the options for the British government to pursue either a single majority Arab state of Palestine or create a system of provincial autonomy had to be dropped. Establishing the terms of reference for the joint committee illustrated a mistaken perception in Westminster that British politicians held sway over the American government; these initial negotiations also exposed an underlying American antagonism to the British position in Palestine more generally. Predictably, the two governments were then unable to agree on the report of the Anglo-American Committee or the subsequent Morrison-Grady proposals.

First, it is important to recognize that early in the postwar trans-Atlantic relationship, Attlee and Bevin tried to exert influence over the US president and failed repeatedly. Truman's initial request for the immigration permits, for example, arrived in the form of a letter to Attlee.[37] This was not immediately made public, but US secretary of state James Byrnes informed Foreign Secretary Ernest Bevin that it was going to be published, causing Attlee to write to the president warning "that such action could not fail to do grievous harm to relations between our two countries."[38] It was published nevertheless. Additionally, Truman and the US State Department could not be persuaded over Bevin's proposed terms of reference for the Anglo-American Committee. Framing the committee's central purpose demonstrated Washington and London's fundamentally opposed positions on even investigating solutions to the Palestine problem.

Bevin and Attlee wanted a commission focused on the problem of DPs in Europe and the possibility of their immigration to countries other than Palestine; this would have prevented the appearance of British double-dealing against the Arabs in favor of Zionism and would have provided greater scope for dealing with the actual DP problem. There was, however, a real danger that Truman would end the whole idea of a joint commission if Bevin insisted on redirecting the spotlight away from Palestine, where a large number of the DPs professed a desire to go.[39] Lord Halifax—Britain's foreign secretary when the MacDonald White Paper was published and subsequently the British ambassador in Washington—spied Truman's personal hand in the negotiations over terms of reference. Halifax wrote to Bevin that "[t]his is very annoying but I got a hint late last night that rats were at work. This is the President himself."[40]

Part of Truman's desire to highlight the Palestine issue in 1945 had been the upcoming New York mayoral election in November, but this meant Truman needed to delay the announcement of the Anglo-American Committee: the Democrats needed to avoid criticism from New York's Jewish community about further delay in dealing with the DP issue.[41] In 1945, it was estimated that only half of the American electorate had even heard of the Palestine issue, but of those, three to one were in favor of the creation of a Jewish state there, and the number was disproportionately high in New York.[42] As a result of these electoral considerations, the best compromise Bevin could achieve on the terms was that the committee would investigate DPs' ability to migrate to Palestine "or other countries outside Europe."[43] Even after this agreement, it was difficult for the Foreign Office to predict what further requirements could yet emerge. Attlee was scheduled to visit Washington in November, and Halifax, perhaps naively, noted that "there will be value in the Prime Minister's presence here to keep the President straight."[44]

When the Anglo-American Committee returned its report, a cabinet committee made up of experts from the Colonial, Foreign, and India Offices, as well as the chiefs of staff and cabinet offices, agreed "that a policy based on the recommendations of the Anglo-American Committee is not one which His Majesty's Government should attempt to carry out alone."[45] This was because "such a policy would have disastrous effects on our position in the Middle East and might have unfortunate repercussions in India."[46] Added to this, the Anglo-American Committee's binational state approach would not please Zionists either and required a "crippling financial burden."[47] It had been a calculated tactic bringing the United States into a joint commission, but Bevin and ultimately the cabinet recognized it was imperative that America also share in the solution to prevent Britain shouldering all of the blame or the cost.[48]

Bevin believed this was possible, not least because he was under the impression that Secretary of State Byrnes told him American interest in the Palestine problem was to prevent large-scale Jewish immigration to America.[49] As an attempt at a comprehensive plan, however, the Anglo-American Committee's report was recognized as "unhelpful, irresponsible, unrealistic" and suggested that the British government was being "pushed around."[50] Regardless, pride had to be put aside. The necessary next step was to agree to a joint scheme for implementation.[51] The foreign secretary, however, was expecting a spirit of cooperation from Washington that did not materialize. He had written to Byrnes on 28 April to stress, "I trust that we can be sure that the United States government will not make any statement about the policy without consultation with His Majesty's Government."[52] Two days later, on 30 April, Truman unilaterally reiterated his demand for the one hundred thousand immigration permits.[53]

A tense few months then followed in which groups of British and American experts attempted to develop a new scheme for Palestine. In this atmosphere, Bevin and Attlee were trying very delicately to prevent further incidents in Palestine that could upset their courting of presidential opinion. In order to avert indiscretions among British forces, the high commissioner was stripped of the power "to authorise the Military Authorities to take drastic action against Jewish illegal organisations without cabinet consent."[54] Attlee informed the high commissioner specifically that "[i]n present critical circumstances it is essential that nothing should be done to alienate U.S. sympathy."[55] President Truman's attitude toward the problem—one naturally centered on his own political requirements rather than the British predicament—should perhaps have alerted Attlee and Bevin that solutions acceptable to them were unlikely to excite the Americans. In need of both a Palestine policy and United States' support, however, the British government had to pursue the show of cooperation and conciliation and hope the president could be persuaded.

To this end, the Jewish Agency, the Higher Arab Executive, and the Arab states were invited to submit their views on the Anglo-American Committee report within one month following 20 May, and then British and American experts would convene to discuss.[56] Vitally, Attlee and Bevin tried to convince Truman that whatever solution the experts created, it had "to consider not only the physical problems involved but also the political reactions and possible military consequences."[57] This also applied to individual stages of the negotiations. Truman, for example, pushed for a preliminary team of American experts to travel to London in advance of the main group, specifically to discuss the practicalities of moving one hundred thousand DPs to Palestine.[58] Bevin resisted, fearing Arabs would interpret such discussions as meaning Britain had already decided on the policy of mass immigration.[59] The foreign secretary relented as long as these preliminary talks remained confidential. Unfortunately, before US State Department official Averell Harriman and his colleagues could begin talks, Bevin made a highly impolitic speech from the Labour Party Conference in Bournemouth on 12 June 1946.

Bevin remarked how the American desire for one hundred thousand immigrants to Palestine "was proposed with the purest of motives. They did not want too many Jews in New York."[60] While this comment betrayed more of what Bevin assumed was American anti-Semitism than his own, this comment in conjunction with earlier statements—such as his warning at a press conference in 1946 that Jews wanted "to get too much at the head of the queue," meaning this attitude would incite further anti-Semitism—only made the foreign secretary himself appear Nazi-like in the tense post-Holocaust atmosphere.[61] Bevin was even rebuked in Parliament for these "hasty, ill-timed remarks," and Labour MP Sydney Silverman reminded him that "[t]he Jews have been at the head of the queue since 1933. They were at the head of the queue in Warsaw, in Auschwitz, in Buchenwald, in Belsen and in Dachau and in all the other spots of unutterable horror that spattered the European mainland."[62] Bevin's chief crime in these instances was a decided lack of tact, sympathy, or emotional understanding of the tragedy that had taken place, which only made agreement with the profoundly saddened President Truman even more difficult.

By declaring that the United States only wanted immigration to Palestine to prevent the arrival of thousands more Jews in New York, Bevin unwisely made the president appear foolish when his goodwill and understanding were crucial.[63] Bevin never retracted his statement—he had meant it—though he instructed the Bournemouth remarks to be circulated so they could be read in context.[64] The second group of American experts arrived to begin a second phase of conversations in July, just as the US Congress was discussing the United Kingdom loan.[65] As a sweetener, Secretary of State Byrnes asked Attlee to issue "a reassuring statement on Palestine," but the cabinet refused.[66] This was because the transparency of such a statement would be obvious to all and because they doubted it would have the desired effect.[67] The talks over the Anglo-American Committee were scheduled to continue, and the chancellor of the exchequer, Hugh Dalton, believed that "according to the latest reports from Washington, the prospects of Congress approving the United Kingdom loan were now more favourable" and so "it would be a mistake for His Majesty's Government to issue any further public statement on Palestine until the debate on the loan was completed."[68] At least the appearance of Anglo-American cooperation was perceived in Westminster to be doing some good in Washington. (See figs. 5.1 and 5.2.)

152 | *Unexpected State*

Fig. 5.1. First public sitting of the Anglo-American Committee of Inquiry in 1946. These hearings took place in Palestine, after the commissioners had visited remains of concentration camps in Europe and met with Arab leaders in Cairo. © The National Archives.

When the US-UK negotiations produced the Morrison-Grady plan of provincial autonomy, Bevin hoped this would secure the president's support as a fulfillment of the Anglo-American Committee's recommendation that Palestine exist as neither an Arab nor a Jewish state and would allow DPs to immigrate to the Jewish province. It was attractive to the British cabinet because provincial autonomy was a short-term policy that could see them through the immediate postwar diplomatic crisis in Palestine, which was just one of many to be dealt with.[69] Then the subject could be revisited outside of an emergency atmosphere. While partition was an inexpedient and diplomatically challenging solution in 1946, provincial autonomy was considered "a constructive and imaginative plan" that "should be commended to the favourable consideration of the Jews and the Arabs if United States support for it could be secured."[70]

Neither Bevin nor Attlee nor the rest of the cabinet were fundamentally opposed to partition. It was merely the timing of it that was wrong, when Britain was at its weakest, and this was something they hoped the American president would understand. Bevin, for example, had Sir Norman Brook advise the cabinet that it may "be practicable to adopt, as our long-term aim, a scheme under which the major part of the Arab province would be assimilated in the adjacent Arab States of Trans Jordan and the Lebanon, and the Jewish province established as an independent Jewish State, with perhaps a somewhat larger territory than that

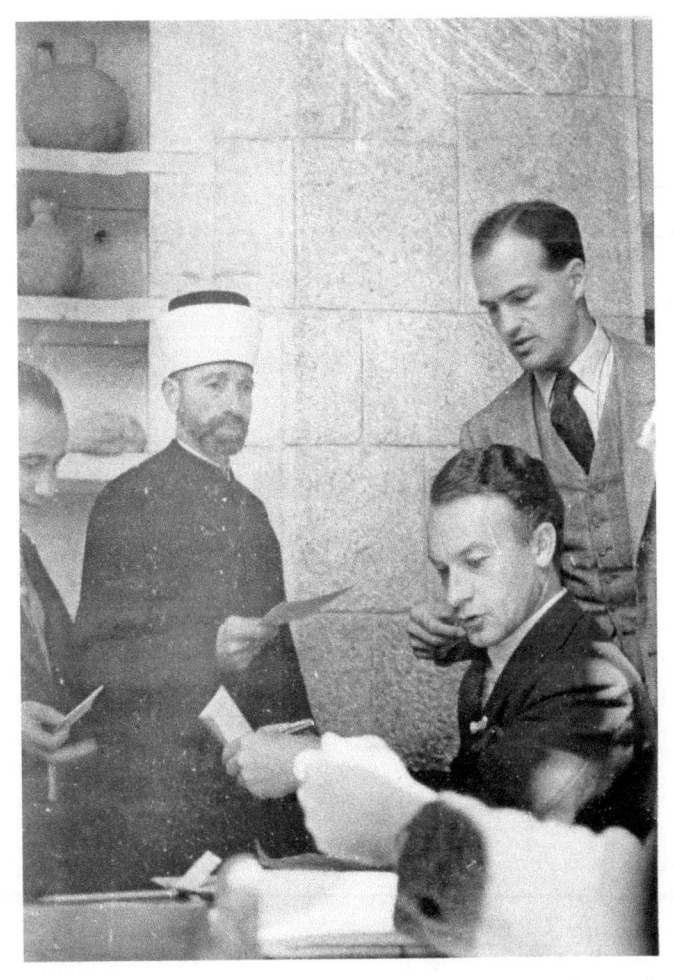

Fig. 5.2. Reporters at the Anglo-American Committee of Inquiry in 1946 having their identities checked. This was necessary due to the high number of terrorist attacks in Palestine. © The National Archives.

suggested for the Jewish province proposed in [the Peel Commission]. He hoped that any intermediate solution [. . .] would contain nothing which was inconsistent with this long-term aim."[71] Provincial autonomy was officially submitted for US approval on 30 July 1946, though Truman had already heard the proposals beforehand from his own team.[72] A debate on the plan was scheduled in Parliament for 31 July and 1 August, and Bevin and Attlee were determined to press ahead despite receiving no word from the White House until the day before the debate.[73] It was a rejection.

Principally, this was because the Morrison-Grady proposals, though relatively practical, violated the spirit of what both Zionists and Truman's humanitarian concerns wanted to achieve. Although provincial autonomy would have allowed the immigration of one hundred thousand Jewish DPs to Palestine, it reflected no urgency on the matter. Such mass immigration would need to wait for the negotiations on constitutional development necessary to create a Jewish province, and, like the 1939 white paper, was still dependent on Arab acquiescence.[74] Agreeing to the plan meant postponement of the DP problem indefinitely and admitting there was going to be a cap on the Jewish community's future growth in Palestine.[75]

On the day of Britain's parliamentary debate, the British ambassador in Washington wrote that "it is acutely embarrassing for us that, on the eve of debate in Parliament, the President should have rejected the proposed statement approved both by Grady and Byrnes."[76] Truman also intended to recall his delegation from London immediately, and this "can hardly be otherwise interpreted than as denoting that, as at present advised, the administration intend drastically to recast the recommendations jointly agreed upon in London, if not to reject them in toto."[77] The newly appointed British ambassador Lord Inverchapel labeled this a "deplorable display of weakness" that was, he feared, "solely attributable to reasons of domestic politics which, it will be recalled, caused the Administration last year to use every artifice of persuasion to defer the announcement about the establishment of the Anglo-American Committee until after the New York elections."[78] This opinion was based on a conversation with the director of the US State Department's Near East Division, who "frankly admitted as much in talk with me this evening."[79]

Rather than telling Parliament about Truman's rejection of the Morrison-Grady proposals, however, Morrison was instructed to inform the Commons that the government "had hoped before the Debate to receive from President Truman his acceptance, but we understand that he has decided, in view of the complexity of the matter, to discuss it in detail with the United States expert delegation who are returning to Washington for the purpose. The President is thus giving further consideration to the matter, and we hope to hear again from him in due course."[80] This avoided the appearance of a total political failure for which there was no time before the debate to prepare, but it also left "the door ajar for the Americans to shut" so that "part at any rate of the onus for the sequel will then rest with them."[81]

The prime minister tried to persuade Truman that the plan devised by US and UK experts was the best prospect for a settlement, that it allowed the introduction of DPs to Palestine "without disturbing the peace of the whole Middle East and imposing on us a military commitment which we are quite unable to discharge."[82] Truman continued to deny support for the plan, which forced

Attlee to remind him that "you will appreciate that any solution must, as matters stand, be one which we can put into effect with our resources alone."[83] Provincial autonomy was the only plan the British had at that point as a reasonable basis for negotiations. Crucially, however, the government did not consider its position immovable on this plan or any of its features.[84] It was merely stuck between the Arabs' steadfast appeal for a single independent Palestinian state, on one hand, and the Jewish Agency's unwavering demand for partition with the creation of a Jewish state (discussed more below), on the other.

A formal conference was opened with the Arab states in London in September, but informal talks with representatives of the Jewish Agency had already begun in Paris in August. A new moment of tension between the transatlantic powers then emerged as Truman intended to make a statement on the evening of Yom Kippur, the Jewish Day of Atonement. Just as Bevin believed he was starting to reach a breakthrough with Zionist negotiators, Attlee received the text of Truman's proposed statement on Palestine at midnight on 3 October 1946. The text reiterated Truman's earlier demand for one hundred thousand Jewish DP immigration visas to Palestine and gave his reason as the suspension of official conference talks until December, which forced DPs to face a harsh German winter without hope or succor.[85] As discussed below, however, the suspension of talks was entirely innocent and actually intended to allow Jewish participation in the official conference. Attlee requested that Truman allow him a little time to discuss the message with Bevin in Paris, and this was denied. Attlee wrote:

> I have received with great regret your letter refusing even a few hours grace to the Prime Minister of the country which has the actual responsibility for the government of Palestine in order that he might acquaint you with the actual situation and the probable results of your action. These may well include the frustration of the patient efforts to achieve a settlement and the loss of still more lives in Palestine. I am astonished that you did not wait to acquaint yourself with the reasons for the suspension of the conference with the Arabs. You do not seem to have been informed that so far from negotiations having been broken off, conversations with leading Zionists with a view to their entering the conference were proceeding with good prospects of success.[86]

Although Truman denied that political calculations were behind his statement, 1946 was an election year. Undersecretary of State Dean Acheson seemed to confirm British suspicions. He informed Britain's ambassador in Washington, Lord Inverchapel, that "Truman had reluctantly yielded to intense pressure from elements within the Democratic Party and from the Jewish groups in and about New York, which had been 'pestering and harassing' him for some time past and which had 'blown up' when the news had come that the conference in London had been adjourned until December 16th."[87] The key to this pressure, Acheson told Inverchapel, was that "the President had been much stirred on hearing that all the candidates nominated for the coming elections in New York were preparing an open attack on him."[88] Complicating the Palestine issue for Democratic congressional candidates was the American Federation of Labor and a general fear among the American voter about Jewish immigration to the United States.[89]

By 1946, American opinions about immigration had hardened, with less than 10 percent of voters outside the clergy favoring immigration.[90] Among the 90 percent against, roughly half opposed immigration for economic reasons—they remembered the hardship of the 1930s, for example—and the rest possessed feelings against Jews or foreigners more broadly and the "threat" they posed to the American way of life.[91] An AIPO poll in January 1946 found even fewer in favor of immigration from Europe, less than 5 percent, and for the same reasons.[92] In a poll specific to Iowa in 1946, about one in seven respondents volunteered an opinion on Palestine—about half were critical of Britain and half believed the United States should expedite sending DPs "'back' to Palestine" rather than admit them to the United States.[93] Conversely, there was almost a complete consensus on the need for a Jewish haven. The majority favored immigration to Palestine but disagreed with any active US military participation in settling the problem.[94]

In addition, between 1946 and 1949, the Truman administration received just under a million campaign cards on the Palestine issue.[95] More than half of these cards came from New York, which contained 47 percent of America's Jews.[96] This meant the cards did not represent the American population as a whole but betrayed the existence of a sophisticated and highly mobilized pressure group campaign.[97] Similarly, Zionist organizations issued letter templates for various age and socioeconomic groups, including school children, to rewrite in their own words to the president and encourage policies such as selling arms to Palestine's Jews.[98] The White House only realized the letters were orchestrated because many had neglected to change the wording adequately enough to avoid detection.[99] These polling statistics and Zionist campaigning made judging the Palestine issue in terms of public opinion confusing at best, and this environment must have weighed on Truman and congressional candidates' minds.

Sensing this atmosphere when in New York for the Council of Foreign Ministers in November 1946, Bevin began to consider any means that might make partition a workable solution, which would strengthen the vital US-UK relationship. Agreeing to consider partition, Bevin believed, was simply an invitation for greater Zionist demands that had the potential to provoke US support for allotting Palestine in its entirety to the Jews.[100] This meant that "before His Majesty's Government could move openly from their present position they would have to await an undertaking by the Jews and by the American government that partition would satisfy them and not be merely the first of a series of demands."[101]

Support from both Republican and Democratic Parties would be necessary to avoid Palestine becoming "a subject for bargaining and vote-catching in the Presidential election."[102] Then, finally, partition would require approval by the United Nations.[103] Secretary of State Byrnes advised Bevin that the president would approve of such a plan.[104] The foreign secretary even seems to have initiated the diplomatic foundations for such a scheme, attempting to scare his counterparts a little. "In all these talks," Bevin wrote back to the Foreign Office, "I have taken the line that there are three courses open to us; to settle the problem ourselves if we can, to offer the Mandate to the United States or to return it to the United Nations," adding gleefully, that "my frank statement of these alternatives has been received with a certain amount of consternation on all sides."[105] After he returned home from New York, however, these ideas seem to have been discarded, most likely due to fundamental Arab opposition.

In January 1947, Bevin told the cabinet that he was not fundamentally opposed to partition but that the difficulty was in imposing that solution against the will of either or both communities; instead, some middle ground should be sought through further negotiations.[106] At this meeting, the cabinet declined to specify a course of action in the event that negotiations broke down, but they acknowledged that referral to the UN "was bound to be embarrassing" because "[t]here would be much discussion of the various promises that had been made on behalf of His Majesty's Government, not all of which were easy to reconcile with one another, and critics would dwell on the long history of our failure to find a solution of the problem by ourselves."[107] When Bevin finally did ask the cabinet to approve referral to the United Nations, he "recalled the various stages of the negotiations over the past eighteen months, and explained how the problem had become progressively more intractable."[108] He blamed the influence of American Jewry both in Washington and within the Jewish Agency, and despite having "made every effort to secure the assistance of the United States government, [. . .] their interventions had only increased our difficulties."[109] The UN was not an avenue of investigation to be taken lightly, but it provided one potential way to secure, at last, a modicum of American acquiescence.

When talks did break down and the cabinet approved referral to the United Nations in February 1947, Bevin held informal talks in New York with the US ambassador to the UN and the secretary general before seeking approval also from Chinese, French, and Soviet delegates.[110] Between them they agreed that a special session of the General Assembly would be called to select the member states of a committee on Palestine, which would report back to the regular assembly.[111] British ambassador to the UN, Sir Alex Cadogan, issued a formal note to the secretary general on 2 April 1947, making it official.[112] In the end, even Truman admitted that "[w]e could have settled this Palestine thing if U.S. politics had been kept out of it."[113] During the process, however, the British government had been rendered incapable of following a course of policy that conflicted with Zionist interests due to the level of support offered to their cause in the United

States. This meant that both provincial autonomy and the option for a single independent Palestinian state, due to the American opposition detailed above, had to be eliminated from consideration.

Talking to the Zionists

As well as negotiations with the United States, diplomacy was also undertaken between Britain and representatives of the Jewish Agency. While this was not necessary on a purely strategic level, as the joint chiefs agreed Palestine's Jewish rebellion could be ended, like the Arab Revolt, with enough reinforcements, the political consequences of a war against "the Jews" following the Holocaust were too ludicrously damaging to consider.[114] As noted above, US opinion was firmly in support of Zionist goals, and it was American, rather than strictly Zionist, goodwill that was perceived as crucial to Britain's postwar recovery. Provincial autonomy was the plan Bevin advanced following the Anglo-American Committee, and securing Zionist agreement to it or any otherwise viable plan implied backing from the United States would be forthcoming as well. Crucially, Zionist acquiescence would have mended the diplomatic fissure that Palestine had opened between London and Washington.

It was not, however, forthcoming, and this failure meant the option to create a system of provincial autonomy disappeared from deliberations, placing Britain in an increasingly tightening diplomatic vice. Provincial autonomy received limited objections in Parliament, and Britain's politicians treated the issue surprisingly calmly considering Jewish paramilitary activities in Palestine. The plan for provinces was never in any way acceptable to the Jewish Agency, however, even as the basis for negotiations through 1946 and 1947.

It is important to understand that the provincial autonomy plan, which provided Bevin's basis for talks with Jews and Arabs, was presented to Parliament very soon after Zionist paramilitary groups bombed the King David Hotel on 22 July 1946. This building housed the British Palestine administration's headquarters. Perhaps counterintuitively, however, rather than driving policy, this attack seemed to create a certain amount of fatigue toward Palestine, so that its mention during parliamentary politics was not overly heated. Serving as chancellor of the exchequer at this time, Hugh Dalton was even flippant about the violence. "There must be a Jewish State" he said, "it is no good boggling at this—and, even if it is small, at least they will control their own immigration, so that they can let in lots of Jews, which is what they madly and murderously want."[115] When the House of Commons met to debate provincial autonomy on 31 July, the death toll was still unknown and a large number of people were still missing. Other than the expected condemnations of terrorist activities, combined with expressions of sympathy for Jews killed by the Nazis, mention of the event itself was surprisingly absent. (See fig. 5.3.)

Fig. 5.3. People run for cover as the King David Hotel in Jerusalem is bombed, 22 July 1946. © IWM.

An exception was Labour backbencher Mr. Wilkes, who declared that the "Irgun represents a right wing, Fascist, terrorist, brutal, murdering organisation controlled by a terrorist and Fascist Right Wing party."[116] After this a number of Conservatives questioned the exact denotation of the term *right wing* and Wilkes agreed to retract that particular phrase from his assessment, which he stated again for good measure. The only MP to note how the bombing might cause political ramifications at home was Mr. Evans. He expressed that it was "a most unpleasant business to be hunted, stalked and ambushed by evilly disposed persons armed with sticks of dynamite, tommy-guns and other lethal weapons, a very unpleasant business indeed. I have had some. And it does not console the victims of these attacks to know that their assailants are Zionist gentlemen with political ambitions. Neither does it console their bereaved mothers and wives, our constituents."[117]

Instead of focusing on the bombing itself, or even the merits of provincial autonomy, a great deal of this discussion surrounded the necessity of guarding against carelessly anti-Semitic language—as used by both the foreign secretary and Palestine's general Evelyn Barker—and mostly criticizing the government for delay but not actual policy. Barker's anti-Semitic indiscretions were somewhat more vehement than Bevin's, as the general had circulated a "restricted" letter to his officers following the King David Hotel bombing. This communiqué ordered them to "put out of bounds to all ranks all Jewish places of entertainment, cafes, restaurants, shops and private dwellings. No British soldier is to have any intercourse with any Jew [. . .]"; he concluded by calling on the army to begin "punishing the Jews in a way the race dislikes as much as any—by striking at their pockets."[118]

Although the government distanced itself from these comments, the accumulated damage was done. Additionally, it had been a year since Bevin had initiated the creation of the Anglo-American Committee, and the debate was soured because MPs had learned of the provincial autonomy plan through leaks to the press rather than an official press release. Lieutenant-Colonel Morris, for example, remarked how "the Lord President of the Council comes along like a conjuror producing a rabbit out of a hat—a rabbit which has, apparently, already escaped and created a certain amount of mischief."[119] The lack of attention Attlee's government paid to Parliament, however, reflects its low level of political importance regarding Palestine policy in the late 1940s. Even when presented with policy initiatives that would satisfy neither Zionists nor Arabs and, therefore, based on previous experience, should have provoked outrage among pro-Zionist or pro-Arab MPs, there was hardly a murmur. "It is remarkable," Colonial Secretary George Hall noted on 1 August, "that we should have a two days' Debate on the question of Palestine with so little political feeling displayed, so many constructive speeches made and so much agreement as to the policy before the House."[120] Equipped with parliamentary acquiescence, Attlee's government pressed ahead with persuading the Jewish Agency and the Arab states to accept provincial autonomy.

Negotiations with representatives of the Jewish Agency were informal, unofficial, and unfruitful, and Ernest Bevin publicly blamed President Truman for the deadlock. One of the key problems was that the Jewish Agency refused to participate in a conference in which the basis for discussion was not partition. As such, when talks began in Paris on 17 August 1946 they were, to a large degree, spontaneous.[121] Principally, Bevin wanted to get the Jewish Agency into official negotiations, but they continued to refuse any framework that did not center on partition proposals. Both the foreign and colonial secretaries "regarded the condition as an impossible one," and this deadlock continued through September 1946.[122] As late as 1 October, Bevin met with Agency representatives Weizmann, Fishman, Goldman, Locker, Brodetsky, Kaplan, and Linton, and they reiterated that attendance at the conference was only possible if its object was to establish a Jewish state in, or as part of, Palestine.[123] They also requested an act of good faith such as releasing Zionist detainees or stopping arms searches in Palestine.[124] Bevin refused, telling them that "British bayonets would not force partition on resisting Arabs."[125] Nevertheless, the foreign secretary did express the hope that provincial autonomy could be an agreed "*modus vivendi* that might lead to partition."[126] This idea of autonomy as merely a transition period before the creation of a Jewish state seemed more appealing to the Jewish Agency representatives.

To Bevin, the situation suddenly seemed promising.[127] Regarding detainees and searches, Bevin also scored a small victory by convincing the Jewish Agency representatives to enter separate talks on law and order, assuring them "there would be no difficulty in reaching some sort of an arrangement about detainees. The British government had not taken the initiative in blowing people up."[128] As Bevin found himself "groping towards a conclusion," he "felt that the best answer would be a trial transitory period on the basis of a unitary state ensuring proper rights for every citizen."[129] As had been the practice since August, the Agency representatives agreed to meet with Bevin again after considering the questions of law and order in Palestine separately.[130] Meanwhile, talks with the Arab states had been postponed until 16 December, after the UN General Assembly and Council of Foreign Ministers.[131] Far from approaching a settlement, Bevin's 1 October meeting with the Zionists was merely the first sign that the Jewish Agency might enter the official conference when it reopened.[132] It provided Bevin with a very small glimmer of hope that was dashed following the statement by President Truman on 4 October 1946.

On the eve of Yom Kippur, Truman publicly reiterated his earlier demand for the immediate immigration of one hundred thousand Jewish DPs to Palestine. Attlee had received only hours of notice before the announcement. Since Bevin was in Paris negotiating with the Jewish Agency, Attlee requested a delay in order to confer with his foreign secretary. This was denied, despite the fact that postponement was partly decided in hope that the Jewish Agency would agree to join, which might be prejudiced by Truman's statement.[133] This is precisely what Attlee wrote to the president, as well as trying to explain that modifying Britain's immigration policy during the adjournment would be tantamount to a breach of faith toward the Arabs.[134] Further complicating the relationship were Zionist interpretations of Truman's speech. He ended the statement with a call for compromise between British and Jewish negotiators, but this was widely viewed as an endorsement of partition.[135] For his part, Truman believed the statement contained nothing new.[136]

Fearing a resurgence of Zionist intransigence, Bevin seized the initiative and set in motion the good faith gesture they had requested. If an agreement regarding detainees could be found, Bevin advised the cabinet, "we shall be able to bring Jewish representatives into the Conference on future policy in Palestine, and there is no reason why this should be deferred until the Delegates of the Arab States return to London on the 16th December."[137] The result was a Colonial Office subcommittee formed to find means of cooperation between the Jewish Agency and the Palestine administration over issues such as detainees, arms searches, and emergency regulations with the aim of securing a truce.[138]

In October, Arthur Creech Jones replaced George Hall as colonial secretary. A known Zionist sympathizer, Creech Jones's appointment was also an act of good faith.[139] The next month, in line with Bevin's earlier discussions with Agency representatives, the new colonial secretary recommended the release of members of the Jewish Executive detained in Palestine since Operation Agatha in June 1946.[140] Agatha had been a forcible search and seizure maneuver ordered by General Barker. It involved more than one hundred thousand soldiers and police surrounding Jewish settlements, including Jerusalem and Tel Aviv, and imposing a curfew. Renamed locally as the "Black Sabbath," the operation resulted in more than three thousand arrests and considerably exacerbated the already tense situation between Jews and Britons in Palestine.[141] The King David Hotel was then bombed only a few weeks later, and this meant that negotiators on both Zionist and British sides spent the autumn and winter of 1946 engaging in tentative talks while being entirely unsure of who they could trust. (See figs. 5.4–5.6.)

Additionally, the conference scheduled for 16 December was postponed again until after Christmas. This was because an upcoming election at the Zionist Conference in Basel, which would not be complete by 16 December, would decide whether the Jewish Agency could enter official negotiations.[142] This meant that, in the meantime, the Jewish Agency pushed very strongly for Bevin to admit partition to the conference proceedings in order to sway the Basel vote.[143]

The problem was, however, that Bevin was attempting to secure an agreement based on provincial autonomy in the short term that may lead in the future to partition. This was because agreeing to consider partition in the first instance would only invite greater demands and place Britain in an intolerable position with the Arab states.[144] At the Twenty-Second Zionist Conference in Basel, Chaim Weizmann lost his presidency to Rabbi Silver, and attendance at the London conference in January was refused unless Britain made significant concessions in the direction of partition—an attitude that US secretary of state Byrnes told Silver was "frankly silly."[145] This marginalization of Weizmann had begun with the Peel Commission's proposals in 1937, when the Zionist Labour leader David Ben-Gurion had ascended to prominence. The power in international Zionism then continued to shift away from its British representatives and more toward

Fig. 5.4. Internees at the Rafa Camp in Palestine, 1947–1948. British counterinsurgency efforts in Palestine included imprisoning large numbers of Jews while the police and military screened for terrorists. © The National Archives.

American leaders, such as Rabbi Silver, when Weizmann's failure to secure the longevity of the Jewish national home became clear in 1939.[146] The postwar Zionist attitude in negotiations became less conciliatory and more militant. Informal talks, however, did continue, though Bevin noted that "[t]errorism is poisoning the relationship between Great Britain and the Zionist movement."[147]

Meeting several times in January and February 1947, representatives of the Jewish Agency, Foreign Secretary Bevin, Colonial Secretary Creech Jones (new), and additional secretary to the cabinet Norman Brook still could not reach any points of consensus.[148] The two secretaries agreed to one last effort, hoping to agree on provincial autonomy leading to independence after a transition period

Fig. 5.5. Press interview with a Jewish man formerly interned by British forces in Palestine, 1947–1948. This was following an exposé about torture practices at these camps. © The National Archives.

of five years.[149] If this failed, then they recommended referral to the United Nations—the statesmen had run out of ideas.[150]

Another problem, however, was that the Jewish Agency could not accept provincial autonomy (even as an interim measure before partition) because it was viewed as merely a small alteration to the 1939 white paper and deprived the Jewish people of their rights in their homeland as promised by the Balfour Declaration, the Mandate, and the prior policy of the Labour Party.[151] Considering the Zionists' Biltmore Declaration, which called for the remaking of Palestine into a Jewish commonwealth (rather than the traditional demand for a Jewish national home within Palestine), Agency representative Moshe Shertok told Creech Jones "he would like the British Delegation to understand the magnitude of the sacrifice

Fig. 5.6. A police station in Jaffa following a terrorist attack, 1945–1947. © IWM.

which the Jews were prepared to make in offering to accept a reasonable partition."[152] When shown British maps of the proposed Jewish province, for example, the Zionists rejected them "as a mockery of their just claims."[153] Instead, they insisted that a Jewish state "must include, over and above the area shown on the map, Galilee, the Gaza Sub-district, the Beersheba Sub-district and the eastern portions of the Hebron and Jerusalem Sub-districts, up to and including the Jerusalem-Jericho road."[154] The colonial secretary noted how "[i]n other words, they claimed the whole of Palestine except the central Judean hills."[155] After the Anglo-American Committee, Ernest Bevin had engaged in Anglo-Jewish negotiations for more than five months and achieved absolutely nothing. As provincial autonomy, even as an interim measure, required cooperation from both sides, the Jewish Agency's constant and unwavering rejection of this plan meant it was also eliminated from consideration.

Negotiations with Arab States

Precarious diplomacy on the Palestine problem also took place between representatives of the British government and leaders of the Arab states. This was, in a nutshell, because communications and oil supplies "depended on retaining the goodwill and co-operation of the Arab peoples."[156] Like the relationship with America, full consequences of any broken ties were difficult to predict, lending the subject an air of greater risk. Crucially, diplomacy with the wider Middle East seems to have been viewed on roughly equal terms as the US-UK relationship, and, by extension, as more important than British-Zionist relations. Bevin and Atlee agreed, for example, that "if the Jews refuse to participate in the Conference owing to their demands not being met, the Conference must go on without them."[157] Although representatives of the Arab states were, ostensibly, willing to negotiate, their basic requirements nullified the option to partition Palestine and made a system of provincial autonomy impracticable. A regional desire for independence was complicated by ongoing Anglo-Egyptian talks, and the Arab leaders' position remained just as immovable as that of their Jewish counterparts.

It is important to note that Arab leaders' opinions were highly important to British politicians. The years 1946–1947 were a time of British weakness and Middle East ascendancy, and the Arab leaders were aware of their value. This placed Britain in a similar situation to 1939, when the white paper was formulated to appeal to regional Arab statesmen who then negotiated in support of their own interests as well as those of Palestinian Arabs. The fate of Palestine, however, was an even trickier subject to discuss with Arab leaders after the war because it was tied to wider impatience for full independence in the Middle East. During the war, Churchill had called for Syria and Lebanon to have full independence. Once this was achieved in 1943, it was entirely unrealistic to expect other Arab states to forfeit the right.[158]

Complicating the situation were ongoing talks between Britain and individual Arab states on other issues. Negotiations over Palestine, for example, coincided with Anglo-Egyptian talks for revising the 1936 treaty of alliance.[159] British ambassador to Egypt, Sir Ronald Campbell, argued that the Anglo-American Committee proposals "will add another serious element of disturbance to the troubled situation in the Middle East at an inopportune moment when in view of the treaty revision problems in Egypt and Iraq, we need to secure as much goodwill as possible from Egyptian-Arab world."[160] Campbell suggested that accepting the committee's proposals should be deferred until after the treaty negotiations with Egypt were complete.[161] Likewise, the Joint Intelligence staff warned that the committee report would create unrest throughout the Arab and Muslim world, endangering a settlement of the India question.[162] This conflict of interests only worsened as negotiations dragged on. January 1947 witnessed Anglo-Egyptian negotiations stall, Britain withdrawing from responsibility in Greece and Turkey, and the beginning of a phased withdrawal from India.[163] This only heightened the strategic importance of the rest of the Middle East, and Arab states recognized their leverage.

When invited to begin talks on the Palestine issue by the British government, the foreign ministers of the Arab states met first in Alexandria to agree on the minimum requirements.[164] They would attend, but only if the subjects of partition, federalization, and Jewish immigration remained off the agenda.[165] Nothing was said about the participation of Palestine's Higher Arab Executive, but the Arab states were not willing to consider any proposals that endangered their counterpart's goal of independence.[166] The Arabs of Palestine did not engage in separate talks over their future because the former mufti of Jerusalem, Haj Amin al-Husseini, was specifically excluded. In addition, the Higher Arab Executive—formed during the Arab Revolt in the 1930s—refused to continue negotiating on a subject that was supposed to have been settled by the 1939 white paper.[167] This atmosphere of protonationalism was something that Attlee found difficult to understand, commenting in his memoirs that "you might think that an Arab struggling to keep alive on a bare strip of sand would jump at the chance of going to Iraq or somewhere else where there was more opportunity for a better life. But oh no. One patch of desert doesn't look very different from another patch of desert but that was the one they wanted—their own traditional piece."[168]

The London Conference opened on 9 September 1946 and, like private talks with the Jewish Agency, showed little ground for compromise on the subject of provincial autonomy. The additional secretary to the cabinet, Norman Brook, wrote to Attlee that the chiefs of staff believed "any solution of the Palestine problem must satisfy two conditions. First, it must give us the power to control and co-ordinate the defense of the country and to maintain forces and military facilities in it as, when and where we require; and secondly, it must not alienate the Arab States."[169] They doubted very much whether provincial autonomy satisfied the second of these conditions.[170] As the chiefs expected, all of the Arab states opposed provincial autonomy because they viewed it as a transition to partition and feared Jewish autonomy would lead to overall population majority and expansionist policies.[171]

In response to this plan, the Arab states proposed an independent unitary Palestine with safeguards for the Jewish minority but a prohibition on further Jewish immigration.[172] It was essentially a fulfillment of the MacDonald White Paper, an option that had already been rejected due to the need for good diplomatic relations with America. When the conference resumed in 1947, Bevin had to admit to the cabinet that negotiations with the Arab states "have confirmed our fear that there is no prospect of finding such a settlement."[173] This was because the absolute minimum requirements for both parties were incompatible—Arabs could not, under any circumstances, endorse the creation of a Jewish state in Palestine and the Zionists could not agree to anything less.[174] This meant Bevin could not secure either full American or Arab backing for any plan and instead searched for another potential source of ideas in the United Nations.[175]

When UNSCOP returned its verdict in August in favor of partition, Bevin immediately understood that Britain could in no way be associated with implementing this plan due to its fragile relationship with the Arab states. He informed the cabinet, contradicting an earlier opinion, that partition would have a destabilizing impact on the Middle East as a whole. "It would probably not be long," Bevin wrote, "before the Jewish government, faced as it would be in the course of time with a problem of over-population and driven by the ultra-nationalist political parties which will not accept partition as a final settlement, would try to expand its frontiers."[176] Partition created a Jewish state with a large Arab minority surrounded by Arab territory, and so Bevin supposed that "the Arab population of this State would play a part in history not unlike that of the Sudeten German minority in pre-war Czechoslovakia. Thus the existence of a Jewish State might prove to be a constant factor of unrest in the Middle East, and this could hardly fail to have a damaging effect on Anglo-Arab relations."[177] Fundamentally, Bevin asserted, partition was not possible. As well as producing an economically unviable Arab state, and in the process putting British soldiers in danger, it would severely sour relations with the Arab states.[178]

Redefining the Realms of Possibility

As diplomacy with the United States prevented fulfillment of the MacDonald White Paper, and since both Jews and Arabs rejected provincial autonomy while the Arab states refused to consider partition, the British government was left in a situation in which all available options were poisonous. This is when the potential to withdraw from Palestine completely entered the realm of possibility. After the UNSCOP proposals were returned in September 1947, but long before the General Assembly voted in favor of partition on 29 November, withdrawal became politically viable simply because all avenues of negotiation had failed and withdrawal threatened to damage neither US nor Arab state relations.[179] (See fig. 5.7.)

As early as January 1947, before the conference with Arab states resumed, Bevin was advising Attlee that success was unlikely and that they were running out of alternatives. Bevin wrote to Attlee, "I think this decision should be taken in full realisation that the Conference has very little chance of success, and before taking it we should look ahead and consider what we should have to do in the event of a breakdown."[180] They had two options: to impose a solution by force, which, as already noted was impossible on a diplomatic level alone before considering the cost, or to give up responsibility for Palestine.[181] Considering this dilemma, the referral to the United Nations should be viewed as a stalling tactic, a desperate search for more options. In February 1947, Bevin told Parliament that "[w]e have carefully studied this matter, and put forward proposal after proposal. They are there, and I personally do not think that we can offer to the United Nations

Fig. 5.7. "Who's Taking Who for a Ride?": a cartoon, published in the *Daily Mail* on 6 January 1947, depicting Prime Minister Attlee as the terrified nanny of militant Zionism. © Leslie Gilbert Illingworth / Solo Syndication.

any more proposals. We shall leave them on the table. They, in turn, may have better ones, but this is the best we can do."[182] Colonial Secretary Creech Jones, however, specifically told the House, "We are not going to the United Nations to surrender the Mandate. We are going to the United Nations setting out the problem and asking for their advice as to how the Mandate can be administered."[183] As well as buying time, the foreign secretary believed this action could bully Palestine's communities into accepting some compromise.

Bevin advised the cabinet that he "thought that both Jews and Arabs were anxious to avoid discussion of the problem" in the UN, and "our firm intention to take the matter to the United Nations Assembly [. . .] might bring them to a more reasonable frame of mind."[184] Bevin believed that "[e]ven though we gave notice of our intention to submit the matter to the United Nations, we could subsequently withdraw it from the agenda of the Assembly if between now and September a solution could be found which was acceptable to both parties."[185] Therefore, rather than "dumping" the issue on the UN in February 1947, Bevin intended to use the new circumstances as a negotiating ploy to Britain's advantage: "[e]ven after such an announcement had been made, he would certainly continue his efforts to find a solution."[186] The foreign secretary and the prime minister even extended this logic after the UNSCOP report was returned. Bevin advised the cabinet that "unless His Majesty's Government announced their intention of abandoning the Mandate and of withdrawing from Palestine, there was no prospect of an agreed settlement."[187] Attlee concurred, hoping that the threat posed to both Jews and Arabs by an unpredictable UN vote on partition might scare the two groups sufficiently to extract concessions.[188] Ultimately, however, no additional overtures from either Jews or Arabs were forthcoming.

As well as seeking more options or more fruitful negotiations, this tactic was intended to prevent Britain from taking on the responsibility for implementing whatever scheme the General Assembly approved. To avoid unwelcome obligations, Bevin inserted a key section in Creech Jones's statement to the UN saying Britain would not implement a solution that was not acceptable to both parties.[189] The additional proviso was intended to ensure that no other UN member put forward ludicrous counterproposals expecting Britain to implement them, but it also allowed Britain to cede responsibility for Palestine under a guise of moral abstention.[190] This stipulation was based on a valid fear. Rumors were spreading at the General Assembly before the vote on 29 November "that the strategic importance of Palestine to our oil interests in the Middle East and to defence of Suez Canal is so great that Great Britain is bound to implement whatever United Nations decides, regardless of consequences to ourselves."[191] In cabinet, however, this was far from the general consensus, and withdrawal had been considered a viable option since at least mid-September: "[O]ur withdrawal from Palestine," Bevin informed the cabinet, "even if it had to be effected at the cost of a period of bloodshed and chaos in the country, would have two major advantages. British lives would not be lost, nor British resources expended, in suppressing one Palestinian community for the advantage of the other. And (at least as compared with enforcing the majority plan or a variant of it) we should not be pursuing a policy destructive of our own interests, in the Middle East."[192] There was clearly only one course of action that satisfied the British government's political needs in 1947. In order to become a fully viable plan, withdrawal also had to satisfy the Treasury and the military.

Another Postwar Economy

In the postwar environment, it was inevitable that considerations of the economy would form some part of any policy decision-making. Discussed briefly here, the economic situation played an important role, but one that was somewhat intertwined with military/strategic needs discussed below. When, in 1947, the British government was presented with an option to withdraw from Palestine, it was facing a disastrous year for the economy, most notably in the form of a sterling crisis. In this context, withdrawing from Palestine was fine as long as it avoided incurring additional costs.

It is important to note that when 1947 began, and during ongoing negotiations with both Arabs and Jews over Palestine, Britain was trapped in a profound energy shortage. A terribly cold winter highlighted the already short supply of coal, and this vital resource slipped below the stock levels considered necessary for national survival.[193] As coal could not be transported to power stations, the lack of electricity throughout the country shut down industry and home consumption; livestock died and people froze in their homes.[194] This was the domestic economic setting in which Attlee, Bevin, and the cabinet agreed to refer the Palestine problem to the UN in February. To complicate their deliberations further, another—potentially devastating—financial crisis hit Westminster in August, just before the completion of the UNSCOP report, and was the direct result of Britain's loan conditions with the United States.

In December 1945, the Attlee government had secured a loan from the United States that began in July 1946. By 1947, however, the funds were diminishing far too quickly.[195] A global shortage of food and raw materials effectively made the United States a sole supplier, and a sharp rise in American prices in early 1947 decreased the original loan's value by approximately $1 billion.[196] As the dollar drain continued, the Treasury estimated the loan might last until 1948 rather than the original estimate of 1951; by July, the Treasury was losing $500 million every month and there were major depletions of gold and silver reserves.[197]

Additionally, part of the loan's terms had been a British commitment to the free convertibility of sterling into dollars, and this initiative was scheduled to commence on 15 July 1947.[198] The result was disastrous. Free convertibility and the global demand for dollars—as well as speculating in foreign markets—meant that Britain was suddenly hit by a massive outflow of capital.[199] In order to meet the demand for dollars, it was necessary to use funds from the American loan, which meant it was unlikely to last even throughout 1947. Britain was losing dollar reserves at a rate between $100 million and $200 million each week.[200]

On 17 August, the cabinet decided that, financially, the situation was too dire and agreed to halt convertibility. In response, the remaining US loan was frozen.[201] Only after tense but rapid negotiations did the US agree to a temporary emergency suspension on 20 August.[202] The situation was bleak, and Britons faced cuts in their food rationing by November 1947.[203] This provided the economic context of the cabinet's decision to withdraw.

Moreover, the military expenditure associated with rebellion in Palestine had exceeded £82 million (approximately £3 billion today) by May 1947, and although this was largely borne by the Palestinian rather than the British taxpayer, there was still a perception of Palestine incurring high costs in times of austerity.[204] Palestine's financial burden was mentioned rarely in cabinet discussions in comparison to the all-encompassing diplomatic problems associated with both American and Arab demands, but Ernest Bevin did specifically recommend withdrawal to avoid the further loss of British lives and waste of resources.[205] Britain's very limited financial reserves were a constant, well-known constraint. Withdrawal removed a costly responsibility following a year of economic uncertainty and privation, not least by removing the one hundred thousand troops needed to fight a Jewish insurgency. This meant that unnecessary additional economic hardship could be avoided.[206]

No Longer a Stronghold

A recurrent theme in Palestine policy discussions during the Mandate was the military or strategic national interest. This was also an important consideration in the postwar environment and was tied very closely to economic needs. Palestine was a strategic imperial outpost and at no point did the chiefs of staff ever explicitly renounce its geographic military importance. The undeclared state of war in Palestine, however, was financially draining and possessed the explosive potential to create equally expensive unrest elsewhere in the Middle East, especially if Britain attempted to enforce either of the UNSCOP proposals. Crucially, when Foreign Secretary Bevin recommended withdrawal to the cabinet on 18 September 1947, he did so with the specific understanding that Palestine lost its strategic value when constantly engaged in, or under the threat of, violent internal conflict and civil war.[207]

British strategic and military planning continued after 1945 as though Britain was still a great world power and a strong empire.[208] The option to withdraw had been mentioned in passing before the UNSCOP report, but it had always been the consensus that leaving Palestine "would have serious effects on our strategic position in the Middle East and on our prestige throughout the world"; the foreign secretary specifically asked the cabinet not to consider such alternatives in October 1946.[209] Throughout consideration of the Palestine problem, the chiefs of staff stressed that "strategic considerations should not be overlooked."[210] Palestine's location gave Britain its strategic hold in the Mediterranean close to the Suez Canal, both of which were made more important in 1947 by the plan to withdraw from Greece and remove troops from Egypt following Anglo-Egyptian talks.

As prospects for negotiations with the Jewish Agency and the Arab states seemed bleak in January 1947, the chiefs of staff outlined the three cardinal requirements of future defense of the British Commonwealth: "(i) the defence of the United Kingdom and its development as a base for an offensive; (ii) the maintenance of our sea communications; and (iii) the retention of our existing position and influence in the Middle East."[211] These "vital props" of Britain's defensive position were all interdependent, and "if any one were lost the whole structure would be imperilled."[212]

Specifically, with regard to Palestine, the territory was considered to hold "special importance in this general scheme of defence. In war, Egypt would be our key position in the Middle East; and it was necessary that we should hold Palestine as a screen for the defence of Egypt."[213] Following the stalled Anglo-Egyptian talks, however, and Britain's commitment to withdraw from Egypt unless it was threatened, the chiefs saw in Palestine the "base for the mobile reserve of troops which must be kept ready to meet any emergency throughout the Middle East."[214] This was because Transjordan was not a good enough outpost on its own, and the Jerusalem enclave would not suffice in the event of partition.[215] Even when the foreign and colonial secretaries suggested merely referring the Palestine problem to the UN, the joint chiefs reacted defensively against this proposal. They believed that "[t]he Preservation of our strategic position in the Middle East as a whole would be gravely prejudiced if our right to station British forces in Palestine were not retained."[216] It was strategically imperative to keep some form of base in the Mediterranean because if all bases there and in the Middle East were lost, the "defence of the United Kingdom and the Commonwealth would be undermined."[217]

However, this preoccupation with long-term strategic planning was combined with an awareness of Britain's very limited short-term resources. This reality meant that hostilities in Palestine, and their potential to create wider instability across the Middle East, were financially costly and strategically dangerous.[218] Colonial Secretary George Hall, for example, stressed that implementing the Anglo-American Committee's recommendations was likely "to involve us in military and financial commitments beyond our capacity to bear."[219] In a joint memorandum, the foreign and colonial secretaries emphasized that "[i]f we were to undertake it, or to be associated in any way with the enforcement of a settlement as unpopular with one of the parties as that now recommended by the United Nations, the whole responsibility would fall on us, as the only armed forces on the spot are ours."[220]

This potential commitment was more than a little daunting. In February 1947, Colonial Secretary Creech Jones, who had professed sympathy for Zionism and favored partition, admitted to the cabinet that it was an unworkable plan. The colonial secretary "confessed" that "the enforcement of Partition was, he was now convinced, bound to involve conditions of rebellion and disorder in Palestine which might last for a considerable time and would involve a substantial military commitment for us."[221] This recognition of limited resources combined with ongoing hostilities in Palestine then gradually altered opinions among Britain's military elites over the summer of 1947, causing them to question whether Palestine was really worth the expense and lives lost. These casualties amounted to 141 members of the Palestine police, 368 servicemen from the army, navy, and air force, and 21 British civilians—lost to both Arab and Jewish violence.[222] An important consideration of British well-being may have been the hanging of two sergeants in July 1947—kidnapped and murdered by the Irgun, their bodies were then booby trapped to injure others.[223] This was only the latest in a line of incidents involving kidnap or ambush, but it was considered particularly shocking.[224]

By 18 September, after the UNSCOP report was complete, a new attitude emerged. The same day Bevin dated his recommendation of withdrawal for the cabinet, the defense secretary outlined the impossibility of fulfilling almost any plan in Palestine. The UNSCOP Majority proposals for partition would involve "[t]he imposition by force of some Colonial type of government in the Arab State, the safeguarding of the Jewish State and the protection of British life," which entailed "appreciable reinforcement of the existing Middle East garrison with appropriate naval and air supports."[225] Long term, it would "render impossible of achievement the firm strategic hold in the Middle East which is an indispensable and vitally important part of Imperial defence policy."[226] Similarly, the Minority Plan for a single binational state "would be impossible to implement [...] against greatly increased opposition from the Jews and it would be necessary to impose by force a Colonial type of government."[227] Agreeing to implement either one of these plans, on a purely military level, would "entail a drastic revision of our Defence Policy."[228] Critically, although the defense secretary advised against any "demonstration of weakness in withdrawing in the face of difficulty" and also added that withdrawal "might be impossible to implement," he did not at any point object to withdrawal from Palestine on the basis of its military importance.[229] The strategic value perceived only months earlier had simply dissipated. Exemplifying this new consensus were opinions expressed by the chancellor of the exchequer, Sir Hugh Dalton.

Dalton, another professed Zionist sympathizer within the cabinet, wrote to Attlee in August 1947:

> I am quite sure [...] that the time has almost come when we must bring our troops out of Palestine altogether. The present state of affairs is not only costly

to us in man-power and money, but is, as you and I agree, of no real value from the strategic point of view—you cannot in any case have a secure base on top of a wasps' nest—and riot is exposing our young men, for no good purpose, to most abominable experiences, and is breeding anti-Semites at an alarming speed. [. . .] It is high time that either we left the Arabs and Jews to have it out in Palestine, or that some other Power or Powers took over the responsibility and the cost.[230]

Dalton also raised the issue in the cabinet on 20 September: "If an agreed settlement could not be reached in Palestine," he said, "that country was of no strategic value to His Majesty's Government and the maintenance of British forces in it merely led to a heavy drain on our financial resources and to the creation of a dangerous spirit of anti-Semitism."[231] The decision to withdraw was approved that day, more than two months before the UN officially adopted partition.

A Rock and a Hard Place

After completion on 31 August and then months in committee and plenary meetings, the partition resolution was finally ready for a vote in the General Assembly. It achieved the necessary two-thirds majority on 29 November 1947, inaugurating the famous Resolution 181.[232] Five days later, on 4 December, the cabinet approved a withdrawal plan drafted jointly by the foreign and colonial secretaries and approved by the Defence Committee.[233] It was presented to Parliament on 11 December and received barely a hint of criticism except on the most minute of procedural details.[234] Although in Parliament, the arrival of this policy seems to have been entirely expected, neither the Jews nor the Arabs nor even the Americans believed it was real, and their UN representatives had to be informed privately in order to be convinced.[235] British forces and administrative staff would only stay in Palestine long enough to aid Jews and Arabs through a limited transition period and planned to withdraw fully by 1 August 1948.[236] This was revised later, and the last member of the British administration left Palestine on 15 May 1948.[237]

Ultimately, the need to protect diplomatic relationships with both the United States and the Arab states left the Attlee government between two policies—partition and independence—that were bitterly opposed on each side. When first assuming office in 1945, Bevin even highlighted Britain's new dual obligation with regard to Palestine: "I consider the Palestine question urgent," he wrote, "and when I return to London I propose to examine the whole question, bearing in mind the repercussions on the whole Middle East and U.S.A."[238] The American relationship with Zionism and President Truman's desire to intervene on behalf of DPs suffering a humanitarian crisis, as well as the need to consider his own domestic political situation, meant there could be no repeat of 1939.

Attlee and Bevin's problem in dealing with Truman, as well as American public opinion molded by Holocaust newspaper headlines, was that British politicians attempted to deal with the tragedy of DPs as entirely separate from the fate of Palestine. The tide of global opinion viewed them as one and the same—not least due to very effective Zionist campaigning. Attlee expressed this to Truman, explaining, "We are giving deep thought to means of helping the Jews in Europe and to the question of Palestine. The two problems are not necessarily the same [. . .]."[239] Bevin then attempted to "sell" the plan of provincial autonomy to both Zionists and Arabs on the basis that it would be an interim solution, though this was a scheme with two diametrically opposed outcomes depending on who constituted the foreign secretary's audience. Bevin's initial search for a long-term settlement became a desperate attempt to create almost any short-term agreement, enough to see the British government through the whirlwind of postwar crises elsewhere.

Attlee later wrote in his memoirs that "[i]t was one of those impossible situations for which there is no really good solution. One just had to cut the knot."[240] Hector McNeil, Foreign Office minister and subsequently vice president of the UN General Assembly, in 1947 summed up the legacy such knot cutting was going to leave for two peoples locked in conflict: "We have failed," he said, "and we must confess our failure. Beyond doubt when the historians come to look at our record of administration in Palestine, they will find many errors, and I hope that they will learn from those errors."[241]

Notes

1. Pappe, *History of Modern Palestine*; Shlaim, *Iron Wall*.
2. Mintz and Geva, "Poliheuristic Theory of Foreign Policy Decision Making."
3. Hugh Dalton, *High Tide and After: Memoirs 1945–1960* (London: Frederick Muller, 1962), 145.
4. Ibid.
5. Ibid., 146.
6. Ibid., 147.
7. Department of State Bulletin, vol. XIII, no. 327, 30 September 1945, *Report of Earl G. Harrison on Conditions and Needs of Displaced Persons*, 456.
8. Dalton, *High Tide and After*, 148.
9. Michael J. Cohen, "The Genesis of the Anglo-American Committee on Palestine, November 1945: A Case Study in the Assertion of American Hegemony," *Historical Journal* 22, no. 1 (1979): 185–207, 185.
10. Cmd. 6806, 1946, *Report of the Anglo-American Committee of Enquiry regarding the Problems of European Jewry and Palestine*, 2–10.
11. Cmd. 6806, *Report of the Anglo-American Committee of Enquiry*, 2–10.
12. Ibid., 39, 42.

13. Ibid.
14. Ibid.
15. Cmd. 7044, 1947, *Palestine No. 1 (1947). Proposals for the Future of Palestine*, 4.
16. Ibid., 5.
17. House of Commons Debates, 31 July 1946, series 5, vol. 426, cols. 965–966.
18. House of Commons Debates, 31 July 1946, cols. 978–979.
19. Ibid., cols. 978–980.
20. CAB 66/64/14, 4 April 1945, "The Future of the British Mandate for Palestine," TNA; CAB 66/65/56, 16 May 1945, "Palestine. Memorandum by the Secretary of State for the Colonies," TNA.
21. CAB 66/64/14, 4 April 1945, "Future of the British Mandate for Palestine."
22. Ritchie Ovendale, "The Palestine Policy of the British Labour Government 1947: The Decision to Withdraw," *International Affairs* 56, no. 1 (1980): 73–93, 88.
23. Tessler, *A History of the Israeli-Palestinian Conflict*, 258.
24. S-0611, S-0611-0001, S-0611-0001-02, June 13 1947, J. Husseini to Chairman, United Nations Special Committee on Palestine, UN Archives; Ibid., July 10 1947; S-0611, S-0611-0001, S-0611-0001-04, 17 July 1947, Abdul Aziz Kuheimi to Mr. Victor Ho, UN archives; S-0611, S-0611-0001, S-0611-0001-04, 14 July 1947, Consul General of Transjordan to Dr. Victor Hoo, UN archives; S-0611, S-0611-0001, S-0611-0001-04, 9 July 1947, "Special Committee on Palestine. Communication Addressed by the Personal Representative of the Secretary-General to the Arab League States," UN Archives.
25. S-0611, S-0611-0001, S-0611-0001-06, 11 August 1947, D. C. MacGillivray to the Principal Secretary, United Nations Special Committee on Palestine, UN Archives.
26. S-0611, S-0611-0002, S-0611, S-0611-0002-06, 16 June 1947, "Special Committee on Palestine. Verbatim Record of the Sixth Meeting," UN Archives.
27. "United Nations Special Committee on Palestine Report to the General Assembly, Volume 1," Lake Success, New York, 1947, chap. 6, 3.
28. "United Nations Special Committee on Palestine Report to the General Assembly, Volume 1," chap. 6, 3.
29. Ibid., chap. 6, 2(B) (c), 1.
30. Ibid., chap. 6, pt. I, 1.
31. Ibid., chap. 6, p. II.
32. Ovendale, "Palestine Policy of the British Labour Government 1947," 89.
33. "United Nations Special Committee on Palestine Report to the General Assembly, Volume 1," Lake Success, New York, 1947, chap. 5, 6.
34. House of Commons Debates, 1 August 1946, series 5, vol. 426, cols. 1237–1238.
35. House of Commons Debates, 1 August 1946, cols. 1237–1238.
36. Department of State Bulletin, vol. XIII, no. 327, 30 September 1945, *Report of Earl G. Harrison on Conditions and Needs of Displaced Persons*, 456.
37. PREM 8/89, 31 August 1945, Truman to Attlee, TNA.
38. PREM 8/89, 14 September 1945, Attlee to Truman, TNA.
39. President's Secretary's Files 1945–1953, Subject File—Foreign Affairs, Box 149, Folder—Clement R. Attlee, Miscellaneous, 28 October 1945, Byrnes to Bevin, Truman Presidential Library.
40. PREM 8/627, 7 November 1945, Halifax to Bevin, TNA.
41. Cohen, "Genesis of the Anglo-American Committee," 199–203.

42. Papers of David K. Niles, Box 29, Folder—Israel File 1940–1945, 4 April 1945, Memo from Hadley Cantril to David Niles, Truman Presidential Library.

43. PREM 8/627, 7 November 1945, Halifax to Bevin.

44. Ibid.

45. FO 371/52517/E3842, 26 April 1946, "Palestine. Appointment, Terms of Reference and Constitution of the Committee. Draft report of the Ad Hoc Official Committee," TNA.

46. FO 371/52517/E3842, 26 April 1946, "Palestine. Appointment, Terms of Reference and Constitution of the Committee."

47. Ibid.

48. CAB 195/4, 29 April 1946, Cabinet Minutes, TNA; CAB 128/5, 29 April 1946, Cabinet Minutes, TNA.

49. CAB 195/4, 29 April 1946, Cabinet Minutes.

50. Ibid.

51. CAB 128/5, 29 April 1946, Cabinet Minutes.

52. FO 371/52517/E3815G, 28 April 1946, Bevin to Byrnes, TNA.

53. Papers of David K. Niles, Box 29, Folder—Israel File 1946, January–June, 30 April 1946, "Statement by the President," Truman Presidential Library.

54. FO 371/52525/E4623G, 4 May 1946, Chief of Staff in Middle East to War Office, TNA.

55. FO 371/52525/E4623G, 8 May 1946, Ismay to Attlee, TNA.

56. FO 371/52525/E4775G, 20 May 1946, Cabinet Minutes, TNA.

57. President's Secretary's Files 1945–1953, Subject File—Foreign Affairs, Box 149, Folder—Clement R. Attlee, Miscellaneous, 10 June 1946, Attlee to Truman, Truman Presidential Library.

58. PREM 8/627, 10 June 1946, Inverchapel to Bevin, TNA.

59. PREM 8/627, 10 June 1946, Inverchapel to Bevin.

60. Louis, *British Empire in the Middle East*, 428.

61. Ibid., 389.

62. House of Commons Debates, 21 February 1946, series 5, vol. 419, cols. 1373–1374.

63. FO 371/52529, 13 June 1946, Inverchapel to FO, TNA.

64. Louis, *British Empire in the Middle East*, 428.

65. PREM 8/627, 25 June 1946, Attlee to Truman, TNA.

66. CAB 128/6, 8 July 1946, Cabinet Minutes, TNA.

67. CAB 128/6, 8 July 1946, Cabinet Minutes.

68. Ibid.

69. CAB 128/6, 11 July 1946, Cabinet Minutes, TNA, 189–191.

70. CAB 128/6, 11 July 1946, Cabinet Minutes, 189–191.

71. Ibid.

72. CAB 128/6, 30 July 1946, Cabinet Minutes, TNA.

73. CAB 128/6, 30 July 1946, Cabinet Minutes.

74. Papers of David K. Niles, Box 29, Folder—Israel File 1946, July–December, 24 July 1946, "Memorandum. Commentary on Some Aspects of the Proposals with Respect to Palestine and the Jewish Problem Submitted to the U.K. and U.S. Governments by the London Conference," Truman Presidential Library.

75. Papers of David K. Niles, Box 29, Folder—Israel File 1946, July–December, 24 July 1946.

76. PREM 8/627, 31 July 1946, Washington (British Embassy) to United Kingdom Delegation, TNA.

77. PREM 8/627, 31 July 1946, Washington (British Embassy).
78. Ibid.
79. Ibid.
80. House of Commons Debates, 31 July 1946, cols. 969–970.
81. PREM 8/627, 31 July 1946, Washington (British Embassy) to United Kingdom Delegation, TNA.
82. President's Secretary's Files 1945–1953, Subject File—Foreign Affairs, Box 149, Folder—Clement R. Attlee, Miscellaneous, 9 August 1946, Attlee to Truman, Truman Presidential Library.
83. President's Secretary's Files 1945–1953, Subject File—Foreign Affairs, Box 149, Folder—Clement R. Attlee, Miscellaneous, 18 August 1946, Attlee to Truman, Truman Presidential Library.
84. President's Secretary's Files 1945–1953, Subject File—Foreign Affairs, Box 149, Folder—Clement R. Attlee; PREM 8/627, 29 November 1946, Creech Jones to Attlee, TNA.
85. President's Secretary's Files 1945–1953, Subject File—Foreign Affairs, Box 149, Folder—Clement R. Attlee, Miscellaneous, n.d., Truman to Attlee, Truman Presidential Library.
86. President's Secretary's Files 1945–1953, Subject File—Foreign Affairs, Box 149, Folder—Clement R. Attlee, Miscellaneous, 4 October 1946, Attlee to Truman, Truman Presidential Library.
87. PREM 8/627, 3 October 1946, Inverchapel to Foreign Office, TNA.
88. PREM 8/627, 3 October 1946, Inverchapel to Foreign Office.
89. President's Secretary's Files 1945–1953, Subject File—Foreign Affairs, Box 162, Folder—Palestine Jewish Immigration, 15 July 1946, Niles to Connelly, Truman Presidential Library.
90. Papers of David K. Niles, Box 28, Displaced Persons and Immigration File 1945–June 1947, 21 October 1946, "Opinions about Immigration: Preliminary Report," Truman Presidential Library.
91. Papers of David K. Niles, Box 28, Displaced Persons and Immigration File 1945–June 1947.
92. Ibid.
93. Ibid.
94. Ibid.
95. Papers of George M. Elsey, Box 115, Folder—Palestine, 26 June 1951, "Philleo Nash to Andie Knutson, Report on Unsolicited Cards on Palestine Situation Stored in Room 65," Truman Presidential Library.
96. Papers of George M. Elsey, Box 115, Folder—Palestine, 26 June 1951, "Philleo Nash to Andie Knutson."
97. Ibid.
98. Ibid.
99. Ibid.
100. PREM 8/627, 26 November 1946, United Kingdom Delegation to Council of Foreign Ministers to Foreign Office, TNA.
101. PREM 8/627, 26 November 1946, United Kingdom Delegation to Council.
102. Ibid.
103. Ibid.
104. PREM 8/627, 26 November 1946, Inverchapel to Foreign Office, TNA.

105. PREM 8/627, 26 November 1946, United Kingdom Delegation to Council.
106. CAB 128/11, 22 January 1947, "Confidential Annex," TNA.
107. CAB 128/11, 22 January 1947, "Confidential Annex."
108. CAB 128/9, 14 February 1947, Cabinet Minutes, TNA.
109. CAB 128/9, 14 February 1947, Cabinet Minutes.
110. PREM 6/626, 1 April 1947, Christopher McAlpine to Addis, TNA.
111. PREM 6/626, 1 April 1947, Christopher McAlpine to Addis.
112. PREM 8/626, 5 April 1947, J. M. Addis to Miss E. A. Gilliatt, TNA.
113. Confidential File 1938 (1945)-1953, Box 43, Folder—State Department, Palestine 2 of 2, 13 May 1947, Truman to Niles, Truman Presidential Library.
114. CAB 128/11, 15 January 1947, "Confidential Annex," TNA.
115. Dalton, *High Tide and After*, 189.
116. House of Commons Debates, 1 August 1946, cols. 1280–1282.
117. House of Commons Debates, 31 July 1946, cols. 1056–1057.
118. Anthony Julius, *Trials of the Diaspora: A History of Anti-Semitism in England* (Oxford: Oxford University Press, 2010), 334.
119. House of Commons Debates, 31 July 1946, cols. 1032–1033.
120. House of Commons Debates, 1 August 1946, cols. 1308–1309.
121. PREM 8/627, 19 August 1946, Foreign Office to Cairo, Beirut, Jedda, Baghdad, Jerusalem, TNA.
122. PREM 8/627, 19 August 1946, Foreign Office; PREM 8/627, 25 September 1946, Goldman to Hall, TNA.
123. FO 371/52560, 1 October 1946, Cunningham to Secretary of State for the Colonies, TNA.
124. FO 371/52560, 1 October 1946, Cunningham to Secretary of State for the Colonies.
125. Ibid.
126. Ibid.
127. FO 371/52560, 1 October 1946, "Note of a Meeting Held in the Foreign Office at 12 O'Clock on Tuesday 1 October 1946," TNA.
128. FO 371/52560, 1 October 1946, "Note of a Meeting Held in the Foreign Office."
129. Ibid.
130. Ibid.
131. PREM 8/627, 4 October 1946, Attlee to Truman, TNA.
132. CAB 129/13, 5 October 1946, "Palestine Conference, Memorandum by the Secretary of State for Foreign Affairs and the Secretary of State for the Colonies," TNA.
133. PREM 8/627, 4 October 1946, Attlee to Truman.
134. Ibid.
135. Cohen, *Palestine to Israel*, 223.
136. White House Central Files 1945–1953, Official File 1945–1953, OF 204, Box 913, Folder—OF 204 (May 1946–53), n.d., Note by Byrnes, Truman Presidential Library.
137. CAB 129/13, 5 October 1946, "Palestine Conference, Memorandum by the Secretary of State."
138. FO 371/52560, 5 October 1946, Colonial Secretary to Cunningham, TNA.
139. Youssef Chaitani, *Dissension among Allies: Ernest Bevin's Palestine Policy between Whitehall and the White House, 1945–47* (London: Saqi, 2002), 84.
140. CAB 129/14, 1 November 1946, Cabinet Minutes, TNA.
141. Segev, *One Palestine, Complete*, 476.

142. CAB 128/6, 21 November 1946, Cabinet Minutes, TNA.
143. PREM 8/627, 26 November 1946, United Kingdom Delegation to Council.
144. Ibid.
145. FO 371/61762, 9 January 1947, Inverchapel to Foreign Office, TNA.
146. Fraser, "Crisis of Leadership," 657–680.
147. FO 371/61762, 4 January 1947, Draft telegram, Bevin to Inverchapel, TNA.
148. FO 371/61873, 29 January 1947, "Note of Meeting between United Kingdom Representatives and a Delegation Representing the Jewish Agency for Palestine Held at the Colonial Office," TNA; FO 371/61873, 3 February 1947, "Note of the Second Meeting between United Kingdom Representatives and a Delegation Representing the Jewish Agency for Palestine Held at the Colonial Office," TNA; FO 371/61873, 10 February 1947, "Note of Fourth Meeting between United Kingdom Representatives and a Delegation Representing the Jewish Agency for Palestine Held at the Colonial Office," TNA; FO 371/61873, 13 February 1947, "Note of Fifth Meeting between United Kingdom Representatives and a Delegation Representing the Jewish Agency for Palestine Held at the Colonial Office," TNA.
149. CAB 129/16, 6 February 1947, "Palestine. Joint Memorandum by the Secretary of State for Foreign Affairs and the Secretary of State for the Colonies," TNA.
150. CAB 129/16, 6 February 1947, "Palestine. Joint Memorandum by the Secretary of State.
151. FO 371/61873, 5 February 1947, "Memorandum by the Jewish Agency," TNA.
152. FO 371/61873, 6 February 1947, "Note of the Third Meeting between United Kingdom Representatives and a Delegation representing the Jewish Agency for Palestine held at the Colonial Office," TNA.
153. FO 371/61873, 13 February 1947, Creech Jones to General Cunningham, TNA.
154. FO 371/61873, 13 February 1947, Creech Jones to General Cunningham.
155. Ibid.
156. CAB 128/6, 11 July 1946, Cabinet Minutes, 189–191.
157. PREM 8/627, 18 August 1946, Foreign Office to United Kingdom Delegation to Peace Conference, TNA.
158. Louis, *British Empire and the Middle East*, 124.
159. F. S. Northedge, "Britain and the Middle East," in *The Foreign Policy of British Labour Governments 1945–1951*, ed. Ritchie Ovendale (Leicester, UK: Leicester University Press, 1984), 167.
160. FO 371/52517/E3757G, 25 April 1946, Campbell (Cairo) to Foreign Office, TNA.
161. FO 371/52517/E3757G, 25 April 1946, Campbell (Cairo) to Foreign Office.
162. FO 371/52517//E3941G, 25 April 1946, "Recommendations of the Anglo-American Committee of Enquiry into Palestine and the Condition of Jews in Europe. Preliminary Report by the Joint Intelligence Staff," TNA.
163. Ovendale, "Palestine Policy of the British Labour Government 1947," 87.
164. Haim Levenberg, "Bevin's Disillusionment: The London Conference, Autumn 1946," *Middle Eastern Studies* 27, no. 4 (1991): 615–630, 620.
165. CAB 128/6, 22 July 1946, Cabinet Minutes, TNA; Levenberg, "Bevin's Disillusionment," 620.
166. Levenberg, "Bevin's Disillusionment," 620.
167. CAB 129/12, 27 July 1946, "Cabinet Conference on Palestine. Invitations to Jews and Palestine Arabs. Memorandum by the Secretary of State for the Colonies," TNA; CAB 129/13, 5 October 1946, "Palestine Conference, Memorandum by the Secretary of State."

168. Clement Attlee and Francis Williams, *Twilight of Empire: Memoirs of Clement Attlee* (London: Barnes, 1962), 183.
169. CAB 129/11, 20 July 1946, "Palestine. Note by the Additional Secretary," TNA.
170. CAB 129/11, 20 July 1946, "Palestine. Note by the Additional Secretary.
171. CAB 129/13, 5 October 1946, "Palestine Conference, Memorandum by the Secretary of State."
172. Ibid.
173. CAB 129/16, 6 February 1947, "Palestine. Joint Memorandum by the Secretary of State.
174. Ibid.
175. CAB 129/17, 13 February 1947, "Palestine. Memorandum by the Secretary of State for Foreign Affairs and the Secretary of State for the Colonies," TNA.
176. CAB 129/21, 18 September 1947, "Palestine. Memorandum by the Secretary of State for Foreign Affairs," TNA.
177. CAB 129/21, 18 September 1947, "Palestine. Memorandum by the Secretary of State for Foreign Affairs.
178. CAB 129/16, 6 February 1947, "Palestine. Joint Memorandum by the Secretary of State.
179. CAB 129/21, 18 September 1947, "Palestine. Memorandum by the Secretary of State for Foreign Affairs."
180. FO 371/61761, 1 January 1947, Bevin to Attlee, TNA.
181. FO 371/61761, 1 January 1947, Bevin to Attlee.
182. House of Commons Debates, 18 February 1947, series 5, vol. 433, cols. 994–995.
183. House of Commons Debates, 25 February 1947, series 5, vol. 433, cols. 2007–2008.
184. CAB 128/9, 14 February 1947, Cabinet Minutes.
185. Ibid.
186. Ibid.
187. CAB 128/10, 20 September 1947, Cabinet Minutes, TNA.
188. PREM 8/859/1, 20 October 1947, Attlee and Bevin to Colonial Secretary, TNA.
189. PREM 8/859/1, 21 September 1947, Henniker to Colonial Office, TNA.
190. PREM 8/859/1, 20 September 1947, "CM (47) 76th Conclusions, Minute 6 Confidential Annex," TNA.
191. FO 371/61878, 17 September 1947, Permanent United Kingdom Representative to United Nations to Foreign Office, TNA.
192. CAB 129/21, 18 September 1947, "Palestine. Memorandum by the Secretary of State for Foreign Affairs."
193. Kenneth O'Morgan, *Labour in Power 1945–1951* (Oxford: Oxford University Press, 1984), 331–332.
194. Ravndal, "Exit Britain," 424; O'Morgan, *Labour in Power*, 332–333.
195. O'Morgan, *Labour in Power*, 339.
196. Ibid.
197. Ibid., 213, 340.
198. Ibid., 342.
199. C. S. S. Newton, "The Sterling Crisis of 1947 and the British Response to the Marshall Plan," *Economic History Review* 37, no. 3 (1984): 391–408, 401.
200. O'Morgan, *Labour in Power*, 344.
201. Ibid., 346.
202. Ibid.

203. Ibid., 348.
204. CAB 129/19, 18 May 1947, "Financial Situation. Cost of Terrorist Damage and Other Illegal Activities, Memorandum by the Secretary of State for the Colonies," TNA; CAB 128/9, 20 May 1947, Cabinet Minutes, TNA.
205. CAB 129/21, 18 September 1947, "Palestine. Memorandum by the Secretary of State for Foreign Affairs."
206. Ravndal, "Exit Britain," 424.
207. CAB 129/21, 18 September 1947, "Palestine. Memorandum by the Secretary of State for Foreign Affairs."
208. Raymond Smith and John Zametica, "The Cold Warrior: Clement Attlee Reconsidered, 1945-7," *International Affairs* 61, no. 2 (1985): 237–252, 246.
209. CAB 128/6, 25 October 1946, Cabinet Minutes, TNA.
210. CAB 128/6, 11 July 1946, Cabinet Minutes, 189–191.
211. CAB 128/11, 15 January 1947, "Confidential Annex."
212. Ibid.
213. Ibid.
214. Ibid.
215. Ibid.
216. PREM 8/627, 6 February 1947, "Note by LC Hollis. Top Secret," TNA.
217. CAB 128/9, 11 February 1947, Cabinet Minutes, TNA.
218. CAB 129/21, 18 September 1947, "Palestine. Memorandum by the Secretary of State for Foreign Affairs."
219. CAB 129/11, 8 July 1946, "Report of the Anglo-American Committee of Enquiry Regarding the Problems of European Jewry and Palestine. Memorandum by the Secretary of State for the Colonies," TNA.
220. CAB 129/22, 3 December 1947, "Palestine. Memorandum by the Secretary of State for Foreign Affairs and the Secretary of State for the Colonies," TNA.
221. CAB 128/9, 7 February 1947, Cabinet Minutes, TNA.
222. House of Lords Debates, 9 June 1948, series 5, vol. 156, cols. 528–529.
223. Ravndal, "Exit Britain," 424.
224. Ibid.
225. CAB 129/21, 18 September 1947, "Palestine: Report of United Nations Special Committee. Military and Strategic Implications. Memorandum by the Secretary of State for Defence," TNA.
226. CAB 129/21, 18 September 1947, "Palestine: Report of United Nations Special Committee. Military and Strategic Implications."
227. Ibid.
228. Ibid.
229. Ibid.
230. PREM 8/623, 11 August 1947, Dalton to Attlee, TNA.
231. CAB 128/10, 20 September 1947, Cabinet Minutes.
232. Pappe, *Making of the Arab-Israeli Conflict*, 41; Caplan, *Contested Histories*, 108.
233. CAB 129/10, 4 December 1947, Cabinet Minutes, TNA; PREM 8/859/1, 27 November 1947, "CAB DO (47) 25th Meeting," TNA; CAB 129/22, 3 December 1947, "Palestine. Memorandum by the Secretary of State for Foreign Affairs and the Secretary of State for the Colonies."

234. House of Commons Debates, 11 December 1947, series 5, vol. 445, cols. 1223–1224.
235. PREM 8/859/1, 4 October 1947, Foreign Office to Cadogan, TNA.
236. PREM 8/859/1, 14 October 1947, Foreign Office to Colonial Secretary, TNA; PREM 8/859/1, 27 November 1947, "CAB DO (47) 25th Meeting."
237. Tessler, *History of the Israeli-Palestinian Conflict*, 261.
238. FO 800/484, 30 July 1945, Bevin to Attlee, TNA.
239. FO 800/484, 6 October 1945, Attlee to Truman, TNA.
240. Attlee and Francis, *Twilight of Empire*, 182.
241. House of Commons Debates, 10 March 1948, series 5, vol. 448, cols. 1364–1365.

The Last Word

More than thirty years of British rule in Palestine witnessed a seemingly unshakable commitment to Zionism crumble under the weight of varying pressures that threatened the political survival of successive prime ministers and cabinets. The events covered in this book represent four distinct periods of policy making, which reflect the only instances when the central government for the British Empire became embroiled in a small nationalist conflict in Palestine. Charting these British attempts, ostensibly at reconciliation between Jews and Arabs, reveals how the distinct leaders' feelings, biases, and passions about Zionism or Arab nationalism, as well as their intents and goals for the tiny territory, were continually shaped and undermined by the necessity of maintaining their own political positions. In every case, the politicians in power were confronted with only a single viable option or an extremely narrow selection of alternatives. Rather than "choosing" which policy to pursue in Palestine, they consistently found themselves cornered into a suboptimal decision. This realization has changed the focus of study entirely, away from questioning what the British government hoped to achieve in Palestine and toward asking, first and foremost, what ramifications it was trying to avoid.

As the incidents featured in this book are organized chronologically and reflect distinct episodes, they constitute the individual puzzle pieces that fit together to form a more complete image of British policy making. During the Balfour Zeitgeist, when Britain committed itself to supporting the creation of a Jewish national home in Palestine—following the Balfour Declaration, the draft Mandate, and, finally, the Churchill White Paper—ample evidence showed that this policy was fomenting violent unrest. Such disturbances had the potential to undermine the strategic value of Palestine and were draining financially. Under these circumstances, ending the British involvement with the Jewish national home would have been an understandable decision, as demonstrated by both the Palin Commission and the Haycraft Commission. Instead, the British government found itself in a position where either renouncing or wholeheartedly supporting the policy of the Balfour Declaration was politically untenable. The calm in Palestine that followed the Churchill White Paper in 1922 seemed to vindicate Britain's middle course, but the riots of 1929 threw it into question yet again.

Circumstances that led to a reversal of the Passfield White Paper in 1931 are possibly the most misunderstood elements of the Palestine Mandate. Rather than a simple equation of Zionist pressure achieving a change in policy, an alignment of political interests among Zionists, Liberals, and the Conservative Party threatened the unity and survival of the Labour government. This episode has received startlingly little scholarly attention, perhaps because the myth of an all-powerful Jewish lobby in interwar Westminster has suited both Israeli and Palestinian historical narratives. However, such simplification is not useful for understanding policy making in Britain, making a more complete analysis of the Passfield White Paper a crucial component of this research.

When Palestine's tensions remained unsolved in the early 1930s and erupted into the Arab Revolt of 1936–1939, the preferences voiced by politicians became simpler to identify. Pending war presented such an obvious risk to the government's political survival that the strategic importance of Arab leaders outside of Palestine's diminutive boundaries was, in 1939, readily apparent. The policy of the MacDonald White Paper, which called for Palestinian independence, has been labeled a "betrayal," but loyalty to the Zionist cause never drove British cabinet discussions at any stage of the Mandate. Rather than the beginning of Realpolitik, this episode was merely a continuation of it.

Ultimately, the withdrawal from Palestine involved many of the same considerations about political risk that had been present in earlier British deliberations. Through highlighting the details of their diplomatic entanglements, it becomes clear that perfectly reasonable explanations for Britain's withdrawal (such as the cost of troops in a dwindling postwar economy) played a lesser role than expected. Inconclusive negotiations with the United States, Zionists, and the Arab states left the British government's proverbial hands tied. Even before the UN General Assembly voted for partition, there was no viable alternative except to withdraw.

Looking at these turning points—from the Churchill White Paper in 1922, to the reversal of the Passfield White Paper in 1931, the MacDonald White Paper in 1939, and, finally, Britain's decision to withdraw from Palestine in 1947—it becomes possible to identify how every decision made about Palestine was molded by a range of mundane political problems. There were changes in British policy during the course of the Mandate, but there was perfect continuity in the decision makers' preferences. Although this self-interested and risk-averse behavior may seem predictable for politicians in general, detailing how this conduct affected British policy in Palestine adds an important element to the existing scholarship. Rather than an assessment of British intents and goals based on individual politicians' capricious allegiances or aversions to Zionism, the politics-first approach reveals a predictable pattern.

Historical Lessons of the Politics-First Approach

Although the focus of this book has been on British policy making toward Palestine through the lens of a politics-first perspective, its four main sections yield several additional points to consider in terms of historical importance. As well as the central theme that personal biases had less to do with policy than individual career prospects, three further potential conclusions can be raised.

The first is that Britain's sponsorship of the Jewish national home, which significantly contributed to Israeli statehood in 1948, was to some degree an accident, not least because Zionism's infamous hold on British politicians was tenuous and dependent on context. The British sponsorship of a Jewish national home evolved out of a combination of ambition and necessity. The original overtures toward Zionism were conducted by Sir Mark Sykes. He believed in national self-determination for small ethnic groups and was searching for a political rather than strictly military means to legitimize British invasion and occupation of Palestine. After World War I, this championing of a grand cause helped Prime Minister David Lloyd George secure Britain's hold on Palestine, which was necessary to protect the routes to Egypt and India. The international approval required for this arrangement, however, meant that it was nearly impossible for Britain to extract itself from the pledge to support a Jewish national home, despite many warnings that this was potentially a dangerous commitment. This is where the "accidental" British support for Zionism became entrenched and was demonstrated in multiple governments' tacit commitment to the policy throughout the 1920s.

Although it was frustrated relatively quickly, the Passfield White Paper also represented an attempt to roll back the unintended policy that was causing unrest among Palestine's majority Arab population. Evidently, the effort was undermined by the inherent weakness of James Ramsay MacDonald's minority Labour government. Again, the continuation of Britain's commitment to a Zionist enterprise was merely a short-term fix, a policy that lacked real intent. The next policy-making episode witnessed yet another retreat from the idea of a Jewish national home. The white paper named for Colonial Secretary Malcolm MacDonald promised independence to Palestine and demonstrated the British government's collectively unsentimental attitude toward the future of Zionism. Interestingly, the most dedicated British effort to maintain the Jewish national home arguably came during the tenure of Foreign Secretary Ernest Bevin, who relentlessly tried to keep the territory and court President Truman's approval but, ultimately, helped engineer Britain's withdrawal.

From this perspective, the British sponsorship of Zionism over a thirty-year period, which allowed the Yishuv to develop enough strength in terms of population numbers, organizational ability, and military training to engage in the first Arab-Israeli War in 1948 and establish the State of Israel, might be considered an accident of history. Even the raging Jewish insurgency in Palestine and the threat of further Arab disturbances that necessitated a final departure could be attributed to the British failure in preceding years to "clarify" internally what endured as an undefined and often inadvertent British responsibility toward Zionism. Mission creep and the use of Palestine as a political football allowed the commitment to continue far longer and more deeply than multiple British governments intended.

On a similar note, the accidental nature of Britain's commitment to Zionism undermines more conspiratorial ideas of Jewish power or, in less controversial terms, the influence of Zionist lobbying. A closer look at British policy making reveals that while Dr. Weizmann was a well-liked, respected, and adroit negotiator among Britain's political elite, his influence owed as much to luck and the virtue of representing the right cause at the right time as to his personal skill in British politics. He and other Zionist leaders, however, did have to battle against periodic British governments' attempts at incomplete reconciliation between Zionism and developing Arab nationalism that would have led to the creation of self-governing institutions in Palestine.

At first, the logical course of action regarding these animosities would have been for Britain to simply abandon the policy of a Jewish national home. This was implied in the first commissions chaired by Major General Palin and Sir Thomas Haycraft and suggested by multiple officials, including Winston Churchill, during the initial stages of British rule. As it was in the empire's best interest to avoid rioting in Palestine, the Churchill White Paper of 1922 did represent a concerted effort to assuage what were considered to be unfounded fears about the nature of Zionism—restricting Jewish immigration in line with economic capacity and assuring the world that the aim was not to create a solely Jewish Palestine.

Then again, in 1930, the Passfield White Paper represented an honest if somewhat naive attempt at redressing a perceived imbalance in Palestine, between the Jewish community, which seemed to be benefiting largely from British rule, and the Arab population, which was suffering far more as a result of economic depression. The same was true in the negotiations leading to the MacDonald White Paper in 1939—the aim was a quiet Palestine. Although the policy of promising independence was hardly driven by altruistic motives, it still demonstrated an attempt at settlement that many British politicians who professed Zionist sympathies, including Colonial Secretary MacDonald, hoped would not be necessary. Following World War II, Ernest Bevin staked his reputation on finding a solution to the Jewish-Arab conflict in Palestine and worked tirelessly to secure some compromise from both sides. It was only because these negotiations repeatedly stalled that Britain's Mandate for Palestine came to an end.

In addition, a second derivative conclusion might be that successive British negotiators did committedly try to solve the conflict they had helped provoke in Palestine but found the issue constrained severely by their own domestic politics. While it is very easy to dismiss a succession of British politicians' policy decisions as inept, dithering, or worsening the conflict, there was also a concerted and consistent effort to end and prevent violence. The counterinsurgency methods of the 1930s are today considered unacceptable, brutal, and in many cases illegal, but the Arab Revolt was a turning point in the British government's attitudes toward Palestinian nationalism. Early British negotiators had really lacked a sympathetic understanding of Arab complaints. Herbert Samuel, for example, formerly the high commissioner of Palestine, seemed to scoff at the idea that Jewish immigration could become unreasonable: "If there were any question that the 600,000 Arabs should be ousted from their homes in order to make room for a Jewish national home; if there were any question that they should be kept in political subordination to any other people; if there were any question that their Holy Places should be taken from them and transferred to other hands or other influences, then a policy would have been adopted which would have been utterly wrong. It would have been resented and resisted—rightly—by the Arab people. But it has never been contemplated."[1]

The Arab rebellion, and later the Jewish insurgency, meant that subsequent mediators were forced to recognize both Zionist and Arab concerns, but they were simply unable to reconcile what they realized far too late was a conflict between nations within one strip of land. It is possible to conclude, therefore, that there were some good intentions but an inability or unwillingness to understand the situation with unmitigated clarity.

These efforts at negotiation are relevant to the discussion of one final potential conclusion about the Mandate: the British political predicament ultimately aided the Jewish insurgency's cause following World War II, specifically with reference to the Holocaust's impact on international diplomacy. A common opinion is that international sympathy for the Zionist cause, following the Holocaust, led to Israel's creation. Such a simplistic argument is easy to refute,[2] but chapter 5 of this book reveals how outrage and distress, particularly in the United States following World War II, severely constrained both British counterinsurgency efforts against Zionists in Palestine and options for dealing with the crisis diplomatically. The policy of granting Palestinian independence, for example, became untenable chiefly because the British economy needed American money. At the same time, maintaining the intended British presence in Palestine endangered relations with the Arab states and would have required a stronger and politically unviable counterinsurgency campaign. While it is simplistic, therefore, to draw a direct link between international sympathy and the creation of Israel, it did play a vital role in the British decision to withdraw that prompted Israel's early leaders to proclaim statehood.

Notes

1. House of Commons Debates, 17 November 1930, series 5, vol. 245, cols. 120–121.
2. Evyatar Friesel, "On the Myth of the Connection between the Holocaust and the Creation of Israel," *Israel Affairs* 14, no. 3 (2008): 446–466.

Bibliography

Unpublished Primary Sources

Cadbury Research Library: Special Collections

Papers of Austen Chamberlain AC39/2/1-56–AC4/1/1-1358.

Churchill Archives Centre

Papers of Leopold Amery AMEL 1/5/3–AMEL 1/5/46.

Durham University Library

Papers of Malcolm MacDonald MAC 2/5/95–MAC 9/9/10.

London School of Economics Archives

Papers of Sidney Webb LSE/PASSFIELD/1/2/9.

The National Archives, Kew

Cabinet Documents CAB 21/77–CAB 195/4.
Colonial Office Documents CO 733/182/8–CO 733/406/7.
Foreign Office Documents FO 371/21873–FO 800/484.
Prime Minister's Documents PREM 1/102–PREM 8/859/1.
War Office Documents WO 32/9614.

Parliamentary Archives

Papers of David Lloyd George LG/F/9/2/54–LG/F/39/2/28.

Truman Presidential Library

Confidential File 1938 (1945)–1953.
Papers of David K. Niles.
Papers of George M. Elsey.
President's Secretary's Files 1945–1953.
White House Central Files 1945–1953.

United Nations Archives

S-0611, S-0611-0001-S-0611, S-0611-0002.
"United Nations Special Committee on Palestine Report to the General Assembly," Vol. 1, Lake Success, New York, 1947.

Published Primary Sources

Cmd. 1540, 1921, *Palestine. Disturbances in May, 1921. Reports of the Commission of Inquiry with Correspondence Relating Thereto*, 21.

Cmd. 1581, 1922, *Committee on National Expenditure. First Interim Report of Committee on National Expenditure.*
Cmd. 1582, 1922, *Committee on National Expenditure. Second Interim Report of Committee on National Expenditure.*
Cmd. 1589, 1922, *Committee on National Expenditure. Third Report of Committee on National Expenditure.*
Cmd. 1700, 1922, *Palestine. Correspondence with the Palestine Arab Delegation and the Zionist Organisation.*
Cmd. 1785, 1923, *League of Nations. Mandate for Palestine, Together with a Note by the Secretary-General Relating to Its Application to the Territory Known as Trans-Jordan, under the Provisions of Article 25.*
Cmd. 3530, 1930, *Report of the Commission on the Palestine Disturbances of August 1929,* 164.
Cmd. 3686, 1930, *Report on Immigration, Land Settlement and Development or Hope-Simpson Report,* 141.
Cmd. 3692, 1930, *Statement of Policy by His Majesty's Government in the United Kingdom.*
Cmd. 5479, 1937, *Report of the Royal Commission,* 370.
Cmd. 5513, 1937, *Statement of Policy by His Majesty's Government in the United Kingdom.*
Cmd. 5854, 1937–1938, *Palestine Partition Commission Report,* 14.
Cmd. 5893, 1938, *Palestine. Statement by His Majesty's Government in the United Kingdom.*
Cmd. 5957, 1939, "From Sherif Hussein to Sir Henry McMahon, 14 July 1915," *Miscellaneous No. 3, Correspondence between Sir Henry McMahon G.C.M.G., G.C.V.O., K.C.I.E., C.S.I. His Majesty's High Commissioner at Cairo and the Sherif Hussein of Mecca.*
Cmd. 6019, 1938–1939, *Palestine. Statement of Policy.*
Cmd. 6806, 1946, *Report of the Anglo-American Committee of Enquiry regarding the Problems of European Jewry and Palestine,* 2–10.
Cmd. 6808, 1945–1946, *Report of the Anglo-American Committee of Enquiry regarding the Problems of European Jewry and Palestine.*
Cmd. 7044, 1947, *Palestine No. 1 (1947). Proposals for the Future of Palestine,* 4.
Department of State Bulletin, vol. XIII, no. 327, 30 September 1945, *Report of Earl G. Harrison on Conditions and Needs of Displaced Persons.*
Labour Party and Trades Union Congress, *Memorandum on War Aims* (London: Inter-Allied Labour and Socialist Conference, 1917).

Hansard

House of Commons Debates, 15 July 1920, series 5, vol. 131.
House of Commons Debates, 2 December 1920, series 5, vol. 135.
House of Commons Debates, 3 March 1921, series 5, vol. 138.
House of Commons Debates, 14 June 1921, series 5, vol. 143.
House of Commons Debates, 9 March 1922, series 5, vol. 151.
House of Commons Debates, 4 July 1922, series 5, vol. 156.
House of Commons Debates, 3 April 1930, series 5, vol. 237.
House of Commons Debates, 17 November 1930, series 5, vol. 245.
House of Commons Debates, 19 June 1936, series 5, vol. 313.
House of Commons Debates, 24 November 1937, series 5, vol. 329.
House of Commons Debates, 22 May 1939, series 5, vol. 347.
House of Commons Debates, 23 May 1939, series 5, vol. 347.

House of Commons Debates, 21 February 1946, series 5, vol. 419.
House of Commons Debates, 31 July 1946, series 5, vol. 426.
House of Commons Debates, 1 August 1946, series 5, vol. 426.
House of Commons Debates, 18 February 1947, series 5, vol. 433.
House of Commons Debates, 25 February 1947, series 5, vol. 433.
House of Commons Debates, 11 December 1947, series 5, vol. 445.
House of Commons Debates, 10 March 1948, series 5, vol. 448.
House of Lords Debates, 8 June 1921, series 5, vol. 45.
House of Lords Debates, 15 June 1921, series 5, vol. 45.
House of Lords Debates, 21 June 1922, series 5, vol. 50.
House of Lords Debates, 27 March 1923, series 5, vol. 53.
House of Lords Debates, 9 June 1948, series 5, vol. 156.

Newspapers

Baldwin, Stanley, Austen Chamberlain, and Leopold Amery, "British Policy in Palestine, the White Paper, Conservative Leaders' Comments," *The Times*, 23 October 1930, 15.
Hailsham, Lord, and John Simon, "British Policy in Palestine," *The Times*, 4 November 1930, 15.
MacDonald, James Ramsay, "The Palestine White Paper, an Interpretation, Prime Minister's Letter," *The Times*, 14 February 1931, 8.

Books

Allison, Graham. *Essence of Decision: Explaining the Cuban Missile Crisis*. Boston: Little, Brown, 1971.
Amery, Leopold. *The Empire at Bay: The Leo Amery Diaries 1929–1945*. London: Hutchinson, 1988.
Amery, Leopold. *My Political Life: War and Peace 1914–1929*, Vol. 2. London: Hutchinson, 1953.
Attlee, Clement, and Francis Williams. *Twilight of Empire: Memoirs of Clement Attlee*. London: Barnes, 1962.
Ball, Stuart. *Baldwin and the Conservative Party: The Crisis of 1929–1931*. London: Yale University Press, 1988.
Ben-Ami, Shlomo. *Scars of War, Wounds of Peace: The Israeli-Arab Tragedy*. London: Weidenfeld and Nicolson, 2005.
Bickerton, Ian. *The Israeli-Palestinian Conflict: A History*. London: Reaktion Books, 2009.
Brecher, Michael. *Decisions in Crisis: Israel, 1967 and 1973*. Berkeley: University of California Press, 1980.
Brecher, Michael. *The Foreign Policy System of Israel: Setting, Image, Process*. New Haven, CT: Yale University Press, 1972.
Bueno de Mesquita, Bruce, and David Lalman. *War and Reason: Domestic and International Imperatives*. New Haven, CT: Yale University Press, 1992.
Campbell, John. *Lloyd George: A Goat in the Wilderness, 1922–1931*. Aldershot, UK: Gregg Revivals, 1993.
Caplan, Neil. *The Israel-Palestine Conflict: Contested Histories*. Chichester: Wiley-Blackwell, 2010.
Ceserani, David. *Major Farran's Hat: The Untold Story of the Struggle to Establish the Jewish State*. Cambridge, MA: Da Capo, 2009.

Chaitani, Youssef. *Dissension among Allies: Ernest Bevin's Palestine Policy between Whitehall and the White House, 1945-47.* London: Saqi, 2002.
Cohen, Michael J. *Palestine: Retreat from the Mandate—The Making of British Policy, 1936-45.* London: Paul Elek, 1978.
Cohen, Michael J. *Palestine to Israel: From Mandate to Independence.* Oxon: Routledge, 1988.
Constantine, Stephen. *The Making of British Colonial Development Policy, 1914-1940.* Cambridge: Routledge, 1984.
Cottam, Richard. *Foreign Policy Motivation: A General Theory and a Case Study.* Pittsburgh, PA: University of Pittsburgh Press, 1977.
Craig, Frederick Walter Scott, ed. *British General Election Manifestos 1900-1974.* London: Macmillan, 1975.
Dalton, Hugh. *High Tide and After: Memoirs 1945-1960.* London: Frederick Muller, 1962.
Danilovic, Vesna. *When the Stakes Are High: Deterrence and Conflict among Major Powers.* Ann Arbor: University of Michigan Press, 2002.
Darwin, John. *Britain, Egypt and the Middle East: Imperial Policy in the Aftermath of War 1918-1922.* London: Macmillan, 1981.
De Bondt, Werner, and Richard Thaler. *Financial Decision Making in Markets and Firms: A Behavioral Perspective.* Cambridge, MA: National Bureau of Economic Research, 1994.
Defries, Harry. *Conservative Party Attitudes to Jews, 1900-1950.* London: Frank Cass, 2001.
Doerr, Paul. *British Foreign Policy 1919-1939.* Manchester: Manchester University Press, 1998.
El-Eini, Roza. *Mandated Landscape: British Imperial Rule in Palestine 1929-1945.* New York: Routledge, 2006.
Friedman, Isaiah. *British Pan-Arab Policy, 1915-1922.* New Brunswick, NJ: Transaction, 2010.
Friedman, Isaiah. *The Question of Palestine 1914-1918.* New York: Schocken Books, 1973.
Gelvin, James L. *The Israel-Palestine Conflict: One Hundred Years of War.* Cambridge: Cambridge University Press, 2005.
George, Alexander, and Andrew Bennett. *Case Studies and Theory Development in the Social Sciences.* Cambridge, MA: MIT Press, 2004.
Gerber, Haim. *Remembering and Imagining Palestine: Identity and Nationalism from the Crusades to the Present.* Basingstoke, UK: Palgrave Macmillan, 2008.
Ghandour, Zeina B. *A Discourse on Domination in Mandate Palestine.* Oxon: Routledge, 2010.
Gomm, Roger, ed. *Case Study Method.* London: Sage, 2000.
Gopal, Sarvepalli. *The Viceroyalty of Lord Irwin 1926-1931.* Oxford: Clarendon, 1957.
Gorny, Joseph. *The British Labour Movement and Zionism 1917-1948.* London: Routledge, 1983.
Grayson, Richard. *Austen Chamberlain and the Commitment to Europe: British Foreign Policy 1924-29.* London: Frank Cass, 1997.
Grief, Howard. *The Legal Foundation and Border of Israel under International Law.* Jerusalem: Mazo, 2008.
Hadawi, Sami. *Bitter Harvest: A Modern History of Palestine.* Buckhurst Hill: Scorpion Publishing Ltd, 1990.
Hadawi, Sami. *Palestine: Loss of a Heritage.* San Antonio, TX: Naylor Company, 1963.
Halperin, Morton. *Bureaucratic Politics and Foreign Policy.* Washington, DC: Brookings Institution, 1974.
Hanna, Paul Lamont. *British Policy in Palestine.* Washington, DC: American Council on Public Affairs, 1942.

Harms, Gregory. *The Palestine-Israel Conflict: A Basic Introduction*. London: Pluto Books, 2008.
Hill, Christopher. *The Changing Politics of Foreign Policy*. London: Palgrave Macmillan, 2003.
Hilsman, Roger. *The Politics of Policy Making in Defense and Foreign Affairs: Conceptual Models and Bureaucratic Politics*. Englewood Cliffs, NJ: Prentice Hall, 1987.
Hollis, Martin, and Steve Smith. *Explaining and Understanding International Relations*. Oxford: Clarendon, 1990.
Hudson, Valerie. *Foreign Policy Analysis: Classic and Contemporary Theory*. Lanham, MD: Rowman and Littlefield, 2007.
Hughes, Matthew. *Allenby and British Strategy in the Middle East*. London: Frank Cass, 1999.
Hughes, Matthew. *British Foreign Secretaries in an Uncertain World, 1919–1939*. Oxon: Routledge, 2006.
James Lowe, Cedric, and M. L. Dockrill. *The Mirage of Power: British Foreign Policy 1914–1922*, Vol. 2. Cambridge: Routledge, 1972.
Janis, Irving. *Groupthink*. Boston: Houghton Mifflin, 1982.
Jervis, Robert. *Perception and Misperception in International Politics*. Princeton, NJ: Princeton University Press, 1976.
Jones, Bryan. *Reconceiving Decision-Making in Democratic Politics: Attention, Choice, and Public Policy*. Chicago: University of Chicago Press, 1994.
Julius, Anthony. *Trials of the Diaspora: A History of Anti-Semitism in England*. Oxford: Oxford University Press, 2010.
Kedourie, Elie. *In the Anglo-Arab Labyrinth: The McMahon-Husayn Correspondence and Its Interpretations, 1914–1939*. Cambridge: Cambridge University Press, 1976.
Keith-Roach, Keith. *Pasha of Jerusalem: Memoirs of a District Commissioner under the British Mandate*. London: Radcliffe, 1994.
Kenworthy, Joseph. *India: A Warning*. London: E. Matthews and Marrot, 1931.
Khalidi, Rashid. *The Iron Cage: The Story of the Palestinian Struggle for Statehood*. Oxford: OneWorld, 2007.
Khalidi, Walid. *From Haven to Conquest: Readings in Zionism and the Palestine Problem until 1948*. Washington DC: Institute for Palestine Studies, 1987.
Kimche, Jon. *Both Sides of the Hill: Britain and the Palestine War*. London: Secker and Warburg, 1960.
Kinnear, Michael. *The Fall of Lloyd George: The Political Crisis of 1922*. London: Macmillan, 1973.
Knopf-Newman, Marcy Jane. *The Politics of Teaching Palestine to Americans: Pedagogical Strategies*. New York: Palgrave Macmillan, 2011.
Koestler, Arthur. *Promise and Fulfilment: Palestine 1917–1949*. London: Macmillan, 1949.
Kramer, Gudrun. *A History of Palestine: From the Ottoman Conquest to the Founding of the State of Israel*. Princeton, NJ: Princeton University Press, 2008.
Laquere, Walter, and Barry Rubin, eds. *The Israeli-Arab Reader*. New York: Penguin, 2008.
Lewis, Geoffrey. *Balfour and Weizmann: The Zionist, the Zealot and the Emergence of Israel*. London: Continuum, 2009.
Louis, William Roger, ed. *The End of the Palestine Mandate*. London: I. B. Tauris, 1986.
Louis, William Roger. *The British Empire in the Middle East 1945–51*. Oxford: Clarendon, 1984.
Makovsky, Michael. *Churchill's Promised Land: Zionism and Statecraft*. London: Yale University Press, 2007.

Marlowe, Christopher. *Seat of Pilate: An Account of the Palestine Mandate.* London: Cresset, 1959.
Matthews, Weldon C. *Confronting an Empire, Constructing a Nation.* London: I. B. Tauris, 1988.
Meinertzhagen, Richard. *Middle East Diary 1917–1956.* London: Cresset, 1959.
Middleton, Charles Ronald. *The Administration of British Foreign Policy 1782–1846.* Durham, NC: Duke University Press, 1977.
Mintz, Alex, and Karl DeRouen. *Understanding Foreign Policy Decision Making.* Cambridge: Cambridge University Press, 2010.
Monroe, Elizabeth. *Britain's Moment in the Middle East 1914–1956.* London: Methuen, 1965.
Morris, Benny. *The Birth of the Palestinian Refugee Problem Revisited.* Cambridge, Cambridge University Press, 2004.
Morris, Benny. *Righteous Victims: A History of the Zionist-Arab Conflict, 1881–1999.* London: John Murray, 2000.
O'Morgan, Kenneth. *Consensus and Disunity: The Lloyd George Government 1918–1922.* Oxford: Clarendon, 1979.
O'Morgan, Kenneth. *Labour in Power 1945–1951.* Oxford: Oxford University Press, 1984.
Pappe, Ilan. *A History of Modern Palestine: One Land, Two Peoples.* Cambridge: Cambridge University Press, 2006.
Pappe, Ilan. *The Making of the Arab-Israeli Conflict 1947–1951.* London: I. B. Tauris, 1992.
Peled-Elhanan, Nurit. *Palestine in Israeli School Books: Ideology and Propaganda in Education.* London: I. B. Tauris, 2012.
Peters, Anthony R. *Anthony Eden at the Foreign Office, 1931–1938.* London: St. Martin's, 1986.
Porath, Yehoshua. *The Emergence of the Palestinian-Arab National Movement, 1918–1929.* London: Frank Cass, 1974.
Porath, Yehoshua. *The Emergence of the Palestinian-Arab National Movement, 1929–1939: From Riots to Rebellion.* London: Frank Cass, 1977.
Reynolds, Philip. *British Foreign Policy in the Inter-War Years.* London: Longmans, Green, 1954.
Rose, Norman. *The Gentile Zionists.* London: Frank Cass, 1973.
Rotberg, Robert I., ed. *Israeli and Palestinian Narratives of Conflict: History's Double Helix.* Bloomington: Indiana University Press, 2006.
Schindler, Colin. *A History of Modern Israel.* Cambridge: Cambridge University Press, 2008.
Schneer, Jonathan. *The Balfour Declaration: The Origins of the Arab-Israeli Conflict.* London: Bloomsbury, 2010.
Segev, Tom. *One Palestine, Complete: Jews and Arabs under the British Mandate.* London: Abacus, 2000.
Self, Robert, ed. *The Neville Chamberlain Diary Letters,* Vol. 3. Aldershot, UK: Ashgate, 2000.
Shepherd, Naomi. *Ploughing Sand: British Rule in Palestine, 1917–1948.* London: John Murray, 1999.
Shlaim, Avi. *The Iron Wall: Israel and the Arab World.* London: Penguin Books, 2001.
Shlaim, Avi. *Israel and Palestine: Reappraisals, Revisions, Refutations.* London: Verso, 2009.
Shlaim, Avi. *The Politics of Partition: King Abdullah, The Zionists, and Palestine 1921–1951.* Oxford: Oxford University Press, 1998.
Snyder, Richard, H. W. Bruck, and Burton Sapin. *Decision Making as an Approach to the Study of International Politics.* Princeton, NJ: Princeton University Press, 1954.

Sprout, Harold, and Margaret Sprout. *Man-Mileu Relationship Hypotheses in the Context of International Politics*. Princeton, NJ: Princeton University Press, 1956.
Stake, Robert E. *The Art of Case Study Research*. London: Sage, 1995.
Stein, Leonard. *The Balfour Declaration*. London: Valentine Mitchell, 1961.
Steinbruner, John. *The Cybernetic Theory of Decision: New Dimensions of Political Analysis*. Princeton, NJ: Princeton University Press, 2002.
Sternhell, Zeev. *The Founding Myths of Israel: Nationalism, Socialism and the Making of the Jewish State*. Princeton, NJ: Princeton University Press, 1998.
Storrs, Ronald. *Orientations*. London: Nicholson and Watson, 1937.
Swedenburg, Ted. *Memories of Revolt: The 1936–1939 Rebellion and the Palestinian National Past*. Fayetteville: University of Arkansas Press, 2003.
Sykes, Christopher. *Cross Roads to Israel*. London: Collins, 1965.
Tessler, Mark. *A History of the Israeli-Palestinian Conflict*. Bloomington: Indiana University Press, 2009.
Van Creveld, Martin. *The Land of Blood and Honey: The Rise of Modern Israel*. New York: St. Martin's, 2010.
Waltz, Kenneth. *Theory of International Politics*. Reading, MA: Addison-Wesley, 1979.
Weizmann, Chaim. *The Letters and Papers of Chaim Weizmann, October 1930–June 1933*, Series 3, Vol. 15. New Brunswick, NJ: Transaction Books, 1978.
Weizmann, Chaim. *Trial and Error: The Autobiography of Chaim Weizmann*. London: Hamish Hamilton, 1949.
Westrate, Bruce. *The Arab Bureau: British Policy in the Middle East 1916–1920*. University Park: Pennsylvania State University Press, 1992.
Williamson, Philip, ed. *Baldwin Papers: A Conservative Statesman, 1908–1947*. Cambridge: Cambridge University Press, 2004.
Williamson, Philip. *National Crisis and National Government*. Cambridge: Cambridge University Press, 1992.
Yin, Robert. *Case Study Research: Design and Methods*. 4th ed. London: Sage, 2008.

Articles and Edited Chapters

Abboushi, W. F. "The Road to Rebellion, Palestine in the 1930s." *Journal of Palestine Studies* 6, no. 3 (1977): 23–46.
Anderson, Paul. "Decision Making by Objection in the Cuban Missile Crisis." *Administrative Science Quarterly* 28, no. 2 (1983): 201–222.
Anderson, Paul. "What Do Decision Makers Do When They Make a Foreign Policy Decision? The Implications for the Study of Comparative Foreign Policy." In *New Directions in the Study of Foreign Policy*, edited by Charles Hermann, Charles Kegley, and James Rosenau, 285–308. Boston: Allen and Unwin, 1987.
Anglim, Simon. "Orde Wingate and the Special Night Squads: A Feasible Policy for Counter-terrorism?" *Contemporary Security Policy* 28, no. 1 (2007): 28–41.
Ashley, Richard. "Noticing Pre-Paradigmatic Progress." In *In Search of Global Patterns*, edited by J. Rosenau, 150–157. New York: Free Press, 1976.
Astorino-Courtois, Allison, and Brittani Trusty. "Degrees of Difficulty: The Effect of Israeli Policy Shifts on Syrian Peace Decisions." In *Integrating Cognitive and Rational Theories of Foreign Policy Decision Making*, edited by Alex Mintz, 29–54. New York: Palgrave Macmillan, 2002.

Bar-On, Mordechai. "Conflicting Narratives or Narratives of a Conflict?" In *Israeli and Palestinian Narratives of Conflict: History's Double Helix*, edited by Robert I. Rotberg, 142–173. Bloomington: Indiana University Press, 2006.

Bar-Tal, Daniel, and Gavriel Salomon. "Israeli-Jewish Narratives of the Israeli-Palestinian Conflict." In *Israeli and Palestinian Narratives of Conflict: History's Double Helix*, edited by Robert I. Rotberg, 19–46. Bloomington: Indiana University Press, 2006.

Baxter, Pamela, and Susan Jack. "Qualitative Case Study Methodology: Study Design and Implementation for Novice Researchers." *Qualitative Report* 13, no. 4 (2008): 544–559.

Brulé, David. "The Poliheuristic Research Program: An Assessment and Suggestions for Further Progress." *International Studies Review* 10, no. 2 (2008): 266–293.

Brulé, David, and Alex Mintz. "Blank Check or Marching Orders? Public Opinion and Presidential Use of Force in the United States." In *Approaches, Levels, and Methods of Analysis in International Politics: Crossing Boundaries*, edited by H. Starr, 157–172. New York: Palgrave Macmillan, 2006.

Brummer, Klaus. "The Reluctant Peacekeeper: Governmental Politics and Germany's Participation in EUFOR RD Condo." *Foreign Policy Analysis* 9, no. 1 (January 2013). https://doi.org/10.1111/j.1743-8594.2011.00174.x

Carlsnaes, Walter. "Foreign Policy." In *Handbook of International Relations*, edited by Walter Carlsnaes, Thomas Risse, and Beth Simmons, 331–349. London: Sage, 2002.

Christensen, Eben, and Steven Redd. "Bureaucrats versus the Ballot Box in Foreign Policy Decision Making: An Experimental Analysis of the Bureaucratic Politics Model and the Poliheuristic Theory." *Journal of Conflict Resolution* 48, no. 1 (2004): 69–90.

Cohen, Michael J. "British Strategy and the Palestine Question 1936–1939." *Journal of Contemporary History* 7, nos. 3–4 (1972): 157–183.

Cohen, Michael J. "The Genesis of the Anglo-American Committee on Palestine, November 1945: A Case Study in the Assertion of American Hegemony." *Historical Journal* 22, no. 1 (1979): 185–207.

Cohen, Michael J. "Secret Diplomacy and Rebellion in Palestine, 1936–1939." *International Journal of Middle East Studies* 8, no. 3 (1977): 379–404.

Cohen, Michael J. "Sir Arthur Wauchope, the Army, and the Rebellion in Palestine, 1936." *Middle Eastern Studies* 9, no. 1 (1973): 19–34.

Dawn, C. Ernest. "Elie Kedourie, in the Anglo-Arab Labyrinth." *International Journal of Middle East Studies* 9, no. 1 (1978): 128–130.

DeRouen, Karl. "The Decision Not to Use Force at Dien Bien Phu: A Poliheuristic Perspective." In *Integrating Cognitive and Rational Theories of Foreign Policy Decision Making*, edited by Alex Mintz, 11–28. New York: Palgrave Macmillan, 2002.

DeRouen, Karl, and Christopher Sprecher. "Initial Crisis Reaction and Poliheuristic Theory." *Journal of Conflict Resolution* 48, no. 1 (2004): 56–68.

Drezner, Daniel. "Ideas, Bureaucratic Politics, and the Crafting of Foreign Policy." *American Journal of Political Science* 44, no. 4 (2000): 733–749.

Druckman, James, and Rose McDermott. "Emotion and the Framing of Risky Choice." *Political Behavior* 30, no. 3 (2008): 297–321.

El-Eini, Roza. "Government Fiscal Policy in Mandatory Palestine in the 1930s." *Middle Eastern Studies* 33, no. 3 (1997): 570–596.

Fair, John D. "The Conservative Basis for the Formation of the National Government of 1931." *Journal of British Studies* 19, no. 2 (1980): 142–164.

Feige, Michael. "Introduction: Rethinking Israeli Memory and Identity." *Israel Studies* 7, no. 2 (2002): v–xiv, vii–viii.

Fraser, T. G. "A Crisis of Leadership: Weizmann and the Zionist Reactions to the Peel Commission's Proposals, 1937–8." *Journal of Contemporary History* 23, no. 4 (1988): 657–680.

Friedman, Isaiah. "The McMahon-Hussein Correspondence and the Question of Palestine." *Journal of Contemporary History* 5, no. 2 (1970): 83–122.

Friesel, Evyatar. "On the Myth of the Connection between the Holocaust and the Creation of Israel." *Israel Affairs* 14, no. 3 (2008): 446–466.

Friesel, Evyatar. "Through a Peculiar Lens: Zionism and Palestine in British Diaries, 1927–31." *Middle Eastern Studies* 29, no. 3 (1993): 419–444.

Gerring, John. "What Is a Case Study and What Is It Good For?" *American Political Science Review* 98, no. 2 (2004): 341–354.

Gil-Har, Yitzhak. "British Intelligence and the Role of Jewish Informers in Palestine." *Middle Eastern Studies* 39, no. 1 (2010): 117–149.

Gross Stein, Janice, and David Welch. "Rational and Psychological Approaches to the Study of International Conflict: Comparative Strengths and Weaknesses." In *Decisionmaking on War and Peace: The Cognitive-Rational Debate*, edited by Alex Mintz and Nehemia Geva, 51–80. Boulder, CO: Lynne Rienner, 1997.

Hansen, David, and James Helgeson. "Choice under Strict Uncertainty: Processes and Preferences." *Organizational Behavior and Human Decision Processes* 66, no. 2 (1996): 153–164.

Hermann, Charles. "Decision Structure and Process Influences on Foreign Policy." In *Why Nations Act: Theoretical Perspectives for Comparative Foreign Policy Studies*, edited by Maurice East, Stephen Salmore, and Charles Hermann, 69–102. Beverly Hills, CA: Sage, 1978.

Hermann, Margaret. "Assessing Leadership Style: Trait Analysis." In *The Psychological Assessment of Political Leaders*, edited by Jerrold Post, 178–214. Ann Arbor: University of Michigan Press, 2003.

Hughes, Matthew. "The Banality of Brutality: British Armed Forces and the Repression of the Arab Revolt in Palestine, 1936–39." *English Historical Review* 124, no. 507 (2009): 313–354.

Hughes, Matthew. "From Law and Order to Pacification: Britain's Suppression of the Arab Revolt in Palestine, 1936–1939." *Journal of Palestine Studies* 39, no. 2 (2010): 6–22.

Hughes, Matthew. "The Practice and Theory of British Counterinsurgency: The Histories of the Atrocities at the Palestinian Villages of al-Bassa and Halhul, 1938–1939." *Small Wars and Insurgencies* 20, nos. 3–4 (2009): 528–550.

James, Patrick, and John Oneal. "The Influence of Domestic and International Politics on the President's Use of Force." *Journal of Conflict Resolution* 35, no. 2 (1991): 307–332.

James, Patrick, and Enyu Zhang. "Chinese Choices: A Poliheuristic Analysis of Foreign Policy Crises, 1950–1996." *Foreign Policy Analysis* 1, no. 1 (2005): 31–54.

Jawad, Saleh Abdel. "The Arab and Palestinian Narratives of the 1948 War." In *Israeli and Palestinian Narratives of Conflict: History's Double Helix*, edited by Robert I. Rotberg, 72–114. Bloomington: Indiana University Press, 2006.

Johnson, Gaynor. "Curzon, Lloyd George and the Control of British Foreign Policy, 1919–22: A Reassessment." *Diplomacy and Statecraft* 11, no. 3 (2000): 49–71.

Kahneman, Daniel, and Amos Tversky. "Choices, Values, and Frames." *American Psychologist* 39, no. 4 (1984): 341–350.

Kahneman, Daniel, and Amos Tversky. "Prospect Theory: An Analysis of Decision under Risk." *Econometrica* 47, no. 2 (1979): 263–291.

Keleman, Paul. "Zionism and the British Labour Party: 1917–39." *Social History* 21, no. 1 (1996): 71–87.

Kent, Marian. "Asiatic Turkey, 1914–1916." In *British Foreign Policy under Sir Edward Grey*, edited by F. H. Hinsley. Cambridge: Cambridge University Press, 1977.

Khalidi, Walid. "A Palestinian Perspective on the Arab-Israeli Conflict." *Journal of Palestine Studies* 14, no. 4 (1985): 35–48.

Khalidi, Walid. "The Palestine Problem: An Overview." *Journal of Palestine Studies* 21, no. 1 (1991): 5–16.

Khalidi, Walid. "Plan Dalet: Master Plan for the Conquest of Palestine." *Journal of Palestine Studies* 18, no. 1 (1988): 4–33.

Kinne, Brandon. "Decision Making in Autocratic Regimes: A Poliheuristic Perspective." *International Studies Perspectives* 6, no. 1 (2005): 114–128.

Klieman, Aaron. "Bureaucratic Politics at Whitehall in the Partitioning of Palestine, 1937." In *Great Powers in the Middle East, 1919–1939*, edited by Uriel Dann, 128–154. New York: Holmes and Meier, 1988.

Klieman, Aaron. "The Divisiveness of Palestine: Foreign Office versus Colonial Office on the Issue of Partition, 1937." *Historical Journal* 22, no. 2 (1979): 423–441.

Kozak, David. "The Bureaucratic Politics Approach: The Evolution of the Paradigm." In *Bureaucratic Politics and National Security: Theory and Practice*, edited by David Kozak and James Keagle, 3–15. Boulder, CO: Lynne Rienner, 1988.

Leana, Carrie. "A Partial Test of Janis' Groupthink Model: Effects of Group Cohesiveness and Leader Behavior on Defective Decision-Making." *Journal of Management* 11, no. 1 (1975): 5–18.

Levenberg, Haim. "Bevin's Disillusionment: The London Conference, Autumn 1946." *Middle Eastern Studies* 27, no. 4 (1991): 615–630.

Levene, Mark. "The Balfour Declaration: A Case of Mistaken Identity." *English Historical Review* 107, no. 422 (1992): 54–77.

Levin, Noam, Ruth Kark, and Emir Galilee. "Maps and the Settlement of Southern Palestine, 1799–1948: An Historical/GIS Analysis." *Journal of Historical Geography* 36, no. 1 (2010): 1–18.

Levy, Jack. "Prospect Theory and the Cognitive-Rational Debate." In *Decisionmaking on War and Peace: The Cognitive-Rational Debate*, edited by Alex Mintz and Nehemia Geva, 33–50. Boulder, CO: Lynne Rienner, 1997.

Lui, Xinsheng. "The Poliheuristic Theory of Decision and the Cybernetic Theory of Decision: A Comparative Examination." In *Integrating Cognitive and Rational Theories of Foreign Policy Decision Making*, edited by Alex Mintz, 159–168. New York: Palgrave Macmillan, 2002.

MacDonald, Paul. " Useful Fiction or Miracle Maker: The Competing Epistemological Foundations of Rational Choice Theory." *American Political Science Review* 97, no. 4 (2003): 551–565.

Maoz, Zeev, and Allison Astorino. "The Cognitive Structure of Peacemaking: Egypt and Israel, 1970–78." *Political Psychology* 13, no. 4 (1992): 647–662.

May, Larry. "Killing Naked Soldiers: Distinguishing between Combatants and Noncombatants." *Ethics and International Affairs* 19, no. 3 (2005): 39–53.

McTague, John J. "The British Military Administration in Palestine 1917–1920." *Journal of Palestine Studies* 7, no. 3 (1978): 55–76.

Mearsheimer, John. "The False Promise of International Institutions." *International Security* 19, no. 3 (1995): 5–49.

Melka, Robert Lewis. "Nazi Germany and the Palestine Question." *Middle Eastern Studies* 5, no. 3 (1969): 221–233.

Miller, Rory, ed. "Introduction." In *Britain, Palestine and Empire: The Mandate Years*, 1–14. Farnham, UK: Ashgate, 2010.

Miller, Rory. "The Other Side of the Coin: Arab Propaganda and the Battle against Zionism in London." *Israel Affairs* 5, no. 4 (1999): 198–228.

Mintz, Alex. "Applied Decision Analysis: Utilizing Poliheuristic Theory to Explain and Predict Foreign Policy and National Security Decisions." *International Studies Perspectives* 6, no. 1 (2005): 94–98.

Mintz, Alex. "The Decision to Attack Iraq: A Noncompensatory Theory of Decision Making." *Journal of Conflict Resolution* 37, no. 4 (1993): 595–618.

Mintz, Alex. "Foreign Policy Decisionmaking: Bridging the Gap between the Cognitive Psychology and Rational Actor 'Schools.'" In *Decisionmaking on War and Peace: The Cognitive-Rational Debate*, edited by Alex Mintz and Nehemia Geva, 1–10. Boulder, CO: Lynne Rienner, 1997.

Mintz, Alex. "How Do Leaders Make Decisions? A Poliheuristic Perspective." *Journal of Conflict Resolution* 48, no. 1 (2004): 3–13.

Mintz, Alex. "Integrating Cognitive and Rational Theories of Foreign Policy Decision Making: A Poliheuristic Perspective." In *Integrating Cognitive and Rational Theories of Foreign Policy Decision Making*, edited by Alex Mintz, 1–10. New York: Palgrave Macmillan, 2002.

Mintz, Alex, and Nehemia Geva. "The Poliheuristic Theory of Foreign Policy Decision Making." In *Decisionmaking on War and Peace: The Cognitive-Rational Debate*, edited by Alex Mintz and Nehemia Geva, 81–102. Boulder, CO: Lynne Rienner, 1997.

Mintz, Alex, Nehemia Geva, Steven Redd, and Amy Carnes. "The Effect of Dynamic and Static Choice Sets on Political Decision Making: An Analysis Using the Decision Board Platform." *American Political Science Review* 91, no. 3 (1997): 553–566.

Morrow, James. "A Rational Choice Approach to International Conflict." In *Decision Making on War and Peace: The Cognitive-Rational Debate*, edited by Nehemia Geva and Alex Mintz, 11–32. Boulder, CO: Lynne Rienner, 1997.

Newton, C. S. S. "The Sterling Crisis of 1947 and the British Response to the Marshall Plan." *Economic History Review* 37, no. 3 (1984): 391–408.

Norris, Jacob. "Repression and Rebellion: Britain's Response to the Arab Revolt in Palestine of 1936–39." *Journal of Imperial and Commonwealth History* 36, no. 1 (2008): 25–45.

Northedge, F. S. "Britain and the Middle East." In *The Foreign Policy of British Labour Governments 1945–1951*, edited by Ritchie Ovendale. Leicester, UK: Leicester University Press, 1984.

Ostrom, Charles, and Brian Job. "The President and the Political Use of Force." *American Political Science Review* 80, no. 2 (1986): 541–566.

Ostrom, Thomas, John Lingle, John Pryor, and Nehemia Geva. "Cognitive Organization of Person Impressions." In *Person Memory: The Cognitive Basis of Social Perception*, edited by Reid Hastie, Thomas Ostrom, Ebbe Ebbeson, Robert Wyer, David Hamilton, and Donal Carlston, 55–88. Hillsdale, NJ: Erlbaum, 1980.

Ovendale, Ritchie. "The Palestine Policy of the British Labour Government 1947: The Decision to Withdraw." *International Affairs* 56, no. 1 (1980): 73–93.

Payne, John, James Bettman, and Eric Johnson. "Adaptive Strategy Selection in Decision-Making." *Journal of Experimental Psychology: Learning, Memory and Cognition* 14, no. 3 (1988): 534–552.

Payne, John, James Bettman, and Mary Frances Luce. "When Time Is Money: Decision Making Behavior under Opportunity-Cost Time Pressure." *Organizational Behavior and Human Decision Processes* 66, no. 2 (1996): 131–152.

Pederson, Susan. "The Impact of League Oversight on British Policy in Palestine." In *Britain, Palestine and Empire: The Mandate Years*, edited by Rory Miller, 39–66. Farnham, UK: Ashgate, 2010.

Putnam, Robert. "Diplomacy and Domestic Politics: The Logic of Two-Level Games." *International Organization* 42, no. 3 (1988): 427–260.

Quattrone, George, and Amos Tversky. "Contrasting Rational and Psychological Analyses of Political Choice." *American Political Science Review* 82, no. 3 (1988): 719–736.

Ravndal, Ellen J. "Exit Britain: British Withdrawal from the Palestine Mandate in the Early Cold War 1947–1948." *Diplomacy and Statecraft* 21, no. 3 (2010): 416–433.

Redd, Steven. "The Influence of Advisers and Decision Strategies on Foreign Policy Choices: President Clinton's Decision to Use Force in Kosovo." *International Studies Perspectives* 6, no. 1 (2005): 129–150.

Redd, Steven. "The Influence of Advisers on Foreign Policy Decision Making: An Experimental Study." *Journal of Conflict Resolution* 46, no. 3 (2002): 335–364.

Renshon, Jonathan, and Stanley Renshon. "The Theory and Practice of Foreign Policy Decision Making." *Political Psychology* 29, no. 4 (2008): 509–536.

Renton, James. "Flawed Foundations: The Balfour Declaration and the Palestine Mandate." In *Britain, Palestine and Empire: The Mandate Years*, edited by Rory Miller, 15–37. Farnham, UK: Ashgate, 2010.

Roberts, Nicholas E. "Re-Remembering the Mandate: Historiographical Debates and Revisionist History in the Study of British Palestine." *History Compass* 9, no. 3 (2011): 215–230.

Roosevelt, Kermit. "The Partition of Palestine: A Lesson in Pressure Politics." *Middle Eastern Journal* 2, no. 1 (1948): 1–16.

Rosenau, James. "Pre-Theories and Theories of Foreign Policy." In *Approaches in Comparative and International Politics*, edited by B. Farrell, 27–92. Evanston, IL: Northwestern University Press, 1966.

Ruddin, Lee Peter. "You Can Generalize Stupid! Social Scientists, Bent Flyvbjerg, and Case Study Methodology." *Qualitative Inquiry* 12, no. 4 (2006): 797–812.

Semmel, Andrew, and Dean Minix. "Small Group Dynamics and Foreign Policy Decision-Making: An Experimental Approach." In *Psychological Models in International Politics*, edited by L. Falkowski, 251–287. Boulder, CO: Westview, 1979.

Sheffer, Gabriel. "British Colonial Policy-Making towards Palestine (1929–1939)." *Middle Eastern Studies* 14, no. 3 (1978): 307–322.

Sheffer, Gabriel. "Intentions and Results of British Policy in Palestine: Passfield's White Paper." *Middle Eastern Studies* 9, no. 1 (1973): 43–60.
Shlaim, Avi. "Britain and the Arab-Israeli War of 1948." *Journal of Palestine Studies* 16, no. 4 (1987): 50–76.
Simon, Herbert. "Human Nature in Politics: The Dialogue of Psychology with Political Science." *American Political Science Review* 79, no. 2 (1985): 294–304.
Simon, Herbert. "Theories of Decision Making in Economics and Behavioral Science." *American Economic Review* 49, no. 3 (1959): 253–283.
Sinanoglou, Penny. "The Peel Commission and Partition, 1936–1938." In *Britain, Palestine and Empire: The Mandate Years*, edited by Rory Miller, 119–140. Farnham, UK: Ashgate, 2010.
Smith, Charles D. "The Invention of a Tradition: The Question of Arab Acceptance of the Zionist Right to Palestine during World War I." *Journal of Palestine Studies* 22, no. 2 (1993): 48–61.
Smith, Raymond, and John Zametica. "The Cold Warrior: Clement Attlee Reconsidered, 1945–7." *International Affairs* 61, no. 2 (1985): 237–252.
Snidal, Duncan. "Rational Choice and International Relations." In *Handbook of International Relations*, edited by Walter Calsnaes, Thomas Risse, and Beth Simmons, 73–94. London: Sage, 2002.
Stake, Robert E. "Naturalistic Generalization." *Review Journal of Philosophy and Social Science* 7, nos. 1–2 (1982): 1–12.
Steiner, Miriam. "The Search for Order in a Disorderly World: Worldviews and Prescriptive Decision Paradigms." *International Organization* 37, no. 3 (1983): 373–413.
Tetlock, Philip. "Identifying Victims of Groupthink from Public Statements of Decision-Makers." *Journal of Personality and Social Psychology* 37, no. 8 (1979): 1314–1324.
Thorpe, Andrew. "Arthur Henderson and the British Political Crisis of 1931." *Historical Journal* 31, no. 1 (1988): 117–139.
Townshend, Charles. "The Defence of Palestine: Insurrection and Public Security, 1936–1939." *English Historical Review* 103, no. 409 (1988): 917–949.
Toynbee, Arnold. "The McMahon-Hussein Correspondence: Comments and a Reply." *Journal of Contemporary History* 5, no. 4 (1970): 185–201.
Utting, Kate. "The Strategic Information Campaign: Lessons from the British Experience in Palestine 1945–1948." *Contemporary Security Policy* 28, no. 1 (2007): 48–62.
Vereté, Mayir. "The Balfour Declaration and Its Makers." *Middle Eastern Studies* 6, no. 1 (1970): 48–74.
Walker, Stephen. "Foreign Policy Analysis and Behavioral International Relations." In *Rethinking Foreign Policy Analysis: States, Leaders, and the Microfoundations of Behavioral International Relations*, edited by Stephen Walker, Akan Malici, and Mark Schafer, 3–20. Oxon: Routledge, 2011.
Walker, Stephen. "The Integration of Foreign Policy Analysis and International Relations." In *Rethinking Foreign Policy Analysis: States, Leaders, and the Microfoundations of Behavioral International Relations*, edited by Stephen Walker, Akan Malici, and Mark Schafer, 267–282. Oxon: Routledge, 2011.
Wasserstein, Bernard. "Herbert Samuel and the Palestine Problem." *English Historical Review* 91, no. 361 (1976): 753–775.

Wilson, Trevor. "The Coupon and the British General Election of 1918." *Journal of Modern History* 36, no. 1 (1964): 28–42.
Winkler, Henry. "The Emergence of a Labour Foreign Policy in Great Britain, 1918–1929." *Journal of Modern History* 28, no. 3 (1956): 247–258.
Yazbak, Mahmoud. "From Poverty to Revolt: Economic Factors in the Outbreak of the 1936 Rebellion in Palestine." *Middle Eastern Studies* 3, no. 3 (2000): 93–113.

Index

Page numbers in italics refer to figures.

Abdullah, Emir of Transjordan, 14, 20, 21, 42, 44, 108
Achdut HaAvoda, 36
Alexander, Lord, 83, 87
Allenby, General Edmund, 35, 40
Amery, Leopold, 53, 54, 72, 74, 76, 77–89, 128–131
Anglo-American Committee of Inquiry, 27, 142–173
anti-Semitism, 24, 36, 79, 83, 151, 175
Anti-Waste League, 47–53, 89
appeasement, 1, 101, 121, 128–129, 134
Arab Delegation, 53, 111–112
Arab Ladies of Jerusalem, 120
Arab Revolt, 20, 21, 22, 26, 62, 90, 101–131
Arab Women's Society, 116
Asquith, Sir Herbert Henry, 46, 78
Attlee, Clement, 27, 142–144, 148–176

Baldwin, Stanley, 53–54, 72–91
Balfour, Arthur James, 1, 16, 40, 45, 77
Balfour Declaration, 1, 5, 14, 17–18, 20, 21, 22, 24, 28, 34, 35, 37, 38, 39, 42, 46, 48, 49, 53, 54, 55, 63, 68, 69, 76, 79, 81, 91, 101, 102, 164, 185
Barstow, George, 44
Basel, Zionist Conference in, 164
Beaverbrook, Lord, 48, 52–53, 76–77, 89. *See also* press barons
Bellows, Private, 119
Ben Gurion, David, 3, 162
Bevin, Ernest, 27–28, 142–176
Biltmore Declaration, 164
Black Letter, 20, 62, 101, 133. *See also* Passfield White Paper
Black Watch, 116
Bonar Law, Andrew, 23, 40, 46, 53

British Zionist Organization, 17
Brittain, Sir Harry, 46
Brook, Sir Norman, 152, 163, 167
Burr, Constable, 115, 116, 118, 120
Bushe, Sir G., 129
Byrnes, James, 148, 150, 151, 154, 157, 162

Cadogan, Sir Alex, 157
Cafferata, Raymond, 61
Campbell, Sir Ronald, 166
Carr, Lieutenant General, 116
Chancellor, Sir John, 19, 64, 75, 80, 81
Chamberlain, Austen, 71, 73, 74, 76–80
Chamberlain, Neville, 21, 53, *106*, 112, 126, 128, 129, 133, 143
Churchill White Paper, 4, 5, 19, 23, 25, 34, 39, 40, 49, 52, 55, 63, 64, 101, 133, 185, 186, 188
Churchill, Winston, 20, 35, 37, 38, 40, 41, 43, 44, 45, 47–49, 52–55
Clemenceau, Georges, 38
Cocks, Frederick, 83
collective punishment, 103, 114–117, 118
Colonial Office. *See* Middle Eastern Department; turf wars
Committee on Imperial Defence, 108, 109, 110, 126
committees of inquiry. *See* Anglo-American Committee of Inquiry; Haycraft Commission; Hope-Simpson Commission; Palin Commission; Peel Commission; Shaw Commission; UN Special Committee on Palestine; Woodhead Commission
Conference of the Principal Allied Powers, 38, 39
Congreve, General Walter Norris, 45
Coupon Election, 46

Creech Jones, Arthur, 162, 163, 164, 169, 170, 174
Cripps, Sir Richard Stafford, 147
Crosland, J. B., 44
Curzon, Lord, 40, 41, 44, 53, 124

Dalton, Sir Hugh, 143, 151, 158, 174, 175
Daily Express, 48
Daily Mail, 48, *169*
Daily Mirror, 48
Davidson, Lady Francis, 68
Deir Yassin, 10
Devonshire, Duke of, 53, 54
Dill, General, 114
discrimination, 114–117
displaced persons, 144–156, 161, 175–176
Dugdale, Baffy, 77

Eastern Department, 41, 82, 124. *See also* Foreign Office
Eden, Anthony, 108–110, 121, 123–128
el Haddad, Mohammed, 120
Egypt, 17, 21, 38, 43, 45, 51, 52, 102, 108–110, 128, 131, 132, 146, 147, 166, 173, 187. *See also* Suez Canal
Evening Standard, 62, 106, 111, 130

Foreign Office. *See* Eastern Department; turf wars
France, 14–15, 16, *16*, 18, 24, 38

Gallacher, William, 108
Geddes Committee on National Expenditure, 45, 48
Geddes, Sir Eric Campbell, 48
General Officer Commanding (GOC), 40, 122
Georges-Picot, Francois, 15, 17
Germany, 17, 21, 42, 43, 46, 90, 102–103, 109, 110, 113, 121, 123, 125, 128, 142, 144, 148
Ghazi, King of Iraq, 108
Grady, Henry F., 145, 154
Grey, Sir Edward, 14
Gurney, Sir Henry, 146

Haganah, 23, 142
Hague Convention, 114
Hague, The, 25, 79, 81

Hailsham, Lord, 25, 65, 78–81, 85
Haining, Lieutenant General R., 114, 115, 117, 122
Halifax, Lord, 22, 124, 126, 149
Hall, George, 160
Hall, James, 25
Hall, Sir Frederick, 46
Harmsworth, Sir Esmond, 47
Harrison, Earl G., 144, 148
Haycraft Commission, 19, 35, 36, 42, 49, 185, 188
Haycraft, Sir Thomas, 36, 188
Hebron Riots, 61
Henderson, Arthur, 68, 71, 80–81, 84–88, 90, 91
Higher Arab Executive, 146, 150, 167
Holocaust, 23, 26, 134, 142, 144, 148, 151, 158, 176, 189
home demolition, 114–116
Hope-Simpson Commission, 20, 63–67, 70, 75, 79, 81, 83–85, 89–91
Hope-Simpson, Sir John, 63
Hopkin, Daniel, 83
Horne, Sir Robert, 53
Howard-Bury, Colonel Charles, 82
Hussein-McMahon Correspondence, 14–15, 18, 21, 45, 103
Hussein, Sharif, 14–15, 103
Husseini, Haj Amin al, 129, 167
Husseini, Jamal al, 120

Ibn Saud, of Arabia, 108, 132
Imperial Conference, 73
independence: Egyptian, 109; Indian, 73, 142; Israeli, 2, 8; Palestinian, 6, 22, 106, 111, 128, 129, 132, 134, 142, 147, 163, 167, 175, 186–189; regional, 21, 102, 166
India, 1, 17, 38, 43, 45, 48, 49, 51, 68–69, 72–79, 82, 84, 88, 90, 91, 107–109, 118, 126, 128, 131, 132–134, 142, 146, 166, 187
India Conference, 72–79
India Office, 41, 149
India Secretary, 41, 48, 109, 118, 133
Inverchapel, Lord, 154, 155
Iraq, 20, 21, 41, 102, 108, 109, 112, 146, 166, 167. *See also* Mosul

Irgun, 23, 134, 142, 159, 174
Irwin Declaration, 73, 75, 77, 79, 82
Irwin, Lord, 73, 76, 90, 124. *See also* Lord Halifax
Islington, Lord, 49, 53
Italy, 38, 39, 110, 121, 123, 125, 131, 132

Jaffa: Arab Revolt, 103, 115, 116, 120, 121; Jaffa Riots, 18–19, 35–36, 44–55, 90–91; terrorism, 165
Jewish Agency, 23, 64, 67, 85, 142, 144, 145, 146, 148, 150, 155, 157, 158, 160–167, 173
Jewish Chronicle, 130
Jones, Sir George, 82
Joynson-Hicks, Lord, 47, 49, 53

Keith-Roach, Edward, 116, 118, 120
Kenworthy, Joseph, 69, 71, 83
King David Hotel, 27, 158, 159, 160, 162
Kitchener, Lord Horatio Herbert, 15
Kitson, Constable, 117

Lamington, Lord, 47
Lampson, Miles, 109–110, 128
Lane, Arthur, 119
League of Nations, The, 19, 26, 37, 38, 39, 43, 45, 53, 63, 64–65, 67–69, 71, 79, 80, 84, 85, 107, 112–113, 118, 120, 121, 123, 125, 132
Lees, Aubrey, 115, 121
Lloyd George, David, 17, 23, 38, 40–53, 72, 73, 75–80, 83, 88–91, 187
Lord Advocate, 70, 87, 88

Macdonald, James Ramsay, 20, 25, 61, 62, 65, 66–73, 77–80, 83, 84, 87–91, 128–129, 187
Macdonald Letter. *See* Black Letter
Macdonald, Malcolm, 22, 72, 82, 84, 87, 88, 110, 124, 126, 187
Macdonald White Paper, 4, 6, 22–23, 26, 101, 106, 110, 112, 128–133, 142–147, 149, 167–168, 186, 188
MacMichael, Sir Harold, 105, 115, 117, 122, 129
Macquistan, Frederick, 48
McMahon, Sir Henry, 14–15
Meinertzhagen, Colonel, 40, 44

Mesopotamia, 17, 38, 41, 42, 45, 51, 53. *See also* Iraq; Mosul
Middle East Department, 37, 40, 43, 44, 53, 80, 122
Miflagat Poalim Sozialistim, 36
Montagu, Sir Edwin, 41, 48, 73
Montagu-Chelmsford Act, 73
Montgomery, Major General B., 114
Morning Post, 48
Morris, Lieutenant-Colonel, 160
Morris, Sir Rhys Hopkin, 82
Morrison-Grady Proposals, 145, 147–148, 152, 154
Morrison, Sir Herbert, 117, 145
Mosul, 38, 41, 51, 52
Moyne, Lord, 146
Munich Agreement, 101, 110, 124, 128, 129, 130, 134. *See also* appeasement

Namier, Sir Lewis, 77, 87
Nebi Musa Riots, 18, 35, 43, 55
necessity, 114, 117–119
Newton, Frances, 120–121
Northcliffe, Lord, 48. *See also* press barons

Occupied Enemy Territories Administration (OETA), 40, 44
O'Connor, Major General R., 114
O'Donnell, Sir Simon, 66
Ogden, Mr, 121, 123
oil, 38, 109, 131, 165, 170
Oliphant, Sir Lancelot, 124, 127
Operation Agatha, 162
Ormsby-Gore, William, 108, 110, 112–113, 123–128
Ottoman Empire, 14, 15, 20

Page-Croft, Sir Henry, 46
Palestine Royal Commission. *See* Peel Commission
Palin Commission, 19, 35–36, 42, 47, 185, 188
Palin, Major General P. C., 19
Parkinson, Sir Cosmo, 124
partition, 6, 8, 21, 22, 27, 101–113, 123–134
Pasha, Mahmoud, 128
Pasha, Nahas, 110

Pasha, Nuri, 20, 112
Passfield, Lady, 68, 73, 74, 78, 79, 83, 85, 86, 88, 108
Passfield, Lord, 6, 20, 64, 69, 70, 80, 81, 84–86, 87
Passfield White Paper, 4, 6, 20, 23–26, 61–82, 84, 86, 88, 89–91
Peel Commission, 21, 102, 103, *104*, 105, 108, 109, 118, 123, 125, 126, 132, 144, 146, 153, 162
Peel, Lord Robert, 21, 73, 103
Permanent Mandates Commission (PMC), 67, 68, 69, 79–80, 85, 113, 118
Plumer, Sir Herbert, 19, 54
Poalei Zion, 25
Pond, Major Bertrude Augustus, 119
press barons, 47, 52, 76, 77, 89. *See also* Lord Beaverbrook; Lord Northcliffe; Lord Rothermere
proportionality, 114, 119–123. *See also* torture
provincial autonomy, 142, 144, 145, 147, 148, 152–158, 160–168, 176

Radcliffe, Major General, 44
Reading, Lord, 73
Rees, Sir J. D., 48
Rendel, George, 124, 127
Rothermere, Lord, 47, 48, 53, 76, 77, 89. *See also* press barons
Royal Ulster Regiment, 119

Samuel, Sir Herbert, 19, 24, 35, 36, 40, 48, 49, 54, 89, 130, 189
Saudi Arabia, 38, 41, 108, 109, 146
Sèvres, Treaty of, 38–39
Shaw, Sir Walter, 20, 63, 87
Shaw Commission, 20, 63–64, 67–68, 70, 72, 79, 83, 85, 91
Shertok, Moshe, 164
Shiels, Sir Drummond, 68, 69, 80, 81, 83, 86, 87
Shuckburgh, Sir John Evelyn, 80, 124, 128
Silver, Rabbi, 162, 163
Silverman, Sidney, 151
Simon Commission, 73, 78–79
Simon, Sir John, 25, 73, 78–81
Sokolow, Nahum, 17, 18

Snell, Harry (later Lord), 64, 130
special interrogation centers, 120
Spectator, The, 48
Stanley, Oliver, 145
Stein, Leonard, 85, 87
Stern Gang, 23, 134, 142, 146
St James Conference, 106, 111–112
Storrs, Sir Ronald, 14, 37, 39
Sunday Express, 48
Suez Canal, 17, 51, 107, 109, 132, 170, 173. *See also* Egypt
Sykes-Picot Agreement, 14–15, 16, *16*, 17
Sykes, Sir Mark, 15, 17, 18, 187
Syria, 10, 14, 15, 16, 21, 38, 44, 102, 146, 166

Tegart, Sir Charles, 120, 121
Times, The, 1, 25, 48, 65, 68, 77, 78, 79, 80, 81, 85
torture, 114, 119–123, *164*. *See also* proportionality
Transjordan, 19, 20, 21, 44, 51, 102, 103, *104*, 108, 146, 173
Trenchard, Sir Hugh, 44
Truman, President Harry, 26, 27, 144–145, 148–158, 160, 161, 175–176, 187
turf wars, 37, 39–42, 123–127

United Nations Special Committee on Palestine (UNSCOP), 6, 27, 142, 143, 145–148, 168, 170, 171, 172, 174
United Nations, The, 27, 143, 144, 146, 157, 164, 167–169, 170, 173

War Office, 17, 39, 40, 43–45, 51–52, 55, 114–123
Waqf, 49, 61
war crimes. *See* proportionality; torture
Wauchope, Sir Arthur, 91, 103, 122
Wavell, Major General, 114
Webb, Beatrice. *See* Lady Passfield
Webb, Sydney. *See* Lord Passfield
Wedgewood, Josiah, 69
Weizmann, Chaim, 3, 17–18, 20, 24, 25, 48, 61, 65–70, 75, 77–78, 80, 84–91
Wailing Wall, 20, 61

Whitechapel by-election, 25, 72, 84, 88, 91
white papers, *See* Churchill White Paper; Passfield White Paper; MacDonald White Paper
Williams, O. G. R., 80, 81, 124
Winterton, Lord, 133
Woodhead Commission, 21, 102, 105, 106, 110, 126, 145–147
Woodhead, Sir John, 105, 106, 125, 127
World Zionist Organization, 17, 53

Worthington-Evans, Sir Worthington Laming, 52, 53, 75

Yemen, 108, 109

Zetland, Lord, 109, 110
Zionism, 1, 2, 9, 13, 16, 17, 18, 23, 24, 26, 35, 44–46, 53, 67–69, 71, 77, 78, 84, 85, 101, 102, 105, 107, 108, 112, 113, 133, 143, 148, 149, 162, *169*, 174, 175, 185–188

CARLY BECKERMAN is Assistant Professor in the School of Government and International Affairs at Durham University.

CW01280725

SECCIÓN DE OBRAS DE POLÍTICA Y DERECHO

JUGADORES CON VETO

Traducción de
José Manuel Salazar

GEORGE TSEBELIS

JUGADORES CON VETO

Cómo funcionan las instituciones políticas

Fondo de Cultura Económica

Primera edición en inglés, 2002
Primera edición en español, 2006

Tsebelis, George
　　Jugadores con veto. Cómo funcionan las instituciones políticas / George Tsebelis ; trad. de José Manuel Salazar. — México : FCE, 2006
　　409 p. ; 23 × 17 cm — (Colec. Política y Derecho)
　　Título original Veto Players. How Political Institutions Work
　　ISBN 978-968-16-8164-7

　　1. Instituciones políticas 2. Sistemas políticos 3. Política I. Salazar, José Manuel, tr. II. Ser III. t.

LC JF51　　　　　　　　　　　　　Dewey 320.4 T844j

Disribución mundial en español

Comentarios y sugerencias:
editorial@fondodeculturaeconomica.com
www.fondodeculturaeconomica.com
Tel. (55) 5227-4672 Fax (55) 5227-4694

🄵🄲🄴 Empresa certificada ISO 9001:2000

Diseño de portada: Teresa Guzmán Romero

Título original: *Veto Players. How Political Institutions Work*

D. R. © 2002, Russell Sage Foundation
Published by Princeton University Press

D. R. © 2006, Fondo de Cultura Económica
Carretera Picacho-Ajusco, 227; 14200 México, D. F.

Se prohíbe la reproducción total o parcial de esta obra
—incluido el diseño tipográfico y de portada—,
sea cual fuere el medio, electrónico o mecánico,
sin el consentimiento por escrito del editor.

ISBN 10: 968-16-8164-9
ISBN 13: 978-968-16-8164-7

Impreso en México • *Printed in Mexico*

Para Alexander y Emily
por su indispensable apoyo

ÍNDICE GENERAL

Prefacio y agradecimientos xiii
Introducción 1
    Jugadores con veto, estabilidad política y consecuencias 2
    Razones sustantivas y metodológicas para el análisis de los jugadores con veto 6
    Una historia parcial de las ideas de este libro 11
    Visión general 13

Primera parte
TEORÍA DE LOS JUGADORES CON VETO [21]

I. *Jugadores con veto individuales* 27
    1. Jugadores con veto y estabilidad política 27
    2. Número de jugadores con veto y estabilidad política 33
    3. Reglas de cuasiequivalencia y de absorción, distancias entre jugadores con veto y estabilidad política 35
    4. Secuencia de movimientos 44
    5. Conclusiones 49

II. *Jugadores con veto colectivos* 50
    1. Introducción 51
    2. Jugadores con veto colectivos y mayorías simples 59
    3. Jugadores con veto colectivos y mayorías calificadas 67
    4. Secuencia de movimientos 72
    5. Conclusiones 79

Segunda parte
JUGADORES CON VETO Y ANÁLISIS INSTITUCIONAL [83]

III. *Regímenes: no democrático, presidencial y parlamentario* 89
    1. Los regímenes autoritario, presidencial y parlamentario en la bibliografía 90

2. La perspectiva de los jugadores con veto 100
3. Críticas a la teoría de los jugadores con veto 113
4. Conclusiones 118

IV. Gobiernos y parlamentos 120
1. Ventajas posicionales del control de la agenda 123
2. Medios institucionales de control gubernamental de la agenda 130
3. Jugadores con veto contra otros enfoques en política comparada 137
4. Conclusiones 149

V. Referéndums 151
1. Democracia directa y representativa 152
2. Instituciones que regulan los referéndums 161
3. Referéndums de jugador con veto 164
4. Las iniciativas populares 170
5. Los vetos populares 171
6. Conclusiones 173

VI. Federalismo, bicameralismo y mayorías calificadas 175
1. El federalismo 176
2. El bicameralismo 184
3. Las mayorías calificadas 191
4. Bicameralismo y mayorías calificadas combinadas 196
5. Conclusiones 201

Tercera parte
EFECTOS POLÍTICOS SOBRE LOS JUGADORES CON VETO [207]

VII. La legislación 213
1. Los datos 214
2. Jugadores con veto y legislación importante 221
3. Jugadores con veto y legislación incremental 231
4. Conclusiones 237

VIII. Políticas macroeconómicas 239
1. Acción colectiva *versus* explicación de inercia de los déficits presupuestarios 240

ÍNDICE GENERAL xi

  2. La estructura de los presupuestos 246
  3. Otros resultados macroeconómicos 258
  4. Conclusiones 262

Cuarta parte
EFECTOS SISTÉMICOS DE LOS JUGADORES CON VETO [263]

IX. *La estabilidad gubernamental* 269
  1. La bibliografía sobre estabilidad gubernamental 270
  2. Jugadores con veto y estabilidad gubernamental 276
  3. Estabilidad gubernamental y predominio ejecutivo 281
  4. Conclusiones 283

X. *El poder judicial y las burocracias* 285
  1. Cómo evitar la invalidación legislativa 286
  2. Jugadores con veto y poder judicial 289
  3. Jugadores con veto y burocracias 300
  4. Conclusiones 315

XI. *Análisis de jugadores con veto en instituciones de la Unión Europea* 316
  1. Bibliografía sobre la Unión Europea 317
  2. Procedimientos legislativos en la Unión Europea 321
  3. Análisis de jugadores con veto de los procedimientos legislativos 330
  4. La evidencia empírica 347
  5. Conclusiones 358

Conclusión 361
Bibliografía 371
Índice de gráficas 395
Índice de cuadros 399
Índice analítico 401

PREFACIO Y AGRADECIMIENTOS

Los orígenes de este libro se pueden rastrear, mucho antes del inicio de mi vida profesional en ciencias políticas, hasta mis días de estudiante en el Institut des Sciences Politiques de París, cuando leí a Duverger y Sartori acerca de partidos y sistemas de partidos, y a Riker sobre coaliciones políticas. Al igual que los dos primeros autores, me interesaba comprender cómo funcionan los sistemas políticos, y al igual que el tercero, me interesaba entenderlo de una manera sencilla.

Recuerdo haber tratado de entender las distinciones que hacían las clasificaciones oficiales: ¿cuál es la diferencia entre un sistema parlamentario y uno presidencial, además del hecho de que, en el primero, los poderes ejecutivo y legislativo pueden disolverse uno al otro mientras que en el segundo no pueden? ¿Cuál es la diferencia entre un sistema bipartidista y uno multipartidista, además de que el primero conduce a un gobierno de un solo partido y el segundo no? (De hecho, siendo originario de Grecia, país con un sistema multipartidista y gobiernos de un solo partido, yo sabía que este factor estilizado es incorrecto.) Estos temas rápidamente se complicaron más e incluso se hicieron incomprensibles cuando consideré las democracias multipartidistas como lo hizo Sartori, debido al multipartidismo "moderado" y "polarizado": no podía entender por qué menos de cinco partidos estaban asociados con un sistema moderado y más de seis con uno polarizado.

Los años pasaron y me trasladé a la Universidad Washington en St. Louis para continuar mis estudios, donde aprendí las ideas básicas acerca de cómo funciona al menos un sistema político (el Congreso de los Estados Unidos). Shepsle y Weingast me enseñaron que los políticos son racionales y tratan de alcanzar sus metas, que las instituciones son restricciones al despliegue de estrategias humanas, y que por ende el estudio de las instituciones habitadas por jugadores racionales nos lleva a entender diferentes resultados (equilibrios institucionales, según Shepsle).

Aunque estas consideraciones eran reveladoras y exactas en su descripción de las instituciones estadounidenses, no respondían a mis preguntas iniciales sobre diferentes partidos y sistemas. Buscaba respuestas que no existían en esa época, ya que el análisis de elección racional estaba completamente establecido en la política estadounidense, pero completamente subdesarrollado en política comparada (como lo descubrí el año en que entré al mercado laboral). De hecho, mis clases comparativas estaban repitiendo esencialmente a Duverger y Sartori, en vez de ir más allá de ellos.

En los inicios de mi vida profesional abordé problemas específicos que pude resolver, en vez de preguntas comparativas globales (siendo como son los requisitos de tenencia del cargo, no estaría escribiendo estas líneas en caso contrario). Las preguntas siguieron conmigo durante mucho tiempo, sin ninguna respuesta hasta que vi a Thomas Hammond presentar una versión preliminar de un ensayo que estaba escribiendo con Gary Miller, y que publicaría más tarde en la *American Political Science Review* como "The Core of the Constitution". Hammond y Miller presentaban un argumento acerca de la Constitución de los Estados Unidos: que agregar jugadores con poder de veto hace aumentar el conjunto de puntos que no pueden ser derrotados (el núcleo); que proporcionar el poder para anular tales vetos hace disminuir el tamaño del núcleo, y que el tamaño del núcleo aumenta con la distancia entre las cámaras. En cuanto escuché el argumento empecé a preguntarme si se podría generalizar a otros sistemas políticos, en particular a los parlamentarios con partidos fuertes. De ser así, tendríamos una forma general de comprender la legislación en todos los sistemas políticos.

Mi pensamiento se concentró entonces en una serie de preguntas generadas por este artículo. Primero, el análisis se presentó en un espacio de dos dimensiones. ¿Qué pasaría si aumentáramos el número de dimensiones de importancia política? ¿Continuaría existiendo el núcleo, o desaparecería? Segundo, ¿puede aplicarse el análisis a sistemas parlamentarios que por definición no tienen división de poderes? Tercero, ¿puede el modelo aplicarse a partidos políticos en vez de a congresistas en particular?

Para mis propósitos, se necesitaban respuestas afirmativas en las tres preguntas. Traté de encontrar las respuestas en 1992-1993, mientras era *National Fellow* en la Institución Hoover. En lo tocante a la pregunta 1, leí una respuesta afirmativa en un artículo, el cual sostenía que siempre y cuando dos cámaras en un sistema bicameral no tengan miembros con preferencias coincidentes, el núcleo existe en cualquier número de dimensiones. Sin embargo, quedé desilusionado en lo que consideré la muy poderosa suposición (es decir, no realista) de los autores sobre preferencias no coincidentes. Al considerar la prueba, descubrí que estaba equivocada y que el núcleo no existía salvo en condiciones extremadamente restrictivas. Este descubrimiento me llevó prácticamente a la desesperación. Me parecía (dejando a un lado las preferencias no coincidentes) que había estado muy cerca de responder a preguntas que me habían intrigado por tantos años, pero que ahora la respuesta me eludía de nuevo.

El siguiente paso en el proceso fue una serie de modelos que ya había incluido en mi libro anterior, *Bicameralism*, donde demostraba que incluso cuando el núcleo no existe, otro concepto de la teoría de la elección social, el "conjunto descubierto" (véase capítulo I), produce resultados muy similares.

Encontré una pista a las respuestas de las preguntas 2 y 3 en el artículo de 1992 de Riker, "The Justification of Bicameralism", en el cual argumenta que los partidos en gobiernos de coalición funcionan esencialmente igual que las cámaras en un sistema bicameral; en ambos casos se necesita un acuerdo para lograr un cambio del *statu quo*.

Con estos resultados en mente, escribí un artículo intentando comparar sistemas políticos al cotejar el tamaño del conjunto no revelado de cada sistema. El artículo (¡qué pena!) era demasiado técnico y poco menos que incomprensible. Miriam Golden, quien suele ser una muy tolerante lectora de mi trabajo, me hizo entender muy bien esos problemas: "¿Por qué haces esto? ¿Qué me dice acerca del mundo?" La claridad de sus palabras me hizo entender que necesitaba emprender otro plan de acción para obtener los resultados pertinentes.

Decidí considerar el conjunto ganador del *statu quo* (véase capítulo I) en vez del conjunto descubierto, y esto me dio una asombrosa simplificación, que mostró a los lectores la pertinencia de mi análisis. Redactar de nuevo el ensayo sobre la base de jugadores con veto y conjunto ganador del *statu quo* no cambió los resultados sustantivos, pero los hizo mucho más comprensibles y útiles. El ensayo era largo, así que después de averiguar qué revista aceptaría un artículo más largo de lo habitual, lo presenté al *British Journal of Political Science*. Fue aceptado de inmediato, publicado en 1995, y recibió el premio Luebbert como el mejor artículo sobre política comparada de 1996.

Al mismo tiempo, participaba en un grupo organizado por Herbert Doering que estudiaba las legislaturas de Europa Occidental. Doering me prometió que si escribía un artículo sobre jugadores con veto para el volumen editado por él, se aseguraría de que se me proporcionaran los datos utilizables sobre legislación del proyecto para poner a prueba el entramado de los jugadores con veto. Su propuesta dio lugar a un segundo artículo sobre jugadores con veto, así como a un conjunto de datos que sometían a prueba el argumento principal propuesto por mí: que muchos jugadores con veto hacen que los cambios políticos importantes sean difíciles o imposibles. Doering tuvo la brillante idea de identificar las leyes que producen "cambios importantes", empleando una enciclopedia de derecho laboral escrita para abogados laboralistas internacionales que practican la jurisprudencia en diferentes países y necesitan conocer los ejemplos importantes de legislación en esas naciones. La prueba corroboró la teoría y fue publicada en la *American Political Science Review* en 1999; obtuvo el segundo lugar para el premio Luebbert como el mejor artículo sobre política comparada en 2000.

Mientras trabajaba en estos temas, me dediqué constantemente a extender la teoría de los jugadores con veto, ya fuera por mi cuenta o junto con otros investigadores. Escribí un artículo para un número especial de *Governance*, dedicado a las instituciones políticas. En ese artículo calculé un eslabón perdido: qué sucede con los resultados políticos cuando los jugadores con veto colectivos deciden por mayorías calificadas y no por mayorías simples; además, describí varias de las consecuencias de la estabilidad política. Demostré que la estabilidad política afecta la inestabilidad del gobierno en sistemas parlamentarios, así como el papel de los jueces y burócratas independientemente del régimen político. Más tarde, leyendo la bibliografía sobre burocracias y poder judicial, descubrí que hay una diferencia entre los indicadores que miden la independencia institucional del poder judicial y de las burocracias del sistema político y la independencia conductual de los mismos actores. Mi interpretación fue que unas expectativas aparentemente contradictorias de independencia judicial y burocrática pueden ser compatibles después de todo. Cuando trabajé con Simon Hug analicé las consecuencias de los jugadores con veto sobre los referéndums; al hacerlo con Eric Chang, descubrí otra indicación de estabilidad política: la estructura de los presupuestos en los países de la OCDE cambia más lentamente cuando el gobierno está compuesto por muchos jugadores con veto.

Mis resultados sobre los jugadores con veto también quedaron confirmados por mi labor sobre la Unión Europea (UE), donde descubrí la importancia no sólo de los actores que pueden vetar, sino también de los actores que pueden determinar la agenda. No hubo nada nuevo en cuanto a la importancia del argumento del establecimiento de agenda (McKelvey había dicho todo lo que había que decir en su artículo de 1976), excepto que las instituciones europeas eran muy complicadas y resultaba difícil ver cómo interactuaban los diferentes actores en una situación de dimensiones múltiples. Habiendo escrito un artículo sobre ese tema, procedí a identificar las diferencias introducidas consistentemente por tratados europeos en periodos de tres años a partir de 1987 hasta la actualidad. He publicado alrededor de docena y media de artículos sobre el tema de las instituciones en la Unión Europea, algunos por mi cuenta, otros con mis estudiantes, y algunos con Geoff Garrett, tratando de ir más allá de la declaración de que las instituciones de la UE son complicadas. Gran parte de este trabajo creó polémicas, y los resultados se presentan de forma resumida en un capítulo de este libro. La importancia de la Unión Europea en la estructura de ideas de los jugadores con veto, que se presenta en este libro, consiste en que sus instituciones son demasiado complicadas y demasiado variables para ser analizadas de alguna otra manera.

Deseo agradecer a los editores del *British Journal of Political Science* y de la *American Political Science Review*, así como a Blackwell Publishing, editores de *Governance*, el permitirme reproducir algunas de las ideas incluidas en los artículos originales. Aunque este libro tuvo un periodo de gestación demasiado largo, fui muy afortunado al recibir los útiles consejos de personas extremadamente confiables. Deseo dar las gracias a Barry Ames, Kathy Bawn, Lisa Blaydes, Shaun Bowler, Eric Chang, William Clark, Herbert Doering, Jeffrey Frieden, Geoffrey Garrett, Barbara Geddes, Miriam Golden, Mark Hallerberg, Simon Hug, Macartan Humphreys, Anastassios Kalandrakis, William Keech, Thomas König, Amie Kreppel, Gianfranco Pasquino, Ronald Rogowski, Kaare Strom, Daniel Treisman, Jim Vreeland y Paul Warwick por haber leído el manuscrito, en su totalidad o en parte, y por sus extensos comentarios, que a veces dieron lugar a largas discusiones y a revisiones aún más extensas.

Deseo agradecer a la Russell Sage Foundation el proporcionarme una beca que hizo posible el trabajo intensivo en el proyecto. Eric Wanner y su equipo (en especial Liz McDaniel, que editó todo el manuscrito) hicieron que mi vida allí fuera muy agradable. ¡Tan sólo desearía que fueran posibles muchas repeticiones! (De hecho, me esforcé mucho, aunque en vano, por convencer a Eric de revocar la vigésima segunda enmienda local y considerar segundas solicitudes.) Disfruté cada minuto pasado en Nueva York, y la emoción de vivir en la "capital mundial del milenio" mejoró mi productividad (si no es que mi producción).

Chuck Myers, de la Princeton University Press, leyó versiones sucesivas del manuscrito y me hizo muchas sugerencias útiles. Fue de gran ayuda y confianza durante todo el proceso de publicación. Gracias, como siempre, a Wolfgang Amadeus Mozart por proporcionarme un ambiente estimulante mientras trabajaba. Finalmente (para dejar al último la culminación ingeniosa), quiero agradecer a mis hijos, Alexander y Emily, el haberme brindado el respaldo emocional necesario para terminar este extenso proyecto.

INTRODUCCIÓN

Este libro trata sobre instituciones políticas: cómo pensamos acerca de ellas de manera constante en diversos países; cómo afectan las medidas políticas, y qué efecto tienen sobre otras características importantes de un sistema político, tales como la estabilidad de los gobiernos y el papel del poder judicial y de las burocracias. Mi meta no es hacer una declaración acerca de cuáles instituciones son mejores, sino identificar las dimensiones a lo largo de las cuales es distinta la toma de decisiones en diferentes formas de gobierno, y estudiar los efectos de esas diferencias.

La mayor parte de la bibliografía sobre instituciones políticas se vale de un solo criterio para identificar las principales características de una forma de gobierno. Por ejemplo, los regímenes políticos se dividen en presidenciales y parlamentarios, las legislaturas en unicamerales y bicamerales, los sistemas electorales en de mayoría o pluralidad y en proporcionales, los partidos en fuertes y débiles, los sistemas de partido en bipartidistas y multipartidistas. Las relaciones entre todas estas categorías están insuficientemente desarrolladas. Por ejemplo, ¿cómo vamos a comparar a los Estados Unidos, régimen bicameral presidencial con dos partidos débiles, con Dinamarca, régimen unicameral parlamentario con muchos partidos fuertes? ¿Qué tipos de interacciones producen las combinaciones de diferentes regímenes, legislaturas, partidos y sistemas de partido?

Observamos tales interacciones en el caso de la Unión Europea, que toma decisiones legislativas con el consenso de dos o tres actores (el Consejo de Ministros, el Parlamento Europeo y, la mayor parte del tiempo, la Comisión Europea). Cada uno de estos actores decide mediante una regla distinta de toma de decisiones. Desde el Tratado de Niza de 2001, el Consejo de Ministros emplea una mayoría triple para tomar decisiones: una mayoría calificada de los votos importantes de sus miembros; una mayoría de los miembros de la UE, y una mayoría calificada de la población (62%). El Parlamento Europeo decide por mayoría absoluta (la cual, como se verá, es *de facto* una mayoría calificada). La Comisión Europea decide por mayoría simple. El Consejo de Ministros es nombrado por los países miembros, el Parlamento Europeo es elegido por los pueblos de Europa, y la Comisión Europea es nombrada por los países miembros y aprobada por el Parlamento Europeo. Este sistema político no es un régimen presidencial ni parlamentario. A veces es unicameral, a veces es bicameral, y en otras ocasiones tricameral y, además, una de sus cámaras decide de acuerdo con varios criterios de mayoría calificada. Ni siquiera intentaré comenzar una descripción del sistema de partidos, que se compone de varias ideologías y un número todavía mayor de nacionalidades. Así, la Unión Europea es una excepción clara a todas las clasificaciones tradicionales. De hecho, se la describe a menudo en la bibliografía pertinente como *sui generis;* sin embargo, las instituciones europeas se pueden analizar muy bien y con gran exactitud sobre la base de la teoría que se presenta en esta obra.

Este libro le permitirá al lector estudiar y analizar sistemas políticos cualquiera que sea su nivel de complejidad institucional. Y lo hará de una manera *consecuente* así como *consistente*. "Consecuente" significa que iniciaremos nuestro análisis a partir de las consecuencias, y trabajaremos retrocediendo hacia las instituciones que las producen. "Consistente" significa que se aplicarán los mismos argumentos a diferentes países en distintos niveles de análisis a lo largo de este libro. El objetivo consiste en formar una teoría del análisis institucional, someterla a múltiples pruebas y, como resultado, tener un alto nivel de confianza al corroborarla en varias situaciones distintas.

Jugadores con veto, estabilidad política y consecuencias

En breves palabras, el argumento fundamental de este libro es el siguiente: con el propósito de cambiar políticas —o, como diremos de aquí en adelante, para cambiar el *statu quo* (legislativo)—, un cierto número de actores individuales o colectivos tiene que estar de acuerdo en el cambio propuesto. Llamaré *jugadores con veto* a tales actores. Los jugadores con veto son especificados en un país por la constitución (el presidente, la Cámara y el Senado en los Estados Unidos) o por el sistema político (los diferentes partidos que son miembros de una coalición gubernamental en Europa Occidental). A estos dos tipos distintos los denomino jugadores con veto *institucionales* y *partidarios,* respectivamente. Ofrezco las reglas para identificar a los jugadores con veto en cada sistema político. De acuerdo con estas reglas, cada sistema político tiene una configuración de jugadores con veto (un cierto número de jugadores con veto, con distancias ideológicas específicas entre ellos, y una cierta cohesión cada uno). Todas estas características afectan el conjunto de resultados que pueden remplazar al *statu quo* (el *conjunto ganador* del *statu quo*, como llamaremos al conjunto de estos puntos). El tamaño del conjunto ganador del *statu quo* tiene consecuencias específicas sobre la creación de las política: unas desviaciones importantes del *statu quo* son imposibles cuando el conjunto ganador es pequeño —es decir, cuando los jugadores con veto son numerosos—; cuando tienen distancias ideológicas importantes entre ellos y cuando poseen cohesión interna. Denominaré *estabilidad política* a esta imposibilidad de desviaciones importantes del *statu quo*.

Además, las instituciones políticas ordenan a los jugadores con veto en secuencias específicas a fin de tomar decisiones políticas. Los jugadores con veto específicos que presentan propuestas de "tómalo o déjalo" a los otros jugadores con veto tienen un control importante sobre las políticas que remplazan al *statu quo*. A estos jugadores con veto les llamo *establecedores de agenda*, los cuales tienen que hacer propuestas aceptables a los otros jugadores con veto (de otro modo las propuestas serán rechazadas y el *statu quo* se conservará). De hecho, seleccionarán entre los resultados factibles aquél que prefieran. Como consecuencia, los poderes que establecen de agenda quedan relacionados inversamente con la estabilidad política. Cuanto mayor sea la estabilidad política (es decir, cuanto más pequeño sea el conjunto de resultados que puedan remplazar al *statu quo*), más pequeño será el papel del establecimiento de agenda. En el caso límite, en que no es posible el cambio desde el *statu quo*, no importa quién controle la agenda.

Si conocemos las preferencias de los jugadores con veto, la posición del *statu quo* y la identidad del establecedor de la agenda (la secuencia de movimientos de los diferentes actores), podremos vaticinar muy bien el resultado del proceso de creación de la política.[1] Sin embargo, con gran frecuencia el establecedor de agenda será un actor colectivo (en cuyo caso las preferencias no están bien definidas)[2] o no conoceremos su ubicación exacta. Por ejemplo, veremos (en el capítulo III) que en sistemas parlamentarios el gobierno establece la agenda, pero no sabemos exactamente cómo; de modo similar, en sistemas presidenciales el establecimiento de agenda corre a cargo de la legislatura, pero, de nueva cuenta, no lograremos identificar las preferencias exactas del comité de consulta que establece las propuestas. En todos estos casos, la única predicción posible se basaría en la estabilidad política, que no requiere definir tanta información.

[1] Véase el capítulo XI.
[2] En el capítulo II defino el concepto de preferencias "cíclicas" y demuestro que los actores colectivos que deciden según el dominio de la mayoría tienen tales preferencias.

La estabilidad política afecta una serie de características estructurales de un sistema político. La dificultad que un gobierno encuentra en su intento por cambiar el *statu quo* puede conducir a su renuncia y a su remplazo en un sistema parlamentario. Esto significa que la estabilidad política conducirá a la inestabilidad del gobierno, como se indica en la gráfica 1. De modo similar, en un sistema presidencial, la imposibilidad de que el sistema político resuelva problemas puede conducir a su remplazo por un régimen militar ("inestabilidad del régimen" en la gráfica 1). Finalmente, la imposibilidad de cambiar el *statu quo* legislativo puede llevar a los burócratas y a los jueces a ser más activos e independientes del sistema político. Ofreceré argumentos teóricos y pruebas empíricas de estas afirmaciones en los capítulos siguientes. La gráfica 1 nos da una descripción visual de los vínculos causales en el argumento.

Las implicaciones de mi argumento, a diferencia de aquellas más frecuentes en la bibliografía especializada, se pueden bosquejar en el ejemplo siguiente. Consideremos cuatro países: el Reino Unido, los Estados Unidos,

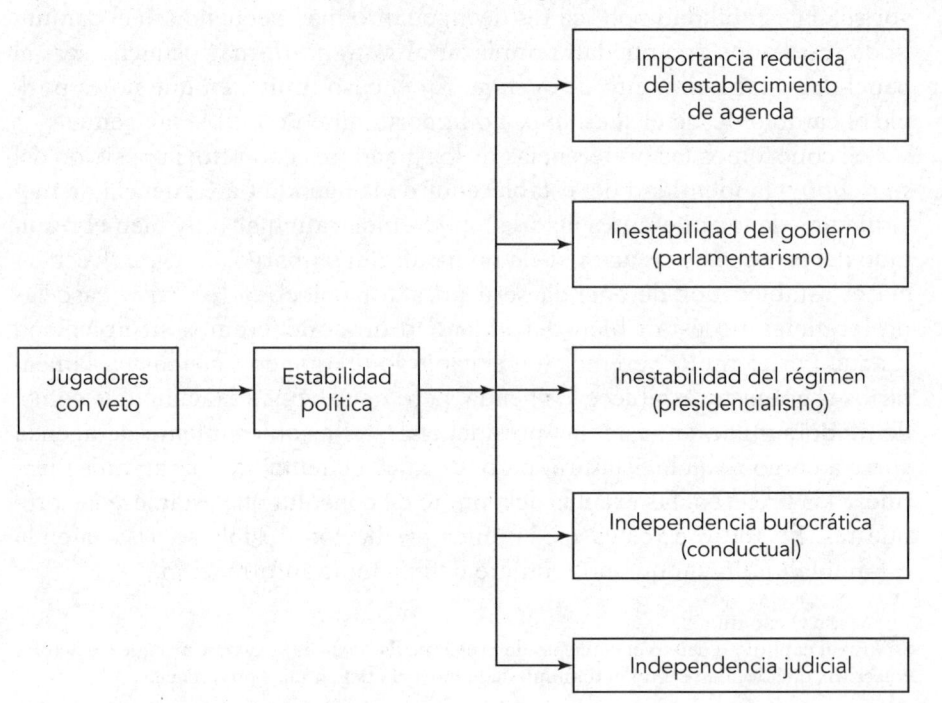

GRÁFICA 1. *Efectos de muchos jugadores con veto.*

Italia y Grecia. Si vemos las teorías existentes en política comparada, estas naciones se agrupan de diferentes maneras. Para los defensores del análisis sobre la base de regímenes distintos (Linz, 1994; Horowitz, 1996), Estados Unidos es el único régimen presidencial, mientras que los otros tres son parlamentarios. Para los patrocinadores de los análisis más tradicionales sobre la base de sistemas de partido, los Estados Unidos y el Reino Unido quedan agrupados como sistemas bipartidistas, mientras que Italia y Grecia son multipartidistas (Duverger, 1954; Sartori, 1976). Los enfoques culturales (Almond y Verba, 1963) también pondrían en el mismo grupo a los sistemas anglosajones, en contraposición a los países de Europa continental. El enfoque de consociacionalismo de Lijphart (1999) considera al Reino Unido como un país mayoritario, a Italia y Grecia como países de consenso y a los Estados Unidos en algún punto intermedio.[3]

En este libro, Italia y los Estados Unidos son países con muchos jugadores con veto, y como tales tendrán alta estabilidad política, mientras que Grecia y el Reino Unido tendrán un solo jugador con veto, y por ende acaso tengan gran inestabilidad política.[4] Obsérvese que Italia y los Estados Unidos no comparten ninguna característica según las clasificaciones tradicionales (ni el tipo de régimen ni el sistema de partidos sin mencionar la cultura o el consociacionalismo). Sin embargo, la teoría de los jugadores con veto espera encontrar características similares en ambos países. Como resultado de la estabilidad política o de la falta de ésta, la inestabilidad gubernamental será mayor en Italia y más baja en el Reino Unido y en Grecia; y el papel del poder judicial y de la burocracia será mucho más importante en los Estados Unidos y en Italia que en el Reino Unido y en Grecia. Algunas de estas expectativas quedarán comprobadas mediante los análisis de los datos en este libro. En la gráfica 2 se presenta la forma en que la teoría de los jugadores con veto abarca las clasificaciones existentes. Ni los regímenes ni los sistemas de partido por sí solos captan las características que capta la teoría de los jugadores con veto. De hecho, el argumento principal de este libro es que cada configuración de variables tradicionales se traza sobre una constelación específica de jugadores con veto, de modo que es posible que dos países sean diferentes en todas las variables tradicionales (regímenes, sistemas de partidos, sistemas electorales, tipo de legislatura,

---

[3] Por una parte, Estados Unidos tiene dos partidos; por otro, es un sistema federal.

[4] Obsérvese la asimetría en la expresión: los países con muchos jugadores con veto *tendrán* estabilidad política, mientras que aquellos con un jugador con veto *pueden* tener inestabilidad. Explico las razones de esta diferencia en el capítulo I.

GRÁFICA 2. *Diferencias en clasificaciones entre regímenes, sistemas de partido y jugadores con veto.*

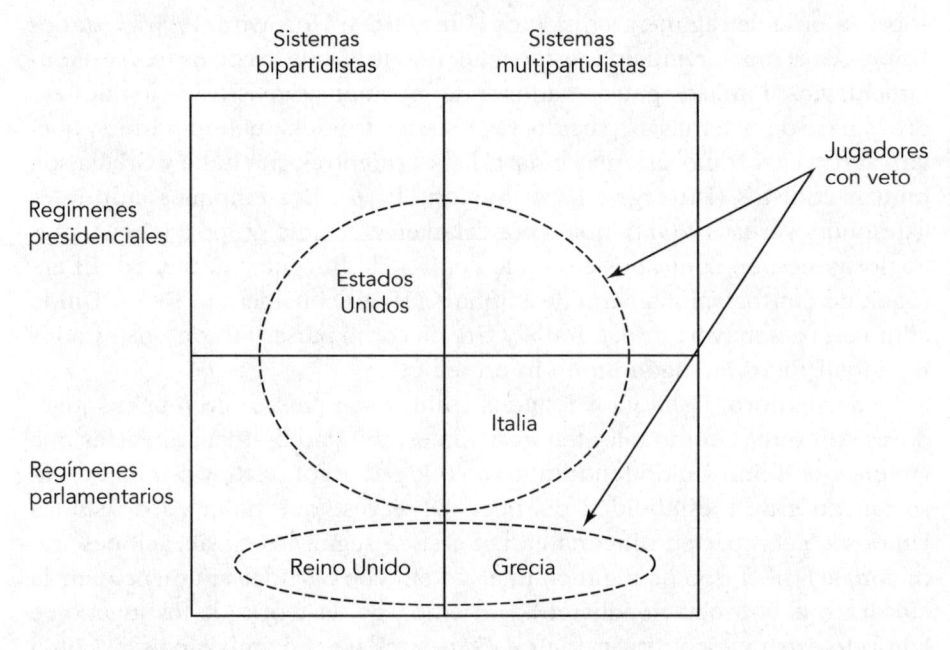

tipos de partidos) y aun así tengan constelaciones iguales o similares de jugadores con veto. Es la constelación de jugadores con veto la que mejor capta la estabilidad política, y es la estabilidad política la que afecta una serie de otras características políticas e institucionales.

En las páginas siguientes se examinarán tanto las causas como los efectos de la estabilidad política. Consideraremos la estabilidad política como una variable tanto dependiente como independiente. Identificaré las constelaciones de jugadores con veto que la causan, y consideraré su impacto sobre otras características tales como estabilidad gubernamental, burocracias y judicatura.

Razones sustantivas y metodológicas para el análisis de los jugadores con veto

¿Por qué empiezo desde las políticas y no desde otros puntos posibles, tales como instituciones, cultura política, características conductuales o normas? Incluso si empezamos a partir de las políticas, ¿por qué concentrarnos en la estabilidad política en vez de la dirección de los resultados de las políticas? Por último, una pregunta metodológica importante: ¿por qué empleo el conjunto ganador del *statu quo* en vez del concepto común de equilibrio? ¿Y cómo afecta mi análisis esta sustitución de los equilibrios por el conjunto ganador del *statu quo*?

Comienzo mi análisis a partir de la creación de políticas (o, más exactamente, a partir de la legislación y la creación de leyes) debido a que las medidas políticas son el principal resultado de un sistema político. El pueblo participa en un sistema político con el fin de promover los resultados (las políticas) que prefiera. Como resultado, la creación de políticas es importante para los actores políticos (partidos o representantes individuales), ya sea que estos actores tengan preferencias directas sobre las políticas (como supone De Swaan, 1973) o si sólo se preocupan por la reelección (esta es la suposición simplificadora de Down, 1957), o si están motivados ideológicamente (para seguir el enfoque de Bawn, 1999a).

Los actores políticos proponen diferentes medidas y son elegidos sobre la base de las políticas que recomienden. Los políticos o los partidos son sustituidos en su cargo cuando las políticas que proponen conducen a resultados indeseables, o cuando no aplican las medidas que prometieron antes de la elección. Obviamente, las declaraciones anteriores son simplificaciones, pero su idea es que el sistema político genera preferencias políticas y asegura que se implanten estas preferencias. No quiero decir con esto que otras características como culturas, ideologías, normas o instituciones no sean objetos legítimos de estudio *per se*. Lo que afirmo es que estamos mejor sintonizados con un sistema político si empezamos nuestro estudio a partir de las políticas que se apliquen, y entonces trabajamos hacia atrás para descubrir cómo estas políticas derrotaron a las alternativas. ¿Cuáles son las preferencias que llevaron a estos resultados, y cómo el sistema político seleccionó ciertas preferencias en lugar de otras?

Pero incluso si nos concentramos en las medidas políticas como base de la empresa intelectual, ¿por qué concentrarnos en la "estabilidad política", la imposibilidad de cambiar significativamente el *statu quo* en vez de ser más ambiciosos y estudiar la dirección del cambio? Hay tres razones para mi elección.

Primero, la estabilidad política afecta una serie de otras características del sistema político, incluyendo características institucionales, como se indica en la gráfica 1. Segundo, es una variable esencial en la bibliografía sobre el tema. Los politólogos a menudo se interesan en el carácter decisivo de un sistema político, en su capacidad de resolver problemas cuando se presenten. Por ejemplo, en un análisis profundo de los efectos de las instituciones políticas, Weaver y Rockman (1993: 6) establecen una distinción entre

> diez diferentes capacidades que todos los gobiernos necesitan para *establecer y mantener prioridades* entre las numerosas demandas en conflicto que se les hacen de modo que no sean sobrepasados ni caigan en bancarrota; para *destinar recursos* donde sean más efectivos; para *innovar* cuando las políticas antiguas hayan fracasado; para *coordinar objetivos en conflicto* en un todo coherente; para ser capaces de *imponer* pérdidas a grupos poderosos; para *representar intereses difusos y no organizados* además de otros concentrados y bien organizados; para *asegurar la implantación efectiva* de las políticas gubernamentales una vez que hayan sido aprobadas; para *asegurar la estabilidad política* de modo que las políticas tengan tiempo de funcionar; para *hacer y mantener compromisos internacionales* en los campos del comercio y la defensa nacional para asegurar su bienestar a largo plazo; y, por encima de todo, para *resolver las divisiones políticas* a fin de asegurar que la sociedad no degenere en guerra civil.

Aunque Weaver y Rockman se interesan en las capacidades de los gobiernos, un gran volumen de la bibliografía sobre economía, empezando con Kydland y Prescott (1977), se ocupa del compromiso creíble del gobierno de *no* interferir en la economía. Barry Weingast (1995) lleva el argumento un paso más allá e intenta diseñar instituciones que producirían tal compromiso creíble. Propone "federalismo de conservación del mercado", un sistema que combina frenos y equilibrios (poderes complementarios o equilibrados entre las ramas de un gobierno) que impiden la interferencia del gobierno en la economía, con competencia económica entre las unidades para asegurar el crecimiento. De manera similar, Witold Henisz (2000a, 2000b) utiliza una serie de datos de largo tiempo para descubrir que las tasas de crecimiento y de inversión son más altas cuando el sistema político no puede cambiar las reglas de juego de la economía.

Bruce Ackerman (2000) adopta una posición intermedia en un artículo profundo y estimulante. Sugiere que la configuración institucional óptima no es aquella con muchos jugadores con veto, como es el caso del sistema estadounidense, o con pocos, como sucede en el Reino Unido. En vez de ello, defiende el caso intermedio de un sistema parlamentario con un senado que no puede vetar todo el tiempo, y con la posibilidad de referéndums que sean convocados por un gobierno y realizados por otro a fin de difuminar el poder del gobierno para establecer la agenda.

Todos estos autores consideran la flexibilidad o la estabilidad de la política como una variable importante. Algunos académicos consideran la flexibilidad como una característica deseable (a fin de resolver más pronto los problemas); otros señalan que intervenciones frecuentes pueden empeorar la situación.

Adopto una posición más agnóstica con respecto a la estabilidad política. Es razonable suponer que aquellos a quienes les desagrada el *statu quo* preferirán un sistema político con capacidad para hacer cambios rápidamente, mientras que los defensores del *statu quo* preferirán un sistema que produzca estabilidad política. No está claro que exista un consenso (ni que sea posible) acerca de si es deseable un ritmo más rápido o más lento de respuesta institucional. La firmeza para producir cambio político es buena cuando el *statu quo* es indeseable (ya sea porque una pequeña minoría domina el gobierno, como el *ancien régime* en Francia o más recientemente Sudáfrica), o porque una crisis exógena desequilibra un proceso deseable (crisis petrolera y crecimiento en la década de 1970). El compromiso de no interferencia puede ser preferible cuando el *statu quo* es deseable (como cuando se establecen derechos civiles), o si una crisis exógena es beneficiosa (como un aumento en el precio del petróleo en una economía productora de crudo). Pero ya sea que la estabilidad política resulte deseable o indeseable, la bibliografía anterior indica que es importante estudiar en qué condiciones se obtiene, lo cual es una meta de este libro.

La tercera razón de enfocar la estabilidad política y no la dirección del cambio es que mi argumento se concentra en instituciones y sus efectos. Aunque algunos investigadores tratan de concentrarse en las implicaciones políticas específicas de ciertas instituciones, creo que los resultados específicos son el resultado de las instituciones dominantes y de las preferencias de los actores implicados. En otras palabras, las instituciones son como conchas, y los resultados específicos que producen dependen de los actores que las ocupen.[5]

[5] Como ejemplo de mi argumento considérese el caso siguiente, desarrollado en el capítulo VIII: una parte importante de la bibliografía sobre economía política argumenta que los gobiernos divididos (que en mi vocabulario significan múltiples jugadores con veto) causan déficits presupuestarios, o inflación más alta. En contraste, mi argumento es que múltiples jugadores con veto causan estabilidad política, es decir, producen déficits altos si el país está acostumbrado a déficits altos (Italia), pero producen déficits bajos si el país está familiarizado con déficits bajos (Suiza o Alemania).

Estas son las tres razones por las cuales usaré la estabilidad política como mi variable principal. Sin embargo, habrá ocasiones cuando sea asequible la información acerca de la identidad y preferencias del establecedor de la agenda, lo cual permitirá la formación de expectativas mucho más exactas acerca de los resultados políticos. El lector verá en el capítulo XI que la bibliografía institucional sobre la Unión Europea ha establecido y alcanzado tales metas.

En cuanto a la variable principal de este libro, la estabilidad política, veremos que es definida por el tamaño del conjunto ganador del *statu quo*.[6] ¿Por qué empleo este concepto en vez de la noción ampliamente aceptada de equilibrio (Nash)? La falta de análisis del equilibrio se debe al hecho de que en los espacios políticos multidimensionales raras veces existen equilibrios. De hecho, aunque en una sola dimensión se garantiza la existencia de equilibrios de modelos de votación, Plot (1967) ha demostrado que en dimensiones múltiples las condiciones para la existencia de equilibrio son extremadamente restrictivas. McKelvey (1976) y Schofield (1977) continuaron con el estudio demostrando que en la ausencia de equilibrio cualquier resultado es posible.

Por otro lado, el conjunto ganador del *statu quo* tiene la cualidad autoimpuesta de que es la intersección de las restricciones que cada participante impone al conjunto de resultados. Ningún jugador racional si pudiese elegir aceptaría cualquier resultado que no prefiriera sobre el *statu quo*.[7]

---

[6] La expresión más apropiada sería "conjunto ganador del resultado por *default*". Sin embargo, casi todo el tiempo la solución por *default* es el *statu quo*. Rasch (2000) ha identificado los países donde esta disposición es parte de las reglas formales. Incluso en casos donde no hay tal regla formal, los votos con que compara el *statu quo* con la alternativa naciente se toman en el parlamento. Por ejemplo, en el estudio que hizo Herbert Doering de 18 países de Europa Occidental en el periodo de 1981 a 1991, de 541 proyectos de ley, un voto final contra el *statu quo* se había tomado 73% de las veces (Doering, *http://www.uni-postdam.de/u/ls_vergleich/research*). En todos estos casos, el resultado final está, por definición, dentro del conjunto ganador del *statu quo*. En los casos donde no se haga una votación final comparando la alternativa con el *statu quo*, la alternativa por *default* queda especificada, ya sea por reglas o por un voto en el parlamento. Si una mayoría en el parlamento puede prever un resultado que no prefiere sobre el *statu quo*, podrá dar pasos para hacer abortar todo el proceso de votación. Por lo tanto, de aquí en adelante empleo la expresión "conjunto ganador del *statu quo*" en vez de "conjunto ganador de la alternativa por *default*".

[7] Aquí excluyo los casos en que un jugador recibe retribuciones específicas por hacer eso. Por ejemplo, puede recibir promesas de que en el futuro serán decisivas sus preferencias sobre otro asunto. No afirmo que tales casos sean imposibles, pero sí sostengo que si se incluyen, provocan que casi todos los resultados posibles sean aceptables sobre la base de tal convenio de ayuda mutua, y hacen imposible cualquier análisis sistemático.

En este sentido, mi análisis es mucho más general que ningún otro modelo (como negociación, jurisdicciones exclusivas de ministros, o primer ministro) que introduzca una serie de restricciones adicionales a fin de producir un solo resultado de equilibrio.[8]

Una historia parcial de las ideas de este libro

Algunos de los argumentos de este libro ya se han planteado incluso hace siglos. Por ejemplo, dejando a un lado la terminología, la importancia de los jugadores con veto se puede encontrar en la obra de Madison y de Montesquieu. Según Montesquieu (1977: 210-11): "El cuerpo legislativo se compone de dos partes, una controla a la otra, por el privilegio mutuo de negarse. [...] Basta para mi propósito observar que [la libertad] se establece por sus leyes". Para Madison, la distinción entre las dos cámaras se vuelve más activa mientras mayores diferencias tengan cada una de ellas. En tales casos, "la improbabilidad de combinaciones siniestras estará en proporción con la disimilitud de los dos cuerpos" *(El Federalista*, núm. 62). La relación entre la longevidad del gobierno y los jugadores con veto se puede encontrar en la obra de A. Lawrence Lowell (1896: 73-74). Él identificó un "axioma en política" como el hecho de que "cuanto mayor sea el número de grupos discordantes que formen la mayoría, más difícil será la tarea de complacerlos a todos, y más débil e inestable será la posición del gabinete".

Más recientemente, la bibliografía sobre "gobiernos divididos" ha presentado argumentos acerca de múltiples jugadores con veto y estabilidad política (Fiorina, 1992; Hammond y Miller, 1987). La bibliografía sobre burocracias ha conectado la producción legislativa con la independencia burocrática (por ejemplo, McCubbins, Noll y Weingast, 1987, 1989; Hammond y Knott, 1996). La bibliografía sobre la independencia judicial ha conectado decisiones judiciales con la capacidad del cuerpo legislativo para invalidarlas (Gely y Spiller, 1990; Ferejohn y Weingast, 1992a, 1992b; Cooter y Ginsburg, 1996). McKelvey (1976) fue el primero en introducir el papel del establecedor de agenda en los juegos de votación multidimensionales y en demostrar que un establecedor de agenda puede tener poderes cuasidictatoriales.

[8] Huber y McCarty (2001) han producido un modelo con resultados considerablemente distintos dependiendo de si el primer ministro puede introducir directamente la pregunta de confianza, o si tiene que obtener antes la aprobación del gobierno.

12 INTRODUCCIÓN

Lo más lejos que me he remontado rastreando las ideas contenidas en este libro fue a una declaración acerca de la importancia del establecimiento de agenda en comparación con el poder de veto que aparece en la *Historia romana*, de Tito Livio (6: 37), escrita hace más de dos mil años:

> Los tribunos de la plebe eran ahora objeto de desdén, dado que su poder se resquebrajaba por su propio veto. No podía haber una administración imparcial o justa mientras el poder ejecutivo estuviera en manos del otro partido, mientras ellos sólo tuvieran el derecho de protestar mediante su veto; ni lograría la plebe tener jamás una participación igual en el gobierno hasta que la autoridad del ejecutivo se les abriera de par en par.

En cuanto a la importancia de la competencia para el establecimiento de la agenda (un tema distinto que se examinará en el capítulo III), recuerdo una cita de Tucídides que podría considerarse como la primera expresión de ideas downsianas en la bibliografía sobre ciencias políticas:

> Pericles en verdad, por su rango, capacidad y conocida integridad, fue habilitado para ejercer un dominio independiente sobre la multitud, es decir, para conducirla en vez de ser conducido por ella; ya que como nunca buscó poder por medios inapropiados, nunca se sintió obligado a halagarla sino que, por el contrario, disfrutaba de una estima tan grande que podía atreverse a encolerizarla por contradicción. Cuandoquiera que los veía a todos exaltados de manera irrazonable e insolente, con una palabra los reducía a la alarma; por otro lado, si caían víctimas del pánico, al punto les haría recobrar la confianza. En suma, *lo que era nominalmente una democracia, en sus manos se convirtió en gobierno por el primer ciudadano*. Con sus sucesores fue diferente. *Más nivelados unos con otros, y cada uno aferrándose a la supremacía, terminaron por comprometer hasta la dirección de los asuntos públicos a los caprichos de la multitud.*[9]

Finalmente, después de que terminé el capítulo V, en que arguyo que la posibilidad de referéndum introduce a un jugador adicional con veto (el "votante medio"), y como resultado los referéndums provocan que sea más difícil

---

[9] Tucídides, *Historias*, libro II, 65.8-10; cursivas agregadas. Agradezco a Xenophon Yataganas haberme recordado la cita, así como indicarme la referencia. Tucídides analiza aquí la capacidad de un jefe para convencer al pueblo (como un presidente "estableciendo la agenda"). En el capítulo III hago una distinción entre esta capacidad y la característica institucional más precisa de cuál jugador con veto hace una propuesta a quién.

cambiar el *statu quo* y llevar los resultados más cerca de las posiciones de la media, descubrí que esta conclusión o variación de ella (dependiendo del significado de las palabras) puede tener al menos un siglo de antigüedad. Albert Venn Dicey (1890: 507) decía que el referéndum "es al mismo tiempo democrático y conservador".[10]

Es probable que la mayoría de las ideas presentadas en este libro no sean originales; algunas han sido propuestas hace siglos, incluso milenios. El valor reside en la síntesis del argumento. Esto significa que mi tarea en este libro es explicar por qué las propuestas que presento encajan unas con otras, y entonces tratar de corroborar las expectativas con pruebas reales o referencias a los análisis empíricos producidos por otros investigadores. Dado que las proposiciones presentadas en este libro son parte del cuadro global, la confianza o la incredibilidad de cualquiera de ellas habrá de fortalecer o minar la confianza en todas las demás.

Visión general

Este libro está organizado deductivamente. Empiezo con principios sencillos, obtengo sus implicaciones (primera parte), y entonces las aplico a situaciones más concretas y complicadas (segunda parte). Primero someto a prueba las implicaciones políticas de la teoría (tercera parte) y después las implicaciones estructurales (cuarta parte). Es posible que esta organización sorprenda a los comparativistas que gustan de argumentos inductivos. De hecho, los lectores primero tendrán que pasar por algunos modelos sencillos antes de entrar al análisis de situaciones más realistas y antes de los resultados empíricos.

¿Es necesaria esta secuencia? ¿Por qué no enumero las expectativas generadas por mi enfoque y entonces sigo adelante y las someto a prueba? La respuesta es que tengo que convencer al lector de que las conclusiones de este libro son lados distintos del mismo constructo mental. Este constructo implica jugadores con veto y establecedores de agenda. Conocer sus ubicaciones, la regla de toma de decisiones de cada uno de ellos y sus interacciones es algo que genera expectativas similares a lo largo de varios temas, que van desde el tipo de régimen (presidencial o parlamentario), hasta interacciones entre gobierno y parlamentos, referéndums, federalismo, legis-

---

[10] Citado en Mads Qvortrum (1999: 533).

lación, presupuestos, independencia de burócratas y jueces. Y los mismos principios de análisis se pueden aplicar no sólo a países que hemos estudiado y analizado muchas veces, sino también a casos en que no encajan los modelos existentes (como la Unión Europea). El lector no apreciaría el bosque si sólo se concentra en los árboles de cada capítulo. Y espero que sea la descripción del bosque la que pueda ayudar a algunos lectores a identificar y analizar árboles que no incluí en este libro.

La primera parte presenta la teoría de los jugadores con veto tanto para jugadores con veto individuales (capítulo I) como colectivos (capítulo II). En el primer capítulo defino jugadores con veto, establecedores de agenda y estabilidad política, concentrándome en jugadores con veto individuales. Explico por qué más jugadores con veto conducen a niveles más altos de estabilidad política. Además muestro que, conforme aumenta la distancia entre jugadores con veto, la estabilidad política aumenta y el papel del establecimiento de agenda disminuye. Explico también por qué todas estas proposiciones que presento son condiciones suficientes pero no necesarias para la estabilidad política, es decir, por qué muchos jugadores con veto con distancias ideológicas grandes entre ellos producirán estabilidad política elevada, mientras que pocos jugadores con veto pueden producir o no inestabilidad política. Finalmente, demuestro que el número de jugadores con veto se reduce si uno de ellos es ubicado "entre" los otros. Muestro las condiciones en las cuales la adición de un jugador con veto no afecta la estabilidad política ni los resultados de la política. Denomino regla de la absorción a esta condición y demuestro su importancia para los pasos ulteriores del análisis. Como resultado de la regla de absorción, una segunda cámara puede tener poder de veto pero no afectar los resultados de la política, o un partido adicional en un gobierno de coalición tal vez no tenga consecuencias políticas debido a que sus preferencias están ubicadas entre las preferencias de los otros socios de la coalición. Una implicación importante de la regla de absorción es que el sólo contar el número de jugadores con veto puede ser engañoso, dado que una gran proporción de ellos puede ser absorbida. Muestro que la mejor manera de tomar en cuenta a los jugadores con veto es considerando no sólo su número, sino sus ubicaciones relativas, y demuestro exactamente cómo se puede hacer esto.

En el capítulo II se generalizan los resultados cuando los jugadores con veto son colectivos. Pasando de jugadores con veto individuales a colectivos, me concentro en la regla de la toma de decisiones de un grupo: mayoría calificada o mayoría simple. Así, el capítulo II se centra en reglas conocidas de toma de decisiones. Explico que los jugadores con veto colectivos en principio pueden generar problemas graves para el análisis debido a que no pueden necesariamente decidir lo que quieren. Sus preferencias son "intransitivas", de modo que diferentes mayorías pueden preferir, al mismo tiempo, la alternativa A en vez de la B, la B en lugar de la C, y la C en vez de la A, lo cual hace que el jugador con veto colectivo prefiera A en lugar de B directamente, pero B en vez de A indirectamente (si C se introduce en la comparación). Encuentro una forma realista de eliminar el problema y calcular los resultados de la elección colectiva cuando las decisiones de los jugadores con veto son tomadas por una mayoría simple o por una calificada.

Como resultado de estos dos capítulos teóricos, podemos formarnos expectativas acerca de la estabilidad política y de los resultados de la toma de decisiones legislativa en cualquier sistema político, ya sea presidencial o parlamentario, ya tenga una legislatura unicameral o bicameral, ya haya dos o más partidos, o si estos partidos son débiles o fuertes. Hay una configuración de jugador con veto de cada combinación de estas variables comparativas tradicionales, y más: el análisis de los jugadores con veto toma en cuenta las posiciones y preferencias de cada uno de estos actores, de modo que la exactitud del análisis y de las expectativas aumenta conforme se introducen preferencias políticas más exactas en los datos.

En la segunda parte se aplican estos conceptos teóricos y expectativas al cuerpo de la bibliografía sobre política comparada, y se cotejan las expectativas generadas por la bibliografía tradicional con las proposiciones generadas en la primera parte. El argumento principal de la segunda parte es que los análisis y variables tradicionales ejercen impacto sobre los jugadores con veto, pero este impacto varía según las situaciones institucionales específicas, y varía incluso más en función de las preferencias de los diferentes jugadores con veto, debido a la regla de absorción.

En el capítulo III se comparan diferentes tipos de regímenes y se argumenta que las diferencias entre regímenes democráticos y no democráticos es la competitividad del proceso de establecimiento de agenda. Como resultado de la competencia política, las élites que tienen éxito político se aproximan más a las preferencias del votante medio. Los regímenes democráticos se clasifican en presidenciales y parlamentarios; la versión de la teoría de los jugadores con veto de la diferencia es que el parlamento controla la agenda legislativa en sistemas presidenciales, mientras que el gobierno controla la agenda en los parlamentarios. Esta concentración en el establecimiento de la agenda genera expectativas opuestas a la bibliografía tradicional: el parlamento es el poderoso en temas legislativos en los sistemas presidenciales, y es el gobierno el que controla el poder en regímenes parlamentarios.

El capítulo IV se concentra aún más en la relación entre gobierno y parlamento en los regímenes parlamentarios. Se explica por qué la mayor parte del tiempo la configuración de jugador con veto de un país está compuesta por los partidos que participan en una coalición gubernamental, y no por los partidos que participan en el parlamento (el enfoque tradicional de sistemas de partido que proponen Duverger y Sartori). También se explica por qué el "predominio ejecutivo", una variable fundamental en el análisis de consociacionalismo de Lijphart, se puede interpretar como el poder institucional atribuido al gobierno para establecer la agenda parlamentaria.

El capítulo V se concentra en el referéndum y explica por qué la inclusión de la posibilidad de un referéndum aumenta el número de jugadores con veto en un país, y produce resultados finales más cercanos al votante medio, incluso si los referéndums no ocurren. También argumenta que las principales diferencias entre referéndums giran en torno al tema del control de la agenda. Este control se divide en dos partes: quién activa el referéndum y quién formula las preguntas. Un jugador con veto existente puede controlar ambas partes del proceso de establecimiento de agenda y, en este caso, aumenta su influencia en la legislación. O puede ser que el referéndum no sea activado por un jugador con veto, pero la pregunta puede ser formulada por un jugador con veto (veto popular) o no (iniciativa popular). Cada uno de estos métodos tiene diferentes consecuencias políticas sobre el papel de los jugadores con veto y el votante medio. Por ejemplo, cuando un mismo jugador controla ambas dimensiones del establecimiento de la agenda (referéndum de jugador con veto o iniciativa popular), quedan eliminados los jugadores con veto legislativos existentes.

El capítulo VI trata sobre federalismo, bicameralismo y mayorías calificadas. Cada uno de estos términos se traduce en la teoría de los jugadores con veto con el fin de sacar implicaciones acerca de las consecuencias de estas instituciones sobre la creación de política. El federalismo suele ir acompañado por el bicameralismo (una segunda cámara representa a los estados y tiene poder de veto sobre piezas importantes cuando no sobre todas las piezas de legislación), o toma de decisiones de mayoría calificada. Como resultado, el federalismo aumenta el número de jugadores con veto, y por lo tanto la estabilidad política. Comparo las propiedades de la toma de decisiones bicameral con mayorías calificadas, así como con la combinación de ambas (que existe en los Estados Unidos así como en la Unión Europea).

La tercera parte se concentra en las implicaciones políticas del análisis anterior. Esperamos una mayor estabilidad política como función de los jugadores con veto después de tomar en cuenta la regla de absorción. La identificación de estabilidad política no es un asunto trivial; dos capítulos se dedican, por tanto, a este tema.

El capítulo VII se concentra en las desviaciones importantes del *statu quo*. Considero la legislación sobre horas de trabajo y condiciones laborales en democracias parlamentarias, y encuentro que se introduce legislación importante en países con uno o unos cuantos jugadores con veto, con más frecuencia de la que ocurre en países con muchos jugadores con veto, particularmente si hay grandes distancias ideológicas entre ellos. Este resultado se contrasta con el número total de leyes en diferentes países; este número se correlaciona positivamente con el número de jugadores con veto. Como resultado, los países con pocos jugadores con veto producen varias leyes de importancia y pocas sin importancia, mientras que las naciones con muchos jugadores con veto producen pocas leyes de importancia y muchas leyes sin ella. El capítulo termina con la expectativa de que tales diferencias sistemáticas conduzcan a un concepto distinto de "ley" en diferentes países.

En el capítulo VIII se examinan los resultados macroeconómicos. Una vasta gama de bibliografía económica postula que el número de jugadores con veto está correlacionado con déficits más altos, ya que diferentes jugadores con veto requieren porciones importantes del presupuesto. En contraste, de acuerdo con la teoría de los jugadores con veto, más jugadores con veto conducen a mayor inercia, y por ende los países con altos niveles de deuda (Italia) continuarán teniendo altos déficits, mientras que los países con bajos niveles de deuda (Suiza) continuarán teniendo bajos niveles de déficit. De modo similar, la composición del presupuesto cambiará más en los países con pocos jugadores con veto, mientras que los países con muchos jugadores con veto dependerán más de un piloto automático.

En la cuarta parte se examinan las consecuencias institucionales de la estabilidad política. De acuerdo con la teoría, la estabilidad política conducirá a una inestabilidad gubernamental en los sistemas parlamentarios, a inestabilidad de régimen en los sistemas presidenciales, y a una independencia de jueces y burócratas. En los capítulos de esta parte se examinan estas afirmaciones.

En el capítulo IX se verá el tema de la estabilidad del gobierno. Además volveremos a considerar las afirmaciones en la bibliografía, según las cuales el sentido de que el sistema de partidos de un país (es decir, características del parlamento) afecta la supervivencia del gobierno. En contraste, la teoría de los jugadores con veto sostiene que son las características del gobierno las que afectan la supervivencia del mismo. Las dos expectativas están sumamente correlacionadas debido a que los sistemas bipartidistas producen gobiernos de un solo partido —un solo jugador con veto—, mientras que los sistemas multipartidistas producen gobiernos de coalición: jugadores con veto múltiples. Sin embargo, la correlación no es perfecta. Los sistemas de muchos partidos pueden producir gobiernos de mayoría de un solo partido así como gobiernos minoritarios. Como resultado, las implicaciones de las dos teorías se pueden separar empíricamente, y trabajos recientes (principalmente de Warwick) han mostrado que lo que importa son las características del gobierno.

En el capítulo X se establecen las razones por las que la estabilidad política afecta el papel de los burócratas y el poder judicial, y se examina la evidencia empírica. Aunque son similares los argumentos para la independencia de la burocracia y el poder judicial en relación con el sistema legislativo, hay más evidencia empírica disponible sobre jueces que sobre burócratas.

En el capítulo XI se aplica todo el análisis desarrollado en el libro a un nuevo sistema político: la Unión Europea. La Unión Europea es algo extraordinario, ya que no es un país ni una organización internacional y ha alterado frecuentemente su constitución (cuatro veces en los últimos quince años). Además, la estructura institucional de la Unión Europea es muy complicada (Ross, 1995) y no encaja en las clasificaciones existentes (no es ni presidencial ni parlamentaria y tiene una cámara que decide con tres diferentes mayorías calificadas). Además de todo eso, la legislatura es con mucha frecuencia tricameral, y el número de partidos es extraordinario si se tiene en cuenta que están definidos tanto por nacionalidad como por ideología. Por consiguiente, la Unión Europea constituye un reto abrumador para la mayoría de las teorías existentes. Incluso para la teoría de los jugadores con veto, la Unión Europea es un desafío importante: tuve que extender la teoría presentada en la primera parte (como el análisis del "establecimiento de agenda condicional" y el cálculo de un núcleo multicameral) con el fin de estudiar las instituciones de la Unión Europea. Por lo tanto, someter a prueba pronósticos de jugadores con veto con datos de la Unión Europea será un difícil examen para la teoría.

En la conclusión regreso a las características distintivas del libro. El modo deductivo de presentación permite que los mismos principios sencillos se combinen en el análisis de fenómenos complicados. Con la introducción de las nuevas variables (jugadores con veto) se rastrea el proceso legislativo con el nivel de detalle que sea necesario, y es significativamente más exacto que en cualquiera de las teorías tradicionales. Como resultado, las expectativas se pueden formular en forma más clara, y someterse a prueba con mayor facilidad.

La evidencia empírica presentada cubre una vasta gama de políticas, procesos y países. La calidad de los datos es a veces muy confiable (capítulos VII y VIII), otras veces no tanto (capítulo X); a veces se origina en el trabajo de un solo autor (capítulo VII) o de dos autores (capítulo VIII), mientras que en otras ocasiones se basa en los resultados de otros investigadores (capítulo IX). Finalmente, la posición del establecedor de agenda se conoce con mucha exactitud en algunos casos, lo cual permite hacer pronósticos exactos sobre los resultados (capítulo XI), mientras que en otros casos ignoraremos la identidad del establecedor de agenda a fin de hablar únicamente acerca de la estabilidad política de los resultados (capítulos VII y VIII). Sin embargo, toda esta evidencia diversificada hace que la teoría investigada sea corroborada en toda una diversidad de condiciones.

PRIMERA PARTE

TEORÍA DE LOS JUGADORES CON VETO

En la primera parte se analiza el impacto de diferentes instituciones políticas sobre la política. Fundamento mi análisis en la política porque podemos pensar en un sistema político como el medio para la toma de decisiones colectiva. En consecuencia, todos los actores en un sistema político, ya se trate de votantes, representantes o partidos, se preocupan por los resultados políticos, ya sea de modo directo o indirecto, ya sea porque prefieren algunos resultados o porque otras cosas que les gustan (como la reelección) dependen de los resultados de la política.

Sin embargo, los resultados de la política son producto de dos factores: las preferencias de los actores implicados y las instituciones predominantes. Dado que la identidad de los jugadores y sus preferencias son variables, mientras las instituciones son más estables, los resultados de la política habrán de variar dependiendo de quién controle el poder político así como en dónde esté el *statu quo*. Por el momento, consideraremos como dado el *statu quo* y analizaremos su ubicación más a fondo cuando se haga necesario.

En este libro nos concentraremos en la parte más estable de la interacción y trataremos de evaluar los resultados enfocando únicamente las instituciones, con un *conocimiento limitado* sobre la identidad de los actores que los producen. Haremos pronósticos acerca de las consecuencias del número de actores implicados o sus posiciones relativas, sin conocer números o ubicaciones con exactitud. Dado que sabemos poco acerca de las identidades y elecciones de los actores implicados, sólo estaremos capacitados para hacer declaraciones sobre el tipo de cambio, o cuántos medios institucionales diferentes *permiten* el cambio del *statu quo*. Hay una consecuencia inmediata de este método de estudio. Lograré identificar las condiciones en que el cambio del *statu quo* es difícil o imposible (la estabilidad política es grande), pero no podré vaticinar el cambio real. Cuando el cambio político es posible, el que ocurra o no se deberá a las elecciones específicas de los actores mismos. Incluso si el cambio es posible, puede ser que no ocurra. En otras palabras, todas las proposiciones que siguen ofrecen condiciones necesarias pero no suficientes para cambiar el *statu quo*. Demostraré en el primer capítulo que las implicaciones de esta declaración están lejos de ser triviales.

En esta parte ofrezco las reglas de acuerdo con las cuales todas las instituciones políticas (tipos de régimen, parlamentos, sistemas de partido, partidos, etc.) se traducen en una serie de jugadores con veto: actores cuyo consenso se requiere para un cambio en el *statu quo*. El número y la ubicación de los jugadores con veto afecta la estabilidad política, o lo difícil que es cambiar el *statu quo*. La secuencia en la cual los jugadores con veto toman sus decisiones (quién hace propuestas a quién) afecta la influencia que estos jugadores con veto tienen en el proceso de toma de decisiones. El que estos jugadores con veto sean individuales o colectivos afecta la forma en que toman decisiones acerca de política. Si se trata de individuos (un presidente o un partido político monolítico), pueden decidir fácilmente sobre la base de sus preferencias. Si son colectivos (un parlamento o un partido político débil), la ubicación del resultado depende de la regla interna de toma de decisiones (unanimidad, mayoría calificada o simple) y de quién controla la agenda. Por lo tanto, las instituciones políticas tradicionales como tipos de régimen, o número de cámaras de parlamento, o número, cohesión y posiciones ideológicas de los partidos, o reglas de toma de decisiones de todos estos actores, se traducirán en alguna constelación de jugadores con veto, que a su vez determinará la estabilidad política de un sistema político.

Este enfoque establece la posibilidad de diferentes medios institucionales para causar el cambio político, pero no identifica ni puede identificar la dirección del mismo. Para la identificación de la dirección del cambio, se requieren las preferencias de los jugadores con veto, así como la identidad del establecedor de la agenda y la ubicación del *statu quo*. En otras palabras, las instituciones en este libro se asemejarán a conchas, y sólo cuando sean identificados los ocupantes de estas conchas y el *statu quo*, será posible hacer pronósticos específicos sobre los resultados. Sin embargo, como lo demuestro, hay resultados importantes que se pueden obtener incluso si ignoramos las elecciones específicas de los diferentes actores. Tales resultados cubren, como lo he argumentado, no sólo la estabilidad política, sino también una serie de consecuencias de la estabilidad política sobre otras variables, como la estabilidad de gobierno o de régimen, la importancia e independencia del poder judicial y el papel de las burocracias.

Esta parte está dividida en dos capítulos. En el primer capítulo se analizan jugadores con veto individuales, mientras que en el segundo nos concentramos en jugadores con veto colectivos. Hay dos razones para esta división. Primero, para fines didácticos, la división de los capítulos facilita una mejor comprensión, dado que la teoría de jugadores con veto individuales es sencilla, directa e intuitiva, mientras que los jugadores con veto colectivos introducen complicaciones en el análisis (dependiendo de las reglas que regulan su toma de decisiones) y, como lo muestro, aproximaciones dentro de los resultados. Segundo, la división es útil porque los jugadores con veto colectivos, como lo explico, tienen problemas particularmente serios como establecedores de la agenda, debido a que diferentes mayorías pueden preferir hacer diferentes propuestas, problema que abordaré a fondo en el capítulo II.

I. JUGADORES CON VETO INDIVIDUALES

EN ESTE capítulo defino los conceptos fundamentales que empleo en este libro, en particular *jugadores con veto* y *estabilidad política*. Demuestro las conexiones entre estos dos conceptos usando modelos espaciales euclidianos sencillos. El capítulo presenta una serie de proposiciones que relacionan el número y la distancia de los jugadores con veto con la estabilidad política. En esencia, el argumento presentado en las secciones 2 y 3 de este capítulo es que cuanto mayor sea la distancia entre los jugadores con veto y su número, más difícil será cambiar el *statu quo*. La última sección introduce una secuencia de movimientos en el cuadro y plantea el argumento de que el primero que actúe (el establecedor de agenda) tiene una ventaja importante. Sin embargo, esta ventaja disminuye conforme aumenta la estabilidad política, es decir, conforme aumenta el número de jugadores con veto y la distancia entre ellos.

1. Jugadores con veto y estabilidad política

Los *jugadores con veto* son actores individuales o colectivos cuyo consenso es necesario para un cambio del *statu quo*. De ahí se deduce entonces que un cambio en el *statu quo* requiere una decisión unánime de todos los jugadores con veto.

La constitución de un país puede asignar la condición de jugador con veto a diferentes actores individuales o colectivos. Si los jugadores con veto son generados por la constitución, se les denomina jugadores con veto *institucionales*. Por ejemplo, la Constitución de los Estados Unidos especifica que la legislación, para ser aplicada, requiere de la aprobación del presidente, la Cámara de Representantes y el Senado (dejemos por el momento la anulación de un veto presidencial). Esto significa que los tres actores (uno individual y dos colectivos) son los jugadores con veto institucionales en los Estados Unidos.

Analizar el juego político por sus jugadores con veto institucionales es algo que puede aclarar algunas ideas. Si los jugadores con veto son generados por el juego político, se les denomina jugadores con veto *partidarios*. Por ejemplo, puede ocurrir que en la Cámara de Representantes haya diferentes mayorías, lo cual hace que la Cámara ya no pueda ser reducida como un jugador con veto. Alternativamente, puede ser que la Cámara esté controlada por un solo partido cohesivo, y que las únicas piezas de legislación aprobadas sean aquellas respaldadas por dicho partido. En este caso, aunque la Cámara sea el jugador con veto institucional, el partido con mayoría es el jugador con veto real (partidario). De modo similar, en Italia, aunque la legislación puede ser generada por la aprobación de ambas cámaras de la legislatura (dos jugadores con veto institucionales), un examen más detenido indica que los jugadores con veto partidarios son los partidos que componen la coalición de gobierno. Retornaremos a este punto en el capítulo II.

Cada jugador con veto individual está representado aquí por su punto ideal en un espacio político de n dimensiones. Además, presupongo que cada jugador con veto tiene *curvas de indiferencia circulares* y que es indiferente entre alternativas que tienen la misma distancia de su punto ideal. La gráfica I.1 presenta un espacio bidimensional, donde las dimensiones 1 y 2 podrían ser el monto del presupuesto para seguridad social y defensa, respectivamente. En estas dos dimensiones un jugador con veto (1) está representado en el centro del círculo. La gráfica también representa cuatro puntos, P, X, Y y Z, en diferentes ubicaciones. El jugador con veto es indiferente

GRÁFICA I.1. *Curvas de indiferencia circular de un jugador con veto.*

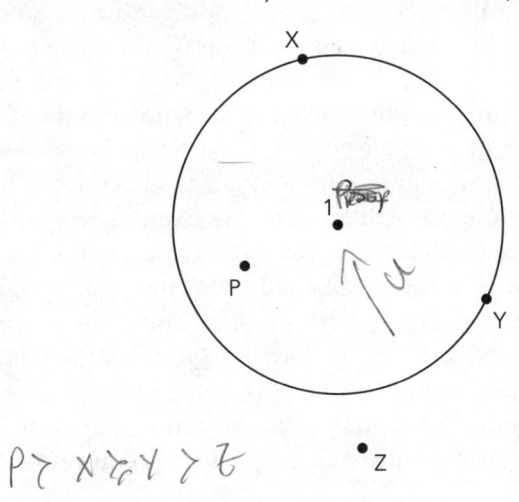

entre los puntos X y Y, pero prefiere P en vez de cualquiera de éstos. También prefiere a cualquiera de ellos en vez de Z. Como tal, el círculo con el centro 1 y el radio 1X —de aquí en adelante (1, 1X)—, o "la curva de indiferencia que atraviesa a X", también pasa a través de Y, mientras que el punto P está ubicado dentro del círculo y el punto Z está ubicado afuera.

Ambas suposiciones incluyen varias simplificaciones. Por ejemplo, un actor individual puede estar interesado en una sola dimensión en vez de dos o más. En un tema redistributivo puede ser que un actor esté interesado en maximizar su parte, y ser completamente indiferente a quién más obtiene cuánto. Por añadidura, las curvas de indiferencia circulares indican la misma intensidad de preferencias en cada tema. Si estas suposiciones no son válidas, se tendrán que reevaluar las declaraciones relacionadas con las distancias ideológicas entre los jugadores con veto. Sin embargo, las afirmaciones que dependen sencillamente del número de jugadores con veto sí se sostienen, cualquiera que sea la forma de las curvas de indiferencia. De aquí en adelante representaré a un jugador con veto mediante un punto (es decir, A), el *statu quo* con otro (SQ), y A preferirá cualquier cosa que haya dentro del círculo (A, ASQ) en vez del *statu quo*.

Ahora defino dos conceptos más. El primero es el conjunto ganador del *statu quo (W(SQ))*, el conjunto de resultados que puede derrotar al *statu quo*. Piénsese en el *statu quo* como la política corriente. El conjunto ganador del *statu quo* es el conjunto de políticas que puede remplazar el existente.[1] El segundo concepto es el *núcleo*, el conjunto de puntos con conjunto ganador vacío: los puntos que no pueden ser derrotados por ningún otro punto si aplicamos la regla de la toma de decisiones. Suelo hacer referencia al núcleo junto con la regla de toma de decisiones que lo produce. Por ejemplo, el "núcleo de unanimidad" se refiere al conjunto de puntos que no pueden ser derrotados si la decisión es unánime. Otro nombre que también utilizo para el "núcleo de unanimidad" es el "conjunto de Pareto". En la gráfica I.2, presento un sistema con tres jugadores con veto, A, B y C, y dos diferentes posiciones del *statu quo*, SQ1 y SQ2. Como se podrá observar, todas las decisiones deben tomarse por unanimidad, dado que A, B y C son jugadores con veto.

Con el fin de identificar el conjunto ganador de SQ1 (W(SQ1)), trazamos las curvas de indiferencia de A, B y C que pasan a través de SQ1, e identificamos su intersección. He sombreado esta intersección en la gráfi-

---

[1] En las partes III y IV se examinan formas más interesantes y productivas para conceptuar el concepto de *statu quo*, pero aquí no las necesitamos.

GRÁFICA I.2. *Conjunto ganador y núcleo de un sistema con tres jugadores con veto.*

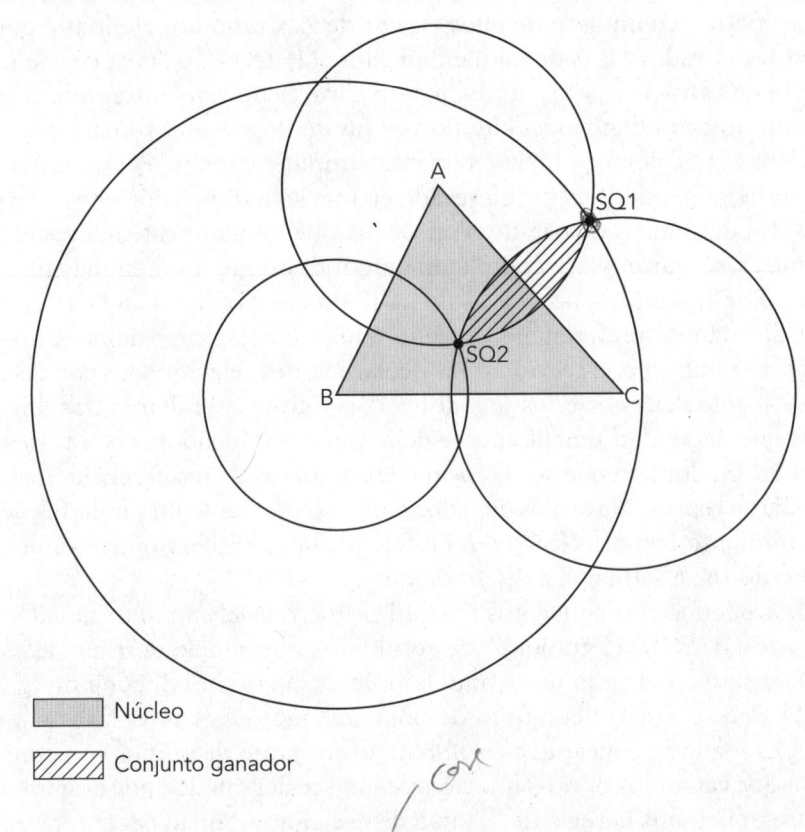

ca I.2. Una operación similar indica que $W(SQ2) = \emptyset$, siempre y cuando SQ2 esté ubicado dentro del triángulo ABC.[2] Así, el núcleo de unanimidad es el triángulo completo ABC como está sombreado en la gráfica.

Utilizo la pequeñez del conjunto ganador de SQ y el tamaño del núcleo de unanimidad como *indicadores de estabilidad política*. En la sección 3 demuestro formalmente que estos dos indicadores son casi equivalentes (proposición I.3). Aquí, sin embargo, ofrezco argumentos en favor de cada uno, independientemente.

En cada proposición, "el conjunto ganador en el caso A es más pequeño que el conjunto ganador en el caso B" significa que el conjunto ganador en el caso A es un subconjunto del conjunto ganador en el caso B. De modo

---

[2] Si, no obstante, SQ2 está ubicado fuera del triángulo ABC, entonces puede ser derrotado por su proyección sobre el lado más cercano, de modo que su conjunto ganador no está vacío.

similar, "el conjunto ganador se contrae" significa que en condiciones nuevas se convierte en un subconjunto de lo que era antes. La *estabilidad política* de un sistema, pues, es la dificultad de efectuar un cambio importante del *statu quo*.

La definición de núcleo de unanimidad conduce lógicamente a la conclusión de que su tamaño es un sustituto de estabilidad política. De hecho, un mayor núcleo de unanimidad produce un mayor conjunto de puntos que no se pueden cambiar. Por el momento, observemos que el argumento en favor de la pequeñez del conjunto ganador parece más complicado. Empleo la pequeñez del conjunto ganador del *statu quo* como un agente de la estabilidad política por las razones siguientes:

1. Cuanto mayor sea el conjunto ganador del *statu quo*, más probable será que algún subconjunto del mismo satisfaga algunas restricciones externas adicionales.
2. Si hay costos de transacción al cambiar el *statu quo*, entonces los jugadores no emprenderán un cambio conducente a una política que sólo sea ligeramente distinta, lo cual significa que subsistirá el *statu quo*.
3. Incluso sin costos de transacción, si los jugadores emprenden un cambio, un pequeño conjunto ganador del *statu quo* significa que el cambio será incremental. En otras palabras, un pequeño conjunto ganador del *statu quo* excluye grandes cambios políticos.

Cada una de estas razones es suficiente para justificar el uso de la pequeñez del conjunto ganador del *statu quo* como agente de la estabilidad política.

Los dos agentes de la estabilidad política son complementarios para diferentes posiciones del *statu quo*. Cuando el *statu quo* está muy alejado de todos los jugadores con veto, su conjunto ganador es grande (la estabilidad política es baja). A medida que el *statu quo* se aproxima a uno de los jugadores con veto, la estabilidad política aumenta (dado que el conjunto ganador del *statu quo* incluye únicamente los puntos que este jugador con veto prefiera por encima del *statu quo*). Desplazar el *statu quo* todavía más y ubicarlo entre los jugadores con veto puede eliminar por completo el conjunto ganador del *statu quo* (como lo indica el caso de SQ2 en la gráfica I.3).

El análisis anterior indica que la estabilidad política depende crucialmente de la posición del *statu quo*. No obstante, son de especial interés las

GRÁFICA I.3. *Conjunto ganador y núcleo de un sistema con cuatro jugadores con veto.*

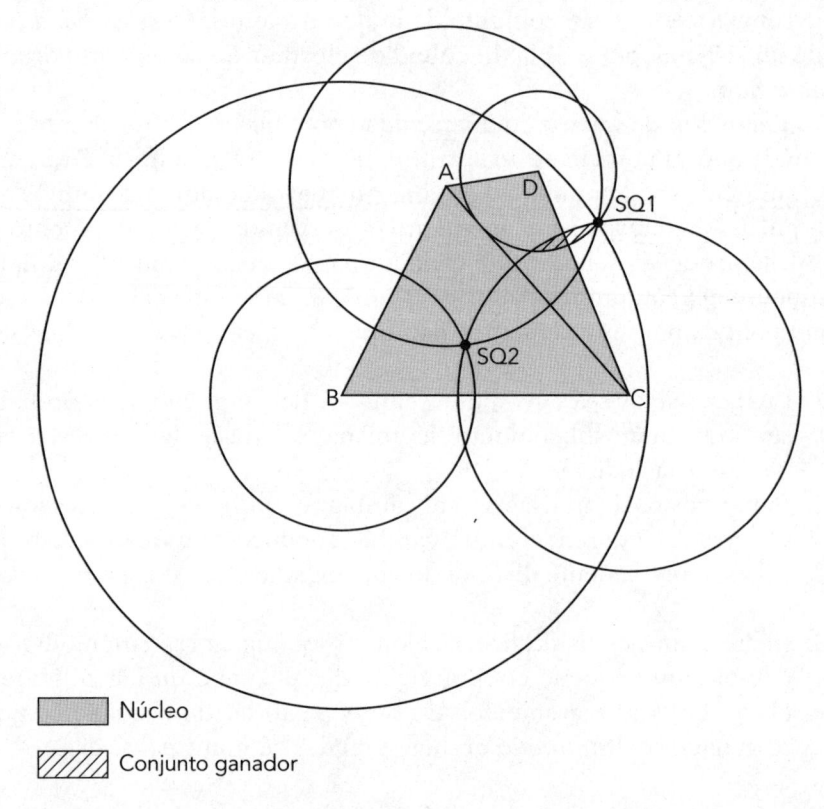

proposiciones *independientes* de la posición del *statu quo*, y ello por dos razones. Primera, en el análisis de la ciencia política no siempre es fácil empezar localizando el *statu quo*. Por ejemplo, cuando se introduce una propuesta de ley sobre atención a la salud, no conocemos al *statu quo* hasta *después* de votado el proyecto de ley. De hecho, una serie de medidas relacionadas con la salud mental, por ejemplo, pueden incluirse o no en el *statu quo* dependiendo de si fueron incluidas en el proyecto de ley mismo.[3]

Segunda, el análisis político que depende de la posición del *statu quo* tiene necesariamente un carácter en extremo contingente y volátil (exacta-

[3] Un enfoque alternativo consideraría un espacio político de dimensionalidad extremadamente alta, y consideraría el *statu quo* como el resultado generado por *toda* la legislación existente y las desviaciones causadas por algún proyecto de ley particular. Entonces pasamos por alto las dimensiones que no han sido afectadas por el cambio. En mi opinión, éste es un procedimiento mucho más complicado.

mente como el *statu quo* del que depende). El análisis de la legislación anterior puede convertirse en una empresa extremadamente difícil (en especial si consideramos esta legislación con el paso del tiempo). No soy de la opinión de que tal análisis sea superfluo o irrelevante, sino todo lo contrario. No obstante, me gustaría ver si se pueden hacer algunas afirmaciones comparativas independientemente de la posición del *statu quo*, si son posibles afirmaciones que sean características de un sistema político y no del *statu quo*.[4]

En lo que resta de este capítulo me concentraré en otros factores que afectan la estabilidad política. En la sección 2 desarrollo el análisis en dos partes complementarias: el caso en que el conjunto ganador de SQ no está vacío, y el caso en que está vacío (cuando SQ está ubicado dentro del núcleo de unanimidad). En la sección 3 demuestro la alta correlación de los dos enfoques.

2. Número de jugadores con veto y estabilidad política

2.1. El conjunto ganador del statu quo *no está vacío*

La gráfica I.3 reproduce la gráfica I.2 y agrega otro jugador con veto: D. Es fácil ver por comparación de las dos gráficas que el conjunto ganador de SQ1 se contrae con la adición de D como jugador con veto. De hecho, D veta algunos de los puntos que eran aceptables para los jugadores con veto A, B y C. Éste es el caso genérico. En condiciones espaciales singulares la adición de un jugador con veto tal vez no afecte el resultado. Con objeto de ahorrar espacio no presento aquí otra gráfica, pero el lector puede imaginarse lo siguiente: si D está ubicado sobre la línea BSQ entre B y SQ de modo que el círculo en torno de D se incluya dentro del círculo en torno de B, la adición de D como jugador con veto no influirá en el tamaño del conjunto ganador de SQ1.[5] Podría continuar con el proceso de agregar jugadores con veto y contemplar el conjunto ganador del *statu quo* que se contrae o permanece igual ("no expandiéndose") con cada nuevo jugador con veto. Es posible que conforme se desarrolla el proceso de agregar jugado-

---

[4] Analizo el concepto mismo de *statu quo* que es omnipresente en modelos formales y tan evasivo en estudios empíricos en el capítulo IX como el fundamento de mi análisis de la estabilidad gubernamental.
[5] Abordo el punto de cuándo "cuentan" los jugadores adicionales con veto, es decir, cómo afectan el tamaño del conjunto ganador del *statu quo*, en la siguiente sección.

res con veto, el conjunto ganador del *statu quo* quede vacío en algún punto, de tal suerte que ya no haya un punto que pueda derrotar al *statu quo*. Este habría sido el caso si D estuviera ubicado en un área tal que SQ1 quedase rodeado por jugadores con veto. Trataremos este caso en los párrafos siguientes. Permítaseme resumir aquí los resultados del análisis hecho hasta el momento. *Si el conjunto ganador del* statu quo *existe, su tamaño disminuye o permanece igual con la adición de nuevos jugadores con veto.*

2.2. El conjunto ganador del statu quo *está vacío*

Concentrémonos ahora en SQ2 en la gráfica 1.3. Allí se presenta el caso en que está vacío el conjunto ganador del *statu quo* con tres jugadores con veto. Dado que W(SQ2) = ∅, el tamaño de W(SQ) no va a cambiar, por muchos jugadores con veto que agreguemos. Sin embargo, la adición de D como nuevo jugador con veto tiene otro resultado interesante: expande el núcleo de unanimidad. El lector puede verificar que el núcleo de unanimidad es ahora el área completa ABCD. De nueva cuenta, no es necesario que un jugador adicional con veto expanda el núcleo de unanimidad. Es posible que deje igual el tamaño del núcleo de unanimidad, como hubiera sido el caso si D estuviera localizado dentro del triángulo ABC. Trataremos este caso en la siguiente sección. Por el momento, la conclusión de este párrafo es ésta: *si hay un núcleo de unanimidad, su tamaño aumenta o permanece igual con la adición de nuevos jugadores con veto.*

Combinando las conclusiones de los párrafos anteriores se llega a la siguiente proposición:

Proposición 1.1: La adición de un nuevo jugador con veto aumenta la estabilidad política o la deja igual (ya sea disminuyendo el tamaño del conjunto ganador del *statu quo*, o acrecentando el tamaño del núcleo de unanimidad, o dejando iguales a ambos).

La estática comparativa que la proposición 1.1 respalda es muy restrictiva. Obsérvese que hablo de la *adición* de un nuevo jugador con veto. La frase implica que los otros jugadores con veto seguirán siendo los mismos en la comparación. Por ejemplo, sería una aplicación inapropiada de la proposición 1.1 el considerar que si eliminamos un jugador con veto determinado y agregamos dos más, el resultado sería un aumento de la estabilidad política. No menos erróneo sería comparar dos diferentes sistemas, uno con tres jugadores con veto y otro con cuatro, y sacar la conclusión de que el segundo produce más estabilidad política que el primero. Así, aunque la proposición I.1 permite hacer comparaciones del mismo sistema político con el paso del tiempo, usualmente no nos permite comparar entre sistemas.

La siguiente proposición, que denominaré "criterio numérico", aumenta la sencillez pero reduce la exactitud de la proposición I.1. La razón es que pasa por alto los casos en que agregar un jugador con veto no causa ninguna diferencia sobre la estabilidad política.

> *Criterio numérico:* La adición de un nuevo jugador con veto aumenta la estabilidad política (ya sea al disminuir el tamaño del conjunto ganador del *statu quo* o al aumentar el tamaño del núcleo de unanimidad).

El "criterio numérico" tiene las mismas restricciones para la estática comparativa que la proposición I.1. Por añadidura, puede conducir a expectativas erróneas, ya que un nuevo jugador con veto *no* siempre aumenta la estabilidad política. Este punto se debe subrayar dado que, como se verá en los capítulos empíricos, la investigación empírica frecuentemente emplea el criterio numérico ya sea para producir expectativas o para someterlas a prueba. Las proposiciones que se presentan en la siguiente sección relajan algunas de las restricciones anteriores.

3. Reglas de cuasiequivalencia y de absorción, distancias entre jugadores con veto y estabilidad política

Esta sección trata de las condiciones en las cuales agregar un jugador con veto afecta (aumenta) la estabilidad política. Si no lo hace, diremos que el nuevo jugador con veto es "absorbido" por los existentes, lo que da el título "regla de la absorción" a esta sección. Como interesante producto secundario del análisis, veremos que los dos distintos agentes de estabilidad política (el tamaño del núcleo de unanimidad y el tamaño del conjunto ganador) son casi equivalentes, así como en qué condiciones alterar las distancias entre los jugadores con veto afecta la estabilidad política.

3.1. Reglas de cuasiequivalencia y de absorción

Empiezo por presentar el argumento en una sola dimensión por razones de sencillez. Considérese la situación que se presenta en la gráfica I.4. Tres individuos (todavía no son jugadores con veto) están ubicados en la *misma línea recta*, y el *statu quo* se encuentra en cualquier parte en un espacio de n dimensiones (un espacio bidimensional vasto para describir la situación). En lo que resta de esta sección hago un índice de los diferentes conjuntos ganadores de los jugadores con veto, no por la posición del *statu quo*, ya que mis resultados son válidos para cualquier posición posible del *statu quo*.

La gráfica I.4 presenta las curvas de indiferencia de los tres actores A, B y C. Las etiquetas D, E y F son las intersecciones de las curvas de indiferencia de A, B y C con la línea AC. Considérese primero que los actores A y B (pero no C) son jugadores con veto, e identifiquemos el conjunto gana-

GRÁFICA I.4. *El conjunto ganador de jugadores con veto A y C está contenido en el conjunto ganador de jugadores con veto y B (B es absorbido).*

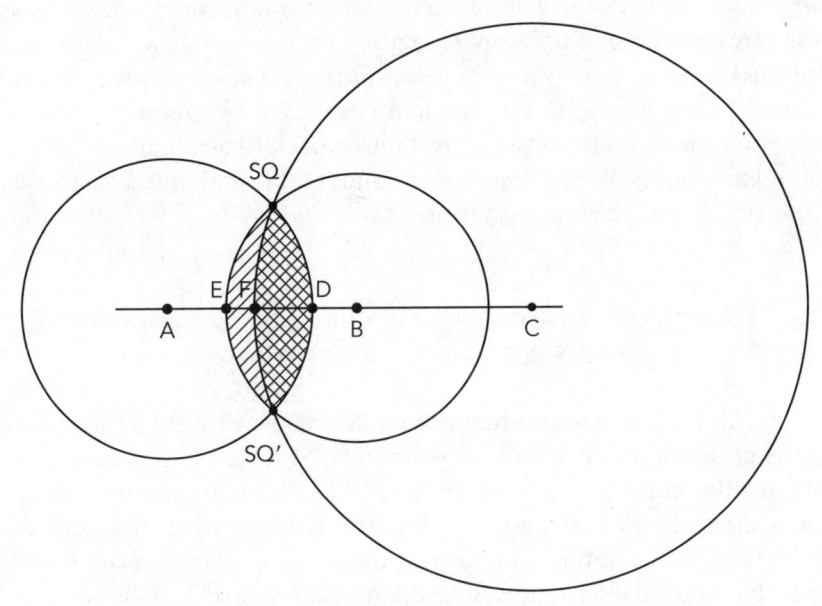

Conjunto ganador de A y B

Conjunto ganador de ABC o AC

dor del *statu quo* (W(AB)). Agreguemos C al conjunto de jugadores con veto; es decir, demos a C la capacidad de vetar los resultados que no le gusten. Es fácil ver que el conjunto ganador del *statu quo* se contrae a W(ABC) (al pasar por los puntos D y F). En este caso agregar un jugador con veto aumenta la estabilidad política del sistema.

Ahora sigamos un diferente curso temporal y presupongamos que los jugadores con veto iniciales son A y C. El conjunto ganador del *statu quo* es W(AC) (pasando a través de D y F). Agregar B como un jugador con veto no afecta su tamaño. En otras palabras, W(ABC) = W(AC).

¿Por qué se restringía la creación de política en el primer caso pero no en el segundo? La razón es que si B está ubicado entre A y C, entonces F está ubicado entre E y D.[6] En otras palabras, es imposible que A y C tengan preferencias conjuntas sobre el *statu quo* que B no compartirá.

Podemos llegar a conclusiones similares en lo tocante al núcleo de unanimidad: agregar B a los jugadores con veto A y C no afecta el núcleo de unanimidad del sistema (que es el segmento AC), mientras que agregar C a A y B expande el núcleo de unanimidad de AB a AC.

De hecho, las dos condiciones son equivalentes: cuando un nuevo jugador con veto es agregado dentro del segmento que conecta a los jugadores con veto existentes (su núcleo de unanimidad), eso no afecta al conjunto ganador del *statu quo*, y cuando no afecta al conjunto ganador del *statu quo* (para cualquier posición de SQ), está ubicado dentro del segmento definido por los jugadores con veto existentes (su núcleo de unanimidad). De hecho, la única manera en que las tres curvas de indiferencia pasarían por los dos mismos puntos (SQ y SQ') sería que los tres puntos A, B y C estuvieran sobre la misma línea recta.

Estos argumentos se pueden generalizar en cualquier número de dimensiones. La gráfica 1.5 presenta un ejemplo bidimensional. A los tres jugadores con veto iniciales A, B y C se agrega un cuarto, D. Si el punto ideal de D está localizado dentro del núcleo de unanimidad de A, B y C (el triángulo ABC), entonces D no tiene ningún efecto sobre el núcleo de unanimidad o sobre el conjunto ganador de A, B y C, cualquiera que sea la posición del *statu quo*. Si, por otro lado, D está fuera del núcleo de unanimidad de A, B y C, expande el núcleo de unanimidad y restringe el conjunto ganador del *statu quo* (al menos para algunas posiciones SQ).

[6] Es fácil ver por el triángulo SQBC que la suma de los dos lados es más larga que la tercera, de modo que BC + BSQ > CSQ. También es verdad que BSQ = BE y CSQ = CF. Sustituyéndolo obtenemos BC + BE > CF, o CE > CF, o F está ubicado entre E y D.

GRÁFICA I.5. *El conjunto ganador de jugadores con veto A, B y C está contenido en el conjunto ganador de D (D es absorbido).*

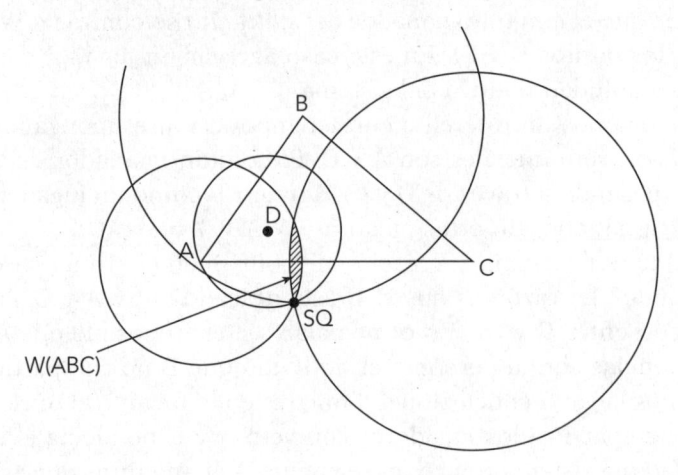

Proposición I.2 (regla de la absorción): Si un nuevo jugador con veto D se agrega dentro del núcleo de unanimidad de cualquier conjunto de jugadores con veto previamente existentes, D no tiene efecto sobre la estabilidad política.

Prueba (por contradicción): Supongamos que un nuevo jugador con veto D pertenece al núcleo de unanimidad de un sistema de jugadores con veto S, y para algunos SQ afecta el tamaño del conjunto ganador del *statu quo*. Sobre la base de la proposición I.1, en este caso se contrae el conjunto ganador del *statu quo*. Las proposiciones previas implican que hay un punto X que prefieren todos los jugadores con veto en S por encima del *statu quo*, pero D prefiere SQ en vez de X. Denominemos X' la parte media del segmento de SQX y tracemos a través de X' el hiperplano que es perpendicular a SQX. Por construcción, todos los jugadores con veto en S están ubicados en un lado de este hiperplano, mientras que D está localizado sobre el otro; en consecuencia, D no está en el núcleo de unanimidad de S.[7]

La proposición I.2 es esencialmente lo que se distingue entre la exactitud verbalmente desmañada de la proposición I.1 y la sencillez aproximada del *criterio numérico*. Explica en qué condiciones un jugador adicional con

---

[7] Agradezco a Macartan Humphreys esta elegante prueba, que es mucho más breve que la mía.

veto va a establecer una diferencia o va a ser absorbido. Esta proposición causa una diferencia importante en aplicaciones empíricas, ya que identifica cuáles jugadores con veto cuentan. Aquí se tiene que señalar un punto importante: todo el análisis se lleva a cabo según la suposición de que no hay costos de transacción en la interacción de diferentes jugadores con veto. La razón por la que hago esta suposición es que resulta difícil encontrar alguna manera de operacionalizar tales costos a través de países y tiempo. Sin embargo, esto no significa que tales costos no existan. Si relajamos la suposición de que no hay costos de transacción, hasta un absorbido jugador con veto agregaría dificultad para cambiar el *statu quo*.

La gráfica I.5 también nos puede ayudar a entender la relación entre los dos criterios de estabilidad política que hemos adoptado. Ya se ha visto sobre la base de la regla de la absorción que agregar un jugador con veto dentro del núcleo de unanimidad de otros no afecta el conjunto ganador del *statu quo*. Ahora veremos que lo contrario también es verdad (que si agregamos un jugador con veto y no reducimos el tamaño del conjunto ganador para cualquier oposición al *statu quo*, el nuevo jugador con veto queda ubicado dentro del núcleo de unanimidad de los anteriores). Como resultado, los dos criterios de estabilidad política son casi equivalentes.

Proposición 1.3 (regla de la cuasiequivalencia): Para cualquier conjunto de jugadores con veto existentes S, la condición necesaria y suficiente para que un nuevo jugador con veto D no afecte el conjunto ganador de ningún SQ es que D esté ubicado en el núcleo de unanimidad de S.

Prueba: La prueba de la regla de la absorción es también la prueba de necesidad. Supongamos que D no pertenece al núcleo de unanimidad de S. Demostraré que hay algunas posiciones de SQ para las cuales el conjunto ganador de SQ se reduce si agregamos D como jugador con veto. Consideremos un hiperplano H que separa a S y D, y seleccionemos un punto SQ en el lado de D. Consideremos la proyección SQ' de SQ sobre H, y extendamos la línea a un punto X de modo que SQX = 2SQSQ' (X es la simétrica de SQ con respecto a H). Por construcción, todos los jugadores con veto en S prefieren a X que a SQ, pero D prefiere a SQ y no a X, así W(SQ) se contrae con la adición de D.

Denomino regla de la cuasiequivalencia a la proposición 1.3 porque demuestra que los dos criterios de estabilidad política que usamos son casi equivalentes: si agregar un jugador con veto no aumenta el tamaño del núcleo, tampoco reducirá el tamaño del conjunto ganador de ningún *statu quo*. De modo similar, si agregar un jugador con veto no reduce el tamaño de W(SQ) para ningún SQ, tampoco aumentará el tamaño del núcleo. Sin embargo, la proposición 1.3 no implica que para *cualquier posición* de SQ aumentar el núcleo disminuya a W(SQ). La razón es que los dos criterios de estabilidad política que usamos tienen una diferencia importante: el tamaño del núcleo no depende de la posición del *statu quo*, mientras el conjunto ganador del *statu quo* (por definición) sí. Como consecuencia de la proposición 1.3, incluso si el tamaño del conjunto ganador del *statu quo* no parecía un criterio muy convincente de estabilidad política como el tamaño del núcleo de unanimidad (en la introducción a esta parte), ahora sabemos que las dos están estrechamente correlacionadas.

3.2. Distancias entre jugadores con veto y estabilidad política

La meta de esta sección es inferir proposiciones que impliquen las distancias entre jugadores con veto que sean *independientes de la posición del* statu quo. En la gráfica 1.4 hemos demostrado que *agregar* B como jugador con veto no tiene ningún efecto, mientras que agregar C sí tiene consecuencias. Ahora podemos cambiar el argumento y considerar un escenario en que *movemos* jugadores con veto en lugar de agregarlos. Si solamente tenemos dos jugadores con veto, A y B, y movemos el punto ideal del segundo de B a C, entonces el conjunto ganador del *statu quo* se contraerá (sin importar en dónde esté el *statu quo*) y el núcleo de unanimidad se expandirá, de modo que aumentará la estabilidad política. En este caso, aumentar la distancia de los dos jugadores con veto (mientras permanecen en la misma línea recta) aumenta la estabilidad política, cualquiera que sea la posición del *statu quo*.

De modo similar, en la gráfica 1.5, agregar D no tiene ningún efecto sobre la estabilidad. En otras palabras, el sistema de los jugadores con veto ABC produce mayor estabilidad política que el sistema ABD. Por lo tanto, si sólo tuviéramos tres jugadores con veto, A, B y un tercero, y pasáramos al tercer jugador con veto del punto C al punto D, la estabilidad política del sistema disminuiría independientemente de la ubicación del *statu quo*. Podemos generalizar estos argumentos de la siguiente manera:

JUGADORES CON VETO INDIVIDUALES

Proposición 1.4: Si Ai y Bi son dos conjuntos de jugadores con veto, y todos los Bi se incluyen en el núcleo de unanimidad del conjunto Ai, entonces el conjunto ganador de Ai se incluye dentro del conjunto ganador de Bi por cada *statu quo* posible y viceversa.

Prueba: Consideremos dos conjuntos de jugadores con veto Ai y Bi, de modo que todos los Bi se incluyan dentro del núcleo de unanimidad de Ai. En ese caso, sobre la base de la proposición 1.2, cada uno de los Bi habría sido absorbido por los jugadores con veto en Ai. Como resultado, la intersección de conjuntos ganadores de todos los Ai es un subconjunto del conjunto ganador de cada Bi, lo cual significa que la intersección de conjuntos ganadores de todos los Ai es un subconjunto de la intersección de conjuntos ganadores de todos los Bi.

La gráfica 1.6 ofrece una representación gráfica de la proposición cuando Ai es un sistema de tres jugadores con veto, y Bi es un sistema de cinco jugadores con veto incluidos en el núcleo de unanimidad de Ai. Obsérvese que a pesar del mayor número de jugadores con veto en el sistema B, el conjunto ganador de cualquier punto SQ con respecto al sistema de juga-

GRÁFICA 1.6. *Los jugadores con veto A1-A3 producen más estabilidad política que B1-B5 (sin importar en dónde esté el* statu quo).

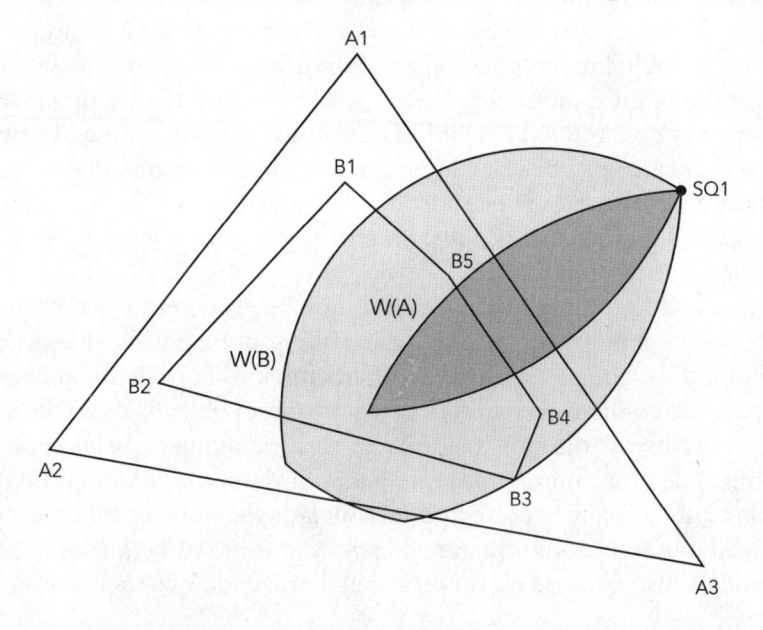

dor con veto A —indicado por W(A) en la gráfica— está contenido dentro del conjunto ganador con respecto al sistema de jugador con veto B —indicado por W(B)—; así, la estabilidad política en el sistema A es mayor. De hecho, podemos llevar B1 más "afuera" hasta que coincida con A1, después llevar B2 a A2, y entonces B3 a A3. La estabilidad política del sistema Bi aumenta con cada movimiento (dado que el núcleo de unanimidad se expande). En el nuevo sistema, B4 y B5 son absorbidos como jugadores con veto.

La proposición 1.4 es la declaración más general de este libro acerca de jugadores con veto en espacios multidimensionales. Permite hacer comparaciones a través de sistemas políticos, siempre y cuando estemos analizando el mismo *rango* de posiciones del *statu quo*. Permítaseme explicar este punto más a fondo. Todos los argumentos que he planteado se sostienen, cualquiera que sea la posición del *statu quo*, pero una vez seleccionado el *statu quo*, se supone que permanece fijo. Hasta ahora, no he comparado la estabilidad política de diferentes sistemas para diferentes posiciones del *statu quo*. Por ejemplo, es una razonable inferencia de la proposición 1.4 esperar que la estabilidad política de un sistema que incluya los partidos comunista, socialista y liberal sea mayor que la estabilidad política de una coalición de partidos socialdemócratas y liberales. Sin embargo, esta proposición no implicaría diferentes posiciones del *statu quo*. Si el *statu quo* en el primer caso resulta muy lejos de los puntos ideales de todos los tres partidos, mientras el *statu quo* en el segundo está ubicado entre las posiciones de los socios en la coalición, entonces el primer sistema puede producir un cambio importante en el *statu quo*, y el segundo no producirá ningún cambio. Para ser más concretos, la estabilidad política no implica que la primera coalición será incapaz de responder a una explosión en una planta de energía nuclear movilizando al ejército si es necesario. Es únicamente en lo tocante a posiciones similares del *statu quo* como tienen sentido las declaraciones de estática comparativa.

Ninguna de las cuatro proposiciones que he presentado hasta aquí identifica la posición política que derrota al *statu quo*. Es posible que el conjunto ganador del *statu quo* sea grande, y sin embargo la posición que se selecciona para ser comparada con él (y derrotarlo) está ubicada cerca del mismo. Es inapropiado sacar la conclusión (a partir de cualquiera de las cuatro proposiciones) de que como el conjunto ganador del *statu quo* es grande en un caso particular, la nueva política estará alejada de él. La conclusión correcta es que cuando el conjunto ganador del *statu quo* es pequeño, la política adoptada estará cerca de él. En otras palabras, cada una de las proposiciones anteriores se debe leer en el sentido de que presenta una condición *necesaria pero no suficiente* para la proximidad de la nueva política al *statu quo:* si la nueva política está lejos del *statu quo*, esto significa que el conjunto ganador es grande, pero si está cerca no quiere decir que el conjunto ganador sea pequeño. De modo similar, si estamos dentro del núcleo de unanimidad no habrá cambio de política, pero si no hay cambio de política no estamos necesariamente dentro del núcleo de unanimidad.

Los puntos señalados en el párrafo anterior son de extrema importancia para los análisis empíricos. Denominemos SQ y SQ' al *statu quo* y su remplazo. Las proposiciones 1.1 a 1.4 indican lo siguiente: cuando el conjunto ganador del *statu quo* es pequeño, también será pequeña la distancia entre SQ y SQ' (representada por |SQ-SQ'|). Cuando el conjunto ganador de SQ es grande, |SQ-SQ'| puede ser grande o pequeño. Agregar transversalmente muchos casos presentará por tanto el cuadro siguiente. *En promedio,* suponiendo que todas las distancias posibles sean igualmente plausibles,[8] conjuntos ganadores grandes presentarán |SQ-SQ'| más grandes que conjuntos ganadores chicos. Además, conjuntos ganadores grandes presentarán una mayor variancia de |SQ-SQ'| que conjuntos ganadores pequeños.

La gráfica 1.7 presenta la relación entre el tamaño del conjunto ganador y la distancia |SQ-SQ'| y da lugar a dos pronósticos. Primero, en promedio, la distancia |SQ-SQ'| aumentará con el tamaño del conjunto ganador del *sta-*

GRÁFICA I.7. *Distancia de la nueva política al* statu quo *en función del tamaño de* W(SQ).

[8] Ésta es una suposición discutible, pero que se necesita aquí y no encuentro nada mejor para sustituirla.

tu quo; y segundo, la variancia de |SQ-SQ'| también aumentará con el (mismo) tamaño del conjunto ganador del *statu quo*.

Debido a la alta variancia de |SQ-SQ'|, cuando el conjunto ganador del *statu quo* es grande, la importancia estadística de una correlación simple entre el tamaño del conjunto ganador y |SQ-SQ'| será baja, debido a la heteroesquedasticidad. Sin embargo, la forma apropiada para someter a prueba la relación entre el tamaño del conjunto ganador y |SQ-SQ'| no es una correlación o regresión simple, sino una prueba doble que incluye la regresión bivariable y también los residuales de esta regresión.[9]

Después de estudiar las proposiciones I.1 a I.4 y la manera como se deberían someter a prueba empíricamente, necesitamos concentrarnos en un tema importante que se ha omitido por completo hasta aquí: el tema de la secuencia.

4. Secuencia de movimientos

Hasta el momento hemos tratado a los jugadores con veto de manera simétrica. Todos ellos eran igualmente importantes para nosotros. Como resultado, sólo identificamos el conjunto de soluciones factibles: el conjunto ganador del *statu quo*. Sin embargo, en los sistemas políticos ciertos actores políticos hacen propuestas a otros, quienes pueden aceptarlas o rechazarlas. Si consideramos tales secuencias de movimientos, podemos reducir considerablemente los pronósticos de nuestros modelos. Sin embargo, con el fin de poder reducir el número de resultados, necesitamos conocer no sólo la identidad precisa, sino también las preferencias del establecedor de la agenda. Como se verá, estos requerimientos son muy restrictivos.[10] Esta sección intenta dilucidar qué diferencia hay si un jugador con veto propone y otro acepta o rechaza.

---

[9] De hecho, ésta es una idea mucho más general. Muchas relaciones presentadas en política comparada y en relaciones internacionales son condiciones necesarias pero no suficientes (piénsese en "no burguesía, no democracia" de B. Moore). La prueba apropiada para tales teorías no es una regresión simple, sino una prueba doble, que incluye heteroesquedasticidad de residuos. En los capítulos empíricos empleo regresión heteroesquedástica multiplicativa para comprobar expectativas de condición necesarias pero no suficientes.

[10] Por ejemplo, veremos en el capítulo IV que en los sistemas parlamentarios los gobiernos controlan la agenda; sin embargo, no sabemos quién dentro de un gobierno es el establecedor de agenda. De hecho, diferentes investigadores han planteado la hipótesis de diferentes actores (primer ministro, ministro de finanzas, ministro correspondiente, negociación entre diferentes actores, importancia proporcional, etcétera).

GRÁFICA I.8. *Importancia del establecimiento de agenda.*

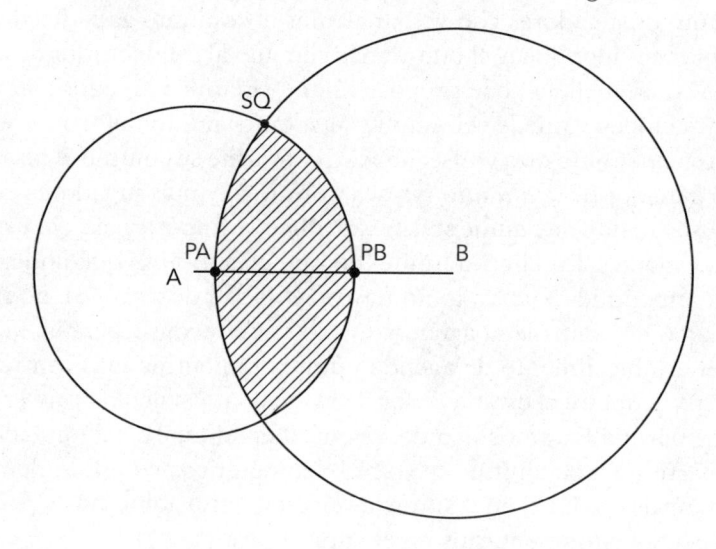

La gráfica I.8 presenta el caso más sencillo posible: dos jugadores con veto. Dado que ambos tratan de alcanzar su punto ideal, o acercarse a él lo más posible, si el jugador con veto A hace una oferta a B, A seleccionará del conjunto ganador completo el punto PA, el que le queda más cerca. De modo similar, si B hace una oferta a A, B seleccionará el punto PB. Es fácil verificar que hay una ventaja importante en hacer propuestas. De hecho, el jugador que hace propuestas considerará el conjunto ganador de todos los otros jugadores con veto como su restricción, y seleccionará de entre todos los puntos contenidos en este conjunto ganador aquél que prefiera. Esta es la ventaja del establecedor de agenda, que McKelvey (1976) identificó por primera vez.[11]

Proposición I.5: El jugador con veto que establece la agenda tiene una ventaja considerable: puede considerar el conjunto ganador de los otros como su restricción, y seleccionar de éste el resultado que prefiera.

La proposición I.5 deja en claro que el análisis de las tres secciones anteriores es válido incluso si conocemos la secuencia de movimientos e inclui-

---
[11] Pero como ya hemos dicho, la idea de la ventaja del establecedor de agenda se puede atribuir a Tito Livio.

mos secuencia en el análisis: podemos sustraer al establecedor de agenda del conjunto de jugadores con veto, calcular el conjunto ganador de lo restante y entonces identificar el punto más cercano al establecedor de agenda.

Como consecuencia de la proposición 1.5, un único jugador con veto no tiene restricciones y puede seleccionar cualquier punto dentro de su curva de indiferencia. Como otra consecuencia, conforme se contrae el tamaño del conjunto ganador del *statu quo* (ya sea porque hay más jugadores con veto o porque sus distancias aumentan), se reduce la importancia del establecimiento de agenda. En el caso límite, en que el *statu quo* queda dentro del núcleo de unanimidad (cuando no hay posibilidad de cambio), no importa para nada quién controle la agenda. Como tercera consecuencia, la importancia del establecimiento de agenda aumenta mientras más centralmente ubicado se encuentre el establecedor de la agenda. Particularizaré estos tres corolarios porque haremos uso del primero en el análisis de gobiernos de un solo partido en el capítulo III (tanto democráticos como no democráticos), y los otros dos en el análisis de la relación entre gobiernos y parlamentos en sistemas parlamentarios en el capítulo IV.

Corolario 1.5.1: Un solo jugador con veto es también el establecedor de la agenda y no tiene restricciones en la selección de resultados.

Corolario 1.5.2: La importancia del establecimiento de agenda disminuye conforme aumenta la estabilidad política.

La gráfica 1.9 brinda una representación gráfica de los corolarios 1.5.2 y 1.5.3, que usaremos con frecuencia. Consideremos primero el conjunto de dos jugadores con veto A y X, y el *statu quo* SQ. El conjunto ganador del *statu quo* está sombreado, y si X es el establecedor de agenda seleccionará el punto X1 que está tan cerca como es posible de su punto ideal. Ahora agreguemos B como otro jugador con veto en el sistema. El conjunto ganador del *statu quo* se contrae (el área de líneas entrecruzadas), y si X continúa siendo el establecedor de agenda, él tiene que seleccionar el punto que prefiera dentro de este conjunto ganador más pequeño. Es claro que el nuevo resultado X2 estará *al menos* tan alejado del punto X como lo estaba el punto X1.[12]

---

[12] En un estudio empírico del bicameralismo alemán, Braeuninger y König (1999) encuentran que los poderes de establecimiento de agenda del gobierno alemán disminuyen cuando la legislación tiene que ser aprobada por la cámara alta (Bundesrat).

JUGADORES CON VETO INDIVIDUALES 47

GRÁFICA I.9. *La importancia del establecimiento de agenda disminuye con más jugadores con veto y aumenta con la ubicación central del establecedor de agenda.*

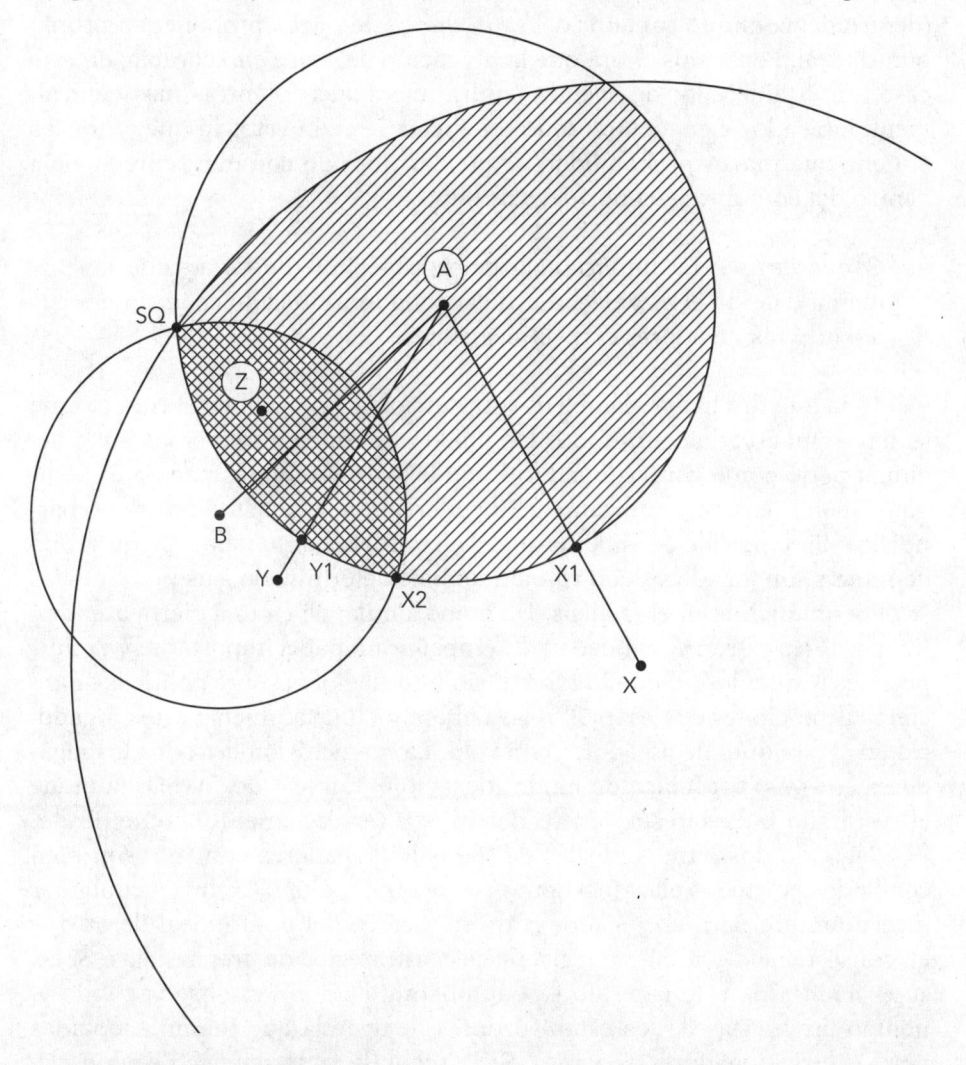

El poder del establecedor de agenda depende también de su ubicación con respecto a otros jugadores con veto. En la gráfica I.9 el establecedor de agenda X estaba más distante de A y de B que del *statu quo;* por eso tuvo que hacer la propuesta X2, que estaba muy lejos de su punto ideal. Si el establecedor de agenda es Y en vez de X, éste tiene que preocuparse únicamente por el jugador con veto A y hacer la propuesta Y1 (dado que él ya está cerca del punto ideal de B). Finalmente, si el establecedor de agenda es Z (dentro del conjunto ganador del *statu quo*) éste puede proponer su propio punto ideal. Pensemos ahora que la ubicación del *statu quo* cambia; en este caso, un establecedor de agenda tendrá más poder mientras más centralmente ubicado se encuentre entre los jugadores con veto, ya que entonces él tiene una mayor probabilidad de quedar ubicado con mayor frecuencia dentro del conjunto ganador del *statu quo*.

Corolario 1.5.3: La importancia del establecimiento de agenda aumenta cuando el establecedor de agenda está ubicado centralmente entre los jugadores con veto existentes.

Toda esta discusión plantea dos suposiciones importantes. Primero, que se han tomado en cuenta todos los jugadores con veto. Veremos en la segunda parte cómo contar jugadores con veto en diferentes países. Sin embargo, consideraremos únicamente jugadores con veto institucionales o partidistas. Si es posible considerar que el ejército, la burocracia o algún grupo de interés son jugadores con veto en un país determinado, sus preferencias se deberán incluir en el análisis. De modo similar, si en una cierta área política actores extranjeros pueden desempeñar un papel importante y excluir posibles resultados (el Fondo Monetario Internacional sobre políticas financieras de naciones en desarrollo), se deberá incluir también a estos jugadores en el conjunto de jugadores con veto. La no inclusión de todos los jugadores con veto especifica de modo inexacto el tamaño del W(SQ), aunque el resultado todavía está dentro del W(SQ) (erróneamente) conjeturado.

Segundo, los puntos ideales de todos los jugadores con veto son bien conocidos por todos ellos (así como por el observador). Excluyen cualquier incertidumbre para un jugador con veto acerca del punto ideal de otro, y en consecuencia cualquier tergiversación estratégica de preferencias. Si las suposiciones de este capítulo se cumplieran, se podrían observar todo el tiempo propuestas de los establecedores de agenda que fueran aceptadas por los otros jugadores con veto. Si la segunda suposición no se cumple, entonces las propuestas pueden fracasar y el proceso de creación de política tal vez empiece de nuevo. Sin embargo, veremos en la segunda parte que las instituciones reales tienen estipulaciones para el intercambio de información entre jugadores con veto.

5. Conclusiones

En éstas se da una visión muy general de toda la teoría que se presenta en el libro. Los jugadores con veto son actores cuyo consentimiento es necesario para un cambio del *statu quo*. La estabilidad política es el término que expresa la dificultad para un cambio importante del *statu quo*. La estabilidad política aumenta en general con el número de jugadores con veto y con las distancias entre ellos (pero véanse las proposiciones I.1 a I.4 para pronósticos más exactos). La comprobación empírica de estos pronósticos requiere no de una regresión sencilla, sino también de pruebas de la variancia de la distancia entre políticas antiguas y nuevas. El jugador con veto que controla el proceso de establecimiento de agenda tiene una importante ventaja redistributiva: puede seleccionar el punto que prefiera de entre el conjunto ganador completo de los otros (proposición I.5). Sin embargo, esta ventaja declina en función de la estabilidad política del sistema (corolario I.5.2), es decir, con el número de jugadores con veto y sus distancias unos de otros. Finalmente, la importancia del establecimiento de agenda aumenta cuando el establecedor de agenda está ubicado centralmente dentro de los jugadores con veto existentes (corolario I.5.3).

Los corolarios I.5.2 y I.5.3 proporcionan las dimensiones posicionales del establecimiento de agenda. El establecimiento de agenda se hace menos importante conforme aumenta el número de jugadores con veto, y más importante cuando el establecedor de agenda está ubicado centralmente dentro de los jugadores con veto. En el capítulo IV estudiaremos (algunas de) las dimensiones institucionales del establecimiento de agenda, es decir, reglas específicas que permiten a algunos autores hacer propuestas e impedir que otros las cambien. La combinación de dimensiones institucionales y posicionales del establecimiento de agenda es necesaria para comprender su importancia.

Este capítulo ha tratado todos los temas que se estudiarán en este libro. Conceptualmente habremos de abundar en los puntos aquí presentados y empíricamente someteremos a prueba los pronósticos formulados. Empezamos con la introducción de una dosis importante de realismo en estos modelos sencillos. ¿Se aplica este análisis a jugadores con veto colectivos, dado que las constituciones de diferentes países no hablan de jugadores con veto sino de actores colectivos tales como parlamentos, partidos y comités?

II. JUGADORES CON VETO COLECTIVOS

Sobre la base del capítulo I podemos analizar situaciones en que los jugadores con veto son personas (como el presidente de los Estados Unidos), o tienen mayorías monolíticas (como un partido comunista), o deciden por unanimidad (como el parlamento polaco de comienzos del siglo XVIII). Sin embargo, tales situaciones son poco comunes. Con mucha frecuencia la toma de decisiones implica la participación de algún jugador con veto colectivo tal como un comité, un partido o un parlamento. Raros son los casos en que esos actores son monolíticos o tienen siquiera una mayoría homogénea dentro de ellos. Y en la actualidad son excepcionales los casos que exijan una toma de decisiones unánime. Por lo tanto, necesitamos generalizar y ver si las intuiciones obtenidas en el capítulo I se sostienen en configuraciones más familiares de preferencias y modos de toma de decisiones.

Aunque este capítulo es esencial para apartarnos de simplificaciones y aumentar la correspondencia entre conceptos teóricos y realidad política, es considerablemente más difícil en el aspecto técnico que el anterior. Por añadidura, aunque las conclusiones presentadas en el capítulo I eran intuitivas hasta el punto de haber podido parecer obvias a los lectores, algunas de las ideas aquí presentadas son contrarias a la intuición. Este capítulo llega a la conclusión de que el análisis del capítulo I proporciona una aproximación muy buena a los fenómenos políticos, pero seguir su argumento es algo más complicado.

El lector no versado en la técnica puede verse tentado a saltarse un capítulo que es considerablemente más difícil que el anterior, que tiene resultados contrarios a la intuición y que, no obstante, llega a las mismas conclusiones. Para disuadir al lector de adoptar tal estrategia, antes de exponer el tema presento una larga introducción que explica los problemas generados por los jugadores con veto colectivos. Espero que esto despierte suficiente interés en los problemas conceptuales. Empero, por si no logro convencer al lector, compendio en la conclusión las ideas más importantes presentadas en este capítulo. Así, un lector no técnico podrá leer la introducción y la conclusión de este capítulo y seguir entonces el resto del libro. El lector que quiera aplicar la teoría de los jugadores con veto a casos no abordados en este libro (países que no analizaremos aquí o toma de decisiones al nivel estatal o local) deberá leer este capítulo completo.

1. INTRODUCCIÓN

La transición de jugadores con veto individuales a colectivos genera dos problemas. Primero, la configuración del conjunto ganador del *statu quo* puede volverse muy complicada, es decir, los *resultados de la toma de decisiones se hacen más complicados*. Necesitaremos abordar estos resultados de alguna manera sencilla. Segundo, los jugadores con veto colectivos violan una suposición importante que hicimos acerca de los individuos: según el dominio de la mayoría, los jugadores con veto colectivos no pueden escoger sin ambigüedad el resultado que prefieran. En otras palabras, *las elecciones de los jugadores con veto colectivos son ambiguas*. Este es obviamente más que un mero inconveniente, o una falta de exactitud descriptiva; puede hacer que los jugadores con veto colectivos sean incapaces de realizar una propuesta y así socavar completamente el análisis del capítulo I. Explicaré en qué condiciones es factible eliminar este problema y argumentaré que estas condiciones se dan con frecuencia.

1.1. Los resultados de la toma de decisiones son más complicados

Consideremos los siete jugadores con veto individuales (1, 2, ..., 7) y el *statu quo* (SQ) que se presentan en la gráfica II.1. ¿Cuáles puntos pueden derrotar al *statu quo* por una decisión unánime de los siete jugadores con veto?

Los puntos capaces de derrotar al *statu quo* pueden ser precisados si consideramos los puntos que cada jugador con veto individual prefiere en vez del *statu quo*. Se le recuerda al lector que tales puntos están ubicados dentro de círculos que pasan a través del *statu quo* y tienen en el centro las preferencias de cada jugador con veto. La intersección de todos estos círculos es la lente más sombreada de la gráfica II.1. De modo similar, así identificamos todos los puntos que no pueden ser derrotados por una decisión unánime de los siete jugadores con veto (el núcleo de unanimidad). Estos

GRÁFICA II.1. *Conjunto ganador y núcleo de unanimidad (7/7), mayoría calificada (6/7) y mayoría simple (4/7).*

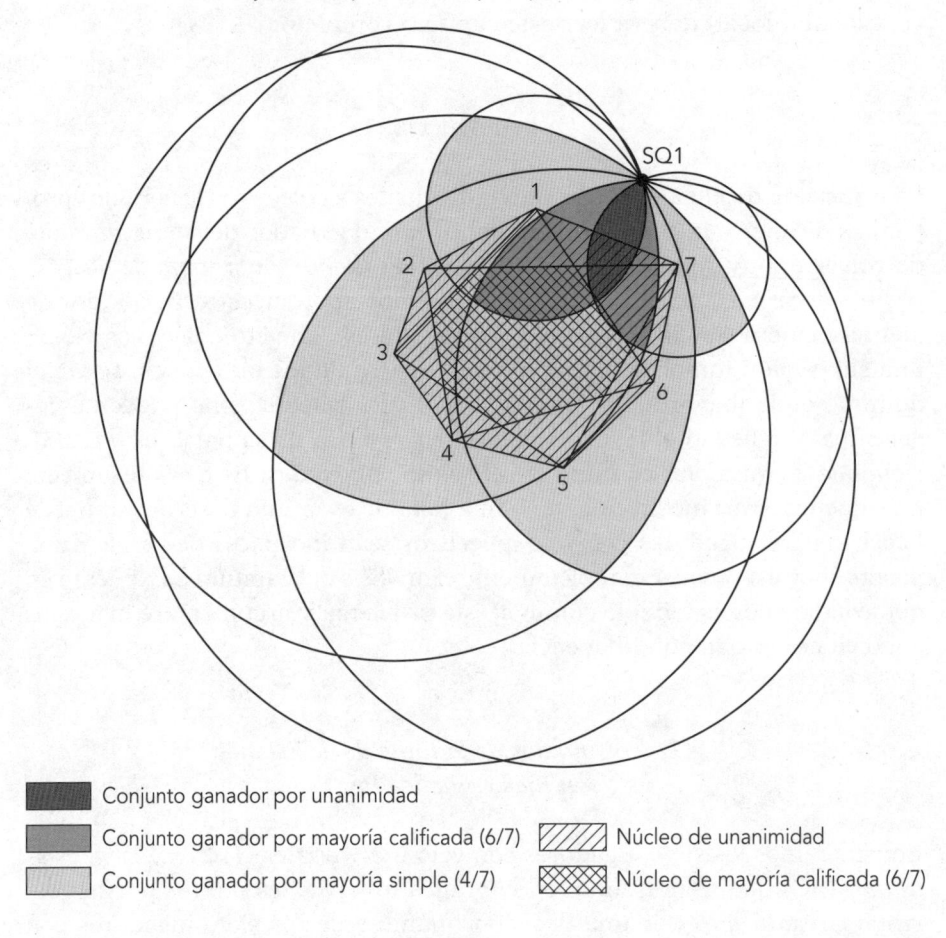

■ Conjunto ganador por unanimidad
■ Conjunto ganador por mayoría calificada (6/7)   ▧ Núcleo de unanimidad
□ Conjunto ganador por mayoría simple (4/7)   ▨ Núcleo de mayoría calificada (6/7)

puntos forman el heptágono completo 1234567.[1] De hecho, no se puede remplazar ningún punto dentro del heptágono sin que objete uno de los jugadores con veto. El área sombreada en la gráfica II.1 representa el núcleo de unanimidad de este jugador con veto colectivo.

¿Qué sucede si este jugador con veto colectivo emplea reglas menos restrictivas de toma de decisiones? ¿Qué pasa si las decisiones las toma una

[1] Los he seleccionado de tal modo que ninguno de ellos esté incluido en el núcleo de unanimidad de los demás, pues de otro modo el núcleo de unanimidad habrá sido un polígono diferente (con menos lados).

mayoría calificada o una mayoría simple en vez de tomarlas por unanimidad? Las intuiciones generadas en el capítulo I indican que la estabilidad política debería disminuir, es decir, que más puntos podrían derrotar al *statu quo* (el conjunto ganador del *statu quo* debería expandirse), y menos puntos deberían ser invulnerables (el núcleo debería contraerse). Consideremos un caso de cada regla; primero, una decisión de mayoría calificada por seis de los siete actores y, segundo, una mayoría simple (cuatro de los siete miembros).

Los puntos capaces de derrotar al SQ por una mayoría calificada de seis séptimos (el conjunto ganador del *statu quo* de la mayoría calificada de los seis séptimos) se pueden identificar si consideramos la intersección de seis de los siete círculos alrededor de los puntos 1, 2, ..., 7 de la gráfica II.1. Presento esta área con sombreado más ligero que los puntos que podrían derrotar al SQ según la regla de unanimidad (el conjunto ganador de unanimidad del SQ) y, como el lector puede verificarlo, incluye este conjunto ganador del *statu quo* de unanimidad. Con el fin de ubicar los puntos que no pueden ser derrotados por una mayoría de seis séptimos (el núcleo de seis séptimos), consideraremos todas las combinaciones posibles de seis de los siete jugadores y tomaremos la intersección de sus núcleos de unanimidad.[2] En la gráfica II.1 esta intersección está representada por el área sombreada con líneas entrecruzadas. El lector puede verificar que está incluida en el núcleo de unanimidad de los siete jugadores.

¿Qué sucede si los siete jugadores deciden de acuerdo con la regla de la mayoría? Con el fin de calcular el conjunto de resultados que derrotan al *statu quo* (el conjunto ganador del *statu quo*), tenemos que considerar las intersecciones de cualesquiera cuatro círculos. El área de sombreado ligero en la gráfica II.1 muestra el área del conjunto ganador del SQ de mayoría, y esta área incluye el conjunto ganador de la mayoría calificada (que incluye el conjunto ganador de unanimidad). Si tratamos de identificar el núcleo de la toma de decisiones por mayoría veremos que este núcleo está vacío, es decir, no hay punto que no pueda ser derrotado por el dominio de la mayoría. Como se verá más adelante, las condiciones en que hay un punto que no pueda ser derrotado por ningún otro bajo el dominio de la mayoría son en realidad muy excepcionales.

---

[2] Una forma más rápida sería conectar los siete jugadores saltándose a uno de ellos cada vez (conectar 1 y 3, 2 y 4, 3 y 5, y así sucesivamente) y considerar el polígono generado por la intersección de estas líneas.

La gráfica II.1 demuestra dos puntos importantes. Primero, la estabilidad política generada por los jugadores con veto colectivos sigue las intuiciones generadas en el capítulo I: disminuye (es decir, el conjunto ganador del SQ se expande y el núcleo se contrae) conforme la regla de la toma de decisiones pasa de ser unanimidad a mayoría calificada y a mayoría simple. Segundo, los cálculos se hacen más complicados cada vez que las preferencias de un jugador con veto colectivo no se expresan con círculos y el conjunto ganador de los jugadores con veto colectivos adopta formas insólitas. Este capítulo intenta identificar una forma sencilla para estimar los resultados del proceso de la toma de decisiones (los puntos que pueden derrotar al *statu quo)* cuando un jugador con veto es colectivo.

1.2. Las elecciones de los jugadores con veto colectivos son ambiguas

Cuando un jugador con veto individual compara tres posibles posiciones de SQ, podemos presuponer que sus preferencias son *transitivas:* si él prefiere SQ1 por encima de SQ2, y a SQ2 en vez de SQ3, entonces también preferirá SQ1 por encima de SQ3. Esta transitividad de preferencias capacita al jugador con veto individual para seleccionar sin ambigüedad entre cualquier conjunto de alternativas, para identificar la alternativa que más prefiera.[3] Sin embargo, los jugadores con veto colectivos que deciden según el dominio de la mayoría no tienen la misma transitividad de preferencias. Las gráficas II.2 y II.3 muestran en dos pasos la intuición en que se basa el argumento.

En la gráfica II.2 hay tres tomadores de decisiones individuales y el *statu quo* ubicado en la mitad del triángulo 123. Intentemos primero identificar los puntos que derrotan al *statu quo* según el dominio de la mayoría simple. Siguiendo el conjunto de reglas del capítulo, trazamos las curvas (círculos) de indiferencia de los tres jugadores y consideramos las intersecciones de cualquier par de ellas. En la gráfica he sombreado W(SQ), que tiene una forma parecida a una flor. Los bordes del área sombreada son los puntos de indiferencia de distintas mayorías. En la gráfica II.1 represento las preferencias de la coalición 1 y 3 con un patrón distinto, y selecciono

---

[3] El individuo puede ser indiferente entre dos alternativas. La indiferencia es distinta de la ambigüedad de preferencias, como quedará claro más adelante. Paso por alto los casos de indiferencia para mayor sencillez de la exposición.

GRÁFICA II.2. *SQ1 derrota a SQ por mayoría (de 1 y 3)*.

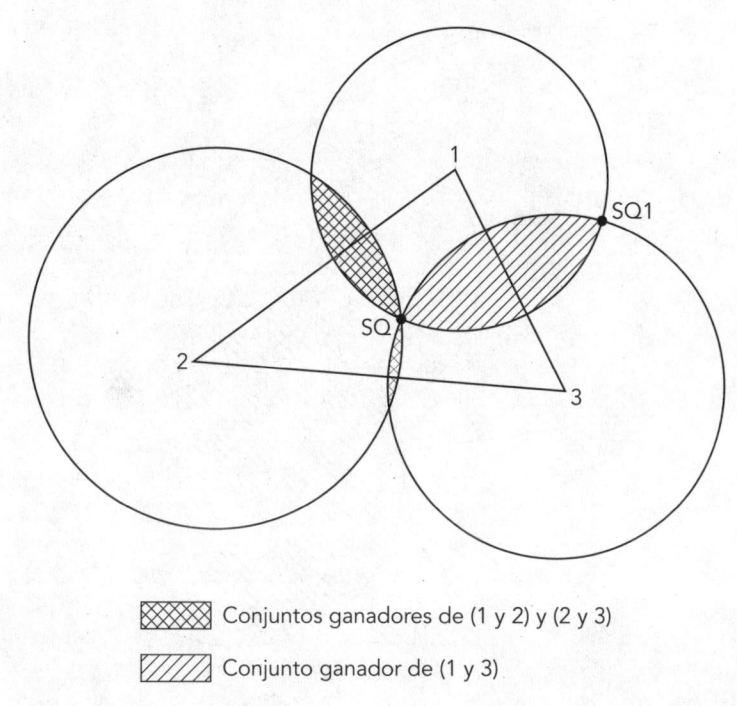

⟨⟨⟨⟨⟨ Conjuntos ganadores de (1 y 2) y (2 y 3)

▨▨▨▨ Conjunto ganador de (1 y 3)

un punto SQ1 que derrote a SQ porque estos dos tomadores de decisiones lo prefieren. Obsérvese que he seleccionado SQ1 al borde del pétalo. La única razón para hacer esta elección es reducir al mínimo los trazos subsecuentes, pero esto no afecta para nada la generalidad del argumento que presento.

Pasemos ahora a una segunda etapa: identificar el conjunto de puntos que derrotan a SQ1. En la gráfica II.3 he trazado el círculo adicional requerido para esta operación, el círculo alrededor del punto 2 (los otros dos círculos ya existen debido a la selección de SQ1). El área sombreada en la gráfica II.3 es la de los puntos que derrotan a SQ1 por diferentes mayorías (conjunto ganador de SQ1: (W(SQ1)).

Le recuerdo al lector que empezamos a partir de SQ e identificamos los otros dos puntos de la manera siguiente: SQ1 era un punto que derrota a SQ por dominio de la mayoría (los tomadores de decisiones 1 y 3 prefieren SQ1 a SQ). De modo similar, SQ2 era un punto que derrota a SQ1 por dominio de la mayoría (los tomadores de decisiones 1 y 2 preferían a SQ2 en

GRÁFICA II.3. *SQ2 derrota a SQ1 por dominio de la mayoría.*

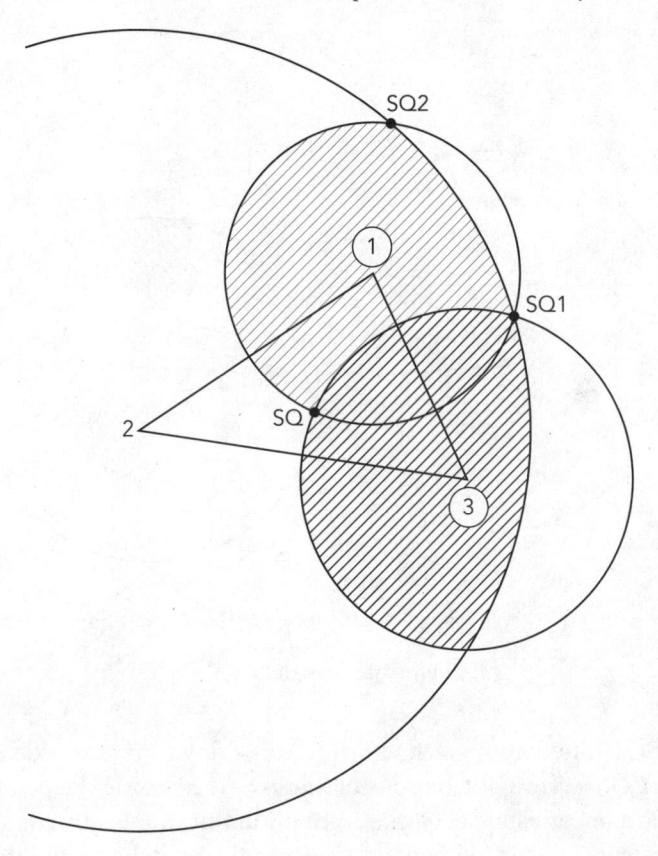

vez de SQ1). Si la colectividad de 1, 2 y 3 fuera un solo individuo que prefiriera a SQ2 sobre SQ1 y a SQ1 sobre SQ, entonces *por transitividad este individuo preferiría también SQ2 por encima de SQ*. Sin embargo, éste no es el caso de nuestra colectividad. Ésta prefiere a SQ sobre SQ2. En otras palabras, nuestra colectividad tiene preferencias ambiguas generadas por el dominio de la mayoría:[4]

$$SQ2 \; \pi \; SQ1 \; \pi \; SQ \; \pi \; SQ2 \tag{1}$$

---

[4] En el análisis anterior paso por alto las relaciones de indiferencia para mayor sencillez de la exposición.

en donde π significa "mayoría preferida". Obsérvese que las tres preferencias no son generadas por las mismas mayorías. Los tomadores de decisiones 1 y 2 son responsables de la primera elección, 1 y 3 por la segunda y 2 y 3 de la tercera. Esta ambigüedad de preferencias, esta "intransitividad" del dominio de la mayoría (para usar el término técnico), ya la conocía Condorcet, pero Arrow (1951)[5] la exploró y generalizó extensamente y en un contexto espacial lo hicieron también McKelvey (1976) y Schofield (1977, 1978).

Para nuestros fines la mejor manera de observar el patrón ambiguo de preferencias generado por el dominio de la mayoría y que se describe en la fórmula 1 es resaltar el hecho de que la colectividad no puede decidirse entre SQ y SQ2: SQ derrota a SQ2 por comparación directa pero es derrotado por SQ2 en una comparación mediada o indirecta (si SQ1 se compara con ambos, elimina a SQ y es eliminado por SQ2).

¿Por qué debe preocuparnos la ambigüedad de las preferencias colectivas, el hecho de que SQ derrota directamente a SQ2, mientras es derrotado indirectamente por SQ2? Porque no sabemos de qué manera se compararán SQ y SQ2. No sabemos cuál está primero en la agenda. Más concretamente, si la colectividad no puede decidirse, los emprendedores estratégicos presentarán una secuencia de elecciones que conduzca a uno u otro resultado. En realidad, McKelvey (1976, 1978) y Schofield (1977, 1978) han mostrado que el problema es mucho más grave que como lo presenta mi descripción; estas "intransitividades" pueden cubrir todo el espacio de tal modo que un sagaz establecedor de agenda pueda presentar a una sociedad una serie de elecciones estructuradas apropiadamente y conducirla a *cualquier* resultado que desee.

Este análisis puede socavar por completo los argumentos que presenté en el capítulo I. Los jugadores con veto colectivos no pueden escoger sin ambigüedad por el dominio de la mayoría. Esto significa que si un jugador con veto colectivo controla la agenda y hace una oferta a otro jugador con veto, *no* se deberá esperar una elección clara ya que los jugadores con veto colectivos llegan a resultados contradictorios cuando tienen que comparar dos puntos (ya no digamos la infinidad contenida en el conjunto ganador de los otros).

En secciones ulteriores demostraré que estas objeciones, que podrían haber sido fatales para mis argumentos, son en realidad meros inconvenien-

---

[5] Arrow ha demostrado, por supuesto, la imposibilidad de que *cualquier* regla de toma de decisiones se ajuste a cinco requerimientos plausibles y deseables.

tes. El conjunto ganador de un jugador con veto colectivo tal vez no sea un círculo, pero el círculo que contiene puede ser identificado, y es posible realizar el análisis de una forma aproximada. Los jugadores con veto colectivos tal vez no sean capaces de hacer elecciones en general, pero en condiciones empíricamente viables pueden seleccionar un área pequeña entre todas las alternativas disponibles. Así, el análisis del capítulo I también se sostiene aproximadamente para los jugadores con veto colectivos.

Sin embargo, hay un precio a pagar. Estas aproximaciones, aunque sean casi precisas en promedio, no siempre son verdaderas. Por ejemplo, como lo demostré en el capítulo anterior, mientras el conjunto de puntos que derrota al *statu quo* se contrae con la distancia de dos jugadores con veto individuales (a lo largo de la misma línea, como demuestra la gráfica 1.4), con los jugadores con veto colectivos es posible acortar la distancia y disminuir el tamaño del conjunto ganador del *statu quo*. Esto puede suceder bajo distribuciones específicas de los jugadores individuales y/o posiciones del *statu quo*. No es un fenómeno frecuente, pero es posible. Como resultado, no puedo presentar como teoremas las afirmaciones que se hacen en este capítulo, pues es posible descubrir que las posiciones de los actores individuales refutan tales teoremas. Las afirmaciones se presentarán como "conjeturas" y examinaremos los argumentos en favor de la validez de esas conjeturas.

El capítulo está organizado para reflejar el capítulo I (el análisis de los conjuntos ganadores primero, de la secuencia después). He interpolado una sección: discutir jugadores con veto colectivos que deciden por mayoría calificada, que resulta ser muy diferente de la mayoría simple. Así, la organización global de este capítulo es la siguiente. En la sección 2 identifico el conjunto ganador de un jugador con veto colectivo por la regla de la mayoría simple. En la sección 3 considero jugadores con veto colectivos que deciden por mayorías calificadas y explico la importante diferencia entre toma de decisiones de mayoría simple y calificada. En la sección 4 trato el tema de la secuencia donde los jugadores con veto colectivos pueden generar más problemas debido a su incapacidad para maximizar. La conclusión general de este capítulo es que el análisis del capítulo I se sostiene con ajustes muy pequeños.

2. Jugadores con veto colectivos y mayorías simples

Supongamos que es necesario el acuerdo de una cámara de legislatura (como la Cámara de Representantes de los Estados Unidos) para un cambio del *statu quo*, y que la cámara decide por mayoría simple de sus miembros. En nuestra terminología la cámara es un jugador con veto colectivo. Sin embargo, ningún miembro individual dentro de la legislatura tiene poder de veto sobre la legislación. Con el fin de encontrar el conjunto ganador del *statu quo* tenemos que identificar las intersecciones de las curvas de indiferencia de todas las mayorías posibles.

La gráfica II.4 presenta el conjunto ganador del *statu quo* para un comité de cinco miembros (uso la palabra comité debido al reducido número de miembros que presento a fin de simplificar la gráfica).[6] El juego político dentro de este comité puede respaldar coaliciones variables o estables. Analizaremos extensamente la diferencia en la segunda parte. Supongamos aquí que cualquier coalición es posible y tratemos de localizar W(SQ). Dado que W(SQ) es generado por la intersección de una serie de círculos, tiene una forma insólita que dificulta el estudio de sus propiedades espaciales. Ferejohn, McKelvey y Packell (1984) ubicaron un círculo donde se puede incluir el conjunto ganador del SQ por dominio de la mayoría. Veamos seguidamente cómo identificar este círculo en tres pasos:

1. *Trazado de líneas medianas*.[7] La *mediana* es una línea que conecta dos puntos y tiene mayorías en cualquiera de sus lados (incluyendo puntos sobre la línea). Por ejemplo, en la gráfica II.4, AC, BE, BD, EC y AD son líneas medianas, ya que tienen en un lado tres puntos y en el otro cuatro (dos de ellos están en las líneas mismas).
2. *Identificación de la "yema"*. La *yema* es el círculo más pequeño[8] que interseca todas las medianas. En la gráfica este círculo tiene el centro Y y el radio r. Es tangente sobre las líneas medianas AD, AC y EC. Interseca las otras dos líneas medianas (BE y BD). El centro Y está a una distancia d de SQ.

---

[6] Como lo demuestro en el capítulo V, muchos miembros en realidad simplifican la situación al menos al nivel conceptual, aunque el trazado de las gráficas se puede volver difícil.
[7] Planos o hiperplanos en tres o más dimensiones.
[8] Esfera o hiperesfera en tres o más dimensiones.

GRÁFICA II.4. *Círculo (Y, d + 2r) contiene el conjunto ganador del* statu quo *de un jugador con veto colectivo (ABCDE).*

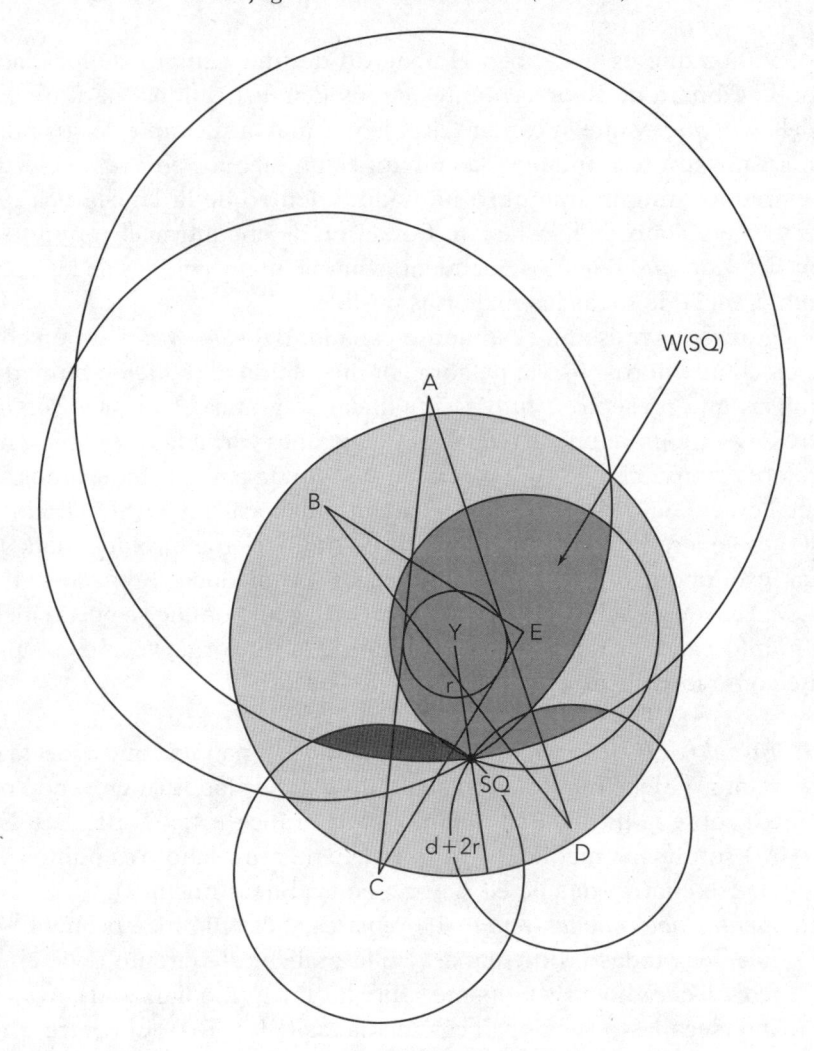

3. *Trazado del círculo (Y, d + 2r).* La gráfica II.5 presenta la yema (Y, r), el *statu quo* SQ a la distancia d del centro de la yema Y y dos diferentes líneas medianas: L1 y L2. Dado que hay mayorías en ambos lados de estas líneas, los puntos SQ1 y SQ2 (simétricos a SQ con respecto a estas medianas) pertenecen también al conjunto ganador del

GRÁFICA II.5. *W(SQ) está contenido dentro del círculo ganador (Y, d + 2r).*

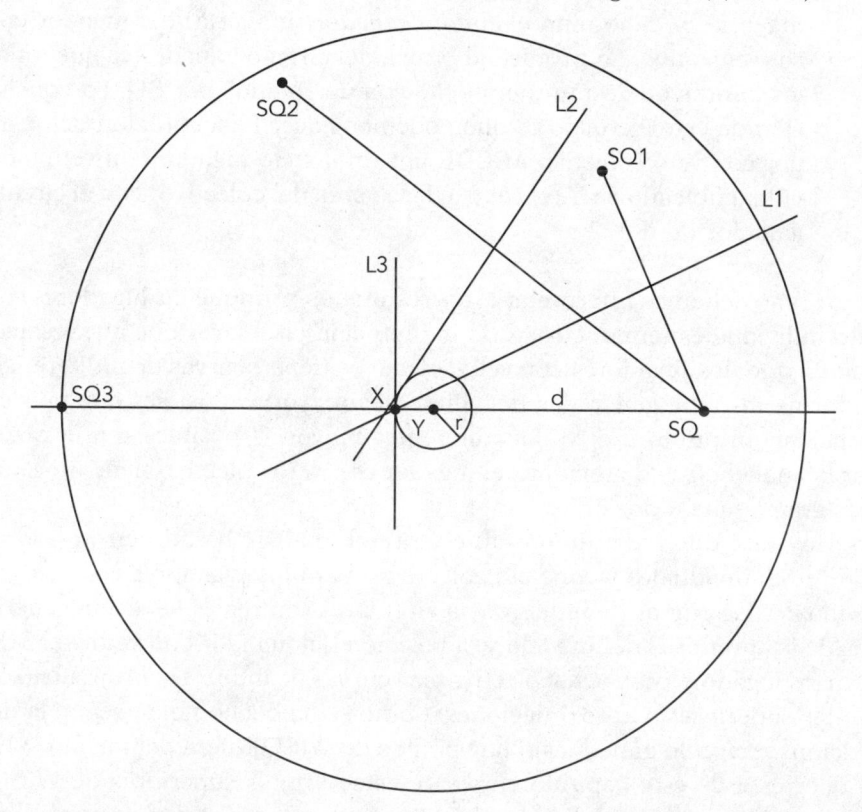

statu quo (se les prefiere sobre SQ por la mayoría de puntos que están en el lado opuesto de estas líneas que SQ). Mi meta es trazar un círculo que incluya todos estos puntos. Para ese propósito, tengo que incluir la ubicación más distante de SQ que puede obtener un punto simétrico al mismo con respecto a una línea mediana. Tal punto es SQ3, que es simétrico con respecto a una línea mediana tangencial a la yema en el punto más distante de SQ (punto X en la gráfica). Este punto está a la distancia d + r de SQ, de modo que la distancia YSQ3 es d + 2r.[9] En consecuencia, el círculo (Y, d + 2r) incluye SQ y todos los puntos simétricos con respecto a todas las líneas medianas posibles. A este círculo que incluye el conjunto gana-

---

[9] La distancia SQSQ3 es 2(d + r), mientras YSQ es d. Mediante una resta sacamos el resultado.

dor del *statu quo* de un jugador con veto colectivo por dominio de la mayoría lo denomino el *círculo ganador* (mayoría) del jugador con veto colectivo. La propiedad básica del círculo ganador es que todos los puntos que están fuera de él son derrotados por SQ. La conclusión de este ejercicio es que podemos hacer la sustitución del jugador con veto colectivo ABCDE por un ficticio jugador con veto individual ubicado en Y (el centro de la yema del colectivo) con el círculo ganador (Y, d + 2r).

¿Cómo debemos interpretar estos resultados? Aunque los jugadores con veto individuales tenían curvas de indiferencia circulares que atravesaban el *statu quo*, los jugadores con veto colectivos tienen curvas de indiferencia de forma insólita, generadas por diferentes mayorías posibles que pueden respaldar un punto u otro. Las diferentes mayorías posibles son la razón por la cual el círculo ganador del jugador con veto colectivo tiene un radio más grande que d por 2r.

Hay una diferencia importante entre el análisis basado en jugadores con veto individuales y con veto colectivos: para los jugadores con veto individuales las curvas de indiferencia circulares son reales (es decir, generadas de las premisas del modelo y la posición del jugador con veto y el SQ); para los jugadores con veto colectivos las curvas de indiferencia circular son límites superiores o aproximaciones. Como se ha hecho notar, según la definición de círculo ganador no hay puntos de W(SQ) fuera del mismo.[10] En lo que resta de este capítulo emplearé estos límites superiores de W(SQ) para aproximar la estabilidad política, ya que pueden proporcionar información acerca de cuáles puntos *no pueden* derrotar al *statu quo* (donde W(SQ) *no* está ubicado). Se le recuerda al lector que las proposiciones I.1 a I.4 proporcionaron condiciones suficientes pero no necesarias para la estabilidad política, de tal manera que el uso del límite superior de W(SQ) es consistente con los argumentos presentados en el capítulo I y mantiene sus conclusiones.

En cuanto al radio de la yema de un jugador con veto colectivo, es una indicación de su *cohesión-m*, o de lo bien que está representada la mayoría por el punto Y ubicado en el centro del jugador con veto colectivo. Así, con-

---

[10] Sin embargo, dado que los círculos en torno de los jugadores con veto colectivos son los límites superiores de W(SQ), es posible que dos de esos límites superiores se intersequen mientras W(SQ) está vacío. Agradezco a Macartan Humphreys el haberme presentado ejemplos concretos de este punto.

forme disminuye el radio de la yema, aumenta la cohesión-m de un jugador con veto colectivo.

Conforme aumenta el radio de la yema (la cohesión-m disminuye), aumenta el círculo ganador del jugador con veto colectivo. Aunque no siempre se da el caso de que un círculo ganador acrecentado implicará un aumento en el tamaño del conjunto ganador del *statu quo*,[11] la estabilidad política aumenta cuando el círculo ganador se contrae, ya que no hay puntos que puedan derrotar al SQ fuera del círculo ganador.

Conjetura II.1: La estabilidad política aumenta conforme se incrementa la cohesión-m de un jugador con veto colectivo (conforme disminuye el radio de la yema).

Es interesante observar que en promedio r *disminuye* conforme *aumenta* el tamaño (el número de individuos) del jugador con veto colectivo. Éste es un resultado contrario a la intuición. La razón de que suceda es que unos puntos adicionales sustituyen algunas de las líneas medianas antes existentes por otras ubicadas más al centro. Hasta donde sé, no hay una solución exacta al problema, pero las simulaciones por computadora han indicado que este es el caso en una diversidad de condiciones (Koehler, 1990). Por ello usaré de nuevo el término "conjetura".

Conjetura II.2: Un aumento en el tamaño (número de individuos) de un jugador con veto colectivo *(ceteris paribus)* aumenta su cohesión-m (disminuye el tamaño de su yema), y en consecuencia aumenta la estabilidad política.

En este libro no someto a prueba las conjeturas relacionadas con la cohesión de los jugadores con veto colectivos. Hasta donde sé, no hay datos sistemáticos sobre la cohesión interna de partidos en regímenes parlamentarios. Incluso en los Estados Unidos, donde la posición de diferentes miembros del Congreso puede precisarse sobre la base de puntuaciones proporcionadas por diferentes grupos interesados, los distintos métodos

---

[11] De hecho, podemos construir ejemplos opuestos donde el conjunto ganador se incrementa conforme el círculo ganador se contrae. Considérense por ejemplo las dos situaciones siguientes: un triángulo ABC y SQ está ubicado sobre A. En este caso W(SQ) es la intersección de los dos círculos (B, BA) y (C, CA). Si metemos A dentro del triángulo BCSQ, entonces el radio de la yema se contrae mientras el conjunto ganador se expande.

plantean controversias metodológicas.[12] Una vez resueltas tales controversias, si podemos usar registros de votaciones en legislaturas para identificar las posiciones políticas de parlamentarios individuales, tales datos se emplearán para identificar la cohesión de partido en los modelos que presento aquí. Por el momento, empleo el análisis anterior sencillamente para establecer dos puntos cualitativos. El primero tiene que ver con el hecho de que la mayoría de los jugadores políticos son colectivos. El segundo implica la dimensionalidad del espacio político subyacente.

Primero, considérense las implicaciones del hecho de que la mayoría de los jugadores con veto son colectivos y no individuales. Un ejemplo lo encontramos en la Constitución de los Estados Unidos: la legislación requiere la aprobación de la Cámara, el Senado y el presidente (las primeras dos por dominio de la mayoría; no entraremos en obstruccionismo, veto y veto presidencial anulado hasta la próxima sección).

En la gráfica II.6 se comparan dos casos diferentes: primero, si los tres jugadores con veto fueran individuos (o si la Cámara y el Senado estuvieran

GRÁFICA II.6. *Posibilidad de cambio incremental cuando dos jugadores con veto son colectivos (EUA).*

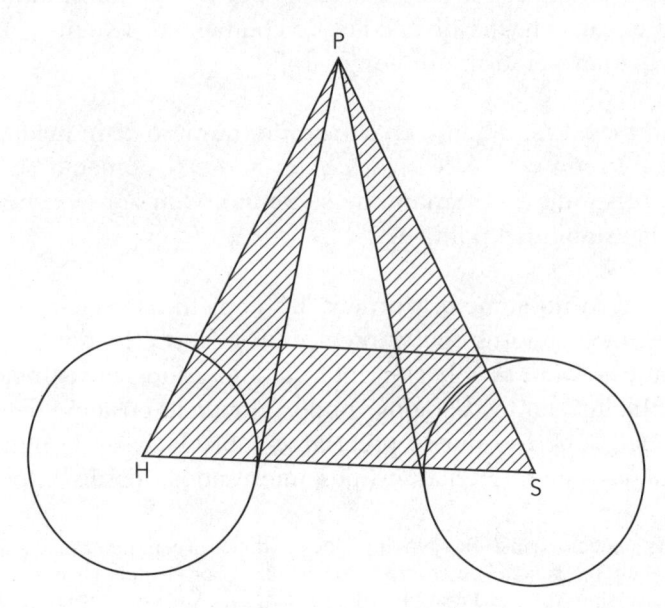

[12] Para un debate reciente véase McCarty, Poole y Rosenthal (2001), y Snyder y Groseclose (2001).

cada uno dominado por un solo partido monolítico) y, segundo, la situación real en que la Cámara y el Senado son jugadores con veto colectivos que deciden por el dominio de la mayoría, en cuyo caso quedan representados por los centros de sus yemas H y S.

Cuando todos los tres jugadores con veto son individuos, la imagen producida por la gráfica II.6 queda en empate mientras el SQ se ubique dentro del triángulo PHS. De hecho, estamos ubicados dentro del núcleo de unanimidad del sistema de los tres jugadores con veto, y ningún cambio es posible.

No obstante, si H y S son jugadores con veto colectivos, hay una *posibilidad* de cambio incremental. Humphreys (2001) ha demostrado que existe esta posibilidad *únicamente* en las áreas cercanas a los lados del triángulo PHS como se indica mediante el área sombreada en la gráfica II.6.[13] Recalco "posibilidad" ya que el hecho de que los conjuntos ganadores de los dos jugadores colectivos se intersequen depende en realidad de las preferencias de miembros individuales del Congreso. Por tanto, en vez del inmovilismo absoluto presentado en el análisis con jugadores con veto individuales, los jugadores con veto colectivos *pueden* presentar la posibilidad de un cambio *incremental* para ciertas ubicaciones del *statu quo*.

Este análisis indica que la posibilidad de cambio se vuelve más pronunciada cuanto menos cohesivas sean las dos cámaras, como lo indica la conjetura II.1. La implicación política es que variaciones pequeñas del SQ *pueden* ser aprobadas por el sistema político, y que tales cambios serán más importantes conforme aumenta la falta de cohesión de cada una de las cámaras. Otra forma de pensar acerca de esta situación es que cuanto más dividida esté cada una de las dos cámaras, más posibilidades se presentarán al presidente de lograr un consenso acerca de alguna alternativa particular. De hecho, si las dos cámaras están políticamente muy cerca una de la otra, el cambio incremental siempre puede ser posible.[14]

Mi segunda observación aborda el tema de la multidimensionalidad del espacio político. En un seminal artículo sobre la Constitución de los Estados Unidos, Hammond y Miller (1987) señalan que en dos dimensiones invariablemente habrá un núcleo siempre y cuando las áreas cubiertas por

---

[13] Esta área queda definida por los lados del triángulo y la tangente a las yemas de las dos cámaras así como las líneas a través de la tangente del punto ideal del presidente a cada una de las dos yemas.
[14] Técnicamente, cuando las yemas de las dos cámaras se intersecan, el núcleo del sistema político *puede* estar vacío.

los miembros de cada cámara no se sobrepongan. Humphreys (2000) descubrió que es grande la probabilidad de que exista un núcleo bicameral en dos dimensiones incluso si las preferencias de los miembros de las dos cámaras se sobreponen.[15] Tsebelis y Money (1997) demostraron que en un espacio político de más de dos dimensiones el núcleo de una legislatura bicameral rara vez existe.

Los actores políticos suelen estar compuestos de muchos individuos que tienen preferencias en dimensiones múltiples. Cada uno de estos factores acrecienta la probabilidad de que cada *statu quo* posible pueda ser derrotado en un sistema político.[16] Los análisis en una sola dimensión conducen a resultados de votante promedio: el votante promedio en una sola dimensión no puede ser derrotado (tiene un conjunto ganador vacío o constituye el núcleo); los modelos multidimensionales por otro lado no tienen votante promedio, cada punto puede ser derrotado, y no hay equilibrio ni núcleo. Riker (1982) incluyó esta propiedad de los sistemas políticos en la esencia misma de la política. De acuerdo con su análisis, la diferencia entre economía y política era que los análisis económicos siempre alcanzaban un equilibrio, mientras que los análisis políticos multidimensionales demuestran que un equilibrio no existe. La implicación de este argumento era que al no existir tal equilibrio, los perdedores siempre andan en busca de nuevos temas para dividir a las coaliciones ganadoras y adueñarse del poder.

Mi análisis muestra que incluso si existen puntos que derroten al *statu quo*, éstos pueden estar ubicados muy cerca de éste, en cuyo caso la estabilidad política del sistema será elevada. Los jugadores con veto sustituyen la cruda dicotomía de si hay un núcleo o no (o si el conjunto ganador del *statu quo* está vacío) por una visión más continua de la política donde la variable dependiente es la estabilidad política, la cual puede existir incluso cuando no haya un núcleo, tan sólo debido a que los posibles cambios son incrementales. El resultado de este enfoque es que seremos capaces de generalizar en múltiples dimensiones en vez de detenernos porque no haya equilibrio.

---

[15] En una simulación por computadora, se valió de dos cámaras de tres miembros, y la probabilidad de un núcleo bicameral fue de más de 50 por ciento.
[16] Técnicamente el núcleo está vacío.

3. Jugadores con veto colectivos y mayorías calificadas

En esta sección examinaremos el proceso de toma de decisiones de los jugadores con veto por el dominio de la mayoría calificada. El interés sustantivo de la sección es evidente: con mucha frecuencia los jugadores con veto colectivos deciden por mayorías calificadas, como las decisiones de pasar por alto vetos presidenciales por el Congreso de los Estados Unidos (dos tercios), o veredictos del Consejo de Ministros de la Unión Europea (aproximadamente cinco séptimos), o conclusiones acerca de asuntos institucionales o constitucionales importantes en otros países (como en Francia o Bélgica).

Argumento que la verdadera importancia de las mayorías calificadas es incluso mayor por dos razones. Primero, si una secuencia de toma de decisiones incluye al final una mayoría calificada (como suele suceder; véase por ejemplo el caso de pasar por alto un veto presidencial en los Estados Unidos o resoluciones en el Consejo de Ministros de la Unión Europea o algunos casos de invalidación del Bundesrat por el Bundestag), entonces el análisis de esta secuencia requiere además una revisión hacia atrás que *empieza* a partir de los resultados de este procedimiento.[17] Segundo, hay una serie de casos en que las reglas oficiales especifican que las decisiones se tomarán por mayoría simple o por mayoría absoluta, pero las condiciones políticas transforman este requerimiento en un verdadero umbral de mayoría calificada (examinaremos estos casos con detalle a lo largo del capítulo VI).

Aunque conceptualmente una mayoría calificada ocupa la categoría intermedia entre la regla de unanimidad que examinamos en el capítulo I y la regla de la mayoría simple que se vio en la sección anterior, es muy diferente la mecánica para localizar un círculo que incluya el conjunto ganador del *statu quo* por mayoría calificada. Dada la importancia sustantiva de la toma de decisiones por mayoría calificada y dadas las diferencias técnicas entre toma de decisiones por mayoría y por mayoría calificada, dedico toda una sección a este procedimiento de toma de decisiones.

Consideremos el centro de la yema (Y, cuya definición aparece en la sección anterior) de un jugador con veto colectivo y el *statu quo* como se presenta en la gráfica II.7. Defino como *divisores q* las líneas que deja en un lado de ellas (incluyendo la línea misma) una mayoría q calificada de puntos in-

---

[17] El proceso se denomina inducción hacia atrás. Para tal análisis del procedimiento de cooperación en la Unión Europea, véase Tsebelis (1994) así como el análisis en el capítulo XI.

GRÁFICA II.7. *Comparación de círculo ganador de mayoría simple (4/7) con círculo ganador de mayoría calificada (5/7).*

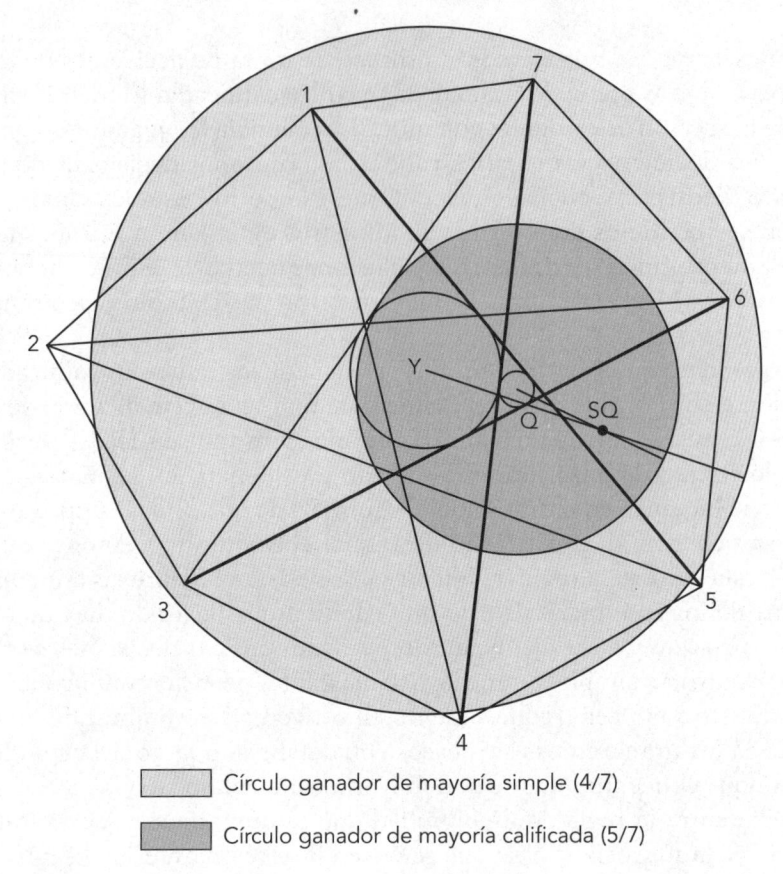

▮ Círculo ganador de mayoría simple (4/7)
▮ Círculo ganador de mayoría calificada (5/7)

dividuales. Obsérvese la diferencia entre divisores q y líneas medianas (o divisores m): las líneas medianas dejan mayorías de puntos individuales *en cada lado* de ellas, mientras que los divisores q dejan una mayoría calificada *solamente en un lado*. Defino como *divisores q pertinentes* los divisores q que dejan SQ y la mayoría q en lados opuestos. La identificación de un círculo que incluye el conjunto ganador de mayoría calificada del *statu quo* QW(SQ) se hace, de nueva cuenta, en tres pasos:

 1. Trazar todos los divisores q pertinentes. En la gráfica II.7 he seleccionado un heptágono, y estoy interesado en mayorías calificadas de cinco séptimos. La selección de un heptágono presenta la simplificación gráfica de que las líneas medianas (dejando al menos cuatro puntos en cada lado) y los divisores q (dejando cinco puntos en uno de los lados) son los mismos, así que no necesito complicar el cuadro. También selecciono el *statu quo* SQ e identifico los divisores q pertinentes (las tres líneas gruesas en la gráfica). Obsérvese que los divisores q pertinentes pasan entre SQ y Y, y los divisores q que dejan Y y SQ en el mismo lado no son pertinentes.

2. Denominar yema q al círculo (esfera o hiperesfera) que se interseca con todos los divisores q, y *círculo q* al círculo (esfera o hiperesfera) que se interseca con todos los pertinentes. En la gráfica II.6 la yema q es idéntica a la yema, y el círculo q es el círculo pequeño entre la yema y el *statu quo*. Obsérvese que aun cuando los centros de la yema y de la yema q están cerca uno de otro (en nuestra gráfica son idénticos por definición), el centro del círculo q se desplaza hacia el *statu quo* porque consideramos únicamente los divisores q pertinentes.

3. Denominar Q y q al centro del radio del círculo q y trazar el círculo (Q, d' + 2q). Éste es el círculo ganador q del *statu quo:* contiene el conjunto ganador de mayoría calificada del *statu quo* (QW(SQ)). La prueba es idéntica a la de los círculos ganadores de mayoría (desarrollados en torno de la gráfica II.5). La gráfica indica que el círculo ganador q es significativamente más pequeño que el círculo ganador de mayoría (como era de esperarse).

Podemos usar el radio de la yema q de un jugador con veto colectivo para definir su *cohesión-q* de una forma similar a la cohesión-m anterior. Conforme el radio de la yema q aumenta, la cohesión-q disminuye. Sin embargo, como lo indica la gráfica II.7, un aumento en el radio de la yema q indica que el centro del círculo q avanzará aún más hacia el *statu quo*, y que, en promedio, reducirá el tamaño del círculo ganador q. De nueva cuenta, esto es conjetura ya que podemos imaginar ejemplos contrarios en que el radio de la yema q aumenta y no obstante el tamaño del conjunto ganador también aumenta. El argumento anterior indica que las estáticas comparativas generadas por la cohesión-q son exactamente lo contrario de la cohesión-m. De hecho, mientras cohesión-q tenga un jugador con veto colectivo (cuanto más pequeño sea el radio de la yema q), mayor será el tamaño del círculo ganador q, mientras que cuanto más cohesión-m tenga un jugador con veto colectivo (cuanto más pequeño sea el radio de la yema), más pequeño será su círculo ganador de mayoría.

Otra manera de pensar sobre la cohesión-q y la estabilidad política es que un jugador con veto en cohesión-q tendrá un núcleo pequeño, lo cual quiere decir que habrá pocos puntos en el espacio que sean invulnerables, y cuanto más lejos de este punto nos vayamos, más grande se volverá el conjunto ganador q. En el caso límite en que los miembros q de un jugador con veto colectivo estén concentrados en el mismo punto, éste es el único punto del núcleo, y el conjunto ganador q aumenta en función de la distancia entre SQ y la ubicación del jugador con veto.

Conjetura II.3: La estabilidad política disminuye conforme aumenta la cohesión-q de un jugador con veto colectivo.

Hay una razón esencial por la cual las conjeturas II.1 y II.3 corren en direcciones opuestas: por definición, las líneas medianas tienen una mayoría en ambos lados, mientras que los divisores q tienen sólo en un lado una mayoría calificada. Como resultado hay una serie de diferencias. Primero, todas las líneas medianas son pertinentes para la construcción del círculo ganador, mientras que sólo los divisores q pertinentes definen el círculo ganador q. Segundo, la yema tiene que estar intersecando con todas las líneas medianas, mientras que el círculo q interseca sólo con los divisores q *pertinentes* que están localizados cerca de SQ (ya que por definición están entre SQ y diferentes mayorías q). Tercero, el círculo ganador tiene que incluir todos los reflejos de SQ con respecto a las medianas, mientras que el círculo ganador q tiene que incluir únicamente los reflejos con respecto a los divisores q pertinentes (véase gráfica II.7).

El resultado siguiente de la estática comparativa se obtiene cambiando el umbral de la mayoría calificada. Al aumentar el umbral, requerimos uno o más tomadores de decisiones individuales para consentir a un cambio del *statu quo*, lo cual acrecienta la estabilidad política.

Proposición II.4: la estabilidad política aumenta o permanece igual conforme se incrementa el umbral q de la mayoría calificada requerida.

La afirmación anterior se puede comprobar formalmente: se sostiene cualquiera que sea la distribución de las preferencias de los miembros de un jugador con veto colectivo. Como ya se observó en el capítulo I, es posible aumentar el umbral de la mayoría calificada y mantener el tamaño del conjunto ganador de la mayoría calificada (piénsese, por ejemplo, en tres jugadores que deciden por dominio de la mayoría por tres quintos o dos tercios).

La gráfica II.7 nos da una representación visual de los círculos que contienen los conjuntos ganadores del *statu quo* de mayoría calificada de cuatro séptimos y cinco séptimos. El lector puede verificar que el conjunto ganador así como el círculo ganador se contraen conforme aumenta la mayoría requerida. Esta gráfica puede ayudarnos a obtener discernimientos de situaciones en que se modifica un umbral de mayoría calificada, como sucede a la regla de limitación del tiempo de debate en el Senado de los Estados Unidos.[18] Un voto de limitación del tiempo de debate solía requerir una mayoría de dos tercios, mientras que ahora necesita sólo tres quintas partes. ¿Qué diferencia marca este cambio de reglas para la estabilidad política? Dado que cuatro séptimos (= 0.57) está cerca de tres quintos (= 0.60) y cinco séptimos (= 0.71) está cerca de dos tercios (= 0.67), la gráfica II.7 sugiere que la estabilidad política disminuye significativamente con este cambio de la regla de la limitación del tiempo de debate.

Estas cuatro conjeturas y proposiciones indican no sólo que los principios que identificamos en el capítulo I se aplican también a jugadores con veto colectivos, sino que dan un paso más allá y analizan la importancia de la cohesión m y q de los jugadores colectivos. Lo que dijimos en el capítulo I acerca de que el tamaño del conjunto ganador del *statu quo* es una condición necesaria pero no suficiente para la distancia entre el *statu quo* y la nueva política, también se sostiene en el caso de los jugadores con veto colectivos, ya que usamos el círculo que incluye el conjunto ganador del *statu quo*. Cuando este círculo es pequeño, la distancia entre SQ y SQ' será pequeña; cuando el círculo es grande, la distancia |SQ-SQ'| puede ser grande o pequeña. Estos resultados se compendian en la conclusión.

---

[18] A diferencia de la Cámara de Representantes de los Estados Unidos, no hay límite de tiempo para que los senadores hagan uso de la palabra, de modo que los senadores pueden obstruir la adopción de cualquier proyecto de ley que les desagrade. La única manera para interrumpir a un senador obstruccionista es mediante un voto de limitación del tiempo de debate en el senado.

4. Secuencia de movimientos

En las dos secciones anteriores se resolvió el problema de la ubicación del conjunto ganador de mayoría simple y calificada de jugadores con veto colectivos. Esta sección trata un problema más serio. Dados los círculos que caracterizan a la toma de decisiones por dominio de la mayoría, ¿puede un jugador con veto colectivo identificar el punto o los puntos que sean los más preferidos entre el conjunto de alternativas factibles (el conjunto ganador de los jugadores con veto individuales o colectivos restantes)?

Con el fin de resolver este problema vamos a *suponer* que un jugador con veto colectivo puede hacer propuestas dentro de un área específica denominada un *conjunto descubierto*. Restringir la ubicación de posibles propuestas no es una suposición inocua. Como se verá, elimina muchos resultados del conjunto factible. Así, será necesaria una justificación de esta premisa antes de que hagamos uso de ella. Esta sección está organizada en cuatro partes. Primero, defino el conjunto descubierto de un jugador con veto colectivo que decide por dominio de la mayoría. Segundo, examino la naturaleza restrictiva de esta suposición. Tercero, le doy una justificación para la misma. Cuarto, calculo la ubicación de una propuesta mediante un jugador con veto colectivo cuando éste usa el conjunto descubierto de las soluciones factibles.

4.1. Definición del conjunto descubierto

La gráfica II.8 indica la forma como resolvemos el problema de la elección de actores colectivos. En esta gráfica dos puntos, X y Y, se presentan junto con sus conjuntos ganadores respectivos, W(X) y W(Y). En bien de la sencillez, omito la representación de los tomadores de decisiones individuales. Supongamos (de nueva cuenta sin menoscabar la generalidad) que Y derrota a X —representado en ambos paneles de la gráfica por el hecho de que Y está dentro de W(X)—. Dado que Y ∈ W(X), hay dos posibilidades acerca de W(X) y W(Y). O los dos conjuntos ganadores se intersecan como en la gráfica II.8 A, o bien W(Y) ⊆ W(X) (léase "es un subconjunto de") como en la gráfica II.8 B.[19]

---

[19] Los casos en que los dos conjuntos ganadores no tienen nada en común o en que W(X) ⊆ W(Y) se excluyen debido a la suposición Y ∈ W(X).

JUGADORES CON VETO COLECTIVOS

GRÁFICA II.8. *(A) Y no cubre a X; (B) Y cubre a X.*

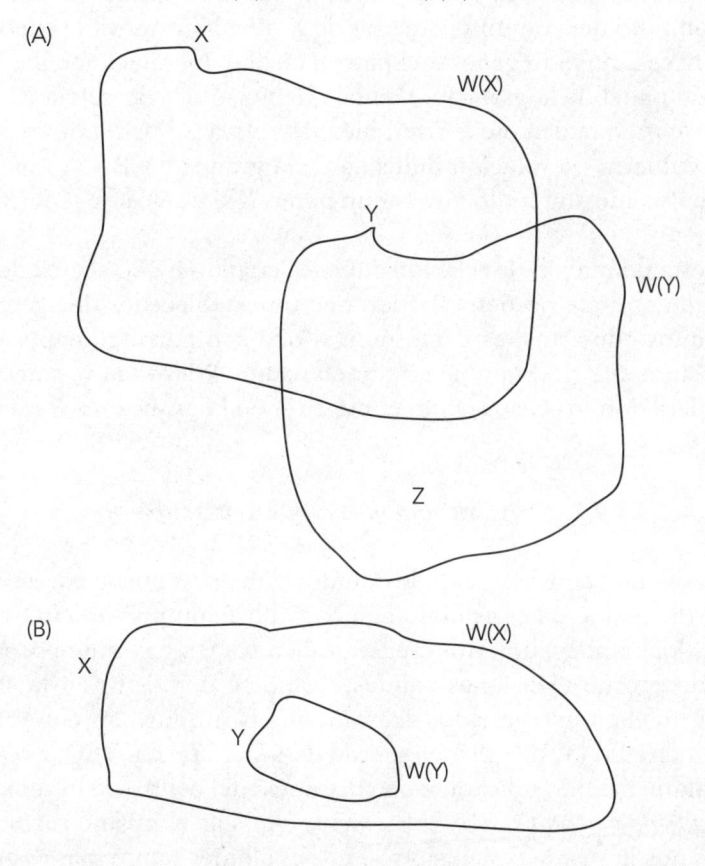

Concentrándonos en la gráfica II.8 A, dado que los dos conjuntos ganadores se intersecan, siempre podemos seleccionar un punto Z de tal modo que $Z \in W(Y)$ y $Z \notin W(X)$. Para ese punto Z tenemos:

$$Z \pi Y \pi X \pi Z \qquad (2)$$

En otras palabras, en la gráfica II.8 A podemos crear un patrón cíclico de preferencias entre X, Y y Z. Este patrón puede ser muy útil para actores estratégicos, ya que los partidarios de X, en vez de reconocer que su solución preferida fue derrotada, pueden introducir Z y pedir una comparación indirecta, de acuerdo con la cual Z derrota a Y, y X derrota a Z, de modo que X prevalece.

Como contraste, en la gráfica II.8 B, donde el conjunto ganador de Y es un subconjunto del conjunto ganador de X, resulta imposible encontrar un punto Z necesario para generar el patrón cíclico. La relación entre X y Y en el segundo panel de la gráfica II.8 es tal que no sólo Y derrota a X, sino que cualquier cosa que derrote a Y también derrota a X. Denominaremos "una relación cubierta" la relación indicada en la gráfica II.8 B.

Formalmente, un punto Y *cubre* un punto X si y sólo si $Y \in W(X)$ y $W(Y) \subseteq W(X)$.

Uso esta definición de relación cubierta cuando hablo acerca de secuencia. Argumento que no tiene sentido que un establecedor de agenda seleccione puntos cubiertos, es decir, puntos que son derrotados por otros no sólo directamente sino también indirectamente. Por lo tanto, son excluidos de consideración los casos como el punto X en la gráfica II.8 B (pero no en II.8 A).

4.2. La restricción del conjunto descubierto

Eliminar de toda consideración los puntos cubiertos puede parecer una suposición razonable. Pero es también una suposición muy restrictiva. Si eliminamos los puntos cubiertos (véase gráfica II.8 B), hay muy pocos puntos que queden como elecciones válidas. Como se demostró en la sección 1 (gráfica II.5), el círculo ganador del *statu quo* de un jugador con veto colectivo es un círculo (Y, d + 2r), en donde d es la distancia YSQ. Como resultado, cualquier punto ubicado a una distancia del centro de la yema de *más de 2r no puede derrotar a SQ directamente*. Aplicar el mismo razonamiento dos veces nos lleva a la conclusión de que cualquier punto más distante que 4r *del centro de la yema no puede derrotar a SQ indirectamente*. Como resultado, todos los puntos con distancia de Y mayor que d + 4r *son cubiertos por SQ*.

McKelvey (1980) utilizó este argumento con el fin de ubicar el conjunto de puntos que no son cubiertos por otro, que se llama el *conjunto descubierto*. Partió del centro de la yema Y y argumentó que todos los puntos fuera del círculo (Y, 4r) son cubiertos por Y. En consecuencia, este círculo contiene el conjunto descubierto, o todos los puntos que no son cubiertos por ningún punto.

El conjunto descubierto es una suposición restrictiva muy poderosa. Traslada el resultado desde cualquier lugar en el espacio a un círculo pequeño ubicado centralmente dentro del jugador con veto colectivo. De hecho, sobre la base de la discusión que rodeaba a la conjetura II.2, conforme aumenta el tamaño de un jugador con veto colectivo, se contrae en promedio el conjunto descubierto, de modo que mientras más grande sea el jugador con veto, más exacto será el pronóstico. ¿Cuán razonable es la suposición del conjunto descubierto?

4.3. ¿Podemos presuponer que el resultado estará en el conjunto descubierto?

El conjunto descubierto es un concepto de la teoría de juegos cooperativos. Seguidamente explicaré primero las suposiciones fundamentales de la teoría de juegos cooperativos y proporcionaré argumentos que respaldan su uso para el problema que tenemos en mano. Segundo, defiendo el uso del concepto particular de conjunto descubierto.

La teoría de juegos cooperativos presupone que son aplicables unos acuerdos concertados entre diferentes jugadores. Las consecuencias de esta suposición son enormes. Cuando los acuerdos son aplicables, las características institucionales dentro de los jugadores con veto colectivos tales como el establecimiento de agenda se vuelven irrelevantes. Las agendas tan sólo determinan la secuencia en la cual se toman las diferentes decisiones y los jugadores estratégicos actúan en cada etapa de una manera que promueve su acuerdo (exigible). Manteniendo constante el conjunto de alternativas factibles, la única institución que importa en un análisis de la teoría de juegos cooperativos es la regla misma de la toma de decisiones. En este sentido, la teoría de juegos cooperativos queda casi exenta de institución.

¿Es razonable presuponer que los acuerdos son exigibles dentro del establecedor de agenda? Hay un argumento que puede defender lo obligatorio de los acuerdos: la reputación. Si los actores están interesados en sus reputaciones y sufren una suficiente pérdida de reputación si no cumplen con su palabra, los acuerdos serán exigibles. Condiciones probables que pueden llevar a la exigibilidad de los acuerdos son grupos pequeños, interacción repetida o la existencia de partidos políticos responsables. La obra de Robert Axelrod (1981) ha cubierto principalmente las primeras dos razones: con interacciones repetidas es importante la sombra del castigo futuro. De modo similar, grupos pequeños pueden mantener una estrategia de castigar a los que deserten. Desarrollaré un poco más el caso de los partidos: si unos individuos dentro de un jugador con veto colectivo pertenecen a partidos e interactúan unos con otros como representantes de estos partidos, hay en juego significativamente más que reputaciones individuales. La deserción de un acuerdo será denunciada a los otros partidos y a la población en general, y las consecuencias serán importantes para el desertor. Como resultado, la suposición de acuerdos obligatorios no es improbable en el mundo real de la política.

Sin embargo, incluso si los acuerdos fueran exigibles, ¿por qué conducirían al conjunto descubierto? Ofrezco tres argumentos. El primero es que restringir el resultado al conjunto descubierto equivale a pasar por alto otros puntos cubiertos, tales como X en la gráfica II.8 B. ¿Por qué los jugadores racionales acordarían cubrir puntos cuando una mayoría de ellos puede hacer un acuerdo que conducirá a Y y derrotará a X no sólo directamente sino también indirectamente? Y si la elección entre dos contratos, uno especificando X y otro Y, es obvia, entonces la suposición de exigibilidad antes examinada conducirá en realidad a Y.

El segundo argumento es que una serie de otros conceptos como el conjunto Banks (Banks, 1985) o el *Tournament Equilibrium Set* de Schwartz (TEQ; Schwartz, 1990) produce resultados en algún subconjunto del conjunto descubierto. Para nuestros fines, lo más importante es el TEQ de Schwartz. Éste presupone que los contratos entre legisladores son exigibles pero los legisladores son libres de recontratar; es decir, si encuentran una propuesta que una coalición mayoritaria prefiera, pueden redactar un contrato exigible para respaldarla. Presupone también que dos propuestas cualesquiera pueden ser comparadas directamente. Calcula el conjunto más pequeño dentro del cual es probable que produzca resultados este proceso de recontratación cooperativa. Denomina TEQ a este conjunto y prueba que es un subconjunto de un conjunto descubierto.

El tercer argumento es que incluso los juegos no cooperativos conducen a equilibrios ubicados centralmente. Por ejemplo, Baron (1996) ofrece un modelo de votación infinitamente repetida, y el equilibrio se aproxima al votante medio. Los resultados en dimensiones múltiples conducen a expectativas de convergencia hacia el centro del espacio político (donde está ubicado el conjunto descubierto). Por ejemplo, Baron y Herron (1999), usando un modelo bidimensional con tres legisladores, producen resultados localizados centralmente cuando el horizonte temporal se expande.

Estos argumentos indican (aunque no prueban) que el conjunto descubierto es una suposición razonable cuando tratamos de una toma de decisiones dentro de comités (grupos pequeños con interacciones frecuentes) o con interacciones entre partidos. A su vez, las decisiones de actores más grandes como una cámara de un parlamento se basan en propuestas de tales actores pequeños (ya sea un comité formal o una reunión informal de líderes de partidos, o el gobierno), de modo que suponer que los resultados cubiertos serán excluidos no es algo arbitrario, dadas las circunstancias. Si el lector está en desacuerdo con esta afirmación, será incapaz de restringir el pronóstico del resultado más allá del conjunto ganador del *statu quo* como se calculó en las secciones 2 y 3.

4.4. Cálculo del conjunto descubierto inducido

Para los lectores que están de acuerdo en que restringir los resultados a los puntos descubiertos del establecedor de agenda (dentro del conjunto ganador del *statu quo*) es una restricción razonable, la tarea no está terminada. Ahora tenemos que identificar estos puntos.

Cabría pensar que la intersección del conjunto descubierto del establecedor de agenda con el conjunto ganador de los otros jugadores con veto resolvería nuestro problema. Sin embargo, esta no es una solución, dado que tal vez los dos conjuntos no se intersequen. Además, algunos puntos en el conjunto ganador de los otros jugadores con veto pueden ser cubiertos por puntos que en sí mismos no son factibles (no pertenecen al conjunto ganador).

El problema de la toma de decisiones de los miembros individuales del establecedor de agenda colectivo es el siguiente: identificar, dentro de los puntos del conjunto factible (el conjunto ganador de los otros jugadores con veto), a aquellos que no estén cubiertos por otros puntos factibles. Llamaremos a la solución para este problema la identificación del *conjunto descubierto inducido (o el conjunto ganador de los otros jugadores con veto)*.

La gráfica II.9 nos ayuda a resolver este problema sobre la base del análisis presentado hasta aquí. Llamemos W al área donde ha de hacerse una propuesta ganadora (el conjunto ganador de los otros jugadores con veto existentes). Llamemos Y al centro de la yema del establecedor de agenda. Si Y fuera un jugador con veto individual, haría la propuesta PI (el punto de W más cercano a su preferencia Y). Si denominamos la distancia YY' = d sabemos que cualquier punto fuera del círculo (Y, d + 4r) queda cubierto por PI (véase sección 4.2).

Tsebelis y Money (1997) estrecharon aún más el área de la propuesta al usar cálculos más precisos. Demostraron que el conjunto descubierto indu-

GRÁFICA II.9. *Área propuesta por un jugador con veto colectivo.*

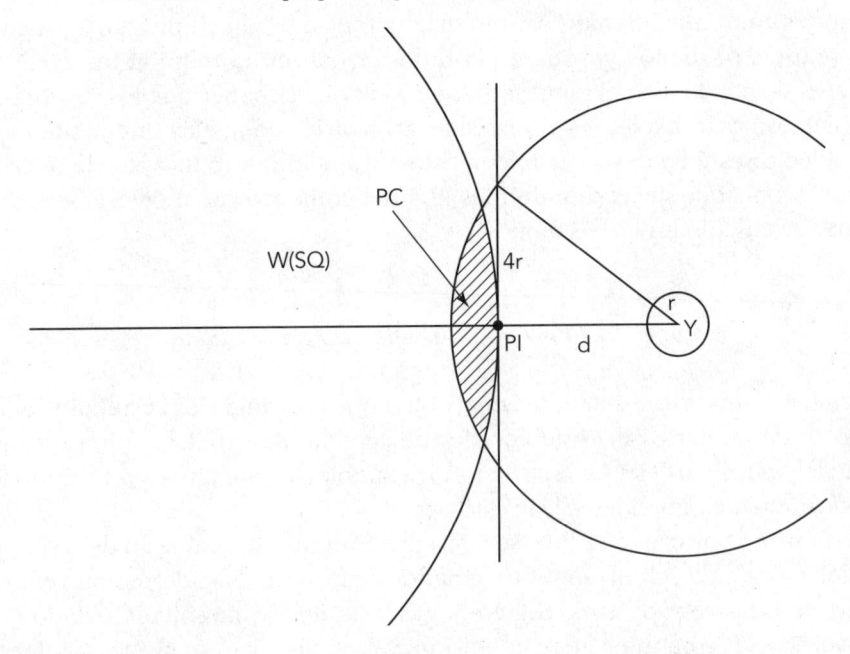

cido está incluido en un círculo (Y, raíz cuadrada (d^2 + ($4r^2$))). Ésta es el área sombreada en la gráfica II.9, denominada PC (propuesta por un colectivo). El lector puede verificar que la propuesta de un jugador con veto colectivo que decida por dominio de la mayoría estará en el área que propondría un individuo ficticio ubicado en el centro de la yema del jugador con veto colectivo.

Proposición II.5: Si los jugadores con veto colectivos hacen propuestas dentro de su conjunto descubierto inducido, harán aproximadamente las mismas propuestas que los individuales (ubicados en el centro de su yema).

La proposición anterior también se sustenta para jugadores con veto colectivos que deciden por mayorías calificadas, dado que una propuesta de mayoría calificada no puede ser ubicada fuera de las propuestas hechas por una mayoría. Así, los jugadores con veto colectivos se comportarán aproximadamente como los individuales no sólo en las propuestas que aceptarán (como se vio en las secciones 2 y 3) sino también en las propuestas que hacen. La suposición necesaria para la última afirmación es que los jugadores con veto colectivos no hacen propuestas cubiertas (es decir, propuestas que sean derrotadas tanto directa como indirectamente por una alternativa).

5. Conclusiones

Comencé este capítulo presentando la diferencia entre jugadores con veto individuales y colectivos. Los jugadores con veto individuales deciden por la regla de la unanimidad (dado que el desacuerdo de parte de cualquiera de ellos puede abortar un cambio del *statu quo*), mientras que los jugadores con veto colectivos aplican mayoría calificada o mayoría simple para sus decisiones. Vimos en la gráfica II.1 que todas las intuiciones generadas por el capítulo I eran válidas, pero que el conjunto de puntos que derrota al *statu quo* (W(SQ)) deja de tener la forma circular simple de los jugadores con veto individuales. El primer objetivo de este capítulo fue encontrar una aproximación simple de las decisiones según mayoría y mayoría calificada.

Calculé el *círculo ganador* de un jugador con veto colectivo, un círculo que contiene el conjunto ganador del *statu quo* por dominio de la mayoría.[20] Según mis cálculos, la estabilidad política *disminuye* si los actores que intervienen en la decisión son jugadores con veto colectivos en oposición a individuales. Los jugadores con veto colectivos pueden alcanzar resultados cuando los individuales no llegan a ponerse de acuerdo. Éste puede ser el caso de las instituciones estadounidenses, donde los desacuerdos entre los miembros de la Cámara y entre senadores pueden proporcionar el espacio necesario para llegar a compromisos mientras los tomadores de decisiones individuales (tales como partidos rígidos que controlen la mayoría de cada cámara) no podrían ponerse de acuerdo.

[20] Para la toma de decisiones por mayoría simple he utilizado análisis anteriores de Ferejohn, McKelvey y Packell (1984), quienes identificaron la yema de una colectividad que decide por dominio de la mayoría como el círculo más pequeño que interseca todas las líneas medianas, líneas que tienen mayorías en cada uno de sus lados. El centro de la yema Y está ubicado centralmente dentro del jugador con veto colectivo. Podemos pensar en él como la aproximación más cercana a una mediana multidimensional. El radio de la yema es una medición de la dispersión de los miembros de la colectividad: un radio pequeño significa que las preferencias en ambos lados están concentradas o simétricamente distribuidas. En general el radio de la yema disminuye conforme aumenta el número de miembros de un jugador con veto colectivo. He demostrado que los jugadores con veto colectivos aceptarán alternativas para el SQ sólo si estas alternativas están ubicadas dentro de un círculo (Y, d + 2r), en donde Y es el centro de la yema, r es el radio de la yema y d es la distancia YSQ.

Repetí estos cálculos para la toma de decisiones por mayoría calificada y calculé el *círculo ganador q* del *statu quo*.[21] Según lo esperado, el círculo ganador q se contrae conforme aumenta la mayoría requerida. Además, el círculo ganador q cambia con la ubicación del *statu quo*.

Como resultado de estos cálculos, puedo sustituir jugadores con veto colectivos por individuales ficticios y usar los círculos ganadores de estos últimos para analizar la estabilidad política. Sin embargo, estos círculos ofrecen las condiciones necesarias aunque no suficientes para que un resultado derrote al *statu quo*. De hecho, todos los puntos fuera de un círculo ganador o un círculo ganador q son derrotados por SQ, pero no todos los puntos dentro de esos círculos derrotan a SQ. La aproximación del conjunto ganador del *statu quo* por círculos ganadores no afecta las pruebas empíricas que realizaremos: un círculo ganador pequeño es una condición necesaria pero no suficiente para una distancia pequeña |SQ-SQ'|. Una prueba de la variancia de |SQ-SQ'| también es necesaria como en el capítulo I. Dado que los círculos ganadores son aproximaciones, se reducirá la exactitud de las pruebas correspondientes.

Mi análisis demuestra que hay una diferencia importante entre la toma de decisiones por mayoría simple o calificada. En las decisiones por dominio de la mayoría, la estabilidad política aumenta con la cohesión;[22] en las decisiones por mayoría calificada, la estabilidad política disminuye con la cohesión.[23]

Con el fin de pasar a temas de secuencia de decisiones, necesitamos suposiciones adicionales. Las suposiciones requeridas intentan abordar el problema genérico de los tomadores de decisiones colectivos según el dominio de la mayoría: sus preferencias colectivas pueden ser ambiguas. De hecho, es posible que diferentes mayorías puedan tener el siguiente perfil de preferencia sobre tres posibles resultados:

---

[21] He identificado los divisores q pertinentes (las líneas que dejan una mayoría q calificada en un lado de ellas y el *statu quo* en la otra). Consideré el círculo más pequeño que se interseca con todos los divisores q relevantes. Denominé este círculo el círculo q con centro Q y radio q. Demostré que el conjunto ganador de mayoría calificada del *statu quo* está ubicado dentro de un círculo (Q, d' + 2q), en donde Q y q son el centro y el radio del círculo q, y d' es la distancia QSQ. Estas afirmaciones se hacen más concretas si consultamos la gráfica II.7.

[22] La cohesión-m más grande significa un radio más pequeño de la yema, lo cual conduce a un círculo ganador más pequeño, de modo que aumenta la estabilidad política.

[23] La cohesión-q más grande contribuye a un círculo-q más grande, lo cual da lugar a un círculo ganador-q mayor, de modo que disminuye la estabilidad política.

Z π Y π X π Z (en donde π significa mayoría preferida)

Este perfil de preferencia indica que aunque Y es preferida sobre X directamente, es derrotada por X indirectamente (si introducimos Z en la comparación, X es preferida sobre Z, la cual es más preferida sobre Y). Esta ambigüedad de elecciones (discrepancia entre preferencias directas e indirectas) puede inducir a los actores estratégicos a proponer alternativas adicionales con el fin de desequilibrar resultados que les disgusten. La suposición que presento no limita estas consideraciones estratégicas de los tomadores de decisiones. Sencillamente estipula lo siguiente: si un jugador con veto colectivo tiene que escoger entre X y Y, la preferencia de una mayoría es Y, y no hay alternativa Z tal como Z π Y π X π Z, entonces la elección será Y. Esto puede parecer una suposición sencilla y obvia, pero tiene consecuencias restrictivas importantes: tan sólo sobreviven las propuestas localizadas centralmente, y si el establecedor de agenda colectivo hace una propuesta dentro del conjunto ganador de los jugadores con veto existentes, esta propuesta se aproximará mucho a la propuesta que hubiera hecho un establecedor de agenda individual.[24]

Hay dos puntos en este capítulo que son contrarios a la intuición, y que necesito señalar. El primero se relaciona con la cohesión de los jugadores con veto colectivos y la estabilidad política: cuanto más cohesivo sea un jugador con veto colectivo que decida por regla de la mayoría, mayor será la estabilidad política, y cuanto más cohesivo sea un jugador con veto colectivo que decida por mayoría calificada, menor será la estabilidad política. El segundo punto se refiere a las restricciones con las cuales los jugadores con veto colectivos harán propuestas similares con los individuales: deberán hacer propuestas que no sean derrotadas tanto directa como indirectamente por otras alternativas disponibles.

En conclusión, los jugadores con veto colectivos se aproximan a la conducta de jugadores individuales. Podemos aproximar sus preferencias mediante un círculo ganador (que incluye al conjunto ganador real) ya sea que decidan por mayoría simple o calificada. También tenemos buenas razones para suponer que ellos harán aproximadamente las mismas propuestas con jugadores con veto individuales ubicados en el centro de su yema.

El objetivo de este capítulo ha sido pasar de los jugadores con veto individuales a los colectivos. La introducción y las conclusiones proporcio-

[24] Localizado en el centro de la yema Y del colectivo.

nan la intuición que sustenta mi enfoque. La parte principal del capítulo proporcionó el algoritmo de identificación de círculos ganadores y círculos ganadores q, de propuestas que pueden ser aceptadas por jugadores con veto colectivos ya sea por mayoría simple o calificada, así como el algoritmo para identificar las propuestas que harán los jugadores con veto colectivos (suponiendo que los puntos cubiertos no serán escogidos). Ahora pasaremos al análisis de sistemas políticos existentes sobre la base de la teoría presentada.

Segunda parte

JUGADORES CON VETO Y ANÁLISIS INSTITUCIONAL

En la parte anterior identificamos diferencias en sistemas abstractos de jugador con veto. Vimos lo que sucede si agregamos jugadores con veto, si los nuevos jugadores con veto están cerca o lejos de los ya existentes, y si el núcleo de unanimidad de un sistema de jugadores con veto incluye el núcleo de unanimidad de otro. Vimos también qué diferencia hay si enfocamos con seriedad la toma de decisiones colectiva y examinamos todas las diferentes reglas de toma de decisiones: mayoría, mayorías calificadas y unanimidad. En esta parte aplico el marco de referencia a estructuras institucionales específicas de interés en los análisis de política comparada: regímenes democráticos y no democráticos, presidencialismo y parlamentarismo, unicameralismo y bicameralismo, sistemas bipartidistas y multipartidistas, así como partidos débiles y fuertes.

Tengo dos distintas metas en esta parte. La primera es desarrollar reglas específicas para los análisis empíricos que siguen: cuáles instituciones o partidos cuentan como jugadores con veto bajo qué condiciones, cómo incluimos las interacciones de gobiernos y parlamentos en el análisis, y el efecto de referéndums o de decisiones de mayoría calificada para un sistema político. El segundo es volver a examinar, sobre la base de este análisis, las ideas dominantes en la política comparada.

Los descubrimientos de esta parte serán tanto positivos como negativos. Algunas partes de la sabiduría popular se confirman, otras son falsas, mientras que otros aspectos son discutibles. Por ejemplo, la distinción de regímenes en presidencial y parlamentario se puede superar, y dentro de cada una de las categorías es grande la varianza entre sistemas específicos. Por lo tanto, los sistemas políticos reales, en vez de pertenecer a dos distribuciones distintas, forman un continuo donde las similitudes pueden ser más grandes a través de los sistemas que dentro de ellos. Como resultado, la teoría de los jugadores con veto desafía algunas distinciones tradicionales como presidencialismo *vs.* parlamentarismo, que se usaban en la política comparada.

Por añadidura, nos concentraremos en diferentes características de algunas de las clasificaciones convencionales y estudiaremos propiedades adicionales de los sistemas políticos. Por ejemplo, en vez de concentrarnos en el sistema de partido de países con sistemas parlamentarios, la teoría de los jugadores con veto se concentra en la estructura de las coaliciones gubernamentales así como en algunas características institucionales (existencia de un presidente o de una segunda cámara capaz de vetar legislación) con resultados significativamente distintos.

Esta parte está organizada a lo largo de las líneas del análisis institucional tradicional. El capítulo III trata de regímenes: democráticos y no democráticos, presidenciales y parlamentarios. El capítulo IV trata la relación entre gobiernos y parlamentos. En el capítulo V se verá la legislación directa de los ciudadanos por medio del referéndums. En el capítulo VI veremos el federalismo, el bicameralismo y las mayorías calificadas. Los títulos (con la posible excepción de las mayorías calificadas) son términos comunes en cualquier libro de política comparada. Agregué las mayorías calificadas como tema de estudio porque, como sostengo, son mucho más frecuentes *(de facto)* que como se pensaría tras una consideración superficial del texto de los arreglos institucionales.

Aunque los títulos sean familiares, la lógica del análisis habitualmente marcará un contraste con los análisis tradicionales, mientras toma los conceptos que son congruentes con los jugadores con veto. Los ángulos principales del análisis serán las propiedades de diferentes constelaciones de jugadores con veto, y la identidad del establecedor de agenda en cada proceso de toma de decisiones. Los capítulos III y IV plantean el argumento de que podemos entender la mayoría de las diferencias entre regímenes, o en la interacción entre gobiernos y parlamentos, concentrándonos en el tema del establecimiento de la agenda. En el capítulo III se argumenta que a pesar de las expectativas generadas acerca de la ubicación del poder político por los adjetivos "presidencial" y "parlamentario" asociados con diferentes regímenes, el control de la agenda pertenece habitualmente al jugador contrario (el gobierno en el sistema parlamentario y el parlamento en el sistema presidencial). En el capítulo IV, que trata sobre las relaciones entre gobierno y parlamento, se analizan las instituciones de control de la agenda y se sostiene que son estas instituciones las que regulan la interacción y no la duración del gobierno, como se afirma en la bibliografía (Lijphart, 1999). En el capítulo V, sobre referéndums, se arguye que todos los referéndums agregan un jugador con veto más (la población), y que sus diferencias se basan en la pregunta de quién controla cada parte de la agenda. En el capítulo VI se tocan los temas de federalismo, bicameralismo y mayorías calificadas desde la perspectiva del número de jugadores con veto. En ese capítulo se presenta el argumento de que el federalismo suele tener instituciones distintivas que regulan la toma de decisiones al nivel nacional, y que el bicameralismo y las mayorías calificadas aumentan el número de jugadores con veto, pero de maneras que producen resultados políticos diferentes.

III. REGÍMENES: NO DEMOCRÁTICO, PRESIDENCIAL Y PARLAMENTARIO

EN ESTE capítulo le presento al lector los debates de la bibliografía tradicional. Posteriormente explico la diferencia entre regímenes como diferencia en características esenciales del proceso de establecimiento de la agenda: los regímenes democrático y no democrático difieren en que el proceso de establecimiento de la agenda puede ser competitivo o no (una diferencia en el *proceso* del establecimiento de la agenda); los regímenes presidencial y parlamentario difieren en la identidad del establecedor de la agenda (gobierno en sistemas parlamentarios, parlamento en sistemas presidenciales; exactamente lo contrario de las expectativas que sus nombres sugieren). Por añadidura, presidencialismo contra parlamentarismo se basa en lo que es el cambio endógeno permitido (cambios en gobierno en comparación con cambios en las coaliciones legislativas). Como resultado de esta diferencia, en los sistemas parlamentarios los partidos son más homogéneos o al menos más disciplinados que en los sistemas presidenciales. Mi argumento general es que la mayor parte de las diferencias entre los regímenes que se examinan en la bibliografía tradicional se pueden estudiar como diferencias en número, posiciones ideológicas y cohesión de los jugadores con veto correspondientes, así como la identidad, preferencias y poderes institucionales de los establecedores de la agenda. Los argumentos desarrollados en este capítulo conducen a la conclusión de que los adjetivos "presidencial" y "parlamentario" asociados con diferentes regímenes generan impresiones erróneas acerca de la distribución del poder: el control de la agenda pertenece muy a menudo al gobierno en los sistemas parlamentarios y al parlamento en los sistemas presidenciales.

El capítulo está organizado en tres partes. Primero, analizo los principales argumentos de la bibliografía sobre los regímenes no democráticos, en comparación con los democráticos y presidenciales, en comparación con el parlamentario. Seguidamente ofrezco la perspectiva de la teoría de los jugadores con veto acerca de los temas que se plantean en la bibliografía tradicional. Por último, reviso algunas de las críticas de la teoría de los jugadores con veto en lo tocante a este análisis.

1. Los regímenes autoritario, presidencial y parlamentario en la bibliografía

Cabría argumentar que un análisis que utilice el número y las propiedades de los jugadores con veto como sus variables independientes equivale a desconocer las distinciones más fundamentales que se hacen en la bibliografía: la que existe entre regímenes democrático y no democrático, o entre regímenes presidencial y parlamentario. De hecho, tanto un régimen democrático como uno autoritario pueden tener un solo jugador con veto, o un régimen presidencial y uno parlamentario pueden tener varios jugadores con veto. ¿Hay alguna diferencia? Con el fin de responder esta pregunta resumiré primero la bibliografía sobre regímenes democráticos y autoritarios, y algo sobre presidencialismo y parlamentarismo. Por supuesto, el espacio no permite un estudio más profundo de tales temas, cada uno de los cuales cuenta con una extensa bibliografía.

1.1. Regímenes democráticos vs. autoritarios

Según muchos teóricos, la democracia converge, o debería converger, hacia el bien común, como lo expresa Jean-Jacques Rousseau en *El contrato social*. Rousseau cree que empezamos con deseos individuales y los acumulamos, y "la suma de la diferencia es la voluntad general". Esta sencilla formulación de la voluntad general ha sido criticada por Kenneth Arrow (1951) en su teorema de la "imposibilidad", lo que ha dado lugar a una extensa bibliografía.[1]

Por esos mismos años, Joseph Schumpeter criticó también a Rousseau, y sustituyó su concepto de democracia por la competencia de la élite por el gobierno. Según la definición de Schumpeter, "el método democrático es aquel arreglo institucional para llegar a decisiones políticas en el cual los individuos adquieren el poder de decidir mediante la pugna competitiva por el voto del pueblo" (1950: 269).

De acuerdo con modelos subsecuentes de la democracia (Downs, 1957), la competencia de la élite conduce a la moderación, al menos cuando hay

---

[1] Véase Riker (1982b) para una revisión de esta bibliografía, y la conclusión de que el concepto de la voluntad general de Rousseau no puede sobrevivir a la crítica generada por esta bibliografía.

dos partidos políticos de modo que cada uno de ellos trata de atraer al "votante promedio". Giovanni Sartori (1976), considerando los sistemas de partido existentes, amplió el argumento de Downs hacia los sistemas de menos de cinco partidos. Afirmó que tales sistemas representan un pluralismo "moderado", mientras que los sistemas con más de seis partidos son propensos a incluir partidos "extremistas" con tendencias centrífugas. Además, la competencia de la élite da lugar a responsividad de los gobiernos por temor a perder la siguiente elección.

La definición de Joseph Schumpeter tuvo una profunda repercusión sobre la teoría política y las ciencias sociales en general. Se le considera una definición mínima de la democracia y una condición necesaria para la misma. De hecho, análisis subsecuentes han ensanchado, en general, los requerimientos. La primera y probablemente la extensión más prominente de requerimientos de democracia (debido a su utilización por parte de instituciones internacionales para evaluar cuáles países son democráticos) es creación de Robert Dahl.

Dahl (1971: 2) reserva el término de democracia "para un sistema político, una de cuyas características es la cualidad de ser casi por completo responsivo a todos los ciudadanos". Plantea cinco requerimientos para la democracia. Éstos incluyen igualdad en las votaciones, participación efectiva, comprensión ilustrada, control final sobre la agenda e inclusión (Dahl, 1982: 6). Dado que es difícil lograr estos requerimientos en cualquier circunstancia, Dahl crea un nuevo término: "poliarquía" (1971: 8), y propone una serie de siete restricciones necesarias para la misma (1982: 10-11). Estas restricciones incluyen reglas acerca de la libertad de información para los ciudadanos, la libertad de expresión y de asociación, el derecho a votar y a ser candidato, la libertad de elección y decisiones políticas tomadas por funcionarios elegidos.

Otros autores han criticado a Dahl por ser demasiado formal. Algunas de estas críticas introducen criterios adicionales sobre desigualdades (particularmente en riqueza e ingreso). Estas concepciones expanden la democracia desde la esfera política hasta la social y económica.[2]

Por otro lado, Adam Przeworski (1999) ha hecho una defensa minimalista de la democracia de Schumpeter. Junto con toda la bibliografía que proviene de Arrow, reconoce que la democracia no es "racional en el sentido que se daba al término en el siglo XVIII" (Przeworski, 1999: 25). En otras

---

[2] Véanse Macpherson (1973), Marshall (1965) y, más recientemente, Rueschemeyer, Huber Stephens y Stephens (1992).

palabras, no hay nada que se pueda definir como el bien común a ser maximizado (existencia). Si lo hubiese, el proceso democrático no lo identifica necesariamente (convergencia), y si lo hiciera, la democracia es el único sistema que lo hace (unicidad). "Parece, por tanto, que escoger mandatarios por elecciones no asegura ni la racionalidad, ni la representación ni la igualdad" (Przeworski, 1999: 43). Pero según este análisis hay algo más que hace deseable la noción de democracia de Schumpeter, y es aquí donde el análisis de Przeworski se aleja de todos los demás enfoques que agregan requerimientos a la definición de Schumpeter.

Przeworski quita la parte de la competencia de la élite y la remplaza por una lotería. De esta manera hace abortar cualquier conexión entre elecciones y representación.

> Obsérvese que cuando la autorización para gobernar es determinada en una lotería, los ciudadanos no tienen sanción electoral, es prospectiva o retrospectiva, y los que ocupan puestos no tienen incentivos electorales para comportarse bien mientras están en el puesto. Dado que elegir gobiernos mediante una lotería hace que sus oportunidades de sobrevivencia sean independientes de su conducta, no hay razones para esperar que los gobiernos se conduzcan de una manera representativa porque quieran ganar la reelección [Przeworski, 1999: 45].[3]

Przeworski pasa a demostrar que incluso este sistema subestándar en ciertas condiciones presenta una ventaja importante: que los perdedores en una elección pueden preferir esperar hasta el siguiente *round* en vez de rebelarse en contra del sistema. Esta característica de conservación pacífica *a fortiori* es aplicable a la democracia según Schumpeter, donde los ciudadanos controlan las sanciones electorales, y los representantes saben que la reelección depende de su capacidad de respuesta.

Esta es una definición muy breve y parcial de la bibliografía sobre democracia. He pasado por alto completamente temas polémicos, es decir, cuestiones sobre la transformación de las preferencias de los ciudadanos.[4] Mi relación demuestra que la mayor parte de la bibliografía gira en torno de la idea de Schumpeter de competencia de la élite por el gobierno, que genera responsividad del gobierno hacia el pueblo. Por otro lado, los regímenes no democráticos carecen de la transparencia de selección de liderazgo, y pueden carecer de representación, pero (¿sorprendentemente?) en pro-

[3] Para un análisis más detallado de la democracia, véase Przeworski (1991).
[4] Para un estudio actualizado de tales problemas, véase Shapiro (2001).

medio no producen un desempeño económico inferior al de los regímenes democráticos (Przeworski y Limongi, 1997; Przeworski *et al.*, 2000).

1.2. Presidencialismo y parlamentarismo

Por definición, la distinción entre los regímenes presidencial y parlamentario es la independencia o interdependencia política de las ramas legislativa y ejecutiva. Según Stepan y Skach (1993: 3-4):

> Un régimen parlamentario puro en una democracia es un sistema de dependencia mutua: *1*. El jefe del poder ejecutivo debe estar apoyado por una mayoría en la legislatura y puede caer si recibe un voto de no confianza. *2*. El poder ejecutivo (normalmente en conjunción con el jefe del Estado) tiene la capacidad de disolver la legislatura y convocar a elecciones. Un régimen presidencial puro en una democracia es un sistema de independencia mutua: *1*. El poder legislativo tiene un mandato electoral fijo que constituye su propia fuente de legitimidad. *2*. El jefe del poder ejecutivo tiene un mandato electoral fijo que es su propia fuente de legitimidad.

Stepan y Skach consideran que estas definiciones aportan "las características necesarias y suficientes" y que son "más que clasificatorias". Lo que tiene importancia aquí es que articulan el consenso que hay en la bibliografía. A partir de Bageot (1867) (en Norton, 1990) y pasando por Linz (1996), Lijphart (1992, 1999), hasta Shugart y Carey (1992), la dependencia política entre el legislativo y el ejecutivo es la característica que define al parlamentarismo. Elgie (1998) ha criticado la distinción tachándola de ambigua y de conducir a diferentes clasificaciones del mismo país, y Strom (2000) ha tratado de abordar los problemas ofreciendo una definición mínima de parlamentarismo que se basa únicamente en la posibilidad de que el parlamento separe al gobierno de sus funciones.

La mayor parte de la bibliografía se ha concentrado en las consecuencias de estas distinciones para diferentes regímenes. ¿Son los sistemas presidenciales mejores o peores que los parlamentarios? En particular, ¿es el presidencialismo una base estable para la democracia? El debate más famoso se originó en un artículo de Juan Linz (1996), donde criticaba la capacidad del presidencialismo para sustentar regímenes democráticos: "Quizás la mejor manera de resumir las diferencias básicas entre sistemas presidencial y parlamentario consiste en decir que mientras que el parlamentarismo imparte flexibilidad al proceso político, el presidencialismo lo hace muy rígido" (Linz, 1996: 128). La razón de la flexibilidad del parlamentarismo y la rigidez del presidencialismo es la endogeneidad de la formación del gobierno en un sistema parlamentario. Una vez que se han celebrado elecciones, o bien hay un partido mayoritario que forma el gobierno, o bien los distintos partidos entablan negociaciones acerca de la formación del gobierno. El resultado de estas negociaciones es un gobierno que cuenta con el respaldo del parlamento, y si en algún momento este respaldo es socavado o desafiado, un voto de confianza resuelve el problema. En cambio, en los sistemas presidenciales no hay un mecanismo de solución de conflictos entre el ejecutivo y el legislativo. Como resultado, el conflicto puede resolverse a través de medios extraconstitucionales:

> Sustituir a un presidente que ha perdido la confianza de su partido o del pueblo es una proposición extremadamente difícil. Incluso cuando la polarización se ha intensificado hasta el punto de la violencia y la ilegalidad, un presidente empecinado puede seguir en el puesto. Para cuando los lentos mecanismos que hay para echarlo fuera e instalar a un sucesor más capaz y conciliador hayan funcionado, puede ya ser demasiado tarde [Linz, 1996: 137-138].

Sin embargo, el análisis de Linz ha sido tildado de parcial y de extrapolar las experiencias de los países latinoamericanos, de Chile en particular. Donald Horowitz rebatió los resultados de Linz basándose en los casos de Sri Lanka y de Nigeria (1996: 149):

> El pleito de Linz no es con la presidencia, sino con dos características que ejemplifican la versión de la democracia según Westminster: primero, elecciones por pluralidad o mayoría de votos que producen una mayoría de escaños al excluir competidores de todo tercer partido; y segundo, democracia de adversarios, con su marcada división entre ganadores y perdedores, gobierno y oposición. Dado que éstas son las objeciones fundamentales de Linz, no es difícil invertir sus argumentos y aplicarlos a sistemas parlamentarios, al menos donde produzcan mayorías y minorías coherentes. [...] La tesis de Linz se reduce a un argumento no en contra de la presidencia sino en contra de la elección por pluralidad, no en favor de los *sistemas* parlamentarios sino en favor de las *coaliciones* parlamentarias.

Es interesante notar dos cosas en esta polémica. Primero, los argumentos presentados en ambas partes están expuestos a sesgos en la selección del caso. En realidad, cada uno de los dos polemistas extrapola de un número muy limitado de casos, y aunque ambos presentan atisbos extremadamente interesantes acerca de la forma como funcionan los sistemas políticos, los dos son vulnerables a extrapolaciones inexactas de casos parciales. Segundo, es interesante notar cómo se asemeja el argumento de Horowitz al argumento de este libro, donde lo que importa no es el tipo de régimen sino el número de jugadores con veto. Regresaremos a este punto en la siguiente sección.

Análisis empíricos más recientes han corroborado las expectativas de Linz. Por ejemplo, Stepan y Skach (1993) examinaron 75 países y descubrieron que la democracia sobrevivía 61% del tiempo en sistemas parlamentarios y sólo 20% en sistemas presidenciales. De modo similar, Cheibub y Limongi (2001), después de examinar "99 periodos de democracia" entre 1950 y 1990, llegan a la conclusión de que la vida esperada de la democracia bajo el presidencialismo es de aproximadamente 21 años, mientras que bajo el parlamentarismo es de 73 años. La introducción de una serie de controles del nivel económico no altera los resultados. Cheibub y Limongi (2001: 5) llegan a esta conclusión:

> Así, está claro que las democracias presidenciales son menos durables que las parlamentarias. Esta diferencia no se debe a la riqueza de las naciones en las cuales se observaron estas instituciones, ni a su desempeño económico. Tampoco se debe a ninguna de las condiciones políticas en las cuales funcionaban. Las democracias presidenciales son sencillamente más frágiles en todas las condiciones económicas y políticas consideradas antes.

De mayor interés para el análisis que se presenta en este libro es el resultado de Shugart y Carey (1992: 154-58), según el cual los poderes presidenciales fuertes (tanto legislativo como no legislativo) son más proclives a llevar al colapso. De acuerdo con sus datos (que incluyen regímenes presidenciales y semipresidenciales desde comienzos de siglo), los regímenes donde el presidente tenía poderes legislativos débiles se colapsaron 23.5% del tiempo (cuatro de cada 17), mientras que la probabilidad de un colapso era de casi el doble (40% de las veces, o seis de cada 15) en regímenes con presidentes legislativamente fuertes (Tsebelis, 1995a). El descubrimiento de Shugart y Carey es congruente con la teoría de los jugadores con veto que se presenta aquí. Como decíamos en la introducción, los regímenes con presidentes legislativamente fuertes tienen un jugador adicional con veto, de modo que la estabilidad política aumenta. Como resultado de esa mayor estabilidad política el régimen puede ser incapaz de proporcionar cambios políticos cuando sea necesario, lo cual conduciría al colapso. Un argumento similar se encuentra en Przeworski y colaboradores (2000: 134), quienes descubrieron que cuando el partido de un presidente tiene entre un tercio y una mitad de los escaños en el parlamento, la probabilidad de colapso aumenta, y el régimen presidencial se hace "particularmente vulnerable", dado que el presidente puede vetar legislación aprobada en el parlamento y la situación puede conducir a un *impasse* político.

Sin embargo, la supervivencia no es la única característica que divide a los regímenes presidencial y parlamentario, según la bibliografía. La mayoría de los académicos, al menos en la década de 1980 y comienzos de la de 1990, cuando el debate se efectuó, creían que hay una distinción importante que genera un sinnúmero de diferentes peculiaridades. Linz (1994: 5) es tan sólo un ejemplo cuando argumenta: "Todos los sistemas presidenciales y parlamentarios tienen un núcleo común que permite su diferenciación". Tal vez Moe y Caldwell (1994: 172) hayan expresado la idea con más determinación: "Cuando las naciones escogen una forma presidencial o una parlamentaria, eligen un sistema completo, cuyas diversas propiedades surgen endógenamente [...] de la dinámica política que su forma adoptada pone en movimiento". Mencionaré las más importantes de ellas tal como se presentan en diferentes partes de la bibliografía.

Stepan y Skach (1993) presentan evidencia de que los sistemas presidenciales no pueden manejar el multipartidismo. De hecho, sus datos indican que no hay democracias exitosas con más de tres partidos que sean presidenciales. También observaron que el parlamentarismo tiene una "mayor tendencia a proporcionar carreras partido-gobierno duraderas, que añaden lealtad y experiencia a la sociedad política" (Stepan y Skach, 1993: 22).

Strom (2000) proporciona fundamentos teóricos para esta última observación acerca de los horizontes de tiempo del personal. En su análisis, "la democracia parlamentaria implica una gran confianza en mecanismos de control *ex ante*, especialmente antes del tamizaje relativo a rendición de cuentas *ex post*" (Strom, 2000: 273). En realidad, en la mayoría de las democracias parlamentarias los ministros tienen que ser miembros del parlamento o tienen que contar con experiencia parlamentaria, de manera que los ministros potenciales ya hayan sido seleccionados antes de su nombramiento.⁵ Como contraste, en los Estados Unidos no sólo hay incompatibilidad entre membresía en el gabinete y el Congreso, sino que la experiencia legislativa es difícilmente un requerimiento para un miembro del gabinete. Según Strom, el que mayor sea la confianza del parlamentarismo en la selección en vez de la rendición de cuentas *ex post* se debe al papel más grande de los partidos políticos. Como resultado, el parlamentarismo se concentra en la selección del personal apropiado, pero es posible que no preste tanta atención como el presidencialismo a las acciones específicas de los representantes seleccionados: "Los regímenes parlamentarios pueden estar mejor equipados para tratar con problemas de selección adversa [...] a costa de otro [problema]: el peligro moral" (Strom, 2000: 278-279).

El papel de los partidos políticos es otro punto de diferencia entre presidencialismo y parlamentarismo que emerge en la bibliografía. Como lo indica Strom en el análisis anterior, generalmente se considera que los partidos son más cohesivos en sistemas parlamentarios que en sistemas presidenciales. Diermeier y Feddersen (1998) argumentan que es la relación de confianza, la amenaza de perder las elecciones y el puesto, y de perder poderes de establecimiento de agenda, lo que hace a los partidos ser más cohesivos en los sistemas parlamentarios que en los presidenciales; de hecho, la cohesión interpartido en los sistemas parlamentarios debería ser mayor que la cohesión intrapartido en sistemas presidenciales (véase también Persson, Roland y Tabellini, 2000).

Sin embargo, análisis más recientes plantean dudas acerca de la fortaleza de este hecho estilizado. Con respecto a los sistemas parlamentarios, Wornall (2001) ha descubierto que los partidos del Bundestag alemán sufren colapsos ocasionales en cohesión, como puede verse en el registro de votación de pasar lista. En su análisis de 615 votaciones tomadas entre 1965 y 1995, Wornall encuentra que la cohesión de partido disminuyó debajo del nivel de 90%⁶ sobre 28.5% de las votaciones de pasar lista. Cuando el análisis se limita a la constante de los tres partidos durante todo el periodo (el CDU/CSU, SPD y FDP), la cohesión se violó en 17.4% de los casos. Por añadidura, hay casos en los cuales los miembros disidentes determinaron el resultado de la votación. De 13 votaciones (que representaban 2.1% de los ca-

⁵ La Quinta República francesa es una excepción que Strom no cita en su análisis. De acuerdo con su análisis, así como en este libro, Francia es un caso de sistema parlamentario.
⁶ La medición de la cohesión se calcula como 1 − (número de disidentes)/(número total de participantes del partido). El número de disidentes se determina identificando a todos los miembros que no votaron con la mayoría (o pluralidad) de su partido.

sos), la legislación habría seguido la línea de pluralidad de partido si los disidentes hubiesen cooperado y votado de acuerdo con las líneas del partido. Esto sugiere que hay considerable disidencia dentro de los partidos legislativos alemanes, incluso en votaciones de pasar lista *(roll call)*, cuando los partidos deberían estar más unificados que nunca. De modo similar, en lo tocante a sistemas presidenciales, Cheibub y Limong (2001) encontraron votos disciplinados respaldando el programa presidencial en Brasil.

Una diferencia más que se ha examinado en la bibliografía entre los dos tipos de regímenes es la visibilidad de las decisiones políticas. En los sistemas parlamentarios la influencia de diferentes actores está oculta (principalmente en la secrecía de las deliberaciones del consejo de ministros), mientras que en los sistemas presidenciales hay transparencia en el proceso de toma de decisiones. Por ejemplo, Peter Cowhey (1993) argumenta que la política exterior de los Estados Unidos tiene más credibilidad que la japonesa, precisamente debido a que el sistema presidencial estadounidense conduce a una divulgación más sistemática de información acerca de la creación de política, y acrecienta la transparencia de las elecciones de política exterior tanto para los votantes en casa como para los aliados extranjeros.

En una línea de pensamiento similar, Vreeland (2001) encuentra que los acuerdos gubernamentales con el Fondo Monetario Internacional son más probables cuando más jugadores con veto participan en un gobierno, y cuando el régimen es presidencial. El primer argumento es congruente con el argumento que se plantea en este libro: mientras más jugadores con veto haya, más difícil es cambiar el *statu quo*, de modo que el gobierno puede tratar de usar un incentivo adicional. El segundo argumento es acerca de la base de la independencia del ejecutivo de la legislatura: es posible que un presidente quiera imponer el resultado a la legislatura en un estilo de "tómenlo o déjenlo", mientras que un gobierno parlamentario no puede hacer lo mismo, dado que todos los jugadores con veto participan en el gobierno.

Finalmente, ha habido cierta discusión (no sistemática) acerca de la provisión de bienes públicos en los diferentes sistemas. Los politólogos estadounidenses han examinado la legislación de partidas del presupuesto usadas para patronazgo político,[7] y han encontrado que los costos difusos y los beneficios concentrados de proyectos geográficamente enfocados hacen ra-

---

[7] Véase Ferejohn (1974); véanse también Weingast, Shepsle y Johnsen (1981), Shepsle y Weingast (1981), y Cohen y Noll (1991).

cional que los congresistas individuales los propongan a pesar de su ineficiencia. La única manera como tales proyectos serán adoptados es mediante legislación colectiva, proyectos de ley que incluyen todos esos proyectos de modo que sean adoptados todos juntos en vez de ser rechazados uno por uno. De hecho, el argumento se puede extender aún más: si un presidente veta tales proyectos debido a la ineficiencia de los mismos, el Congreso puede empeorar la situación al expandir la coalición y hacerla a prueba de vetos (al incluir los proyectos favoritos de dos tercios de los legisladores de cada cámara).

Linz (1994: 63) extiende este argumento a los partidos en el Congreso de sistemas presidenciales en general debido a la debilidad de los partidos: "Al no tener responsabilidad por la política nacional, recurrirían a la representación de intereses especiales, intereses localizados y redes clientelares para sus distritos electorales". Otros académicos, como Ames (1995), atribuyen las partidas del presupuesto usadas para patronazgo político a los sistemas electorales, no al tipo de régimen. Sin embargo, más recientemente Persson y Tabellini (1999, 2000)[8] han presentado el argumento contrario al afirmar que los regímenes presidenciales tendrán un gobierno más pequeño, dado que el juego legislativo en esos regímenes es más competitivo: prevalecen diferentes coaliciones de una pieza de legislación a otra. Como resultado, los votantes tienen un mayor control de sus representantes y se reduce el nivel de divisiones. El argumento no es convincente a nivel teórico porque Persson y Tabellini (1999) ignoran en su análisis (así como en sus modelos) la implicación básica de una división de poderes: la mayoría de los sistemas presidenciales le proporcionan poder de veto legislativo al presidente, lo cual reduce la competencia política dado que un actor específico tiene que ser parte de *cualquier* coalición ganadora (el presidente es un jugador con veto de acuerdo con la terminología de este libro). Por añadidura, una suposición crucial en sus modelos es que el establecimiento de agenda en regímenes presidenciales se divide en dos partes, sobre el monto del presupuesto, por un lado, y sobre la distribución del mismo, por el otro, y la agenda está controlada por dos instituciones o legisladores diferentes, mientras que el establecimiento de la agenda en proyectos de ley sobre finanzas pertenece al ejecutivo en sistemas tanto presidenciales como parlamentarios. No obstante, Persson y Tabellini (1999) presentan evidencia empírica que sustenta su argumento. Sus resultados empíricos son co-

---

[8] Véase también Persson, Roland y Tabellini (2000).

rroborados (cualitativamente) por Charles Boix (2001), quien encuentra un coeficiente negativo muy poderoso de regímenes presidenciales en el tamaño del sector público.

En conclusión, hay un resultado en la bibliografía que es corroborado en todos los análisis: la democracia sobrevive mejor bajo el parlamentarismo que bajo el presidencialismo. Sin embargo, parece que todas las demás características descritas en la bibliografía, aunque se basan en análisis profundos, no son corroboradas todo el tiempo. La distinción rigurosa entre parlamentarismo y presidencialismo que existe en Linz (1994) o en Moe y Caldwell (1994) no es el final de los análisis más recientes. Por ejemplo, Eaton (2000: 371) concluye su revisión de la bibliografía más reciente sobre el tema de las diferencias de régimen de la siguiente manera: "en la mayoría de los casos, las distinciones fundamentales entre parlamentarismo y presidencialismo tienden a diluirse". De modo similar, Cheibub y Limongi (2001: 25) argumentan:

> La realidad de los regímenes parlamentario y presidencial es más compleja de lo que sería si tratásemos de inferir la conducta entera de esos sistemas a partir de sus primeros principios. Así, ¿qué explica la diferencia? Sospechamos que la diferencia principal entre los dos regímenes se debe a la forma como está organizado el proceso de la toma de decisiones.

A ese conjunto de interrogantes nos abocaremos ahora.

2. La perspectiva de los jugadores con veto

La forma como los jugadores con veto abordan estas interrogantes es muy diferente. Con el fin de entender las diferencias no sólo entre regímenes democráticos y no democráticos, sino también entre presidencialismo y parlamentarismo, tenemos que concentrarnos en el proceso de producción de leyes:

- ¿Cómo son seleccionados los jugadores con veto?
- ¿Quiénes son los jugadores con veto? (¿Quién necesita estar de acuerdo para un cambio del *statu quo?*)
- ¿Quién controla la agenda legislativa? (¿Quién hace propuestas a quién y bajo qué reglas?)

- Si estos jugadores son colectivos, ¿bajo qué reglas decide cada uno de ellos (mayoría simple, mayoría calificada o unanimidad)?

Estas tres categorías de regímenes tienen diferencias importantes en al menos una de estas dimensiones. Por ejemplo, el proceso competitivo de la selección de jugador con veto es la definición mínima de democracia que vimos en la primera sección. Argumentaré más adelante que los temas de control de la agenda y cohesión de diferentes jugadores con veto son, en principio, distinciones entre sistemas presidencial y parlamentario.

2.1. ¿Cómo son seleccionados los jugadores con veto?

El proceso que se requiere en la definición de Schumpeter de la democracia hace que las diferentes élites compitan por el poder político más representativo de las opiniones del pueblo a quienes representan. Downs (1975) ha presentado un modelo de espacio político unidimensional de este proceso competitivo. Su modelo es tan ampliamente conocido que no lo presentaré aquí otra vez. En el capítulo sobre referéndums (capítulo v) planteo una generalización multidimensional de este modelo.[9]

Hay varias conclusiones que se han inferido de los modelos de Downs que se deben discutir y moderar. Por ejemplo, se podría sacar la conclusión de que debido a la competencia, los regímenes democráticos son más representativos de la voluntad del público. Por añadidura, cabría afirmar que la competencia entre dos partidos da lugar a una mejor representación del público. Finalmente, se puede pensar que aunque muchos regímenes democráticos tienen múltiples jugadores con veto, los regímenes autoritarios tienen necesariamente uno solo. Todas éstas son inferencias razonables, pero argumentaré que no son de ninguna manera conclusiones necesarias del modelo de Downs (o verdaderas en cuanto a eso).

Primero, aunque la competencia electoral es una condición inherente para la introducción de las preferencias del público en política, no es ni una condición necesaria ni suficiente para la representación. Se le recuerdan al lector los argumentos de Przeworski (1999), que se presentaron en la sección anterior. Además, vimos en la introducción de este libro que hace ya

---

[9] Me disculpo con los lectores que conocen la diferencia entre un análisis unidimensional (que lleva siempre a un resultado de votante medio) y un análisis multidimensional (donde el votante medio casi nunca existe) por haber tenido que esperar hasta entonces por la respuesta.

más de dos mil años, Tucídides presentaba argumentos similares acerca de la democracia ateniense. Sus gustos entraban en conflicto con el votante medio y admiraba la capacidad de Pericles para desviarse de las preferencias del público, mientras culpaba a sus sucesores por seguir "los caprichos de la multitud".[10] En consecuencia, las democracias no representan necesariamente las preferencias del votante medio.

Por otro lado, los regímenes autoritarios no se desvían necesariamente de las preferencias del votante medio. Es posible que las preferencias del público estén muy cerca o sean incluso idénticas a las preferencias de la persona a cargo. Por ejemplo, regímenes populistas, como el de Perón en Argentina, pueden presentar tales similitudes en preferencias.

Segundo, otra conclusión inapropiada que la gente sacaría de los modelos de Downs es que la competencia de dos equipos de élites puede conducir a un sistema más representativo o moderado que la competencia de múltiples equipos. La razón es que con dos partidos en una sola dimensión, el resultado es necesariamente la posición del votante medio, mientras que con más de dos partidos o con más de dos dimensiones la mayor parte del tiempo, no hay un resultado de equilibrio. De hecho, como afirma Lijphart (1999), el argumento de que sistemas bipartidistas conducen a la moderación política ha sido, por largo tiempo, la sabiduría dominante en la ciencia política anglosajona. De nueva cuenta, ésta no es una conclusión necesaria. De hecho, análisis empíricos más recientes (por ejemplo, Huber y Powell, 1994; Powell, 2000) han demostrado que un sistema multipartidista proporciona una planimetría más exacta entre las preferencias del votante medio y las preferencias del gobierno.

Finalmente, no es verdad que los sistemas no democráticos tengan necesariamente un solo jugador con veto. Mientras que el proceso de toma de decisiones en los sistemas democráticos es usualmente más transparente para los observadores externos (como periodistas o científicos de la política), que tienen una buena idea de la forma como se toman las decisiones políticas, éste no es el caso en los regímenes no democráticos. Sin embargo, la transparencia no significa necesariamente múltiples jugadores con veto, y la carencia de la misma no implica a un solo jugador con veto. Remmer (1989) ha presentado un poderoso argumento de que diferentes regímenes autoritarios en América Latina tienen estructuras muy distintas y en algunos de ellos un individuo es responsable por las decisiones políticas,

---

[10] Véase la cita completa en la introducción.

mientras que en otros muchos jugadores están investidos con el poder para vetar decisiones. Afirmo que la situación no es diferente a la toma de decisiones dentro de partidos políticos en las democracias.

Los partidos políticos en regímenes democráticos usualmente se aproximan por un solo punto ideal inferido de su manifiesto político. Sin embargo, no sabemos cómo se originó esta preferencia. ¿Era la preferencia del líder del partido? ¿Se trataba del compromiso concertado en una institución con pocos miembros (como un secretariado o un politburó) o en una entidad más grande (como un grupo parlamentario)? En el segundo caso, ¿cuál fue la regla de la toma de decisiones? ¿Estaban todos o algunos de los miembros investidos con el poder para vetar la discusión? Las respuestas a todas estas preguntas no son consecuentes en lo tocante a ambos regímenes no democráticos y partidos políticos, y en vez de ello presuponemos un solo tomador de decisiones. Me limito a señalar nuestra falta de información acerca de la forma como se toman ciertas decisiones en regímenes tanto democráticos como no democráticos y argumento que, como se demostró en el capítulo II, sustituir jugadores con veto colectivos por individuales es una aproximación razonable a la ausencia de tal información.

Por lo tanto, lo que distingue a los regímenes democráticos de los no democráticos es si los jugadores con veto son decididos por competencia entre las élites, por votos o mediante algún otro proceso, y no hay una distinción necesaria en términos de representación o en términos del número real de jugadores con veto. Debemos estudiar el régimen específico con el fin de tomar decisiones sobre estos asuntos.

2.2. Jugadores con veto en diferentes regímenes

Identifiquemos primero qué cuenta como un jugador con veto. Si la constitución identifica a algunos actores individuales o colectivos que deben ponerse de acuerdo para un cambio del *statu quo*, éstos obviamente son jugadores con veto. Por ejemplo, la Constitución de los Estados Unidos especifica que se requiere un consenso de la Cámara, el Senado y el presidente (excluyendo vencer en la votación un veto presidencial) para promulgar leyes. Como resultado, la constitución especifica que hay tres jugadores con veto. En aras de la sencillez en esta sección pasaremos por alto que dos de ellos son colectivos (en el capítulo II se demostró que tal simplificación es permisible). Consideremos ahora el caso especial de que estos tres jugadores con veto tienen puntos ideales sobre una línea recta. Sobre la base del análisis del capítulo I, uno de ellos es absorbido, de modo que en este caso los Estados Unidos tendrían de hecho dos jugadores con veto. O considérese la situación donde los tres jugadores con veto están controlados por el mismo partido disciplinado (como fue el caso en los primeros cien días de la administración de Roosevelt); entonces, dos de los tres jugadores con veto son absorbidos y, en consecuencia, en este periodo hay únicamente un jugador con veto.

Consideremos ahora un sistema parlamentario unicameral. La constitución no define quiénes son los jugadores con veto ni especifica el número de éstos. Las leyes son votadas por el parlamento, de modo que, en cierto sentido, el único jugador con veto que la constitución especifica es el parlamento. Sin embargo, supongamos que en este país un solo partido controla al gobierno (como es generalmente el caso en el Reino Unido o en Grecia). Entonces, este partido, por definición, es el único jugador con veto en el sistema político. Puede implementar cualquier cambio político que desee, y no se implementará ningún cambio político con el cual este partido esté en desacuerdo. Supongamos que como resultado de circunstancias políticas extraordinarias, el gobierno de un solo partido es sustituido por un gobierno bipartidista, como fue la coalición de la derecha y la izquierda en Grecia en 1989 o el pacto entre liberal y laborista en el Reino Unido. Ahora ninguna ley será promulgada a no ser que ambos socios en el gobierno estén de acuerdo con ella. En otras palabras, durante este periodo Grecia o el Reino Unido se transformarán en un sistema político de dos jugadores con veto. Pero por lo general, la dinámica de un sistema parlamentario requiere del consenso de un partido (sistemas Westminster) o de más partidos (gobiernos de coalición) para la modificación del *statu quo*. Cada uno de estos partidos decidirá por mayoría de su grupo parlamentario: en consecuencia, cada uno de estos partidos es un jugador con veto (colectivo).

Llamaré *jugadores con veto institucionales* a los jugadores con veto individuales o colectivos que la constitución especifique. Se espera que el número de estos jugadores con veto permanezca constante, pero sus propiedades pueden cambiar. Por ejemplo, se pueden transformar de colectivos a individuales (si una institución, que decide por mayoría simple, está controlada por un partido disciplinado) y viceversa. Asimismo, es posible que sus distancias ideológicas muestren variaciones y que uno o más de ellos sean absorbidos.

Llamaré *jugadores con veto partidarios* a los jugadores con veto que el juego político genera dentro de jugadores con veto institucionales. Por ejemplo, la sustitución de una mayoría de un solo partido por una mayoría de dos partidos dentro de cualquier jugador con veto institucional transforma la situación de un solo jugador con veto partidario a dos jugadores con veto partidarios. Tanto el número como las propiedades de los jugadores con veto partidarios cambian con el tiempo. Los partidos pueden perder mayorías, tal vez se dividan o se fusionen y tales transformaciones *pueden* tener un efecto sobre el número de jugadores con veto partidarios. Este es el punto que profundizaré en lo que resta de esta sección.

Consideremos un parlamento de cinco partidos en un sistema parlamentario unicameral. Según la constitución, la legislación es promulgada cuando una mayoría de este parlamento acuerda sustituir el *statu quo*. Supongamos (para simplificar las cosas) que los cinco partidos son cohesivos y que tres de ellos controlan una mayoría. El lector puede consultar la gráfica II.4 para visualizar tal sistema. La situación especificada por la constitución es un solo jugador con veto colectivo institucional. Según el capítulo II, si conocemos el *statu quo* SQ podemos identificar al círculo ganador (mayoría). Esta es el área circular con sombreado ligero en la gráfica. Podemos identificar también el conjunto exacto de puntos que derrotan al SQ —el área con sombreado más oscuro W(SQ)—.

Consideremos ahora que no todas las coaliciones son posibles y que tres de los partidos, A, B y C, forman un gobierno. Esta alianza asegura que ninguno forme coaliciones con los partidos D o E. Esta información adicional altera el número de jugadores con veto partidarios y las expectativas de las soluciones factibles. Los únicos puntos que pueden derrotar al SQ están ubicados en la lente de sombreado más oscuro. Por lo tanto, la nueva información transformó el análisis del sistema político de un jugador con veto colectivo a tres individuales y redujo el conjunto ganador del *statu quo*.

En la suposición anterior pasamos desde cualquier coalición posible a una y solamente una, y omitimos el caso intermedio cuando varias coaliciones son posibles siempre y cuando no incluyan a un determinado partido. Podemos pensar en tal escenario político cuando los comunistas, o algún otro partido específico, sean excluidos de todas las mayorías posibles. De hecho, tal caso sería equivalente a un requerimiento de mayoría calificada impuesto a la legislatura, caso que estudiamos teóricamente en el capítulo II, y que se abordará de nuevo en los capítulos IV y VI cuando veamos las mayorías calificadas.

Estos ejemplos pueden ayudarnos a analizar situaciones políticas específicas. Por ejemplo, ¿cuál es la configuración total de jugador con veto en un país con muchos jugadores con veto institucionales, si dentro de cada uno de ellos hay muchos jugadores con veto partidarios? Los análisis anteriores indican que avanzamos en tres etapas.

Primero, ubicamos jugadores con veto institucionales en un espacio multidimensional. Segundo, procedemos a disgregarlos en los jugadores partidarios que los componen con el fin de identificar los jugadores con veto individuales o colectivos dentro de cada uno de ellos. Tercero, aplicamos a este sistema las reglas de absorción: si algunos de los jugadores con veto están ubicados en el núcleo de unanimidad de los otros, podemos eliminarlos porque no restringen al conjunto ganador del *statu quo*. Por ejemplo, si tenemos un sistema bicameral presidencial donde una de las cámaras decide por dominio de la mayoría y la otra por regla de la mayoría calificada (ejemplo seleccionado a propósito debido a que Estados Unidos se le aproxima, pues las decisiones importantes requieren limitar en el debate a los potenciales obstruccionistas por una mayoría de tres quintos en el Senado), entonces ubicaremos el área de intersección de los conjuntos ganadores de los dos jugadores colectivos y la intersecaremos con el conjunto ganador del presidente. Si existe un sustituto del *statu quo*, tiene que estar ubicado en la intersección.

Vayamos a una situación menos complicada: algunas leyes en Alemania *(Zustimmungsgesetze,* o leyes de conformidad) requieren el consenso tanto del Bundestag como del Bundesrat; mientras que para otras *(Einspruchsgesetz)* una mayoría del Bundestag basta para la aprobación.[11] ¿Cuál es la diferencia entre los dos tipos de leyes? A fin de responder la pregunta tenemos que diferenciar entre dos posibles situaciones, dependiendo de si las mayorías en las dos cámaras son las mismas o son diferentes. Si los partidos que controlan la mayoría en ambas cámaras son los mismos, no hay diferencia entre los dos tipos de legislación (en aras de la sencillez, presupongo que las posiciones de los partidos en cada cámara son idénticas). Si las mayorías son diferentes, entonces la coalición del gobierno que consta de dos partidos tendrá que solicitar la aprobación de un partido de la oposición, lo cual elevará a tres el número de jugadores con veto en Alemania. En este caso, habrá una diferencia importante entre *Zustimmungsgesetze* y

---

[11] A veces se requiere una mayoría de dos tercios en el Bundestag para poder invalidar una mayoría de dos tercios en el Bundesrat.

Einspruchsgesetz, y será mucho más difícil adoptar las primeras que las segundas.

De modo similar, en un sistema presidencial hay una diferencia entre leyes y decretos ejecutivos. Las primeras requieren participación de muchos jugadores con veto (los que existen en una o dos cámaras legislativas y el presidente), mientras que los segundos sólo necesitan la aprobación presidencial. Retornaremos a esta distinción en el capítulo siguiente.

Hay también una diferencia entre ley y decreto gubernamental en Francia, pero funciona en la dirección exactamente opuesta. Las leyes requieren una votación en el parlamento, mientras que los decretos gubernamentales requieren un acuerdo en el gobierno. El presidente de Francia es parte del gobierno pero no tiene poder de veto sobre la legislación. Como resultado, el presidente puede vetar un decreto gubernamental pero no puede vetar leyes. Si el presidente no cuenta con el respaldo de la mayoría parlamentaria (una situación que en Francia se denomina cohabitación), es más fácil aprobar leyes que decretos gubernamentales. Esto es exactamente lo que hizo el primer ministro Chirac en el primer periodo de cohabitación (1986-1988). Cuando se enfrentó a la negativa del presidente Mitterrand a firmar decretos gubernamentales, convirtió los mismos documentos en leyes, haciendo imposible que el presidente las vetara.

Me he concentrado deliberadamente en actores institucionales y partidarios que existen en todo sistema democrático, y he pasado por alto a otros jugadores con veto potenciales, tales como tribunales o individuos específicos (ministros con influencia, posiblemente oficiales del ejército) que pueden existir o no en determinados sistemas políticos. Abordo el tema de los tribunales en el capítulo x. En lo que respecta a otros actores, los consideraré como ruido aleatorio al nivel de este análisis, pero afirmo que deberían estar incluidos en los análisis de áreas políticas específicas, o estudios de caso. Por ejemplo, en países corporativistas los jugadores con veto del sistema político pueden ser sustituidos por trabajadores y empresarios, los verdaderos negociadores de contratos laborales específicos. De modo similar, en los análisis de la política de defensa de los Estados Unidos en la década de 1980 y principios de la década de 1990, tal vez tendríamos que incluir al presidente del Senado sobre Servicios Armados, Sam Nunn, como jugador con veto, dado que era capaz de anular decisiones tanto del presidente Bush (el nombramiento del secretario de Defensa) y al presidente Clinton (legislación sobre homosexuales en las fuerzas armadas). De modo similar, el presidente de Relaciones Exteriores del Senado, Jesse Helms, logró hacer abortar muchas de las iniciativas del presidente Clinton (en particular nombramientos de embajadores). Sin embargo, no deberíamos saltar de la consideración de un presidente de comité específico como jugador con veto a la inclusión de todos los presidentes de comité en el Congreso como jugadores con veto, y ciertamente no a todos los presidentes de comités en otros sistemas como jugadores con veto.

En los casos en que se pueda plantear el argumento de que ciertas instituciones o individuos tienen poderes de veto (ya sea formalmente como los comités o informalmente como en algunos casos de representantes de las fuerzas armadas), los análisis de la toma de decisiones deberían incluir a estos jugadores con veto y sus preferencias. El capítulo VI se concentra en los diferentes modos de tomar una decisión (por ejemplo, jugadores con veto colectivos múltiples, mayorías calificadas) que se pueden aplicar para el análisis de tales casos.

2.3. Establecimiento de agenda en el presidencialismo y el parlamentarismo

En la proposición 1.5 hemos analizado el poder del establecimiento de agenda. Podemos aplicar esta proposición para identificar diferencias entre los regímenes presidenciales y los parlamentarios. En lo tocante a los proyectos de leyes hacendarias, la iniciativa corresponde al ejecutivo en ambos sistemas, el presidencial y el parlamentario. Sin embargo, en lo tocante a leyes no financieras, por regla general en los sistemas parlamentarios, el gobierno hace una propuesta al parlamento para aceptarla o rechazarla, mientras que en los sistemas presidenciales el parlamento hace una propuesta al ejecutivo para aceptarla o vetarla. En este sentido, los papeles del establecimiento de agenda se invierten en los dos sistemas. Además, los nombres dados a cada uno de estos sistemas no reflejan la realidad legislativa: se espera que los presidentes sean poderosos en sistemas presidenciales, y el parlamento en los parlamentarios. El análisis que presento invierte los papeles en la arena legislativa. Mi argumento es que si el parlamento es fuerte en sistemas parlamentarios esto no se debe a la legislación; es así porque puede retirar su respaldo del gobierno y sustituirlo. Si el presidente es fuerte en sistemas presidenciales, esto no es debido a su poder para legislar, sino a decretos ejecutivos y al poder para tomar decisiones sobre política exterior y otros asuntos.

Otros autores han identificado esta evaluación extraña y sorprendente, pero, hasta donde sé, la causa (establecimiento de agenda) nunca ha sido señalada. Por ejemplo, Seymour Martin Lipset (1996: 151) ha argumentado:

> El hecho de que las presidencias contribuyen a partidos débiles y ejecutivos débiles, mientras que los parlamentos tienden a tener el efecto contrario, ciertamente afecta la naturaleza y posiblemente las condiciones de la democracia. Pero en gran parte de la bibliografía se presupone erróneamente lo contrario: que un presidente es inherentemente más fuerte que un primer ministro, y que el poder está más concentrado en el primero.

De modo similar, Stepan y Skach (1993: 18) arguyen: "Aquí, entonces, está la paradoja. Muchas democracias nuevas seleccionan el presidencialismo porque creen que es una forma fuerte de gobierno ejecutivo. Sin embargo [...] las democracias presidenciales disfrutan de mayorías legislativas menos de la mitad del tiempo. [...] Los ejecutivos y las legislaturas en esos países estaban 'empatados' unos con otras". De manera más pintoresca, Lyndon Johnson dijo lo siguiente: "Ser presidente equivale a ser un asno en una tormenta de granizo. No hay nada qué hacer más que quedarse allí y aguantarla" (citado en Ames, 2001: 158). La teoría de los jugadores con veto argumenta que si los parlamentos son débiles en sistemas parlamentarios y fuertes en sistemas presidenciales, si los presidentes son débiles y los primeros ministros fuertes, no es por idiosincrasia o por razones aleatorias, sino porque el establecimiento de la agenda está controlado por el gobierno en sistemas parlamentarios y por el parlamento en sistemas presidenciales. Esta es una declaración general que habremos de condicionar en el siguiente capítulo.

Por último, una consideración importante: el hecho de que el establecedor de agenda tenga los poderes que la proposición I.5 identifica no quiere decir que los demás jugadores con veto quedan al margen, como se demostró en la elección presidencial de los Estados Unidos en 2000. Si aceptamos el argumento de que el Congreso controla la agenda, ¿se desprende de esto que el resultado de la elección no importaría mucho, o que importaría más si el presidente controlara la agenda? No necesariamente, ya que el resultado final depende de las posiciones de los otros jugadores con veto y del *statu quo*.

La gráfica III.1 presenta una posible configuración de diferentes jugadores con el fin de ilustrar el punto. Consideremos que el establecedor de la

GRÁFICA III.1. *Diferencia entre la presidencia de Gore y de Bush cuando el presidente controla o no la agenda.*

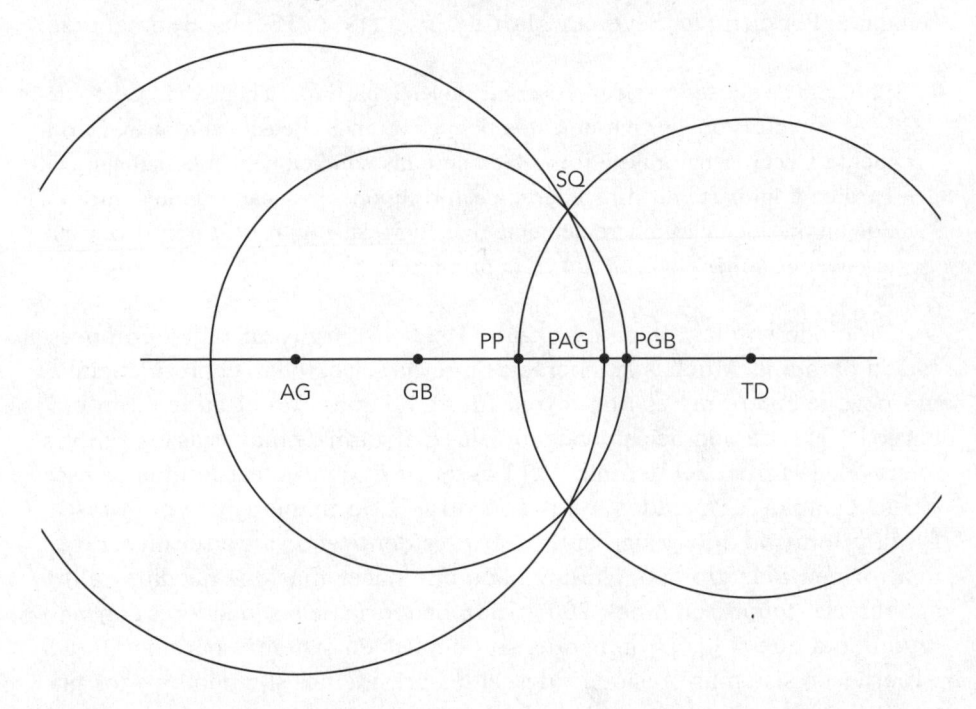

agenda del Congreso es el líder de la mayoría de la Cámara, Tom DeLay, y que el punto ideal del candidato George Bush está ubicado entre el punto ideal del candidato Al Gore y el republicano DeLay. Para un *statu quo* indicado en la gráfica, DeLay (TD) haría a George Bush (PGB) una propuesta diferente que a Al Gore (PAG, de haber sido éste el elegido). De hecho, el resultado electoral estableció una diferencia según la configuración de la gráfica III.1 *porque* la Cámara controla la agenda. Si el presidente controlara la agenda, ambos candidatos harían la misma propuesta (PP) a la Cámara.

Este ejemplo se basa en muchas suposiciones discutibles: paso por alto al Senado para simplificar la representación; supongo que DeLay haría la propuesta, aunque él tendría que negociar con los republicanos más moderados (cercanos a Bush). Sin embargo, capta una parte importante de la situación política en el periodo de 1994 a 2000. Bill Clinton se hizo más conocido por su habilidad para frustrar la agenda republicana (principalmente el "Contrato con los Estados Unidos" de los republicanos) que por promover sus propios planes. Sin embargo, podemos pensar en unas cuantas medidas positivas, tales como el alza de impuestos en 1993 (aprobada en una Cámara y un Senado dominados por los demócratas) y algunas medidas en comercio (como el TLCAN y China, que se dieron porque Clinton llevó a algunos demócratas a una coalición con los republicanos) que no fueron simplemente planeadas para bloquear las políticas de los republicanos.

Tal vez le sorprenda al lector que, de acuerdo con el análisis anterior, el resultado de la elección presidencial de 2000 sea más significativo si el presidente no tiene poderes de establecimiento de agenda que cuando sí los tiene. ¿Cómo concuerda este análisis con los poderes del establecimiento de agenda que examinamos en la proposición 1.5? Aquí comparo dos diferentes jugadores, en la suposición de que no controlan la agenda, mientras que en la proposición 1.5 se compara el poder de los jugadores con veto cuando controlan la agenda o cuando no. La proposición 1.5 de nuestro ejemplo implica que tanto Bush como Gore preferirían controlar la agenda que dejársela a DeLay, lo cual es verdad sin duda alguna.

En suma, en esta sección se ha argumentado que el control de la agenda para proyectos de leyes no hacendarias corresponde al parlamento en los sistemas presidenciales y al gobierno en los parlamentarios. En el capítulo siguiente abundaremos en esto, y demostraré que esta aparente diferencia de establecimiento de agenda tiene que ser analizada y documentada país por país. La diferencia de un país a otro puede ser importante: algunos sistemas presidenciales pueden dar tantos poderes de establecimiento de agenda al presidente que parecen parlamentarios, y algunos sistemas parlamentarios pueden quitarle tantas iniciativas de establecimiento de agenda al gobierno que parecen presidenciales.

2.4. Cohesión del jugador con veto en presidencialismo y parlamentarismo

La bibliografía sobre presidencialismo y parlamentarismo ha identificado otra diferencia importante (desde el punto de vista de los jugadores con veto) entre los dos tipos de regímenes. Los partidos son más disciplinados en los sistemas parlamentarios que en los presidenciales, aunque, como se vio en la sección 1, la evidencia empírica disputa la fortaleza de esta relación.

La bibliografía sobre sistemas electorales ha ofrecido una causa distinta de la variabilidad de la disciplina de partido: el voto personal. De hecho, en los sistemas electorales en que los candidatos compiten por un voto personal, son propensos a prestar atención en las demandas de sus votantes así como a las exigencias de su partido, mientras que en las situaciones en que las posibilidades del candidato dependen únicamente de la lealtad al partido, la lealtad al partido debería ser la regla.[12] Así, la cohesión y disciplina de partido serán mayores en sistemas sin un voto personal.

Como hemos visto en el capítulo II, la cohesión interna de los jugadores con veto colectivos afecta el tamaño del área dentro de la cual está ubicado el conjunto ganador. Cuanto menor sea la cohesión de partido, menor será la estabilidad política. Si combinamos este argumento con los resultados de la bibliografía sobre cohesión de partido en diferentes regímenes, concluiremos que *ceteris paribus* los sistemas presidenciales tienen una estabilidad política menor. Esta es una cláusula *ceteris paribus* muy poderosa porque probablemente es imposible mantener constante todo lo demás. El hecho de que los partidos carecen de disciplina en sistemas presidenciales hace difícil o incluso imposible identificar los orígenes de votos particulares. Como resultado, es difícil identificar a los jugadores con veto partidarios en sistemas presidenciales. Siempre que éste sea el caso, nos confinaremos al estudio de los jugadores con veto institucionales.

Por ejemplo, en los Estados Unidos, con un gobierno dividido, si los partidos fueran cohesivos, únicamente se aprobarían los proyectos de ley bipartidarios, incluso desatendiendo la posibilidad de obstruccionismo (que se verá en el capítulo VI). Dado que los partidos no son cohesivos, se hace posible la creación de política. Por ejemplo, Clinton aprobó su reforma fiscal en 1993 sin votos republicanos, aunque logró aprobar su acuerdo del TLCAN principalmente con votos republicanos. Si estos virajes en coalición no fueran posibles, habría habido menos aplicaciones de política en la presidencia de Clinton. Pero como resultado de estos virajes, no podemos sustituir a los jugadores con veto institucionales por partidarios en un sistema presidencial.

Por otro lado, no todos los sistemas presidenciales tienen la misma moderación de partidos que vemos en los Estados Unidos, donde es posible casi cualquier coalición. En algunos sistemas presidenciales ciertos partidos no apoyarán las medidas del gobierno en ninguna circunstancia. Si éste es el caso, tal vez no seamos capaces de sustituir a jugadores con veto ins-

---

[12] Véase Carey y Shugart (1995) para distinciones de diferentes sistemas electorales a lo largo de estos lineamientos.

titucionales por otros partidarios, pero sí podríamos excluir a algunos de los partidos como posibles jugadores con veto. Esta información aumentaría la estabilidad política, pero no proporcionaría la precisión que podríamos tener si supiésemos que una combinación específica de partidos respaldaría algún proyecto de ley en particular. Analizamos esta situación como un caso de toma de decisiones bajo mayoría calificada en el capítulo VI.

3. Críticas a la teoría de los jugadores con veto

La diferencia en el análisis entre tipos de régimen por un lado y jugadores con veto por el otro ha sido uno de los aspectos más poderosos así como de los más criticados de la teoría de los jugadores con veto. Ha sido tan poderoso porque al nivel teórico podemos analizar diferentes tipos de regímenes u otras situaciones institucionales dentro del mismo marco. Ha sido el más criticado porque distintos autores niegan que los jugadores con veto institucionales y partidarios puedan ser tratados de igual manera. Por lo tanto, aquí trataré algunas de las críticas formuladas en presentaciones anteriores de la teoría de los jugadores con veto y explicaré la forma como las he abordado en este libro.

El principal argumento crítico fue que aun cuando es un desarrollo positivo la conceptualización de diferentes situaciones institucionales en un marco unificado en mi formulación original de la teoría de los jugadores con veto (Tsebelis, 1995a), existe una distinción importante entre jugadores con veto institucionales y partidarios, y no se debería juntar a los dos. Strom (2000) ha presentado el argumento teórico más convincente, y por ello empiezo por abordar su punto.

Strom analiza temas de delegación y rendición de cuentas en los sistemas parlamentarios e indica que la cadena de delegación es una sola en sistemas parlamentarios (de los votantes al parlamento, al primer ministro, a los ministros, a los burócratas); mientras que la delegación en sistemas presidenciales ocurre con principios y agentes competidores (votantes de múltiples representantes —presidente, Cámara, Senado— y estos representantes supervisan colectivamente a los burócratas). Abordo el tema de la delegación a burocracias en el capítulo X. Aquí quiero concentrarme en la crítica que Strom presenta acerca de la distinción entre jugadores con veto institucionales y partidarios. Esta es su crítica, en su forma más general:

Aunque Tsebelis identifica así similitudes intrigantes entre parlamentarismo presidencial y multipartidista, la distinción sigue siendo importante para nuestros fines. [...] Pero generalmente, es engañoso tratar a los jugadores con veto institucionales y partidarios en forma aditiva, dado que los partidos y las instituciones en las cuales operan no son mutuamente independientes, sino en cambio sumamente interdependientes. Un jugador con veto creíble debe tener tanto oportunidad como motivo para ejercer su veto. Los jugadores con veto partidarios pueden tener un motivo (aunque éste no siempre sea evidente), pero por lo general no tienen oportunidad. Los jugadores con veto institucionales por definición tienen oportunidad, aunque no necesariamente motivo. Es interesante que Tsebelis (1995: 310) descarte a los jugadores con veto institucionales que no tienen motivo discernible, es decir, cuando sus preferencias son idénticas a las de los otros jugadores con veto, por ejemplo en legislaturas bicamerales congruentes. El mismo trato se les debería dar a los jugadores partidarios que no tienen oportunidad demostrable de ejercer el veto [Strom, 2000: 280].

Con el fin de respaldar su argumento, Strom presenta el ejemplo de coaliciones "de tamaño exagerado", o partidos extremistas que tal vez no quieran vetar una política gubernamental y abandonen al gobierno. En su opinión es posible evitar a estos jugadores y no deben contar de la misma manera que los jugadores con veto institucionales.

Strom señala una serie de puntos correctos en el párrafo anterior. Es verdad, por ejemplo, que en el artículo al que hace referencia yo había identificado sólo jugadores con veto idénticos como casos para la aplicación de la regla de absorción y, por consiguiente, yo aplicaba esta regla únicamente a jugadores con veto institucionales. En la actual versión de mi argumento, he presentado la regla de la absorción más general posible, la proposición 1.2, donde no importa si los jugadores absorbidos son institucionales o partidarios. Por ejemplo, si en la gráfica 1.6 el sistema de jugadores con veto A está en una cámara de una legislatura mientras el sistema de jugadores con veto B está en otra cámara, el sistema B será absorbido sin importar que esta segunda cámara sea la Cámara o el Senado. La legislación que es aprobada por el sistema A de jugadores con veto recibirá necesariamente la aprobación del sistema B. De modo similar, si un país tuviera una legislatura bicameral con una cámara compuesta únicamente de los jugadores con veto en el sistema A, y la otra compuesta del sistema de A's y un B, la situación entera sería equivalente a una legislatura unicameral compuesta de los tres jugadores con veto en el sistema A. Por ejemplo, en Japón el Partido Demócrata Liberal (PDL) perdió la mayoría en el Senado en 1999. Como resultado, el PDL incluyó en el gobierno a representantes de los liberales y el Komeito (Partido de Gobierno Limpio), aunque hablando técnicamente sus votos no eran requeridos para una mayoría en la Cámara. De modo similar en Alemania, si el Bundesrat está dominado por la oposición la situación no es políticamente distinta de una gran coalición: la legislación que no es aprobada por ambos partidos mayoritarios no será aceptada. O, en un sistema presidencial, si el partido del presidente tiene las mismas preferencias que el presidente será parte de cualquier coalición de creación de política, ya que si un proyecto de ley no obtiene su apoyo, será vetado por el presidente. La versión actual de la regla de absorción es así mucho más general que la que criticaba Strom y toma en consideración algunas de sus objeciones.

También es verdad que los miembros de partido de gobiernos de tamaño exagerado pueden ser dejados a un lado como jugadores con veto, no así los jugadores con veto institucionales, como argumenta Strom. Trato esta objeción teóricamente en el capítulo IV y presento pruebas empíricas que respaldan mi argumento en los capítulos VII y VIII.

Donde Strom no está en lo correcto, a mi parecer, es en la última parte de su argumento: "El mismo tratamiento [es decir, absorción] se debería dar a los jugadores partidarios que *no tienen una oportunidad demostrable de ejercer el veto*". Los partidos en el gobierno están allí para acordar un programa de gobierno. De hecho, como veremos en el siguiente capítulo, negociar tales programas es algo que exige mucho tiempo, y los gobiernos hacen esfuerzos serios para hacer que se vote e implemente todo lo incluido en ellos, como lo ha demostrado cuidadosamente De Winter (de próxima aparición). Además, si nuevos temas aparecen en el horizonte político, los integrantes de los diversos partidos en el gobierno tienen que abordarlos en común. Si tal plan político no es factible, la coalición de gobierno se disolverá, y se formará un nuevo gobierno. Por lo tanto, la solicitud de que los partidos en el gobierno tengan "oportunidad demostrable de ejercer el veto" es, o bien equivalente a la participación en el gobierno, o bien irrazonable. De hecho, la participación en un gobierno otorga a los partidos el derecho a vetar legislación y a provocar una crisis de gobierno si así lo desean. Esta es una condición suficiente para que un partido califique como jugador con veto. Si la "oportunidad demostrable" se da en una base de caso por caso, es imposible satisfacerla empíricamente, ya que incluso los casos en que el veto fue ejercido en realidad, y la legislación fue abortada como resultado, tal vez no sean "demostrables" dado el secreto de las deliberaciones gubernamentales.

Otro tipo de crítica tiene una base empírica. El argumento es que en algunos temas específicos, diferentes tipos de jugadores con veto tienen efectos conflictivos, de modo que los jugadores con veto no deberían estar incluidos en el mismo marco. Birchfield y Crepaz (1998: 181-182) presentaron el argumento de la siguiente manera:

> No todos los puntos de veto son creados igual. Argumentamos que [...] es necesario distinguir entre "puntos de veto competitivos" y "colectivos" que no sólo son institucionalmente diferentes sino que conducen también a resultados sustancialmente distintos. Los puntos de veto competitivos ocurren cuando diferentes actores políticos operan por medio de instituciones separadas con poderes de veto mutuos, tales como federalismo, bicameralismo fuerte y gobierno presidencial. Estas instituciones, basadas en sus poderes de veto mutuos, tienen una enorme capacidad de restringir al gobierno. [...] Los puntos de veto colectivos, por otro lado, surgen de instituciones donde los diferentes actores políticos operan en la misma entidad y cuyos miembros interactúan sobre una base de cara a cara. Ejemplos típicos de puntos de veto colectivos son los sistemas electorales proporcionales, legislaturas multipartidistas, gobiernos multipartidistas y regímenes parlamentarios. Estos son puntos de veto que comportan medios colectivos y responsabilidad compartida.

Estos argumentos parecen similares a los de Strom, en el sentido de que tienen la intención de diferenciar los sistemas presidencial y parlamentario, pero son considerablemente menos precisos. Por ejemplo, la "base cara a cara" no distingue la interacción entre gobierno y parlamento por un lado y comités de conferencia en legislaturas bicamerales por el otro. En ambos casos existe interacción personal pero no es muy frecuente, así que no está claro por qué el parlamentarismo se distingue del bicameralismo sobre esta base.

Apoyándose en los resultados, los autores argumentan que la mayor desigualdad económica está asociada con jugadores con veto competitivos, y la más baja asociada con los colectivos. En otro artículo, Crepaz (2002) encuentra resultados similares asociados con la primera y la segunda dimensiones del consociacionalismo de Lijphart (1999), la "dimensión de ejecutivo-partidos" y la "dimensión federal-unitaria". En el mismo artículo, Crepaz equipara las dos distinciones: la primera dimensión de Lijphart con los "puntos de veto colectivos" de Birchfield y Crepaz y la segunda dimensión de Lijphart con los "puntos de veto competitivos" de Birchfield y Crepaz.

Encuentro algunas incongruencias en estos argumentos y considero discutible la generalización de sus resultados. Las distinciones de Lijphart no son equivalentes a las que hicieran Birchfield y Crepaz. Por ejemplo, el primero incluye las cinco características siguientes en su dimensión federal-unitaria: *1)* gobierno unitario o gobierno federal; *2)* legislatura unicameral o bicameral; *3)* constituciones flexibles e inflexibles; *4)* ausencia o presencia de revisión judicial; *5)* dependencia o independencia del banco central. No hay referencia al gobierno presidencial, que Birchfield y Crepaz consideran una característica de "jugadores con veto competitivos", y no se hace referencia a bancos centrales, constituciones o revisión judicial en el concepto de jugadores con veto competitivos de Birchfield y Crepaz. De modo parecido, el parlamentarismo es una característica de los jugadores con veto colectivos según Birchfield y Crepaz, pero no una característica de la primera dimensión de Lijphart; el corporativismo es una característica para Lijphart pero no para Birchfield y Crepaz. Como resultado de estas diferencias, no estoy seguro de cuáles características son responsables de los resultados de desigualdad.

Si eliminamos las características que no son comunes en los diferentes índices (que incluirían presidencialismo y parlamentarismo, que no está en la lista de Lijphart), el común denominador de los resultados es que el federalismo aumenta las desigualdades pero el multipartidismo las reduce. Puedo entender por qué el federalismo es propenso a acrecentar las desigualdades: algunas transferencias de recursos están restringidas dentro de los estados. En consecuencia, si la federación incluye estados ricos y pobres, las transferencias de los primeros a los segundos son reducidas en comparación con un estado unitario. Desconozco por qué los gobiernos multipartidistas reducen la desigualdad, y no sé si este resultado se repetiría en muestras más grandes que los países de la OCDE. Si hay una conexión, en mi opinión, ésta debería incorporar las preferencias de diferentes gobiernos. No está claro que todos los gobiernos traten de reducir las desigualdades, de modo que los gobiernos multipartidistas están "habilitados" (como afirma Crepaz) para hacer más que los gobiernos de un solo partido. El argumento habitual en la bibliografía es que la izquierda (como gobierno de un solo partido o como coalición) aspira a reducir las desigualdades, no alguna estructura institucional en particular.

Finalmente, incluso si hay respuestas para todas estas preguntas, la relación entre desigualdad y características institucionales específicas no es una negación de los argumentos presentados en este libro. En ninguna parte he argüido que los jugadores con veto producen o reducen las desigualdades. Por añadidura, en este capítulo se sostiene que aunque puede haber similitudes entre los regímenes no democrático, presidencial y parlamentario en lo tocante al número de jugadores con veto y las distancias ideológicas entre éstos, hay diferencias en el establecimiento de agenda y la cohesión de partido. Tampoco he afirmado nunca que el federalismo no tiene un efecto independiente además del que opera a través de los jugadores con veto. Como lo demuestro en el capítulo VI, el federalismo está correlacionado con los jugadores con veto porque puede agregar uno o más jugadores con veto mediante la segunda cámara fuerte de un país federal, o por medio de decisiones por mayoría calificada. Como resultado, el federalismo se puede usar como sustituto de los jugadores con veto cuando no se tiene información sobre jugadores con veto.[13] Sin embargo, éste no es el único efecto posible del federalismo y también puede operar independientemente. Por ejemplo, en el capítulo X veremos que los países federalistas son más propensos a tener un poder judicial activo dado que estas instituciones resolverán problemas de conflicto entre niveles de gobierno.

En conclusión, Strom ha ayudado a identificar algunas debilidades en versiones anteriores de mi argumento. La expansión de la regla de absorción que se presenta en este libro incluye a los jugadores con veto institucionales y partidarios. Strom tiene un argumento válido en lo tocante a las coaliciones de ganancia no mínima, que abordaremos en el capítulo siguiente. Pero introduce una restricción demasiado severa en los sistemas parlamentarios cuando requiere que para que un partido cuente como un jugador con veto deberá presentar una "oportunidad demostrable para ejercer el veto". Argumento que la participación en el gobierno es una condición suficiente.

4. Conclusiones

Hemos pasado revista a las diferencias entre los sistemas no democrático y democrático, así como entre los sistemas presidencial y parlamentario, y hemos examinado de nuevo la bibliografía sobre la base de la teoría de los

---

[13] En el capítulo X se analiza un artículo de Treisman (2000c) usando exactamente esta estrategia.

jugadores con veto. Este análisis me llevó a presentar los conceptos de jugadores con veto institucionales y partidarios, y a identificar a tales jugadores en una serie de situaciones. Resulta que con el tiempo el número de jugadores con veto puede cambiar en un país (si algunos de ellos son absorbidos porque modificaron sus posiciones), o que el mismo país puede tener diferentes constelaciones de jugadores con veto dependiendo del tema motivo de su legislación (como Alemania).

En lo tocante a jugadores con veto, aunque los regímenes no democráticos son considerados generalmente como regímenes de un solo jugador con veto, un análisis más detenido revelaría la existencia de múltiples jugadores con veto. Por lo tanto, el número de jugadores con veto tampoco es una diferencia fundamental entre regímenes democrático y no democrático.

Mi revisión de la bibliografía sobre presidencialismo y parlamentarismo ha señalado que aunque hay una diferencia concluyente en la probabilidad de supervivencia de la democracia, todas las otras diferencias son motivo de debate en el análisis político actual. El análisis del presidencialismo y el parlamentarismo revela que la diferencia más importante entre estos regímenes es la interacción entre el poder ejecutivo y el legislativo en sistemas parlamentarios y su independencia en los presidenciales. Las otras diferencias parecen borrosas. En cuestión de jugadores con veto hay similitudes entre sistemas presidencial y parlamentario multipartidista, y contrastan con gobiernos de un solo partido en sistemas parlamentarios. Hay diferencias entre los sistemas parlamentario y presidencial, sobre quién controla la agenda, los gobiernos en sistemas parlamentarios, los parlamentos en sistemas presidenciales (que se examinarán más detenidamente en el siguiente capítulo), y en la cohesión de los partidos en cada sistema (el presidencialismo está en promedio asociado con cohesión más baja). En el siguiente capítulo nos concentraremos en la pregunta de quién controla la agenda y cómo.

IV. GOBIERNOS Y PARLAMENTOS

EN ESTE capítulo enfocaremos con mayor detalle los mecanismos de establecimiento de agenda. Se demostrará que hay dos variables importantes que es necesario examinar para comprender el poder del gobierno como establecedor de agenda en sistemas parlamentarios. La primera es posicional, la relación entre la posición ideológica del gobierno y el resto de los partidos en el parlamento. La segunda consiste en las disposiciones institucionales que permiten al gobierno proponer sus proyectos legislativos y hacer que sean votados en la tribuna del parlamento: las reglas del establecimiento de agenda. Estas dos cuestiones se originan del análisis realizado en la primera parte. Se concentran en el establecimiento de agenda y estudian las condiciones posicionales e institucionales para la misma. Resulta que mi análisis tiene algunas diferencias importantes con respecto a la bibliografía existente.

La primera diferencia es que nos concentraremos en las características de los *gobiernos* en sistemas parlamentarios en vez de concentrarnos en la visión tradicional del *sistema de partidos* (Duverger, Sartori). De acuerdo con la bibliografía tradicional, los sistemas bipartidistas generan gobiernos de un solo partido, donde el parlamento se reduce a una aprobación rutinaria de las actividades del gobierno, mientras que los sistemas multipartidistas generan parlamentos con mayor influencia. El análisis del sistema de partidos se concentra en los parlamentos porque éstos son la fuente de la cual se originan los gobiernos; en términos técnicos, los "principales" que seleccionan a sus "agentes". La teoría de los jugadores con veto se concentra en gobiernos porque éstos son los establecedores de agenda de la legislación, como se observa en el capítulo III. Los gobiernos de un solo partido tendrán toda la discreción para cambiar el *statu quo*, mientras que los gobiernos multipartidistas únicamente harán cambios incrementales.

Una segunda diferencia entre mi análisis y la bibliografía existente es la pregunta acerca de quién, dentro del gobierno, controla la agenda. Sobre la base de mi análisis, el establecimiento de agenda pertenece al gobierno en su conjunto. Es posible que en algunas áreas sea el primer ministro, en otras, el ministro de finanzas, en otras más el ministro correspondiente.

También se puede hacer mediante negociaciones entre los diferentes partidos en el gobierno. Todas estas posibilidades son congruentes con mi enfoque, mientras que otros enfoques asignan los derechos de establecimiento de agenda a actores gubernamentales específicos (Laver y Shepsle, 1996; por ejemplo, al ministro correspondiente).

Una tercera diferencia se refiere a las interacciones entre gobiernos y parlamentos. Aunque gran parte de la bibliografía señala una diferencia entre los regímenes presidencial y parlamentario, un investigador (Lijphart, 1999), en su influyente análisis de las democracias consociacionales en comparación con las mayoritarias, combina los tipos de régimen (como se hace en este libro) y se concentra en el concepto de "predominio ejecutivo" como una diferencia importante entre y dentro de regímenes. El predominio ejecutivo, en palabras de Lijphart, capta "el poder relativo de las ramas ejecutiva y legislativa del gobierno" (Lijphart, 1999: 129) y se le calcula por la durabilidad del gabinete en los sistemas parlamentarios. Argumento que la interacción entre ejecutivo y legislatura está regulada por una variable institucional: *las reglas del establecimiento de agenda*. Permítaseme explicar en qué consisten estas diferencias.

Puede parecer trivial la diferencia de un análisis basado en sistemas de partido (es decir, partidos en el parlamento) o coaliciones gubernamentales (es decir, partidos en el gobierno). Después de todo, los sistemas multipartidistas suelen conducir a gobiernos de coalición, y los sistemas bipartidistas a gobiernos de un solo partido. Sin embargo, la correlación no es perfecta. Por ejemplo, Grecia (país multipartidista) tiene un gobierno que controla completamente la legislatura. Además de las diferencias en expectativas empíricas (se espera que los gobiernos griegos sean fuertes sobre la base de los jugadores con veto, mientras que su composición de un solo partido es una falla de comprensión de la relación entre gobiernos y parlamentos generada por el análisis del sistema de partidos), la diferencia principal estriba en la identificación de mecanismos causales que configuren la interacción entre gobiernos y parlamentos.

Argumento también que la variable de los jugadores con veto no depende tan sólo de instituciones o de sistemas de partidos, sino que se deriva de ambos. Por ejemplo, los jugadores con veto incluyen no sólo a asociados en el gobierno, sino también a una segunda cámara de la legislatura o a presidentes de la república (si tienen poder de veto). Además, un partido puede ser importante en el parlamento y contar en el sistema de partidos de un país, pero su aprobación de una medida legislativa tal vez no sea necesaria, en cuyo caso no será un jugador con veto. Finalmente, uno o más jugadores con veto, ya sea un asociado gubernamental, una segunda cámara o un presidente de la república pueden ser absorbidos y no contar como jugadores con veto, como se demostró en el capítulo I.

La interrogante de si son ministros quienes controlan la agenda o si es todo el gobierno es una pregunta menor; sin embargo, dado que mi enfoque comparte con el de Laver y Shepsle la importancia atribuida al establecimiento de agenda, necesito aclarar que alguna prueba empírica que entra en conflicto con las expectativas de ellos no afecta mi análisis.

Igualmente trivial puede parecer la diferencia de si la relación entre gobiernos y parlamentos está determinada sobre la base de la duración del gobierno o por las reglas de establecimiento de la agenda. Pero la duración del gobierno varía únicamente en sistemas parlamentarios, y en consecuencia no se puede usar como un agente sustituto del predominio ejecutivo en los sistemas presidenciales, o en otros tipos de sistemas; las reglas del establecimiento de agenda se pueden usar en diferentes tipos de sistemas. Además, argumento que no hay relación lógica entre predominio ejecutivo y duración del gobierno, de modo que para el estudio de la relación entre legislativo y ejecutivo se necesita una variable diferente. Demuestro que esta relación se puede captar mediante las reglas que regulan el establecimiento de la agenda legislativa.

El capítulo está organizado en tres secciones. En la sección 1 se estudian las condiciones posicionales del establecimiento de agenda. Me concentro en diferentes tipos de gobiernos parlamentarios (coaliciones de ganancia mínima, gobiernos de tamaño exagerado y gobiernos minoritarios) y estudio su capacidad de imponer sus preferencias al parlamento. Demuestro que cuando el establecedor de agenda está ubicado centralmente entre los otros jugadores, él será capaz de producir resultados muy cercanos a su punto ideal incluso si no controla una mayoría parlamentaria. La sección 2 se concentra en las disposiciones institucionales del establecimiento de agenda. Aunque todos los gobiernos parlamentarios son capaces de formular la pregunta sobre la confianza con el fin de obligar al parlamento a acatar sus preferencias, también tienen a su alcance una serie de otras armas que les permiten cambiar los resultados a su favor. Estudiaremos estos arreglos institucionales. En la sección 3 se comparan los resultados de las secciones 1 y 2 con enfoques alternativos en la bibliografía y se muestran las diferencias del análisis de los jugadores con veto con descripciones de sistemas de partidos, discreción ministerial o duración del gobierno como medida de predominio ejecutivo. En la mayor parte de este capítulo se estudian los sistemas parlamentarios, debido a restricciones en la bibliografía. Sin embargo, no pierdo la oportunidad de mostrar cómo se aplican los argumentos también a regímenes presidenciales.

1. Ventajas posicionales del control de la agenda

Como se dijo en el capítulo III, en los sistemas parlamentarios es el gobierno quien controla la agenda para legislación no financiera. Una de las razones principales es su capacidad de asociar un voto sobre un proyecto de ley con la pregunta sobre la confianza (Huber, 1996). Tal iniciativa gubernamental obliga al parlamento a aceptar el proyecto del gobierno, o bien sustituye al gobierno. Como resultado, desde nuestro punto de vista cada gobierno, *siempre y cuando esté en su poder,* es capaz de imponer su voluntad al parlamento (las palabras en cursivas no son triviales). Mi declaración se sostiene para cualquier tipo de gobierno parlamentario, ya sea que controle o no una mayoría de los votos legislativos.

Algunos datos estadísticos sencillos sugieren que es correcta la evaluación general de que los gobiernos controlan la agenda en democracias parlamentarias. En más de 50% de todos los países, los gobiernos introducen más de 90% de los proyectos de ley. Además, la probabilidad de ser aprobados estos proyectos de ley es muy alta: más de 60% de los proyectos de ley pasan con probabilidad mayor de 0.9 y más de 85% de los proyectos de ley pasan con probabilidad mayor de 0.8 (Inter-Parlamentary Union, 1986; cuadro 29).

Sin embargo, incluso si los gobiernos tienen el control de la agenda, puede ser que los parlamentos introduzcan restricciones importantes a sus elecciones. O puede ser que los parlamentos enmienden los proyectos gubernamentales de tal manera que el resultado final tenga escaso parecido con el original proyecto de ley. Afirmo que la mayor parte del tiempo, ninguno de estos casos se presenta. Los problemas entre gobierno y parlamento surgen únicamente cuando el gobierno tiene una composición política diferente de la mayoría en el parlamento. Examinando todos los casos posibles de relaciones entre el gobierno y una mayoría parlamentaria, demuestro que tales diferencias no existen, o en el caso de existir, el gobierno es capaz de prevalecer debido a las armas posicionales o institucionales de que dispone.

Hay tres configuraciones posibles que sustentan la relación entre gobierno y parlamento: coaliciones de ganancia mínima (que constituyen el caso de libro de texto), gobiernos de tamaño exagerado (gobiernos que incluyen más partidos de los necesarios para formar una mayoría) y gobiernos minoritarios (gobiernos que no cuentan con el respaldo de una mayoría). Estas tres categorías constituyen formas de gobierno mutuamente excluyentes y colectivamente exhaustivas en sistemas parlamentarios.

1.1. Coaliciones de ganancia mínima

Éste es el caso más frecuente (si incluimos los gobiernos de un solo partido en sistemas bipartidistas que son, por definición, coaliciones de ganancia mínima) y el menos interesante para nuestro estudio. El gobierno coincide con la mayoría en el parlamento y, en consecuencia, no hay desacuerdo en temas importantes. Como lo indica la gráfica II.4, la coalición de ganancia mínima representada en el gobierno restringe el conjunto ganador del *statu quo* desde toda el área sombreada de la gráfica hasta el área que hace a los socios de la coalición estar en mejores condiciones que el *statu quo*. Hay una excepción que considerar: si los partidos en el gobierno son débiles e incluyen miembros con grandes desacuerdos acerca de un proyecto de ley, la propuesta puede ser derrotada en el parlamento. Esto, sin embargo, es sólo una posibilidad marginal porque los votos son públicos y los líderes de partido poseen grandes mecanismos coercitivos que previenen la disensión pública (Italia era la única excepción a la regla hasta que el gobierno dio entrada a votaciones abiertas en 1988 y terminó con el problema de los *franchi tiratori*, parlamentarios que votaban para derrotar y ridiculizar a su propio gobierno). El más fuerte de estos mecanismos es la eliminación de la lista.

Incluso en los casos en que se requiere un voto secreto, el liderazgo de partido puede arreglárselas para estructurar la votación de alguna forma que le permita vigilar a sus parlamentarios. Un buen ejemplo de tal estructuración proviene de Alemania. En 1972 el canciller Willy Brandt estuvo a punto de perder la mayoría que respaldaba su coalición debido a deserciones de su propio partido, el SPD, y su partido de coalición, el FDP. El 27 de abril se enfrentó a un voto constructivo de no confianza en el Bundestag.[1] Según las reglas del parlamento, un voto de no confianza es una votación

---

[1] De acuerdo con el artículo 67 de la ley básica alemana, no puede haber una votación para destituir al canciller del puesto si antes no se ha votado a su sucesor.

secreta, y el canciller temía perder su mayoría. Por esta razón, instruyó a los miembros de su coalición para que se quedaran en sus lugares y no participaran en la votación, con lo cual controló efectivamente a los posibles desertores. La medida de no confianza fue rechazada por un voto: 247 de los 496 miembros del Bundestag respaldaron al jefe de la oposición, Rainer Barzel (Tsebelis, 1990).

En general, el proceso de formación de coalición proporciona una ventaja importante a los gobiernos. En el gobierno se incluye el liderazgo o las principales personalidades del partido, de modo que cuando llegan a un acuerdo es difícil que otros miembros del parlamento lo desafíen o lo anulen. Un ejemplo de esto último es la siguiente declaración de la primera ministra noruega Kare Willoch, acerca de su gobierno de coalición: "Yo quería a sus personalidades principales en el gobierno. Mi exigencia era que sus líderes de partido estuvieran en el gobierno porque yo no quería fortalecer los otros centros que estarían en el parlamento. Esa fue mi condición absoluta para tener tres partidos en el gobierno" (Maor, 1992: 108).

1.2. Coaliciones de tamaño exagerado

Los gobiernos mayoritarios de tamaño exagerado son muy comunes en Europa Occidental. Laver y Schofield (1990) calculan que el 4% del tiempo (de los 218 gobiernos que examinaron), un partido que por sí solo forma una mayoría le pedirá a otro partido que se una al gobierno; 21% de las veces, en tanto que no hay partido mayoritario, la coalición formada contiene uno o más partidos más de lo necesario. En tales casos, algunos de los socios de la coalición pueden ser pasados por alto y las medidas políticas se seguirán aprobando por mayoría en el parlamento. ¿Deben contar estos partidos como jugadores con veto o se les debe pasar por alto?

Pasar por alto a los socios de coalición, aunque es posible desde un punto de vista numérico, impone costos políticos porque si el desacuerdo es grave, el socio pequeño puede renunciar y el proceso de formación de gobierno debe empezar de nuevo. Incluso si se pueden evitar los costos de formación de gobierno (mediante la formación de un gobierno que incluya a todos los socios de la coalición anterior sin el partido que está en desacuerdo), el argumento sigue siendo válido, ya que la reforma propuesta será presentada en el parlamento por una coalición que no incluye al partido en desacuerdo. Maor reporta de la siguiente manera la posición de un líder del Partido Liberal, miembro de la coalición de gobierno en Dinamarca: "Podíamos detener todo lo que no nos gustaba. Ese es un problema con un gobierno de coalición entre dos partidos con principios muy diferentes. Si no puedes llegar a un acuerdo, entonces tal gobierno tiene que permanecer alejado de la legislación en tales áreas" (Maor, 1992: 107).[2]

La aritmética más sencilla hace caso omiso del hecho de que hay factores políticos que necesitan coaliciones de tamaño exagerado. Cualquier cosa que estos actores pudieran ser, para que la coalición permanezca intacta se debe respetar la voluntad de sus diferentes asociados. En consecuencia, aunque la aritmética del proceso legislativo pueda ser distinta que la aritmética del gobierno, un alejamiento del *statu quo* habitualmente debe ser aprobado por el gobierno antes de ser presentado en el parlamento y, en esa etapa, los participantes en una coalición de gobierno son jugadores con veto. Este análisis indica que, en general, los gobiernos de tamaño exagerado tendrán las mismas regularidades que las coaliciones de ganancia mínima, pero sus relaciones serán más débiles porque no tienen que sostenerse en cada situación.

Sin embargo, los argumentos anteriores no han convencido a Strom (2000), como se vio en el capítulo III. Su argumento es que algunos de los partidos en coaliciones de tamaño exagerado no tendrán la "oportunidad de ejercer el veto". Si éste es el caso, deberíamos contar únicamente a los partidos que se requieren para obtener una mayoría. No es difícil modelar los requerimientos numéricos y localizar el conjunto ganador de una coalición de tamaño exagerado en el marco de los jugadores con veto: podemos pensar que los partidos que componen la coalición de gobierno de tamaño exagerado no deciden por unanimidad (como lo implica el argumento político) sino por mayoría calificada (como el número de votos lo permita). Si, pongamos por caso, se requieren tres de cuatro partidos en una coalición de tamaño exagerado para lograr una decisión por mayoría, entonces podemos identificar el conjunto ganador de las tres cuartas partes de la coalición de gobierno. El capítulo II muestra que el conjunto ganador de mayoría calificada (tres cuartos) es más grande que el conjunto de unanimidad de la coalición de gobierno y en donde estarán ubicados los posibles resultados.

En resumen, proporciono un argumento político para explicar por qué la voluntad de los socios en la coalición se deberá respetar siempre y cuan-

---

[2] El gobierno en este caso es un gobierno minoritario, pero la lógica se aplica por igual a coaliciones de ganancia mínima o de tamaño exagerado.

do el gobierno permanezca en su lugar: porque los socios en la coalición que estén en desacuerdo pueden irse del gobierno. Strom se basa en un argumento numérico según el cual en los gobiernos de tamaño exagerado los votos de algunos partidos tal vez no sean necesarios, por lo cual estos partidos no insistirán en su posición y los proyectos de ley se aprobarán sin sus votos. Cierto es que a veces los partidos permanecen en coaliciones y votan en contra de medidas políticas específicas (por ejemplo, en Israel el Partido Laborista se mantuvo dentro de la coalición Likud, pero hizo saber que estaba en contra de represalias por el atentado con bomba a Sbarro en Jerusalén en agosto de 2001).[3] Si este fenómeno no sucede con frecuencia, entonces contar a todos los socios en la coalición de gobierno como jugadores con veto será un buen enfoque para los análisis empíricos. Si, por un lado, los asociados en la coalición votan a menudo en contra de su propio gobierno, entonces un argumento de votación por mayoría calificada se debería aplicar en los análisis empíricos. En los capítulos VII y VIII el lector puede verificar que contar a todos los socios de la coalición como jugadores con veto proporciona una buena aproximación para la estabilidad política.

1.3. Gobiernos minoritarios

Los gobiernos minoritarios son todavía más frecuentes que las coaliciones de tamaño exagerado. Strom (1990) ha analizado gobiernos minoritarios y descubiertos que son comunes en los sistemas multipartidistas (alrededor de un tercio de los gobiernos en su muestra). Además, la mayor parte de ellos (79 de 125) son gobiernos de un solo partido que se asemejan a gobiernos mayoritarios de un solo partido. Laver y Schofield han argumentado que hay una diferencia entre una mayoría gubernamental y una legislativa. Aunque su argumento es técnicamente correcto, sostendré que esta diferencia no tiene mayor importancia empírica. La razón es que los gobiernos (ya sean minoritarios o no) poseen la capacidad de establecer la agenda. En particular, los gobiernos poseen no sólo ventajas institucionales sobre sus parlamentos respectivos (que se verán en la sección 3) sino que también tienen ventajas posicionales de establecimiento de agenda, que se examinaron en el capítulo I (corolarios I.5.2 y I.5.3). Concentrémonos un poco más en estas ventajas posicionales. El partido que forma un gobierno

---

[3] Agradezco este ejemplo a Ron Rogowski.

minoritario suele estar ubicado centralmente en el espacio. Por esta razón puede seleccionar entre muchos asociados diferentes para hacer que el parlamento apruebe su programa (Downs, 1957; Laver y Schofield, 1990; Strom, 1990). Con el propósito de ahondar más en este punto, consideremos un parlamento de cinco partidos en un espacio bidimensional como el de la gráfica IV.1. Lo que sigue es una ilustración del argumento, no una prueba formal.

En la gráfica IV.1 se examina si las preferencias gubernamentales (G) pueden contar con la aprobación del parlamento. Se le recuerda al lector que cualquier propuesta presentada en la tribuna del parlamento tendrá que ser preferida por una mayoría por encima de G o derrotada por G.[4] Identifiquemos los conjuntos de puntos que derrotan a G. Estos puntos están ubicados dentro de las lentes GG' y GG". Si el parlamento está interesado en cualquier otro resultado y el gobierno propone su propio punto ideal, una mayoría de parlamentarios se pondrá del lado del gobierno.

GRÁFICA IV.1. *Un gobierno minoritario ubicado centralmente puede evitar derrotas graves (resultados en áreas X).*

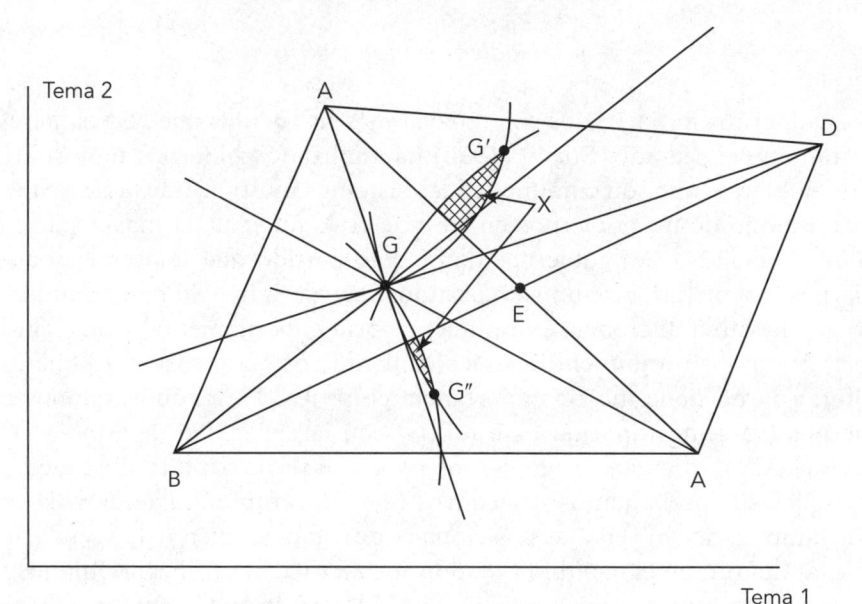

[4] La indiferencia entre los dos también es una posibilidad. Continuaré pasando por alto este caso, como en el pasado.

Para recapitular, si un gobierno minoritario está ubicado centralmente en el espacio, puede ser parte de las mayorías parlamentarias más probables y, en consecuencia, mover el *statu quo* dentro de su propio conjunto ganador. De hecho, la mayor parte del tiempo es posible que no tenga que comprometerse en absoluto, y puede localizar el resultado final sobre su propio punto ideal. Por lo tanto, presuponiendo que el gobierno controla la agenda, puede cambiar el *statu quo* de la manera que prefiera. Este argumento es muy parecido pero no idéntico al corolario 1.5.3. La diferencia es que allí se suponía que todos los actores eran jugadores con veto, mientras que aquí no.

Pero si un punto es seleccionado entre una de las dos lentes GG' y GG", el gobierno perderá la votación. La situación sería tolerable para el gobierno si SQ se moviera en el área de esas lentes que está cerca de G, pero las áreas sombreadas llamadas X son una derrota seria para el gobierno. Ahora mismo podemos afirmar que tal es un evento de escasa probabilidad, pero este es un argumento pobre. En realidad, aunque pueda darse el caso de que *al azar* no es muy probable que el resultado esté ubicado en las dos áreas sombreadas X de la gráfica, los resultados legislativos no son aleatorios. Una coalición de partidos A, C y D seleccionaría un punto en X con el fin de derrotar y poner en ridículo al gobierno. ¿Puede el gobierno evitar tal humillación?

Esto nos lleva a la segunda categoría de ventajas de un gobierno minoritario sobre el parlamento, las ventajas institucionales. Esta categoría de ventajas no se limita a gobiernos minoritarios. Cada gobierno parlamentario tiene a su disposición algún medio constitucional, así como otros procesales o políticos, para imponer al parlamento su voluntad en temas importantes. Tales ventajas institucionales son mucho más importantes para los gobiernos que no disfruten del respaldo de una mayoría estable en el parlamento, por razones obvias. El gobierno puede obligar a la mayoría del parlamento a acatar su propuesta. Sin embargo, hay una razón adicional generada por la teoría que se presenta en este libro: la mayor parte del tiempo los gobiernos minoritarios tienen un solo jugador con veto. Como resultado, la estabilidad política es escasa, y la importancia del establecimiento de agenda es grande (como lo indica la gráfica 1 de la Introducción). Así, sobre la base de la teoría presentada en este libro, si los gobiernos minoritarios tienen poderes institucionales de establecimiento de agenda, harán uso de ellos con más frecuencia que otras formas de gobierno (particularmente las coaliciones de tamaño exagerado).

Concentrémonos en un mecanismo particular que existe en diversos países, como lo demuestra Heller (1999). Weingast (1992) describió el mecanismo como "combatir el fuego con fuego", y lo identificó por primera vez en el Congreso de los Estados Unidos. Los detalles son muy sencillos: el gobierno puede hacer la última enmienda al proyecto de ley que esté en consideración. En consecuencia, cuando vea que alguna enmienda hostil está a punto de ser adoptada, puede modificar esta enmienda de tal modo que proteja su propio proyecto de ley. Usemos la gráfica IV.1 para ver cómo puede prevalecer el gobierno de minoría. Supongamos que el gobierno de minoría presenta un proyecto de ley sobre su propio punto ideal G y que en la tribuna del parlamento se propone una enmienda en el área indeseable X. Esta enmienda significaría una derrota política importante para el gobierno. Sin embargo, el gobierno puede "combatir el fuego con fuego" y proponer una enmienda en la parte no sombreada de las dos lentes (simétrica a la propuesta hostil con respecto a la línea AC; de hecho, ligeramente más cerca a A y a C). Esta enmienda tendría una mayoría en el parlamento (sería votada por G, A y C) y está localizada muy cerca de la preferencia del gobierno (G). Estudiemos ahora tales mecanismos de establecimiento de agenda.

2. Medios institucionales de control gubernamental de la agenda

Varias constituciones proporcionan a los gobiernos una serie de poderes de establecimiento de agenda, tales como una prioridad de proyectos de ley del gobierno, posibilidad de reglas cerradas o restrictivas, conteo de abstenciones a favor de proyectos de ley del gobierno, posibilidad de proponer enmiendas en cualquier punto del debate (incluso antes de la votación final) y otros. El caso más extremo a este respecto es la Constitución de la Quinta República francesa. En esta constitución se aplican las restricciones siguientes al parlamento: de acuerdo con el artículo 34, el parlamento legisla por excepción (únicamente en las áreas que este artículo especifica, mientras que en todas las demás áreas el gobierno legisla sin pedir el consenso del parlamento); el artículo 38 permite la legislación por decreto (después del acuerdo del parlamento); de acuerdo con el artículo 40, no puede haber aumento de desembolsos ni reducción de tributación sin el consenso del gobierno; el artículo 44.3 da al gobierno el derecho a presentar votos según regla cerrada (no se aceptan enmiendas); el artículo 45 permite al gobierno declarar que un proyecto de ley es urgente, con lo cual reduce el número de vueltas en las cuales las dos cámaras se pasarán una a otra el proyecto de ley;[5] finalmente, el arma más poderosa de todas: el artículo 49.3 permite al gobierno transformar la votación sobre cualquier proyecto de ley en una cuestión de confianza (Huber, 1992; Tsebelis, 1990: cap. 7). El retrato de un parlamento impotente está completo si consideramos que el gobierno controla la agenda legislativa, que el parlamento está en sesión menos de la mitad del año (las sesiones especiales se limitan a dos semanas y deben tener una agenda especificada),[6] que la estructura de comité estaba diseñada para ser ineficaz (seis grandes comisiones cortando transversalmente las jurisdicciones de ministros) y que las discusiones se basan en proyectos gubernamentales y no en informes de comisiones. Finalmente, incluso las mociones de censura son difíciles porque requieren la solicitud de una décima parte de los parlamentarios (el derecho no es reutilizable durante la misma sesión) y una mayoría absoluta de votos *en contra* del gobierno (las abstenciones se cuentan en favor del gobierno).

El gobierno francés es una excepción por la amplitud, profundidad y diversidad de las armas institucionales que tiene a su disposición. Sin embargo, el gobierno alemán posee también armas institucionales interesantes, como la posibilidad de pedir un voto de confianza cuando quiera que lo considere apropiado (artículo 68) o la posibilidad de declarar necesidad legislativa y legislar con el consenso de la segunda cámara (el Bundesrat) por seis meses (artículo 81). Hasta el gobierno italiano tiene el derecho de emitir decretos ejecutivos (conocidos como ordenanzas; Kreppel, 1997). Por añadidura, en lo que toca a la legislación parlamentaria, tiene el derecho de ofrecer la última enmienda en la tribuna del parlamento (Heller, 1999). El propósito de esta sección es examinar la bibliografía sobre medidas que dotan al gobierno con poderes legislativos de establecimiento de agenda.

Como quedó claro en el capítulo III, la más importante de estas medidas es la vinculación de la pregunta de confianza a un proyecto de ley, que es equivalente a la amenaza de la renuncia del gobierno, seguida por la disolución del parlamento (Huber, 1996). Esta medida existe en todos los sistemas parlamentarios excepto en Noruega. Sin embargo, esta medida es como una amenaza de armas nucleares en disputas internacionales: es ex-

[5] Para un análisis del sistema de *navette* en Francia, véase Tsebelis y Money (1997). Su argumento es que reducir el número de vueltas aumenta el poder de la Asamblea Nacional (que tiene posiciones más cercanas al gobierno).

[6] Los socialistas, que tenían una pesada agenda de reformas, necesitaron 17 de tales sesiones en su primer periodo (1981-1986).

traordinaria y no se puede usar con frecuencia. Aquí me concentraré en las armas de menor alcance y mayor frecuencia. La principal referencia a lo que sigue es una serie de artículos de Doering (todos de 1995) sobre las instituciones que asignan al gobierno poderes legislativos de establecimiento de agenda. Doering (1995a) identifica y evalúa las siete variables que presentaré. El análisis de Doering cubre 18 países de Europa Occidental y combina datos de análisis anteriores de sistemas parlamentarios como *Parliaments of the World* (1986) con investigación original dirigida por un grupo internacional de académicos. Lo que sigue es la lista de variables con explicaciones acerca de sus valores numéricos.

a) Autoridad para determinar la agenda plenaria del parlamento

Esta variable tiene siete modalidades; los dos extremos son que la agenda puede ser determinada por el gobierno o solamente por el parlamento. Veamos la lista entera de posibilidades:

i. El gobierno establece la agenda por sí solo (Reino Unido e Irlanda).
ii. En reunión de los comités con el presidente, el gobierno tendrá una mayoría más grande que su porción de asientos en la cámara (Francia y Grecia).
iii. Decisión por regla de la mayoría en reunión de las comisiones con el presidente, donde los grupos de partidos están representados proporcionalmente (Luxemburgo, Portugal y Suiza).
iv. Consenso de los grupos de partidos buscado en la reunión de comités con el presidente, pero la mayoría plenaria puede echar abajo la propuesta (Austria, Bélgica, Alemania, Noruega y España).
v. La cámara no puede impugnar la decisión del presidente después de consultar con grupos de partidos (Dinamarca, Finlandia, Islandia y Suecia).
vi. La fragmentación del establecimiento de agenda se centra si no se puede alcanzar la votación unánime de líderes de partido (Italia).
vii. La cámara misma determina la agenda (Holanda).

Ésta es la variable más importante, aunque sólo garantiza que se discutirán los temas que el gobierno proponga, no el resultado de los debates parlamentarios.

b) Proyectos de leyes hacendarias como prerrogativa del gobierno

Aunque esta prerrogativa pertenece al gobierno en todos los países, en algunos de ellos los miembros del parlamento tienen vedado el presentar proyectos de leyes hacendarias. Por ejemplo, en el Reino Unido,

> ningún miembro de la Cámara de los Comunes puede proponer un proyecto de ley que tenga el propósito central de aumentar el gasto o la tributación; tampoco avanzarán más las estipulaciones relevantes de un proyecto de ley que plantee alguno de tales aumentos, de no ser que una resolución que autorice tales incrementos haya sido presentada por el gobierno y acordada por la Cámara de los Comunes [Inter-Parliamentary Union, 1986: 862].

Francia, el Reino Unido, Irlanda, Portugal y España pertenecen a la categoría de países que no permiten a sus parlamentarios presentar proyectos de leyes hacendarias. Grecia aplica algunas restricciones, mientras que el resto de los países aplica muy pocas o ninguna restricción a los parlamentarios en proyectos de ley hacendaria.

c) ¿Está restringida la etapa de un proyecto de ley en comités por una decisión plenaria anterior?

Algunos de los primeros resultados que se encuentran en la bibliografía comparativa sobre los parlamentos eran que la importancia de los comités depende de si éstos consideran un proyecto de ley antes o después de ser presentado en el parlamento por primera vez.

> Si un comité puede considerar un proyecto de ley antes de que éste sea abordado en el parlamento, las probabilidades de que el comité influya en o determine el resultado suelen ser mayores que cuando los frentes de batalla han sido fijados de antemano en juntas plenarias. Por lo general, cuando exista un fuerte compromiso para utilizar comités, éstos reciben primero los proyectos de ley [Shaw, 1979: 417].

La mayoría de los países permiten a los comités desempeñar un papel importante en el proceso legislativo, mientras que en tres naciones (Irlanda, España y el Reino Unido) el parlamento remite el proyecto de ley a los comités. En Dinamarca la decisión del parlamento no es estrictamente obligatoria.

*d) Autoridad de los comités para volver a redactar
los proyectos de ley del gobierno*

La interrogante que se aborda en esta sección es cuál texto decide la cámara. ¿Llega a la cámara el proyecto de ley del gobierno con comentarios del comité, o enmienda el comité el proyecto de ley del gobierno y presenta su propio proyecto a la cámara? Hay cuatro diferentes respuestas posibles:

> *i.* La cámara considera el proyecto de ley original del gobierno con enmiendas agregadas (Dinamarca, Francia, Irlanda, Holanda y el Reino Unido).
> *ii.* Si el texto redactado de nuevo no es aceptado por el ministro pertinente, la cámara considera el proyecto de ley original (Grecia).
> *iii.* Los comités pueden presentar textos sustitutos, que se consideran comparándolos con el texto original (Austria, Luxemburgo y Portugal).
> *iv.* Los comités están en libertad de redactar de nuevo el texto del gobierno (Bélgica, Finlandia, Alemania, Islandia, Italia, Noruega, España, Suecia y Suiza).

e) Control del calendario en los comités legislativos

Este tema combina las respuestas a dos preguntas diferentes:

> Primero, ¿es establecido el calendario por la entidad plenaria principal o por el propio comité? Segundo, ¿puede la mayoría plenaria turnar el proyecto de ley a otro comité o incluso tomar una votación final sin un informe del comité, o disfruta éste del privilegio exclusivo de debatir un proyecto de ley siempre y cuando piense que no coincide con un derecho de revocación por parte de la plenaria? [Doering, 1995a: 237].

La combinación de las respuestas produce la siguiente clasificación:

i. Los proyectos de ley presentados a la comisión constituyen automáticamente la agenda. En Finlandia, Irlanda y el Reino Unido, donde se aplican estas reglas, el gobierno controla la agenda del comité.
   ii. La autoridad directiva de la entidad plenaria con el derecho de revocación. En Austria, Francia, Grecia, Italia, Luxemburgo, Noruega, Portugal y España la sesión plenaria puede supervisar la agenda del comité.
   iii. Los propios comités establecen su agenda pero existe el derecho de revocación de parte de la plenaria (Bélgica, Alemania y Suiza).
   iv. Puede ser que la cámara no remita los proyectos de ley a otros comités. En Dinamarca, Islandia, Holanda y Suecia los propios comités controlan su agenda.

*f) Abreviar el debate antes de la votación
final de un proyecto de ley en la plenaria*

La siguiente clasificación responde a tres preguntas:

1) ¿Es posible que el gobierno, o su mayoría simple en la plenaria (sobre la cual el gobierno normalmente rige) pueda imponer unilateralmente y con antelación un límite de tiempo demasiado breve para abreviar el debate para la votación final? *2)* ¿Es posible que una limitación del debate sea impuesta únicamente mediante acuerdo mutuo entre los partidos? *3)* ¿No hay limitación por adelantado ni posibilidad de cierre del debate, con lo cual teóricamente se abren oportunidades ilimitadas para el obstruccionismo? [Doering, 1995a: 240].

Los 18 países caen en las siguientes categorías:

   i. Limitación por adelantado mediante voto mayoritario (Francia, Grecia, Irlanda y el Reino Unido).
   ii. Organización por adelantado del debate mediante acuerdo mutuo entre los partidos (Austria, Bélgica, Dinamarca, Alemania, Islandia, Italia, Luxemburgo, Noruega, Portugal, España y Suiza).
   iii. Ninguna limitación por adelantado ni cierre (Finlandia, Holanda y Suecia).

g) Vida máxima de un proyecto de ley pendiente de aprobación, después de lo cual prescribe si no se adopta

Cuanto más corta sea la vida de un proyecto de ley si el parlamento no lo adopta, más imperativo será el poder de establecimiento de agenda del gobierno. La duración máxima de vida de los proyectos de ley varía considerablemente de un país a otro, desde un periodo de seis meses o un año hasta un plazo infinito.

    i. Los proyectos de ley mueren al final de la sesión (seis meses a un año) (Dinamarca, Islandia y el Reino Unido).
    ii. Los proyectos de ley expiran al final del término legislativo de cuatro a cinco años (Austria, Finlandia, Alemania, Grecia, Irlanda, Italia, Noruega y España).
    iii. Los proyectos de ley habitualmente expiran al final del periodo legislativo, pero es posible que duren más (Bélgica, Francia y Portugal).
    iv. Los proyectos de ley nunca prescriben (excepto cuando son rechazados por una votación) (Luxemburgo, Holanda, Suecia y Suiza).

El cuadro IV.1 muestra la puntuación que cada país recibe en cada una de las siete variables de control de la agenda. La columna siguiente ofrece una variable de control de toda la agenda gubernamental que usaremos en éste y otros capítulos.[7] Aunque la variable "control de la agenda" es la más avanzada en la actual bibliografía, las puntuaciones por país en esa variable no se deberían considerar concluyentes. Doering ha hecho un trabajo excelente compilando indicadores objetivos acerca de quién puede colocar incisos en la agenda y si pueden reducir el tiempo de discusión en la cámara o en los comités pertinentes, pero se necesita hacer más. Por ejemplo, el argumento de Heller (1999) y Weingast (1992) de "combatir el fuego con fuego", es decir, proponer una enmienda de último momento (que examinamos en relación con la gráfica IV.1), no fue incluido en la lista de Doering. De hecho, la identificación de tales mecanismos o prácticas que los gobiernos

---

[7] Los valores numéricos atribuidos a cada país fueron calculados de la siguiente manera: usé los componentes de principal y analicé todas las siete mediciones del control de agenda de Doering. Usé las primeras cargas factoriales para asignar valor estadístico a cada una de estas variables (el primer valor específico explica 47% de la varianza) y normalicé la suma cargada con valor estadístico.

CUADRO IV.1. *Control de agenda, duración y predominio ejecutivo del gobierno.*

País	Agenda plenaria	Iniciativa financiera	Comisión	Reescribir	Calendario	Votación financiera	Lapso de propuesta de ley	Control de agenda	Duración del gobierno (Lijphart)	Predominio ejecutivo (Lijphart)
Alemania	4	3	3	4	3	2	2	−0.126	2.82	2.82
Austria	4	3	3	3	2	2	2	−0.044	5.47	5.47
Bélgica	4	3	3	4	3	2	3	−0.170	1.98	1.98
Dinamarca	5	3	2	1	4	2	1	−0.106	2.28	2.28
España	4	1	1	4	2	2	2	0.221	4.36	4.36
Finlandia	5	3	3	4	1	3	2	−0.148	1.24	1.24
Francia	2	1	3	1	2	1	3	0.333	2.48*	5.52*
Grecia	2	2	3	2	2	1	2	0.280	2.88	2.88
Holanda	7	3	3	1	4	3	4	−0.527	2.72	2.72
Irlanda	1	1	1	4	1	2	2	0.519	3.07	3.07
Islandia	5	3	3	1	4	2	1	−0.170	2.48	2.48
Italia	6	3	3	4	2	2	2	−0.219	1.14	1.14
Luxemburgo	3	3	3	3	2	2	4	−0.053	4.39	4.39
Noruega	4	3	3	4	2	2	2	−0.063	3.17	3.17
Portugal	3	1	3	3	2	2	3	0.147	2.09	2.09
Reino Unido	1	1	1	1	1	1	1	0.690	5.52	5.52
Suecia	5	3	3	4	4	3	4	−0.427	3.42	3.42
Suiza	3	3	3	4	3	2	4	−0.135	1*	8.59*

El control de la agenda se calcula en este estudio con las mediciones de Doering (1995b): "Duración del gobierno" y "Predominio ejecutivo" de Lijphart, cuadro 7.1 (1999: 132).
* Francia y Suiza son los únicos países con diferentes cifras para duración del gobierno y predominio ejecutivo.
FUENTE: Columnas 1-7 de Doering (1995b).

pueden usar para controlar la agenda es la vía de estudio más importante del control de la agenda gubernamental, y mejorará las mediciones que tenemos actualmente en el cuadro IV.1. Finalmente, el cuadro incluye dos columnas del análisis de Lijphart (1999), que más adelante examinaremos a fondo.

3. JUGADORES CON VETO CONTRA OTROS ENFOQUES EN POLÍTICA COMPARADA

Haré una comparación del análisis que hasta aquí he presentado con tres enfoques importantes en política comparada. El primero (Duverger, 1954; Sartori, 1976) compara diferentes países sobre la base de las características que prevalecen en su sistema de partidos. El segundo (Laver y Shepsle,

1996) comparte el enfoque del establecimiento de agenda, pero lo atribuye a los ministros correspondientes y no al gobierno en conjunto. El tercero (Lijphart, 1999) estudia la interacción entre el legislativo y el ejecutivo sobre la base de la duración del gobierno en sistemas parlamentarios.

3.1. El número de partidos en el parlamento

En política comparada, el sistema de partidos de un país desempeña un papel crucial para entender la política de esa nación. A partir de Duverger (1951), el sistema de partidos de un país ha estado tradicionalmente conectado con otras características importantes del país, ya sea como causa o como efecto. Según Duverger, el sistema de partidos fue tanto el resultado del sistema electoral de un país como la causa de un cierto tipo de interacción entre su gobierno y su parlamento.[8]

En lo tocante a los efectos del sistema de partidos sobre la formación de coaliciones, el argumento de Duverger era directo: los sistemas bipartidistas dan la mayoría a un solo partido y en consecuencia producen gobiernos estables que dominan el parlamento; los sistemas multipartidistas generan gobiernos de coalición que pueden perder votos en el parlamento (incluyendo votos de confianza), y por tanto son débiles e inestables. Deberá quedar claro en lo anterior que cuando Duverger examina el número de partidos en el sistema de partidos, se refiere al número de partidos importantes en el *parlamento* de un país. Por ejemplo, el Reino Unido es el arquetipo del sistema bipartidista porque los liberales, a pesar de sus votos, no ocupan un número importante de escaños en el parlamento. Esta es una característica común de todos los análisis que he examinado: el número de partidos en el sistema de partidos se define esencialmente como el número de partidos en el parlamento.

Sartori (1976) abundó en el modelo de Duverger y, entre otras cosas, volvió a definir la tipología. En particular, en lo tocante a los sistemas multipartidistas, distinguió entre pluralismo moderado y polarizado. La dinámica de la competencia de partidos en el pluralismo moderado es similar al bipartidismo: dos coaliciones compiten por el puesto, una de ellas gana, y ambas coaliciones están cerca del centro ideológico. Como contraste, el

[8] No analizaré los efectos del sistema electoral sobre el sistema de partidos. El lector interesado puede encontrar esta información en Duverger (1954), Rae (1967), Lijphart (1994), Sartori (1996) y Cox (1997).

pluralismo polarizado incluye un partido que ocupa el centro y al cual se contraponen oposiciones bilaterales a su izquierda y a su derecha. Estas oposiciones son extremas ideológicamente y/o incluyen partidos antisistema. Según Sartori, la línea divisoria entre pluralismo moderado y extremo es "aproximadamente" cinco partidos. A partir de esta exposición, queda claro que el punto de corte es una regularidad empírica, no un argumento teórico. Sea como sea, Sartori, siguiendo los fundamentos que estableció Duverger, espera que el número de partidos en el sistema de partidos de un país afecte las políticas de esa nación.

Podemos encontrar un marco teórico común en todos estos análisis. Sobre la base de las teorías de agente principal, Mathew McCubbins y sus colaboradores (McCubbins, 1985; Kiewiet y McCubbins, 1991; Lupia y McCubbins, 2000) han estudiado la lógica de la delegación de acuerdo con la cual un agente actúa en nombre de otro actor (el principal). En la interacción entre gobierno y parlamento, el principal es el parlamento, dado que éste selecciona al gobierno y puede remplazarlo con un voto de censura (Strom, 2000). Como resultado, un gobierno, al igual que cualquier otro comité parlamentario, se enfrenta al dilema de obedecer a la mayoría en el parlamento o ser echado del poder.

Estas teorías son congruentes y cada una se suma a las otras. También son congruentes con otros organismos de trabajo. Por ejemplo, el análisis cultural de Almond y Verba (1963) separa las democracias anglosajonas de las continentales, distinción que es empíricamente casi idéntica a sistemas bipartidistas contra multipartidistas. Powell (1982) encontró una correlación entre sistemas bipartidistas y estabilidad ejecutiva, pero una relación muy tenue entre sistemas de partido y niveles de violencia.

Todos estos argumentos no reconocen el papel del gobierno para promover legislación. Como argumentábamos, los gobiernos configuran los resultados legislativos debido al poder que tienen de establecimiento de agenda. El que puedan hacerlo regular y extensamente no depende del número de partidos en el parlamento, sino de las estipulaciones institucionales del establecimiento de agenda y de la posición del gobierno frente a las otras fuerzas parlamentarias. Por ejemplo, el gobierno griego está formado por un solo partido y tiene un gran dominio de la agenda (cuadro IV.1). De allí se desprende que el gobierno impondrá su voluntad al parlamento de modo regular y extenso. El hecho de que hay muchos partidos en el parlamento no es relevante en este análisis.

3.2. La discreción ministerial

En la exposición anterior, la diferencia entre los jugadores con veto y la sabiduría convencional era la falta de reconocimiento por los tradicionales analistas del poder de establecimiento de la agenda. Éste no es el caso de análisis más contemporáneos en política comparada. Huber (1996) analiza el poder de los gobiernos parlamentarios para formular la pregunta sobre la confianza; Diermeier y Feddersen (1998) explican la cohesión del gobierno sobre la base de sus poderes de establecimiento de agenda. Persson y Tabellini (2000) se valen de los poderes de establecimiento de agenda para explicar las diferencias entre los sistemas presidencial y parlamentario. Hallerberg y von Hagen (1999, 2001) se concentran en el papel de los ministros de finanzas sobre el control del gobierno. Aquí me concentro en un enfoque influyente, según el cual es el ministro correspondiente quien controla la agenda del gobierno (el modelo de Laver y Shepsle [1996] de discreción ministerial). El argumento de Laver y Shepsle no es que los ministros tengan derechos exclusivos de toma de decisiones en su área (aunque sus modelos se pueden interpretar de ese modo), sino que están haciendo propuestas al gobierno en áreas donde nadie más es competente y, en consecuencia, son capaces de configurar las propuestas del gobierno. En sus palabras: "La discreción ministerial es el resultado de la capacidad del ministro para configurar la agenda de las decisiones colectivas del gabinete en vez de determinar las decisiones del gabinete una vez que la agenda haya sido establecida" (Laver y Shepsle, 1996: 33). A su vez, el gobierno hace estas propuestas al parlamento, que son aceptadas con escasas modificaciones. "Tal vez la característica más distintiva de nuestro enfoque sea la suposición de que las decisiones políticas de mayor importancia las toma el ejecutivo" (Laver y Shepsle, 1996: 13).

Los jugadores con veto y la discreción ministerial comparten así el enfoque en el establecimiento de la agenda, pero están en desacuerdo en cuanto a la identidad del establecedor de la agenda. Creo que aun cuando todo gobierno parlamentario en última instancia controla la agenda al vincular la legislación importante con un voto de confianza, no está claro que dentro del gobierno la agenda esté bajo el control del ministro correspondiente. En primer lugar, el primer ministro también desempeña un papel importante en la formación de la agenda. Segundo, la coalición de gobierno ha negociado un programa de gobierno y un ministro no puede presentar legislación que esté en desacuerdo con este programa. Tercero, los comités del gobierno discuten temas políticos sustantivos, y si los ministros de otros partidos tienen desacuerdos políticos con un proyecto de ley, no lo aceptarán tan sólo porque sea la propuesta del ministro correspondiente. Cuarto, y de mayor importancia hasta el momento, la teoría de la discreción ministerial implica que los cambios de ministros (mientras la misma coalición permanece en el poder) provocarían graves cambios políticos en los ministerios correspondientes. Ésta no es la experiencia de los gobiernos multipartidistas más extremosos como la Cuarta República francesa y la Italia de la posguerra. Por ejemplo, André Siegfried, uno de los padres de la ciencia política francesa, plantea el punto opuesto cuando explica la "paradoja de política estable con gabinetes inestables": "En realidad las desventajas no son tan graves como parecen. [...] Cuando hay una crisis del gabinete, ciertos ministros cambian o sencillamente los mismos ministros son intercambiados de puesto; pero ningún servidor público es desplazado, y la administración cotidiana continúa sin interrupción" (Siegfried, 1956: 399).

Los argumentos anteriores discuten sobre si el establecimiento de agenda corresponde exclusivamente al ministro correspondiente. Podemos plantear un argumento con un plan de acción ligeramente distinto: incluso si presuponemos (incorrectamente) que éste sea el caso, establece poca diferencia. De hecho, como se demostró en el capítulo I, un mayor número de jugadores con veto restringe el conjunto ganador del *statu quo* y, como resultado, disminuye la importancia del establecimiento de agenda (corolario 1.5.2). Así, mientras más partidos participen en el gobierno, menos importante será el papel de los ministros, incluso si presuponemos que éstos tienen jurisdicción exclusiva sobre la agenda. Esto es exactamente lo que Huber y Shipan (de próxima publicación) encuentran en su análisis de las restricciones que múltiples principales (gobiernos divididos en sistemas tanto parlamentarios como presidenciales) imponen a los burócratas y al ejecutivo.

Pruebas empíricas corroboran los argumentos anteriores. La mejor prueba empírica de la tesis de la influencia ministerial sería una prueba de políticas a lo largo de los lineamientos que señala la cita de Siegfried: comparar políticas gubernamentales bajo la misma coalición pero con distintos ministros y verificar si las diferencias son más importantes que las similitudes. Sin embargo, tal prueba no se ha realizado. En cambio, Paul Warwick sistemáticamente puso a prueba una de las implicaciones de Laver y de Shepsle acerca de la duración de las coaliciones de gobierno. Lever y Shepsle identifican los argumentos sobre el equilibrio según su propia teoría y esperan que los gobiernos sin equilibrio sean más inestables.[9] En vez de ello, Paul Warwick descubre que son la condición mayoritaria y el alcance ideológico de los gobiernos y no la condición de equilibrio lo que afecta en forma importante la duración del gobierno. Saca la conclusión de que los partidos en el gobierno tratan de acomodarse unos con otros para formar la política y no permitir que los ministros tomen decisiones independientes acerca de sus portafolios.[10]

De modo similar, Michael Thies (2001) analiza la pauta de nombramientos de ministros nuevos en Italia, Alemania y Japón (con gobiernos de un solo partido y en coaliciones) y averigua que en Italia y Japón los ministros nuevos en su inmensa mayoría son nombrados de diferentes partidos (y en los gobiernos de un solo partido de Japón, de diferentes facciones) de los ministerios correspondientes. La única excepción a la pauta identificada es Alemania, pero en este caso Thies señala la importancia del canciller y una serie de otras medidas que instituyen la toma de decisiones colectiva (y la responsabilidad) del gobierno. Llega a la conclusión de que el modelo de jurisdicción exclusiva no funciona para la creación de política.

Finalmente, Lieven de Winter (2001) explora la forma en que los gobiernos presentan las piezas de legislación incluidas en su programa (usualmente negociadas *antes* de la distribución de ministerios). Tras someter a prueba 500 ejemplos de legislación en 18 países europeos, ha descubierto que los gobiernos "invierten más recursos en garantizar un proceso legislativo rápido y sin tropiezos, cuidando el proyecto de ley desde la cuna [introducción a la legislatura] hasta la madurez [promulgación]" (2001: 3). Más exactamente, Lieven de Winter ha descubierto que los proyectos de ley que cubren el programa del gobierno tienen una serie de características: son más complejos, menos sujetos a una lectura plenaria antes de la fase de comités, con gran frecuencia tratados por los comités que son presididos por un

---

[9] "Si todo lo demás permanece constante, por lo tanto (y en la vida real puede que no suceda así), un sistema de partidos que no tenga un partido fuerte y ningún gabinete de MDD (mediana dimensión por dimensión) de conjunto ganador vacío parece propenso a ser más inestable que uno que sí los tenga" (Laver y Shepsle, 1996: 78).

[10] En palabras de Warwick, sus resultados "claramente ponen en duda la suposición fundamental de la autonomía ministerial. Se expresó considerable escepticismo cuando Laver y Shepsle presentaron el tema frente a un grupo de expertos en países [...] y el escepticismo es respaldado aquí. [...] Los pactos de coalición no pueden afectar solamente la división de carteras, ni ejercer el poder consiste en dejar que cada partido haga lo que le guste en las carteras que reciba" (Warwick, 1999: 391). Laver y Shepsle (1999) ponen en duda las conclusiones de Warwick. El lector interesado debe leer las cuatro partes de la discusión entre estos autores.

parlamentario de la mayoría, tienen parlamentarios mayoritarios como simpatizantes, más a menudo son sometidos a un voto de comités, tienen un índice de aprobación más bajo en comités y en la plenaria y enfrentan diferentes formas de desavenencia de comités u obstrucción plenaria, tienen mayor disciplina de votación entre la mayoría y también entre la oposición, con mayor frecuencia son impugnados frente a tribunales constitucionales y tienen una mayor tasa de éxito general. De Winter informa que estos resultados son congruentes con la responsabilidad gubernamental colectiva e incongruentes con la tesis de la influencia ministerial.

3.3. ¿La duración del gobierno o el establecimiento de agenda definen el predominio ejecutivo?

De acuerdo con el argumento propuesto en este libro, las razones por las cuales los gobiernos que controlan la agenda (ya sean coaliciones de ganancia mínima, gobiernos minoritarios o mayorías de tamaño exagerado) son posicionales (los gobiernos en sistemas multipartidistas tienen una mayoría que los respalda o están ubicados en el centro del espacio de político) o institucionales (una serie de dispositivos mediante los cuales los gobiernos controlan la agenda que fue presentada en la sección anterior y resumida por el indicador "control de agenda"). Hay un enfoque alternativo que resumiré y discutiré en mayor detalle por dos razones: primero, debido a su posición destacada en la bibliografía, y segundo, porque trasciende las divisiones por tipo de régimen, que son tan frecuentes en esa bibliografía. Este análisis nos permite comparar diferentes tipos de regímenes.

En *Patterns of Democracy*, Arend Lijphart (1999: 129) propone un indicador del predominio ejecutivo: "¿Cómo puede medirse el poder relativo de las ramas ejecutiva y legislativa del gobierno? *En sistemas parlamentarios, el mejor indicador es la durabilidad del gabinete*" (cursivas agregadas). Lijphart distingue su enfoque de lo que denomina el punto de vista "prevaleciente", según el cual "la durabilidad del gabinete es un indicador no sólo de la fortaleza del gabinete comparada con la de la legislatura sino también de la estabilidad del régimen" (1999: 129). Lijphart cita la teoría de Warwick como ejemplo de su punto de vista[11] y contrasta este enfoque con los

---

[11] "Un sistema parlamentario que no produzca gobiernos duraderos probablemente no llevará a la creación de una política efectiva para atraer una gran lealtad popular, o tal vez incluso no sobrevivirá a largo plazo" (Warwick, 1994: 139).

análisis de Siegfried (1956) y de Dogan (1989), según los cuales el cambio en el personal ministerial no afecta la política.

Según Lijphart, toda la bibliografía que él cita conviene en que la durabilidad del gabinete es un indicador del predominio del ejecutivo. El desacuerdo estriba en si la estabilidad del gobierno ejerce un efecto sobre el régimen, y Lijphart, Siegfried y Dogan argumentan que no tiene ningún efecto, mientras que Warwick y la mayor parte de la bibliografía sobre coaliciones argumentan lo contrario.

Mi argumento es que la duración del gobierno y el predominio del ejecutivo no tienen la conexión manifiesta que Lijphart da a entender. Si hay tal conexión, el argumento lógico que conduce a ella se debe plantear explícitamente. De hecho, yo iría más allá: que la duración del gobierno es lógicamente independiente del poder del gobierno. La duración del gobierno está en función de cuándo renuncia el gobierno en el poder o cuándo es derrotado por una votación en su contra en el parlamento. La renuncia del gobierno es indicación de un desacuerdo político entre gobierno y parlamento, y cuando quiera que ocurra tal desacuerdo, el gobierno tendrá que renunciar, ya sea fuerte o no, o los partidos que participan en un gobierno por sus propias razones crearán desacuerdos con el fin de llevar a la formación de un nuevo gobierno. Ninguno de estos cálculos tiene una correlación sistemática con el poder del gobierno actual. Pero Lijphart usa el predominio ejecutivo extensamente en la parte teórica de su libro: es uno de sus indicadores de consociacionalismo, y está conectado con otras características de las democracias como son el sistema de partidos, el sistema electoral o la concentración o participación del poder. Además (y lo que tal vez no sea bien conocido), el predominio del ejecutivo entra en *todas* las evaluaciones empíricas del análisis que hace Lijphart de los regímenes democráticos, debido a que emplea técnicas analíticas factoriales, de modo que la variable "predominio ejecutivo" es uno de los indicadores que generan los componentes principales de su análisis, y todas las puntuaciones de los países en cada tema se derivan de esta variable. Dada la falta de justificación teórica, ¿podemos mejorar la medición que hace Lijphart del "predominio ejecutivo"? Con el fin de responder esta pregunta tenemos que seguir de cerca los pasos del argumento de Lijphart.

Lijphart interpreta de la siguiente manera el predominio ejecutivo sobre la base de la duración del gobierno. Primero evalúa la vida promedio del gabinete en los gobiernos donde la única característica que cuenta es la composición del partido (los gobiernos con composiciones de partido idénticas se cuentan como uno, incluso si el primer ministro renuncia o si hay una elección). Utiliza entonces la vida promedio del gabinete empleando varios acontecimientos adicionales que marcan el término de un gobierno: elecciones, cambio de primer ministro, cambio de la ganancia mínima, coaliciones de tamaño exagerado o condición minoritaria de un gabinete. El promedio de estas dos mediciones se presenta en el cuadro 7.1 de Lijphart (1999), pero hay algunos pasos adicionales necesarios para la creación del "índice de predominio del ejecutivo". Véase a continuación la descripción del resto del proceso:

> Se requieren dos ajustes importantes para traducir los promedios en la tercera columna del cuadro 7.1 a un índice satisfactorio del predominio ejecutivo. Primero, algunos de los promedios presuponen valores extremos. Botswana, que tiene gabinetes de un solo partido compuestos del Partido Democrático de Botswana de 1965 a 1996, es el ejemplo más notable. Su ciclo de elecciones cada cuatro años reduce la duración promedio de la tercera columna a 17.63 años, pero de todas formas es el triple que el promedio de 5.52 años en Gran Bretaña, y no hay buenas razones para creer que el gabinete de Botswana sea tres veces más predominante que el gabinete británico. Según esto, cualesquiera valores superiores a 5.52 años en la tercera columna son truncados en este nivel en la cuarta columna. Se necesita un ajuste mucho mayor para los sistemas presidenciales y para el sistema suizo de división de poderes. En cuatro de los seis casos, la duración del gabinete da una impresión completamente errónea del grado de predominio ejecutivo. [...] Suiza es un ejemplo excelente de equilibrio entre ejecutivo y legislativo. Por ende, le asigno impresionistamente un valor de 1.00 año. Lo mismo es apropiado para los Estados Unidos y Costa Rica. En el otro extremo, a Francia se le debe asignar el valor más elevado de predominio ejecutivo, lo mismo que a Gran Bretaña [Lijphart, 1999: 133-134].

A 11 de los 36 países que aparecen en el estudio de Lijphart se les asignan valores impresionistas del índice de predominio ejecutivo, debido a que la duración de sus gobiernos, expresada como promedio de las dos mediciones no tenía nada que ver con un equilibrio de poder entre el legislativo y el ejecutivo.

Sostengo que el predominio ejecutivo es cuestión de control de la agenda, que refleja la capacidad del gobierno para hacer que sus propuestas sean aceptadas tal como son, en vez de que el parlamento las enmiende considerablemente. Si esto es así, el índice de control de la agenda que calculamos en la sección anterior debería tener una correlación alta con la variable del "predominio ejecutivo" de Lijphart. Y así es en verdad: la correlación entre el índice de "predominio ejecutivo" de Lijphart (que aparece en el cuadro IV.1) y el indicador de "control de la agenda" que desarrollé en la sección anterior tiene significación estadística (r = 0.496 significativo al nivel 0.05). Es interesante notar que esta correlación es mucho más alta que la correlación entre "predominio ejecutivo" y "duración" en el propio conjunto de datos de Lijphart. De hecho, para el ejemplo restringido de 18 países derivados del conjunto de datos de Doering, aunque las dos columnas de Lijphart tienen números idénticos para todos los países, con excepción de Suiza (la duración es 8.59 y el predominio ejecutivo es 1) y Francia (la duración es 2.48 y el predominio ejecutivo es 5.52), la correlación de "predominio ejecutivo" y "duración" es 0.29 (que no tiene significación estadística dado que la prueba F proporciona el número 0.24). Por supuesto, los 18 países que cubre el cuadro IV.1 son la mitad más fácil de los países de Lijphart. Todos son de Europa Occidental; todos (con excepción de Suiza) son democracias parlamentarias.[12]

La clasificación de Lijphart tiene la ventaja principal de que cubre regímenes tanto presidenciales como parlamentarios. Este es un punto que no se debe perder de vista en la discusión. Es verdad que la variable de la duración no se puede usar para generar indicadores del predominio ejecutivo en sistemas presidenciales, y Lijphart usa valores "impresionistas". Sin embargo, si consideramos las capacidades legislativas de los presidentes en sistemas presidenciales, obtendremos resultados muy similares a la clasificación que hace Lijphart de los regímenes presidenciales. Shugart y Carey (1992: 155) proporcionan esta información, y sobre la base de su clasificación el presidente de Costa Rica recibe 1 (puntuación de Lijphart 1), el presidente de los Estados Unidos recibe 2 (puntuación de Lijphart 1), Venezuela obtiene 0 (puntuación de Lijphart 2) y Colombia 5 u 8, dependiendo del periodo (puntuación de Lijphart 3). Estos dos conjuntos de números generan un coeficiente de correlación de 0.64, lo cual significa que las capacida-

[12] Puede haber un problema de clasificación dado que la Quinta República francesa así como Finlandia, Portugal, Islandia, Irlanda y Austria son clasificados usualmente como regímenes semipresidenciales. Esto no es un problema para la teoría de los jugadores con veto, porque en todos estos países el número de jugadores con veto se calcula sobre la base de los poderes legislativos, de modo que la Quinta República francesa es exactamente como un país parlamentario. Lijphart emplea el argumento del semipresidencialismo para dar a Francia una puntuación distinta del promedio de duración del gobierno, pero no altera las puntuaciones de duración del gobierno de los otros países semipresidenciales.

des legislativas de los presidentes en países latinoamericanos se correlacionan muy bien con la variable del predominio ejecutivo de Lijphart.

En el capítulo anterior separé los sistemas presidenciales y los parlamentarios sobre la base del control de la agenda legislativa, y afirmé que básicamente, a pesar de su nombre, los sistemas parlamentarios dan la mayor parte del poder legislativo al gobierno, y la mayoría de los sistemas presidenciales da el control de la agenda al parlamento. En este capítulo empezamos investigando esta declaración sumaria y descubrimos diferencias importantes en sistemas parlamentarios. ¿Tienen los sistemas presidenciales varianza elevada también en el establecimiento de la agenda? Lamentablemente no existe un estudio de gran alcance como el que Doering hizo sobre el establecimiento de la agenda en sistemas presidenciales, así que tenemos que dar únicamente una respuesta preliminar.

Basándonos en Shugart y Carey (1992: 155) podemos corroborar que el establecimiento de la agenda en sistemas presidenciales reside principalmente en el Congreso. Estos investigadores se preguntan si los presidentes tienen el derecho de "exclusivamente proponer" legislación. Sus respuestas son negativas para todos los países con presidentes elegidos popularmente, con la excepción de Brasil, Chile (puntuación de 1, proporciona a la asamblea poderes de enmienda ilimitados) y Uruguay (puntuación de 2, da a la asamblea poderes de enmienda restringidos). Sin embargo, estudios más detallados arrojan dudas sobre un cuadro tan uniforme. Por ejemplo, Londregan (2000: 88) argumenta que el presidente chileno tiene importantes poderes de establecimiento de agenda:

> Los artículos 65, 67 y 68 de la constitución permiten al presidente aprobar legislación a pesar de que tope con la oposición de una mayoría en una cámara, siempre y cuando se encuentre con el apoyo de una supermayoría en la otra, mientras que el artículo 70 de la constitución y los artículos 32 a 36 de la ley orgánica del Congreso contienen poderosas estipulaciones de veto que le permiten al presidente tener la última palabra en el debate legislativo al proponer enmiendas junto con su veto, enmiendas que se deben votar en favor o en contra sin mayores cambios de parte del Congreso. Como si estos poderes presidenciales fueran insuficientes, los artículos 62 y 64 de la constitución le permiten al presidente proponer y enmendar legislación, mientras que los mismos artículos más el 24 de la ley orgánica del Congreso limitan la capacidad de los miembros del Congreso para hacer tal cosa.

De modo similar, Cheibub y Limongi (2001) argumentan que varios presidentes de países latinoamericanos tienen el derecho exclusivo de iniciar legislación relacionada con el presupuesto. Además, plantean el argumento de que el presidente de Brasil realmente controla la agenda, y la mayor parte de su legislación es aprobada por el Congreso. Ésta es una posición de la que discrepa Ames (2001). Ames ofrece pruebas de que partes importantes de las agendas presidenciales han sido retiradas, no ratificadas o rechazadas.[13] Sin embargo, ni Cheibub y Limongu (2001) ni Ames (2001) proporcionan detalles institucionales, y una parte importante de su argumento se basa en las divisiones dentro del Congreso mismo. Estos ejemplos específicos indican la necesidad de un estudio detallado de los poderes de establecimiento de agenda en sistemas presidenciales.

Hay dos puntos más generales que se pueden inferir de estos estudios más detallados sobre países. El primero es la importancia de los decretos ejecutivos para los poderes de establecimiento de agenda de los presidentes (Carey y Shugart, 1998). Por ejemplo, en Brasil el presidente puede usar decretos para proponer legislación por 30 días. Tales decretos se convierten en leyes sólo cuando son aprobados por la legislatura, pero el presidente puede volver a emitir indefinidamente esos decretos. Éste es un poder que invierte la situación de múltiples jugadores con veto que caracteriza a los sistemas presidenciales, y lo usa en favor del presidente. Si el presidente emite un decreto ejecutivo, entonces es difícil que el Congreso altere su decisión, en particular si él mantiene poderes de veto legislativo (Eaton, 2000: 362).

Es posible que al presidente se le deleguen poderes de decreto para temas específicos. En Rusia los legisladores votaron para delegar importantes poderes de decreto al presidente Yeltsin en 1991 relacionados con "la banca, el mercado de valores [...] inversiones, actividad aduanera, el presupuesto, formación de precios, tributación, propiedad, reforma de la tierra y empleo" (Parrish, 1998: 72). Es difícil imaginar algún tema excluido de esta lista.

Incluso en los Estados Unidos el presidente tiene a su alcance tales estrategias. Por ejemplo, Bill Clinton dio entrada a su discutida política de "no preguntes, no digas" sobre homosexuales en las fuerzas armadas por decreto ejecutivo, amenazando al mismo tiempo con vetar toda legislación que invalidara su decisión. De modo similar, George W. Bush alteró muchas políticas de Clinton mediante decretos ejecutivos. Cualquier estudio de esta-

[13] Véase Ames (2001), capítulo VII, y en particular los cuadros 15 y 16, que ofrecen páginas de agendas legislativas fallidas de presidentes brasileños.

blecimiento de agenda deberá, por tanto, investigar el alcance y la frecuencia de los decretos ejecutivos.[14]

Otro poder presidencial "oculto" de establecimiento de agenda es la ventaja que tienen los presidentes frente a miembros del Congreso, de posiciones de asesoría para investigar, bosquejar y respaldar sus propuestas. Londregan (2001) argumenta que el respaldo administrativo acrecienta la "valencia" de las posiciones presidenciales y hace que a los miembros del Congreso les resulte difícil rechazarlas. Esta ventaja burocrática puede reducir de hecho los poderes *de facto* de establecimiento de agenda del Congreso. Por otro lado, es posible que los congresistas puedan fácilmente alterar o incluso revertir esta ventaja si se dan cuenta de lo mucho que importa.

4. Conclusiones

El poder legislativo está correlacionado con capacidades de establecimiento de agenda. Estas capacidades se atribuyen en general a los gobiernos en sistemas parlamentarios y a los parlamentos en los presidenciales, como se vio en el capítulo III. Sin embargo, cuando consideramos las cosas más detalladamente, vemos que varía el poder de establecimiento de agenda en sistemas parlamentarios.

En coaliciones de ganancia mínima, cada uno de los partidos en el gobierno es un jugador con veto, y el resultado de los votos en el parlamento (si los partidos pueden controlar a sus parlamentarios) es idéntico a las propuestas del gobierno. En los gobiernos minoritarios y en los de tamaño exagerado, los partidos del gobierno son política pero no aritméticamente jugadores con veto. Los gobiernos minoritarios requieren el respaldo de otros partidos, y los gobiernos de tamaño exagerado pueden pasar por alto las posiciones de los partidos que no sean necesarios para una mayoría parlamentaria. En consecuencia, en gobiernos minoritarios y de tamaño exagerado las expectativas que se han presentado en la primera parte de este libro se mantendrán, pero con márgenes de error mayores que en las coaliciones de ganancia mínima.

Una consideración más detallada de los establecedores de agenda nos revela que el grado de establecimiento de agenda institucional varía. Por ejemplo, en el Reino Unido el gobierno disfruta de privilegios de estableci-

---

[14] Véase Cheibub y Limongi (2001) acerca del uso de estos poderes en Brasil.

miento de agenda considerablemente más altos que el gobierno de Holanda (véase sección 1). Empleé toda la información disponible y construí un índice de poder de establecimiento de agenda que incluye 18 países de Europa Occidental. Este índice se basa en procedimientos reales de actividad legislativa, en contraposición a los enfoques de la duración del gobierno y a los impresionistas.

Desafortunadamente, no existen análisis similares de los sistemas presidenciales. En el capítulo anterior separé diferentes regímenes sobre la base del establecimiento de agenda. Allí me concentré en la varianza en cada categoría, y vimos que si queremos comprender la relación que hay entre la legislatura y el ejecutivo, tenemos que concentrarnos en preguntas específicas de control de la agenda. Si esto se convierte en el foco de investigaciones futuras, seremos capaces de identificar similitudes en la toma de decisiones en países como Italia, Holanda y los Estados Unidos, así como similitudes entre Chile y el Reino Unido o Francia, a pesar de su clasificación oficial en diferentes categorías. De modo parecido, los gobiernos minoritarios en sistemas parlamentarios pueden parecer muy similares a sistemas presidenciales particulares, en que el presidente tiene poderes institucionales fuertes y un respaldo débil dentro del Congreso. Incluso, en gobiernos minoritarios y en regímenes presidenciales el partido en el gobierno y el partido del presidente tienen el privilegio de que serán incluidos en cualquier coalición posible (de hecho, de que ellos seleccionarán la composición de la coalición).

El estudio de los poderes de establecimiento de agenda en regímenes tanto presidenciales como parlamentarios aumentará significativamente nuestra capacidad para entender las instituciones políticas y comparar a los dos. La idea de Lijphart de que diferentes sistemas políticos (presidencial así como parlamentario) deben ser clasificados de acuerdo con el "predominio ejecutivo" es un gran avance en relación con las distinciones tradicionales de tipos de régimen. Sin embargo, no es la duración sino los poderes de establecimiento de agenda lo que determinará cuáles preferencias prevalecerán. La duración del gobierno no es un buen sustituto para los poderes de establecimiento de agenda, no sólo porque no es aplicable a sistemas presidenciales, sino además porque tampoco tiene relación causal con el predominio del ejecutivo en sistemas parlamentarios.

V. REFERÉNDUMS

La mera posibilidad de un referéndum introduce las preferencias de la población en el proceso de creación de política. Argumento que esto es equivalente a la introducción de un nuevo jugador con veto, y los resultados que prevalecen (ya sea que el referéndum se lleve a cabo o no) se aproximan mejor a las preferencias del público. Por añadidura, la estabilidad política en principio incrementa con la introducción de un nuevo jugador con veto.

Sin embargo, lo más interesante de los referéndums es el control de la agenda. Revisaremos temas desarrollados en la introducción de esta parte, es decir, el proceso de establecimiento de agenda es competitivo o exclusivo. El establecimiento de agenda del proceso del referéndum se divide en dos partes: primera, quién hace la pregunta, y segunda, quién activa el referéndum. Si ambas partes de la agenda están controladas por el mismo jugador (ya sea un jugador con veto existente u otro actor en iniciativas populares), el proceso del referéndum elimina a todos los demás jugadores con veto. Así, el efecto global de los referéndums sobre la estabilidad política depende de temas de control de agenda.

Finalmente, el grado en que diferentes tipos de referéndums se aproximen a las preferencias del público también depende de las medidas específicas de control de agenda: si un jugador con veto existente controla ambas partes de la agenda (tanto formulando la pregunta como activando el referéndum), simplemente usará referéndums para eliminar la entrada de otros jugadores con veto; si el control de agenda es delegado a través de un proceso competitivo, entonces se aproximará más a las preferencias del público.

El capítulo está organizado en seis secciones. La sección 1 trata de la interrogante acerca de qué diferencia surge si hay una posibilidad de referéndums. En otras palabras, ¿qué pasa si el pueblo puede participar directamente en el proceso legislativo? La sección 2 trata de las diferencias institucionales entre procesos de referéndum. Algunos de ellos están bajo el control de los jugadores con veto existentes, otros más son delegados a la iniciativa popular, y otros más dividen el proceso de establecimiento de agenda en dos partes (activar y formular la pregunta) y delegan cada una de ellas a un actor diferente. Las secciones finales estudian cada uno de estos procesos con cierto detenimiento.

1. Democracia directa y representativa

¿Qué diferencia hay si los resultados son seleccionados directamente por el pueblo o indirectamente por sus representantes en el parlamento? Para los partidarios de referéndums, las decisiones, por definición, son mejores si el pueblo las toma. El argumento más famoso en ese sentido viene de Rousseau (1947: 85):

> La soberanía no puede ser representada por la misma razón de que no puede ser alienada; su esencia es la voluntad general, y esa voluntad debe hablar por sí sola, o no existirá; o es ella misma o no es ella misma; no hay una posibilidad intermedia. Los delegados del pueblo, por lo tanto, no son y no pueden ser sus representantes; sólo pueden ser sus comisionados, y como tales no están calificados para concluir nada definitivamente. Ninguno de sus actos puede ser ley, a no ser que haya sido ratificada por el pueblo en persona; y sin esa ratificación nada es una ley.

Volveremos a considerar esta cita al final de este capítulo. Por el momento vamos a ser menos normativos y más abstractos, y afirmaremos que los resultados seleccionados por el parlamento serán preferidos al *statu quo* por una mayoría en el parlamento, mientras que los resultados seleccionados por un referéndum serán preferidos por una mayoría de la población. El resultado del referéndum en una sola dimensión sería la preferencia del votante medio, pero en múltiples dimensiones tal votante medio raras veces existe. Como se verá, el número de dimensiones de política implicadas en un referéndum es una pregunta abierta. A veces múltiples temas son agrupados; en otras ocasiones se hacen esfuerzos por separar temas y decidir sobre ellos uno por uno. Por ejemplo, los referéndums se usan a veces para aprobar (o desaprobar) constituciones enteras; por otro lado, el Tribunal Constitucional italiano ha decidido que excluirá las propuestas populares que contengan "tal pluralidad de demandas heterogéneas que haya una falta de matriz racional y unitaria que las coloque bajo la lógica del artículo 75 de la Constitución" (Butler y Ranney, 1994: 63-64).

En esta sección se sostendrá primero que el número de dimensiones implícitas establece muy poca diferencia en el argumento: los resultados selectos del referéndum pueden abordarse extremadamente bien con el argumento del votante medio.[1] El segundo tema que abordaremos es que las preferencias de este votante medio pueden ser significativamente distintas de la política que hayan seleccionado los jugadores con veto existentes.

1.1. Preferencias del "votante medio" en referéndums

En el capítulo II demostramos que el conjunto ganador del *statu quo* cuando toda la gente vota se incluye en un círculo (Y, d + 2r), donde Y es el centro de la yema de la población entera de votantes, d es la distancia entre Y y SQ, y r es el radio de la yema de toda la población. Un argumento que no presenté en el capítulo II, pero que se puede encontrar en Ferejohn *et al.* (1984), es que el conjunto ganador del *statu quo* contiene un segundo círculo (Y, d − 2r). Como resultado, los límites del conjunto ganador del *statu quo* están ubicados entre dos círculos, ambos con centro Y: uno de ellos con radio (d + 2r) y el otro con radio (d − 2r).[2]

Hemos dicho también que cuando el número de votantes aumenta, el radio de la yema (r) disminuye en promedio (capítulo II). En consecuencia, para los millones de personas que son potenciales participantes en un referéndum en la mayoría de los países o estados, r es (la mayor parte del tiempo) excepcionalmente pequeño. Como resultado, el conjunto ganador del *statu quo* está contenido entre dos círculos que difieren poco uno del otro: 4r, cuando r se hace más y más pequeño.

Lo que los dos párrafos anteriores indican es que, para una población numerosa, el votante medio tal vez no exista sino que todas las líneas medianas pasan a través de un área muy pequeña (del radio r), de modo que

---

[1] En este capítulo no analizo los referéndums que requieren mayorías calificadas. Hay pocos casos en los cuales la ley requiera un cierto porcentaje de electores o votantes (por ejemplo, en Dinamarca hasta 1953, 45% de electores; en la República de Weimar, 50% de los electores; en Nueva Zelanda de 1908 a 1914, 60% de los votantes) o una congruencia entre una mayoría de votantes y una mayoría de estados (por ejemplo, Suiza, Australia). En 1911 en Nueva Zelanda, 54% que favorecía la prohibición no tuvo efecto, ya que el requerimiento era de 60% de los votos (Butler y Ranney, 1978: 17). Todos los argumentos del texto se sostienen para las mayorías calificadas también, como se demostró en el capítulo II.

[2] Obviamente, el círculo pequeño existe únicamente si d > 2r, es decir, si el *statu quo* tiene una distancia mayor que el diámetro de la yema desde el centro de ésta.

una mediana "como si" se puede aproximar muy bien por el centro Y de la yema de la población. Además, el conjunto ganador del *statu quo* para una población tan grande se aborda también muy bien mediante un círculo de radio d. En otras palabras, la multiplicidad de votantes simplifica en vez de complicar el problema de identificación del votante medio y el conjunto ganador del *statu quo*. Obsérvese que a lo largo de este análisis el número de dimensiones políticas implícitas pierde importancia. Mientras que en una sola dimensión hay un votante medio, en múltiples dimensiones un votante medio "como si" (el centro de la yema de la población) es una aproximación muy buena.

La gráfica v.1 ofrece una representación visual del argumento. La yema de la población es muy pequeña y tiene el centro Y. El conjunto ganador de

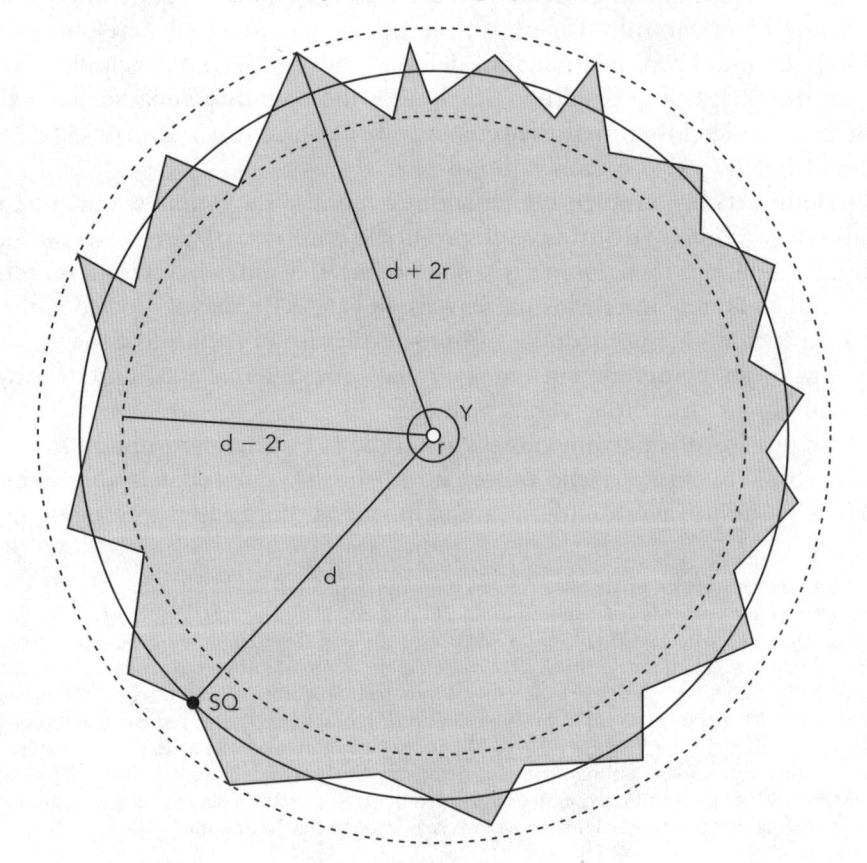

GRÁFICA V.1. *Conjunto ganador de un grupo numeroso de votantes.*

un punto que tiene la distancia d de Y es el área sombreada en la figura, y está ubicado entre los dos círculos con radios (d + 2r) y (d − 2r), así que puede ser aproximado por el círculo (Y, d).

1.2. Democracia directa y mediada

Dinamarca nos da un par de interesantes ejemplos de las diferencias entre democracia directa y mediada. En palabras de Vernon Bogdanor (1994: 72): "Puede parecer una paradoja que el Acta Única Europea, que no hubiese obtenido una mayoría en el Folketing, recibiera una mayoría en el país, mientras que Maastricht, que disfrutaba del respaldo de partidos con 80% de los escaños en el Folketing, fuera rechazado por los votantes en 1992". La gráfica v.2 nos ayuda a reflexionar sobre la paradoja potencial. ¿En dónde estaría ubicada una decisión parlamentaria? Si no sabemos nada sobre la toma de decisiones en el parlamento, excepto que ésta requiere una mayoría simple, entonces según lo que hemos dicho en este libro sería un jugador con veto colectivo, y el conjunto ganador del *statu quo* estaría ubicado dentro del círculo (Y, d + 2r), donde Y y r son el centro y el radio de la yema del parlamento, y d es la distancia entre el *statu quo* y Y. Si necesitamos mayor exactitud, consideraremos la intersección de cualquiera de los tres círculos que representan los diferentes partidos que conducirían al área sombreada en la figura. Si conocemos alguna información adicional acerca de la toma de decisiones parlamentaria, podemos incorporarla en los cálculos e identificar el conjunto ganador del *statu quo* con mayor exactitud. Por ejemplo, si sabemos que hay un partido parlamentario que ciertamente no está incluido en la toma de decisiones parlamentaria, podemos estudiar el parlamento como un jugador con veto colectivo que decide por mayoría calificada. O, alternativamente, si conocemos los partidos que forman el gobierno, identificaremos al conjunto ganador del *statu quo* considerando a cada uno de ellos como un jugador con veto y encontrando la intersección de sus conjuntos ganadores. Si los partidos que forman el gobierno son A, B y C, el resultado estará en la lente de sombreado más oscuro en la gráfica.

No hay razón para creer que los dos procesos (democracia directa y representativa) conducirán al mismo resultado. Bowler y Donovan (1998) han dejado esto perfectamente claro. Además, Lupia (1992, 1993) ha estudiado los atajos de información que puedan informar a los votantes acerca de sus

GRÁFICA V.2. *Diferencia entre democracia directa y mediada.*

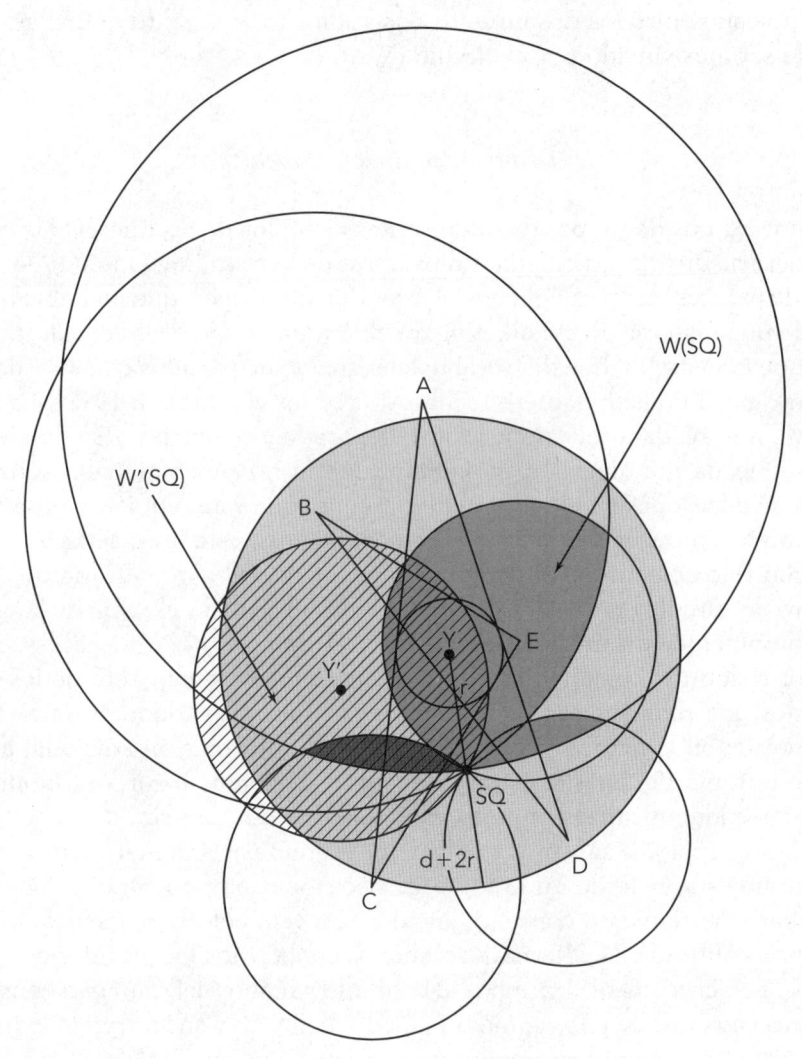

intereses en referéndums. Si denominamos Y' al centro de la yema de la población, no hay garantía de que Y' y Y serán idénticos. Depende del sistema electoral si cada minoría está representada en el parlamento. Ni siquiera los sistemas de representación proporcional más puros, como los de Israel u Holanda, pueden garantizar, por ejemplo, la representación para las minorías de 0.5%. Los sistemas con umbrales más altos, como el de 4% de Suecia o 5% de Alemania, excluyen muchas más. Por último, los sistemas de pluralidad electoral pueden representar apenas a terceros partidos o incluso eliminarlos por completo.

Permítaseme usar un ejemplo conocido como la paradoja del referéndum (Nurmi, 1998: 336-337) para mostrar un mecanismo que genera tal discrepancia. Supongamos que hay 99 votantes y nueve parlamentarios (cada parlamentario representa 11 votos). Por añadidura, hay dos partidos: el partido A con dos tercios de los votos obtiene seis parlamentarios, y el partido B con un tercio de los votos obtiene tres parlamentarios. Esta sociedad tiene que votar sobre el asunto de si X debe sustituir al *statu quo*. Supongamos que los simpatizantes del partido A están divididos seis a cinco, en favor del *statu quo*, y que este patrón aparece en cada distrito electoral, mientras que los seguidores del partido B se muestran unánimemente en favor del cambio. El parlamento del país decidiría, seis votos a tres, conservar el *statu quo*, mientras un referéndum habría producido cambios con 63 votos a favor y 36 en contra. ¡El ejemplo indica que una política que es respaldada por casi dos tercios de los votantes, es rechazada por dos tercios de sus representantes en un país con un sistema electoral de representación proporcional!

En la gráfica he seleccionado un punto diferente como la mediana de la población. Podemos ver que las posibles soluciones según los dos procedimientos tienen varios puntos en común, pero debido a la diferencia entre Y y Y' estas soluciones no coinciden. Esto es solamente parte del problema ya que no hay garantía de que la coalición que prevalece dentro de los votantes sería políticamente la misma que la coalición que prevalece dentro del Parlamento. Por ejemplo, si hay un gobierno de los partidos A, B y C, el resultado tendría que estar ubicado dentro del área de mayor sombreado, mientras que el resultado de un referéndum podría quedar en cualquier parte dentro del área plumeada en la gráfica.

Por tanto, los resultados de la democracia directa y de la representativa pueden ser diferentes en verdad. Pero, ¿podemos localizar estos resultados? ¿O podemos tener un algoritmo que nos ayude a entender en cuáles áreas estarán los resultados? Lo que sabemos del capítulo I es que cuantos más jugadores con veto haya, más pequeño será el conjunto ganador del *statu quo*, y más se respetará la posición de la mediana correspondiente. Pero esta declaración compara resultados dentro de procedimientos, no por medio de democracia directa y representativa. Por ejemplo, si un solo partido tuviera una mayoría parlamentaria en nuestra gráfica v.2, el resultado estaría ubicado en su propio punto ideal. Si los partidos A, B y C son jugadores con veto y comparten el control de la agenda parlamentaria, el conjunto ganador del *statu quo* se contrae y el área de mayor sombreado queda más cerca de la mediana del parlamento.[3]

Hay muchísimos debates en la bibliografía acerca de las ventajas y desventajas presuntas y potenciales de los dos procedimientos. Según los defensores de la democracia directa, hay dos ventajas principales: la primera se relaciona con los resultados que encajen mejor con las preferencias del pueblo (véase Rousseau, *supra*). La segunda corresponde a la educación de ciudadanos en valores democráticos. Tocqueville ha expresado mejor la idea: "Los concejos municipales son para la libertad lo que la escuela primaria es para la ciencia: la ponen al alcance del pueblo, enseñan a los hombres cómo emplearla y cómo gozar de ella". Para sus críticos, desde Platón hasta Stuart Mill, de Schumpeter a Sartori, la pregunta principal es saber si el ciudadano promedio tiene información y capacidad para juzgar lo que sea mejor para los intereses colectivos. Riker (1982) ha agregado un tema adicional: quién controla la agenda es de mayor importancia cuando se formulan preguntas. Finalmente, la legislación por referéndums ha planteado objeciones sobre la base de que las minorías pueden perder sus derechos. Gamble (1997) hace tal afirmación empíricamente, mientras Bowler y Donovan (1998) y Frey y Goette (1998) discrepan acerca de la magnitud de los resultados de Gamble.

Mi meta en esta sección (o en el libro entero, al respecto) no consiste en hacer una declaración acerca de cuál procedimiento es mejor, sino en afirmar que hay diferencias en sus resultados y en estudiar los efectos de tales diferencias sobre la toma de decisiones en sistemas políticos. Si una decisión parlamentaria tiene que ser ratificada por la población (como suele ocurrir en asuntos constitucionales), entonces el resultado tiene que estar ubicado en la intersección de los conjuntos ganadores parlamentario y popular. En otras palabras, los referéndums crean un jugador adicional con veto en el proceso de toma de decisiones: el pueblo. Hay dos resultados de

---

[3] Este argumento es idéntico al resultado formal de Kalandrakis (2000) de que, en equilibrio, los gobiernos de coalición serán menos extremosos que los gobiernos con sistemas bipartidistas. Es también congruente con los resultados empíricos que presentan Huber y Powell (1994) de que los gobiernos multipartidistas son más representativos del votante medio que los gobiernos mayoritarios de un solo partido. Sin embargo, ambos estudios no establecen diferencia entre la mediana del parlamento y la mediana de los votantes.

esta introducción de un nuevo jugador con veto. Primero, en principio, se hace más difícil cambiar el *statu quo*, como se vio en los capítulos I y II. La cortapisa "en principio" se debe a que, como veremos más adelante, a veces los jugadores con veto existentes son eliminados por el proceso de referéndum. Segundo, los resultados finales se aproximarán mejor a las preferencias del votante medio cuando exista la posibilidad de un referéndum (si la decisión auténtica se toma mediante un referéndum o no).

La mayor parte de la bibliografía tradicional sobre referéndums no acepta estos puntos. De hecho, considera la estabilidad como contradictoria a la voluntad del votante medio; las preferencias sobre los referéndums reflejan así a uno o a otro. Butler y Ranney (1994: 21) compendian los conocimientos convencionales:

> Como concluye Magleby en *Direct Legislation*, la gente que cree en democracia representativa no diluida, atribuye el más alto valor a las virtudes de *estabilidad*, acuerdo, moderación y acceso para todos los segmentos de la comunidad, por muy pequeños que sean, y buscan acuerdos institucionales que aíslan principios fundamentales de fluctuaciones a corto plazo en la opinión pública. Quienes creen en acercarse tanto como sea posible a la democracia directa atribuyen el más alto valor a las virtudes del cambio, participación, competencia, conflicto y *dominio de la mayoría*, y buscan acuerdos institucionales que maximicen respuestas rápidas y completas a lo que quieren las mayorías populares.

Hay pruebas empíricas en la bibliografía en favor de mis dos expectativas. En lo tocante a la protección del *statu quo*, tanto Immergut (1992) como Neidhart (1970) argumentan que los referéndums populares dan poder a sus defensores. Immergut arguye que después de que una propuesta política fracasó debido a un referéndum en 1911 en Suiza, los políticos se volvieron prudentes y sólo reformas menores fueron posibles. El gobierno federal y la legislatura permanecieron como rehenes de poderosos grupos de intereses que podían amenazar con un reto de referéndum. Para Neidhart, los referéndums han transformado la democracia suiza en una democracia negociadora donde el gobierno propone primero la legislación a grupos interesados con el fin de evitar el proceso de referéndum.

El primer estudioso que ofreció evidencia empírica del respeto a la voluntad del votante medio fue Pommerehne (1978), quien descubrió diferencias importantes en comunidades de legislación directa y legislación mediada en Suiza. Pommerehne construyó un modelo econométrico basado en una función de la demanda del votante medio para estudiar pautas de desembolso en municipios suizos. Descubrió que el modelo funciona mejor en comunidades con legislación directa que las que carecen de ésta. En un estudio similar, Feld y Savioz (1997) arguyeron que la legislación directa permite poner un freno a los hábitos de derroche de los políticos. Matsusaka (1995) ha producido resultados similares con Feld y Savioz con datos de los estados de la Unión Americana. Para el periodo 1960-1990, su análisis sugiere que los estados con iniciativas populares tenían un más bajo nivel de desembolsos, impuestos y déficits. Su modelo controla los factores económicos y demográficos e incluye una variable ficticia *(dummy)* para los estados con iniciativas. El coeficiente de la variable ficticia de legislación directa resulta ser negativo, lo cual indica que los niveles de gasto en estados con iniciativas son significativamente más bajos. Hay una diferencia política importante en la interpretación de estos estudios. La primera muestra testimonia en favor de la proximidad a los intereses del votante medio; las otras dos demuestran un resultado político específico (independientemente de las preferencias del votante medio). Sin embargo, Matsusaka (2000) extendió más su análisis en el tiempo (abarcando la primera mitad del siglo XX) y descubrió que el desembolso era, de hecho, *más alto* en los estados con iniciativas. Sacó esta conclusión: "Esto parece indicar que la iniciativa no es inherentemente un dispositivo que reduzca el tamaño del gobierno" (Matsusaka, 2000). Sin embargo, los dos resultados de Matsusaka podrían indicar proximidad de resultados a las preferencias del votante medio. De modo similar, Elizabeth Gerber proporciona muestras de que la legislación sobre el aborto en adolescentes (Gerber, 1996) o la pena de muerte (Gerber, 1999) se aproxima mejor a las preferencias del votante medio en estados con referéndums que en estados sin éstos, ya sea que la legislación fuera propuesta, de hecho, por un referéndum o no. Por último, Hug (2001) desarrolló nuevas técnicas estadísticas para estimar modelos de legislación directa y confirmó la expectativa teórica de proximidad de los resultados a las preferencias del votante medio, incluso en casos donde las pruebas no eran concluyentes. Este análisis agota las similitudes entre todos los tipos de referéndums. Ahora me concentraré en las diferencias que se relacionan con quién controla la agenda del proceso de referéndum.

2. Instituciones que regulan los referéndums

La mayor parte de la bibliografía sobre referéndums coincide en que "el nombre de referéndum incluye una diversidad de situaciones y de usos que sólo guardan una relación superficial unos con otros" (Smith, 1975: 294), y las diferentes formas de referéndums pueden implicar consecuencias muy distintas (Finer, 1980: 214). Sin embargo, la similitud de conclusiones termina allí. Los desacuerdos surgen cuando diversos autores tratan de clasificar distintos tipos de referéndums o describen las consecuencias que cada tipo implica.

Por ejemplo, Smith (1975) emplea dos normas para elaborar una "matriz de varianza funcional de los referéndums": por un lado, "control", y por el otro, "efecto hegemónico". Butler y Ranney (1978) usan cuatro categorías distintas: *1)* referéndums controlados por el gobierno, *2)* referéndums requeridos por la constitución, *3)* referéndums por petición popular, y *4)* iniciativas populares. Pier Vincenzo Uleri (1996) recalca los aspectos legales de los referéndums y multiplica la clasificación, empleando términos como *referéndum obligatorio, voto opcional, referéndum de iniciativa, decisión-promoción,* o *control, voto de rechazo, voto de abrogación,* etcétera.

Más recientemente, otros investigadores se han concentrado en los aspectos estratégicos de los referéndums, el grado en que algunos jugadores controlan la agenda. Mi análisis es muy similar a tales enfoques, y usaré una clasificación similar a la que presentó Hug (2001), siguiendo a Mueller (1996), según las normas dicotómicas que propuso Suksi (1993).

Hug distingue los referéndums sobre la base de tres criterios dicotómicos. Primero, observa si se requieren o no. Segundo, subdivide los no requeridos en dos categorías sobre la base de si requieren que el pueblo tome una iniciativa o no (activo y pasivo). Y tercero, subdivide los referéndums activos sobre la base de quién controla la agenda, es decir, si la proposición sobre la votación se origina en el gobierno o en la oposición.

Concuerdo con la lógica que respalda la clasificación de Hug, pero sus normas no se generalizan muy bien a diferentes países. Por ejemplo, en un régimen presidencial, quién está en el gobierno y quién en la oposición es algo que no queda claramente definido, mientras que sí es claro quiénes son los jugadores con veto existentes. Las agendas del referéndum incluyen dos temas distintos por decidir: primero, la decisión de si habrá o no un referéndum, lo que denomino "activación"; y segundo, la redacción exacta de la pregunta. La gráfica v.3 proporciona el algoritmo implícito para mi clasificación.

1. Referéndums requeridos. "Requeridos" significa que el gobierno está obligado a exponer una medida política a los votantes. No se emprende ninguna iniciativa de referéndum. Un documento particular tiene que ser ratificado por el pueblo para poder ser promulgado. En muchos países, los referéndums requeridos se aplican a cambios constitucionales. Tales referéndums existen al nivel estatal en los Estados Unidos y al nivel nacional en Suiza.
2. Referéndum de jugador con veto. Si un referéndum no es requerido, un actor tiene que decidir celebrar un referéndum. Una primera posibilidad es que la decisión de celebrar un referéndum pertenezca a uno de los jugadores con veto existentes. Podría ser el parlamento (un jugador con veto colectivo) o el gobierno (uno o más jugadores con veto) de un país, o algún otro jugador con veto particular, como

GRÁFICA V.3. *Preguntas que definen diferentes categorías de referéndums.*

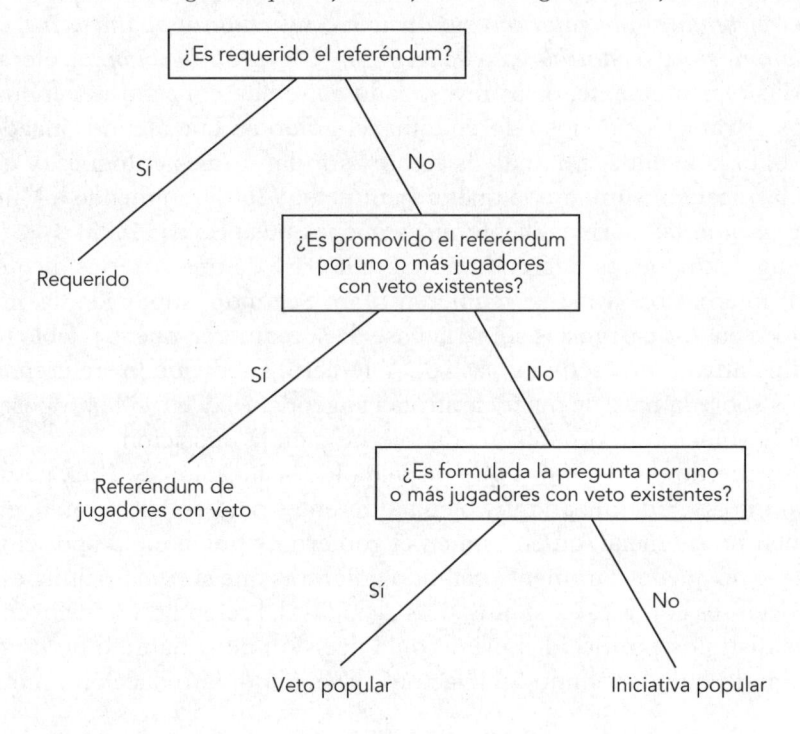

el presidente de la Quinta República francesa.[4] Este referéndum con frecuencia ha sido denominado "plebiscito".

3. Veto popular. Es posible que un jugador con veto existente formule la pregunta, pero la celebración del referéndum es prerrogativa de otro agente. Tales referéndums son esencialmente vetos a políticas decididas por jugadores con veto existentes. El actor activador puede ser la población en conjunto por medio de un proceso de firmas, como se hace en Italia con ciertas leyes (Bogdanor, 1994), o en Suiza para la mayor parte de la legislación federal, o en los Estados Unidos con los "referéndums populares" al nivel estatal, o en Dinamarca con cierta minoría en el parlamento.

4. Iniciativa popular. Es posible que la propuesta colocada en la boleta no se origine en la legislación de jugador con veto existente, sino que sea una propuesta escrita por algún grupo político que recababa las firmas requeridas para colocarlas en la boleta de voto. Este tipo de referéndum existe a nivel estatal en los Estados Unidos y también en Suiza. Hug y Tsebelis (2002) presentan a los actores exactos que activan los referéndums y formulan la pregunta en todos los países del mundo. En las secciones siguientes señalaré las consecuencias estratégicas de diferentes tipos de referéndums no obligatorios.

Nos concentraremos primero en el caso donde ambos temas de la agenda están en manos de uno de los jugadores con veto institucionales o partidarios existentes, y entonces investigaremos el caso de un proceso competitivo de establecimiento de agenda correspondiente a referéndums por iniciativa popular. Por último, se examinarán algunas instituciones más complicadas donde los dos temas del establecimiento de agenda son controlados por jugadores diferentes (uno activa el referéndum y el otro propone la pregunta).

---

[4] Como se observó en el capítulo IV, el presidente francés no es un jugador con veto en los términos de la legislación porque no tiene veto legislativo. Sin embargo, si la mayoría parlamentaria está de su lado, él es en realidad un jefe (o uno de los jefes) de esta mayoría. Por ejemplo, ningún actor político disputaba que De Gaulle o Pompidou fueran los jefes de la mayoría cuando estaban en el poder. Ningún actor político negó que D'Estaing fuera el jefe de uno de los dos socios de la coalición en el gobierno. De modo similar, Mitterrand fue el jefe de la mayoría en cuanto hubo una mayoría de la izquierda. Así, cuando el partido legislativo del presidente es parte de la mayoría, él es un jugador con veto (aunque no uno adicional). La constitución de la Quinta República no permite que un presidente convoque a un referéndum en contra de la voluntad de su gobierno.

3. Referéndums de jugador con veto

Supongamos que un solo jugador con veto controla ambas partes de la agenda del referéndum: él puede formular la pregunta y activar el referéndum. Concentrémonos en la gráfica v.2 y veamos en qué condiciones diferentes posibles establecedores de agenda convocarían en realidad a un referéndum. El establecedor de agenda del referéndum tiene que calcular si prefiere seleccionar su punto preferido de W′(SQ) o arriesgarse con W(SQ). Con el fin de simplificar aquí nuestros cálculos, supongamos que un referéndum no tiene costos políticos para el establecedor de agenda. Obviamente, ésta es una suposición incorrecta, pero podemos abordarla fácilmente agregando tales costos en los cálculos.

Considero dos casos diferentes de toma de decisiones parlamentaria: primero, que hay una estable coalición de partidos A, B y C (denomino esta situación gobierno "parlamentario"); segundo, que es factible cualquier posible coalición ganadora entre A, B, C, D y E (denomino esta situación un sistema "presidencial"). En cada uno de estos casos considero dos posibles establecedores de agenda: el partido A y el partido E (el primero es parte del gobierno de sistema parlamentario, el segundo no lo es).[5]

Con una información completa, el establecedor de agenda del referéndum tiene la garantía de obtener su punto más preferido del conjunto ganador popular del *statu quo* —W′(SQ) en la gráfica v.2—. Dado que tanto A como E están localizados fuera de W′(SQ), pueden alcanzar los puntos A′ y E′, respectivamente, cuando controlan la agenda del referéndum. La pregunta es: ¿puede la democracia indirecta ofrecer a los establecedores de agenda del referéndum una alternativa más atractiva? Para responder esta pregunta tenemos que calcular el conjunto ganador del *statu quo* de estos dos puntos W(A′) (véase gráfica v.4) y W(E′) (véase gráfica v.5).

La gráfica v.4 presenta exactamente la misma configuración de jugadores que la gráfica v.2 e identifica el punto A′, que es el mejor resultado que puede lograr el establecedor de agenda del referéndum —A′ es la intersección de la línea AY con el círculo (Y, YSQ)—. La gráfica v.4 identifica también el conjunto ganador de A′ —en vez de W(SQ)—, dado que el jugador A puede introducir un referéndum y obtener A′ como resultado. Fuera de esto, el conjunto ganador A considerará únicamente los puntos incluidos en el

---

[5] En este caso E no es un jugador con veto. Incluyo este caso contrario a la objetividad para dar una visión completa.

GRÁFICA V.4. *Resultados posibles cuando A controla la agenda del referéndum.*

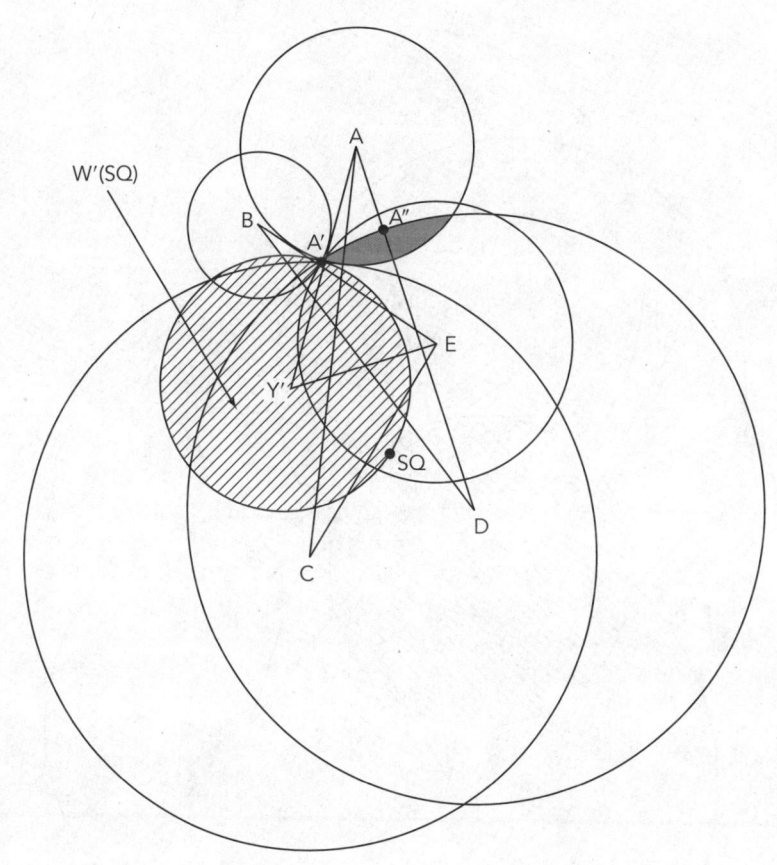

círculo (A, AA′), y activará un referéndum para cualquier punto más alejado que A′. Sólo hay una coalición posible que puede aprobar puntos dentro del círculo (A, AA′): A, D y E. En consecuencia, A tiene que seleccionar esta coalición con el fin de obtener un resultado que él prefiera más que A′ (preferiblemente A″). En nuestro sistema "presidencial" idealizado, esto es lo que sucederá. En el caso de un sistema "parlamentario" con A, B y C en el gobierno, la situación es más complicada. Obsérvese que no hay punto que todos los tres A, B y C prefieran más que A′, dado que A′ es el núcleo de unanimidad de A, B y C. A tiene que escoger entre mantener el gobierno en su sitio o provocar una dimisión del mismo. De modo similar, los partidos B y C pueden ofrecer aprobar el resultado A′ y evitar un referéndum,

GRÁFICA V.5. *Resultados posibles cuando E controla la agenda del referéndum.*

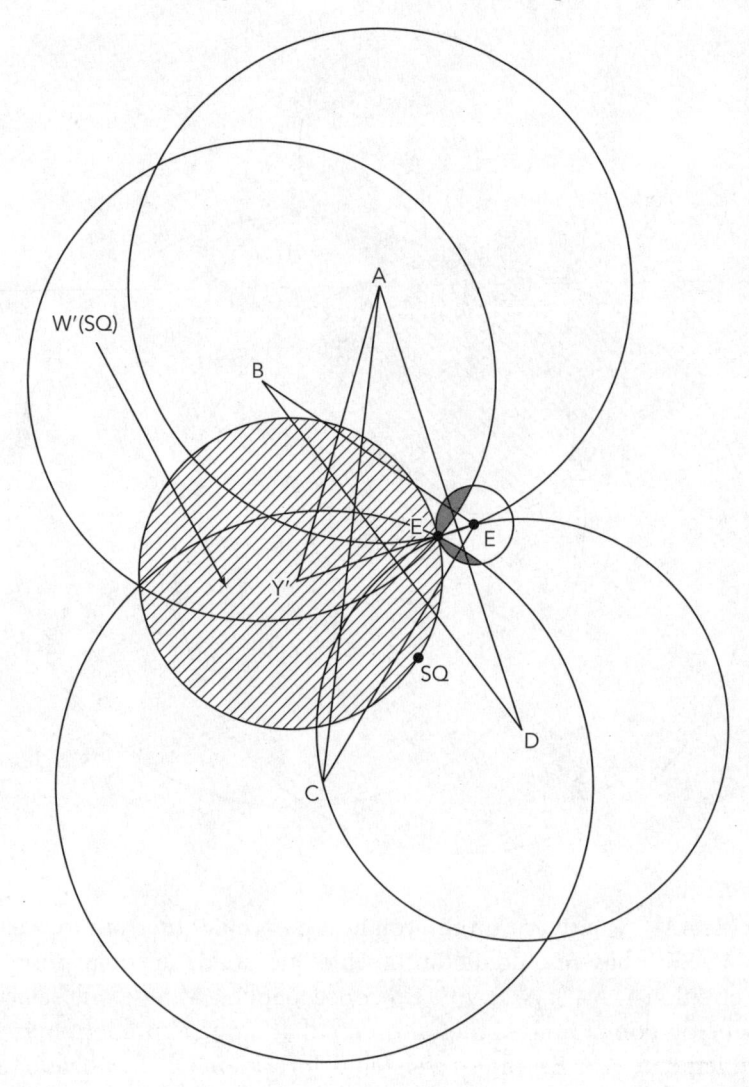

o tal vez prefieran delegar su desacuerdo a un referéndum. Estos cálculos conducen a tres posibles resultados: el gobierno ABC permanece en el poder y adopta A′ sin un referéndum. El gobierno ABC permanece en el poder y se adopta A′ por referéndum. El gobierno renuncia y es remplazado por otra coalición que selecciona un punto factible desde W(A′).

La gráfica v.5 presenta exactamente la misma configuración de jugadores que antes, pero identifica el conjunto ganador del punto E' en vez de SQ, dado que el jugador E puede introducir un referéndum y obtenerlo. Fuera de este conjunto ganador únicamente pueden ser considerados los puntos incluidos en el círculo (E, EE'), ya que E preferiría promover un referéndum que aceptar un punto más alejado que E'. Hay tres posibles coaliciones que pueden aprobar puntos dentro del círculo (E, EE'): (ABE), (ADE), (CDE). En consecuencia, E tiene que seleccionar una de las coaliciones disponibles. En el caso de que cualquier coalición sea posible (el sistema "presidencial" anterior), E seleccionará su propio punto ideal respaldado por (ADE). En el caso contrario a la objetividad (contrafáctico) de un sistema "parlamentario" con (ABC) en el gobierno, la situación sería más complicada. E podría aprovechar su ventaja de establecimiento de agenda del referéndum para tratar de negociar un gobierno diferente: de hecho, los jugadores A, D y E pueden preferir un nuevo gobierno de coalición. Si los partidos en el gobierno quieren mantenerse juntos, E activará un referéndum y el gobierno perderá.

En todos estos cálculos, un sistema presidencial donde los partidos pueden cambiar las coaliciones sobre la base del tema en consideración era un sistema más flexible que uno parlamentario, donde la coalición gubernamental existente era incapaz de adaptarse al nuevo ambiente político generado por el referéndum, incluso cuando el establecimiento de agenda pertenecía a un jugador con veto existente (A).[6] Un sistema parlamentario puede producir resultados similares delegando un tema político a un referéndum, y dejándolo fuera del conflicto político de los principales partidos. Por ejemplo, en el Reino Unido el referéndum sobre participación en la Unión Europea recibió este trato especial debido a que los dos partidos estaban divididos y no podían tratar el tema sin graves daños a su unidad.

Dados estos cálculos, los partidos que piensan estratégicamente en la legislatura (en particular si, por alguna razón, quieren evitar un referéndum) pueden asegurarle al establecedor de agenda del referéndum que harán cualquier cosa que esté a su alcance para hacer que el proceso legislativo termine en un área que sea al menos tan buena para él como el resultado de un referéndum. Estos experimentos mentales conducen a las conclusiones siguientes. Primero, la posición del establecedor de agenda del referéndum se traduce en ventajas políticas importantes. Planteamos este punto

---

[6] Y, por supuesto, lo mismo se puede decir en el caso contrario a la objetividad en que un jugador sin veto (E) controla la agenda.

en los dos primeros capítulos, pero aquí iremos un paso más adelante: si un jugador con veto controla la agenda del referéndum, cancela a otros jugadores con veto como tales. La razón es que el jugador con veto con control de la agenda de un referéndum puede elegir entre emplear los procedimientos de la democracia directa o representativa, y todos los otros jugadores tienen que ofrecerle la solución más ventajosa. Éste es un análisis muy diferente del presentado por los defensores de referéndum que consideran éste como la expresión de la voluntad del pueblo (véase Rousseau, *supra*). Segunda (y ésta es una consecuencia de la primera), los resultados legislativos de la democracia representativa son alterados si es posible la democracia directa.

Permítaseme presentar algunos ejemplos de referéndums de la vida real para mostrar que la primera conclusión es congruente con procesos políticos reales, no sólo con ejercicios mentales. Abordaré la segunda conclusión (la modificación de resultados del proceso parlamentario) en la sección 4.

En Francia, el presidente de la república puede convocar a referéndums según dos diferentes artículos de la constitución. Según el artículo 11: "Sobre la propuesta del gobierno durante sesiones parlamentarias, o sobre la propuesta conjunta de las dos Asambleas, publicado en el *Journal Officiel*, el presidente de la república puede someter a referéndum cualquier proyecto de ley del gobierno que trate de la organización de las autoridades públicas [...] el cual [...] aunque no esté en conflicto con la constitución, afectaría el funcionamiento de las instituciones". El derecho a proponer enmiendas constitucionales de acuerdo con el artículo 89 "pertenece actualmente al presidente de la república, sobre la propuesta del Primer Ministro y los miembros del parlamento. El proyecto o propuesta de enmienda debe ser aprobado por las dos asambleas en términos idénticos".

Durante su mandato (1958-1969), Charles de Gaulle proclamó cinco referéndums. Nunca esperó que el gobierno o el primer ministro se lo propusieran. Las propuestas siempre llegaban *después* del anuncio de De Gaulle. Además, De Gaulle usó el artículo 11 en vez del apropiado artículo 89 para enmiendas constitucionales, tales como el referéndum de 1962, cuando cambió el modo de elección del presidente, de elecciones indirectas a directas. Esta acción no encontró el apoyo de casi ningún experto constitucional, pero después de aceptada la propuesta, la cuestión de la constitucionalidad se volvió nula. De Gaulle pasó por alto así las restricciones constitucionales y empleó la iniciativa del referéndum como su poder propio.

Lo más interesante es cómo De Gaulle agrupó las preguntas propuestas, de modo que no tuviera que aceptar un *no* por respuesta: perdió únicamente en el último de los cinco referéndums que propuso. Ese referéndum, de abril de 1969, formulaba la pregunta: "¿Aprueba usted el proyecto de ley que trata de la creación de regiones y la reforma del Senado?" "El proyecto de ley constaba de más de 14 páginas de letra menuda, comprendía 69 artículos e implicaba la modificación o sustitución de 19 artículos de la constitución" (Wright, 1978: 156). Por añadidura, De Gaulle presentó la votación como un referéndum sobre él mismo, diciéndole al pueblo francés el 10 de abril: "No puede haber la menor duda. [...] La continuación de mi mandato o mi partida dependen obviamente de la respuesta del pueblo a lo que pregunto [...] ¿qué tipo de hombre sería yo [...] si intentara ridículamente seguir en el cargo?" (Wright, 1978: 158). Tal vez la presentación del problema fuera insólito para De Gaulle en 1969, pero ciertamente no la asociación del resultado del referéndum con el hecho de si él seguía en el cargo. En 1961 declaró que "un resultado negativo o incierto me impediría seguir con mi tarea". En 1962 declaró: "Vuestras respuestas me dirán si puedo y debo continuar con mi labor". De las dos declaraciones, la primera fue mucho más efectiva, dado que el presidente de la república es también el comandante en jefe de las fuerzas armadas, y fue hecha en medio de una guerra colonial.

La amenaza de renuncia cuando no había alternativa clara para De Gaulle fue evidentemente el elemento más crítico para el éxito de sus paquetes de referéndum. Cuando en 1969 el ex primer ministro Georges Pompidou declaró que él estaría dispuesto a servir a su país como presidente si fuera necesario, el referéndum de De Gaulle fracasó y, leal a su palabra, éste renunció.

Lo que no se ha subrayado en la bibliografía sobre estos acontecimientos es que todas estas maniobras son casos de control de la agenda, que es el poder del actor que formula la pregunta en referéndums. Este poder tenía tan frustrados a los adversarios de De Gaulle que uno de ellos (el ex primer ministro Pierre Mendes-France) dijo: "¿Plebiscitos? No se discuten; se combaten". Otro fue más tranquilo y filosófico pero igualmente negativo en su evaluación. De Gaulle (1971: 325) citó los pensamientos de Vincent Auriol, presidente de la Cuarta República: "El referéndum es un acto de poder absoluto. [...] Mientras que ostensiblemente se inclina ante la soberanía del pueblo, es, de hecho, un intento para privar al pueblo de su soberanía, en beneficio de un hombre".

4. Las iniciativas populares

Hasta ahora he tratado de los referéndums cuando el establecedor de agenda disfruta del monopolio del poder. Ahora me concentro en referéndums que delegan poderes de establecimiento de agenda al ganador de un proceso competitivo. El argumento que presento aquí es un eco del argumento presentado en el capítulo III acerca de la diferencia entre regímenes democráticos y no democráticos.

Si diferentes grupos pueden convertirse en establecedores de agenda mediante un referéndum, al ganar el derecho a presentar su pregunta al electorado (recabación de firmas), el resultado legislativo dependerá de lo competitivo que sea el proceso de selección. Si todos los establecedores de agenda potenciales están incluidos en el proceso de selección, y si los votantes están informados, entonces la única manera en que podemos seleccionar propuestas capaces de prevalecer (derrotar no sólo al *statu quo* sino también a posibles alternativas) es converger hacia las preferencias del votante medio. Este resultado es una generalización multidimensional del argumento presentado en el capítulo III, y es posible porque el conjunto ganador del *statu quo* puede ser representado por un círculo, como se demostró en la gráfica v.1.

Si algunos de los establecedores de agenda potenciales son excluidos del proceso, entonces los restantes pueden ser más extremosos y el resultado legislativo estará más alejado de las preferencias del votante medio, si a ningún grupo con referencias similares al votante medio se le permite entrar al proceso de establecimiento de agenda. Como se señaló en el capítulo I, hay un poder importante en el establecimiento de agenda.

Como consecuencia de este análisis, tenemos que concentrarnos en el proceso de selección del establecedor de agenda y evaluar lo competitivo que es. Si, por ejemplo, lo que se requiere son *voluntarios* para seleccionar firmas, entonces las demandas que estén apoyadas por una mayoría de la población suelen obtener los voluntarios necesarios para su colocación en la boleta electoral, y las iniciativas que no tengan suficientes voluntarios probablemente no contarán con el respaldo de una mayoría. En consecuencia, tal proceso es competitivo y podemos esperar que el resultado esté localizado cerca de las preferencias del votante medio.

Si, en cambio, lo que se solicita para que un tema sea colocado en la boleta es una selección de firmas por *profesionales* remunerados, los grupos organizados (incluso con puntos ideales alejados del votante medio) serán los únicos capaces de participar. En este caso, el proceso de selección de agenda se traducirá en resultados que pueden ser incongruentes con las preferencias del votante medio. En todos los casos, el resultado seleccionado tiene que estar más cerca de las preferencias del votante medio que el *statu quo*.[7] Así, de nueva cuenta, pese al hecho de que el votante medio toma la decisión final, el resultado depende decisivamente de las preferencias del establecedor de agenda.

Los referéndums de jugador con veto eliminan a los jugadores con veto existentes en las legislaturas, y lo mismo hacen las iniciativas populares. De hecho, por medio de las iniciativas populares, todo el proceso legislativo es sustituido por referéndums. Es posible que los jugadores con veto existentes traten de evitar el desafío del referéndum. Sin embargo, los únicos puntos que no se pueden desafiar son los cercanos al votante medio "como si" (el centro de la yema de la población). Además, podría ser que este punto ni siquiera fuese parte del conjunto ganador del *statu quo* de la democracia mediada, lo cual significa que los jugadores con veto existentes queden cancelados *porque* el mismo jugador controla toda la agenda del referéndum.

5. Los vetos populares

Los referéndums no obligatorios serán promovidos por los actores con jurisdicción, como una función de sus propias preferencias. Los jugadores con veto existentes seleccionarán un referéndum si quieren cancelar a otros jugadores con veto, como argumenté en la sección 2. Los jugadores sin veto seleccionarán un referéndum si el resultado propuesto por el gobierno no está dentro del conjunto ganador del votante medio. De hecho, esto es verdad sólo si ellos así lo creen, como lo indica la siguiente historia de un referéndum sobre el divorcio en Italia.

En diciembre de 1970 se promulgó por primera vez el divorcio legal en Italia. La estipulación más importante de esta ley era que si los cónyuges habían estado "legalmente separados" por cinco años, podían obtener un divorcio. La respuesta de la Iglesia católica fue inmediata. El papa reveló que había enviado notas diplomáticas al gobierno antes de la promulgación

---

[7] Debería repetir aquí que se supone que el radio de la yema es 0; de otro modo, no se podría excluir la selección de un punto que estuviera más alejado del centro de la yema que el *statu quo* hasta en 2r.

de la ley, y los clérigos plantearon la cuestión de un referéndum para abrogar la nueva ley. En la práctica, aunque tales referéndums estaban especificados en el artículo 75 de la constitución italiana, nunca habían tenido lugar y no había legislación alguna sobre sus procedimientos. El gobierno, doblegándose a la presión del Vaticano, aprobó tal ley *antes* de la aprobación de la ley sobre divorcio, de modo que los católicos, si así lo deseaban, podían imponer un referéndum para abrogar dicha ley cuando fuera aprobada. Lo que sucedió fue que en febrero de 1971 los obispos italianos emitieron una declaración de que el matrimonio era indisoluble, y se recabaron 1.4 millones de firmas hasta el mes de junio a fin de imponer el referéndum, casi el triple del número requerido.

Lo interesante fue la reacción del *establishment* político a esta amenaza de referéndum, que no fue bien recibida por el liderazgo de los comunistas ni de los democratacristianos. Primero, en julio de 1971 hubo un intento de presentar una propuesta de ley que hiciera inadmisible todo referéndum que protegiera minorías étnicas o religiosas *o el matrimonio*. Entonces, los comunistas presentaron una nueva propuesta de ley de divorcio mejorada, con la esperanza de que sustituyera la ley de divorcio existente, de modo que el proceso tuviera que empezar de nuevo. Cuando esta maniobra falló (principalmente debido al calendario parlamentario), el parlamento se disolvió un año antes, a fin de evitar que el referéndum se celebrara en 1972. El nuevo parlamento tenía una ligera mayoría derechista, pero los democratacristianos no trataron de revocar la ley pues no querían sustituir su alianza con los socialistas por una alianza con los fascistas, que también estaban en contra de la ley de divorcio. Finalmente, el referéndum se realizó en 1974, tres años después de recabadas las firmas (Butler y Ranney, 1994). Ni los partidarios del referéndum ni el *establishment* político italiano habían previsto este resultado. Fue una derrota de 60 a 40 del procedimiento de abrogación, resultado humillante para la coalición clerical.

Esta historia indica que aunque el jugador activador puede imponer un referéndum, los jugadores con veto existentes pueden aplazarlo de manera que el equilibrio de fuerzas mejorará en su favor, o modificarán el *statu quo* de modo que el referéndum sea cancelado o pospuesto aún más. Estas reacciones de los jugadores con veto existentes apuntan a ganarse las preferencias del votante medio.

Los casos que he presentado hasta aquí presuponen principalmente la existencia de votantes bien informados. La situación es alterada significativamente con la suposición más realista de información incompleta. Como escribió Wolf Linder (1994: 144) en *Swiss Democracy:* "El dinero es [...] el factor singular más importante que determina los resultados de la legislación directa". Según su opinión, las desigualdades en gastos de campaña se elevan a razones de 1:20 o 1:50, y "en Suiza así como en los Estados Unidos, el bando más gastador gana 80-90% de las campañas. Es excepcional que los desposeídos le ganen al 'dinero en grande'". Lowenstein (1982) clarifica esta afirmación para los Estados Unidos, argumentando que cuando el bando que respalda el *statu quo* gasta significativamente más que los partidarios del cambio, las posibilidades están fuertemente en favor del *statu quo*. Estos argumentos se pueden captar mediante un modelo de información incompleta, según el cual el dinero se gasta para convencer a un votante medio desinformado de que una propuesta está más cerca de su punto ideal que otra (cualquiera que sea la verdadera ubicación de los tres puntos).

6. Conclusiones

Los referéndums —la posibilidad de una legislación directa— alteran significativamente las reglas y los resultados del proceso legislativo. La simple posibilidad de presentar una elección legislativa a la aprobación del pueblo introduce un jugador adicional con veto en el proceso de la toma de decisiones: el votante medio de la población. Aunque en dimensiones múltiples tal votante no existe, como argumenté en la sección 1, se puede identificar un votante medio "como si", y los pronósticos serán aproximaciones muy exactas de los resultados. Si el mismo jugador es capaz de activar el referéndum y también controla la redacción de la pregunta, entonces los jugadores con veto legislativo tradicionales son eliminados del proceso de la toma de decisiones, como se vio en las secciones 3 y 4. De hecho, el análisis indicó que en vez del conjunto ganador del *statu quo*, los cálculos pertinentes implicaron al conjunto ganador del punto que puede lograr el establecedor de agenda del referéndum.

Las diferencias entre referéndums dependen de quién controle la agenda (activación y pregunta). Si es un jugador con veto existente, lo fortalece a él a costa de los otros. Si es una iniciativa popular, favorece a los grupos que pueden afectar la agenda. Si el proceso de establecimiento de agenda es competitivo, favorece al votante medio. Como resultado, los jugadores con veto existentes tienen que considerar no sólo al conjunto ganador del *statu quo*, sino también las preferencias del votante medio "como si".

Los proponentes de la democracia directa argumentan que ésta expresa la voluntad del pueblo, mientras que los adversarios hablan de la falta de información de los votantes que les impide tomar las decisiones correctas. Vimos que las preferencias del votante medio en el parlamento y en la población tal vez no coincidan, y que las coaliciones formadas dentro de cada uno de estos organismos pueden ser diferentes de modo que los resultados de la democracia directa y de la representativa pueden ser distintos.

El argumento de que la voluntad popular se expresa a través de referéndums, como lo afirma Rousseau, es desatinadamente optimista.[8] No toma en cuenta el papel del establecimiento de la agenda, la activación y la formulación de la pregunta. Estos dos aspectos del establecimiento de la agenda pueden corresponder a la jurisdicción de un solo jugador (referéndums de jugador con veto, iniciativa popular) o ser compartidos por dos jugadores distintos (referéndums obligatorios, vetos populares).

Como se ha visto, si el establecimiento de la agenda es delegado a un jugador con veto, fortalece a este actor frente a los otros jugadores con veto. Si el proceso de establecimiento de agenda se vuelve competitivo, entonces las preferencias del votante medio serán más respetadas. Como resultado de este análisis, se abordarán mejor las preferencias del votante medio en países o estados con iniciativa popular; la legislación en países con veto popular estará más distante de las preferencias del votante medio, pero no tanto como en países o estados con referéndums obligatorios, o con referéndums de jugador con veto.

---

[8] O, más precisamente, incorrecto. Habría sido optimista que Rousseau se hubiese referido a los referéndums populares. Sin embargo, me sorprendió saber que en realidad se expresó en términos tan elogiosos de los referéndums organizados por el gobierno, como lo documenta Manin (2001). En este caso, tal vez sea más exacta la evaluación de Auriol, citada antes.

VI. FEDERALISMO, BICAMERALISMO Y MAYORÍAS CALIFICADAS

EL TÉRMINO *federal* se emplea para países donde "*1)* dos niveles de gobierno rigen al mismo país y al mismo pueblo; *2)* cada nivel tiene al menos un área de jurisdicción en la cual es autónomo, y *3)* hay alguna garantía (aunque tan sólo sea una declaración en la constitución) de la autonomía de cada gobierno en su propia esfera" (Riker, 1964: 11).

Los investigadores se han concentrado en los efectos del federalismo sobre diferentes resultados políticos, al nivel tanto teórico como empírico. Sin embargo, el consenso ha sido escaso. Por ejemplo, en lo tocante a uno de los temas más intensamente estudiados en economía política, el federalismo fiscal, no hay consenso acerca de si la descentralización tiene consecuencias provechosas o no. Riker (1975: 144) ha planteado el argumento de que no debería haber diferencias de política entre países federales y unitarios, mientras que Rose-Ackerman (1981) y Dixit y Londregan (1998) proporcionan argumentos para explicar por qué la legislación será diferente en estos dos tipos de Estados. En cuanto a la dirección de las diferencias potenciales, académicos como Tiebout (1956), Buchanan (1950), Oates (1972) y Weingast (1995) han descrito los beneficios económicos de la descentralización. Por otro lado, Davoodi y Zou (1998), Prud'homme (1995), Tanzi (1995) y Treisman (2000a, 2000b) señalan problemas asociados con la descentralización. La mayor parte de esta bibliografía examina los resultados (beneficiosos) de la competencia económica entre los Estados.

Este libro adopta una visión distinta del federalismo. Me concentro en la estructura institucional del gobierno federal. Allí observo frecuentemente al menos una de dos características diferentes: el uso del bicameralismo con una segunda cámara que tiene poder de veto efectivo sobre la legislación, o el uso de mayorías calificadas en la creación de política. Argumento que cada una de estas dos estructuras institucionales genera más jugadores con veto, de modo que los países federales tienen *ceteris paribus* niveles más altos de estabilidad política y otras características estructurales (independencia del poder judicial, de las burocracias, e inestabilidad del gobierno si son parlamentarios) que se derivan de la existencia de múltiples jugadores con veto.

Aunque el bicameralismo (con veto efectivo de la segunda cámara) y las mayorías calificadas son más frecuentes en países federales, no es porque estos últimos los empleen en exclusiva. Por ejemplo, Japón, aunque no es un país federal, tiene una cámara alta con derecho de vetar la legislación propuesta por la cámara baja. De modo similar, en Francia (país unitario), el gobierno tiene el poder de decidir si un proyecto de ley será aprobado por consenso de ambas cámaras, o si la cámara baja decide en contra de la cámara alta. De modo parecido, las mayorías calificadas, aunque en muchos países no sean requeridas constitucionalmente, a menudo son el resultado del juego político, como se verá en la tercera sección de este capítulo. Dado que ninguna de estas dos características está necesariamente vinculada con el federalismo, las estudiaremos independientemente una de otra y del federalismo.

El capítulo está dividido en cuatro secciones. En la primera veremos por qué el federalismo ha sido una variable independiente tan elusiva y nos concentraremos en sus implicaciones sobre los jugadores con veto. En la segunda se examinarán las instituciones bicamerales. La tercera está dedicada a un análisis de la toma de decisiones por mayoría calificada. La cuarta aborda la combinación de bicameralismo y mayorías calificadas.

1. El federalismo

Varios análisis han señalado características importantes que unen o separan a los países federales. Por ejemplo, todos ellos incluyen unidades componentes que compiten unas con otras por la atracción de los ciudadanos (Tiebout, 1956). Por otro lado, algunos países federales tienen agencias para la implantación de políticas nacionales al nivel federal (por ejemplo, los Estados Unidos), mientras que otros lo hacen al nivel estatal (Unión Europea, Alemania).[1] En esta sección me concentraré en dos temas: el federalismo fiscal y los jugadores con veto. El federalismo fiscal domina la bibliografía económica. Aquí afirmo que aunque los argumentos teóricos en favor de la descentralización pueden parecer decisivos, la evidencia empírica no parece respaldar estas teorías. Seguidamente me concentro en las instituciones que más a menudo prevalecen en diferentes países federales.

[1] Véase un excelente artículo de Scharpf (1988) sobre el tema.

1.1. El federalismo fiscal

Basándonos en la definición de Riker citada antes, el federalismo es un equilibrio entre unidades constituyentes que desean participar en la federación (y no alejarse de ella) y el gobierno central que no les quite su autonomía. Si alguna de estas condiciones no se mantiene, la federación se desplomará (se transformará en un grupo de estados independientes o en uno unitario). Sin embargo, Riker (1975: 144) no creía que hubiera diferencias políticas entre países federales y no federales debido a este desequilibrio entre centro y periferia. De hecho, él propuso un experimento mental donde ocho pares de países (uno de estos pares era Australia y Nueva Zelanda) estaban divididos por la variable "federalismo" pero tenían políticas muy similares en casi todas las dimensiones.

Pero los economistas que estudian el federalismo señalaron dos diferencias importantes entre países federales y países unitarios. Primero, Hayek (1939) sugirió que, en vista de que los gobiernos y consumidores locales tienen mejor información acerca de las condiciones y preferencias locales, tomarán mejores decisiones que los gobiernos nacionales. Segundo, Tiebout (1956) se concentró en los efectos de la competencia entre jurisdicciones dado que el pueblo puede "votar con los pies" y arguyó que el federalismo ofrece a la gente la elección entre diferentes menús de bienes públicos.

Sin embargo, estos enfoques iniciales pasaron por alto la cuestión de los incentivos de los políticos para ofrecer bienes públicos y mantener los mercados. Weingast (1995: 24) se concentró en el siguiente problema fundamental:

> Los mercados requieren protección y, por esto, también necesitan un gobierno lo bastante fuerte para no responder a las inevitables fuerzas políticas que defienden la intervención en los mercados para ganancia privada. El dilema político fundamental de un sistema económico es que un Estado lo suficientemente fuerte para proteger los mercados privados es lo bastante fuerte para confiscar la riqueza de sus ciudadanos.

Este problema de la producción de instituciones lo bastante fuertes para generar ciertos resultados deseables, pero que al mismo tiempo no puedan abusar de su fuerza, ha aparecido repetidas veces en la bibliografía. Según Przeworski (1991: 37), la *democracia* estable "requiere que los gobiernos sean lo bastante fuertes para gobernar efectivamente, pero lo bastante débiles para no ser capaces de gobernar en contra de intereses importantes". Para Weingast (1997), el *imperio de la ley* es otro mecanismo que sostiene gobiernos fuertes pero limitados. Según los padres fundadores de la Constitución de los Estados Unidos, *frenos y contrapesos* constituían tal mecanismo. Para Ackerman (2000), es una *división limitada de poderes* (que, como se dijo en la Introducción, es un número limitado de jugadores con veto). Weingast aplicó el mismo enfoque analítico al tema del federalismo y creó el concepto de "federalismo conservador del mercado".

El federalismo conservador del mercado agrega tres características a la definición que hace Riker del federalismo político:

1) Los gobiernos subnacionales tienen una *responsabilidad reguladora de la economía;* 2) se asegura *un mercado común* que impide que los gobiernos inferiores usen su autoridad regulatoria para levantar barreras comerciales en contra de bienes y servicios de otras unidades políticas, y *3)* los gobiernos inferiores enfrentan una *dura restricción presupuestaria,* es decir, no tienen ni capacidad de imprimir dinero ni acceso a crédito ilimitado [Weingast, 1995: 5; cursivas en el original].

La originalidad del análisis de Weingast consiste en que las condiciones del federalismo conservador del mercado se introducen implícitamente en vez de ser *derivadas* como características del federalismo. Por ello en su análisis no todos los países federales presentan o tienden hacia estas características, mientras que en otros análisis más teóricos, la competencia fiscal aumenta el costo de un rescate financiero y en consecuencia sirve como dispositivo de compromiso para el gobierno federal, y la combinación de centralización monetaria y descentralización fiscal endurece la restricción presupuestaria (véase Qian y Roland, 1998). Para Weingast, como contraste, países como Argentina, Brasil y la India, aunque son federales, no son países federales conservadores del mercado y tienen un desempeño económico bajo.

Desafortunadamente, Weingast no ha presentado todavía una lista de países que satisfagan los criterios del "federalismo conservador del mercado". La clasificación de países en esta categoría no es directa debido a que a los Estados Unidos, según el análisis de Weingast, se le califica como "conservador del mercado" sólo hasta la década de 1930, mientras que la China contemporánea, a la que Weingast considera como federalismo conservador de mercado, no es un país federal en términos estrictos. Por consiguiente, las intuiciones de Weingast no se pueden someter a prueba directamente. Sin embargo, ciertos análisis empíricos del desempeño económico de los sistemas federales ponen en duda seriamente las conclusiones de los análisis económicos (al menos los de la primera generación; Hayek, 1939; Tiebout, 1956, y Oates, 1972). En el más reciente de estos análisis empíricos, Treisman (2000b) crea un conjunto de datos que abarca 154 países y define cinco tipos diferentes de descentralización, dependiendo de las instituciones políticas que prevalecen en un país, el número de columnas en que diferentes unidades se pueden clasificar, el tamaño de las unidades de nivel inferior, y así sucesivamente. Sus conclusiones son que los países con niveles más altos de descentralización tienen niveles más altos de corrupción, y niveles más bajos de provisión de bienes públicos que indiquen "calidad del gobierno", como vacunación infantil y reducción del analfabetismo en los adultos. Saca esta conclusión: "La idea de Tiebout de que hacer disminuir el tamaño de las unidades del gobierno fortalecerá la competencia entre los gobiernos por el capital, con lo cual se estimularía una mayor eficiencia y honradez, no queda respaldada. Los países con jurisdicciones más pequeñas de primera columna suelen ser percibidos como más corruptos" (Treisman, 2000b: 1). El mismo resultado se mantiene también con otras mediciones de la descentralización: descentralización y corrupción se correlacionan positivamente en los datos de Treisman.

1.2. Las instituciones del federalismo

La definición que hace Riker del federalismo ha sido el punto de partida para el estudio de las instituciones del federalismo. Hicks (1978: 175) emplea esencialmente la definición de Riker y lleva este punto un paso más adelante en lo tocante a sus implicaciones institucionales:

> Si estamos de acuerdo en que un sistema federal tiene el doble propósito de crear una nación y conservar la identidad de sus unidades, es claramente esencial que la Constitución y las instituciones deben estar apropiadamente diseñadas para ambos propósitos. [...] La Constitución proporcionará: *1)* una Asamblea probablemente grande, representativa de todos los ciudadanos y escogida de entre las unidades (o estados), muy probablemente en proporción a sus poblaciones relativas; *2)* una Cámara de estados o Senado, considerablemente más pequeña pero que proporciona normalmente una representación estrictamente igual de todos los estados.

De modo similar, Bednar, Eskridge y Ferejohn (2001: 9) analizan el plan institucional del federalismo:

El oportunismo del gobierno nacional se restringe mejor al fragmentar el poder a nivel nacional. Al hacer que a una voluntad nacional le sea más difícil formarse y mantenerse con el tiempo, estos mecanismos tenderán a frenar a las autoridades nacionales para que no invadan la autoridad estatal, sobre todo en lo referente a temas políticos polémicos (el objetivo más tentador de engaños nacionales al acuerdo federal). La fragmentación anterior se puede lograr mediante un sistema formal de división de poderes y requerimientos extras (tales como aprobación bicameral y presentación al jefe del ejecutivo para veto) para la legislación.

También señalan la importancia de dos mecanismos adicionales: uno informal, la fragmentación del sistema de partidos,[2] y uno formal, un poder judicial independiente para controlar el oportunismo federal. Analicemos estos mecanismos uno por uno.

La mayoría de los analistas asocia el federalismo con "bicameralismo fuerte" (en la terminología de Lijphart), es decir, un sistema donde la segunda cámara tiene veto formal y no tiene la misma composición de la primera. De hecho, la mayor parte de los países federales cuenta con una segunda cámara fuerte. Lo que no es bien sabido es que la forma constitucional bicameral, que después de la adopción de la Constitución de los Estados Unidos se hizo muy frecuente en países federales, no fue la primera disposición institucional característica del federalismo. Federaciones como los Países Bajos Unidos, los Cantones Suizos y la Confederación Alemana decidían por negociación entre los representantes de los diversos estados (Tsebelis y Money, 1997: 31). Sobre la base de estas experiencias, la república confederada ideal de Montesquieu era una asociación de pequeños estados homogéneos que tomaban decisiones por unanimidad (Inman y Rubinfeld, 1997: 76), mientras que la forma de Condorcet de evitar los problemas de la periodicidad de la mayoría que él había descubierto era la toma de decisión por mayorías calificadas (Tsebelis y Money, 1997: 38).

En términos filosóficos, la concepción de Montesquieu del federalismo se basaba en las unidades pequeñas que representaban preferencias similares,

---

[2] Según Bednar, Eskridge y Ferejohn (2001), esta fragmentación es producida por el sistema electoral apropiado. Como se vio en el capítulo III, otros mecanismos (por ejemplo, la falta de voto de confianza en sistemas presidenciales) también pueden producir fragmentación.

y la unanimidad o dominio de la mayoría calificada que reducía la probabilidad de imposición de la preferencia de un estado sobre otro. Para Condorcet, el bicameralismo no tenía ninguna ventaja que no pudiera lograrse de manera más fácil y segura mediante mayorías calificadas en una cámara.[3]

Madison desarrolló su modelo de la república federal establecido en *El Federalista** (especialmente los números 10 y 51) al criticar los defectos de los artículos de la Confederación, con respecto a dos debilidades principales:

> Primero, las debilidades internas y externas de un gobierno basadas en un convenio entre varias repúblicas soberanas pequeñas; y segundo, el meollo del asunto, el peligro de tiranía de la mayoría dentro de tales estados pequeños. Estas dos líneas de argumento contradicen los dos elementos del modelo de la república confederada de Montesquieu: la solución mediante un acuerdo y la teoría de la república pequeña. Madison encuentra el remedio para tales males en la soberanía del pueblo en la gran república compuesta [Beer, 1993: 245].

El argumento de Madison contradice también al análisis de Condorcet, el cual atribuye igual peso a todas las posibles mayorías o mayorías calificadas, punto al que retornaremos en las conclusiones de este capítulo.

En consecuencia, tanto las mayorías calificadas como el bicameralismo se han empleado como bases del federalismo, pero con el tiempo el segundo remplazó a las primeras. En federaciones contemporáneas, la Unión Europea ha empleado la toma de decisiones por mayorías calificadas (o unanimidad) para garantizar las preferencias de sus miembros. De hecho, en el periodo anterior a la elección del Parlamento Europeo (1979), y antes de que recibiera poderes formales (1987), la toma de decisiones por mayoría calificada o por unanimidad en el Consejo de Ministros fue el único mecanismo que protegía los intereses de los países miembros. Desde 1987 la Unión Europea ha aplicado una combinación de bicameralismo y mayorías

---

[3] En "Lettres d'un bourgeois de New-Haven a un citoyen de Virginie" (escrito en 1787), Condorcet afirmaba: "Pero es fácil ver (y este asunto se puede demostrar rigurosamente) que en lo tocante a la veracidad de las decisiones no hay ventaja en multiplicar los cuerpos legislativos, que no conseguiríamos un medio más sencillo y seguro pidiendo una mayoría calificada en una cámara" (Condorcet, 1968, vol. 9: 76). En otras partes de esta obra, ofreció ejemplos de lo que se puede denominar problemas tipo I y tipo II del bicameralismo: si se necesita tomar una decisión por mayoría simple, ésta podría frustrarse por la falta de mayorías congruentes en dos cámaras, y si una decisión requiere una mayoría calificada, ésta se puede obtener con un número menor de votos en un sistema bicameral ("Est-il Utile de diviser une Assemblee nationale en plusieurs chambers?", en Condorcet, 1968, vol. 9: 333-363).

* Publicado en español por el FCE [E.].

calificadas (véase el capítulo XI). Como se verá en la sección 4, en los Estados Unidos se emplea una combinación similar de mayorías calificadas y bicameralismo para la toma de decisiones políticas. De hecho, probablemente sería más apropiado hablar de "multicameralismo" en vez de bicameralismo en el caso de los Estados Unidos y la Unión Europea, ya que además de las dos instituciones parlamentarias (las dos cámaras en el caso de los Estados Unidos, y el consejo y el parlamento en el caso de la Unión Europea), hay un tercer actor con poderes de veto: el presidente en los Estados Unidos y la Comisión[4] en la Unión Europea.

¿Por qué las mayorías calificadas y el bicameralismo o multicameralismo aumentan el número de jugadores con veto? Porque si consideramos la legislatura de un país como un solo jugador con veto colectivo que decide por dominio de la mayoría, entonces tanto el bicameralismo como las mayorías calificadas introducen restricciones adicionales, al especificar que algunas o todas las mayorías simples no bastan para tomar una decisión. Como resultado, algunas partes de lo que solía ser el conjunto ganador del *statu quo* ya no son válidas, y el conjunto ganador del *statu quo* se contrae.

La gráfica VI.1 ofrece la respuesta para el caso del bicameralismo. Supongamos que había seis actores en un parlamento, y por consiguiente cuatro de ellos eran necesarios para llegar a una decisión mayoritaria. Cualquier combinación de cuatro de seis jugadores bastaría para sustituir al *statu quo*. Ahora supongamos que dividimos los seis jugadores iniciales en dos grupos, el grupo L1, L2 y L3 (que representa a la cámara baja), y el grupo U1, U2 y U3 (que representa a la cámara alta). Si el requerimiento para una sustitución del *statu quo* se convierte en mayorías congruentes en las dos cámaras, algunas de las mayorías anteriores —como (L3, U1, U2, U3) en la gráfica— quedan ahora invalidadas, ya que no representan mayorías en ambas cámaras. La gráfica VI.1 muestra el conjunto ganador de un sistema bicameral con sombreado de líneas entrecruzadas y el conjunto ganador de una legislatura unicameral pero no bicameral con sombreado transversal.

Un argumento similar se puede plantear si en vez de bicameralismo introducimos mayorías calificadas. Si consideramos el caso de una mayoría calificada de cinco sextos, la gráfica VI.1 demuestra que está vacío el conjunto ganador del punto seleccionado como *statu quo*. No hay coalición que incluya cinco de los seis jugadores que esté de acuerdo con un remplazo del *statu quo*. En las secciones siguientes me concentro en cada uno de es-

---

[4] Para excepciones y un análisis más detallado, véase el capítulo XI.

FEDERALISMO, BICAMERALISMO Y MAYORÍAS CALIFICADAS   183

GRÁFICA VI.1. *Conjunto ganador de legislaturas bicamerales (por mayorías concurrentes) y unicamerales (por mayorías calificadas).*

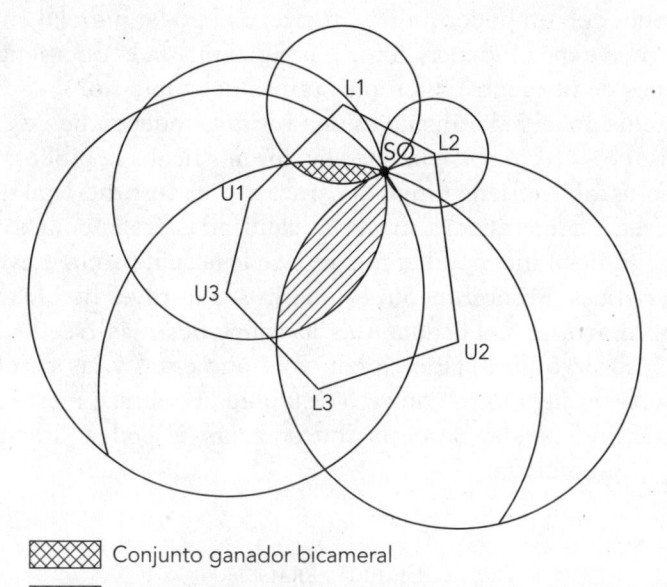

[Figura: diagrama con círculos y polígonos etiquetados L1, L2, L3, U1, U2, U3, SQ]

▨▨▨▨ Conjunto ganador bicameral
▨▨▨▨ Conjunto ganador adicional de legislatura unicameral

tos métodos de acrecentar el número de jugadores con veto: bicameralismo y mayorías calificadas.

Un mecanismo diferente que según Bednar, Eskridge y Ferejohn "hace más difícil que una voluntad nacional se forme y se mantenga con el tiempo" es la fragmentación del sistema de partidos. La idea de que un sistema de partidos fragmentado no será capaz de decidir o mantener sus decisiones puede parecer plausible, pero no es necesariamente correcta. Como se ha visto en el capítulo II, el conjunto ganador de jugadores con veto colectivos puede incluir puntos que no estén incluidos en el conjunto ganador de un jugador con veto individual. Por consiguiente, los sistemas de partidos fragmentados *pueden* producir resultados que los no fragmentados no podrían alcanzar (al tomar algunos disidentes de un partido y formar una mayoría). La fragmentación *per se* puede dificultar aún más la negociación entre diferentes facciones, pero no impide los resultados.

Finalmente, otro mecanismo que debilita al gobierno central, según Bednar, Eskridge y Ferejohn, es la existencia de un poder judicial fuerte e independiente. Como se verá en el capítulo X, hay, de hecho, una asociación entre federalismo y un poder judicial independiente; sin embargo, no está claro cuál es la dirección de la causación. ¿Es que los países federales crean constituciones con un poder judicial fuerte, o el poder judicial en países federales se vuelve más independiente e importante dado que tiene que ejercer funciones de juez entre diferentes ramas del gobierno?

En conclusión, el federalismo es una variable independiente elusiva. No parece causar los efectos beneficiosos que pronosticaba la bibliografía sobre federalismo fiscal. No tiene ninguna característica institucional única o necesaria (ya sea bicameralismo, mayorías calificadas, fragmentación de partidos o poder judicial independiente), pero se le asocia con la mayoría de estas características. Mi argumento es que ya sea a través de bicameralismo o mediante mayorías calificadas (las asociaciones más frecuentes con el tiempo), el número de jugadores con veto aumenta, y las características asociadas con los jugadores con veto (estabilidad política, inestabilidad gubernamental, independencia de las burocracias, el poder judicial, etc.) se hacen más pronunciadas.

2. El bicameralismo

Alrededor de un tercio de los parlamentos del mundo son bicamerales (Tsebelis y Money, 1997). En estas legislaturas bicamerales, varían la composición y el poder de la segunda cámara así como las reglas acerca de la manera como se llega al consenso (si es necesario). Trataré primero estos temas preliminares y después me concentraré en la toma de decisiones según un conjunto de reglas que requieren análisis especial sobre la base de la teoría de los jugadores con veto: el caso donde ambas cámaras tienen poder de veto y están compuestas por partidos débiles.

2.1. Diversidad bicameral y multicameral

El poder de la segunda cámara varía de un país a otro. A veces se requiere el consenso de la cámara alta para la adopción de legislación (Estados Unidos, Suiza, Italia), a veces no (Reino Unido, Austria). Es muy común que los países federales tengan cámaras altas con derecho de vetar legislación.

Otra característica de los países bicamerales es que la segunda cámara puede tener una estructura política similar o diferente de la primera. Las razones de las diferencias en posiciones políticas pueden ser que las dos cámaras sean elegidas por distritos electorales distintos (frecuentemente en países federales una representa a la población y la otra a los estados), o tengan sistemas electorales distintos, o puedan sencillamente tener otras reglas de toma de decisiones. Un ejemplo de reglas diferentes se encuentra en el Congreso de los Estados Unidos, con la regla de obstruccionismo del Senado (que no existe en la Cámara): como resultado de esta regla, una mayoría calificada de tres quintas partes es esencialmente necesaria para que la legislación pase por el Senado, mientras que una mayoría simple es necesaria para la Cámara. Analizaré seguidamente este caso en detalle.

Incluso si ambas cámaras tienen la misma composición partidaria, de allí no se infiere que sean eliminadas las diferencias entre ellas. Aunque sus dos cámaras eran casi idénticas en alineación política, la legislatura italiana necesitó 17 años para adoptar la legislación sobre violación *(violenza sessuale)*. Los temas principales eran si la violación es posible en el matrimonio, y si la víctima siempre debería ser la que decidiera acudir al tribunal y cuándo. Las organizaciones feministas y las mujeres en el parlamento adoptaban posiciones distintas. Como resultado, los líderes de los partidos no quisieron intervenir en la disputa, y la legislación que se presentó primero en 1977 no se adoptó sino hasta 1995-1996.[5]

Por lo tanto, las legislaturas bicamerales pueden introducir un segundo jugador con veto institucional (si la segunda cámara tiene la posibilidad de vetar legislación). Me concentraré en casos que cumplen con este requerimiento de veto. Sin embargo, sería incorrecto suponer que las segundas cámaras sin poder de veto no afectan la legislación. Tsebelis y Money (1997) han demostrado que tales cámaras pueden influir en los resultados y a veces incluso hacer abortar la legislación (como la Cámara de los Lores cuando suspende legislación justo antes de una elección, lo cual conduce a la terminación de los proyectos de ley).

Finalmente, aunque estamos hablando de bicameralismo, desde el punto de vista de este libro es fácil generalizar a cualquier número de cámaras. Por ejemplo, el sistema político estadounidense, debido a la división de poderes entre el presidente y la legislatura por un lado y el federalismo por el otro, es *de facto* un sistema tricameral (requiere el acuerdo de tres jugadores con veto institucionales en vez de dos). En el capítulo II se presentó la gráfica II.5, donde se identifica un área que contiene el conjunto ganador

---

[5] Gianfranco Pasquino, comunicado personal.

del *statu quo* del sistema tricameral estadounidense cuando un jugador con veto (el presidente) es un individuo, mientras que los otros dos (la Cámara y el Senado) son colectivos. De modo similar, una forma de aprobar legislación en la Unión Europea es mediante un acuerdo de la Comisión Europea, el Parlamento Europeo y una mayoría calificada del Consejo de Ministros, lo cual significa también que este sistema se puede interpretar como tricameral.[6] Analizaremos en el capítulo XI el sistema estadounidense según todos los conjuntos de reglas.

Si los partidos tienen cohesión, el diferente número de cámaras puede elevar el número de jugadores con veto, pero esto no complica el análisis. Por ejemplo, si la misma mayoría controla las cámaras alta y baja y si los partidos tienen los mismos puntos ideales, entonces serían raros los casos como el desacuerdo entre las cámaras italianas, y podríamos realizar el análisis en una sola cámara (técnicamente, los jugadores con veto de la segunda cámara son absorbidos). Si una cierta coalición domina la mayoría en una cámara pero no en la segunda, entonces los partidos requeridos para formar una mayoría en la segunda cámara tienen que ser considerados jugadores adicionales con veto. Por ejemplo, como se vio en el capítulo III, si en Japón y en Alemania la coalición gobernante no controla al Senado, tenemos que agregar como jugador con veto al partido requerido para dominar la cámara alta, ya sea que el nuevo jugador con veto sea incluido en la coalición de gobierno (como en Japón en 1999) o no (como en Alemania).[7]

El caso que no hemos incluido en esta discusión preliminar es el caso donde ambas cámaras tienen poder de veto sobre la legislación, y los partidos en cada una de ellas no tienen cohesión, como suele suceder en los regímenes presidenciales bicamerales.

2.2. Bicameralismo fuerte con partidos débiles

Cuando los partidos son débiles, las mayorías que prevalecen en cada cámara no son estables y las mayorías de las dos cámaras no necesariamente coinciden. Como resultado, un análisis de jugadores con veto no puede

---

[6] Braeuninger (2001) estudia sistemas multicamerales teóricamente, aunque su ejemplo aborda la toma de decisiones en organizaciones internacionales.

[7] Una pregunta anterior para el caso de Alemania es si los partidos son cohesivos para ser considerados como poseedores de las mismas preferencias en ambas cámaras. La investigación empírica más reciente sobre el tema (König, 2001) indica que sí lo son.

avanzar más allá del nivel institucional. La gráfica VI.2 ofrece una representación visual del argumento en un caso muy sencillo.

Las dos cámaras (la baja representada por L, la alta con U) están trazadas en dos dimensiones y están localizadas lejos una de otra. Cualquier coalición en cada una de ellas es posible y deciden por mayorías congruentes. En las condiciones anteriores, primero hay algunos puntos que la regla de toma de decisiones actual no puede derrotar. Éstos se denominan el *núcleo bicameral*. Estos puntos están a lo largo del segmento LU. De hecho, cualquier punto por encima o por debajo de este segmento puede ser derrotado por su proyección sobre la línea LU. Por añadidura, cualquier punto a la izquierda de L puede ser derrotado por L1, L3 y una unanimidad de U.

GRÁFICA VI.2. *Núcleo bicameral y conjunto ganador bicameral de SQ.*

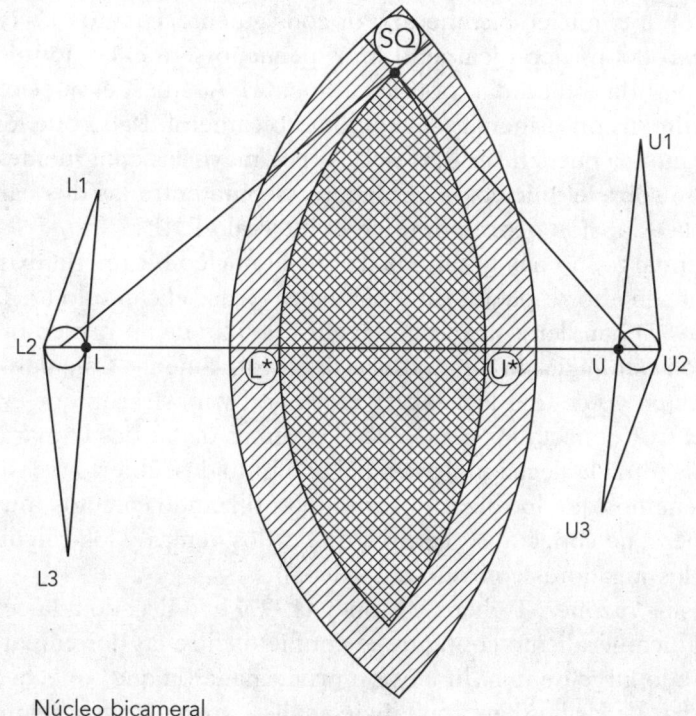

LU Núcleo bicameral

Conjunto ganador calculado con jugadores con veto individuales

Conjunto ganador aproximado a través de jugadores con veto colectivos

De modo similar, cualquier punto a la derecha de U puede ser derrotado por U1, U3 y una unanimidad de L.[8]

La gráfica VI.2 también presenta el conjunto ganador de una posición particular del *statu quo*. El cálculo ha sido realizado de dos maneras distintas: exactamente y por aproximación. Para el cálculo exacto, considero a los miembros individuales de las dos cámaras e identifico todos los puntos que dictan mayorías congruentes en las dos cámaras (área de sombreado cruzado). Para el cálculo aproximado, uso el concepto de jugadores con veto colectivos que se presentó en el capítulo II, trazo los círculos ganadores de cada cámara y considero su intersección. Esta intersección está sombreada con líneas transversales en la gráfica, y tal como se esperaba contiene el conjunto ganador del *statu quo*.

La ubicación del núcleo bicameral en este análisis es importante ya que, como se vio en la gráfica VI.2, el conjunto ganador bicameral está dividido a la mitad por el núcleo bicameral. Por consiguiente, cuanto más cerca esté el *statu quo* del núcleo bicameral, más pequeño será el conjunto ganador del *statu quo* (la estabilidad política aumenta). Además, el núcleo bicameral es la dimensión principal del conflicto bicameral. Dado que los puntos fuera del núcleo pueden ser derrotados (por mayorías congruentes) por su proyección sobre el núcleo, la verdadera disputa entre las dos cámaras se reduce a la adopción de un punto en el intervalo L*U*.

Sin embargo, no hay garantías de que el núcleo bicameral exista particularmente en altos espacios dimensionales (véase el capítulo II). Tsebelis y Money (1997) han demostrado que incluso a falta de un núcleo bicameral, la situación estratégica no se modifica significativamente. Calcularon el *conjunto descubierto* de una legislatura bicameral y mostraron que ésta incluye la línea que conecta los centros de las yemas de las dos cámaras. Por lo tanto, si se toma la decisión dentro del conjunto descubierto (véase el capítulo II), tenemos que localizar el resultado utilizando cálculos muy similares (la línea que conecta los centros de las dos yemas y los cálculos ganadores de los jugadores con veto colectivos).

Por estas razones, Tsebelis y Money (1997) han llegado a la conclusión de que el bicameralismo configura el conflicto entre las dos cámaras en un conflicto a lo largo de una dimensión privilegiada (la que conecta el centro de las yemas de las dos cámaras). Este análisis no es significativamente distinto del que se propone en este libro. Como resultado de cualquiera de esos

---

[8] Véase Hammond y Miller (1987) y Tsebelis y Money (1997). Estos últimos trazaron erróneamente el núcleo más allá de los puntos L y U.

FEDERALISMO, BICAMERALISMO Y MAYORÍAS CALIFICADAS 189

dos análisis, cuanto mayor sea la distancia entre los centros de las yemas de las dos cámaras, más pequeña será la posibilidad de cambio. Otra conclusión que los dos análisis comparten es que el resultado de negociaciones bicamerales depende de cuál cámara controla la agenda. En el análisis de este libro, identifico el resultado cuando una de las dos cámaras controla el proceso de establecimiento de agenda. Sin embargo, como Tsebelis y Money lo demuestran, el establecimiento de agenda real es un proceso significativamente más complicado. La gráfica VI.3 muestra este tema.

Como se analizó en los capítulos I y II, cuando una cámara hace una propuesta a la otra, ambas seleccionan el punto más cercano a ellas desde el conjunto ganador del *statu quo*, de modo que el resultado será L1 (o alrededor de L1) en el caso en que la cámara baja sea la establecedora de agenda, y U1 (o alrededor de U1) si la cámara alta controla la agenda. Sin embargo, la mayoría de los países ha adoptado reglas más complicadas, que se conocen como el sistema de *navette*.[9] El proyecto de ley viene y va de una cámara a la otra, ya sea hasta que se llegue a un acuerdo[10] o hasta que se aplique alguna regla para detenerlo. En algunos países el desacuerdo pro-

GRÁFICA VI.3. *Resultados bicamerales según el sistema de* navette *(alternando ofertas).*

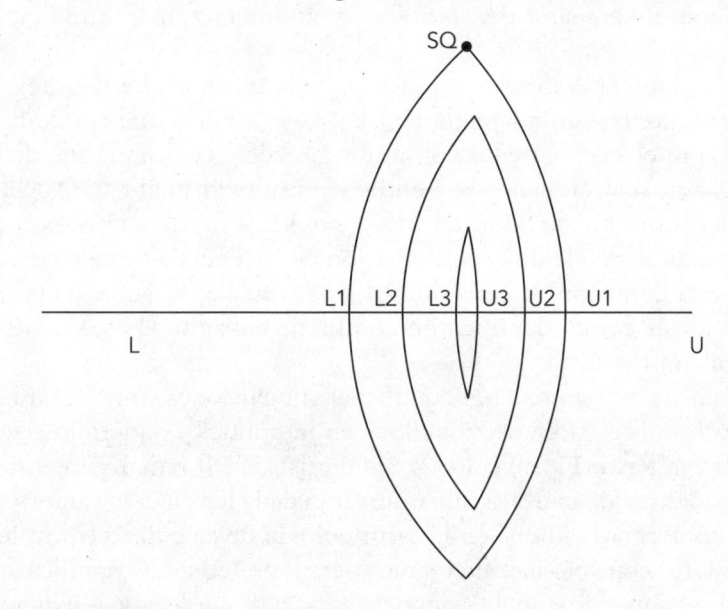

[9] *Navette* es la palabra francesa para lanzadera.
[10] Esto significa que el número de vueltas es potencialmente infinito (Italia).

longado conduce a la formación de un comité de consulta (Francia, Japón, Suiza); en otros la cámara baja toma la decisión final (el Reino Unido, Austria); en otros hay una sesión conjunta de las dos cámaras (Australia).

Tsebelis y Money han identificado las diferencias en resultados políticos que estos arreglos institucionales producen. En su análisis usan la "impaciencia" de cada cámara como variable adicional. Su argumento es que cada cámara prefiere un acuerdo inmediato que un aplazamiento, y con el fin de llegar a este acuerdo inmediato está dispuesta a hacer ciertas concesiones. Las implicaciones cualitativas de este argumento se presentan en la gráfica VI.3. Si la cámara baja hace una oferta y existe la posibilidad de una nueva vuelta de negociaciones después de un rechazo, se pasará al punto L2 con el fin de evitar este rechazo. Si hay dos vueltas de negociación, se acercará aún más al punto L3, y así sucesivamente. De modo similar, si la cámara alta controla la agenda y hay una vuelta de negociaciones en caso de desacuerdo, propondrá U2 con el fin de evitar estas negociaciones; si hay dos vueltas de negociaciones, propondrá U3 con el fin de evitarlas, y así sucesivamente. Obsérvese que la teoría de los jugadores con veto que se presenta en este libro incluye todos estos embrollos institucionales, ya que he adoptado el argumento más general de que el resultado está localizado dentro del conjunto ganador del *statu quo,* y no intento afinar aún más el pronóstico.

Puedo plantear el mismo argumento en lo tocante a los comités de consulta. Éstos controlan la agenda legislativa y deciden cuál resultado particular de la intersección de los conjuntos ganadores del *statu quo* de las dos cámaras será seleccionado. Por ende, el resultado final estará localizado dentro del conjunto ganador del *statu quo* de las dos cámaras, pero la ubicación exacta depende de la composición de la regla de toma de decisiones dentro de la comisión de consulta. El lector puede consultar la gráfica II.9 para visualizar cómo identifica un comité de consulta el área dentro de la cual hará su propuesta.

El análisis en esta sección conduce a conclusiones similares a las de la bibliografía sobre "gobierno dividido" en la política estadounidense. Algunos investigadores (Fiorina, 1992; Sundquist, 1988) han argumentado que el gobierno dividido causará una reducción de la legislación importante. De hecho, "gobierno dividido" en la terminología de este libro equivale a "los dos jugadores con veto institucionales tienen preferencias significativamente distintas". Sin embargo, la evidencia empírica que recabó Mayhew (1991) acerca de leyes importantes no corrobora la expectativa del gobierno dividido.[11] Mayhew encuentra que no hay diferencia importante en la legislación entre periodos de gobierno unificado y dividido. Ha habido una respuesta empírica importante al descubrimiento de Mayhew. Sarah Binder (1999) ha planteado el argumento de que el conjunto de datos de Mayhew requiere de un "denominador", es decir, el conjunto de leyes potenciales (algunas de las cuales no fueron aprobadas debido a un gobierno dividido o alguna otra razón). Ella identifica el conjunto de tales leyes, y cuando mide la proporción de la legislación real acerca de este conjunto de leyes, descubre que la distancia entre los dos partidos así como la distancia entre las dos cámaras tiene un impacto negativo importante sobre el porcentaje de proyectos de ley que se aprueban. En consecuencia, los resultados más recientes que aparecen en la bibliografía estadounidense concuerdan con el argumento de este libro. Hay, sin embargo, una respuesta más teórica al argumento de Mayhew que se concentra en la pregunta de los requerimientos de la mayoría calificada en la toma de decisiones en los Estados Unidos. Abordo este argumento en la última sección, después de un análisis detallado de las mayorías calificadas.

3. Las mayorías calificadas

Como se vio en la primera parte de este capítulo, Condorcet, quien no creía en las virtudes del bicameralismo, arguyó que las mayorías calificadas pueden producir los mismos resultados de estabilidad política, de una manera más sencilla y segura. En esta sección muestro dos puntos: primero, cómo pueden las mayorías calificadas aumentar la estabilidad política; segundo, qué tan omnipresentes son, aunque no estén especificadas explícitamente por instituciones formales.

3.1. *Núcleo y conjunto ganador de mayorías calificadas*

Consideremos un jugador con veto colectivo compuesto de siete miembros (1 ... 7) que decide por una mayoría calificada de cinco séptimos. Podemos dividir varias veces a ese jugador con veto colectivo de la siguiente manera: podemos seleccionar cualquier grupo de cinco puntos (por ejemplo, 1 ... 5),

[11] Para un debate sobre el conjunto de datos de Mayhew, véanse Kelly (1993) y Mayhew (1993).

y entonces considerar el pentágono compuesto de estos cinco puntos (el núcleo de unanimidad de estos cinco jugadores). Cualquier punto incluido en este pentágono no puede ser derrotado por un acuerdo unánime de los cinco jugadores seleccionados. Si ahora seleccionamos todas las combinaciones posibles de cinco jugadores, y hay una intersección de sus núcleos de unanimidad, esto significa que cualquier punto en esta área no puede ser derrotado por cualquier mayoría calificada de cinco séptimos.

La gráfica VI.4 presenta una intersección de los núcleos de unanimidad de todas las combinaciones posibles de cinco miembros. Esta área es un núcleo de cinco séptimos del jugador con veto colectivo. Tal núcleo no siempre existe y, sin embargo, es más frecuente que un núcleo bicameral. De hecho, Greenberg (1979) ha demostrado que tal núcleo siempre existe si $q > \frac{n}{(n+1)}$, donde q es la mayoría requerida y n es la dimensionalidad del espacio político. El lector puede comprobar que el núcleo de unanimidad siempre existe (independientemente del número de dimensiones políticas),[12] y que para los puntos ubicados fuera del núcleo el conjunto ganador del *statu quo* no está vacío. Además, si el núcleo de mayoría calificada existe y el *statu quo* se aproxima a este núcleo, el conjunto ganador del *statu quo* se contrae (la estabilidad política aumenta).

Una comparación del núcleo bicameral y el núcleo de mayoría calificada en un espacio de n dimensiones (suponiendo que ambos existan) indica

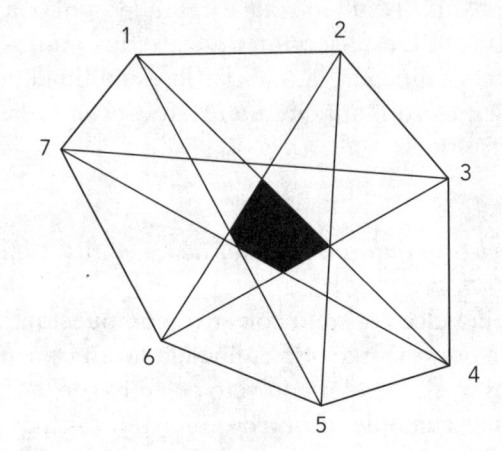

GRÁFICA VI.4. *Núcleo de mayoría 5/7 en dos dimensiones.*

[12] Esto es así porque n puntos se definen cuando mucho como espacio (n − 1)-dimensional.

que el primero es un solo objeto dimensional, mientras que el segundo está en general en n dimensiones. Y la forma del núcleo afecta el tamaño del conjunto ganador del *statu quo* (es decir, la estabilidad política). Para que el conjunto ganador del *statu quo* sea pequeño en un sistema bicameral, el *statu quo* tiene que estar ubicado cerca de una línea particular, mientras que en el dominio de la mayoría calificada, si el *statu quo* está localizado centralmente dentro del jugador con veto colectivo, su conjunto ganador será pequeño o estará vacío (la estabilidad política será alta).

¿Cuál es la implicación de esta diferencia? La toma de decisiones por mayoría calificada suele dejar intactas las políticas centralmente ubicadas o producir cambios incrementales en ellas. La toma de decisiones por mayoría calificada también suele producir resultados ubicados centralmente en el espacio. Los resultados del bicameralismo son más aleatorios. Si los dos jugadores con veto colectivos en un sistema bicameral están localizados en lados opuestos de un tema político, el bicameralismo concentrará la discusión en el tema. Si, no obstante, los dos jugadores con veto están de acuerdo en la cuestión política, no es probable que el tema sea discutido de manera satisfactoria entre las dos cámaras.[13] Veamos algunos ejemplos: si una cámara de una legislatura bicameral es más rural y la otra más urbana, es probable que se discutan los temas de subsidios a la agricultura y que se identifique un acuerdo sobre ese asunto. Si, pese a ello, ambas cámaras representan a jugadores con veto más jóvenes o más viejos, es probable que no se dé una discusión del tema de la seguridad social ni un compromiso que tome en cuenta ambos lados del tema.

3.2. Omnipresencia de las mayorías calificadas

Como se vio en el capítulo II, los requerimientos de mayoría calificada imponen restricciones adicionales al conjunto ganador del *statu quo*. Primero, conforme aumenta el umbral de la mayoría calificada requerida, se contrae el conjunto ganador del *statu quo*. Segundo, a diferencia del conjunto ganador de mayoría del *statu quo*, que casi nunca está vacío, el conjunto ganador de la mayoría calificada del *statu quo* sí puede estar vacío. Tercero, y de extrema importancia para el tamaño del conjunto ganador de mayoría ca-

---

[13] Se puede analizar o no dentro de cada una de las cámaras, dependiendo de la actitud de la mayoría.

lificada del *statu quo* (si éste existe), es la cohesión-q del jugador colectivo. Como estipula la conjetura II.3, la estabilidad política disminuye cuando la cohesión-q aumenta.

Cuando los jugadores con veto colectivos deciden por mayorías calificadas, todos estos cálculos son necesarios para identificar la ubicación del conjunto ganador del *statu quo*. Por ejemplo, éste es el caso del Consejo de Ministros de la Unión Europea, de la anulación de un veto presidencial en los Estados Unidos, de las legislaturas con respecto a temas constitucionales en Bélgica, o de la cámara baja al decidir en contra de la cámara alta en países como Chile y Argentina (véase Tsebelis y Money, 1997, para ejemplos). Sin embargo, lo que no resulta obvio es que los cálculos de mayoría calificada son necesarios en algunos casos adicionales, que denomino "equivalentes de mayoría calificada". Examinemos a continuación tales casos.

1. Requerimientos no constitucionales. Aunque el Senado de los Estados Unidos formalmente toma decisiones por una mayoría simple de sus miembros, la posibilidad de obstruccionismo modifica la situación considerablemente. Si un senador decide obstruir un proyecto de ley, la única posibilidad de terminar con sus esfuerzos es un voto de tres quintas partes del Senado para terminar el debate y votar el proyecto de ley. En consecuencia, 40 senadores pueden evitar que la legislación sea adoptada. Para que cualquier legislación importante sea aprobada en el Senado de los Estados Unidos, se requiere el acuerdo del partido minoritario (a menos que este partido no controle 40 escaños). En otras palabras, el Senado de los Estados Unidos es una institución de mayoría calificada (o supermayoritaria). En la sección 4 veremos la diferencia que ocasiona este "detalle".

2. Mayorías absolutas y abstenciones. A veces los requerimientos constitucionales especifican una mayoría absoluta de los miembros de un parlamento. Por ejemplo, el parlamento europeo tiene que proponer enmiendas por la mayoría absoluta de sus miembros en ciertos procedimientos legislativos. De modo similar, la Asamblea Nacional francesa puede pasar un voto de no confianza solamente por la mayoría absoluta de sus miembros. El canciller alemán es investido (y remplazado) por una mayoría absoluta de los miembros del Bundestag. Si todos los miembros de un cuerpo legislativo están presentes y nadie se abstiene, entonces coinciden una mayoría absoluta y una mayoría simple. Si, en cambio, hay miembros ausentes, o si ciertos miembros se abstienen de votar, entonces el requerimiento de mayoría absoluta es equivalente a una mayoría calificada de los miembros que participan en la votación.

Consideremos que el porcentaje de abstenciones y/o votantes ausentes es A. Del resto, el porcentaje de votos "sí" es Y (y el restante (1 − Y) es votos "no"). Un requerimiento de mayoría absoluta se traduce en $Y > \frac{(1/2)}{(1-A)}$. Esta relación da los siguientes "equivalentes de umbral de mayoría calificada". Si 50% de los miembros del Parlamento Europeo (MPE) están ausentes o se abstienen, se requiere una unanimidad de votos para que pase una enmienda. Si 33.3% no votan o se abstienen, el umbral requerido es de tres cuartos; si el porcentaje de no participantes es de 25%, una decisión requiere dos terceras partes de los MPE presentes, y así sucesivamente. Dado que el requerimiento de mayoría absoluta se traduce en un umbral equivalente de mayoría calificada en el Parlamento Europeo, esta institución es a veces incapaz de presentar enmiendas deseables para una mayoría (absoluta) de sus miembros.

3. *Aliados renuentes o indeseables y mayorías simples.* En la Cuarta República francesa (1946-1958), en plena Guerra Fría, los gobiernos a menudo declaraban que si el Partido Comunista votaba a su favor no contarían los votos comunistas. Una declaración de tal naturaleza equivale a quitar un porcentaje de votos de la columna "sí" y pasarlos a la de abstenciones. De nueva cuenta, estamos hablando de equivalencia de mayoría calificada. Alternativamente, algunos partidos pueden negarse a respaldar cualquier gobierno posible. Se los conoce en la bibliografía como "partidos antisistema". La mera existencia de tales partidos transforma los requerimientos de mayoría simple a mayorías calificadas. Considérese, por ejemplo, que un partido nuevo se agrega a los cinco partidos de un parlamento (como los que aparecen en la gráfica II.4), y que todos los partidos tienen el mismo número de votos (16.67%). Si el partido nuevo es un partido antisistema, es decir, un partido que vota "no" en cada tema, entonces con el fin de obtener una mayoría se necesita que cuatro de los seis partidos voten "sí". Dado que el partido seis siempre vota no, entonces la mayoría requerida es, de hecho, de cuatro quintas partes (cuatro de los cinco partidos restantes tienen que estar de acuerdo). Aplicando el razonamiento que presenté anteriormente en la sección 3 del capítulo II, esta equivalencia de mayoría calificada hace disminuir sustancialmente el conjunto ganador del *statu quo*. De hecho, puede hacer imposible la realización de cualquier cambio en el *statu quo*.

Para modelar algunas legislaturas latinoamericanas se requeriría esta técnica de equivalencia de mayoría calificada. La razón es que los partidos latinoamericanos son más disciplinados que los partidos estadounidenses, pero menos que los europeos; en consecuencia, las coaliciones ganadoras pueden excluir a algunos partidos (que nunca respaldan las políticas predominantes), pero usan a diferentes partidos cada vez. En este caso el analista tiene que excluir los partidos que nunca participan en mayorías y ver cómo los partidos restantes forman mayorías calificadas con el fin de lograr los votos requeridos.

Finalmente, como escribí en el capítulo IV, los gobiernos de tamaño exagerado en sistemas parlamentarios pueden ser modelados como equivalentes de mayoría calificada, debido a que todos los miembros de la coalición son necesarios para que se adopte una medida política particular. Los argumentos de Strom (2000) que se presentaron en el capítulo IV conducirían a tal enfoque. Sin embargo, como el lector verificará por los resultados empíricos de los capítulos VII y VIII, no necesité tal enfoque para modelar los efectos de las coaliciones de tamaño exagerado sobre los temas de horas de trabajo, condiciones laborales y estructuras presupuestarias que estos capítulos cubren.

Para concluir, aunque las mayorías calificadas *per se* no son un requerimiento muy frecuente, el conocimiento de la realidad política predominante dentro de diferentes instituciones o sistemas políticos puede llevar al investigador a usar equivalentes de mayoría calificada, y al análisis que se presentó en la sección 3 del capítulo II para modelar instituciones o sistemas políticos particulares. Cuandoquiera que las mayorías calificadas se convierten en la regla de la toma de decisiones (ya sea *de facto* o *de jure),* la estabilidad política deberá aumentar y cabría esperar que los resultados convergieran hacia el centro de la ubicación de los jugadores con veto.

4. Bicameralismo y mayorías calificadas combinadas

¿Qué sucede si el bicameralismo se combina con mayorías calificadas, de tal modo que una de las cámaras decida por mayoría simple y la otra decida por mayoría calificada? Éste es el caso del Congreso de los Estados Unidos si consideramos que el Senado tiene que tomar decisiones importantes por medio de mayorías a prueba de obstruccionismo (que permiten que una mayoría de tres quintos invoque limitación del tiempo de debate en el parlamento y termine con el obstruccionismo). Es también el caso de instituciones de la Unión Europea, debido a que el Consejo de Ministros decide por mayoría calificada o por unanimidad.

FEDERALISMO, BICAMERALISMO Y MAYORÍAS CALIFICADAS 197

La gráfica VI.5 repite la gráfica VI.2 con la única diferencia de que las decisiones en la cámara alta se toman por unanimidad. Hay dos consecuencias principales de estos requerimientos más estrictos de toma de decisiones en una de las dos cámaras, como se muestra en la gráfica VI.5. Primero, la estabilidad política aumenta (dado que el conjunto ganador del *statu quo* se contrae). Segundo, los resultados se desplazan en favor de la cámara menos flexible (ya sea que consideremos todo el conjunto ganador del *statu quo* o simplemente la intersección con el núcleo o la línea que conecta los centros de las dos yemas [en la gráfica, de todos los puntos L*U*, sólo uno sobrevive]). Emplearé estos resultados para analizar la toma de decisiones en la Unión Europea en el capítulo XI.

Si restringimos el análisis anterior a una dimensión, entonces el núcleo del sistema bicameral se expande, y es más difícil desequilibrar el *statu quo*.

GRÁFICA VI.5. *Conjunto ganador por mayorías concurrentes y por unanimidad en la cámara alta.*

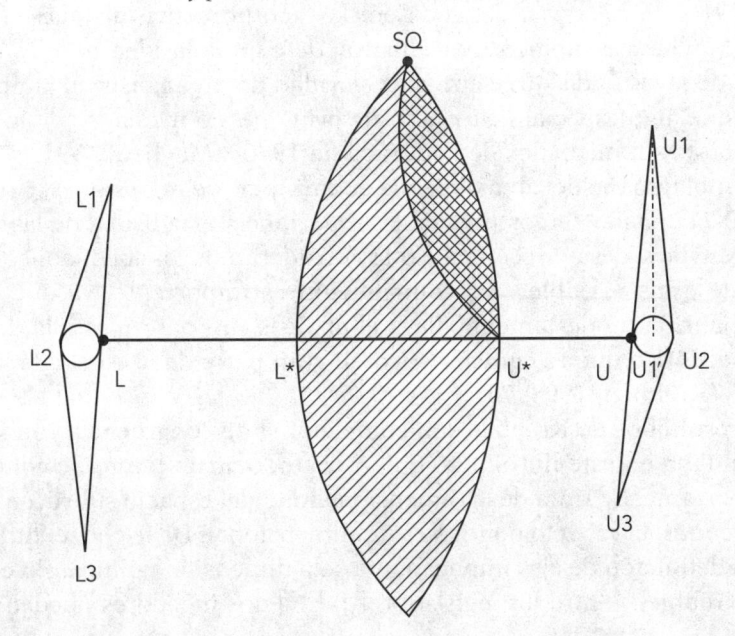

▨ Conjunto ganador por mayorías concurrentes
▩ Conjunto ganador por mayoría en la cámara baja y por unanimidad en la cámara alta

En particular, los puntos entre U1' (la proyección de U1 sobre el núcleo bicameral) y U2 que podrían ser modificados bajo mayorías congruentes son ahora invulnerables bajo la nueva regla de toma de decisiones.

Ésta es la esencia del argumento que Keith Krehbiel (1998) presenta en su importante libro *Pivotal Politics*[14] Al nivel teórico, Krehbiel muestra un modelo unidimensional e identifica los "ejes" de la toma de decisiones (los senadores 40 y 60 para obstruccionismo y los senadores 34 y 66 para anular por votación un veto presidencial) y el tamaño del área incluida entre los dos ejes (el "área de rejilla").[15] Empíricamente, Krehbiel identifica cambios en "el tamaño del área de rejilla" al usar el tamaño de las mayorías en cada cámara y calcular si el respaldo para el presidente aumenta (en cuyo caso el área de rejilla se contrae) o disminuye (en cuyo caso la rejilla aumenta).

Krehbiel usa su modelo para reevaluar los resultados de Mayhew, quien identificó dos variables principales que son responsables por la productividad legislativa: una era la primera mitad de un periodo presidencial (Mayhew, 1991: 176-177), y la segunda era la "actitud activista", que en palabras de Mayhew es una forma "elusiva" de captar la idea de que "en la creación de leyes nada surge con más claridad de un análisis en la posguerra sino que algo especial ocurriría desde principios o mediados de la década de 1960 hasta mediados de la década de 1970" (Mayhew, 1991: 177). Al introducir el tamaño del área de rejilla en una serie de regresiones, Krehbiel (1998: 70-71) puede demostrar que la importancia estadística de las variables de Mayhew desaparece incluso si consideramos las mediciones alternativas de estas variables. La contribución es importante, ya que como Krehbiel afirma modestamente, lleva el análisis "un paso más allá del respaldo anecdótico que es característico de gran parte de la teoría de la presidencia" (Krehbiel, 1998: 75).

Los resultados de Krehbiel son completamente congruentes con la teoría presentada en este libro, pero quiero introducir un punto de comparación importante. Se trata de la dimensionalidad del espacio subyacente. En *Pivotal Politics,* el espacio político es unidimensional. De hecho, el título del libro y la definición de ejes implican una sola dimensión política. En el análisis de Krehbiel, "entre los legisladores n [...] dos jugadores pueden tener

---

[14] Véase también Jones (2001a, 2001b).

[15] Para un modelo unidimensional similar que tome en cuenta las posiciones de los comités véase Smith (1988). Para modelos multidimensionales véanse Shepsle (1979), y Shepsle y Weingast (1981, 1984, 1987).

condición de eje único debido a procedimientos supermayoritarios" (Krehbiel, 1998: 23).

Sin embargo, si agregamos una sola dimensión política al modelo subyacente, los ejes se multiplican. En la gráfica VI.6 A presento el argumento unidimensional, según el cual los ejes siempre son los mismos sin importar en dónde esté el *statu quo* y sin importar en dónde esté la propuesta alternativa (véase también Krehbiel, 1998: 23). En la gráfica VI.6 B agrego una segunda dimensión, y considero únicamente tres votantes, A, B y C. Dependiendo de dónde esté la propuesta alternativa, el jugador eje puede cambiar (la propuesta PA convierte en eje al votante A, la propuesta PB hace eje a B, mientras que la propuesta PC hace eje a C). Podemos aumentar las di-

GRÁFICA VI.6. *(A) Votantes ejes en una dimensión: dos obstruccionistas (F,F) y dos ejes con veto (V,V). (B) Casi cualquier votante puede ser pivotal en múltiples dimensiones.*

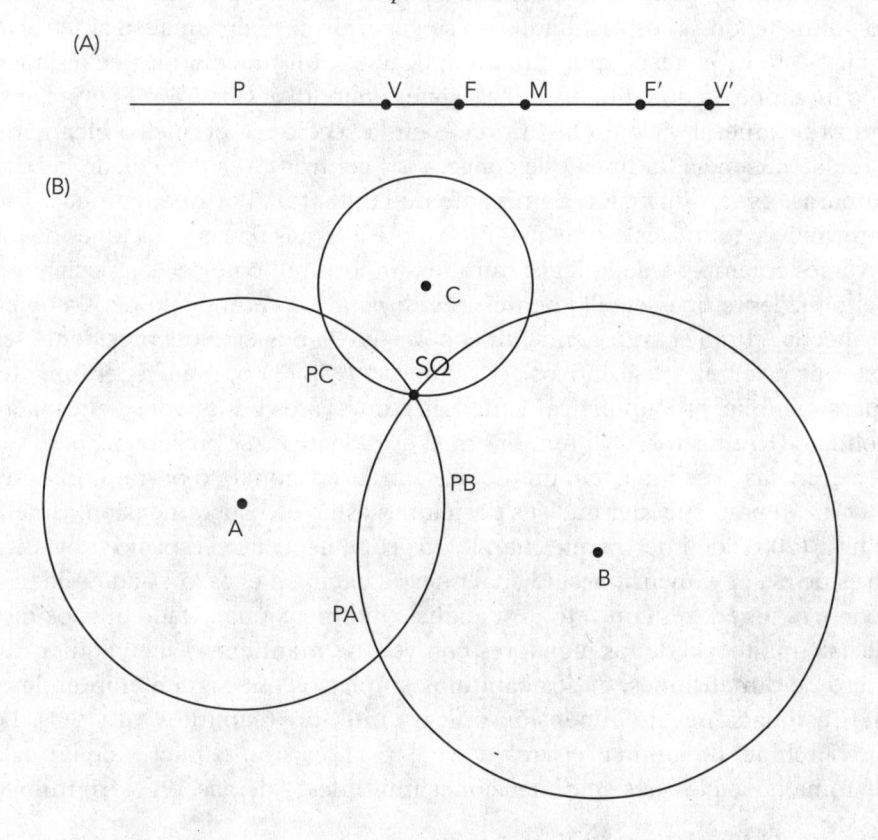

mensiones y las alternativas del *statu quo*, y casi cualquiera de un grupo particular de jugadores se convertirá en eje ("pivotal"). Este cambio fundamental de una dimensión a más de una no es una característica insólita de los modelos de votación o del modelo de Krehbiel. En realidad, hablando acerca de todos los modelos espaciales, Krehbiel (1988) ha argumentado: "El simple hecho de expandir la dimensionalidad del espacio de elección de uno a dos tiene consecuencias profundamente desestabilizadoras". Es una característica distintiva de la teoría de los jugadores con veto el que sus conclusiones se mantengan en cualquier número de dimensiones, ya sea que los jugadores con veto sean individuales o colectivos. El precio que pago por esta capacidad de generalizar es que a veces tengo que restringir las propuestas en el conjunto descubierto, y mis conclusiones se mantienen sólo como aproximaciones (capítulo II).

¿Es razonable expandir la dimensionalidad del espacio? Teóricamente, la respuesta es un claro "sí", pues no podemos confiar en modelos de una sola dimensión si sus resultados no se generalizan. Pero incluso si teóricamente éste es el caso, ¿por qué no apegarse a un modelo más económico que funcione en una dimensión? Después de todo, el Congreso es una legislatura bicameral y, como he afirmado en la sección 2, el núcleo bicameral o, en su ausencia, la línea que conecta los centros de las yemas de las dos cámaras, es la dimensión dominante de conflicto. ¿Por qué, entonces, no informar de todo a esta dimensión? Porque además de las posiciones de los diversos miembros de la legislatura, es importante conocer las posiciones del presidente que sencillamente se *presuponen* en el modelo de Krehbiel. De hecho, como él argumenta, presupone que la posición del presidente "es exterior a los ejes legislativos" (Krehbiel, 1998: 73) o, más generalmente, "para cambiar probabilísticamente entre intervalos designados del espacio político" (Krehbiel, 1998: núm. 27). Si el presidente no se presupone, pero sus preferencias sí se incluyen, un modelo unidimensional no bastará, pues no hay razón para suponer que sus posiciones estén en esta dimensión. Braeuninger (2001) demuestra que cuando un grupo negocia, el espacio subyacente es de n − 1 dimensiones, lo cual querría decir, en el caso estadounidense (con tres jugadores con veto), un análisis bidimensional. Dado que los modelos en la teoría de los jugadores con veto se mantienen en cualquier número de dimensiones, en los capítulos empíricos que siguen emprenderemos estimaciones de dimensión única y múltiple (capítulos VII y VIII). Lo que Krehbiel denomina "el área de rejilla" no es sino el núcleo de la regla de toma de decisiones en dimensiones múltiples. Además, en el capítulo XI examinaré otro caso de tres jugadores con veto institucionales (la Unión Europea) y presentaré modelos multidimensionales del núcleo de procedimientos muy complicados.

Para resumir mi argumento, es verdad que el gobierno de los Estados Unidos no es meramente unido o dividido como varios investigadores han afirmado, sino que también es supermayoritario, debido a que una legislación importante no puede ser aprobada sin quitar los obstáculos obstruccionistas en el Senado, y la mayor parte del tiempo el partido minoritario controla los 40 escaños requeridos. Esto significa que el gobierno dividido está incorporado dentro de las instituciones estadounidenses, no debido al requerimiento de que los tres jugadores con veto estén de acuerdo en un cambio particular del *statu quo*, sino debido a la regla de obstruccionismo que esencialmente impide que una legislación partidista sea aprobada en el Senado. La contribución de Krehbiel (1998) consistió en señalar la importancia de los procedimientos supermayoritarios con el fin de entender la política estadounidense. Empleo el término "supermayoritario" en vez de "pivotal" debido a que el segundo presupone una sola dimensión que no se puede dar por sentada. Sus resultados empíricos son un primer paso importante, pero tienen que ser duplicados sobre la base de modelos multidimensionales.

5. Conclusiones

El federalismo ha sido objeto de estudio en ciencias políticas y en la bibliografía sobre economía. La expectativa era que la descentralización condujera a decisiones más apropiadas para las personas de las cuales se ocupaban. La evidencia empírica no corrobora esta expectativa.

Estudié las instituciones de federalismo, y descubrí que dos reglas particulares así como sus combinaciones son usadas más a menudo en países federales: bicameralismo y mayorías calificadas. Cada uno de estos procedimientos así como su combinación aumenta el número de jugadores con veto, y en consecuencia acrecienta la estabilidad política. La expectativa es que el federalismo no sólo aumentará la estabilidad política sino que tendrá consecuencias estructurales asociadas con múltiples jugadores con veto: independencia de las burocracias y del poder judicial, inestabilidad del gobierno, etc. Por supuesto, es posible que el federalismo tenga también consecuencias independientes. Por ejemplo, puede acrecentar la independencia del poder judicial no sólo porque el número de jugadores con veto aumenta sino también porque a los jueces se les pide que ejerzan sus funciones entre diferentes niveles de gobierno. Examinamos tales efectos en los capítulos empíricos correspondientes.

Aunque las instituciones bicamerales y de mayoría calificada acrecientan el número de jugadores con veto, hay una diferencia importante entre las dos: las instituciones bicamerales funcionan bien sólo si la dimensión subyacente de conflicto es captada por los centros de las yemas de las dos cámaras; las mayorías calificadas suelen mantener los resultados localizados centralmente en el jugador con veto colectivo.

Los cuatro capítulos de la segunda parte cubren fenómenos centrales en el análisis político comparativo: tipos de regímenes, interacciones entre legislativo y ejecutivo, referéndums, federalismo, bicameralismo y mayorías calificadas. He vuelto a examinar los conocimientos existentes y a veces he terminado por estar de acuerdo con la bibliografía (democracia y competencia), en ocasiones en conflicto (el poder del gobierno es un derivado del poder de establecimiento de agenda que no es equivalente a la duración del gobierno), a veces he explicado desacuerdos existentes (papel del establecimiento de agenda en diferentes tipos de referéndums) y en otras ocasiones he presentado una diferente perspectiva de análisis (instituciones de federalismo en vez de federalismo fiscal, composición del gobierno en lugar del análisis de sistema de partidos). En vez de revisar los resultados aquí, me concentro en diferentes mecanismos para aumentar o disminuir el número o las distancias de los jugadores con veto que se examinaron en esta segunda parte.

En la primera parte considero dados el número y las distancias de los jugadores con veto y analizo sus implicaciones sobre la estabilidad política. En la segunda parte estudio diferentes configuraciones institucionales y sus efectos sobre la constelación de jugadores con veto de una política. Aunque está claro que las posiciones políticas de los jugadores con veto afectan la estabilidad política ya sea debido a la absorción (algunos jugadores con veto no afectan los resultados políticos) o debido a las distancias ideológicas de los jugadores con veto (si ellos convergen, la estabilidad política disminuye), hay una fuente adicional de variación que he discutido en cada capítulo pero que quiero resaltar como parte de las conclusiones. Las estipulaciones institucionales específicas no siempre tienen el mismo resultado sobre los jugadores con veto. La misma institución puede agregar o quitar jugadores con veto, o puede mantener igual el número de éstos pero alterar sus distancias, lo cual afectaría la estabilidad política.

En la segunda parte he dejado en claro algunos de estos puntos. Por ejemplo, los referéndums siempre agregan un jugador con veto (el votante medio "como si"), pero según sus reglas de establecimiento de agenda, pueden eliminar los ya existentes. De hecho, cuando el mismo jugador controla tanto la cuestión como la activación de un referéndum, los jugadores con veto existentes quedan eliminados. He demostrado que en referéndums de jugador con veto la posición del *statu quo* deja de tener importancia y el establecedor de agenda puede obtener un resultado en el conjunto ganador del votante medio "como si". Vimos también que en referéndum de iniciativa popular, los diferentes grupos establecedores de agenda potenciales se concentrarán en atraer una mayoría del público y pasarán por alto a los jugadores con veto existentes.

Se pueden plantear argumentos similares acerca del bicameralismo: la segunda cámara puede tener o no tener jugadores con veto. Por ejemplo, el Bundesrat alemán tiene poderes de veto sobre toda legislación que tenga consecuencias para el federalismo, pero no en otras leyes. En lo tocante a las mayorías calificadas, diferentes temas pueden requerir de umbrales distintos.

En sistemas presidenciales, el presidente suele tener el poder de vetar legislación, pero típicamente hay estipulaciones para que la legislatura pueda anular por votación un veto presidencial. Según el grado en que tales medidas se puedan lograr, las condiciones de anular por votación un veto presidencial reducen la estabilidad política, ya que proporcionan un mecanismo según el cual el *statu quo* puede ser modificado a pesar de las objeciones del presidente.

Pero la estipulación institucional más complicada (desde la perspectiva de un jugador con veto) es la de los decretos ejecutivos. Esta institución habitualmente sustrae jugadores con veto, pero también puede agregar jugadores con veto, o dejar igual el número de éstos pero alterar sus distancias ideológicas. El caso arquetípico de decretos ejecutivos sería un decreto presidencial en un sistema presidencial (Carey y Shugart, 1998): el presidente evita a los otros jugadores con veto y toma la decisión final en un área de su jurisdicción.

Sin embargo, hay casos en que los decretos gubernamentales agregan un jugador con veto a los ya existentes: en Francia, por ejemplo, el presidente de la república es parte del gobierno (de hecho, lo preside), de modo que él tiene que estar de acuerdo con un decreto gubernamental. En lo tocante a la legislación ordinaria él no tiene veto; así lo pueden dejar de lado los partidos en el gobierno (suponiendo diferentes mayorías presidenciales y parlamentarias). Examino este punto más a fondo en el análisis empírico del capítulo VII.

Finalmente, los decretos del gobierno pueden conservar el mismo número de jugadores con veto pero alterar sus distancias. Por ejemplo, el gobierno italiano se ha valido a menudo de decretos ejecutivos como una forma para pasar de lado al parlamento (Kreppel, 1997). Sin embargo, como argumentamos en el capítulo IV, los miembros del partido en el gobierno son jugadores con veto en un sistema multipartidista. ¿Por qué resulta más fácil aprobar decretos gubernamentales que legislación parlamentaria si los jugadores con veto son los mismos? La respuesta de Kreppel es que los miembros del gobierno están ideológicamente más cerca unos de otros que el liderazgo de los partidos correspondientes, de modo que la estabilidad política disminuye. La proposición I.4 y la gráfica I.6 plantean el mismo punto en el caso más general: si los tomadores de decisiones están más cerca unos de otros, el conjunto ganador del *statu quo* se expande, y la estabilidad política se reduce.

En resumen, aunque la teoría de los jugadores con veto a veces llega a conclusiones similares a las de la bibliografía existente, también hay muchos desacuerdos. Pero algo todavía más importante: no hay una manera directa de traducir instituciones existentes al número y las distancias de los jugadores con veto. Algunas instituciones tienen efectos similares (el federalismo aumenta el número de jugadores con veto), mientras que otras alteran su impacto sobre los jugadores con veto sobre la base de estipulaciones institucionales específicas (quién controla la agenda sobre referéndums, decretos ejecutivos). Aún más importante, sin embargo, es el hecho de que los resultados del análisis de los jugadores con veto dependen de las posiciones ideológicas de los jugadores con veto: algunos de ellos pueden ser absorbidos; incluso si no son absorbidos, pueden converger o divergir, y esto tendrá implicaciones serias para la estabilidad política. Hasta la importancia del establecimiento de agenda depende de las posiciones de los jugadores con veto y de la ubicación del establecedor de agenda.

Deseo concluir subrayando la consistencia del enfoque de los jugadores con veto. En cada capítulo he analizado distintos enfoques influyentes: tipos de régimen, sistemas de partidos, influencia ministerial, predominio ejecutivo, federalismo fiscal, políticas ejes, para mencionar sólo unos cuantos. Cada uno se basa en diversas suposiciones y conduce a conclusiones pertinentes al tema de estudio para el cual fue desarrollado. Como contraste, la teoría de los jugadores con veto se basa en el mismo conjunto de principios desarrollados en la primera parte, y son estos principios los que nos han conducido a todos los acuerdos o desacuerdos con la bibliografía, así como a todas las declaraciones condicionales o calificadas sobre instituciones.

TERCERA PARTE

EFECTOS POLÍTICOS SOBRE LOS JUGADORES CON VETO

En el conjunto básico de proposiciones que se presentaron en la primera parte se emplea la estabilidad política como la variable dependiente y el número, y las distancias entre los jugadores con veto como las variables independientes. He explicado por qué el aumentar el número de jugadores con veto (proposición I.1) y el núcleo de unanimidad de ellos (proposición I.4) conduce a una estabilidad política mayor. En la tercera parte se someterán a prueba estas proposiciones.

Hay varias dificultades con las pruebas empíricas de estas expectativas. Provienen de la relación entre políticas legislativas y resultados legislativos. El meollo del problema es que los legisladores tienen que diseñar políticas mientras tienen preferencias por los resultados. Por ejemplo, cuando los legisladores de un país aprueban leyes sobre un tema específico, dan una serie de pasos: definen el problema que quieren resolver; definen las condiciones en las cuales ocurre, o el conjunto específico de condiciones que abordarán; definen los medios mediante los cuales intervendrán, y el grado en el cual usarán estos medios. En consecuencia, ocurre una serie de resultados relacionados con la política. En la legislación sobre el desempleo, por ejemplo, algunas personas, pero no otras, reciben compensación por desempleo; personas seleccionadas reciben atención a la salud incluso si no están empleadas; un cierto número de administradores y personal médico se emplean para abordar estos problemas, y cuestan un cierto monto del presupuesto. Todos estos resultados son los temas que preocupan a los legisladores y que tenían en mente al planear la política de desempleo.

Sin embargo, es posible que algunos de estos resultados no fueran previstos cuando se presentó la legislación: la definición de desempleo pudo haber sido tan global que permitiera a una serie de ciudadanos privados pedir ayuda por desempleo mientras tenían algún tipo de trabajo, o puede haber proporcionado exactamente la misma cantidad de cobertura de atención a la salud de modo que aumentara el número de médicos requeridos, o el desempleo puede haber aumentado por razones que la legislatura no consideró. Como resultado de cualquiera de estas condiciones, el número de personal administrativo o médico, o la cantidad de dinero requerido pueden ser diferentes de las preferencias de los legisladores. En este caso los legisladores pueden decidir presentar nuevas leyes que enmienden las políticas especificadas en el pasado, de modo que se aproximen más a los resultados preferidos.

Ésta puede ser una descripción más o menos exacta de la forma como funciona la creación de medidas políticas, pero ¿cómo vamos a introducir en este cuadro la variable de la estabilidad política en la cual estamos interesados? ¿Nos vamos a concentrar en el acto de legislar y ver si las leyes nuevas difieren de las anteriores, incluso si los resultados no difieren, o vamos a concentrarnos en los resultados ya sean éstos producidos por la legislación o por choques exógenos? Supongamos que la legislatura cambia la definición de desempleo, pero como el desempleo es tan bajo causa poca diferencia sobre el presupuesto. ¿Es éste un cambio político importante o insignificante? O bien, supongamos que el desempleo aumenta mientras la legislación ha seguido siendo exactamente la misma. ¿Es ésta una indicación de estabilidad política o de cambio político?[1]

En los dos capítulos que siguen me valgo de ambas interpretaciones y trato de concentrarme en cada una mientras controlo la otra. Por añadidura, los dos capítulos presentan modelos con un número diferente de dimensiones del espacio político implícito. En el capítulo VII la variable dependiente se sigue bien sobre el eje de política izquierda-derecha, de modo que estimo un solo modelo dimensional. En el capítulo VII la variable dependiente es claramente multidimensional, de modo que el modelo que analizo emplea múltiples dimensiones.

El capítulo VII trata de la legislación de horas de trabajo y condiciones laborales y se concentra en cambios legislativos importantes. Definiré cómo evaluar tales piezas importantes de legislación y usaré una medición comprobable intersubjetivamente para esta definición. He dado todos los pasos posibles para definir los cambios políticos importantes en tal forma que sean convincentes, y que ciertamente no dependerán de mis propias mediciones. Sin embargo, por muy exacta que sea esta medición, es completamente imposible que dos países comiencen desde y lleguen a los mismos resultados políticos, uno aplicando cambios políticos importantes y el otro no. Por ejemplo, si un país introduce una ley completa sobre compensación por desempleo, es probable que cualquier observador considere esto

[1] La distinción que aquí establezco entre legislación y resultados es muy similar a la que se hace en la bibliografía de economía política entre instrumentos y resultados (Alt y Crystal, 1985).

como una pieza importante de legislación. Por otro lado, si un segundo país introduce varias docenas de piezas legislativas para diferentes grupos sociales (por ejemplo, trabajadores agrícolas, sector público, industria) sobre aspectos específicos de beneficios por desempleo (por ejemplo, duración, condiciones, montos, atención a la salud), es probable que ninguna de estas piezas de legislación sea considerada importante. El capítulo VII está expuesto a las críticas de los "resultados" de la estabilidad política. Aunque demuestro que un país produce legislación importante y el otro no, es posible que no haya diferencias en los resultados durante un largo tiempo.

En el capítulo VIII se abordan las políticas macroeconómicas y me concentro en los resultados, sin abordar directamente el tema de la política. Los resultados considerados son déficits presupuestarios, inflación y la composición del presupuesto de diferentes países. No hay manera de ver directamente si estos resultados se debían al diseño gubernamental directo o a otras políticas gubernamentales (como el deterioro del comercio provocado por razones de política exterior), o a sucesos aleatorios (cambios en el desempleo debidos a condiciones internacionales), o a una sensibilidad alta o baja del presupuesto a factores externos. Trataré de controlar algunas de estas posibilidades introduciendo variables falsas *(dummy)* para cada país, de modo que cualquiera que sea la razón política que afecte la estructura presupuestaria esté controlada. Sin embargo, este análisis no es inmune a una objeción "de políticas" al argumento de la estabilidad política. Es posible que estos cambios en resultados presupuestarios no reflejen cambios en políticas del presupuesto.

Las variables independientes para los dos capítulos que describen las constelaciones de jugadores con veto con el tiempo en diferentes países se pueden encontrar en *http://www.polisci.ucla.edu/tsebelis/*. Los resultados que estos dos capítulos producen son congruentes. La estabilidad política aumenta con el número de jugadores con veto, o, más exactamente, conforme aumenta el alcance de una coalición de gobierno (el tamaño del núcleo de unanimidad en una sola dimensión, y alguna medición distinta pero equivalente en dimensiones múltiples). Además, cuando sólo se somete a prueba la distancia ideológica, no solamente es negativo el coeficiente, sino que los términos de error son heteroesquedásticos (exactamente como lo indica la gráfica I.7). De hecho, me valí de un procedimiento especial de estimación (regresión heteroesquedástica multiplicativa) para estimar simultáneamente ambos efectos. Cuando se introducen múltiples variables independientes, los resultados adicionales son que la estabilidad política disminuye conforme aumenta la alternación (distancia ideológica) de cada coalición respecto a sus predecesoras. Por último, someto a prueba si diferentes tipos de gobierno (coaliciones de ganancia mínima, minoritario y de tamaño exagerado) afectan la estabilidad política, y encuentro que aunque los gobiernos minoritarios y las coaliciones de tamaño exagerado tienen mayor y menor estabilidad política, respectivamente, que las coaliciones de ganancia mínima, estos resultados son pequeños y estadísticamente insignificantes. Así, el argumento que se plantea en esta sección es que la estabilidad política, ya sea medida en resultados o en políticas, depende de los jugadores con veto, como se especificó en la primera parte.

VII. LA LEGISLACIÓN

La teoría que presento en este libro pronostica que la estabilidad política (definida como la imposibilidad de un cambio importante del *statu quo*) será el resultado de muchos jugadores con veto, en particular si hay diferencias ideológicas importantes entre ellos. Este capítulo apunta a la realización de una prueba directa y en escala nacional de la producción de leyes importantes en función del número y las distancias ideológicas de los jugadores con veto. Sometí a prueba estos pronósticos usando un nuevo conjunto de datos de "leyes importantes" sobre temas de "horario de trabajo y condiciones laborales".[1]

El horario de trabajo y las condiciones laborales constituyen una dimensión legislativa difícilmente correlacionada con la dimensión izquierda-derecha que predomina en los sistemas de partido en toda Europa. Por lo tanto, podemos encontrar las posiciones ideológicas de diferentes partidos sobre la dimensión izquierda-derecha y usarlas como sustitutos de las posiciones ideológicas de los partidos con respecto al horario de trabajo y las condiciones laborales. Según este enfoque, dado que todos los partidos están ubicados a lo largo de la misma dimensión, podemos identificar a los dos partidos más extremosos de una coalición, y todos los demás serán "absorbidos" puesto que están ubicados dentro del núcleo de los más extremosos (proposición 1.2). El resultado de este análisis es que la distancia ideológica de los dos partidos más extremosos en una coalición gubernamental, el *alcance* de esta coalición, será nuestra variable independiente. El número de leyes importantes será una función declinante del alcance. Además, el número de leyes importantes será una función creciente de la distancia entre el gobierno actual y el anterior, de aquí en adelante llamada *alternación*. La razón es que cada gobierno tratará de modificar las políticas con las que esté en desacuerdo, y cuanto mayor sea la distancia entre los dos gobiernos, mayor será la distancia entre los jugadores con veto actuales y el *statu quo*. Asimismo, cuanto más tiempo permanezca en el poder un gobierno, más propenso será a producir legislación importante en el área bajo

---

[1] Agradezco a Herbert Doering haberme proporcionado este conjunto de datos.

consideración (Tsebelis, 1995a: 105). Por último, como expliqué en la gráfica I.7, la varianza del número de leyes importantes será más elevada cuando el alcance de una coalición sea pequeño, y más bajo cuando su alcance sea grande.

El capítulo está organizado en tres secciones. La primera presenta el conjunto de datos que combina información acerca de leyes importantes en diferentes países de Europa Occidental con datos acerca de coaliciones gubernamentales (composición de gobiernos y posiciones ideológicas de los partidos en una escala izquierda-derecha). En esta parte, explico cómo se generaron las diferentes variables usadas en este estudio. La segunda parte presenta los resultados en que los gobiernos son la unidad del análisis, y muestra que las expectativas del modelo quedan corroboradas. La tercera parte emplea países como la unidad de análisis y señala la relación inversa entre legislación importante y piezas de legislación general que se producen en un país.

1. Los datos

Con el fin de probar si el número y la distancia ideológica de los jugadores con veto afecta la producción de leyes importantes, he desarrollado un conjunto de datos combinando información sobre legislación importante (leyes y decretos) sobre "horario de trabajo y condiciones laborales" en 16 países de Europa Occidental para el periodo 1981-1991, con datos sobre gobiernos de coalición para los mismos países y el mismo periodo.[2] En esta sección, explico lo que se incluyó en los conjuntos de datos originales, así como las manipulaciones adicionales necesarias para la construcción de variables específicas.

1.1. La legislación importante

Doering y su equipo identificaron el número de leyes importantes para todos los países de Europa Occidental en el área de legislación laboral (legislación sobre "horario de trabajo y condiciones laborales") para el periodo 1981-1991. Con ese propósito utilizaron la base de datos computarizada NATLEX, compilada por la Organización Internacional de Trabajo (OIT), domiciliada en Ginebra. Aunque la base de datos fue creada a comienzos de

---

[2] Recibí de Herbert Doering los datos sobre legislación importante y de Paul Warwick la información sobre coaliciones de gobierno.

la década de 1970, no llegó a completarse hasta comienzos de la década de 1980. En consecuencia, el comienzo de la base de datos que analicé es del 1º de enero de 1981. Esta base de datos ha sido indexada por tema de estudio, de modo que podemos identificar todas las leyes sometidas a votación y todos los decretos emitidos sobre cualquier tema específico en todos los países europeos. Aunque esta base de datos es de gran utilidad para identificar cualquier tema de legislación laboral, y Doering y su equipo la han usado para generar números confiables de piezas de legislación en diferentes áreas, no nos proporciona indicación alguna de legislación "importante": la variable dependiente para someter a prueba la teoría de los jugadores con veto.

El paso siguiente habría sido identificar algún sustituto de su importancia. Tal sustituto no debía ser el tamaño ni la extensión de la legislación, ya que una ley se puede redactar para enumerar áreas de aplicabilidad (en cuyo caso la extensión está correlacionada con la importancia) o áreas de excepción (en cuyo caso la extensión está correlacionada negativamente con la importancia). Los otros sustitutos que se me ocurren son el monto del presupuesto necesario para la implantación, o el número de personas afectadas por su promulgación. Ambos criterios indicarían que no sería importante un proyecto de ley sobre eutanasia o sobre matrimonios entre personas del mismo sexo. Este breve análisis indica que los criterios para la selección de leyes "importantes" tienen un considerable ingrediente de subjetividad que puede socavar los resultados de cualquier análisis para un lector que no comparta las mismas normas de selección.

Al enfrentar este problema, Doering tuvo la brillante idea de usar la *Encyclopedia of Labor Law* para generar la variable "leyes importantes". La enciclopedia, compilada por Roger Blanpain, fue escrita para abogados laboralistas de un país europeo que desearan ejercer la abogacía en otro. Según la introducción, "*National Legislation* intenta hacer asequibles a suscriptores y usuarios de la Enciclopedia las estipulaciones pertinentes de los *actos más importantes* del Parlamento, *decretos* gubernamentales, grandes *acuerdos colectivos* nacionales e interindustriales y otras fuentes legales, donde abarcan un país en su totalidad" (Blanpain, suppl. 194, julio de 1997: subsección 5; cursivas en el original). Cada país es cubierto por una monografía de 150 a 250 páginas escrita por un profesor de derecho o un juez para explicar a los lectores la legislación importante en el área. Las monografías tienen una pauta común que facilita la identificación del tema de estudio. La enciclopedia no incluye a Noruega ni a Islandia. Las leyes que estaban en la intersección de ambas fuentes (NATLEX y la *Encyclopedia*) se consideran "importantes", mientras que las leyes que sólo existen en la base de datos NATLEX se consideran no importantes.

La *Encyclopedia* de Blanpain ofrece una prueba de validación para la base de datos NATLEX, ya que para el periodo 1981-1991 todas las leyes mencionadas en Blanpain estaban incluidas en NATLEX. Esto no se hizo así para el periodo anterior a 1981, el cual, a su vez, valida el punto de corte para el estudio.[3] Las fechas de promulgación de las leyes importantes de cada país fueron comparadas con las fechas en que los gobiernos estuvieron en el poder, de modo que las leyes fueron atribuidas a los gobiernos que las patrocinaron.

1.2. Los gobiernos

El conjunto de datos sobre gobiernos incluye las fechas de comienzo y terminación de los gobiernos en los 16 países del estudio (Alemania, Austria, Bélgica, Dinamarca, España, Finlandia, Francia, Grecia, Holanda, Irlanda, Italia, Luxemburgo, Portugal, Reino Unido, Suecia y Suiza).[4] Las fechas de comienzo y terminación del estudio (1º de enero de 1981 a 31 de diciembre de 1991) se consideraron como las fechas del comienzo y terminación del gobierno en funciones en esa fecha.[5] Sobre la base de estas fechas de principio y terminación de diferentes gobiernos, calculé la duración en años de cada uno de ellos.

En el conjunto de datos sobre gobiernos se emplearon métodos convencionales para explicar el comienzo y el final de los gobiernos. Warwick (1994: 27) es explícito acerca de qué constituye el principio: "Un gobierno típicamente comienza cuando es nombrado por un jefe de Estado". En cuanto al final, Warwick adopta los criterios que proponen Browne, Glei-

---

[3] Estas elecciones se describen con más detalle, junto con preguntas legales que surgen cuando la descripción de una ley es inadecuada o insuficiente, en la enciclopedia de Blanpain, en un ensayo escrito con Georgios Trantas. Trantas, un jurista, siguió la idea de Doering e identificó de hecho la intersección de Blanpain y NATLEX (Scholtz y Trantas, 1995).

[4] Este capítulo sigue muy de cerca a Tsebelis (1999). Una de las diferencias importantes es que ahora he incluido a Suiza. La adición es importante porque Suiza es la única de estas naciones que no es un sistema parlamentario, y en consecuencia su inclusión sin una diferencia sustantiva en resultados hace más creíble el argumento de los jugadores con veto.

[5] Como resultado, los gobiernos de cada país al comienzo y al final del periodo han sido truncados (duraron más de lo indicado, y pueden haber producido legislación fuera del periodo de este estudio).

ber y Mashoba (1984: 7).[6] Sin embargo, la variable que importa para la teoría de los jugadores con veto es la composición partidaria del gobierno. Por lo tanto, dos gobiernos sucesivos con composición idéntica deben contar como un solo gobierno, incluso si están separados por una elección, la cual modifica la proporción de diferentes partidos en el parlamento.[7] La razón es que la variable que entra en un análisis de jugadores con veto no es la fortaleza relativa de diferentes partidos en el gobierno o en el parlamento, sino el hecho de que cada uno de ellos necesita estar de acuerdo para que la legislación sea aprobada.

Con el fin de operacionalizar el argumento anterior, desarrollé un conjunto de datos de gobiernos "combinados", en el cual gobiernos sucesivos con la misma composición fueron considerados un solo gobierno, estuviesen separados por una renuncia y/o por una elección. Obviamente, la combinación afecta los valores de duración y número de leyes producidas por un gobierno. Para tomar en cuenta este cambio, agregué el número de leyes producidas por diferentes gobiernos para ser combinadas y di el crédito al gobierno resultante con su número total de leyes. La duración se volvió a calcular como la suma de la duración de gobiernos consecutivos (esto excluye posibles gobiernos interinos y periodos en que un gobierno que ha renunciado espera ser remplazado, lo que se debería haber incluido si yo hubiese recalculado sobre la base de las nuevas fechas de principio y terminación). Como resultado de la combinación, el número de casos en el conjunto de datos disminuyó a 59.[8]

La diferencia entre el conjunto de datos gubernamentales combinados que se usa en este estudio y el método tradicional de contar gobiernos que-

---

[6] Según Browne, Gleiber y Mashoda (1984): "Un gobierno se considera terminado cuando: *1)* se llevan a cabo elecciones parlamentarias, *2)* cambia el jefe de gobierno, *3)* cambia la composición de partido del gobierno o *4)* el gobierno presenta su renuncia, la cual es aceptada por el jefe del Estado" (Warwick, 1994: 28). En este cuarto punto Warwick presenta una variación y cuenta como terminación hasta las renuncias que no son aceptadas subsecuentemente por el jefe del Estado.

[7] Para un argumento similar acerca de gobiernos italianos que se sucedieron uno a otro mientras la composición del partido (y en ocasiones la persona) es la misma, véase Di Palma (1977: 31).

[8] Habrían sido 58, pero cuento dos veces al gobierno francés durante el periodo de cohabitación de 1986-1988: considero sólo a los dos partidos participantes como jugadores con veto en lo tocante a la legislación, pero agrego al presidente cuando considero un decreto gubernamental que ellos emitieron. Esto produce un cálculo conservador porque omito todas las veces en que un gobierno de cohabitación no produce decretos como resultado de sus divisiones ideológicas.

dará claro en los dos casos siguientes. Primero, en Grecia el gobierno socialista (PASOK) llegó al poder en 1981 y, según el conjunto de datos, generó cuatro leyes importantes en el área de "horario de trabajo y condiciones laborales". En 1985 los socialistas fueron reelegidos y el nuevo gobierno generó dos leyes importantes adicionales. Según el conjunto de datos gubernamentales combinados, los dos gobiernos PASOK cuentan como uno que no terminó su programa legislativo en el primer periodo y continuó cambiando el marco legislativo de los gobiernos de derecha de 1974 a 1981 durante su segundo periodo.

El segundo ejemplo proviene de Francia. Después de que François Mitterrand fue elegido presidente de la república en 1981, nombró a Pierre Maurois como primer ministro de un gobierno de coalición que incluía a socialistas y comunistas. Ese gobierno generó cuatro leyes importantes en el área en estudio. En 1983 un segundo gobierno de Maurois con la misma composición de partidos sustituyó al existente gobierno de Maurois. Este segundo gobierno permaneció un año en el poder, hasta que los comunistas abandonaron la coalición debido a las políticas de austeridad que Mitterrand estaba a punto de imponer con el fin de permanecer en el sistema monetario europeo. El segundo gobierno de Maurois no generó ninguna ley nueva sobre "horario de trabajo y condiciones laborales". En mi conjunto de datos los dos gobiernos cuentan como uno: en un periodo de tres años la coalición entre socialistas y comunistas generó cuatro leyes importantes. Está implícito en mi descripción que el segundo gobierno de Maurois no generó ninguna ley porque el primero había completado su labor en esta área.[9]

1.3. La ideología

El conjunto de datos sobre el gobierno incluyó también la composición de diferentes gobiernos (los partidos participantes en coaliciones gubernamentales), a los cuales agregué las posiciones del presidente de Portugal, Francia y el Bundesrat en Alemania y sus "puntuaciones ideológicas" sobre la base de tres índices. El primero provino de la obra de Warwick (1994) *Government Survival in Western European Parliamentary Democracies* (él amplió el conjunto de datos recabados por Browne, Gleiber y Mashoba [1984], quienes habían ampliado el conjunto de datos recabados por Dodd,

---

[9] Todos los cálculos de este artículo fueron duplicados con la forma tradicional de contar gobiernos y produjeron los mismos resultados cualitativos.

1976). Este índice fue generado a partir de 40 medidas diferentes desarrolladas por expertos, manifiestos de partidos y fuentes de encuestas. En los gobiernos incluidos en este conjunto de datos, el índice fluctuó desde un nivel bajo de −6 (izquierda) a un alto de 5 (derecha).

El segundo índice lo proporcionaron Castles y Mair (1984) en "Left-Right Political Scales: Some 'Expert' Judgments". Estas puntuaciones ideológicas fueron generadas a partir del cuestionario de una encuesta de más de 115 politólogos de Europa Occidental y los Estados Unidos (Castles y Mair, 1984: 75). El cuestionario pedía a cada respondente que colocara todos los partidos que poseyeran escaños en su legislatura nacional sobre el espectro político izquierda-derecha que fluctúa desde 0 (ultraizquierda) a 10 (ultraderecha), con 2.5 representando a la izquierda moderada, 5 al centro y 7.5 a la derecha moderada. Castles y Mair presentan los resultados de los países que tuvieron al menos tres respondientes. La puntuación ideológica reportada para cada partido fue el promedio de respuestas disponibles. Dada la escala de diez puntos, el rango potencial de respuestas era (0, 10). Sin embargo, de los partidos analizados aquí, la puntuación baja fue 1.4, recibida por el Partido Comunista de Francia, y la alta fue de 8.2 para el Partido Gaullista.

El tercer índice proviene de la variable de primera dimensión de Laver y Hunt (1992): "aumentar servicios o reducir impuestos". Los respondientes fueron politólogos profesionales (Laver y Hunt, 1992: 38-41, 122). A cada respondente se le pidió ubicar las posiciones políticas de los líderes de partido y de los votantes para cada partido en su país sobre el espectro izquierda-derecha. Además de los partidos que ganaron escaños en la elección más reciente, se les pidió a los respondientes que evaluaran cada partido que obtuviera al menos 1% del voto nacional, así como cualquier partido regional importante. La escala que adoptaron Laver y Hunt fue de 20 puntos (para acomodar el hecho de que los países incluidos en su estudio contenían hasta 14 partidos para colocar en la escala). En la primera dimensión (impuestos o servicios públicos) los respondientes asignaron a cada partido una puntuación que iba de 1 ("promover la elevación de impuestos para acrecentar los servicios públicos") a 20 ("promover la reducción de servicios públicos para reducir impuestos"). Entre los casos incluidos en el conjunto de datos, la variable (primera dimensión) de Laver-Hunt fluctuó desde un mínimo de 2.1 hasta un máximo de 17.4.

Suiza no estuvo incluida en ninguno de los conjuntos de datos. Ha tenido un gobierno que incluía cuatro partidos principales (socialistas, liberales, democratacristianos y el Partido de los Agricultores) durante el periodo en estudio. Utilicé los datos generados para un gobierno similar en Finlandia (cuatro jugadores con veto incluyendo el Partido Social Democrático, los partidos Rural y Agrario y el Partido Popular) para los datos faltantes sobre Suiza. Sobre la base del conjunto de datos de Sani y Sartori (1983) del que informan Laver y Schofield (1990: 255, 265), el gobierno suizo tenía una gama de 3.4 (= 7.1 − 4.7) en su escala, mientras que la finlandesa era mayor[10] de 2.4 (= 6.3 − 3.9).

Laver y Hunt incluyeron los 15 países restantes en su estudio. Warwick no clasificó los partidos de la Quinta República francesa y Grecia. Por añadidura, algunos partidos gobernantes en Irlanda, Italia, España y Suecia no fueron registrados. Castles y Mair no incluyeron Luxemburgo, Portugal ni Grecia.

Sobre la base de cada una de estas mediciones de ideología, logré construir nuevas variables que representan el "rango" de cada gobierno según el índice, así como la "alternación" de un gobierno al siguiente. La variable del rango fue creada tomando el valor absoluto de la distancia entre los partidos más extremosos de una coalición. Estos dos partidos solían ser (pero no siempre) los mismos para diferentes índices. Sin embargo, las correlaciones entre las variables del rango calculadas sobre la base de los casos cubiertos por los tres índices fueron muy altas.[11]

La variable de alternación fue calculada descubriendo la posición de rango medio de cada gobierno, y tomando las diferencias entre dos gobiernos sucesivos.[12] Dado que esta medición fue calculada usando el gobierno anterior, necesité información sobre el gobierno anterior al que estaba en el poder en 1981. De nueva cuenta, los tres diferentes índices produjeron valores muy correlacionados de alternación para los casos que los tres índices cubrían.[13]

---

[10] Sani y Sartori no informan de la posición de todos los partidos incluidos en el gobierno francés, de modo que no podría hacer el cálculo exacto.

[11] Las correlaciones entre cualquier pareja de estos índices fueron superiores a 0.8.

[12] La fórmula que usé fue la siguiente: (maxgovt1 + mingovt1) − (maxgovt2 + mingovt2), donde max- y min-govt1 son las puntuaciones ideológicas del gobierno anterior, y max- y min-govt2 son las puntuaciones ideológicas del gobierno "actual".

[13] Las correlaciones entre cualquier par de estos índices también eran superiores a 0.8.

1.4. Las nuevas variables de "rango" y de "alternación"

Estas tres variables de rango y alternación cubrían distintos países y se calcularon sobre la base de diferentes preguntas, que eran pertinentes para la división izquierda-derecha. Con el fin de conservar el tamaño de mi conjunto de datos, así como para usar toda la información asequible, construí nuevas mediciones de rango y alternación, con base en los valores de *todos* los índices disponibles. Para lograr esto, estandaricé cada uno de los índices y entonces tomé el promedio de las puntuaciones estandarizadas que estaban disponibles para cada gobierno. Para lograr la estandarización, usé únicamente los valores de las variables para los países cubiertos por los tres índices. Este procedimiento se aplicó separadamente sobre las tres variables de rango y alternación, lo cual dio lugar a tres variables de rango estandarizadas y tres variables de alternación estandarizadas. Las variables promedio de rango y alternación usaron toda la información disponible de la siguiente manera: en el caso de que los tres indicadores existieran, el promedio se calculó sobre la base de las tres; para los países con dos índices, únicamente el promedio se calculó sobre la base de los dos índices estandarizados; en los casos cubiertos por un solo análisis (Grecia), usé esa puntuación estandarizada. En las regresiones apliqué el valor absoluto de la alternación calculada antes, ya que no hay diferencia si un gobierno de izquierda es sustituido por un gobierno de derecha, o viceversa.

2. Jugadores con veto y legislación importante

En esta sección someto a prueba los pronósticos que se hicieron en la introducción de este capítulo. Veremos si el rango afecta negativamente el número de leyes importantes mientras que al mismo tiempo produce una relación heteroesquedástica. Construyo la variable *rango* (distancia ideológica normalizada promedio de asociados extremos de una coalición de gobierno, corregida para tomar en cuenta reglas institucionales como el presidente de Portugal o el Bundesrat en Alemania). Someto a prueba si esta relación es al mismo tiempo negativa y heteroesquedástica (véase gráfica I.7). También pongo a prueba si la alternación y la duración del gobierno afectan positivamente el número de leyes importantes al introducir una serie de variables adicionales: *alternación* (valor absoluto de la diferencia normalizada promedio entre dos gobiernos sucesivos), *duración* (años de un gobierno en funciones), así como otras variables que no resultaron ser tan importantes (como se había pronosticado).

2.1. Someter a prueba el efecto negativo de rango y heteroesquedasticidad

La relación esperada entre *rango* y *leyes* es que la primera es una condición necesaria pero no suficiente para la segunda: un rango grande impedirá una legislación importante, pero un rango pequeño no garantizará la existencia de legislación importante. Como se hizo notar en el capítulo I, la implicación de este análisis es que *rango* y *leyes* tendrán una correlación negativa, y los residuos al cuadrado (o el valor absoluto de los mismos) de la relación estimada también se correlacionarán negativamente con el *rango*. La heteroesquedasticidad tiene un impacto negativo sobre la importancia de coeficientes estadísticos (ya que genera grandes errores estándar). Sin embargo, la existencia de la heteroesquedasticidad pronosticada deberá estar a favor de mi teoría, no en contra. Dicho de otro modo, la prueba apropiada para una teoría que pronostica una condición suficiente pero no necesaria es una combinación de una prueba de medios (regresión) con escasa importancia estadística y una prueba de la varianza (residuos) para heteroesquedasticidad. Si ambos pronósticos resultan ser corroborados (como lo son), entonces la confianza en la teoría que pronosticaba ambas relaciones debe ser significativamente más alta que el valor p de cualquier coeficiente.

En el cuadro VII.1 se someten a prueba estas dos expectativas con un modelo de regresión heteroesquedástica multiplicativa.[14] Las dos ecuaciones siguientes se someten a prueba simultáneamente mediante la estimación de la probabilidad máxima:

$$\text{Ecuación 1: } leyes = a - b\ rango + \varepsilon$$

$$\text{Ecuación 2: } \varepsilon^2 \exp(p - q\ rango)$$

---

[14] En una versión anterior (Tsebelis, 1999) estimé tres modelos independientes: uno el número promedio de leyes importantes, otro estimando el término de error, y uno más "para corregir" por heteroesquedasticidad. El desarrollo de modelos de regresión heteroesquedástica multiplicativa permite hacer comprobaciones simultáneas.

CUADRO VII.1. *Modelo de regresión heteroesquedástica multiplicativa de legislación importante.*

	Modelo 1 (*incluye* rango)	Modelo 2 (*excluye* rango)
Variable dependiente: número de leyes importantes		
Constante	1.1935**** (0.2017)	1.2711*** (0.2246)
Rango	−0.4837**** (0.0133)	
Variable dependiente: el término de error al cuadrado del número de leyes importantes		
Constante	0.7110**** (0.1852)	1.0910*** (0.1841)
Rango	−0.7471**** (0.1919)	
N	59	59
Prob. $> \chi^2$	0.000	0.000
Prueba de probabilidad-razón:	$\chi^2_2 = 17.85$	Prob. $> \chi^2_2 = 0.0001$

Nota: Errores estándar en paréntesis.
 * $p < 0.1$ nivel.
 ** $p < 0.05$ nivel.
 *** $p < 0.01$.
 **** $p < 0.001$.
Todas las pruebas son de una cola.

Como lo indica el cuadro VII.1, los coeficientes de *rango* para las ecuaciones 1 y 2 son sumamente significativos. Sin embargo, la hipótesis de nulidad es que ambos coeficientes son 0. Por esta razón estimo un segundo modelo que omite el *rango* como variable explicativa de ambas ecuaciones y realizo una prueba de razón probable que proporcione un chi² = 17.85, que da un valor p de 0.0001.

Las gráficas VII.1 y VII.2 proporcionan más evidencia visual. La gráfica VII.1 presenta la relación entre *leyes* y *rango*. En esta gráfica he separado los

GRÁFICA VII.1. *Número de leyes importantes por rango ideológico de la coalición.*

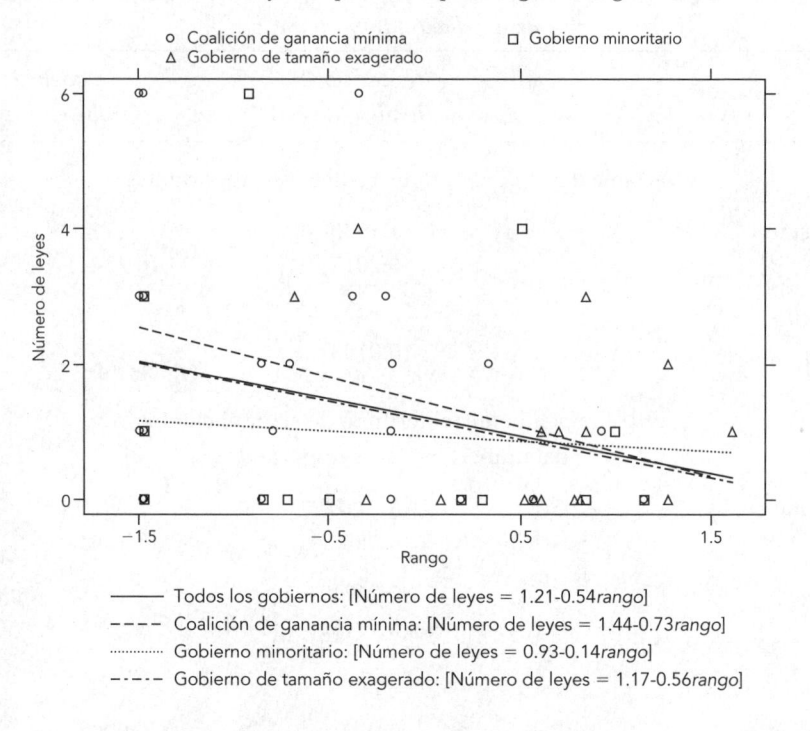

———— Todos los gobiernos: [Número de leyes = 1.21-0.54*rango*]
- - - - Coalición de ganancia mínima: [Número de leyes = 1.44-0.73*rango*]
·········· Gobierno minoritario: [Número de leyes = 0.93-0.14*rango*]
–·–·– Gobierno de tamaño exagerado: [Número de leyes = 1.17-0.56*rango*]

gobiernos de coalición de ganancia mínima (indicados con O en la gráfica) de gobiernos minoritarios (□ en la gráfica) y de coaliciones de tamaño exagerado (△ en la gráfica). La razón de esta distinción se explicó en el capítulo IV. La lógica política en todos estos casos indica que los partidos en el gobierno son jugadores con veto. Sin embargo, las restricciones aritméticas son diferentes entre coaliciones de ganancia mínima, donde el apoyo de todos los partidos es aritméticamente necesario; gobiernos minoritarios, donde más votos son necesarios, y coaliciones de tamaño exagerado, donde no son necesarios todos los votos. Mi expectativa (en el capítulo IV) era que el argumento del jugador con veto se sostendría de una manera aproximada en el caso de gobiernos minoritarios y de tamaño exagerado. Los datos en general confirman mis expectativas. Presento cuatro líneas de regresión bivariable. La línea superior resume la relación entre leyes y rango que ocurre en coaliciones de ganancia mínima. La relación es muy fuerte y significativa. Las dos líneas intermedias resumen la relación global y las

GRÁFICA VII.2. *Residuos (valor absoluto) de leyes importantes por rango ideológico de la coalición.*

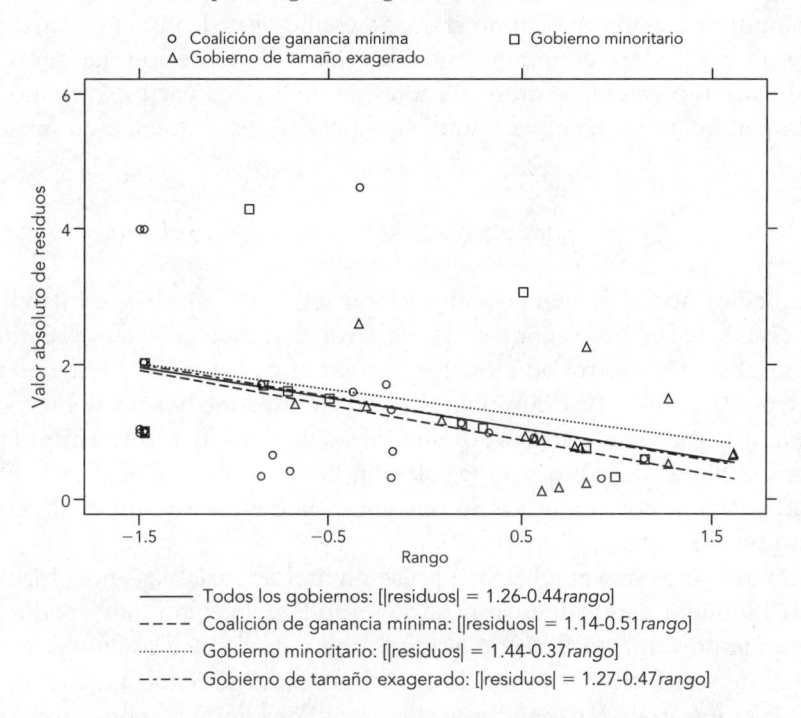

——— Todos los gobiernos: [|residuos| = 1.26-0.44*rango*]
- - - - Coalición de ganancia mínima: [|residuos| = 1.14-0.51*rango*]
············ Gobierno minoritario: [|residuos| = 1.44-0.37*rango*]
–·–·– Gobierno de tamaño exagerado: [|residuos| = 1.27-0.47*rango*]

coaliciones de tamaño exagerado. Ambas relaciones tienen significación estadística. La última línea representa gobiernos minoritarios y tiene una pendiente negativa pero muy débil y sin significación estadística. Este resultado indica que sería preferible[15] conocer las condiciones exactas de cada uno de estos gobiernos minoritarios, como argumenta Strom (2000) (véase capítulo III). La comparación de la gráfica VII.1 con la I.7 (utilizada en el capítulo I para indicar qué esperar de resultados empíricos) indica el alto grado de concordancia entre teoría y datos (que también aparecía en las regresiones del cuadro VII.1).

La gráfica VII.2 ofrece una representación visual del valor absoluto de los residuos de una regresión OLS de *leyes* y *rango* significativos. He seleccionado el valor absoluto para esta gráfica debido a que la gráfica de residuos

[15] Por ejemplo, sería interesante saber si la mayor parte del tiempo se buscó respaldo para las propuestas del gobierno entre los mismos partidos, en cuyo caso aumenta el número de jugadores con veto.

al cuadrado es visualmente engañosa (elimina residuos pequeños y se exacerban los grandes). De nueva cuenta, divido gobiernos en coaliciones de ganancia mínima, gobiernos minoritarios y coaliciones de tamaño exagerado, pero esta vez no hay diferencia entre las líneas de regresión que representan al conjunto entero de datos y cada una de las dos partes. Podemos ver que la pendiente es negativa y muy significativa, exactamente como se esperaba.

2.2. Prueba para alternación y duración del gobierno

Los modelos que aparecen en esta sección son multivariables e introducen una serie de variables de control. De acuerdo con mi análisis, se espera que dos variables de control adicionales *(duración y alternación)* tengan signo positivo. *Alternación* (la diferencia entre los puntos medios del gobierno actual en relación con el anterior) es una forma de introducir un sustituto para el *statu quo,* en caso de que la legislación haya sido introducida por el gobierno anterior. Por supuesto, no hay garantía de que éste fuera el caso en verdad (véase *supra).*

El modelo 1 en el cuadro VII.2 presenta ambas variables en su forma lineal. El modelo 2 introduce la idea de un índice declinante de producción de leyes importantes utilizando el logaritmo natural de duración como variable independiente. Este modelo corrobora todas las expectativas generadas por la teoría de los jugadores con veto. Por ello la sometí a tres pruebas adicionales. La primera prueba consiste en examinar si los resultados se mantienen para diferentes subconjuntos de datos. Los modelos 2A, 2B y 2C separan los diferentes gobiernos en coaliciones de ganancia mínima (23 casos), gobiernos minoritarios (15 casos) y coalición de tamaño exagerado (21 casos), y volví a someter a prueba el modelo para cada una de estas categorías. La segunda prueba es introducir una serie de variables de control con el fin de someter a prueba el carácter espurio de los resultados. El modelo 3 introduce tres variables de control plausibles: *control de agenda, corporativismo* e *ideología de izquierda* del gobierno. La bibliografía existente sugiere éstas como explicaciones alternativas para los resultados. La última prueba es volver a correr el modelo con y sin variables de control como una regresión binomial negativa (dado el hecho de que mi variable dependiente es una "cuenta", los coeficientes OLS pueden estar sesgados).

Como se muestra en el cuadro VII.2, todas las relaciones hipotetizadas salen con el signo correcto (negativo para rango y positivo para alternación

CUADRO VII.2. *Modelos multivariables de legislación importante (lineal y binomio negativo).*

Variable	Modelo 1	Modelo 2	Binomio negativo M2	Modelo 2A CGM[1]	Modelo 2B minoritario	Modelo 2C de tamaño exagerado	Modelo 3	Binomio negativo M3
Constante	−0.18 (0.26)	0.25 (0.24)	−0.89*** (0.26)	−0.27 (0.47)	0.29 (0.85)	0.81*** (0.36)	0.25 (0.25)	−0.9*** (0.27)
Rango	−0.27* (0.17)	−0.33** (0.18)	−0.20* (0.15)	−0.63** (0.33)	−0.06 (0.50)	−0.57* (0.36)	−0.35** (0.19)	−0.24* (0.17)
Abs (altern.)	0.54*** (0.23)	0.65**** (0.23)	0.23* (0.16)	0.85*** (0.33)	0.73 (0.83)	−0.08 (0.42)	0.65*** (0.24)	0.25* (0.18)
Duración	0.35*** (0.06)							
Ln (duración)		0.84**** (0.16)	0.83**** (0.16)	0.91*** (0.27)	0.73* (0.45)	0.84*** (0.23)	0.85**** (0.17)	0.83**** (0.17)
Agenda							−0.19*** (0.80)	−0.09 (0.69)
Corporativismo							0.01 (0.27)	0.07 (0.24)
Izquierda							−0.01 (0.16)	0.01 (0.11)
N	59	59	59	23	15	21	59	59
R^2	0.525	0.504		0.635	0.299	0.493	0.506	
R^2 ajustado	0.499	0.477		0.577	0.108	0.404	0.449	
Seudo R^2			0.205					0.207

[1] CGM: coalición de ganancia mínima.
Errores estándar entre paréntesis.
* $p < 0.05$.
** $p < 0.05$.
*** $p < 0.01$.
**** $p < 0.001$.
Todas las pruebas son de una cola.

y duración). Sobre la base del modelo 2, podemos convenir que la producción de leyes importantes es afectada negativamente por el rango del gobierno, positivamente por la diferencia entre gobiernos actuales y anteriores (alternación), y que la duración aumenta el número de leyes pero a un índice declinante.

Los modelos 2A, 2B y 2C repiten el análisis para coaliciones de ganancia mínima, gobiernos minoritarios y gobiernos de tamaño exagerado, respectivamente. Todos los signos de los coeficientes están como se hipotetizaron, sin embargo los niveles convencionales de significación estadística se pierden, excepto en el caso de las coaliciones de ganancia mínima.[16]

El modelo 3 introduce tres diferentes variables de control. La primera es *control de agenda*. Doering (1995b) ha identificado la importancia del establecimiento de agenda del gobierno para la cantidad tanto como para la calidad de la legislación producida en un país. En pocas palabras, su argumento es que el control de la agenda que tiene el gobierno aumenta el número de proyectos de ley importantes y reduce la inflación legislativa (escasos proyectos de ley pequeños). Doering definió el control de la agenda de dos diferentes maneras: cualitativa y cuantitativamente.[17] Planteó la hipótesis de una relación positiva entre leyes importantes y control de la agenda. Sin embargo, Doering examinó países como unidades del análisis, y sus mediciones (que yo uso) se refieren a países. En consecuencia, la varianza de la legislación importante dentro de cada país no puede ser captada por las variables de Doering. Examinaré este análisis más a fondo en la siguiente sección.

Corporativismo fue la segunda variable introducida para fines de control. Usé *corporativismo* como variable tricotómica (con Bélgica, Alemania, Luxemburgo y Suiza como casos ambiguos) y como dicotómica (con los países anteriores considerados como corporativistas). Al igual que *control de agenda*, se considera constante por país. A este respecto, sigo gran parte de la bibliografía sobre corporativismo, pese al hecho de que la investigación contemporánea encuentra fluctuaciones importantes en las varia-

[16] Agradezco una referencia anónima para la sugerencia de subdividir el conjunto de datos. La división aplicó los criterios estándar en la mayoría de los países. Sin embargo, en Alemania tuve que tomar en cuenta al Bundesrat si está dominado por la oposición, en Portugal al presidente si su partido no fue incluido en el gobierno, y en el caso de un decreto gubernamental en Francia, tomé en cuenta al presidente de la república. En todos estos casos el error estándar del gobierno fue alterado para tomar en cuenta la teoría de los jugadores con veto: por ejemplo, en Alemania un gobierno de coalición de ganancia mínima fue codificado como de tamaño exagerado si se requería el respaldo de un Bundesrat dominado por la oposición.

[17] La medición cualitativa de control de la agenda es el primero de los indicadores que define Doering (véase análisis en el capítulo III). La medición cuantitativa proviene de mis cálculos en el mismo capítulo y se encuentra en el cuadro IV.1. En mis análisis he usado ambas mediciones con resultados similares.

bles que componen el concepto a lo largo del tiempo (Golden, Wallerstein y Lange, 1999).

En los países corporativistas, sigue diciendo el argumento, las máximas asociaciones de empleadores y sindicatos negocian los temas que cubre este artículo; y sólo si no concuerdan interviene y legisla el parlamento o el gobierno emite decretos. Debido a esto, los países corporativistas (donde los rangos del gobierno son generalmente altos) presumiblemente producen menos leyes laborales importantes. Hay dos problemas en este argumento. Primero, en los países corporativistas se produce legislación, independientemente de si los asociados están de acuerdo o no. Si lo están, el parlamento o el gobierno emiten legislación o decretos que confirmen el acuerdo. De no ser así, las instituciones legislativas del país deciden acerca del desacuerdo. Por ejemplo, a fines de la década de 1980 el problema tanto de Noruega como de Suecia era la necesidad de recortar salarios para impedir que aumentara el desempleo. En Noruega, los asociados (sindicatos y empleadores) acordaron un congelamiento de salarios y pidieron al gobierno minoritario socialdemócrata que lo integrara en la legislación, de modo que fuera universalmente obligatorio. La legislación fue aprobada por el parlamento, en tanto que los sindicatos independientes (es decir, los no afiliados a la confederación principal) se quejaron de ser las víctimas, pues los sueldos habían bajado, y el desempleo no creció mucho. En Suecia, al mismo tiempo, los asociados no lograron llegar a un acuerdo para controlar los salarios, de modo que el gobierno de minoría socialdemócrata presentó legislación para congelarlos. En el caso sueco, todos los sindicatos protestaron, la propuesta fue derrotada, el gobierno cayó, los sueldos siguieron aumentando rápidamente y el desempleo subió mucho más que en Noruega. Segundo, si el argumento fuera correcto, se esperaría menos legislación laboral *general* en países corporativistas, no tan sólo menos legislación *importante*. Sin embargo, los países corporativistas tienen más legislación completa en el área de horario de trabajo y condiciones laborales.

La tercera variable fue la *ideología* de cada gobierno. Dado que la variable dependiente es la legislación laboral, podemos suponer que los gobiernos de izquierda producen más de ella. En mi opinión, esta interpretación desconoce la posibilidad de que gobiernos de derecha revoquen leyes laborales, o que deshagan lo que hayan hecho los gobiernos de izquierda. *Ideología de izquierda* se midió exactamente de la misma manera que *rango* y *alternación*, de modo que varía por gobiernos y los resultados empíricos serán concluyentes.

Como lo indica el modelo 3, ninguna de las tres variables de control anteriores tiene algún impacto sobre los resultados del modelo 2. Las tres variables adicionales llegan muy cerca de cero y son completamente insignificantes. Por añadidura, no hay ningún aumento en el R^2 del modelo, y el R^2 ajustado se contrae. Es seguro decir que, estadísticamente, estas variables nada explican (aunque conceptualmente tengamos que hacer referencia al análisis de párrafos anteriores para entender por qué es así).

Para asegurar que estos resultados no están generados por peculiaridades de algún país, examiné los puntos de mayor influencia (los cuatro casos —tres puntos, pero uno de ellos es doble— en la cuarta parte superior izquierda de la gráfica VII.1) con el fin de que no reflejaran situaciones insólitas. Estos cuatro puntos representan a gobiernos de Bélgica, Suecia, Grecia y el Reino Unido. En el caso de los dos primeros países, los gobiernos producen una cantidad extraordinaria de leyes ya que su rango era sumamente pequeño. En el caso de los dos últimos, la regla fue gobiernos de un solo partido, y dos de ellos (compuestos de dos o más gobiernos reales) generaron un alto número de leyes importantes. Incluso sin estos casos, se conserva la relación negativa entre rango y leyes importantes, aunque se pierde la significación estadística.

Finalmente, los modelos de regresión binomial negativa no alteran en ningún sentido las conclusiones de los modelos anteriores. En vista de que la interpretación de los coeficientes lineales es más fácil y más intuitiva, y dado que las variables de control adicionales no la mejoran, debemos sacar conclusiones del modelo 2. Prevengo al lector de que el número parecerá "pequeño" puesto que trato con una sola área de legislación. Tendríamos que agregar diferentes áreas para encontrar el efecto global.[18]

Dado que el coeficiente del logaritmo natural de duración es positivo, podemos decir que el efecto de la duración sobre la legislación del gobierno es doble. Por un lado, la duración tiene un efecto positivo sobre la legislación; por el otro, la tasa de producción de leyes se reduce con la duración.

---

[18] En este agregado tendríamos que repetir la lógica de este análisis, no extrapolar mecánicamente los resultados. Por ejemplo, las posiciones de los partidos en el gobierno acerca de temas ambientales se deberían considerar con el fin de pronosticar la legislación ambiental, no la escala izquierda-derecha usada aquí. Por lo tanto, es perfectamente razonable esperar que un gobierno compuesto de partidos cercanos unos a otros en la escala izquierda-derecha y que produce muchas leyes importantes sobre asuntos laborales pueda producir pocas leyes ambientales importantes si los jugadores con veto están muy alejados unos de otros en la dimensión de política ambiental. De otro modo tendríamos que realizar un análisis multidimensional (capítulo VIII).

Examinemos la importancia política de estos resultados. Los resultados empíricos tomados en su conjunto indican que las coaliciones de rango grande no son propensas a producir legislación importante, mientras que las coaliciones de rango pequeño y los gobiernos de un solo partido pueden producir o no tales leyes y decretos. En otras palabras, la estabilidad política es la característica de las primeras, mientras que la *posibilidad* de un cambio político importante es la característica de las segundas. Así, los resultados de esta sección son que, dependiendo de la composición del gobierno (o de estructuras institucionales que produzcan continuamente jugadores con veto únicos o múltiples), podemos obtener estabilidad política o bien el potencial para el cambio político, pero no ambas cosas.[19]

3. Jugadores con veto y legislación incremental

Tras haber establecido la relación entre jugadores con veto, rango y legislación importante (falta de estabilidad política), veamos ahora la legislación incremental (no importante) y el número total de leyes. Mi expectativa ha sido que

> *ceteris paribus*, leyes importantes y sin importancia deberían variar inversamente, debido a limitaciones de tiempo. La cláusula *ceteris paribus* presupone que el parlamento tiene tiempo limitado y lo usa para aprobar legislación (ya sea importante o trivial). Si hay otros usos de tiempo como preguntas a ministros, debates generales, etc., o si el tiempo de las reuniones es variable en sí mismo, se deben introducir controles sobre estos factores [Tsebelis, 1995b: 104].

En esta sección, la unidad de análisis se convierte en el país en vez del gobierno, ya que los datos a nivel de gobierno no están disponibles.

Ya hemos visto en el capítulo IV el análisis que hace Doering del establecimiento de agenda del gobierno en democracias parlamentarias. Doering (1995b) ha establecido la importancia del establecimiento de agenda guber-

---

[19] A menos que un gobierno de un solo partido encuentre una tecnología para comprometer su credibilidad: nombrando una agencia independiente y asignándole jurisdicción o afirmando que el *statu quo* es su propio punto ideal. No voy a analizar las tecnologías de compromiso, pero el punto final es que los gobiernos pluripartidistas tienen dificultades para modificar el *statu quo*, pero no así los gobiernos de un solo partido (véase análisis sobre tributación en el capítulo VIII).

namental tanto para la cantidad como para la calidad de la legislación producida en un país. En breves palabras, su argumento es que el control gubernamental de la agenda acrecienta el número de proyectos de ley importantes y reduce la inflación legislativa (pocos proyectos de ley pequeños).

Doering (1995c) se valió de datos legislativos reales para someter a prueba sus ideas. Las pruebas no sólo corroboraron su intuición de que el control gubernamental de la agenda reduce la inflación legislativa, sino que también eliminan otras explicaciones plausibles (incluyendo el tamaño de la población de un país, barreras electorales al ingreso de partidos, número de partidos en el parlamento y legislación adicional al nivel subnacional) a lo largo del camino. Entonces, desde una perspectiva diferente, Doering ha llegado a las mismas conclusiones que la teoría de los jugadores con veto: conforme aumenta el número de leyes importantes, disminuye la inflación legislativa; mas para él, es el control gubernamental sobre la agenda legislativa lo que conecta ambas cosas.

Con el fin de revisar los resultados de Doering usaré la medida compuesta de control gubernamental de la agenda legislativa que desarrollé en el capítulo IV a partir de los siete indicadores de Doering (véase el cuadro IV.1). Sin embargo, todo lo que digo también se sostiene si usamos el primer indicador de Doering del control de la agenda gubernamental, o su índice cuantitativo.

El cuadro VII.3 introduce una serie de variables para cada país: el número de leyes y decretos importantes (la suma de tales instrumentos legislativos para el periodo completo en escrutinio), el número promedio de leyes por país (del cuadro 18.1 de Doering, 1995a), un número promedio de jugadores con veto por país, una medición cualitativa de jugadores con veto, así como mi índice de control gubernamental calculado sobre la base de los siete indicadores de Doering.

Es necesaria una explicación de estos datos. Para la variable del número de leyes por país, Suecia tiene dos números: uno tomado del cuadro 18.1 de Doering (1995c), mientras que el otro es el número promedio de leyes nuevas, que proporciona Ingvar Mattson, del Departamento de Ciencias Políticas de la Universidad Lund (Doering, 1995c: 596). Aparentemente, en Suecia cuentan cada enmienda como una ley separada. Por lo tanto el número en el cuadro de Doering, como él lo analiza, aunque técnicamente correcto, está inflado por normas comparativas. En cuanto a los jugadores con veto, he usado dos variables diferentes. Una proporciona el número promedio de jugadores con veto para el periodo que examiné. La otra es

LA LEGISLACIÓN

CUADRO VII.3. *Número de leyes, leyes importantes, jugadores con veto y control gubernamental de la agenda legislativa.*

País	Leyes importantes (horas de trabajo)	Leyes/año	Jugadores con veto (cual.)	Jugadores con veto (núm.)	Control de la agenda (cual.)	Control de la agenda (núm.)
Alemania	2	83	3	2.19	−4	−0.126
Austria	3	121	2	1.79	−4	−0.044
Bélgica	7	49	3	4.29	−4	−0.170
Dinamarca	5	165	3	3.57	−5	−0.106
España	3	56	1	1	−4	0.221
Finlandia	4	343	3	3.89	−5	−0.148
Francia	8	94	2	1.57	−2	0.333
Grecia	10	88	1	1	−2	0.280
Holanda	1	134	3	2.13	−7	−0.527
Irlanda	2	35	2	1.78	−1	0.519
Italia	1	264	3	4.70	−6	−0.219
Luxemburgo	6	66	2	2	−3	−0.053
Portugal	5	69	2	2.34	−3	0.147
Reino Unido	6	62	1	1	−1	0.690
Suecia	9	375 (56 nuevos)	2	1.82	−5	−0.427
Suiza	3	32	3	4	−3	−0.135

Número de leyes y control cualitativo de la agenda (con signo opuesto) de Doering (1995).

una medición cualitativa de los jugadores con veto, establecida de la manera siguiente: los países con gobiernos de un solo partido reciben una puntuación de 1, los países con una mezcla de uno o dos partidos en el gobierno reciben una puntuación de 2, y los países con más de dos partidos en el gobierno reciben una puntuación de 3. Estas puntuaciones reflejan la situación prevaleciente en estos países por un periodo considerablemente más largo que los 10 años que hemos estado estudiando hasta aquí. El único país que requiere una explicación adicional es Alemania. El número 3 refleja el hecho de que, aunque las coaliciones gubernamentales desde comienzos de la década de 1950 implican sólo dos partidos, el Bundesrat ha estado dominado por una mayoría de la oposición durante periodos importantes.

El cuadro VII.4 presenta los coeficientes de correlación de las variables incluidas en el cuadro VII.3. Las tres partes dependen de si Suecia es incluida con 375 leyes anuales (cuadro VII.4, parte A), con 56 de tales leyes (cuadro VII.4, parte B), o excluida de los datos por completo (cuadro VII.4, parte C).

CUADRO VII.4. *Correlaciones entre jugadores con veto, establecimiento de agenda y legislación.*

	Leyes importantes	Leyes/año	Jugadores con veto (cual.)	Jugadores con veto (prom.)	Control de la agenda (cual.)	Control de la agenda (cuadro VI.1)
A. Suecia incluida con 375 proyectos de ley por año						
Leyes importantes	1.000					
Leyes/año	0.084	1.000				
Jugadores con veto (cual.)	−0.454	0.285	1.000			
Jugadores con veto (prom.)	−0.307	0.305	0.836	1.000		
Control de la agenda (cual.)	0.386	−0.594	−0.620	−0.490	1.000	
Control de la agenda (cuadro IV.1)	0.213	−0.529	−0.704	−0.528	0.889	1.000
B. Suecia incluida con 56 proyectos de ley al año						
Leyes importantes	1.000					
Leyes/año	−0.278	1.000				
Jugadores con veto (cual.)	−0.454	0.436	1.000			
Jugadores con veto (prom.)	−0.307	0.506	0.836	1.000		
Control de la agenda (cual.)	0.386	−0.552	−0.620	−0.490	1.000	
Control de la agenda (cuadro IV.1)	0.213	−0.328	−0.704	−0.528	0.889	1.000
C. Suecia excluida						
Leyes importantes	1.000					
Leyes/año	−0.235	1.000				
Jugadores con veto (cual.)	−0.461	0.430	1.000			
Jugadores con veto (prom.)	−0.279	0.496	0.835	1.000		
Control de la agenda (cual.)	0.527	−0.606	−0.654	−0.534	1.000	
Control de la agenda (cuadro IV.1)	0.424	−0.419	−0.791	−0.623	0.893	1.000

El lector puede verificar que la correlación entre todas las leyes y las leyes importantes es negativa en dos de las tres partes del cuadro, más especialmente en la que excluye a Suecia. Así, en dos de las tres partes se corrobora la expectativa de correlación negativa entre legislación importante y general.

Sin embargo, son más interesantes las relaciones entre los jugadores con veto y el número de leyes, así como la relación entre jugadores con veto y control de agenda en manos del gobierno. Los jugadores con veto se correlacionaron positivamente con el número de todas las leyes, y negativamente con el número de leyes importantes en todas las tres partes del cuadro VII.4. De modo similar, como lo ha demostrado Doering convincentemente, el control de agenda en manos del gobierno se correlaciona negativamente con la inflación legislativa. Por último, el resultado más interesante es que el número de jugadores con veto está sumamente correlacionado con el control de la agenda (de nueva cuenta, en todas las partes del cuadro VII.4).

¿Cómo podemos interpretar estos resultados? Creo que la correlación positiva de los jugadores con veto y la falta de control de la agenda con el número total de leyes y la correlación negativa de las mismas variables con el número de leyes importantes apuntan hacia una diferencia en el concepto mismo de "ley" entre países. Las "leyes" en países con muchos jugadores con veto y control gubernamental bajo de la agenda producen cambios incrementales del *statu quo*, mientras que en países con pocos jugadores con veto y un importante control gubernamental de la agenda, producen cambios completos y generales.

Pero, ¿por qué está correlacionada la falta de establecimiento de agenda de parte del gobierno con el número de jugadores con veto? El lector deberá volver a consultar la gráfica 1 en la Introducción, donde planteo el argumento de que muchos jugadores con veto conducen a una importancia menor del establecimiento de agenda, ya que el conjunto ganador del *statu quo* es más pequeño, y de este modo el control de la agenda pierde importancia. ¿Y estos resultados apoyan dicha suposición? La respuesta a esta pregunta es negativa, ya que los indicadores de Doering (1995a, b, c) se refieren a la estructura institucional de estos países, no a la frecuencia con la que gobiernos específicos aplican tales medidas de control de agenda (en la medida en que existan).

¿Hay algún argumento diferente para la correlación entre jugadores con veto y control gubernamental de la agenda? De hecho, ¿es una relación coincidental o una causal? Se pueden plantear varios argumentos de que no es una mera correlación. En tanto que es difícil un argumento causal que atribuya la existencia de jugadores con veto a la falta de control de la agenda, es posible un argumento estratégico que va del control de la agenda a jugadores con veto. En países con un poderoso control gubernamental de la agenda, las negociaciones de partido para gobiernos de coalición terminarán en un gobierno de minoría o en un gobierno con escasos jugadores con veto. A la inversa, en países sin control gubernamental de la agenda, los partidos formarán coaliciones de gobierno de tamaño exagerado con el fin de controlar la legislatura. Por otra parte, un argumento causal que va de jugadores con veto a control de la agenda es directo: la existencia de muchos jugadores con veto los hace incapaces de hacer aprobar en el parlamento las numerosas e importantes piezas de legislación requeridas para el control de la agenda. Este argumento considera el control de la agenda como una colección de piezas importantes de legislación. En consecuencia, esperamos *no verla* en países con muchos jugadores con veto. Finalmente, se puede plantear un tercer argumento: los jugadores con veto y el control de agenda tienen orígenes comunes. Los mismos factores sociológicos e históricos que fragmentan a un país en muchos partidos competidores (ninguno de los cuales tiene una mayoría) hacen a estos partidos lo bastante desconfiados unos de otros, por lo cual rechazan la idea de permitir que quienquiera que esté en el gobierno tenga un control importante sobre la legislación.

¿Cuál de las tres explicaciones está más cerca de la verdad? Esta es una pregunta central para investigaciones futuras. Con el fin de abordar esta interrogante, tendríamos que recabar datos sobre la adopción (y el posible rechazo) de los diferentes mecanismos de control de agenda y analizarlos en relación con los gobiernos que los producen. En otras palabras, tendríamos que duplicar este estudio con control de la agenda como el tema de estudio.

Por último, ¿qué hay acerca del uso real de las mediciones de control de la agenda por parte de diferentes gobiernos? La expectativa que se presentó en este libro (gráfica 1) es que más jugadores con veto reducen la importancia del control de agenda; en consecuencia, los gobiernos con más jugadores con veto harán menos uso de tales medidas. ¿Hay alguna prueba empírica que respalde esta expectativa? De nueva cuenta, la referencia se encuentra en el libro de Doering, quien más recientemente ha ampliado su investigación para incluir el uso real de mediciones de control de la agenda. Doering (próxima publicación) examina unas 500 piezas de legislación de 18 países de Europa Occidental con gobiernos pluripartidistas (ya sea mayoría o minoría) y encuentra que hacen menos uso de medidas de control de la agenda (13.7%) que los gobiernos de un solo partido (20.7%).[20]

4. Conclusiones

He presentado las implicaciones de la teoría de los jugadores con veto cuando los partidos están localizados en un espacio unidimensional y he analizado datos sobre piezas importantes de legislación en 16 países de Europa Occidental. Todas las expectativas relevantes de la teoría presentada en la introducción y en el capítulo I fueron corroboradas por los datos: el número de leyes importantes varía inversamente al rango de los gobiernos que las producen y en proporción directa a la diferencia entre posiciones ideológicas del gobierno actual y el anterior. La duración del gobierno aumenta el número de leyes importantes, pero con rendimientos decrecientes. Además, los residuos de la relación anterior son heteroesquedásticos y varían inversamente al rango de las coaliciones de gobierno. La razón de esta relación es que un rango amplio es una condición suficiente (aunque no necesaria) para la ausencia de legislación importante.

El número de jugadores con veto está correlacionado positivamente con el número de piezas generales de legislación en un país. Esto genera la expectativa de que el concepto mismo de "ley" difiera de un país a otro, y los países con un gran número de jugadores con veto aplican más legislación incremental. La relación positiva entre los jugadores con veto y las piezas totales de legislación y la relación negativa entre jugadores con veto y piezas importantes implica una relación negativa general entre número total de leyes y piezas importantes de legislación.

La conclusión de este análisis es que ahora se ha establecido el eslabón empírico perdido entre jugadores con veto y una serie de características importantes de los sistemas parlamentarios. Muchos jugadores con veto con grandes distancias ideológicas entre ellos significan que la legislación sólo puede ser incremental. Si ocurre un choque exógeno, un gobierno con muchos jugadores con veto con grandes distancias ideológicas entre ellos no puede resolver la situación y no puede estar de acuerdo con las políticas ne-

---

[20] Cálculos nuevos de Doering (próxima publicación), cuadro 9.

cesarias (excepto si la opinión pública es unánime al respecto). Finalmente, la relación entre jugadores con veto y control de la agenda que identificamos aquí, junto con la relación entre control de la agenda y poder ejecutivo que se identificó en el capítulo IV, nos llevan a la conclusión de que muchos jugadores con veto afectan la relación entre gobierno y parlamento en países de Europa Occidental. Muchos jugadores con veto están correlacionados con falta de control de la agenda institucional por parte del gobierno, y la falta de control de la agenda significa gobiernos más débiles y parlamentos más fuertes. Las razones de la relación entre jugadores con veto y control de la agenda por parte del gobierno tienen que ser investigadas más a fondo en el futuro. Finalmente, pocos jugadores con veto conducen al uso del arsenal existente de control de la agenda con mayor frecuencia que muchos jugadores con veto, debido a que la importancia del establecimiento de agenda se reduce con el número de jugadores con veto pues el conjunto ganador del *statu quo* se contrae (y la estabilidad política por lo tanto se incrementa).

VIII. POLÍTICAS MACROECONÓMICAS

EN ESTE capítulo veremos temas tales como déficits, presupuestos, inflación y crecimiento. Un título más apropiado habría sido "resultados macroeconómicos". La razón es que los fenómenos que se estudian en este capítulo son el resultado no sólo de elecciones gubernamentales conscientes (como políticas ambientales o laborales), sino también de una serie de otros factores que escapan del control de los gobiernos nacionales. Por ejemplo, en condiciones específicas las políticas sobre desempleo decididas por un gobierno anterior podrían pesar sobre el presupuesto de un país, aumentar el déficit, elevar la inflación, etc., sin ninguna acción por parte del gobierno en el poder. De modo similar, un choque exógeno como un cambio del precio del petróleo puede ejercer un impacto sobre el desempleo sin la intervención de ninguna decisión gubernamental específica.

En tanto que en el capítulo anterior logramos concentrarnos en la creación de leyes por parte del gobierno y pasamos por alto los resultados específicos, aquí haremos lo contrario. Consideraremos los resultados directamente, y trataremos de inferir el efecto de decisiones políticas específicas (instrumentos) al introducir una serie de variables de control para eliminar tanto "ruido" como sea posible.

En este capítulo hay dos resultados importantes de la teoría de los jugadores con veto como se presentó en las dos partes anteriores. Primero, que la estabilidad política no se refiere únicamente a la legislación sino también a los resultados (estados del mundo). Segundo, que la teoría de los jugadores con veto permite investigar no sólo los fenómenos unidimensionales, sino también los multidimensionales. De hecho, aunque la mayoría de los estudios a los que se hace referencia en este capítulo son, de hecho, pruebas empíricas de una sola dimensión de la teoría de los jugadores con veto, un fenómeno particular que estudiaremos en este capítulo, la estructura de los presupuestos, es multidimensional. Así, en este capítulo se ofrece una metodología para la comprobación empírica de los modelos multidimensionales. Esta metodología se puede usar en el estudio de los fenómenos que no pueden reducirse a una sola dimensión.

Este capítulo se basa en bibliografía existente, y se dividirá en tres partes. La primera se concentra en los déficits presupuestarios. La segunda y más larga aborda la composición de los presupuestos. La última revisa los efectos de los jugadores con veto sobre crecimiento, tributación e inflación.

1. Acción colectiva *versus* explicación de inercia de los déficits presupuestarios

A finales de la década de 1970 y a lo largo de la década de 1980 casi todos los países de la OCDE empezaron a tratar de reducir los déficits presupuestarios generados por sacudidas en los precios del petróleo. Algunos de ellos estabilizaron sus políticas y redujeron sus déficits más pronto que otros. La bibliografía sobre macroeconomía estudió la estabilización y produjo una serie de explicaciones que clasificaré en dos enfoques principales. El primero (que denomino "acción colectiva") argumenta que cuantos más partidos participen en el gobierno, mayores serán los déficits presupuestarios, ya que cada uno de ellos quiso servir a sus propios votantes privilegiados, y, como resultado, aumentar el gasto (y los déficits) era el único compromiso factible entre diferentes asociados en el gobierno. El segundo (al que llamo "inercia") argumenta, junto con la tesis presentada en este libro, que un mayor número de asociados gubernamentales tiene más dificultades para *cambiar* (reducir) el tamaño del déficit y estabilizarlo. Es interesante observar que el primer enfoque hace pronósticos más claros que el segundo: de acuerdo con la acción colectiva, más socios en el gobierno implica déficits (y deuda) más altos, y menos socios implica déficits y deuda más bajos; sin embargo, la inercia espera que haya más asociados en el gobierno para desacelerar el ritmo de los ajustes. Dado que el periodo en estudio se caracteriza por un intento de reducir déficits, las implicaciones empíricas de las dos teorías son idénticas, y a veces los investigadores no prestan atención a las diferencias teóricas subyacentes.

1.1. *Enfoque de acción colectiva*

La idea clave en la bibliografía sobre acción colectiva es el problema del fondo común. La esencia del problema del fondo común es que en un gobierno de creación de política descentralizada, donde cada ministro que gasta sólo tiene autoridad sobre su propia cartera, el costo de gastar en exceso se comparte con otros ministerios. Por lo tanto, cada ministro es motivado para gastar en exceso a fin de complacer a sus votantes a costa de otros ministerios. En otras palabras, dado que cada ministro internaliza sólo una parte del costo de elevar el gasto sobre sus propios bienes, todos los grupos tienen un incentivo para gastar más de lo óptimo a fin de apropiarse de más recursos por sus beneficios. Así, la racionalidad individual conduce a una irracionalidad colectiva, donde el déficit presupuestario resultante es radicalmente distinto de la solución cooperativa. En suma, la bibliografía sobre acción colectiva argumenta que cuanto más dispersa esté la autoridad de toma de decisiones, mayor será el déficit presupuestario. La solución propuesta, por lo tanto, es centralizar completamente la autoridad de toma de decisiones, delegando el poder de toma de decisiones a un agente independiente, como un fuerte ministro de hacienda.

El enfoque de acción colectiva ha recibido cierto apoyo empírico. Por ejemplo, en un estudio de panel que incluyó 20 países de la OCDE de 1960 a 1995, Perotti y Kontopoulos (1998) descubrieron que el gasto gubernamental y la deuda pública son significativamente más altos en países donde hay más socios de coalición y ministros que gastan en el gobierno. Roubini y Sachs (1989b) argumentan que los gobiernos de coalición tendrán un sesgo hacia niveles más altos de gasto gubernamental, en relación con gobiernos de partido mayoritario. Además, la idea del problema de la bolsa común también se ha estudiado extensamente en procedimientos presupuestarios. Por ejemplo, la evidencia empírica en von Hagen y Harden (1995) y Hallerberg y von Hagen (1999) sugiere que los países en los cuales las autoridades en toma de decisiones presupuestarias están centralizadas son menos propensos a sufrir déficits presupuestarios.

1.2. Enfoque de inercia política

A diferencia del enfoque de acción colectiva, que se basa en el dilema del prisionero de n-personas, el enfoque de inercia política recalca la posibilidad de que tal vez no exista un consenso para cambiar un *statu quo* insostenible cuando hay demasiados partidos en el gobierno. Alesina y Drazen (1991) desarrollaron primero un modelo de "guerra de desgaste" de estabilización retrasada, y demostraron la dificultad para llegar a una decisión colectiva a fin de implementar ajustes fiscales debidos al desacuerdo entre diferentes grupos sociales acerca de cómo distribuir la carga fiscal. Spolaore

(1993) extendió el modelo de guerra de desgaste al gobierno de coalición y mostró que un gobierno de coalición es más propenso a retrasar el ajuste fiscal que un gobierno de un solo partido. La razón fundamental es que a diferencia del partido en el poder en un gobierno de un solo partido, que puede fácilmente desplazar los costos a miembros externos, los partidos gobernantes en un gobierno de coalición muy probablemente estarán en desacuerdo o vetarán cualquier política fiscal que vaya en contra de los intereses de sus votantes. Así, el enfoque de inercia política argumenta que los retrasos en el ajuste o la eliminación de déficits existentes podrían ser resultado de luchas entre socios de la coalición (o los grupos sociales a los que representan) acerca de quién soportará los costos/recortes necesarios en el gasto presupuestado, incluso si esos jugadores convienen en que la deuda actual requiere ajustes. En suma, la lucha distribucional entre diferentes grupos conduce a un estancamiento en el proceso de creación de política, lo cual, a su vez, retrasa la implantación de políticas dirigidas a eliminar el déficit presupuestario. Además, pronostica que la estabilización retrasada y los déficits prolongados suelen ocurrir más en sistemas sociopolíticos fragmentados y polarizados.

La evidencia empírica en favor del enfoque de inercia política es fuerte, pero de ninguna manera unánime. Roubini y Sachs (1989a) descubrieron que los déficits grandes están asociados positivamente con gobiernos débiles en países de la OCDE. Cosetti y Roubini (1993) y Alesina y Perotti (1995) expanden el modelo de estructura de Roubini y Sachs y confirman sus resultados.

Respecto a la política estadounidense, Poterba (1994) y Alt y Lowry (1994) presentaron pruebas del efecto de los gobiernos divididos en los estados. Consideraron la respuesta política a los choques fiscales y descubrieron que el ajuste es más lento en estados con control dividido que en estados con control unificado. Sus resultados son notablemente similares (en espíritu) a los de Roubini y Sachs en economías de la OCDE: en ambos casos, los gobiernos de coalición o los divididos no crean déficits presupuestarios, sino que retrasan el ajuste a los choques. Krause (2000) se concentra en el desempeño fiscal de los Estados Unidos. Descubre que el grado de divergencia política ideológica entre instituciones políticas (el presidente, la Cámara y el Senado) desempeña un papel notable para explicar déficits presupuestarios fiscales en los Estados Unidos durante el periodo de la posguerra.

Por otro lado, hay cierta evidencia empírica que contradice los resultados de Roubini y Sachs. Por ejemplo, Edin y Ohlsson (1991) sólo encontraron una relación positiva entre deudas públicas y gobiernos minoritarios.

Además, De Haan y Sturm (1997) volvieron a examinar los resultados de Roubini y Sachs (1989a, 1989c) y de Edin y Ohlsson (1991) y encontraron resultados contradictorios: el crecimiento de la deuda del gobierno y el nivel de gasto gubernamental no están relacionados con el índice de Roubini y Sachs de dispersión del poder, ni con su variante como lo sugieren Edin y Ohlsson.

Dado que el conjunto de países que ha estudiado la bibliografía de acción colectiva y de estabilización apuntaba a reducir los déficits presupuestarios, los resultados empíricos de ambos enfoques teóricos fueron idénticos. Sin embargo, un estudio particular logró producir un resultado empírico que contradice a la bibliografía de acción colectiva. Robert Franzese (2002), quien cubrió 21 países durante 35 años, llegó a la conclusión de que múltiples jugadores con veto retrasan los cambios a déficits presupuestarios ya fuese que éstos fueran altos (en países como Italia) o bajos (en países como Alemania y Suiza). Dado el alcance del análisis de Franzese, lo analizaré más a fondo. Primero, Franzese somete a prueba siete diferentes teorías político-económicas de la deuda pública. Segundo, operacionaliza las variables de los jugadores con veto en una forma precisa y de acuerdo con lo que he escrito en este libro. Tercero, produce un resultado de importancia particular, que se describe a continuación.

A. *Diferentes teorías político-económicas.* Franzese presenta las siguientes teorías:

1. Teorías de la composición del gobierno y la estabilización retrasada. En estas teorías incluye dos variaciones diferentes: la teoría de la "influencia", según la cual los partidos en el gobierno ejercen una influencia proporcional a su tamaño, y las teorías de "veto-actor", que se presentan en este libro.
2. Las distribuciones por riqueza y edad en la transferencia de deuda inter e intrageneracional.
3. Los ciclos político presupuestarios electorales y partidarios.
4. La manipulación estratégica de la deuda para alterar políticas gubernamentales futuras.
5. La multiplicidad de grupos de votantes y políticas distributivas.
6. Las complejidades de la estructura tributaria y votantes fiscalmente afectados.
7. La autonomía del banco central y la reducción del financiamiento de la deuda.

Dado que estas teorías no vienen en pareja, es decir, ninguna se puede expresar como restricción de la otra poniendo algunos de los coeficientes en cero, Franzese usa pruebas-J (Davidson y MacKinnon, 1981) para comparar su poder de pronóstico. El procedimiento para las pruebas-J es el siguiente: para dos modelos $Z = f(X,*)$ y $Z = g(Y,*)$, estimamos primero $Z = f(X,*)$ e incluimos sus pronósticos $\hat{Z}$ en el cálculo de la segunda $Z = g(Y, \hat{Z},*)$. Si el coeficiente de $\hat{Z}$ es no significativo, entonces la segunda hipótesis *abarca* la primera: no hay información importante adicional cubierta por la primera hipótesis. El procedimiento se repite invirtiendo las dos teorías. Es posible que ambas abarquen una a otra, o que ninguna de ellas abarque la otra. Así, la única prueba concluyente es cuando una de ellas abarca la otra pero no viceversa. Dado que las teorías que Franzese somete a prueba analizan aspectos completamente diferentes de los déficits presupuestarios, vemos que el resultado comparativo más frecuente es que cada uno de los modelos no abarca los otros o, para usar los términos de Franzese: "Los datos insisten en que cada una de las teorías agrega capacidad explicativa a cualquiera de las otras". Hay, sin embargo, algunas excepciones, y las presentaré en los términos de Franzese (2002: 156):

> Primero, y del mayor interés teórico, los datos *no* niegan que la concepción del veto-actor del modelo de gobierno débil abarque la concepción de la influencia, pero fácilmente pueden rechazar lo contrario de que la concepción de influencia abarca la concepción del veto-actor. Además, si alguien lee a lo largo de las dos primeras columnas, la concepción del veto-actor se niega con más fuerza a ser abarcada por cualquiera de las otras mientras que, si leemos las dos primeras columnas hacia abajo, es rechazada con menos fuerza en el sentido de que cubra las otras. Por tanto, la concepción del veto-actor de Tsebelis (1995) de fraccionalización y polarización claramente domina la concepción de influencia.

La razón de este claro resultado es que mi modelo es más general que otras explicaciones que compiten con él, como influencia, negociaciones o jurisdicciones exclusivas de ministros. De hecho, cada una de estas teorías impone restricciones adicionales y llega a pronósticos más claros que los jugadores con veto (véase la Introducción).

B. *Operacionalización de los jugadores con veto*. Aunque gran parte de la bibliografía trata de gobiernos minoritarios en forma idiosincrásica (algunos como variable falsa [Edin y Ohlsson, 1991; Haan y Sturm, 1997], algunos como un caso peor de gobiernos de coalición [Roubini y Sachs, 1989a, 1989b]), Franzese aplica el número o la distancia de diferentes jugadores con veto en una sola dimensión como sus variables independientes. Como resultado, su análisis es congruente con los argumentos de este libro, y sus resultados corroboran la teoría de los jugadores con veto.

C. *Efectos de "fraccionalización" y "polarización".* Éstos son los nombres que Franzese da al número de jugadores con veto y al rango de la coalición de gobierno (en una sola dimensión). Franzese sometió a prueba ambas variables al mismo tiempo y descubrió que el ajuste del déficit es una función negativa del número de jugadores con veto, pero no depende del rango de coaliciones de gobierno. Dado que las dos variables están correlacionadas, posiblemente cada una de ellas sería significativa si se sometiera a prueba por sí sola. También puede ser que el fenómeno subyacente sea multidimensional (en este caso el número de jugadores con veto puede ser un mejor sustituto que el rango de una coalición en una sola dimensión).

Pero el resultado más interesante es que cuando se somete a prueba el monto de un déficit como función del monto de la deuda (que de hecho no es más que déficits acumulados), el investigador saca la conclusión de que "la desviación estándar se eleva en una fraccionalización centrada en la media (es decir, = + 1.2 partidos, desde 1.5 hasta 2.7), aumenta los déficits 0.2% de PIB a deuda promedio, pero el mismo aumento en NdP [número de partidos] induce un 0.2% de *reducción* del déficit del PIB a deuda baja y un 0.55% de aumento de PIB en deuda alta" (2002: 176, cursivas en el original). En otras palabras, Franzese encuentra que varios partidos en el gobierno conservan el *statu quo* más efectivamente, ya sea que esto signifique que los déficits continuarán siendo altos (en países como Italia) o bajos (en países como Suiza). Este resultado es prueba en contra de las teorías de acción colectiva y en favor de los enfoques de inercia. Dado que ambos enfoques se sometieron a prueba con datos de un periodo en que los gobiernos estaban intentando reducir déficits, es muy difícil encontrar experimentos cruciales entre los dos enfoques, de modo que el estudio de Franzese es el único con este atributo adicional.

En tanto que la bibliografía anterior se concentra exclusivamente en el monto del déficit (con la excepción de Alesina y Perotti, 1995), nos podemos concentrar, en vez de ello, en la composición del presupuesto y en ver cómo son financiadas diferentes partidas en función de la composición del gobierno. Dedicaré la mayor parte de este capítulo a este punto, dado que la composición de los presupuestos es por definición un fenómeno multidimensional y, como resultado, es probable que requiera indicadores multidimensionales para su estudio.

2. La estructura de los presupuestos

Los jugadores con veto esperan que los presupuestos cambien de un año al siguiente a un ritmo más lento conforme aumentan el tamaño de las coaliciones de gobierno y sus distancias ideológicas. Siguiendo este argumento, Bawn (1999b) se concentró en partidas específicas en el presupuesto de la República Federal de Alemania desde 1961 a 1989. La investigadora analizó el presupuesto en categorías de dos dígitos, y a partir de estas categorías identificó partidas favorecidas por el SPD y el CDU-CSU. En la primera categoría incluyó gastos en subvenciones y préstamos educacionales, educación profesional, educación en arte y cultura, política de mercado laboral, deportes, medio ambiente, servicio a la comunidad municipal, renovación urbana, minería y manufacturas, y ayuda para Alemania Oriental. En la segunda, Bawn incluyó defensa, investigación y desarrollo no universitario, vivienda, mejoramiento en estructura agrícola, inversiones en infraestructura, caminos, ríos y puertos, aviación y marina (las últimas partidas, sobre el fundamento de que son partidas de prebenda política de infraestructura/negocios). La investigadora identificó también una serie de partidas ambiguas, pero éstas no afectaron su análisis.

Se suponía que el Partido Liberal quería minimizar el gasto a través de este análisis. Como resultado, en partidas del SPD las preferencias fluctuaron desde los liberales (bajas) hasta los democratacristianos (medias) a los socialistas (altas), mientras en partidas del CDU-CSU las preferencias fluctuaron desde liberales (bajas) hasta socialistas (medias) a democratacristianos (altas). El análisis de Bawn identificó el rango de cada uno de los gobiernos de coalición así como las partidas para las cuales era de esperar un aumento o disminución en el presupuesto con un cambio del gobierno. Por ejemplo, cuando el SPD penetra en el gobierno en 1966, sustituyendo a los liberales, se espera que las partidas presupuestarias en la lista del SPD aumenten debido a que el país pasa de una coalición que desea un gasto bajo en estas partidas a una coalición que requiera gasto elevado. Por el contrario, cuando la coalición SPD-CDU-CSU es sustituida en 1969 por la coalición SPD-Liberal, no se espera ningún cambio en las partidas presupuestarias del SPD (a pesar de que el SPD controla ahora la cancillería). Bawn forma una serie de expectativas sobre la base de este análisis de jugadores con veto en una sola dimensión. Varios de ellos son contrarios a su intuición. Todas sus expectativas son corroboradas en sus análisis empíricos.

König y Tröger (2001) duplican esencialmente los resultados de Bawn para un periodo más largo, usando preferencias estimadas de los diferentes partidos. Su enfoque es una mejora sobre el de Bawn debido a que en vez de presuponer que los liberales quieren minimizar el gasto, les toman la palabra y estiman que están deseosos de gastar en algunas partidas presupuestarias. Sin embargo, el análisis de Bawn y el de König y Tröger cubren sólo un país, y a través de una sagaz selección de partidas presupuestarias reducen el espacio político a una sola dimensión. Tal elección es imposible cuando consideramos todas las partidas presupuestarias. Tsebelis y Chang (2002) consideraron este problema.

Para Tsebelis y Chang (de aquí en adelante TC), la composición de los presupuestos se altera en dos formas distintas. La primera es deliberada en el sentido de que el gobierno actual quiere aumentar o decrecer el monto del gasto (el presupuesto) y gastar un porcentaje más alto o más bajo del mismo en alguna área; por ejemplo, acrecentando el presupuesto de defensa o desplazando el gasto de defensa a educación. La segunda es automática, en el sentido de que la legislación existente (ya sea introducida por el gobierno actual o por los anteriores) tiene consecuencias económicas: acrecentar el desempleo afecta la composición del presupuesto debido a estipulaciones específicas en la legislación de seguridad social. Por supuesto, el monto del cambio presupuestario dependerá de las estipulaciones específicas de la legislación en cada país.

Con el fin de diferenciar entre el cambio estructural de presupuestos deliberado y el automático, TC incluyen una serie de variables de control en su estudio. Primero, incluyen inflación, desempleo, porcentaje de población dependiente (individuos mayores de 65 años) e índices de crecimiento, dado que las fluctuaciones de estas variables pueden afectar el componente de seguridad social del presupuesto. Segundo, incluyen una serie de variables de país falsas, ya que la legislación en un país puede proporcionar diferentes soluciones y tiene diferentes efectos sobre el presupuesto de la nación. Su resultado básico es que el cambio deliberado en la estructura de los presupuestos (es decir, gasto gubernamental) en países industrializados avanzados depende de la composición de los gobiernos y la distancia ideológica entre el gobierno anterior y el actual. Específicamente, cuanto más diversa sea la coalición gubernamental (cuanto mayores sean las distancias ideológicas entre los partidos), menos cambio ocurrirá en la estructura de los presupuestos. Por añadidura, cuanto mayor sea la alternación, más importante será el cambio en la estructura. Estos resultados son congruentes con los resultados del capítulo VII, pero hay una diferencia importante: el estudio de TC es multidimensional. De hecho, consideran las posiciones de partido en dos dimensiones diferentes y calculan las "diferencias ideológicas" y la "alternación" de jugadores con veto en un espacio bidimensional.

Según la proposición 1.4 (y tal como se indica en la gráfica 1.7), si el núcleo de unanimidad de un sistema político contiene el núcleo de unanimidad de otro sistema político, los cambios en el *statu quo* serán más difíciles en el primer caso que en el segundo. Además, dado que los presupuestos son determinados por el gobierno en funciones, es fácil identificar la posición del *statu quo* en lo que se refiere a los presupuestos. Para el problema que nos ocupa, entonces, TC lograron someter a prueba si la posibilidad de cambio es una función de la posición del *statu quo*. De hecho, cuanto más lejos esté ubicado el *statu quo* de las preferencias de los jugadores con veto, más podrán desviarse del *statu quo*.

La variable dependiente que TC usaron en su estudio es la de los cambios en la estructura de los presupuestos en países industrializados avanzados. El presupuesto de cada país asigna recursos a una serie de áreas, por lo que fue conceptualizado como un vector en un espacio euclidiano n-dimensional. Consiste en una secuencia de porcentajes (con el fin de controlar su tamaño) asignados a diferentes jurisdicciones: (a_1, a_2, ... , a_n). Cada año hay una diferente asignación presupuestaria, de modo que TC indexaron cada secuencia por el tiempo en que fue seleccionada. Por consiguiente, la diferencia entre dos presupuestos puede ser representada por la distancia entre la composición de los presupuestos de dos años sucesivos.

TC sometieron a prueba si las diferencias en la composición anual de los presupuestos de cada país eran una función decreciente de las distancias ideológicas de los jugadores con veto existentes (DI), y una función creciente de la distancia ideológica entre gobiernos sucesivos, que en el capítulo VII denominamos "alternación" (A). Obsérvese que DI es la extensión multidimensional de lo que en el capítulo anterior denominamos "rango".

La razón por la que TC usan características gubernamentales *actuales* en vez de las características del gobierno en el poder el año anterior (el cual votó el presupuesto) es que, según la bibliografía, el gobierno actual tiene medios para alterar el presupuesto existente. En particular, en un estudio de gran alcance sobre las reglas en materia de presupuestos en países de la Unión Europea, Hallerberg, Strauch y von Hagen (2001) identifican una serie de maneras mediante las cuales un gobierno puede enmendar la estructura presupuestaria. Primero, los ministros de finanzas en la mayoría de los países de la UE[1] pueden bloquear el desembolso o imponer límites al efectivo. También tienen el poder de asignar fondos para ser transferidos entre capítulos, y el desembolso del presupuesto en la etapa de implantación tiene que estar sujeto a la aprobación de los ministros de finanzas. Segundo, hay un conjunto de reglas formales que permiten a los gobiernos tratar con gastos inesperados y cambios súbitos en las rentas públicas. En particular, 11 de 15 Estados de la Unión Europea otorgan a los gobiernos el poder para emprender acciones necesarias si se topan con cambios fiscales inesperados. Por ejemplo, Dinamarca requiere acción gubernamental para corregir la estructura del presupuesto si el desembolso es mayor de lo esperado o si los ingresos son menores a lo esperado. Finalmente, la mayoría de los países de la Unión Europea (con excepción de Finlandia, Grecia y Luxemburgo) permiten llevar un saldo anterior de fondos al presupuesto del año siguiente. Hallerberg, Strauch y von Hagen (2001) observan también que el grado de discreción gubernamental sobre el presupuesto corriente puede ser muy sustancial: en teoría, el Reino Unido sencillamente permite que 100% de fondos no gastados se pasen al año siguiente.

Los resultados de Hallerberg, Strauch y von Hagen son duplicados en sistemas presidenciales. En el estudio de la política presupuestaria de gobiernos estatales en los Estados Unidos, Alt y Lowry (1994) y Poterba (1994) sugieren que es el gobierno actual quien determina la formación final de la asignación presupuestaria. Su argumento es que después de que un presupuesto ha sido aprobado, es posible que los ingresos y gastos se alejen de lo esperado y conduzcan a déficits inesperados. En tal escenario, el gobierno actual puede alterar la decisión del presupuesto de modo que se puedan evitar los déficits inesperados. Específicamente, Poterba sugiere que muchas constituciones estatales impiden que los gobiernos estatales incurran en déficits, y los estados también varían en cuanto a las políticas que están disponibles para eliminar un déficit y satisfacer reglas de presupuesto equilibrado. Por ejemplo, algunos estados tienen permitido tomar prestado y cerrar el vacío presupuestario actual. Algunos estados también pueden sacar fondos de sus balances generales para cubrir déficits presupuestarios.

[1] Esto sucede en 11 de 15 países de la Unión Europea. Las excepciones son Finlandia, Holanda, España y Suecia.

De modo similar, Alt y Lowry argumentan que los estados tienen una diversidad de leyes sobre presupuesto equilibrado que podrían influir en la política fiscal, y algunas de las leyes anulan explícitamente los gastos sin fondos.[2] Por lo tanto, en el estudio de TC cada gobierno es considerado responsable por el presupuesto realizado durante el año en que estuvo en el poder.

TC derivaron su variable dependiente del *Government Finance Statistics Yearbook* del Fondo Monetario Internacional. En este conjunto de datos, todos los desembolsos presupuestarios de cada país en particular se catalogan en nueve categorías principales: servicio público general, defensa, educación, salubridad, seguridad y bienestar social, vivienda y comodidades comunitarias, otras comodidades comunitarias y sociales, servicios económicos y otros.

Las variables independientes se construyeron exactamente igual que en el capítulo anterior. Además de los datos concernientes a la primera dimensión, TC usaron asimismo una segunda dimensión de Laver y Hunt (1992), quienes calificaron los partidos sobre la base de sus "relaciones amigables pro o anti URSS". Obsérvese que esta dimensión es diferente de la dimensión de izquierda-derecha. De hecho, la correlación por pareja entre las distancias ideológicas basadas en estas dos dimensiones en el conjunto de datos está sólo ligeramente por encima de 0.5. Sin embargo, los partidos que tienen puntuaciones altas en esta segunda dimensión son partidos de izquierda.[3]

---

[2] En realidad, TC sometieron a prueba los gobiernos del año en curso y del anterior y no encontraron ninguna asociación entre el gobierno anterior y los presupuestos actuales, lo cual se puede explicar porque los presupuestos cambian con mucha lentitud (marginalmente) y los gobiernos actuales sin duda tienen los medios para imponer tales modificaciones.

[3] Algunos ejemplos del conjunto de datos de TC: en 1988, cuando el gabinete Schluter de Dinamarca experimentó una reforma del gobierno: de una coalición de conservadores, liberales y centro demócratas a una coalición de conservadores, liberales y liberales radicales, TC encuentran que el rango ideológico en el segundo índice cambia de 1.6 a 5, mientras que el rango ideológico en el primer índice sólo cambia de 5.6 a 4.9. De modo similar, en Australia en 1983 cuando el gabinete Fraser (que consistía en el Partido Nacional y el Partido Liberal) fue sustituido por el gabinete Hawke (el Partido Laborista), la posición ideológica del gobierno en el segundo índice cambió de 12.59 a 7.29, mientras que la posición ideológica en el primer índice sólo cambió de 14.86 a 10.10.

2.1. La "distancia ideológica" bidimensional y las variables de "alternación"

Basándonos en la proposición 1.4, necesitamos saber si el núcleo de unanimidad de un gobierno está incluido en el núcleo de unanimidad de otro. En una sola dimensión, ésta es una tarea sencilla: comparamos la longitud del núcleo de las dos coaliciones (el "rango", como lo hicimos en el capítulo VII). En dos o más dimensiones, en cambio, no es posible una medición tan directa. Por ejemplo, no es verdad que si el núcleo de unanimidad de la coalición A cubre un área más grande que el núcleo de unanimidad de la coalición B, entonces A necesariamente incluye a B (es decir, el criterio pertinente de acuerdo con la gráfica 1.6). Por ejemplo, si una coalición tiene dos miembros distantes (lo que por definición significa que su núcleo de unanimidad es una línea recta y por lo tanto cubre un área de cero), puede tomar decisiones más fácilmente que una coalición con tres miembros ubicados cerca unos de otros (lo cual cubre un área pequeña pero positiva). Como resultado, TC aproximaron las distancias ideológicas de diferentes coaliciones en dos dimensiones usando su rango en cada dimensión y calculando su promedio. Para alternación, la selección del indicador fue más fácil porque se conocía la posición del punto medio del rango en cada dimensión, de modo que la distancia entre dos gobiernos se pudo calcular mediante el teorema de Pitágoras.[4] Obsérvese que esta fórmula produce distancias positivas, ya sea que el gobierno sucesor esté a la izquierda o a la derecha del predecesor en la primera dimensión, o de sus posiciones relativas en la segunda dimensión.

Es interesante comparar este enfoque con el que se empleó en el capítulo VII. Allí el problema era unidimensional, y como resultado fue posible calcular exactamente el rango y la alternación. Aquí el problema es multidimensional, la distancia ideológica (el equivalente en rango) se calcula por aproximación. De hecho, hay varias mediciones posibles de la variable, y ninguna capta la información que la proposición 1.4 requiere exactamente. Aunque es más probable que una configuración de jugadores con veto con una puntuación DI más alta (calculada por TC) incluirá una con puntuación DI más pequeña, no se garantiza la inclusión. Por lo tanto, de acuerdo con mi enfoque, múltiples dimensiones no conducen al "caos" como en la bibliografía de elección social, sino a un modelo más complicado que conser-

[4] $A_{12} = \sqrt{A_1^2 + A_2^2}$, donde A_1 y A_2 son alternación en la primera y la segunda dimensiones.

va las intuiciones unidimensionales, justo como los jugadores con veto colectivos en el capítulo II llevaron a un análisis más complicado que se puede aproximar muy bien mediante el análisis del capítulo I.

La primera prueba que realizaron TC fue en busca de efectos negativos de distancias ideológicas sobre el cambio de presupuestos, junto con resultados heteroesquedásticos (varianza elevada asociada con distancias ideológicas bajas). Usaron regresión heteroesquedástica multiplicativa (como en el capítulo VII) y estimaron dos modelos: el primero incluía distancia ideológica, y la variable dependiente retrasada (tomando en cuenta el componente del tiempo) para el valor esperado de la distancia del presupuesto, y la distancia ideológica para el término de error. Como resulta evidente en el cuadro VIII.1, la distancia ideológica tiene un coeficiente negativo tanto para el valor esperado de la distancia presupuestaria como para el término de error como se pronosticó. El segundo modelo incluyó las mismas variables con excepción de la distancia ideológica (en ambas ecuaciones). Una prueba de razón de probabilidad indica que la probabilidad de que sea falsa la expectativa de coeficientes negativos en ambas ecuaciones es menor de seis por ciento.

TC agregaron entonces dos tipos de variables de control para apartar las modificaciones al presupuesto deliberadas de las automáticas: primero, agregaron (diferencias en) desempleo, crecimiento, inflación y el monto de la población dependiente (individuos mayores de 65 años de edad). Segundo, agregaron falsas variables para todos los países con el fin de eliminar modificaciones automáticas del presupuesto debidas a la legislación existente. Además, agregaron variables falsas de control para el tipo de gobierno (coalición de ganancia mínima, gobierno minoritario o de tamaño exagerado). Le recuerdo al lector que sobre la base de la discusión en el capítulo IV, se espera que estas variables no tengan efecto, mientras que otros investigadores (Strom, 2000) esperan un signo negativo de los gobiernos minoritarios (ya que éstos requieren respaldo de partidos que no están en el gobierno) y un signo positivo para las coaliciones de tamaño exagerado (ya que éstas pueden prescindir del respaldo de algunos asociados en el gobierno).

Los resultados de la estimación se resumen en el cuadro VIII.2, y coinciden con los pronósticos de la teoría de los jugadores con veto: ambos coeficientes de distancia ideológica y alternación en este modelo tienen significancia y llevan el signo que se esperaba. Además, el tamaño de los coeficientes estandarizados de la distancia ideológica (-0.17) y alternación (0.12) sugiere que el efecto de la estructura de los jugadores con veto no

CUADRO VIII.1. *Resultados sencillos sobre estructura presupuestaria en 19 países de la* OCDE, *1973-1995.*
(Modelo estimado por regresión heteroesquedástica multiplicativa.)

	Modelo 1	Modelo 2
Variable dependiente: el valor esperado de la distancia del presupuesto		
Constante	0.2759****	0.2820****
	(0.0199)	(0.0201)
Distancia del presupuesto retrasada	0.1515****	0.1360****
	(0.0349)	(0.0351)
Distancia ideológica	−0.0155	
	(0.0165)	
Variable dependiente: el término de error de la distancia del presupuesto		
Constante	−2.5480****	−2.5243****
	(0.0769)	(0.0769)
Distancia ideológica	−0.2004***	
	(0.0872)	
N	338	338
Prob. $> \chi^2$	0.000	0.000
Prueba de probabilidad-razón entre el modelo 1 y el modelo 2: $\chi^2_2 = 5.74$		
Probabilidad $< \chi^2_2 = 0.0567$		

Nota: Errores estándar entre paréntesis.
* $p < 0.1$ nivel.
** $p < 0.05$ nivel.
*** $p < 0.01$ nivel.
**** $p < 0.001$ nivel.
Todas las pruebas son de una cola.

sólo tiene significancia estadística sino que es también de considerable importancia. Las variables falsas de gobierno minoritario y de tamaño exagerado no tienen significancia, tal como se esperaba de acuerdo con la teoría de los jugadores con veto (y la de tamaño exagerado incluso tiene el signo erróneo). Descartar el tipo de variables de gobierno así como las variables

CUADRO VIII.2. *Resultados multivariables sobre estructura presupuestaria en 19 países de la* OCDE, *1973-1995.*
(Modelo estimado por modelo de series temporales de corte transversal de efecto fijo con errores estándar corregidos por panel.)

	Modelo 1 coeficiente	Modelo 1 coeficiente estándar	Modelo 2
Distancia del presupuesto retrasada	0.0870** (0.0446)	0.1316**	0.0896** (0.0437)
Distancia ideológica	−0.0547** (0.0277)	−0.1665***	−0.0500*** (0.0275)
Alternación	0.0375*** (0.0170)	0.1185**	0.0381*** (0.0172)
Δ desempleo	0.0360** (0.0208)	0.1008**	0.0361** (0.0209)
Δ edad > 65	0.0041 (0.1416)	0.0018	
Δ crecimiento	0.0055 (0.0070)	0.0383	
Δ INF	0.0018 (0.0040)	0.0273	
Minoría	−0.0432 (0.0879)	−0.0596	
Tamaño exagerado	−0.0020 (0.0793)	−0.0024	
N	336		336
R^2 ajustado	0.6154		0.6200
Prob. > χ^2	0.0000		0.0000

Nota: Los coeficientes estimados para variables de país falsas se suprimen para facilitar la presentación. Los errores estándar corregidos por panel están entre paréntesis.
* $p < 0.1$ nivel.
** $p < 0.05$ nivel.
*** $p < 0.01$ nivel.
**** $p < 0.001$ nivel.
Todas las pruebas son de una cola.

económicas ΔPOP65, ΔGROWTH, ΔINF (que tampoco tienen significancia) y volver a dirigir la regresión para verificar la solidez da exactamente los mismos resultados (modelo 2).

En conclusión, toda la evidencia empírica que presentan TC convalida la hipótesis de que, pese a los factores que explican el cambio automático de estructura presupuestaria, el cambio deliberado de estructura presupuestaria se puede explicar mediante la distancia ideológica gubernamental y las diferencias ideológicas entre los gobiernos. Específicamente, una coalición gubernamental está asociada con un cambio más importante en el presupuesto si los miembros de este gobierno son menos diversos ideológicamente o si su posición ideológica es más divergente del gobierno anterior. En otras palabras, la estructura presupuestaria tiende a trabarse dentro del patrón existente en sistemas políticos con jugadores con veto ideológicamente distantes; en contraste, la estructura presupuestaria tiende a ser más flexible en sistemas políticos con jugadores con veto ideológicamente similares.

TC también investigaron la forma en que la distancia ideológica y la alternación afectan la estructura del presupuesto sobre un nivel desagregado. Sus resultados, que se presentan en el cuadro VIII.3, sugieren que la distancia ideológica y la alternación asimismo explican bien el cambio en cada categoría presupuestaria. De hecho, hay sólo una de las nueve partidas del presupuesto (vivienda y comodidades comunitarias) con el signo equivocado en la variable de la distancia ideológica (pero no tiene significancia), y todo el resto tiene los signos esperados en ambas variables. Dos de los ocho casos restantes (defensa y otras comodidades comunitarias y sociales) tienen el signo esperado pero no tienen significancia; y en todos los demás casos ambos coeficientes tienen signos correctos y al menos uno de ellos tiene significancia. La distancia ideológica afecta considerablemente seis de nueve categorías presupuestarias; y la alternación tiene un efecto importante sobre ocho de nueve categorías presupuestarias. En particular, encuentra que entre estas nueves categorías del presupuesto, el cambio de educación, salud y seguridad social es especialmente sensible tanto a los efectos de la distancia ideológica como a los de la alternación.

Finalmente, TC duplican su modelo, verificando por separado cada una de las dimensiones implícitas, y encuentran que el modelo bidimensional tiene esencialmente el mismo desempeño que la primera dimensión, pero supera a la segunda dimensión (véase cuadro VIII.4). Considerando cada partida del presupuesto una por una, el modelo bidimensional presenta me-

Cuadro VIII.3. *Resultados estimados por cada categoría presupuestaria.*

Categoría presupuestaria	Distancia ideológica	Alternación
Servicios públicos generales	−0.0852** (0.0505)	0.0040 (0.0266)
Defensa	−0.0149 (0.0241)	0.0111 (0.015)
Educación	−0.1197** (0.0716)	0.0544** (0.0271)
Salud	−0.2340*** (0.1033)	0.1160*** (0.0477)
Seguridad y bienestar social	−0.2724*** (0.1034)	0.0672 (0.0574)
Vivienda y comodidades comunitarias	0.0826 (0.0953)	0.5096*** (0.0929)
Otros servicios comunitarios y sociales	−0.0119 (0.0126)	0.0026 (0.0047)
Servicios económicos	−0.1804* (0.1306)	0.0612* (0.0432)
Otros	−0.1970 (0.1690)	0.0018 (0.0852)

Nota: Los coeficientes estimados para variables de país falsas, los cambios en tasa de desempleo y la variable dependiente retrasada se suprimen para facilitar la presentación. Los errores estándar corregidos por panel están entre paréntesis.
* $p < 0.1$ nivel.
** $p < 0.05$ nivel.
*** $p < 0.01$ nivel.
Todas las pruebas son de una cola.

joramiento en una dimensión (habitualmente la segunda) en cinco de 10 casos, deterioro en cuatro y ningún impacto en uno. Estos resultados empíricos indican que el mejoramiento del modelo bidimensional es principalmente conceptual en un análisis cuando se usa únicamente la primera división, y tanto conceptual como empírico en la segunda dimensión.

CUADRO VIII.4. *Comparación del poder explicativo de análisis unidimensional y bidimensional.*

Categoría presupuestaria	Distancia ideológica en 1ª dimensión	Alternación en 1ª dimensión	Distancia ideológica en 2ª dimensión	Alternación en 2ª dimensión	Distancia ideológica en dos dimensiones	Alternación en dos dimensiones	Dimensión ideológica 1ª–2	Alternación 1ª–2	Distancia ideológica 2ª–2	Alternación 2ª–2
Total	***	***	*	***	**	***	→		←	
Servicios públicos generales	**	*	C	*	*	*	→		←	
Defensa	C	**	C	**	C	C		→		→
Educación	**	**	C	***	**	**		→	←	→
Salud	***	****	**	****	***	****				
Seguridad y bienestar social	***	*	***	C	***	*			←	←
Vivienda	W	C	W	*	W	C	→	←←		←←
Otros servicios comunitarios y sociales	*	C	C	C	C	**	→	←←		←←
Servicios económicos	**	*	C	**	*	***	→	←	←	←
Otros	C	**	**	*	*	C	←	→	→	→

Notas: W significa "signo equivocado". C significa "signo correcto".
  * $p < 0.1$.
 ** $p < 0.05$.
*** $p < 0.01$.
↑ significa que los resultados mejoran en un paso (de W a C, * a ** etc.).
↑↑ significa que los resultados mejoran en dos pasos (W a * * a *** etc.).
↑↑↑ significa que los resultados mejoran en tres pasos (C a *** etc.).
↓ significa empeoramiento de los resultados.

3. Otros resultados macroeconómicos

En esta sección presento tres diferentes estudios con distintas variables dependientes: inflación, tributación y crecimiento. La expectativa de la teoría de los jugadores con veto es la misma independientemente de la variable dependiente: cambios importantes en los resultados estarán asociados sólo con jugadores con veto ideológicamente congruentes. Entre las variables independientes usadas en estos estudios, hay una (federalismo) que está directamente correlacionada con los jugadores con veto. Además, los argumentos de estos artículos se relacionan de forma implícita o explícita con los argumentos que se plantean en este libro. Presentaré estos estudios en secuencia y explicaré la relación entre sus resultados y la teoría que se presenta en esta obra.

A. *Federalismo e inflación*. La expectativa teórica generada del análisis en este libro es que los cambios en la inflación serán más bajos en países federales que en unitarios. De hecho, como se vio en el capítulo VI, el federalismo está asociado con un creciente número de jugadores con veto *(ceteris paribus)*. Treisman (2000c) estudió la inflación en 87 países durante las décadas de 1970 y 1980. Comparó tres diferentes expectativas para la relación entre federalismo e inflación generada por diferentes teorías (en sus palabras, compromiso, acción colectiva y continuidad). Las teorías del "compromiso" esperan una inflación más baja en países descentralizados, ya que los diversos actores que intervienen en la toma de decisiones reducen la capacidad de un gobierno central para causar inflación con fines políticos. Las teorías de "acción colectiva" esperan una inflación más alta en países federales, ya que los diversos actores implicados se dedicarán a aprovechar las ventajas fiscales. Lo que Treisman denomina teorías de "continuidad" es la teoría de los jugadores con veto que ya hemos descrito.[5] Treisman concluye, pronto en su artículo, que hay

> un fuerte respaldo para la hipótesis de la continuidad. En general, las tasas de inflación promedio tendieron a elevarse durante las décadas de 1970 y 1980 en Estados tanto unitarios como federales. Aunque hubo una tendencia general hacia arriba, el alza fue menor en federaciones con inflación baja en el periodo anterior en comparación con Estados unitarios similares, y el alza fue mayor

[5] De hecho, en este artículo Daniel Treisman utiliza a menudo la terminología de jugadores con veto.

en federaciones que empezaron con inflación alta en comparación con Estados unitarios similares [Treisman, 2000c: 844].

El resto del análisis apunta a identificar los mecanismos necesarios para explicar estos resultados. Según Treisman, hay dos razones principales. Primero, "la estructura federal, al aumentar el número de jugadores con veto requeridos para cambiar el sistema de control sobre banqueros centrales, tiende a coartar el grado de independencia del banco central, ya sea alta o baja" (Treisman, 2000c: 851). Segundo, los sistemas políticos difieren en el grado en que los desequilibrios son empujados del nivel local al regional y luego al nacional (lo que Treisman denomina "conductividad fiscal"). "La descentralización [...] parece reducir el cambio en el grado de conductividad, sea alta o baja" (Treisman, 2000c: 853).

B. *Tributación y jugadores con veto*. De acuerdo con la teoría que se presenta en este libro, cualquier cambio importante de la tributación sólo será posible con pocos jugadores con veto. Hallerberg y Basinger (1998) estudiaron el cambio de tributación que ocurrió en países de la OCDE a fines de la década de 1980. Todos los países de la OCDE redujeron impuestos para los individuos de mayor ingreso y para las empresas. Considerando el monto de cada una de estas dos reducciones como una variable dependiente, Hallerberg y Basinger tratan de identificar la causa de este cambio. En su análisis consideran una serie de variables de la bibliografía económica que debían ejercer un impacto sobre los fundamentos teóricos. Primero, incluyen la movilidad del capital, dado que los países pueden verse obligados a bajar su tasa tributaria para impedir fugas de capital conforme éste se hace más móvil. Segundo, toman en cuenta la dependencia comercial dado que las economías abiertas tienden a ser más sensibles a cambios en tasas tributarias que las economías cerradas. Finalmente, controlan también la inflación y el crecimiento económico. Desde el punto de vista de la bibliografía sobre ciencias políticas, las posibles variables pertinentes eran jugadores con veto (incluidos en su análisis como una variable falsa) y partidismo, este último porque prácticamente toda la bibliografía sobre ciencias políticas argumenta que los partidos de ala derecha reducen impuestos para los estratos de altos ingresos y para las empresas, mientras que la izquierda alza los impuestos con estos dos grupos como sus principales blancos.

Sólo dos de estas variables dieron lugar a resultados consistentes tanto para las reducciones tributarias (la personal y la empresarial): jugadores con veto y crecimiento real. Hallerberg y Basinger interpretan de la siguiente manera su resultado de jugador con veto: "Los resultados en lo tocante a los jugadores con veto fueron extremadamente alentadores. Un movimiento hacia dos o más jugadores con veto desde un jugador con veto reduce el cambio de las tasas empresariales en 18.4 puntos y reduce el cambio en el ingreso neto marginal tope en 20.3 puntos".

El uso que hacen Hallerberg y Basinger (1998) de una variable falsa es consistente con el argumento que se presenta aquí. Como se vio en el capítulo VII, en una sola dimensión lo que importa es la distancia ideológica entre los socios de una coalición. En tanto que los gobiernos de un solo partido tienen, por definición, un rango de cero, el rango de gobiernos de dos partidos o de varios no está necesariamente relacionado con el número de asociados.

C. *Crecimiento y jugadores con veto*. La teoría que presento en este libro no hace ningún pronóstico acerca de una relación entre jugadores con veto y crecimiento. Como se estipuló en la Introducción, la suposición fundamental de muchos argumentos económicos es que muchos jugadores con veto crean la posibilidad de que un sistema político "se comprometa", de que no altere las reglas del juego económico (como sería confiscar repentinamente riqueza mediante tributación). A la inversa, la suposición fundamental de la mayor parte de los análisis políticos es que los sistemas políticos deben ser capaces de responder a choques exógenos. He conectado los dos argumentos y he dicho que "elevado nivel de compromiso" es otra forma de decir "incapacidad de respuesta política". No está claro si muchos jugadores con veto conducirán a un crecimiento más alto o más bajo, ya que "amarrarán" a un país a cualesquiera políticas que hereden, y depende de si dichas políticas inducen o inhiben el crecimiento.

Witold Henisz (2000a) sometió a prueba el habitual argumento económico de que muchos jugadores con veto crean un compromiso creíble para no interferir con los derechos de la propiedad privada que "es un instrumento para obtener las inversiones de capital a largo plazo requeridas para que los países experimenten un rápido crecimiento económico" (Henisz, 2000a: 2-3).

El lector cuidadoso reconocerá que este argumento agrega una suposición importante a mi análisis: que mayor credibilidad conduce a más altos niveles de crecimiento. Henisz (2000a: 6) reconoce que mayor estabilidad también podría prolongar un *statu quo* malo:

Las restricciones que estos factores institucionales y políticos proporcionan pueden paralizar también los esfuerzos del gobierno para responder a choques externos y/o corregir errores políticos. [...] Sin embargo, la suposición de la bibliografía y de este artículo es que, en promedio, el beneficio de unas restricciones a la discreción ejecutiva supera los costos de la flexibilidad perdida.

Para la prueba empírica, Henisz (2000a) crea un conjunto de datos que abarca 157 países para un periodo de 35 años (1960-1995). Identifica cinco posibles jugadores con veto: el ejecutivo, la legislatura, una segunda cámara de la legislatura, el poder judicial y el federalismo. Construye un índice de restricciones políticas, tomando en cuenta si el ejecutivo controla a los otros jugadores con veto (legislatura, poder judicial, gobiernos estatales) y la fraccionalización de estos jugadores adicionales con veto, y promedia sus resultados durante periodos de cinco años. Entonces vuelve a examinar el análisis del crecimiento de Barro (1996) introduciendo su nueva variable independiente. Sus conclusiones son que la variable de las "restricciones políticas" tiene poder explicativo adicional y que sus resultados son significativos: un cambio en la desviación estándar en esta variable produce entre 17 y 31% de un cambio de desviación estándar en el crecimiento.

La variable independiente de Henisz está conceptualmente muy relacionada con los jugadores con veto, y cubre un número abrumador de países. Sin embargo, es discutible la correlación empírica entre las "restricciones políticas" y el número o las distancias entre jugadores con veto. Por ejemplo, el sistema judicial no siempre tiene jugadores con veto (véase el capítulo X) y el federalismo parece haber sido contado por partida doble porque está incluido en la segunda cámara de una legislatura. Además, las restricciones legislativas se incluyen mientras se toma en cuenta a *todos* los partidos en el parlamento. Tal enfoque puede ser correcto para sistemas presidenciales con coaliciones creadas en torno de proyectos de ley específicos; pero en sistemas parlamentarios, el gobierno controla el juego legislativo (como se vio en el capítulo IV) porque se basa (al menos la mayor parte del tiempo) sobre una mayoría parlamentaria estable. Como resultado, los partidos de oposición no imponen restricciones a la legislación.

Estas diferentes reglas de conteo producen evaluaciones significativamente distintas de los países. Por ejemplo, Henisz encuentra que Canadá tiene restricciones políticas muy altas, mientras que en este libro la clasificación es muy diferente (la segunda cámara que representa también a los gobiernos locales es débil o está controlada por el mismo partido que la primera, y el poder judicial no es muy fuerte). De modo similar, se considera que Alemania y Bélgica tienen "restricciones políticas" muy grandes, mientras que en mis análisis Alemania tiene un rango intermedio de jugadores con veto (la distancia ideológica de los jugadores con veto sólo es elevada cuando el Bundesrat está dominado por la oposición).

En suma, la gran ventaja del conjunto de datos de Henisz es que abarca el mayor número de países reportados en este libro; las desventajas son que se introducen algunas restricciones que no reflejan el proceso real de la toma de decisiones, y que aunque se identifica un mecanismo plausible (según el cual las restricciones afectan la credibilidad de los compromisos, de la inversión y del crecimiento), sólo se muestra una correlación entre el primero y los últimos pasos del proceso.

4. Conclusiones

En este capítulo se analizan estudios empíricos de una serie de resultados macroeconómicos. Todo parece estar correlacionado con la estructura de los jugadores con veto de manera importante: cuantos más jugadores con veto y/o cuanto más distantes estén, más difícil será apartarse del *statu quo*. De hecho, los déficits presupuestarios se reducen a un ritmo más lento (cuando su reducción se convierte en una prioridad política importante), la estructura de los presupuestos se hace más viscosa, la inflación permanece en los mismos niveles (ya sean altos o bajos) y la política tributaria no cambia fácilmente. Todos estos resultados indican una alta estabilidad de los resultados. Por añadidura, revisando la bibliografía encontramos la comprobación empírica de un resultado esperado en la bibliografía económica: la existencia de muchos jugadores con veto puede reducir los riesgos políticos asociados con un gobierno activo, aumentar la inversión y conducir a niveles más altos de crecimiento.

La mayor parte de los análisis hechos en este capítulo usan alguna medición correlacionada con los jugadores con veto (como el federalismo de Treisman, 2000c, la variable falsa de los jugadores con veto de Hallerberg y Basinger, 1998) por un indicador unidimensional (Bawn, 1998; Franzese, 2001). Sin embargo, Tsebelis y Chang (2002) en un estudio hacen uso del análisis multidimensional que se presentó en la primera parte de este libro.

CUARTA PARTE

EFECTOS SISTÉMICOS DE LOS JUGADORES CON VETO

En esta última parte analizo los resultados estructurales de la estabilidad política. ¿Por qué debe importarnos que sea fácil o difícil cambiar el *statu quo*? Como se estipula en la Introducción, una forma de concebir la estabilidad política es como un compromiso creíble del sistema político de no intervenir en interacciones económicas, políticas o sociales y reglamentarlas. Otra manera es concebir la estabilidad política como la incapacidad del sistema político para responder a los cambios que ocurren en el ambiente económico, político y social. Estos dos aspectos están intrínsecamente vinculados y son inseparables. Algunos analistas pueden preferir una manera de pensar más que la otra, hasta el momento en que la estructura institucional, alabada por su capacidad de hacer compromisos creíbles, es incapaz de responder a algún choque, o el sistema político con firmeza admirable es incapaz de hacer compromisos creíbles. El argumento, hasta el momento, ha sido el de que estructuras institucionales particulares producirán niveles específicos de estabilidad política, y no es posible tener credibilidad parte del tiempo y cambiar hacia la firmeza cuando se la necesite. Decidirse por una estructura institucional es algo que da a la situación un cierto nivel de estabilidad política. Pero, ¿cuáles son los resultados de diferentes niveles de estabilidad política?

La estabilidad política tiene múltiples efectos. Primero, en regímenes presidenciales, si la estabilidad política es grande, la inestabilidad del régimen aumenta (como se vio en el capítulo III): es posible que el presidente o los militares se vuelvan en contra de las instituciones democráticas que sean incapaces de resolver los problemas del país. En los tres capítulos siguientes examinaremos más a fondo otros resultados de la estabilidad política.

El primer resultado de la estabilidad política que estudiaremos en el capítulo IX es la *inestabilidad* del gobierno en las democracias parlamentarias. Como ya se ha visto, los sistemas parlamentarios tienen la flexibilidad de cambio de gobierno cuando hay un callejón sin salida político. El gobierno decide retar al parlamento con la cuestión de la confianza y pierde o renuncia debido a que no puede hacer aprobar su legislación en el parlamento, o el parlamento que está en desacuerdo con el gobierno quita a éste del poder. Un desacuerdo importante entre gobierno y parlamento conduce a una nueva coalición de gobierno que puede (o no) resolver el callejón sin salida político. Lo interesante de esto es que lo que los jugadores perciben como "callejón sin salida político" es lo que hemos denominado estabilidad política en este libro. Por lo tanto, la estabilidad política acrecienta la probabilidad de sustituir gobiernos, a lo que haremos referencia de aquí en adelante como inestabilidad gubernamental.

En el capítulo IX se aborda el tema de la supervivencia del gobierno. Aunque la mayor parte de los análisis teóricos y empíricos explican la inestabilidad gubernamental mediante características que prevalecen en el parlamento de un país, la teoría de los jugadores con veto se concentra en la composición de los gobiernos para explicar la supervivencia gubernamental. Como se ha demostrado en la obra de Warwick (1994), las explicaciones basadas en la composición gubernamental son más exactas empíricamente. Lo que este capítulo muestra es que este análisis es congruente con la estructura de jugadores con veto presentada en este libro. Demuestro que la teoría de los jugadores con veto combinada con una comprensión teóricamente informada del concepto de *statu quo* puede explicar todos los resultados desconcertantes de la bibliografía empírica.

El capítulo X trata sobre la independencia de las burocracias y el poder judicial. Se verá por qué la estabilidad política conduce a una mayor independencia de estas dos ramas, y se presentarán pruebas empíricas que corroboran estas expectativas. Compararé mis resultados para burócratas y jueces con otros trabajos teóricos o empíricos. Si diferentes teorías generan distintas expectativas, explico las razones de las diferencias y considero la evidencia empírica en busca de comprobación.

El capítulo XI aplica la teoría de los jugadores con veto a un caso insólito: la Unión Europea. Según Alberta Sbragia (1992: 257), la Unión Europea es "única por su estructura institucional [...] no es ni un Estado ni una organización internacional". La Unión Europea también ha cambiado su constitución varias veces en los últimos 15 años. Estas peculiaridades han llevado a los estudiosos de la Unión Europea a describirla como un sistema *sui generis* (Westlake, 1994: 29; Nugent, 1994: 206). Finalmente, las instituciones de la Unión Europea incluyen estipulaciones muy complicadas. Las decisiones del Consejo de Ministros las toma una mayoría triple, mientras que dos instituciones más, el Parlamento Europeo y la Comisión Europea, participan en el proceso de toma de decisiones con mucha frecuencia como jugadores con veto. Por estas razones, considero que un buen análisis de este sistema fluido e insólito es una prueba difícil para la teoría de este libro. Si el análisis de los jugadores con veto nos proporciona atisbos interesantes y exactos acerca de la Unión Europea, la teoría habrá pasado una prueba exigente. El lector verá que la estructura del proceso legislativo ha cambiado varias veces, desplazando al poder entre los principales actores institucionales. Además, estos cambios han afectado el papel de otros actores, por ejemplo la burocracia y el poder judicial, exactamente igual que en otros países, tal como la primera mitad de este libro nos ha llevado a esperar, y exactamente como se demuestra en el capítulo x.

IX. LA ESTABILIDAD GUBERNAMENTAL

COMO se vio en el capítulo IV, la estabilidad gubernamental es una variable importante para el estudio de los sistemas parlamentarios. Por ejemplo, Lijphart (1999: 129) considera la duración del gobierno como un sustituto del "predominio ejecutivo" y distingue este enfoque de lo que él denomina el punto de vista "prevaleciente" según el cual "la durabilidad del gabinete es un indicador no sólo de la fortaleza del gabinete en comparación con la de la legislatura sino también de la estabilidad del régimen". Huber y Lupia (2000) arguyen que la estabilidad gubernamental acrecienta la eficiencia ministerial debido a que un ministro del que se espera siga en su puesto será respetado por la burocracia.

En realidad, la formación de coaliciones gubernamentales y la duración de los gobiernos correspondientes ha sido probablemente una de las ramas más prolíficas en la bibliografía sobre política en democracias industrializadas avanzadas. A partir de la obra de Riker (1962), los teóricos de la coalición descubrieron la importancia de las "coaliciones de ganancia mínima"[1] y entonces procedieron a definir una serie de otros conceptos útiles para el estudio de la formación de coaliciones: "tamaño mínimo", "rango mínimo", "ganancia conectada mínima", "política viable".[2] Floreció el trabajo empírico sobre la durabilidad de diferentes gobiernos (Dodd, 1976; Sanders y Herman, 1977; Robertson, 1983; Schofield, 1987; Laver y Schofield, 1990; Strom, 1988; King *et al.*, 1990; Warwick, 1994). Algunas de estas obras se basaron en la composición "numérica" de diferentes gobiernos (número de escaños que controlaban, estatus mayoritario o minoritario); otras partes incluían las posiciones políticas de los partidos (ya fuera todos ellos o sólo aquéllos que compusieran al gobierno); la mayor parte incluía información adicional pertinente a la formación del gobierno (de si el gobierno tenía que recibir un voto de investidura del parlamento, cuántos intentos de formación de gobierno fueron hechos antes de un gobierno consolidado).

---

[1] Coaliciones que dejan de controlar una mayoría de escaños en el parlamento si pierden a un miembro del partido.
[2] Véase Lijphart (1999: 91-96) para definición y análisis de todos estos conceptos.

En este capítulo reviso esta bibliografía, señalo los resultados más recientes y los confronto con las principales expectativas generadas por la teoría de los jugadores con veto: que la estabilidad política conduce a la inestabilidad gubernamental. Con el fin de poder generar pronósticos específicos a partir de la teoría, analizo a fondo un concepto fundamental (en modelos teóricos de juegos) pero elusivo (en el trabajo empírico): el *statu quo*. Desarrollo más a fondo la diferencia entre políticas (como las que se estudiaron en el capítulo VII) y los resultados (como los del capítulo VIII), y explico por qué lo que en el pasado solía ser una situación satisfactoria en un país puede ahora requerir cambios importantes. Desde este punto de partida estudio las implicaciones para la supervivencia del gobierno. Los gobiernos son los actores responsables de tales ajustes, y dado que su composición afecta su capacidad de actuar, perjudica en última instancia su probabilidad de supervivencia. Como resultado de este análisis, la duración del gobierno en regímenes parlamentarios estará vinculada a la configuración de los jugadores con veto. Una vez establecido este vínculo, reviso el análisis de Lijphart acerca de la conexión entre duración del gobierno y el predominio ejecutivo que se presentó en el capítulo IV, y explico por qué la duración del gobierno se correlaciona empíricamente con el predominio ejecutivo a pesar del hecho de que no hay una conexión lógica, como se vio en el capítulo IV.

Este capítulo está organizado en tres partes. En la primera se revisa la bibliografía sobre la duración del gobierno y se examina si ésta depende de características del parlamento o del gobierno de un país. La segunda emplea la teoría que se presenta en este libro para explicar los resultados empíricos. La tercera se vale de los resultados de capítulos anteriores para explicar por qué la duración del gobierno se correlaciona con el predominio ejecutivo, pese a la falta de conexión lógica.

1. La bibliografía sobre estabilidad gubernamental

La mayor parte de la bibliografía sobre duración de gobierno la correlaciona con las características del parlamento, como el número de partidos y sus distancias ideológicas entre sí. Análisis más recientes se concentran en las características gubernamentales. En esta sección comparo y contrasto los dos enfoques, pero empiezo explicando qué evalúa la bibliografía cuando discute "estabilidad del gobierno".

1. *Estabilidad gubernamental*. Aunque muchos autores han escrito acerca de la estabilidad gubernamental, no han aplicado las mismas condiciones definitorias para saber qué es un remplazo de gobierno. Por ejemplo, diferentes autores no concuerdan en si la situación donde un gobierno es remplazado por otro con la misma composición de partido debe contarse como un solo gobierno o como dos diferentes.

Más exactamente, hay cuatro diferentes criterios que se aplican en la bibliografía: si la composición de partido de un gobierno cambia o no, si hay o no una renuncia formal del gobierno, si hay un cambio de primer ministro, y si hay una elección. Aunque todos los autores aceptan el primer criterio, existen variaciones en lo tocante a todos los demás. Dodd (1976) y Lijphart (1984) aceptan únicamente el primer criterio como condición necesaria y suficiente para un cambio de gobierno. El segundo criterio, y el más frecuentemente usado para la terminación del gobierno, es una elección. Laver y Schofield (1990: 147) justifican este criterio porque una elección cambia el peso de los partidos en el parlamento, y en consecuencia modifica el ambiente de negociación donde se da la formación de coalición. Los otros dos criterios tienen graves desventajas para el análisis comparativo: en algunos países se requiere la renuncia formal y en otros no, y la renuncia de un primer ministro puede obedecer o no a razones políticas, de modo que hay un mayor desacuerdo en lo tocante a estos dos criterios.

¿Cuál de estos criterios es el más apropiado? Creo que cada autor selecciona un criterio que tiene mayor sentido según la base de su propia opinión sobre cómo funciona el proceso. Por ejemplo, si opina que la composición del gobierno depende del poder relativo de los diferentes partidos, la inclusión de elecciones como criterio es una elección muy razonable. Si se percibe que la mayor parte de las renuncias de primeros ministros son acontecimientos políticos, incluso si los implicados afirman que renuncian "por razones personales", la inclusión de la renuncia del primer ministro también tiene sentido. En el capítulo VII adopté el criterio de Lijphart (1984) y Dodd (1976) de la composición de partido de los gobiernos al crear una lista de gobiernos "mezclados" pero repetí los cálculos con las definiciones más tradicionales, obteniendo los mismos resultados cualitativos. Lijphart (1999) promedió los resultados sobre la duración generados por su propio criterio con las normas que se aplican en gran parte de la bibliografía y usó la "duración" promedio generada de este modo para calcular su índice de "predominio ejecutivo". Regresaremos a este punto en la última sección de este capítulo.

2. *Las características parlamentarias afectan la estabilidad gubernamental*. Cualquiera que sea la norma de duración, usualmente está correlacionada con las características parlamentarias. Por ejemplo, incluso en el ímpetu inicial de crear teorías sobre la coalición (Riker, 1962; sobre la base de la teoría del juego cooperativo), una serie de modelos "ciegos a la política" presuponía que las coaliciones formadas serían de "ganancia mínima" en el parlamento, de modo que las carteras ministeriales no serían asignadas a partidos que no fueran necesarios para obtener una mayoría en el parlamento.

Más adelante se introdujeron criterios de posición política, y el modelo subyacente giraba en torno a mejorar la propia posición en el gabinete. La mayor parte del tiempo esto significa aumentar la participación en carteras de un partido, aunque algunos analistas como De Swaan (1973: 88) sostuvieron que "un actor intenta formar una coalición ganadora en la cual esté incluido y que espera adoptar una política que esté tan cerca como sea posible [...] de su propia política preferida".

El argumento implícito o explícito en todos los enfoques fue que diferentes partidos obligarían a un gobierno a renunciar cuando tuvieran una buena oportunidad de ser incluidos en el siguiente gobierno y obtener una mejor posición. Como resultado, entran en escena las características del *parlamento* que producen a los gobiernos. Si un partido está centralmente colocado en el parlamento, si es grande, si otros partidos están dispersos o agrupados, todos estos indicadores son buenos pronósticos de que un partido será incluido en el siguiente gobierno. Aquí están las variables que afectan la duración del gobierno sobre la base de esta bibliografía: el número de partidos en el sistema político (Duverger, 1954), el "número efectivo de partidos" en un sistema, la presencia de partidos antisistema o de partidos "extremistas", el grado de polarización ideológica o "conflicto de fragmentación" (todas estas condiciones hacen más difícil formar y mantener gobiernos). Finalmente, el requerimiento de investidura formal elimina a algunos gobiernos que en caso contrario podrían haber sobrevivido por un tiempo (Laver y Schofield, 1990: 147-148). En lo tocante a las características del gobierno mismo, los resultados de los análisis empíricos indicaron que la condición de "ganancia mínima" aumentaba la longevidad del gobierno, en tanto que Sanders y Herman (1977) y Schofield (1987) no encontraron pruebas de que lo compacto del gobierno en lo ideológico afectara su longevidad.

Todos estos enfoques, según Laver y Schofield (1990: 155), dejan "dos importantes cabos sueltos. [...] El primero es que hay una considerable variación inexplicada entre sistemas en la duración promedio de los gabinetes. El segundo es que la duración de los gabinetes no parece estar relacionada con asuntos políticos, pese al hecho de que la política de partido acrecienta grandemente nuestra capacidad de explicar la formación de gobiernos para empezar". Con el fin de abordar estos dos problemas, Laver y Schofield introducen un "ambiente de negociación" como una variable independiente. Muestran que en un espacio político de una sola dimensión (izquierda-derecha) podemos dividir diferentes países en centrista unipolar, fuera del centro unipolar, bipolar y multipolar. Entonces demuestran que los países con un sistema de negociación centrista unipolar (como Luxemburgo e Irlanda), o con un sistema bipolar (como Austria y Alemania), tienen gobiernos que duran significativamente más que países con ambientes de negociación multipolares (como Holanda, Finlandia, Italia); países con sistemas unipolares (fuera de centro) (como Noruega, Suecia, Islandia) tienen niveles intermedios de longevidad gubernamental. Laver y Schofield (1990) crearon uno de los últimos "modelos deterministas"[3] de duración de gobiernos y llevaron el método hasta donde ha llegado.

El enfoque determinista fue criticado por los modelos de "enfoque en los hechos" que se basan en la idea de que las verdaderas disoluciones de gobiernos son causadas por sucesos aleatorios que los actores no pudieron prever (Browne, Gleiber y Mashoba, 1984). La intención inicial del enfoque en los hechos no era concentrarse en las causas de la duración del gobierno, sino en modelar explícitamente su aleatoriedad. Los modelos en los hechos se concentraban en la probabilidad condicional de que un gobierno termine por haber sobrevivido por un cierto periodo. Esta tasa condicional de terminación (tasa de riesgo) que se suponía constante entre países se convirtió en la variable dependiente en la mayoría de los análisis, pero los resultados empíricos fueron pobres: las tasas de riesgo eran diferentes entre países (las únicas excepciones fueron Bélgica, Finlandia, Italia e Israel).

King y colaboradores (1990) fueron los primeros en presentar un modelo que unificaba los dos enfoques. Incluía los argumentos causales de los enfoques deterministas junto con la metodología superior del enfoque en los hechos: el modelo convertía las tasas de riesgo en una función de las características que los modelos deterministas estudiaban. En otras palabras, el nuevo modelo suponía que los gobiernos caen como resultado de hechos aleatorios, pero la capacidad de diferentes gobiernos para sobrevivir era función

---

[3] Los modelos deterministas son los que suponen que la duración del gobierno es una función de las variables independientes incluidas en el modelo.

de diferentes características que prevalecían en el sistema de partidos del país. Los resultados de este modelo unificado indican que la fragmentación del sistema de partidos y la polarización de la oposición son los atributos del régimen más fuertemente asociados con la duración del gabinete.

Como consecuencia de estos resultados, Laver y Schofield (1990: 161) llegan a la conclusión de que "la fragmentación y polarización del sistema de partidos aparecen como las variables importantes en un análisis que controla una gran variedad de asuntos e incluso toma en cuenta el impacto de choques aleatorios. Éstas, por supuesto, son las variables que identificamos como parámetros importantes de la estabilidad del sistema de negociación, y por lo tanto tendientes a ejercer un impacto sobre la estabilidad del gabinete".

En conclusión, la introducción de metodología más avanzada no alteró las conclusiones de la bibliografía sobre coaliciones para 1990: las dos características principales que afectan la supervivencia del gobierno en sistemas parlamentarios son características del sistema de partidos de un país: fragmentación y polarización. Estas dos variables representan características determinadas por el *parlamento* que selecciona a los diferentes gobiernos, y ambas tienen que ver con el ambiente de negociación que prevalece en este parlamento.

3. *Las características del gobierno afectan la estabilidad del gobierno.* Varios años después, Paul Warwick (1994) presentó una crítica seria de los resultados anteriores, y una especificación alternativa del modelo subyacente. Pasó la explicación de la sobrevivencia del gobierno, del parlamento al *gobierno*. Criticó tanto la variable de polarización del parlamento como la variable de fragmentación del parlamento, y las sustituyó por variables similares que describen a los gobiernos.

En lo tocante a la polarización, Warwick arguyó que ésta no necesariamente afecta la complejidad del ambiente de negociación. De hecho, tenía el efecto contrario:

> Laver y Schofield creyeron que la variable de polarización refleja la complejidad global de las posiciones de partido en el sistema de partidos; cuanto más complicado sea este arreglo, más vulnerable será la distribución del poder de negociación a ligeras perturbaciones. Pero lo que la variable mide en realidad es la proporción de escaños parlamentarios ocupada por partidos extremistas, y dado que los partidos extremistas suelen ser considerados socios indeseables entre los partidos pro sistema ["no coalicionables", en términos de Laver y Scho-

field, 1990: 200-201], su presencia debería estrechar la gama de alternativas de coalición, si todo lo demás permanece constante [Warwick, 1994: 46].

Warwick presenta otra explicación de la polarización:

> Dado el estatus no coalicionable de los partidos extremistas, los gobiernos formados en tales sistemas usualmente deben abarcar un arreglo ideológicamente diverso de partidos pro sistema y/o contentarse con ser minoritarios; en todo caso, son vulnerables a un colapso o terminación temprana. Aparte de aclarar el signo del coeficiente de polarización, esta explicación tiene la ventaja de localizar la causa próxima de supervivencia del gobierno en un atributo gubernamental particular, en vez de asociarla con una característica general del ambiente parlamentario en general [Warwick, 1994: 47].

En lo tocante a la fraccionalización, Warwick sostuvo que la medición debería reflejar la situación dentro del gobierno:

> El interés de King y colaboradores en el tamaño o la fraccionalización se extendió solamente al tamaño del sistema de partidos; nunca sometieron a prueba el tamaño del gobierno. En cambio, una vez que el tamaño del gobierno se toma en consideración, se elimina el papel importante que juega el tamaño efectivo del sistema de partidos, lo cual indica que los sistemas de partido grandes tienden a experimentar mayor inestabilidad debido a que los gobiernos que producen son grandes. Este perfeccionamiento del modelo de King y colaboradores implica que si hay validez en la idea del ambiente de negociación, es el ambiente de negociación dentro del gobierno lo que importa, no el ambiente de negociación parlamentario en general [Warwick, 1994: 47].

Warwick introduce la variable de "diversidad ideológica", similar a la que denominé "rango" en el capítulo VII y "distancias ideológicas" en el capítulo VIII. Ésta mide la diversidad ideológica de la coalición de gobierno sobre la base de una serie de indicadores que incluyen izquierda-derecha, clerical-secular y respaldo al régimen. La introducción de esta variable convierte la polarización (el tamaño de partidos extremistas) en una minúscula variable independiente para gobiernos mayoritarios. En los gobiernos minoritarios ocurre lo contrario: mientras que la diversidad ideológica del gobierno no es importante, la polarización sí lo es. Warwick (1994: 66) explica la diferencia de la siguiente manera:

Aunque la polarización muestra un impacto de gran importancia sobre la supervivencia del gobierno en situaciones tanto mayoritarias como minoritarias antes de introducir la diversidad ideológica (modelos 1 y 3), una comparación de los modelos 2 y 4 muestra que sólo sobrevive a la introducción del índice de diversidad ideológica en situaciones de gobierno minoritario. Por tanto, el efecto importante que el índice de diversidad ideológica transmite queda confinado a gobiernos mayoritarios.

Para resumir los argumentos: la mayor parte de la bibliografía hasta 1990 explicaba la duración del gobierno en democracias parlamentarias sobre la base de características del sistema de partido, principalmente la diversidad ideológica y la fraccionalización. La razón por la cual se concentraron en las características prevalecientes del parlamento era que los partidos determinarían su comportamiento sobre la base de sus probabilidades de ser incluidos en el nuevo gobierno, y estas probabilidades son determinadas por las características del sistema de partido. Warwick (1994) efectuó experimentos cruciales e introdujo ambas características del parlamento y del gobierno. El resultado fue que el número de partidos en el parlamento fue sustituido por el número de partidos en el gobierno, el cual fue sustituido a su vez por las distancias ideológicas entre los partidos en el gobierno para gobiernos mayoritarios. Para gobiernos minoritarios (que suelen ser gobiernos de un solo partido), la diversidad ideológica del parlamento sigue siendo una variable explicativa poderosa. Warwick interpreta sus resultados en el sentido de que indican que lo que determina la supervivencia es la negociación *dentro* de los gobiernos. Reviso ahora estos resultados sobre la base de la teoría de los jugadores con veto.

2. Jugadores con veto y estabilidad gubernamental

Hasta aquí, en este libro hemos presentado resultados sobre la base de modelos espaciales, sin preocuparnos específicamente por la posición del *statu quo*. En el nivel teórico (capítulos I y II) generé proposiciones que se mantienen para cada posición del *statu quo*, en tanto que al nivel empírico usé dos atajos. En el capítulo VII expliqué por qué era difícil identificar el *statu quo*, y usé la posición del gobierno anterior como sustituto. En el capítulo VIII me valí de la misma aproximación pero la justificación fue más apropiada, dado que muy a menudo la solución por ausencia para no votar un presupuesto a tiempo es la adopción automática o cuasiautomática del presupuesto del año anterior.

He explicado ya que cualquier intento de incluir el *statu quo* en trabajos empíricos tiene que ser *a posteriori*, de tal modo que el *statu quo* quede definido sólo *después* de que la nueva legislación haya sido aprobada. La razón es que la legislación nueva en un área (por ejemplo, seguridad social) puede incluir o no estipulaciones para modificar varios proyectos de ley. Por ejemplo, el nuevo proyecto de ley sobre salud mental. Este tema puede haber existido en otros casos de legislación, pero tal vez no se haya abordado legislativamente en el pasado. Si tales estipulaciones se incluyen en el nuevo proyecto de ley, entonces el *statu quo* queda determinado no sólo por las disposiciones del anterior proyecto de ley sobre seguridad social sino también por las medidas de otros proyectos de ley que especifican las definiciones y condiciones apropiadas en relación con la salud mental. Si la salud mental no es incluida en el nuevo proyecto de ley, entonces el *statu quo* no deberá incluir estipulaciones sobre esta área. Además de las dificultades de identificar la posición política específica del *statu quo* que se examinó en el párrafo anterior, hay dificultades teóricas más graves con el concepto, que están relacionadas con los temas de duración del gobierno.

El *statu quo* es un elemento esencial de todo modelo político multidimensional, como los que he presentado a lo largo de este libro. Para empezar, presuponemos las posiciones del *statu quo* y las preferencias ideológicas de diferentes actores, y entonces identificamos la manera en que estos actores se van a comportar. En tanto que el concepto de *statu quo* es esencial en todos los modelos teóricos, se ha prestado poca atención a la manera como el concepto corresponde a situaciones políticas reales. Habitualmente los modelos presuponen un espacio político, información completa y estabilidad del *statu quo*, exactamente igual que todos los demás modelos que presenté en la primera parte. Tales modelos pueden bastar cuando se analizan situaciones sencillas como la legislación en un área política específica. En cambio, resultan inadecuados para analizar temas más complicados como la selección del gobierno o la supervivencia del mismo.

Quiero introducir dos elementos de incertidumbre que serán esenciales para comprender los mecanismos de selección y duración del gobierno. El primero es la incertidumbre entre políticas y resultados; el segundo es la incertidumbre con el paso del tiempo. Analicemos cada uno de ellos.

Incertidumbre entre políticas y resultados. Varios modelos han dado por sentado que hay incertidumbre entre políticas y resultados (Gilligan y Krehbiel, 1987; Krehbiel, 1991). De acuerdo con estos modelos, los actores tienen preferencias acerca de los resultados pero deben seleccionar las medidas políticas. La implicación para el modelado es que los actores están localizados sobre la base de sus preferencias en un espacio de resultados, pero no pueden seleccionar los resultados directamente. Tienen que seleccionar políticas, las cuales incluyen un elemento aleatorio. Sólo algunos expertos tienen conocimiento específico de la correspondencia exacta entre políticas y resultados, y por ende los tomadores de decisiones tienen que extraerles esta información (digo "extraer" porque los expertos tal vez no quieran revelarlo y actúen estratégicamente). Sin embargo, estos modelos no estudian ningunas otras variaciones en los resultados; una vez seleccionada una política, siempre produce los mismos resultados. Pero esta es una simplificación que ha sido disputada por el "enfoque en los hechos" para la formación de coalición.

Incertidumbre entre resultados actuales y futuros. El "enfoque en los hechos" resaltaba el hecho de que acontecimientos inesperados pudieran retar a los gobiernos y dividir las coaliciones que los respaldan. La razón por la cual estos hechos son inesperados es que son determinados exclusivamente por sucesos en el entorno o determinados conjuntamente por tales sucesos y las políticas de los gobiernos. Sin embargo, tales hechos externos modifican la posición del *statu quo* en el espacio de resultados, incluso si no cambia la política. Por ejemplo, cuando se presenta una crisis petrolera, el presupuesto del gobierno (que podría haber sido un compromiso perfecto en el momento en que fue votado) parece completamente inadecuado porque el precio de la energía aumenta enormemente. Tales variaciones de resultados (mientras que la política permanece constante) son causas adicionales de incertidumbre. En su momento la incertidumbre entre políticas y resultados fue abordada durante la votación del presupuesto, pero ahora la misma política produce resultados muy diferentes.

De modo similar, las políticas de importación o exportación pueden tener resultados diferentes cuando un socio comercial modifica cierto componente de su conducta, o cuando cambian las condiciones externas. Si un país está vendiendo a bajo costo sus productos en el mercado internacional, o si está expuesto, por ejemplo, a radiactividad debido a un accidente nuclear, pueden hacerse necesarias unas restricciones al comercio, mientras que tales medidas ni siquiera se habían considerado.

Si los partidos saben que van a enfrentarse con ambos tipos de incertidumbre, ¿cómo van a abordar la situación cuando formen un gobierno? Pri-

LA ESTABILIDAD GUBERNAMENTAL   279

mero considerarán la distancia entre los socios en la coalición como factor muy importante a tomar en cuenta. Reducir la distancia entre los jugadores con veto habilita a los gobiernos a producir un programa de política *antes* de que formen y respondan a choques exógenos *subsecuentes*.

¿Cómo se darían las negociaciones entre jugadores con veto potenciales? La gráfica IX.1 presenta un espacio de *resultado* con tres jugadores con veto potenciales. Éstos analizarán su programa gubernamental e incluirán en el mismo todos los casos donde los resultados (producidos por las políticas existentes) estén muy lejos de sus preferencias. Por ejemplo, si el *statu quo* estaba en la posición SQ, lo llevarán a cierto punto dentro de W(SQ),

GRÁFICA IX.1. *Diferentes efectos de choques sobre coaliciones de gobierno.*

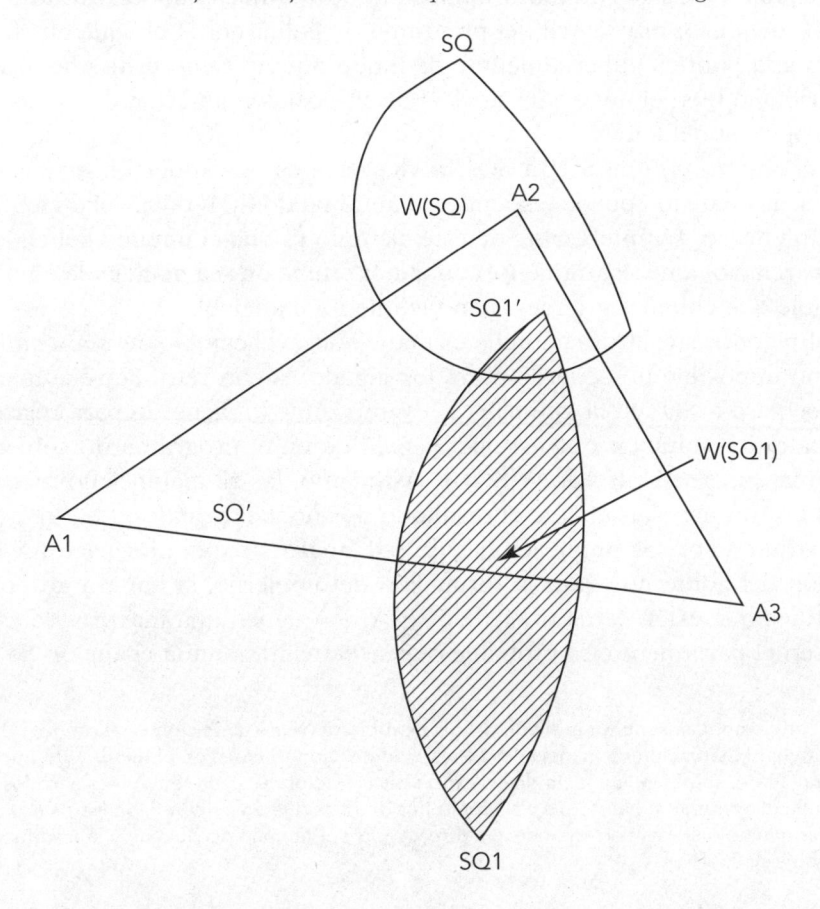

y si estuviera en SQ1, lo moverían dentro de W(SQ1). Podrían incluir más incisos en el programa de gobierno cuanto más lejos esté el *statu quo* y estén más cerca unos de otros, como hemos visto en la primera parte de este libro. En particular la gráfica I.6 y la proposición I.4 demuestran que (dejando a un lado los costos de transacción) lo que importa no es el número de jugadores con veto sino el tamaño de su núcleo de unanimidad.

Supongamos que algún choque exógeno sustituye un resultado existente. La suposición subyacente en la bibliografía de "enfoques en los hechos" es que el tamaño del choque importa, y algunos de ellos son demasiado grandes para que ciertos gobiernos los puedan resolver. Demostraré que ésta es una forma inexacta de pensar acerca del problema. En mi modelo hay dos posibilidades: este movimiento puede ser "manejable" o "no manejable". Con movimiento manejable quiero decir un sustituto de SQ que o bien está muy cerca del programa de gobierno (el choque en efecto simula la política gubernamental, de modo que no se necesita una acción ulterior), o bien el nuevo SQ se aleja de su posición anterior, de modo que el programa del gobierno se sigue incluyendo en W(SQ). En la gráfica IX.1, pasar el *statu quo* de SQ1 a SQ1' o viceversa es una situación manejable, ya que la coalición puede responder abandonando SQ1' o volviendo a SQ1', según el caso. Lo interesante de este ejemplo es que el tamaño del choque no se relaciona necesariamente con que la situación sea manejable o no. Es posible que choques grandes sean fácilmente manejables.[4]

En contraste, la situación no es manejable si el cambio del *statu quo* ha hecho imposible un acuerdo entre los jugadores con veto. Por ejemplo, si SQ se pasa a SQ' en la gráfica IX.1, es imposible un acuerdo para regresar a cualquier solución que estuviera incluida en el programa de gobierno —tenía que ser dentro de W(SQ)—. Asimismo, las situaciones no manejables no son necesariamente el resultado de choques grandes.

¿Cuáles son las implicaciones de este análisis para la formación y duración del gobierno? Para la formación del gobierno, si hay un grupo de partidos que están cerca unos de otros y que tienen una mayoría de escaños en el parlamento, es probable que se conviertan en la coalición de go-

---

[4] Por ejemplo, si la nueva posición del SQ es cubierta (véase definición en el capítulo I) por la antigua, la situación es manejable. El resultado es congruente con el análisis de Lupia y Strom (1995). También han incluido las expectativas electorales de los diferentes partidos con el fin de determinar si habrá una elección o no. Una conclusión común de nuestros dos análisis es que no hay una correspondencia directa entre el tamaño del choque y la terminación del gobierno.

bierno. Si no hay tal grupo, se formará una mayoría de gobierno a partir de los partidos con diferencias grandes o se formará un gobierno minoritario. El gobierno minoritario más probablemente se formará cuando la oposición esté dividida (de otro modo el gobierno podría haber sido formado también por la oposición). Estas expectativas se confirman en el análisis empírico de Martin y Stevenson (2001: 41), quienes encuentran que "cualquier coalición potencial más probablemente se formará cuanto mayor sea la incompatibilidad ideológica de sus miembros, cualquiera que sea su tamaño". Encuentran también que la probabilidad de formación de gobiernos minoritarios aumenta cuando la oposición está dividida.

En cuanto a la duración del gobierno, Warwick ha realizado todas las pruebas cruciales que implica el análisis anterior: ha demostrado que las variables estándar que miden características parlamentarias (fraccionalización y polarización del sistema de partidos) son sustituidas por las distancias ideológicas de los partidos en el gobierno, excepto para gobiernos minoritarios donde la polarización parlamentaria tiene un impacto importante.

Finalmente, una razón adicional por la cual la polarización de los parlamentos puede ejercer un impacto independiente sobre la supervivencia del gobierno es lo que hemos visto en el capítulo VI con el encabezado "equivalentes de mayoría calificada". La existencia de partidos enemigos del sistema hace aumentar esencialmente la mayoría requerida para la toma de decisiones políticas, de mayoría simple a calificada, y como resultado reduce significativamente el conjunto ganador del *statu quo*.

3. Estabilidad gubernamental y predominio ejecutivo

Con base en el análisis anterior, la duración del gobierno es proporcional a la capacidad de éste para responder a choques inesperados, y esta capacidad es función de la constelación de jugadores con veto: el tamaño del núcleo de unanimidad de los jugadores con veto (proposición 1.4). De acuerdo con mi explicación no hay una relación lógica entre duración del gobierno y predominio ejecutivo como argumentaba Arend Lijphart (1999) (véase análisis en el capítulo IV).

Sin embargo, en el capítulo IV sólo argumentamos que la duración del gobierno y el predominio ejecutivo eran lógicamente independientes, y dejamos sin explicar su elevada correlación (la base del argumento de Lijphart). Ahora regresamos a examinar las razones de la correlación entre duración del gobierno y predominio ejecutivo. Mi argumento es que se trata de una correlación espuria, y explicaré qué camino siguen las flechas causales.

En el capítulo IV presenté evidencia de que el predominio ejecutivo es una función de los poderes gubernamentales de establecimiento de la agenda. De hecho, en tanto que cada gobierno parlamentario tiene la posibilidad de vincular una pregunta de confianza a cualquier proyecto de ley particular o, equivalentemente, llegar al compromiso de que si un proyecto de ley particular es derrotado entonces renunciará, ésta es un arma de alto costo político y no se puede usar con frecuencia. De uso más cotidiano son los procedimientos institucionales que restringen las enmiendas en el parlamento, y cuanto más de estas armas controle el gobierno, más podrá presentar preguntas de "tómenlo o déjenlo" al parlamento, y como resultado logrará hacer aprobar más de sus leyes. Por lo tanto, en el capítulo IV se señaló una relación causal entre el establecimiento de la agenda gubernamental y una de las variables de Lijphart: el predominio ejecutivo.

El presente capítulo establece una relación causal entre los jugadores con veto y la otra variable que Lijphart emplea en su análisis: la duración del gobierno. El argumento era que cuanto más cerca estén los jugadores con veto, más capaces serán de resolver choques políticos y, en consecuencia, más larga será la duración del gobierno. De hecho, mi argumento da un paso más adelante y hace pronósticos acerca de la formación del gobierno: cuanto más cerca estén diferentes jugadores con veto potenciales, mayor será la probabilidad de que formen un gobierno.

Lo que se necesita establecer es una relación entre jugador con veto y control gubernamental de la agenda. Pero este tema se abordó en el capítulo VII. Allí señalamos la poderosa correlación entre las dos variables al nivel nacional, y ofrecimos las razones de que esta correlación no sea accidental. No logré establecer la dirección de la causación, pero señalé tres diferentes argumentos que pueden explicar la relación. El primero fue un argumento causal que va de los jugadores con veto al establecimiento de agenda gubernamental: jugadores con veto múltiples no pueden introducir legislación importante y por lo tanto los países con gobiernos de coalición no han sido capaces de introducir tales reglas de establecimiento de agenda. El segundo fue un argumento estratégico que va desde los poderes de establecimiento de agenda hasta los jugadores con veto: si los poderes de establecimiento de agenda están presentes, las negociaciones de coalición son más fáciles ya

GRÁFICA IX.2. *Relaciones causales entre jugadores con veto, establecimiento de agenda gubernamental, duración del gobierno y "predominio ejecutivo".*

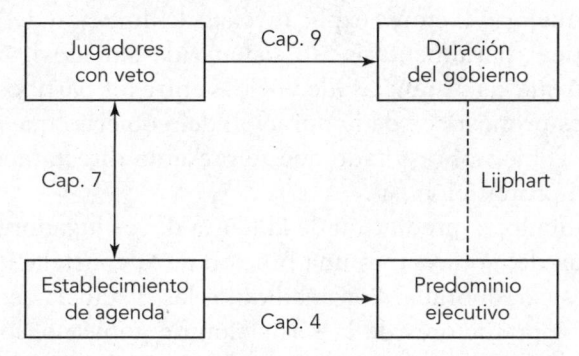

```
   Jugadores      Cap. 9      Duración
   con veto     ─────────►   del gobierno

      ▲
 Cap. 7│                       ┊ Lijphart
      ▼                        ┊

 Establecimiento              Predominio
   de agenda      ─────────►   ejecutivo
                   Cap. 4
```

que los gobiernos pueden hacer lo que quieran con mayorías mínimas o incluso con una minoría de votos. El tercero fue histórico, en el sentido de que las mismas razones sociológicas que generaron jugadores con veto múltiples también los hacía desconfiar unos de otros, de modo que se niegan a proporcionar poderes de establecimiento de agenda a los ganadores del juego de formación de coalición. Cualquier argumento que sea corroborado empíricamente nos muestra la dirección de la relación causal. Por el momento, esta es una pregunta abierta, y por ello en la gráfica IX.2 he incluido una flecha que señala en ambas direcciones entre jugadores con veto y poder de establecimiento de agenda.

Como lo indica esta gráfica, en diferentes partes del libro se examinaron las relaciones entre las diferentes variables y se establecieron los vínculos causales entre establecimiento de agenda y predominio ejecutivo (capítulo IV), jugadores con veto y duración del gobierno (capítulo IX) y jugadores con veto y establecimiento de agenda (capítulo VII). La gráfica IX.2 sigue así los orígenes de la correlación entre duración del gobierno y predominio ejecutivo.

4. CONCLUSIONES

La formación y duración del gobierno en democracias parlamentarias ha sido tema de numerosos estudios. En tanto que la bibliografía empírica ha identificado características de sistema de partido como las variables definitorias de la duración del gobierno, en cambio la teoría de los jugadores con veto se concentra en la composición de los gobiernos. Los experimentos cruciales que Warwick dirigió demuestran que las características del gobierno, particularmente las distancias ideológicas entre los partidos en el gobierno, son mejores factores explicativos de la duración del gobierno que las características parlamentarias (o sistema de partidos). Además, Warwick demostró que las distancias ideológicas entre los partidos en el gobierno son mejores pronósticos de la duración del gobierno que el número de partidos en el gobierno, resultado que se presentó directamente en la gráfica I.6 (y en la proposición I.4).

Como resultado, la predicción de la teoría de los jugadores con veto de que la duración del gobierno es una función de la constelación de jugadores con veto es corroborada. Por añadidura, las distancias entre los partidos son buenos predictores de la formación de gobierno, lo cual es congruente con la idea de que los partidos usan de modo implícito o explícito un razonamiento congruente con el análisis de los jugadores con veto cuando participan en el proceso de formación de gobierno. Finalmente, dado que la duración del gobierno no es un indicador del predominio ejecutivo como argumenté en el capítulo IV, he explicado por qué estas dos variables tenían una poderosa correlación entre ellas.

En la Introducción hice referencia al "axioma en políticas" de A. Lawrence Lowell (1896: 73-74): "cuanto mayor sea el número de grupos discordantes que formen la mayoría, más difícil será la tarea de complacerlos a todos, y más débil e inestable será la posición del gabinete". Las primeras dos secciones de este capítulo demostraron que, 100 años después, hemos confirmado la mitad de este axioma (la parte acerca de los jugadores con veto y la inestabilidad gubernamental). La otra mitad puede ser correcta o no, dependiendo de la interpretación de la palabra "débil". Si "débil" significa un gabinete que no puede hacer cambios importantes en política, esto es exactamente lo que la segunda y la tercera partes de este libro han demostrado. Pero si significa falta de "predominio ejecutivo", se basa en una correlación espuria, como se indica en la última sección de este capítulo.

X. EL PODER JUDICIAL Y LAS BUROCRACIAS

EN LA introducción conecté el juego legislativo y la capacidad de los actores políticos para cambiar el *statu quo* con la independencia e importancia del poder judicial y la burocracia en un país. El razonamiento era sencillo: tanto el poder judicial (cuando hace interpretaciones estatutarias) como las burocracias pueden ser invalidados legislativamente si hacen elecciones con las cuales están en desacuerdo los jugadores con veto (el legislativo), de modo que probablemente deseen evitar tales elecciones. De hecho, tanto el poder judicial como la burocracia tratarán de interpretar la ley de acuerdo con su punto de vista (o tal vez intereses) mientras eliminan la posibilidad de ser invalidados. La mayor estabilidad política dará así mayor discreción tanto a los burócratas como a los jueces.

De acuerdo con la teoría de juegos, describo un juego secuencial donde los burócratas o jueces hacen el primer movimiento (interpretar las leyes existentes) y los jugadores con veto hacen el segundo (decidir invalidar o no y cómo). Esta descripción se puede encontrar con mucha frecuencia en la bibliografía.[1] Analizo únicamente el mecanismo de la invalidación legislativa y no estoy abordando otros factores (como la duración del ejercicio en el cargo) que presumiblemente también afectan la independencia.

En este capítulo mi meta es estudiar esta bibliografía y presentar evidencia empírica que corrobore las expectativas. Se debe hacer notar que estamos en el principio de la búsqueda empírica, y hemos avanzado más acerca de los jueces en una perspectiva comparativa que sobre los burócratas. El análisis empírico depende, por tanto, de indicadores desarrollados como sustitutos o de evaluaciones de expertos que a veces resultan en conflicto. Mi presentación contiene tres partes: en la primera se plantea el problema de la toma de decisiones del primero en mover cuando éste escoge junto con la posibilidad de ser invalidado, en la segunda aplicamos el modelo al poder judicial y en la tercera a las burocracias.

---

[1] Gely y Spiller (1990), Mikva y Bleich (1991), Ferejohn y Weingast (1992a, 1992b), Eskridge (1991), Cooter y Drexl (1994), y Bednar, Ferejohn y Garrett (1996) acerca de jueces; McCubbins, Noll y Weingast (1989), Hammond (1996), Hammond y Knott (1999) acerca de burócratas.

1. Cómo evitar la invalidación legislativa

Supongamos que hay tres jugadores con veto legislativos. El triángulo 123 que ellos definen es su núcleo, el conjunto de puntos que no pueden ponerse de acuerdo en cambiar. En consecuencia, si el primero en mover selecciona uno de los puntos del núcleo, no habrá invalidación legislativa. La gráfica x.1 presenta tres posibilidades diferentes. En los dos primeros casos los puntos ideales de los primeros en mover J y K están fuera del núcleo legislativo y seleccionan el punto del núcleo más cercano a ellos (J' y K', respectivamente). A pesar de que estas dos elecciones son considerablemente distintas una de otra, los jugadores con veto son incapaces de cambiar ninguna de ellas. En el tercer caso, el primero en mover está ubicado dentro del núcleo legislativo pero cambia de opinión y pasa del punto L1 al punto L2. Dado que el primero en mover está dentro del núcleo, puede seleccionar su propio punto ideal.

Estas historias idealizadas están cerca de las realidades políticas. Pensemos en el caso siguiente: en los Estados Unidos (país con tres jugadores con veto) el Tribunal Supremo decidía en varios temas extremadamente importantes que en la mayoría de los demás países habrían sido prerrogativa de la rama legislativa. Integración y elección se nos ocurren de inmediato. Pero tabaco y armas de fuego pueden unirse a la lista de decisiones políticas delegadas a los tribunales debido a que el sistema político es incapaz de legislar sobre el tema.

GRÁFICA X.1. *Selección de una política dentro del núcleo por parte del primero en actuar (burocracia o poder judicial).*

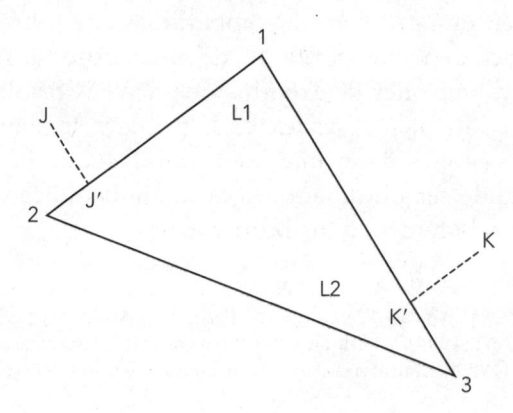

Como ejemplo del cambio de opinión del primero en mover, consideremos el tema del acoso sexual, donde cambian los requerimientos del peso de la prueba. En el pasado, la víctima necesitaba mostrar que como resultado del comportamiento de un superior o compañero de trabajo, ella estuvo muy afligida, perdió días de trabajo, consultó médicos, etc. Después del dictamen en el caso de Harris contra Forklift Systems (1993),[2] cualquier conducta que hubiera preocupado a una persona normal se definió como acoso sexual.

Sin embargo, el modelo que presento aquí es muy sencillo, y el argumento teórico necesita ser apuntalado (además de las historias de apoyo). La primera pregunta es qué sucede si los jugadores con veto no son individuales sino colectivos, si la dimensionalidad del espacio político es alta y si, como una consecuencia, no hay núcleo como en la gráfica x.1. Ningún punto es entonces invulnerable a una invalidación legislativa. ¿Significa esto que el primero en mover (poder judicial o burocracia) no tiene poder de establecimiento de agenda? No exactamente.

En el caso de ausencia de un núcleo legislativo, el conjunto ganador del *statu quo* no está vacío; en lugar de ello, como se demostró en el capítulo II, puede ser de tamaño muy pequeño para ciertas posiciones del *statu quo*. Una decisión burocrática o judicial que tenga un conjunto ganador tan pequeño no valdría el esfuerzo de la invalidación legislativa. De hecho, hay graves costos de transacción para cada decisión legislativa: podemos, por ejemplo, tomar la iniciativa para presentar un proyecto de ley, conformar una coalición para respaldarlo, o eliminar a oponentes que tengan una opinión distinta comprándolos o solidificando alianzas. Si la diferencia entre la decisión judicial y burocrática y el resultado que probablemente obtenga un jugador con veto particular no es lo suficientemente grande, tal empresa tal vez no valdrá la pena.

El análisis de la existencia del núcleo nos lleva a otro punto interesante: la invalidación legislativa puede requerir de diferentes mayorías, en cuyo caso el núcleo legislativo puede tener un tamaño importante. Por ejemplo, en los Estados Unidos las decisiones del Tribunal Supremo pueden ser interpretaciones constitucionales más que estatutarias. Después de que el presidente Clinton firmó la Ley de Libertad Religiosa (ley que prácticamente él había iniciado, y que obtuvo un respaldo casi unánime en ambas cámaras del Congreso), el Tribunal Supremo dictaminó que la ley violaba la

---

[2] Agradezco a Eugene Volokh la referencia.

constitución porque se estaba legislando en un área que era jurisdicción de los estados. Todos los partidarios de la ley cambiaron su curso de acción y decidieron presentar 50 de estas leyes, una en cada estado, en lugar de tratar de modificar la constitución. La razón es que muy pocas personas piensan que la modificación de una decisión constitucional del Tribunal Supremo puede darse de otra manera que de un cambio en la mente colectiva del Tribunal Supremo (la única manera para cambiar *Roe vs. Wade* es esperar que el Tribunal Supremo cambie de parecer o una enmienda constitucional).[3]

Hay dos objeciones más acerca de la anterior descripción de teoría de juegos simple que se plantea en la bibliografía. La primera es que como los primeros en moverse en el juego antes presentado serán capaces de seleccionar una política cerca de o idéntica a su propio punto ideal, ¿qué hará la rama legislativa para impedir que ocurra esto? Abunda la bibliografía donde se arguye que la legislación será más restrictiva cuando haya muchos jugadores con veto (por ejemplo, McCubbins, Noll y Weingast, 1987, 1989; Moe, 1990; Moe y Caldwell, 1994; Epstein y O'Halloran, 1999). Demostraré que mi análisis sólo parece contradecir este argumento. La segunda objeción es que puede haber diferencias importantes entre los sistemas parlamentario y presidencial en lo tocante a la delegación de poderes: los jugadores con veto en sistemas presidenciales, según algunos (Moe, 1990; Moe y Caldwell, 1994; Strom, 2000; Ackerman, 2000), tienen asignaciones explícitas para supervisar a la burocracia, mientras que los jugadores con veto parlamentarios practican colectivamente la supervisión. Como resultado, esta opinión sostiene que los sistemas políticos difieren unos de otros no debido al número de jugadores con veto sino al tipo de régimen.

Es interesante observar que estas objeciones han sido planteadas únicamente acerca de los burócratas y no acerca de los jueces. Hasta donde sé, aunque muchos investigadores estadounidenses han planteado el argumento de que una legislación más detallada está diseñada para restringir el papel de los burócratas, nadie ha planteado el mismo argumento acerca del papel de los jueces.[4] De modo similar, la diferencia entre presidencialismo

---

[3] En la siguiente sección señalaré que la interpretación constitucional puede convertir al tribunal en un jugador adicional con veto.

[4] Para una excepción europea, véase Fritz Scharpf (1970), quien planteó precisamente este argumento acerca de la legislatura alemana. Su idea era que la ley alemana es muy detallada por una serie de razones, entre las cuales están la restricción de los jueces (quienes deciden sobre fundamentos procesales y sustantivos) así como la restricción de las burocracias estata-

y parlamentarismo ha aparecido en la bibliografía sobre burocracias y no en la bibliografía acerca del poder judicial. Dado que mi presentación sobre las burocracias y el poder judicial fue simétrica, no entiendo la razón de este trato diferente en la bibliografía. Sin embargo, lo respetaré y abordaré estos puntos en la tercera sección acerca de las burocracias.

2. Jugadores con veto y poder judicial

2.1. Teorías tradicionales del poder judicial

La distinción habitual en derecho comparativo es entre países con tradiciones de derecho consuetudinario y derecho civil. En los países de derecho consuetudinario (el Reino Unido y todas sus ex colonias como los Estados Unidos, Australia, Nueva Zelanda, Irlanda y Malta), las "leyes" no se consideran tanto los actos del parlamento sino, más bien, la acumulación de decisiones e interpretaciones de los jueces. La regla central en países con derecho consuetudinario es *stare decisis* ("que prevalezca la decisión"), las palabras latinas para la importancia del precedente. Las decisiones tomadas por jueces anteriores en casos similares son obligatorias para un juez. Como resultado, los jueces crean la ley además de aplicarla e interpretarla.

En los países que siguen la tradición del derecho civil, el fundamento de la ley es un código legal completo y autorizado. Sobre este código la legislatura construye una superestructura de estatutos. Los códigos más frecuentemente usados son el Código Napoleónico (que se aplica en Francia, Bélgica, Grecia, Luxemburgo, Holanda, Italia, España y Portugal). Un segundo código es el Código Civil Alemán (que se usa en Alemania, Noruega, Suecia, Finlandia, Dinamarca e Islandia). En los países con derecho civil los jueces interpretan la ley; no la hacen.

Según esta distinción clásica, el papel del poder judicial debe ser más importante en los países con derecho consuetudinario. Sin embargo, análisis más recientes indican la convergencia de los dos sistemas. Gallagher, Laver y Mair (1995: 62) citan una serie de autores que analizan explícitamente la convergencia (Waltman y Holland, 1988: 85), o describen la con-

---

les (que son independientes del gobierno federal). En el análisis de Scharpf, las cortes estadounidenses no tienen una revisión sustantiva de las decisiones burocráticas, y hay burocracias federales. Estas diferencias pueden explicar la ausencia del argumento de que la legislación detallada restringe a los jueces en los Estados Unidos.

ducta del poder judicial en sistemas de derecho consuetudinario en términos de "precedente" y analizan los "estatutos" en sistemas con derecho consuetudinario.

Las teorías de la convergencia concuerdan con el análisis de la primera sección de este capítulo. De acuerdo con la teoría de los jugadores con veto, lo que cuenta para la independencia e importancia del poder judicial no es el sistema jurídico de un país, sino más bien si las cortes son constitucionales o no y la dificultad del sistema político para invalidar una interpretación estatutaria o constitucional.

Ya hemos examinado el tema de la interpretación estatutaria como una cuestión de estabilidad política del sistema político correspondiente; concentrémonos ahora en el asunto de la interpretación constitucional. Este es un tema importante, debido a que las cortes pueden interpretar la constitución y fundamentar sus decisiones en ella, y no pueden ser invalidadas por el sistema político. La única excepción sería mediante una modificación de la constitución, lo cual significaría que el poder judicial de un país sería un jugador con veto, dado que una decisión del poder judicial podría invalidar una ley.

2.2. ¿Son jugadores con veto los jueces?

Aunque está claro que el poder judicial de un país no es un jugador con veto cuando se realizan interpretaciones estatutarias, ya que puede ser invalidado por la legislación, sucede lo contrario en lo tocante a la interpretación constitucional. De hecho, el rechazo por una corte constitucional basta para abrogar una legislación aprobada por la legislatura. Algunos países, como Francia, tienen una revisión de la legislación *a priori y en abstracto*, invalidando leyes por motivos constitucionales antes de que sean aplicadas. En este caso, el Conseil Constitutionel de Francia actúa como una cámara adicional del parlamento y puede hacer abortar piezas completas de legislación o partes de ellas justo antes de que el presidente de la república firme esta legislación y la convierta en ley (Stone, 1992).

Stone-Sweet (2000) argumenta que la introducción del escrutinio por las cortes constitucionales ha alterado profundamente el papel de las cortes y de las legislaturas, y ha introducido una interacción constante entre las dos instituciones. De acuerdo con esta interacción, las legislaturas siempre son conscientes de que sus acciones pueden ser invalidadas por cortes constitucionales, y a veces incluso piden instrucciones a las cortes a fin de inmunizar sus decisiones contra la abrogación judicial. Según Stone-Sweet, a medida que las cortes se hacen cada vez más elaboradas en diferentes áreas, se reduce la discreción de las legislaturas. Como resultado, estamos en el proceso de formación de un gobierno de jueces. Volcansek (2001) plantea argumentos similares en el caso italiano, y explica cómo y por qué la corte constitucional italiana ha intervenido en cuestiones de divorcio y decretos ejecutivos.

La esencia de estos argumentos es correcta: las cortes constitucionales pueden hacer abortar la legislación, y por tanto son jugadores con veto. Sin embargo, las conclusiones y pronósticos acerca de gobiernos de jueces parecen exagerados. ¿Por qué? Mi respuesta se basa en el análisis de la regla de la absorción en el capítulo I. Aunque los jueces constitucionales son jugadores con veto, la mayor parte del tiempo son absorbidos.

Como se vio en el capítulo I, para que un jugador con veto establezca una diferencia política debe estar ubicado fuera del núcleo de unanimidad de los otros jugadores con veto existentes (véase proposición I.3). Argumentaré que las cortes constitucionales muy a menudo están ubicadas dentro del núcleo de unanimidad de los otros jugadores con veto. La razón principal es el proceso de nombramiento a los puestos más altos. El único gran país sin restricciones a un proceso de nombramientos puramente politizado es Francia, donde los nueve miembros del Conseil Constitutionel son nombrados por el presidente de la república (tres), el presidente de la Asamblea Nacional (tres) y el presidente del Senado (tres) sin condiciones o aprobaciones especificadas.

En los Estados Unidos los candidatos que el presidente propone tienen que ser aprobados por el Senado. En Italia un tercio de los miembros de la Corte Constitucional (cinco) son nombrados por el presidente de la república, un tercio por el poder judicial y un tercio por el parlamento mediante una mayoría de dos tercios en una sesión conjunta de la Cámara de Diputados y del Senado; todos los nombramientos tienen que ser para jueces con 20 años de experiencia o profesores de derecho. En Alemania, ocho miembros son elegidos por el Bundestag y los otros ocho por el Bundesrat con una mayoría de dos tercios; todos los miembros deben estar calificados para ser jueces federales (y seis de los 16 deben ser, de hecho, jueces federales). En España dos de los 12 jueces son nombrados por el gobierno, dos por el poder judicial y cuatro por cada cámara del parlamento mediante una mayoría de tres quintas partes; su competencia judicial debe ser bien conocida (Stone-Sweet, 2000: 49).

Las restricciones impuestas a la selección de los miembros de la institución más alta del poder judicial eliminan las posiciones extremas y prácticamente garantizan que la mediana de la corte estará ubicada centralmente en el espacio político. Sin embargo, los medios que usan los politólogos estadounidenses y los académicos judiciales para estudiar al Tribunal Supremo de los Estados Unidos no están disponibles para otras cortes debido a que las deliberaciones son secretas y la mayor parte del tiempo a los disidentes (si hay alguno) no se les llega a conocer y ciertamente no firman ni son publicados.

La descripción anterior genera otra pregunta: ¿cómo es posible que los tribunales constitucionales lleguen a vetar legislación bajo estas condiciones? Es decir, ¿en qué condiciones no se incluye la mediana del Tribunal Supremo en el núcleo de unanimidad de los jugadores con veto existentes? Presentaré dos respuestas verosímiles a esta pregunta, y le recuerdo al lector que la verosimilitud es lo más que podemos esperar mientras no se abra la caja negra de las deliberaciones judiciales.

Primero, los jueces son seleccionados por su competencia y sus posiciones políticas (conocidas). Algunas de sus posiciones tal vez sean desconocidas debido a que no han deliberado sobre cada tema, y otras posiciones se considerarían secundarias, de modo que no están sujetas a pruebas de tornasol. Uno de estos temas puede volverse importante o polémico, como los matrimonios entre personas del mismo sexo o la eutanasia, y el Tribunal Supremo tal vez discrepe de los creadores de políticas, pero éste no era el criterio de selección en el pasado. De hecho, es probable que ésta sea una nueva dimensión que corte a través de líneas de partido.

Segundo, un veto por el Tribunal Supremo no se debe considerar necesariamente como una oposición a la acción gubernamental. Puede ser la expresión de *preferencias de procedimiento* (Rose-Ackerman, 1990; Ferejohn y Weingast, 1992a), como la introducción de restricciones técnicas. La corte podría indicarle al gobierno que esta forma particular de alcanzar sus metas viola la constitución, de modo que es necesario adoptar un diferente curso de acción. Stone-Sweet (1992) presenta varios ejemplos en que el parlamento francés solicitó al Consejo Constitucional que proporcionara la fraseología específica para que la legislación sobreviviera al escrutinio constitucional de la corte. Finalmente, mediante su propia interpretación de la ley, las cortes podrían también provocar una legislación nueva y más deseable. Es así como Van Hees y Steunenberg (2000) explican la famosa decisión de la Suprema Corte Holandesa, que permite la eutanasia en las condiciones específicas que ocurrieron en el caso bajo revisión, que entonces provocó una legislación adicional sobre el tema.

En conclusión, los jueces no son jugadores con veto cuando toman decisiones estatutarias. Son jugadores con veto cuando hacen interpretaciones constitucionales, pero la mayor parte del tiempo son absorbidos por los jugadores con veto políticos existentes. Las únicas excepciones serían si los jugadores con veto existentes están ubicados en posiciones políticas extremas (recordamos el caso de Francia durante el primer gobierno de Mitterrand [1981], donde el gobierno quería implementar una serie de cambios políticos importantes mientras la corte constitucional había sido nombrada por gobiernos de la derecha), o si nuevos temas se pusieran a consideración. En estos casos, las cortes constitucionales deberían contar como jugadores adicionales con veto. Sin embargo, dada la caja negra que contiene la toma de decisiones del poder judicial, sería imposible atribuir esto a las posiciones políticas de jugador con veto. Como resultado, no he incluido el poder judicial (ni siquiera en la forma de cortes constitucionales) como un jugador con veto en mis descripciones en este libro.

2.3. La evidencia empírica

Si el poder judicial no es un jugador adicional con veto, entonces podemos estudiar la discreción judicial como una variable dependiente. Como argumento en este capítulo, los sistemas políticos que muestran estabilidad política también tendrán independencia del poder judicial. ¿Hay alguna prueba empírica que respalde esta afirmación? Varios estudios empíricos han intentado evaluar la independencia del poder judicial. Algunos de ellos han tratado de someter a prueba pronósticos similares a los de este libro.

Lijphart ha introducido una medición de la fortaleza de la revisión judicial "basada primero en la distinción entre la presencia y ausencia de revisión judicial y, segundo, en tres grados de *activismo* en la aserción de este poder por parte de las cortes" (1999: 225-226; cursivas agregadas). Determina también la dificultad mediante la cual se puede enmendar la constitución de un país (por una mayoría superior a dos tercios, por "dos tercios o equivalente", "entre dos tercios y mayorías ordinarias", y por mayorías ordinarias). Califica a los 36 países que estudió sobre la base de estas dos variables y encuentra que la "revisión judicial" tiene una correlación moderada pero de significación estadística con la rigidez constitucional.

De modo similar, Nicos Alivizatos (1995) ha presentado una tipología de cuatro clases de lo que él denomina "politización judicial", el grado en el cual los jueces "influyen en el proceso de la toma de decisiones". Con este propósito, él determina una variable dependiente acerca de si un país tiene una corte constitucional o no, y si los jueces son considerados activistas o no.[5] Los países con una corte constitucional y los jueces activistas alcanzan una puntuación de cuatro, los países con una corte constitucional y jueces no activistas tienen puntuación de tres, los países sin una corte constitucional pero con jueces activos tienen una puntuación de dos, y aquellos sin una corte ni activismo judicial alcanzan la puntuación de uno. Introduce una serie de posibles variables independientes para evaluar qué causa la "politización judicial". Primero clasifica a los países como descentralizados o no (usando de hecho tres categorías, una para países federales, una para federalismo *de facto*, y una para países unitarios); segundo, evalúa el grado de polarización izquierda-derecha (en dos categorías); tercero, introduce una variable cualitativa para expresar a los jugadores con veto (con puntuación de uno para un solo partido, tres para muchos partidos, y dos para una mezcla de las dos); cuarto, introduce una variable que evalúa las anomalías parlamentarias (guerras civiles o dictaduras); quinto, una variable que indica el grado de integración a la Unión Europea (en el momento algunos países eran miembros, otros estaban a punto de convertirse en miembros y otros no lo eran). El investigador encuentra que la decisión de tener una corte constitucional depende principalmente de dos variables: de si el país es federal y de si en el pasado hubo anomalías parlamentarias. La "politización judicial", por el otro lado, depende de la descentralización, la polarización y los jugadores con veto (en niveles p menores de 0.05).

Finalmente, Cooter y Ginsburg (1996) han usado una escala de "discreción judicial" generada por una serie de expertos. Una segunda y mucho más creativa manera de evaluar la discreción judicial es mediante el trámite destinado a restringir la responsabilidad. "Descubrimos que las cortes con pronóstico de gran valentía estaban dispuestas a innovar en esta área del derecho privado más que otras cortes. Las cortes con pronóstico de poca valentía, en cambio, se contentaban con esperar la adopción legislativa de la nueva norma". De hecho, los dos autores clasifican diferentes países sobre la base de si las cortes presentaron ante la legislatura normas de responsabilidad estrictas, o si sencillamente invirtieron la carga de la prueba

---

[5] Para usar la especificación del autor: "dependiendo de si los tribunales han dado en realidad señales inequívocas de activismo judicial en contraposición a la moderación judicial".

del demandante al demandado, o esperaban a que la legislatura cambiara la ley.

Cooter y Ginsburg usan dos variables independientes. La primera es "el número de vetos legislativos" que se determina de la siguiente manera: "En sistemas parlamentarios unicamerales, donde el gobierno está formado por la coalición mayoritaria en la legislatura, hay esencialmente un veto sobre la legislación. [...] Otros sistemas tienen dos vetos sobre la legislación nueva. Tal sería el caso en un sistema parlamentario bicameral (como en Alemania), o en un sistema parlamentario esencialmente unicameral con un presidente fuerte (como en Francia)". La segunda variable independiente que usaron es la duración de la coalición de gobierno como "un indicador más sencillo del predominio de partido" (1996: 299). Encontraron que estas dos variables independientes afectan la discreción judicial, ya sea medida por las evaluaciones de expertos judiciales o por la prueba de responsabilidad estricta.

El lector cuidadoso ya habrá identificado los problemas de cada una de las dos variables independientes empleadas por Cooter y Ginsburg. La variable "número de vetos" usa lo que yo denominé "criterio numérico" en el capítulo I. Declaré allí que ésta es una base discutible para estáticas comparativas entre países. Pasa por alto las diferencias en las posiciones ideológicas de diferentes jugadores con veto, lo cual puede ser muy importante de un país a otro. Además, las puntuaciones particulares no reflejan adecuadamente las instituciones de los diferentes países. Por ejemplo, Francia tiene una puntuación de dos, aunque el presidente no tiene poder de veto; Holanda o Austria, dos, aunque sus respectivas cámaras altas son muy débiles (de hecho, la de Austria es más débil que la del Reino Unido, que tiene la puntuación de un veto). Israel y Dinamarca recibieron una puntuación de uno debido a que son unicamerales, a pesar del hecho de que usualmente tienen gobiernos de coalición. La variable "duración" como medición de predominio de un tipo o de otro también ha sido criticada en la tercera sección del capítulo IV, así que no repetiré aquí mis objeciones.

En estos estudios se han aplicado diferentes formas de medir la independencia judicial, correlacionándola con diversas variables independientes, algunas de las cuales estaban conectadas con jugadores con veto, algunas no, y otras más supuestamente estaban conectadas aunque de manera incorrecta. Usaré las variables independientes en cada uno de estos estudios: *judpol* para la "politización judicial" de Alivizatos, *judrev* para la "revisión judicial" de Lijphart, *expertos* y *responsabilidad estricta* para las dos distintas mediciones de la independencia judicial de Cooter y Ginsburg.

Correlacionaré estas variables con la medición cualitativa de los jugadores con veto que se presentó en el capítulo VII. He extendido esta medición para los países que analizaron Cooter y Ginsburg, pero no para las 36 países de Lijphart. Algunas de las pruebas cubrirán por tanto los 18 países en el conjunto de datos de Alivizatos, algunos de los 20 países de Cooter y Ginsburg y todos los 24 países restantes incluidos en el cuadro.

El cuadro X.1 presenta los datos que se analizarán. Los datos faltantes son generados porque Alivizatos cubre únicamente países de Europa Occidental, en tanto que Cooter y Ginsburg tienen una intersección importante con estos países, pero cubren también otras naciones. Únicamente Lijphart cubre la totalidad de los 24 países. El cuadro X.2 produce las correlaciones de Pearson como medición fácilmente interpretable de la asociación entre

CUADRO X.1. *Independencia judicial.*

País	Judpol	Judrev	Expertos	Responsabilidad estricta	Descentralización	Politización	Jugadores con veto	Duración
Alemania	4	4	3.46	2	3	2	3	6.3
Australia		3	2.33	1	3	1	2	9
Austria	3	3		2	3	2	2	8
Bélgica	3	3	3.5	3	3	1	3	4.8
Canadá		3	2.33	2	3	1	2	8
Dinamarca	1	2		1	1	1	3	8
España	3	3	2	1	3	2	1	6
Estados Unidos		4	4.42	3	3	1	3	6.9
Finlandia	1	1		1	1	1	3	4.8
Francia	4	3	3.7	3	1	2	2	6.8
Grecia	2	2			1	2	1	
Holanda	2	1	4.2	2	1	1	3	2.5
Irlanda	2	2		1	1	2	2	6.4
Islandia	1	2			1	1	3	
Israel		1	4.5	2	1	2	2	2.4
Italia	4	3	3.33	2	2	2	3	1.3
Japón		2	2.17	1	1	1	1	9.4
Luxemburgo	1	1		3	1	1	2	4
Noruega	1	2		1	1	2	2	4
Nueva Zelanda		1	2	1	1	1	1	6
Portugal	3	2			1	2	2	
Reino Unido	2	1	2.1	1	2	2	1	8
Suecia	2	2	2.5	1	1	2	2	4.2
Suiza	2	1			3	1	3	

CUADRO X.2. *Correlaciones entre variables independientes con y sin Australia, Canadá, Israel y Holanda.*

	X.2 A				X.2 B			
	Judrev	Expertos	Responsabilidad estricta	Judpol	Judrev	Expertos	Responsabilidad estricta	Judpol
Judrev (Lijphart)	1.000				1.000			
Expertos	*0.12611*	1.000			*0.6446*	1.000		
Responsabilidad estricta	0.4003	0.7912	1.000		0.5286	0.9132	1.000	
Judpol (Alivizatos)	0.8660	*0.3259*	0.5547	1.000	0.8346	*0.7603*	0.6471	1.000

Nota: Las correlaciones entre diferentes índices son similares ya sea que se incluya o no a los cuatro países, con pocas excepciones (señaladas en cursivas).

las diferentes variables independientes. El lector puede verificar que aunque los datos de Lijphart se correlacionan muy bien con las evaluaciones de Alivizatos en el subconjunto de países de Europa Occidental, tienen diferencias importantes con los juicios de expertos cuando vemos países fuera de Europa. En particular, Israel es clasificado como un poder judicial muy débil por Lijphart (uno) y muy fuerte por los informes de expertos (7.5, todavía más elevado que el Tribunal Supremo de los Estados Unidos), mientras Australia y Canadá son clasificados por Lijphart como muy independientes (tres), pero no muy fuertes según los informes de los expertos (2.33). Finalmente, otro país de desacuerdo es Holanda, donde el poder judicial es considerado por los expertos como muy independiente, nada independiente según Lijphart y en grado intermedio según Alivizatos. Estas observaciones se hacen para indicar que incluso los expertos están en desacuerdo con algunas evaluaciones. Es posible que estos desacuerdos se basen en diferentes propiedades implícitas de la variable que cada uno de ellos examina (como lo indican los diferentes nombres que usan). Si eliminamos estos cuatro países de desacuerdo, las correlaciones entre los juicios de los expertos se vuelven significativamente más altas. Dada la escasez de países y de datos, no intento sacar a los países donde los expertos están en desacuerdo con las pruebas empíricas.

El cuadro X.3 presenta la relación entre las diferentes mediciones que expresan la independencia o importancia del poder judicial y las variables

CUADRO X.3. *Independencia judicial como función de los jugadores con veto.*

Variable independiente	Judpol (Alivizatos)	Judrev (Lijphart)	Responsa-bilidad estricta	Responsa-bilidad estricta	Responsa-bilidad estricta	Expertos	Expertos	Expertos	Judpol (Alivizatos)
Jugadores con veto (z o t)	1.292** (0.6305)	0.4117 (−0.3484)	0.8022** (0.4311)	0.8145** (0.4207)	0.7952** (0.4432)	0.9652***** (0.2125)	0.7212*** (0.2456)	0.8514***** (0.2143)	0.6308** (0.3011)
Polarización (z o t)	3.2597***** (1.0628)	0.9319** (0.5199)	−0.068 (0.5555)	—	—	0.1392 (0.3288)	—	—	1.6745***** (0.4522)
Descentrali-zación (z o t)	0.9234**** (0.3632)	0.9837***** (0.3045)	0.2959 (0.2894)	0.2954 (0.2893)	—	−0.3155* (0.1848)	—	—	0.5093*** (0.1939)
Duración (z o t)	—	—	—	—	−0.0437 (0.1245)	—	−0.0866 (0.0812)	—	—
Número de observaciones	18	24	20	20	20	14	14	14	18
Seudo R² o R² ajust.	0.371	0.234	0.136	0.136	0.113	0.579	0.537	0.532	0.556

Nota: Las columnas con la variable independiente marcadas con *** usan estimados OLS. Errores estándares entre paréntesis.
* $p < 0.10$.
** $p < 0.05$.
*** $p < 0.01$.
**** $p < 0.001$.
Todas las pruebas son de una cola.

dependientes correspondientes, una de las cuales siempre es una expresión cualitativa de los jugadores con veto. Aunque en toda la bibliografía revisada se utiliza una estimación OLS, la técnica es inapropiada debido a que la variable dependiente está compuesta solamente por tres o cuatro grupos de países. En las estimaciones que siguen utilizo una técnica *ordered probit* apropiada cuando la variable dependiente tiene valores discretos. Las últimas cuatro columnas del cuadro x.3 presentan estimaciones OLS debido a que la variable dependiente es continua. Con propósitos de comparación, he estimado dos veces los datos que Nicos Alivizatos generó: una vez mediante el procedimiento correcto *(ordered probit)* y una vez por el procedimiento tradicional (OLS). Obsérvese la diferencia en seudo R^2 de la estimación *probit* en la primera columna desde el R^2 ajustado de la técnica OLS en la última.

He examinado diferentes modelos. En cada caso empecé por incluir dos variables: jugadores con veto y descentralización política. Analicé la variable "jugadores con veto" en el capítulo vii. La variable de descentralización mide si un país es unitario, federal o entre ambos. He incluido esta variable porque en países federales se le puede pedir al poder judicial que adjudique los conflictos entre diferentes niveles de gobierno, de modo que hay una fuente adicional de las decisiones importantes que el poder judicial ha de tomar. De hecho, como se vio en el capítulo vi, algunos autores (Bednar, Eskridge y Ferejohn, 2001) consideran el poder judicial independiente como una condición para el federalismo. Al igual que algunos autores (Alivizatos), he agregado la variable "polarización". Ésta es esencialmente una versión cualitativa de la variable "alternación" que se usó en los capítulos vii y viii. Sin embargo, no está claro que esta variable tendrá un efecto positivo o negativo sobre el papel del poder judicial. Se puede argumentar que el poder judicial moderará extremos de diferentes gobiernos, o que será intimidado por la perspectiva de ser invalidado. De hecho, la variable de Alivizatos resulta positiva o negativa dependiendo del modelo. Cuando sale sin significancia, vuelvo a estimar el modelo descartando "polarización". En el caso de las dos variables independientes del artículo de Cooter y Ginsburg, también integro un modelo que incluye la variable "duración del gobierno" ya que de acuerdo con las expectativas de los autores debería tener significancia. Resulta ser que no. Finalmente, no incluyo en el cuadro pruebas del sistema judicial (derecho civil en comparación con derecho consuetudinario), ya que ninguno de ellos resulta con significancia estadística, y algunos incluso tienen el signo equivocado.

Los resultados presentados en el cuadro x.3 nos llevan a las siguientes conclusiones. En todos los modelos excepto en dos, la significancia estadística de los jugadores con veto es alta (por encima de 0.05 en pruebas de una cola). Las dos excepciones son la que usa la variable independiente de Lijphart sin significancia estadística,[6] y la que somete a prueba la hipótesis de Cooter y Ginsburg sobre la base de datos de confiabilidad estricta (significancia al nivel de 0.10).

Además, la mayor parte del tiempo la descentralización tiene significancia estadística. Por otro lado, la polarización no parece tener significancia excepto para el indicador de Alivizatos, y sale varias veces con un signo diferente. En consecuencia, la evidencia empírica corrobora la expectativa de que la independencia del poder judicial aumenta en función de los jugadores con veto. Además, la mayor parte del tiempo hay respaldo empírico para la idea de que los países federales tendrán un poder judicial más independiente que los unitarios. No hay pruebas de que el sistema judicial de un país (derecho consuetudinario y derecho civil) o la polarización de las fuerzas políticas en éste afecten la independencia judicial.

3. Jugadores con veto y burocracias

En esta sección empiezo por analizar los diferentes argumentos que se presentan en la bibliografía acerca de las burocracias. En particular me concentro en dos argumentos que llegan a diferentes expectativas a partir de la teoría presentada en este libro. El primero tiene que ver con la independencia de las burocracias, ya sea que aumenten o disminuyan con los jugadores con veto; el segundo se refiere a la variable independiente que explica la independencia burocrática: ¿es jugadores con veto o el tipo de régimen?

3.1. Teorías de las burocracias

Mathew McCubbins, Roger Noll y Barry Weingast han escrito una serie de artículos que componen probablemente el estudio más influyente de derecho administrativo. En dos de los más importantes (McCubbins, Noll y Wein-

---

[6] Incluso con la variable de Lijphart, la estadística-z se duplica cuando descartamos los cuatro países donde los expertos legales discrepan significativamente de la puntuación de Lijphart.

gast, 1987, 1989), los autores (de aquí en adelante McNollgast) se concentran predominantemente en la forma como las legislaturas creaban derecho administrativo, que restringe efectivamente a la burocracia para que realice los deberes prescritos por la coalición promulgadora. El problema fundamental de acuerdo con ellos es el *riesgo moral*, la posibilidad de que las burocracias escojan políticas que difieran de las preferencias de la coalición promulgadora.

Con el fin de evitar el riesgo moral, las legislaturas pueden crear leyes administrativas, las cuales tienen tres características principales: primero, la coalición promulgadora deberá crear un ambiente para la burocracia que refleje las políticas en el momento de su promulgación. Segundo, deberán asegurar el resultado en favor de los grupos que sean los más afectados y los más favorecidos por la coalición. Tercero, las políticas de su agencia deberán exhibir una característica de piloto automático: deberán permitir cambios políticos conforme cambien las preferencias de los grupos interesados.

Este análisis tiene ciertas consecuencias para el modelo desarrollado en la primera parte de este capítulo. Dado que los primeros en actuar en el juego que presenté antes serán capaces de seleccionar una política cercana o idéntica a su propio punto ideal, la rama legislativa *se asegurará una ventaja de antemano* para evitar esta posibilidad. McNollgast (1987, 1989) argumentan que ningún actor político concertará un acuerdo a no ser que sus intereses estén protegidos y, como resultado, los legisladores buscarán procurarse tal protección cuando escriban leyes administrativas.

Sobre la base de los argumentos y resultados de esta bibliografía, Terry Moe (1990) y David Epstein y Sharyn O'Halloran (1999) han argumentado que la legislación será más difícil cuando el cuerpo legislativo esté más dividido porque tratará de encerrar dentro de la legislación los intentos de la coalición que la produjo, lo cual lleva a una reducción de la independencia de las burocracias. Este argumento parece contradecir mi relación, de modo que lo abordaré con detalle.

Mi argumento se basa en lo que puede suceder *después* de la decisión burocrática *(ex post)*, mientras que los argumentos de McNollgast se fundamentan en lo que la legislatura hará previamente *(ex ante)*. Espero que, manteniendo constante la legislación, los burócratas y los jueces serán más independientes del gobierno cuando haya muchos jugadores con veto. El argumento de "asegurarse una ventaja de antemano" de McNollgast *no mantiene constante la legislación;* de hecho, la esencia de este argumento consiste en comparar los diferentes tipos de legislación producida con diferentes configuraciones de jugadores con veto. Además, el argumento de "asegurarse una ventaja de antemano" se ocupa de la independencia de los burócratas respecto *de la coalición que promulga la legislación*. Hay dos argumentos diferentes: los veremos uno por uno.

Primero, permítaseme dar mi propia expectativa para la legislación administrativa como función de jugadores con veto. Dada la libertad de las cortes y los burócratas para interpretar la legislación libremente cuando hay múltiples jugadores con veto, estos jugadores con veto preferirán restringirlos *ex ante*, es decir, les gustaría incluir restricciones de procedimiento dentro de la misma legislación (exactamente como arguyen McNollgast). ¿Serán capaces de hacer eso? Depende de sus preferencias por este tipo de legislación. Si sus preferencias son similares, entonces serán capaces de hacerlo. Si, no obstante, tienen preferencias sobre cómo atarles las manos a diferentes burócratas (un partido quiere capacitar a los ciudadanos para que den la voz de alarma, el otro quiere agencias de supervisión fuertes e independientes, para usar un ejemplo bien conocido [McCubbins y Schwartz, 1984]), y puede ser que no haya acuerdo. Así, en caso de múltiples jugadores con veto, el pronóstico real depende de las preferencias de los jugadores con veto existentes. Por otro lado, jugadores con veto individuales pueden invalidar a burócratas o jueces en cualquier momento (suponiendo que no haya ningún costo de transacción o político). Como resultado, tales gobiernos no se preocuparían por introducir restricciones adicionales en la legislación.

Este argumento espera que una legislación burocrática difícil de manejar sea *a veces* el resultado de múltiples jugadores con veto, mientras que la legislación simple sea *siempre* el resultado de jugadores con veto individuales. En otras palabras, múltiples jugadores con veto son una condición necesaria pero no suficiente para una legislación burocrática difícil de manejar. Como resultado, en promedio, cabría esperar una legislación más engorrosa en el caso de múltiples jugadores con veto (como lo pronostica McNollgast), pero también esperaríamos una mayor variación en el caso de múltiples jugadores con veto, exactamente como lo especifica el argumento presentado en el capítulo I (véase gráfica I.7). Huber y Shipan (2002) y Franchino (2000) han descubierto diferentes niveles promedio de legislación restrictiva, pero no han sometido a prueba el componente de varianza de este argumento.

Mi segundo punto es que el argumento de asegurarse una ventaja de antemano es acerca de la independencia burocrática ante la coalición promulgadora, mientras que estoy interesado en la independencia del gobierno, o de los principales actores políticos en el momento de la decisión. Puede darse el caso de que la coalición promulgadora lograra controlar a los burócratas a través de restricciones *ex ante* incorporadas a la ley, pero si esta coalición es remplazada, entonces los nuevos actores principales no serán capaces de obligar a los burócratas a obedecer sus deseos. Con el fin de hacer eso, es posible que tengan que cambiar la ley, y una coalición de múltiples jugadores con veto puede ser incapaz de hacerlo.

La distinción entre la coalición promulgadora y la actual tal vez no sea importante en los Estados Unidos, ya que un gobierno dividido ha sido la regla durante décadas y, en vista de las restricciones supermayoritarias en el Senado (capítulo VI), hasta los periodos de gobierno de un solo partido casi desaparecieron. Sin embargo, en otros países no se puede eliminar la distinción entre coalición promulgadora y coalición en el poder, y es la independencia del liderazgo político actual lo que define a la independencia burocrática o judicial.

En conclusión, mi argumento es que, manteniendo la legislación constante, la independencia burocrática de los jugadores con veto actuales aumenta con el número y las distancias entre jugadores con veto. Además, la legislación se vuelve más engorrosa en promedio (aunque la varianza de este pronóstico está en función de los jugadores con veto). Bajo las mismas condiciones, el argumento de asegurarse una ventaja de antemano espera una legislación más engorrosa, y menos independencia de los burócratas ante las coaliciones promulgadoras. Los dos argumentos son diferentes y no son incompatibles.

El segundo tema que plantea la bibliografía sobre burocracias es si hay problemas específicos de múltiples asociados principales con el régimen presidencial en contraposición a los jugadores con veto. Hay varios artículos que afirman que el parlamentarismo tiene una unidad de dirección de las burocracias en comparación con el presidencialismo. El argumento lo han planteado Moe y Caldwell (1994), quienes comparan el sistema británico con el estadounidense; Ackerman (2000), que critica las burocracias en los Estados Unidos, y Strom (2000), que analiza no sólo las burocracias sino más generalmente las características de delegación de los sistemas parlamentarios. De estas tres piezas, las dos primeras plantean argumentos que no identifican las conexiones causales. En realidad, es posible que el sistema estadounidense presente problemas de unidad de dirección de las burocracias (como lo afirman Ackerman, Moe y Caldwell) y que el sistema británico tenga unidad de dirección (como argumentan Moe y Caldwell), pero la razón de estas características es la distinción entre jugadores con veto individuales o múltiples, no la diferencia en el tipo de régimen. Este argumento, empero, no se puede plantear acerca de Strom, quien explícitamente compara los dos sistemas y aborda el argumento de los jugadores con veto, así que me concentro en su presentación y abordo el tema de la independencia burocrática sobre la base de su análisis.

Según Strom, la característica principal de un régimen parlamentario es la sencillez de su estructura de delegación. De hecho, desde las elecciones, hasta la selección de un primer ministro, la selección de ministros y las instrucciones a los burócratas, toda la vida política es una serie de delegaciones de principales individuales o colectivos hacia agentes individuales o colectivos. Como contraste, la delegación en sistemas presidenciales, dejando aparte el tema de los actores individuales o colectivos, se da de principales individuales a múltiples agentes (la gente selecciona instituciones múltiples), de principales múltiples a actores individuales (las diferentes instituciones legislativas delegan a agencias individuales), o de principales múltiples a agentes múltiples (a veces las instituciones legislativas pueden tener diferentes agencias que compiten por alguna tarea particular).

Sin embargo, éste es el tipo ideal de representación de los dos sistemas, y Strom reconoce que la realidad se puede dar en muchos matices (de hecho, reconoce que algunos de estos matices son determinados por la teoría de los jugadores con veto). Quiero abundar en estos puntos y argumentar que la cadena única de delegación es una simplificación. Esa simplificación puede ser importante con el propósito de resaltar características del presidencialismo, como la supervisión explícita de las burocracias a manos de los diferentes principales, en comparación con la ausencia de audiencias similares en sistemas parlamentarios; sin embargo, no considera la toma de decisiones dentro del gobierno, la cual, en el caso de gobiernos multipartidistas, puede ser un solo principal de una manera muy abstracta y del tipo caja negra.

Tratemos de abrir la caja negra del gobierno: según Strom, el primer ministro delega a los ministros, y los ministros delegan a los burócratas, de modo que los burócratas son parte de la cadena de mando única. Así, en la versión idealizada del argumento de Strom, el primer ministro determina en última instancia el comportamiento de los burócratas.

Comparemos este punto de vista con el argumento de Laver y Shepsle (1996) sobre las jurisdicciones ministeriales, que ya se examinó en el capítulo IV. Según estos autores, el ministro decide qué van a hacer los burócratas. No es así, diría Thies (2001); éste presenta pruebas de gobiernos compuestos de diferentes partidos no sólo entre ministerios, sino también dentro de éstos, de modo que los viceministros son de partidos diferentes al del ministro con el propósito de mantener a éste controlado. En opinión de Thies, la cadena de mando no es inequívoca.

Presentemos ahora el distinto punto de vista de Mark Hallerberg y Jürgen von Hagen (1999), quienes afirman que en lo tocante a los presupuestos, algunos países delegan la autoridad final al ministro de finanzas con el fin de mantener el presupuesto en el nivel que decida el gobierno. Hallerberg y von Hagen presentan las estructuras institucionales de diferentes países y demuestran que en varias delegaciones de creación de política importante, los poderes pertenecen al ministerio de finanzas. Aquí la cadena de mando implica al ministro y al ministerio de finanzas (podría abarcar también al primer ministro).

Sin embargo, cuando el ministerio de finanzas pueda desempeñar un papel clave en temas económicos, otros ministerios pueden participar también en la toma de decisiones correspondientes a sus jurisdicciones. Por ejemplo, no parece probable que en una conferencia internacional sobre el medio ambiente, las delegaciones nacionales incluyan a burócratas del ministerio del medio ambiente sin representantes del ministerio de asuntos exteriores. En la preparación de documentos sobre salud de la mujer, es probable que participen burócratas de salud y trabajo, por ejemplo.

Entra en escena Wolfgang Mueller (2000) con su análisis de sistemas parlamentarios que abarca *partidos* en cada paso del proceso de delegación. En opinión de Mueller, los partidos están más presentes en la formación del gobierno, menos en el proceso que pasa del gobierno a ministros individuales, mientras que la intervención en la delegación de ministros a funcionarios públicos es ilegítima: "Los funcionarios públicos deberán limitarse a implantar reglas generales y deberán hacerlo imparcialmente" (Mueller, 2000: 311). Obsérvese que el punto de Mueller aquí es normativo (nos dice lo que debería suceder, no lo que está sucediendo); sea como fuere, parece limitar severamente el principio de delegación al nivel de la burocracia.

Mi argumento es que cuando tratamos de abrir la caja negra de la delegación, surgen varias teorías plausibles, y cada una de ellas identifica una corriente distinta de "gobierno" a "burócratas". Puede ser directamente del ministro a los burócratas (Laver y Shepsle), o podría implicar a otros actores: el primer ministro (Strom), ministro de finanzas (Hallerberg y von Hagen), u otros ministros o partidos. Mi teoría es la única que abarca todas estas posibilidades sin tomar partido. Tan sólo estipula que si las cosas son importantes, cualquier actor gubernamental implicado deseará que su punto de vista sea respetado, de modo que el resultado sea aceptable para todos ellos. Ésta es una posición minimalista y no toma partido. Puede ser que el resultado quede localizado más cerca del ministro o el primer ministro o cualquier otro de estos actores. Muy probablemente los burócratas hábiles pondrán a cada uno de los principales en contra de los otros.

Como se argumentó en el capítulo IV, es verdad que los sistemas presidencial y parlamentario difieren en varias dimensiones (quién controla la agenda, si las coaliciones son fluidas y emprenden políticas o son rígidas y forman gobiernos). Los argumentos de Strom agregan variaciones interesantes sobre el tema de la delegación: que en sistemas parlamentarios la selección *ex ante* de agentes es más efectiva; que en sistemas presidenciales los controles *ex post* están institucionalizados; que el parlamentarismo se caracteriza por delegación y responsabilidad más indirectas (dado que hay etapas adicionales que implican selección del gobierno). Sin embargo, concentrándonos en las burocracias, las conclusiones se basan en el modelo del "tipo ideal" (o, de acuerdo con Strom, el modelo "maximalista"), el cual pasa por alto la toma de decisiones en el gobierno y la sustituye por el principio de que "los funcionarios públicos tienen un principal único, su respectivo ministro del gabinete" (Strom, 2000: 269). Si vemos que los burócratas en los gobiernos de coalición tienen muchos principales, entonces mientras más principales tengan, más capaces serán de poner a unos en contra de otros, y en mayor medida aumentará su independencia.

3.2. La evidencia empírica

Una serie de estudios empíricos han sometido a prueba el argumento de McNollgast sobre asegurarse una ventaja de antemano y encontraron evidencia que lo respaldaba. Huber y Shipan (2002) corroboraron el argumento con datos de la legislación laboral en dos diferentes casos: por un lado los estados de la Unión Americana y por el otro los países europeos. Encontraron que más jugadores con veto conducen a una legislación más restrictiva. De modo similar, Epstein y O'Halloran (1999) corroboraron el argumento en varias ocasiones con datos de los Estados Unidos. Franchino (2000) analizó la legislación de la Unión Europea y encontró una delegación más extensa a la Comisión Europea (burocracia) cuando la legislación es adoptada por mayoría calificada en el Consejo de Ministros que cuando es adoptada por unanimidad.

Hay, entonces, una importante cantidad de pruebas de que ocurre la práctica de asegurarse una ventaja de antemano y de que los países con muchos jugadores con veto tienen una legislación burocrática más engorrosa. ¿Hay alguna evidencia de que cuando la legislación es fija, los burócratas la interpretan de una manera más independiente cuando aumenta el número de jugadores con veto?

Ésta es una proposición mucho más difícil de demostrar, ya que a fin de hacer pruebas convincentes tendríamos que incluir las preferencias de los burócratas como parte del análisis. Identificar las preferencias de los burócratas en diferentes temas impone un problema casi insuperable para el análisis. Sin embargo, hay un caso donde podemos suponer que las preferencias de los burócratas son conocidas y ver si los resultados se aproximan más o menos a tales preferencias. El caso es la cuestión de la independencia del banco central.

Aquí está mi argumento. A los bancos centrales se les han asignado deberes relativos a políticas monetarias, tipos de cambio e inflación. La bibliografía sobre los bancos centrales y su importancia es abundante y no se revisará aquí.[7] Una serie de artículos sobre economía ha medido la independencia de esta rama particular de la burocracia. Examino la parte de esta bibliografía que conecta la independencia del banco central (IBC) con los pronósticos generados por la teoría que se presenta en este libro. En particular, examino si los bancos centrales pueden ejercer más independencia cuando hay muchos jugadores con veto (y más distantes).

Hay dos corrientes en la bibliografía empírica. La primera utiliza la IBC como variable dependiente y la correlaciona con características institucionales de los países (Bernhard, 1998; Lijphart, 1999; Moser, 1999; Hallerberg, 2001a). La segunda correlaciona el *comportamiento* del banco central con características institucionales (Lohmann, 1998; Keefer y Stasavage, 2000). Veamos cada una de estas corrientes por separado.

Jugadores con veto e IBC. Aunque los artículos sobre los efectos de la IBC abundan en la bibliografía económica, muy pocos de ellos han tratado la IBC como una variable dependiente. La enorme mayoría considera los efec-

---

[7] Véase Berger *et al.* (2001) para una revisión que cubre más de 150 artículos.

tos de la IBC como una serie de otras variables, o la solidez de diferentes indicadores de IBC.

Las medidas de IBC existentes usan cierta combinación de características institucionales para evaluar la independencia de los bancos centrales. Implican nombramiento y duración del ejercicio en el cargo del gobernador del banco central, ya sea que el banco participe en la formulación de la política monetaria, que la estabilidad de precios sea el objetivo principal del banco, y si el banco presta dinero únicamente al gobierno. Las respuestas positivas a las preguntas anteriores indican una IBC más alta.

William Bernhard (1998) examinó la IBC de 18 democracias industrializadas en el periodo de 1970 a 1990 y la correlacionó con una serie de características institucionales. Usó tres diferentes índices de IBC generados por Grilli y colaboradores (1991), Alesina y Summers (1993), y Cukierman (1991), pero informa de resultados únicamente sobre la base del promedio de los tres. Entre sus variables independientes estaba el índice Alford (un indicador de la votación por clase), bicameralismo fuerte, una combinación de polarización, gobierno de coalición e instituciones legislativas que él denominaba "amenaza de castigo". Descubrió que todas sus variables tenían significancia estadística.

De modo similar, Lijphart (1999) examinó varias mediciones de IBC diferentes y las correlacionó con dos variables distintas: federalismo y predominio ejecutivo. Estas dos variables están correlacionadas con los jugadores con veto (véase el capítulo III, que explica la correlación positiva entre jugadores con veto y federalismo; y los capítulos IV y VII, que aclaran la correlación negativa con el predominio ejecutivo). Descubrió que hay una poderosa correlación de la IBC con federalismo pero ninguna correlación con predominio ejecutivo.

Moser (1999) creó una variable tricotómica, que denominó "controles y equilibrios" (o "frenos y contrapesos"), y examinó todos los países de la OCDE. Su argumento es que controles y equilibrios altos generarán bancos independientes debido a que será difícil que el sistema político modifique la carta constitutiva del banco. Descubrió resultados que corroboraban fuertemente su argumento. Sin embargo, la clasificación de Moser ha sido criticada por inconsistente. Por ejemplo, Hallerberg argumenta:

> Los Estados que Moser clasifica como poseedores de controles y equilibrios fuertes (Australia, Canadá, Alemania, Suiza y los Estados Unidos) son los mismos Estados OCDE que Lijphart (1999) clasificó como Estados verdaderamente federa-

listas. Pero uno de ellos, Canadá, no debería ser un caso de "controles y equilibrios fuertes" según el propio esquema de clasificación de Moser, el cual recalca que las cámaras deben tener igual poder y contar con diferentes procedimientos para elegirlos para que los controles sean fuertes. [...] Más generalmente, sobre la escala de federalismo de Lijphart que va de uno a cinco, los Estados de "controles y equilibrios fuertes" de Moser tendrán todos una puntuación de cinco, mientras que el promedio de los Estados restantes es de sólo 1.9.

Estoy de acuerdo con esta evaluación y encuentro además que otros países como Portugal, Grecia, Finlandia e Islandia están clasificados erróneamente en la categoría intermedia.[8] Infiero de esta declaración que el resultado de Moser ofrece cierta evidencia adicional de que el federalismo (pero no la existencia de jugadores con veto partidarios) está correlacionado con la IBC.

Finalmente, Hallerberg (de próxima publicación) brinda una serie de razones por las cuales tanto los jugadores con veto como el federalismo deberían acrecentar la independencia del banco central.[9] Según su argumento, los Estados unitarios con gobiernos de un solo partido prefieren un banco central dependiente y tipos de cambio flexibles; los Estados unitarios con gobiernos de coalición prefieren un banco central independiente (moderadamente) y tipos de cambio fijos; los sistemas federales con gobiernos de un solo partido (como Canadá) prefieren un banco central independiente (moderadamente) y tipos de cambio flexibles, y los gobiernos pluripartidistas en Estados federales prefieren un banco independiente y tipos de cambio flexibles. Hallerberg encuentra una poderosa evidencia empírica de todos sus pronósticos, tanto sobre la variable de la independencia del banco central como sobre el régimen de tipo de cambio.

Por lo tanto, algunas de las investigaciones empíricas (Bernhard, 1998; Hallerberg, 2001) identifican jugadores con veto institucionales y partidarios correlacionados con la IBC, mientras que otros encuentran válida la correlación únicamente con jugadores con veto institucionales (federalismo). Con el fin de ver si hay una distinción entre ellos, usé los cuatro índices IBC de Bernhard (1998) y los correlacioné con federalismo y con jugadores con veto.

[8] Portugal tiene un presidente con poderes de veto, de modo que estaría incluido en los países con controles y equilibrios fuertes, mientras que los otros países tienen un gobierno que está de acuerdo con el parlamento, de modo que se deberían clasificar con controles y equilibrios débiles.

[9] Véase también Clark y Hallerberg (2000).

El cuadro X.4 replica los datos de Bernhard (1998) sobre la IBC y el cuadro X.5 usa estos datos para estimar los efectos de los jugadores con veto y el federalismo. El cuadro X.5 indica que tanto el federalismo como los jugadores con veto tienen correlaciones independientemente altas con la IBC. Sin embargo, ¿cómo podemos interpretar estas correlaciones? Todos los índices de IBC son principalmente variables institucionales, que describen lo que está escrito en las leyes de los países correspondientes. No obstante, las leyes no son siempre específicas en todas las preguntas que la clasificación requiere. Si las respuestas a estas interrogantes las dan no sólo las leyes sino también las prácticas predominantes, entonces el indicador no es una medición puramente institucional.

Dependiendo de si los índices de IBC implican características conductuales o son puramente institucionales, cambia la interpretación de los resultados empíricos. La primera posibilidad es que las mediciones impliquen también características conductuales. En este caso, la evidencia del cuadro X.5 corrobora la teoría de los jugadores con veto: cuantos más jugadores con

CUADRO X.4. *Independencia del banco central.*

País	Descentra- lización	Jugadores con veto	*Grilli* et al. *(1991)*	*Alesina y Summers (1993)*	*Cukierman (1991)*	*Total*
Alemania	3	3	0.87	1	0.66	0.84
Australia	3	2	0.6	0.5	0.31	0.47
Austria	3	2	0.6	0.625	0.58	0.6
Bélgica	3	3	0.47	0.5	0.19	0.39
Canadá	3	2	0.73	0.625	0.46	0.61
Dinamarca	1	3	0.53	0.625	0.47	0.54
España	3	1	0.33	0.375	0.21	0.31
Estados Unidos	3	3	0.8	0.875	0.51	0.73
Francia	1	2	0.47	0.5	0.28	0.42
Holanda	1	3	0.67	0.625	0.42	0.57
Irlanda	1	2	0.47	0.625	0.39	0.49
Italia	2	3	0.33	0.45	0.16	0.33
Japón	1	1	0.4	0.625	0.16	0.4
Noruega	1	2	0.44	0.5	0.14	0.4
Nueva Zelanda	1	1	0.2	0.25	0.27	0.2
Reino Unido	2	1	0.4	0.5	0.31	0.42
Suecia	1	2	0.44	0.5	0.27	0.4
Suiza	3	3	0.8	1	0.68	0.83

FUENTE: Bernhard (1998).

CUADRO X.5. *Diferentes mediciones de la independencia del banco central (IBC) como función de los jugadores con veto y de la descentralización.*

IBC	Grilli et al. (1991)	Alesina y Summers (1993)	Cukierman (1991)	Total IBC
Jugadores con veto	0.126***	0.1316***	0.0842**	0.1161***
(t)	(0.0423)	(0.0508)	(0.0475)	(0.0423)
Descentralización	0.0751**	0.0535*	0.0592*	0.0632**
(t)	(0.0343)	−0.0412	(0.0385)	(0.0343)
Constante	0.1073	0.2025	0.0586	0.1193
	(0.1057)	(0.127)	(0.1188)	(0.1058)
N	18	18	18	18
R^2 ajustado	0.479	0.334	0.232	0.414

Nota: Errores estándar entre paréntesis.
* $p < 0.10$.
** $p < 0.05$.
*** $p < 0.01$.
Todas las pruebas son de una cola.

veto haya, más independiente será esta burocracia particular. No tengo una respuesta a por qué el federalismo en todos los estudios empíricos tiene un impacto independiente sobre la IBC. Una posible respuesta sería que en algunos países (por ejemplo, Alemania, los Estados Unidos), el Estado participa en el nombramiento de miembros de la junta del banco central. Sin embargo, ésta no es una práctica universal.

La segunda posibilidad es que las mediciones de IBC representan características puramente institucionales. En este caso, la IBC no es una respuesta a la pregunta: "Si la legislación se mantiene constante, ¿cuáles bancos centrales son más independientes?", que se abordó en la primera sección de este capítulo. La pregunta pertinente a los datos de la IBC sería: "¿Por qué los creadores de leyes en algunos países prefieren niveles más altos de independencia del banco central?", y la teoría presentada en este libro no nos da una respuesta. La respuesta requiere un tipo de argumento "genético".[10] El de Hallerberg (de próxima publicación) es, hasta donde conoz-

[10] Esto sería un argumento como el que presenta Alivizatos (1995) en lo tocante a las cortes constitucionales (véase la sección anterior), de que *ceteris paribus* tales cortes suelen estar presentes en países con graves violaciones a los derechos humanos en su pasado.

co, el único artículo que ofrece razones de por qué diferentes tipos de gobiernos (federal o unitario) *y* diferentes configuraciones de jugadores con veto (único o múltiples) tendrían diferentes preferencias y generarían resultados distintos en términos de regímenes de IBC y tipo de cambio. Su argumento es completamente independiente del argumento que se presenta en este libro.

Jugadores con veto y comportamiento del banco central. Pasemos ahora a una expresión más precisa de independencia: el comportamiento del banco. ¿Es afectado este comportamiento por el ambiente político en el cual opera el banco? En un importante artículo empírico, Susanne Lohmann (1998) sometió a prueba una serie de teorías relacionadas con el desempeño real del Bundesbank alemán. Sus conclusiones fueron que "la independencia *conductual* del banco central alemán fluctúa a lo largo del tiempo con el control del partido de los puntos de veto federales" (Lohmann, 1998: 401).

Para llegar a esta conclusión, Lohmann examina cinco hipótesis en competencia: primero, que el banco central tiene plena independencia y está compuesto de tecnócratas; segundo, que el banco central no tiene independencia (en cuyo caso no importa de qué esté compuesto); tercero, que el banco central tiene plena independencia y está compuesto de partidarios; y quinto, que tiene independencia parcial y está compuesto de tecnócratas. Cada una de estas combinaciones de composición y nivel de independencia produce una diferente trayectoria temporal de crecimiento monetario como función de la composición del gobierno y el momento oportuno de las elecciones; los gobiernos de izquierda quieren expansión del crecimiento monetario; los bancos partidarios tratan de ayudar a un gobierno de su partido y de dañar a un gobierno opuesto, en particular en época de elecciones, en tanto que los tecnócratas se comportan de la misma manera, independientemente de quién esté en el poder; los bancos independientes no son afectados por las elecciones inminentes, mientras que los bancos no independientes sí lo son.

Con el fin de someter a prueba todas sus hipótesis, Lohmann introduce una serie de variables: económica (crecimiento monetario, crecimiento del PIB, inflación, tipos de cambio), económica institucional (Bretton Woods, sistema monetario europeo), ciclos electorales, composición del gobierno, composición de la cámara alta (Bundesrat), composición del banco central (quién nombra a los distintos miembros), y popularidad del canciller. Sus resultados respaldan las dos conclusiones siguientes:

La política monetaria alemana está sujeta a presiones electorales. No hay prueba de que las preferencias partidarias tengan influencia mediante el poder de nombramiento. El Consejo del Bundesbank está lleno de tecnócratas parcialmente independientes cuya independencia disminuye con el respaldo partidario para el gobierno federal en el Bundesrat. [...] La hipótesis auxiliar de que el punto de veto del Bundesrat protege la independencia del Bundesbank es la única hipótesis congruente con la evidencia compilada tanto en el estudio del caso como en el análisis de regresión [Lohmann, 1998: 440].

Los resultados de Susanne Lohmann son congruentes con la teoría presentada en este libro. Sin embargo, como ella observa, la composición del Bundesrat en Alemania está correlacionada con la popularidad gubernamental, de modo que las mediciones institucionales podrían de hecho reflejar la capacidad del gobierno de controlar la política monetaria. Éste es un problema de colinealidad que no se puede resolver con un conjunto de datos que cubre sólo a un país y 45 años. Sin embargo, dos estudios más recientes (Keefer y Stasavage, 2000) tienen bases de datos mucho más amplias. Philip Keefer y David Stasavage (2000: 17) desarrollan un modelo económico que conduce a los tres pronósticos siguientes:

1) La presencia de un banco central legalmente independiente debería tener un efecto negativo sobre la inflación sólo en presencia de controles y equilibrios (poderes complementarios o equilibrados entre las ramas de gobierno). *2)* La interferencia política, como sustitución de los gobernadores del banco central, es menos probable cuando están presentes los controles y equilibrios. *3)* La presencia de un banco central legalmente independiente tiene un efecto más negativo sobre la inflación cuando diferentes ramas de gobierno tienen preferencias divergentes acerca de la inflación.

Los tres vaticinios son congruentes con la teoría planteada en este libro. De hecho, la proposición 3 de Keefer y Stasavage pone a prueba no sólo el número de jugadores con veto sino también las distancias ideológicas entre ellos (véase proposición 1.4 del capítulo I).

Para someter a prueba sus pronósticos, Keefer y Stasavage usaron un conjunto de datos que abarcaba 78 países durante 20 años (para el periodo 1975-1994). Su variable dependiente es la inflación. Sus variables independientes incluyen la independencia del banco central y una serie de variables institucionales. Utilizan como indicadores de la independencia del banco central tanto la "independencia legal", que mide una serie de indicadores institucionales (véase la sección anterior), como las tasas de sustitución de los gobernadores del banco central (una variable que según la bibliografía refleja mejor la independencia real en países en desarrollo). Sus variables institucionales se pueden encontrar en una base de datos sobre instituciones políticas desarrollada por Beck y colaboradores (1999). La variable *controles* se "basa en un fórmula que primero cuenta el número de jugadores con veto, con base en si el ejecutivo y la(s) cámara(s) legislativa(s) están controlados por diferentes partidos en sistemas presidenciales y sobre el número de partidos en la coalición de gobierno para sistemas parlamentarios" (Keefer y Stasavage, 2000: 19). La *polarización* se mide "de acuerdo con si las fuentes de datos indican que los partidos (los cuatro más grandes) tienen una orientación económica que era de izquierda, de centro o de derecha [...] la diferencia máxima entre esas entidades que comprenden el indicador *controles* explicado antes. Este máximo constituye la medición de *polarización política*" (Keefer y Stasavage, 2000: 20).

El lector puede comprobar que el método usado para la identificación de variables institucionales está estrechamente conectado con los métodos empleados en este libro. La mayor diferencia es que las posiciones ideológicas de diferentes jugadores con veto no son identificadas con exactitud, lo cual queda compensado por el tamaño de la muestra. Keefer y Stasavage usan variables interactivas (jugadores con veto de IBC*) con el fin de ver si importan las instituciones. En su análisis encuentran que la independencia del banco central no tiene efecto alguno sobre la inflación cuando entra linealmente (un resultado reportado con mucha frecuencia en la bibliografía), pero los coeficientes de los términos interactivos son negativos y tienen significancia. Obtienen esta conclusión:

> Más concretamente, en un sistema parlamentario con una coalición gobernante de tres partidos [...] se pronosticaría que un aumento de una desviación estándar en la independencia legal del banco central reduciría la tasa anual de inflación aproximadamente en 20%. Como contraste, en un sistema parlamentario con una mayoría de un solo partido [...] el cambio pronosticado de inflación estaría cerca de cero. [...] Esto sugiere una explicación para el resultado de Cukierman, Webb y Neyapti (1992) de que la IBC está correlacionada significativa y negativamente con la inflación en países industriales avanzados pero no en países en desarrollo: los países en desarrollo, en promedio, tienen niveles más bajos de controles y equilibrios [Keefer y Stasavage, 2000: 23].

Cuando la variable "polarización política" se incluye en las regresiones, los resultados indican que "controles y equilibrios hacen la mayor contribución a la eficiencia del banco central en sociedades más polarizadas" (Keefer y Stasavage, 2000: 33).

4. Conclusiones

En este capítulo he desarrollado un modelo sencillo que genera la expectativa de que para cualquier legislación dada, la independencia de la burocracia y del poder judicial estará relacionada positivamente con los jugadores con veto (número y distancias entre ellos) que controlan el proceso legislativo. Este modelo fue puesto entonces a prueba con datos existentes sobre la independencia del poder judicial y de la burocracia.

En el nivel teórico he hecho la distinción entre países con o sin tribunales constitucionales. Argumenté que los tribunales constitucionales son jugadores adicionales con veto (dado que para todo propósito práctico no pueden ser invalidados legislativamente). Sin embargo, debido a las reglas de elección de estos tribunales, la mayor parte del tiempo son absorbidos como jugadores con veto por los tribunales políticos ya existentes. Los resultados empíricos acerca de los jueces se basaron en cuatro diferentes índices de independencia judicial generados por combinaciones de una veintena de países industrializados avanzados y corroboraron las expectativas del modelo de la primera sección.

En lo tocante a las burocracias, establecí la distinción entre independencia institucional y conductual con el fin de diferenciar el argumento que se presentó en este libro a partir de los argumentos comunes en la bibliografía. Logré identificar un caso (actividades del banco central) donde se pudieran someter a prueba las expectativas generadas por mi argumento. Examinando la evidencia empírica descubrí que la independencia del banco central está correlacionada tanto con los jugadores con veto como con el federalismo. Argumenté que, muy probablemente, la IBC es una variable institucional y como consecuencia la teoría que se presenta en este libro no puede explicar las razones por las cuales el banco central es más independiente en los países con muchos jugadores con veto. Sin embargo, concentrándonos en la independencia conductual (en la lucha en contra de la inflación), presenté evidencia de que las expectativas generadas en la primera parte de este capítulo han sido sólidamente corroboradas por un conjunto de datos que cubren un gran número de países.

XI. ANÁLISIS DE JUGADORES CON VETO EN INSTITUCIONES DE LA UNIÓN EUROPEA

La Unión Europea fascina a observadores y académicos debido a que se trata de un objeto de estudio único. La estructura institucional de la Unión Europea es nueva y, como resultado, se han inventado algunos neologismos para describirla. "No es un Estado ni una organización internacional" (Sbragia, 1992: 257); "menos que una Federación, más que un Régimen" (W. Wallace, 1983: 403); "atrapada entre soberanía e integración" (W. Wallace, 1982: 67); "Intergubernamentalismo institucionalizado en una organización supranacional" (Cameron, 1992: 66); el "terreno medio entre la cooperación de naciones existentes y el nacimiento de una nueva" (Scharpf, 1988: 242). Algunos estudiosos incluso han visto ventajas en la situación: Sbragia (1988: 242) cita con aprobación a Krislov, Ehlermann y Weiler, afirmando: "La ausencia de un modelo claro, por un lado, hace que las analogías *ad hoc* sean más apropiadas y justificables. Si no podemos especificar lo que son analogías claras, las menos claras pueden ser apropiadas".

En este capítulo en vez de utilizar analogías (apropiadas o inapropiadas), aplico la teoría de los jugadores con veto y examino la lógica y los resultados de la toma de decisiones generada por los diferentes procedimientos legislativos adoptados en tratados sucesivos, y establezco comparaciones entre mis conclusiones y otros análisis institucionales. Como resultado, este capítulo cuenta con tres características importantes: primera, estudia diferentes estructuras institucionales que prevalecen en un mismo territorio; segunda, fomenta la aplicación de la teoría de los jugadores con veto ya que las instituciones de la Unión Europea son muy complicadas: comprenden tres instituciones legislativas, cada una de las cuales toma decisiones por diferentes mayorías formales o reales, y el derecho a establecer la agenda en ocasiones incluye restricciones, a veces es compartido y otras veces cambia entre los actores; tercera, dado que el estudio de las instituciones y políticas de la Unión Europea ha progresado más que los estudios de caso, los pronósticos de diferentes teorías son más acertados, y los datos recabados permiten establecer comparaciones sobre una base relativamente sólida. En suma, este capítulo hace comparaciones por medio de diferentes situaciones institucionales (que implican la misma área geográfica), hace que la teoría cubra instituciones más complicadas, y usa pruebas empíricas para corroborar pronósticos empíricos más detallados que cualquiera de los capítulos anteriores.

Este capítulo se divide en cuatro partes. En la primera se analizan algunos de los temas que se estudian en la bibliografía sobre la Unión Europea. Veremos que diferentes partes de esa bibliografía se concentran en la composición nacional o supranacional de diversas instituciones, y que consideran estas instituciones como el marco dentro del cual los actores racionales persiguen sus metas, o en el sentido de que configuran las preferencias e identidades de estos actores. La segunda parte describe lo que se considera en todo este libro como la base de un enfoque institucional de la política, el sistema legislativo de la Unión Europea. La Unión Europea ha adoptado una serie de procedimientos legislativos diferentes. Estos procedimientos son muy complicados y significativamente distintos de otros sistemas políticos (presidencial o parlamentario), de modo que no podemos presuponer que el lector sepa lo que ellos permiten exactamente y lo que impiden. En la tercera parte se analiza la distribución prevista del poder entre las instituciones legislativas (la Comisión Europea, el Consejo de Ministros y el Parlamento Europeo), así como implicaciones de reglas legislativas sobre burocracias y el poder judicial. La última parte considera la evidencia empírica disponible para evaluar la validez de diferentes teorías institucionales.

1. Bibliografía sobre la Unión Europea

La bibliografía sobre la Unión Europea es extensa, quizás por el hecho de que es uno de los pocos ejemplos de desarrollo institucional en escala real y en curso donde observadores y actores por igual consideran los efectos de medidas institucionales y diseñan el siguiente paso. Es imposible resumir esta extensa bibliografía en unas cuantas páginas. Remito al lector interesado a las revisiones que la sintetizan. Algunas de estas revisiones (Hix, 1994) multiplican las diferentes corrientes de pensamiento, dividiéndolas no sólo en enfoques basados en las relaciones internacionales y en política comparada, sino también en enfoques pluralistas, realistas, estructuralistas, sociológicos y de elección racional. Otros (Pollack, 2001; Aspinwall y Schneider, 2000) combinan diferentes enfoques y dividen los estudios en racionales y constructivistas.

Es innegable que la mayor parte de estos estudios adopta una arquitectura racionalista en que se presupone que las instituciones son reglas dentro de las cuales los actores desarrollan sus elecciones con el propósito de lograr el mejor resultado.[1] Limitaré mi discusión en esta sección a tales estudios, en particular el intergubernamentalismo, el neofuncionalismo y el análisis institucional y explicaré sus diferencias. Me concentraré en la bibliografía del análisis institucional en las últimas tres partes de este capítulo.

A riesgo de simplificar demasiado, los intergubernamentalistas se concentran en la negociación de tratados y consideran la estructura institucional de la Unión Europea como la variable dependiente. Además, esta estructura se concibe en términos generales (como el enfoque de Moravcsik, 1998, en las instituciones de la Unión Europea como compromisos creíbles con la integración) en vez de ser analizada en función de las interacciones detalladas entre las cuatro instituciones principales de la Unión Europea y sus probables efectos sobre la política. Sin embargo, el enfoque de tipo láser del intergubernamentalismo sobre los tratados requiere un estudio previo de todas las realidades de la Unión Europea que son generadas (o propensas a ser generadas) por las instituciones que fueron producidas por los tratados anteriores. Como se verá, la Unión Europea ha cambiado con mucha frecuencia su estructura institucional, y por ello la influencia de diferentes actores así como los resultados políticos pueden variar con el paso del tiempo.

Para los neofuncionalistas, en contraste, las instituciones de la Unión Europea no son variables independientes sino actores: la Comisión Europea, el Tribunal Europeo de Justicia (TEJ), y el Parlamento Europeo (PE) emprenden acciones que afectan la dirección que tome la integración europea. Más específicamente, la teoría neofuncionalista argumenta que la integración en Europa está avanzando porque "los actores en diversas situaciones nacionales distintas son persuadidos para que cambien sus lealtades, expectativas y actividades políticas hacia un nuevo centro, cuyas instituciones po-

---

[1] Otros estudios adoptan un marco constructivista y consideran que las instituciones también configuran identidades y preferencias de los actores. Thomas Christiansen, Knud Erik Jorgensen y Antje Wiener (1999: 529) han expresado así la esencia del enfoque: "La integración europea misma ha cambiado con los años, y es razonable presuponer que en el proceso la identidad de los agentes y después sus intereses han cambiado por igual. Aunque este aspecto del cambio puede teorizarse dentro de perspectivas constructivistas, permanecerá en gran parte invisible en los enfoques que descuiden el proceso de formación de identidad y/o presupongan intereses que se dan de manera exógena". Aquí no examinaré tales enfoques, ya que como lo argumenta Moravcsik (1999), la mayoría de ellos no han logrado construir hipótesis distintivas y comprobables.

seen o exigen jurisdicción de los Estados nacionales preexistentes" (Haas, 1961: 366-367). El motor que impulsa este proceso son los "derrames", es decir, situaciones donde "una acción dada, relacionada con una meta específica, crea una situación en la cual la meta original puede ser asegurada solamente emprendiendo más acciones, lo cual a su vez crea una condición ulterior y una necesidad de más, y así sucesivamente" (Lindberg, 1963: 9). Como resultado, los neofuncionalistas evitan el análisis de las estrategias disponibles para diferentes actores y las restricciones con las cuales operan. Es decir, no analizan las instituciones con la intención de generar resultados de equilibrio particulares.

Garrett y Tsebelis (1996) y Tsebelis y Garrett (2001) han diferenciado el enfoque institucionalista del intergubernamentalismo y el neofuncionalismo analizando las obras recientes más representativas en cada uno de estos programas de investigación. No repito aquí sus argumentos, excepto los puntos principales presentados en el cuadro XI.1.

El cuadro presenta las dos dimensiones que distinguen entre estas tres principales corrientes de investigación. La primera es si nos concentramos solamente en las interacciones entre los gobiernos miembros en el sentido de que definen el proceso de integración. Aquí, el enfoque institucional está más cerca del neofuncionalismo que del intergubernamentalismo. Evita el foco inapropiadamente miope de los análisis intergubernamentales sobre revisiones de tratados, prestando mayor atención a la multitud de directrices, reglamentaciones y decisiones judiciales claramente importantes que influyen día a día en el curso de la integración europea.

La segunda dimensión se refiere a la pregunta de si el curso de la integración europea es el producto de elecciones intencionales de parte de los actores correspondientes (y las interacciones estratégicas entre éstos). Para

CUADRO XI.1. *Tres enfoques de la integración europea.*

	Interguberna- mentalismo	Neofuncionalismo	Institucionalismo
¿Son los gobiernos los únicos actores (importantes)?	Sí	No	No
¿Consecuencias no intencionales?	No	Sí	No (con información completa)

los neofuncionalistas, la ley de las consecuencias no intencionales (derrames) es la base del análisis. Para los intergubernamentalistas, en acentuado contraste, los gobiernos que firman tratados no están solamente en el asiento del conductor, también saben exactamente adónde van.

La posición del análisis institucional del tema es más calificada. Si los actores operan con información completa (por ejemplo, si conocen toda la información pertinente unos acerca de los otros), diseñarán instituciones que promoverán muy bien sus preferencias, sujetos a la restricción de que cada uno de los otros actores se comportará de manera similar. No obstante, incluso en condiciones de información completa, el análisis institucional sugiere un tipo diferente de investigación sobre la negociación de tratados que es típica del intergubernamentalismo.

El intergubernamentalismo trata la estructura institucional de la Unión Europea como una variable dependiente; es el producto de negociación de tratados. Sin embargo, los análisis institucionales argumentan que el estudio de los resultados institucionales es lógicamente anterior al análisis de la elección institucional. Para usar la terminología de Shepsle (1986), tenemos que entender los "equilibrios institucionales" antes de pasar al análisis de las "instituciones de equilibrio". El hecho de que los intergubernamentalistas típicamente eviten el análisis de las "instituciones como variables independientes" reduce de manera significativa su capacidad de entender la elección institucional. Incluso si los intergubernamentalistas están en lo correcto al presuponer que la negociación de tratados ocurre con información completa, el hecho de que presten más atención a los objetivos políticos estipulados que a las instituciones creadas para implantarlos es una flaqueza grave en este modo de análisis.

Pero, ¿cuán apropiada es la suposición de información completa para la negociación de tratados? Creo que la realidad se encuentra en algún punto medio entre el negro y el blanco de la línea divisoria entre neofuncionalismo e intergubernamentalismo. La suposición de información completa es estricta. Como verá el lector, la utilizo solamente en las etapas finales de los procedimientos complicados de la Unión Europea después de que los actores hayan intercambiado información. En lo tocante a la implantación y adjudicación, el hecho de que el Protocolo Barber se insertara en el Tratado de Maastricht para contrademandar una decisión del Tribunal Europeo de Justicia constituye una buena prueba de que el Tribunal Europeo de Justicia no siempre pronostica con exactitud las reacciones de los gobiernos miembros (Garrett, Kelemen y Schulz, 1998).

En el caso de la negociación de tratados, el umbral de la información completa es incluso más alto, debido a que los gobiernos toman decisiones que tendrán largas cadenas de efectos dentro del futuro indefinido. Si no conocen toda la información pertinente unos acerca de otros, o si operan bajo presiones cognoscitivas que restringen su capacidad de comportarse de modo perfectamente racional, o si esperan con alguna probabilidad que los choques en el ambiente político cambiarán la capacidad de otros actores, la suposición estricta de la información completa es improbable que resulte de gran ayuda.

Pero como un asunto empírico, vale la pena preguntarse cuánta de la evolución de la Unión Europea desde mediados de la década de 1980 que veremos en la siguiente sección fue prevista por los gobiernos miembros durante los procesos de creación del tratado, y cuánto no fue intencional. Si nos concentramos en los debates acerca de reducir el déficit democrático mediante la reforma de los procedimientos legislativos de la Unión Europea (una de las características más importantes de la integración europea en los últimos 20 años) la balanza parece inclinarse en favor de la suposición de información completa. En general (pero, como se verá, no en todos los aspectos), las modificaciones institucionales introducidas tuvieron el efecto intencional de reducir el papel de la Comisión y acrecentar el del Parlamento Europeo.

En suma, la pretendida "ley de consecuencias no intencionales" ha sido empíricamente acribillada con muchas más excepciones de las que sugiere la mayoría de los comentaristas sobre la integración europea. Así, concentrarnos en las interacciones institucionales formales en la Unión Europea no sólo ayuda a explicar cómo ésta ha operado en diferentes épocas, sino que también nos proporciona atisbos importantes acerca de la forma en que los gobiernos miembros han decidido amalgamar su soberanía en el proceso de integración.

2. Procedimientos legislativos en la Unión Europea

Hay cuatro actores institucionales principales en la Unión Europea: el Consejo de Ministros, la Comisión Europea, el Parlamento Europeo y el Tribunal Europeo de Justicia.[2] Tres de estos actores (todos a excepción del TEJ) componen la rama legislativa de la Unión Europea. La interacción entre

---

[2] A estos cuatro deberíamos agregar el Banco Central Europeo, creado por el Tratado de Maastricht (1991).

ellos quedó definida en una serie de tratados que se iniciaron con el Tratado de Roma en 1957 hasta llegar al Tratado de Niza (2001). Una Conferencia Intergubernamental Europea fue programada para el año 2004.

Las Conferencias Intergubernamentales que introdujeron o alteraron las políticas legislativas en la Unión Europea son las siguientes: el Tratado de Roma (1957), el Compromiso de Luxemburgo (1966), el Acta Única Europea (1987), el Tratado de Maastricht (1991), el Tratado de Ámsterdam (1997) y el Tratado de Niza (2001). En cierto sentido, la Unión Europea ha estado perfeccionando constantemente sus instituciones políticas: seis revisiones en sus 40 años de historia y cuatro de ellas en los últimos 15. Me concentraré en este acelerado periodo de revisión que se inició en 1987 y que produjo una innovación institucional cada tres años. Pero antes se requiere una breve introducción histórica.

2.1. Del Tratado de Roma al Compromiso de Luxemburgo

El Tratado de Roma (1957) fue la cristalización de un compromiso entre los elementos federalistas y antifederalistas de la Unión Europea (en esa época, la Comunidad Económica Europea [CEE]). Las instituciones diseñadas en este tratado introdujeron un nuevo procedimiento legislativo denominado "consulta". El Tratado de Roma especificaba que la toma de decisiones unánime en el Consejo sería remplazada por una toma de decisiones de mayoría calificada en algunas áreas en 1966 (cuando se inició la tercera fase de la integración; Tratado de la CEE, art. 8, puntos 3-6). De hecho, según el procedimiento de consulta, una propuesta de la Comisión requeriría una mayoría calificada en el Consejo para su aceptación, pero necesitaba de unanimidad para ser modificada. Este modo de toma de decisiones, que dio a la Comisión la autoridad de hacer propuestas que eran más difíciles de rechazar o modificar, se ha conservado en tratados ulteriores y se analiza con detalle en la siguiente parte.

Sin embargo, las especificaciones del Tratado de Roma no se aplicaron en 1966 debido a las objeciones del gobierno francés a las estipulaciones de mayoría calificada. Los franceses empezaron a plantear tales objeciones poco después de que el general Charles de Gaulle llegara al poder en 1958. De Gaulle era un reconocido adversario al supranacionalismo, pero en buena medida respaldaba el intergubernamentalismo y la estrecha cooperación de naciones soberanas e independientes (De Gaulle, 1960 y 1971: 189-191).

A raíz de los Tratados de Roma, De Gaulle hizo varios intentos de que sus ideas fueran aceptadas por sus aliados europeos. Los primeros dos, con el nombre de Planes Fouchet I y II, fracasaron, mientras que el tercero, conocido como el Compromiso de Luxemburgo, tuvo éxito.

En 1966, De Gaulle logró poner un fin *de facto* a la votación mayoritaria que iba a durar hasta 1987. La batalla que llevó al Compromiso de Luxemburgo empezó en relación con un plan propuesto por la Comisión para fundar la recién acordada Política Agrícola Comunitaria (PAC). La Comisión propuso un monto que excedía con mucho la cantidad necesaria, y la propuesta de la Comisión sugería que este ingreso "extra" podía ser útil para financiar proyectos que no fueran aquellos ya aceptados por los gobiernos. Por añadidura, la propuesta requería aumentar los poderes presupuestarios del Parlamento Europeo e indirectamente de la Comisión (Tsebelis y Kreppel, 1998: 60-63).

De Gaulle aprovechó la oportunidad y en una conferencia de prensa de 1965 argumentó que el episodio mostraba una Comisión que intentaba excederse de sus poderes, en detrimento de la soberanía nacional de los Estados miembros. A partir de julio de 1965, después de una junta inconclusa del Consejo sobre las crisis presupuestarias inminentes, Francia inició su así llamada política de "silla vacía". De hecho, Francia boicoteó a la Comunidad Europea durante siete meses, causando una profunda crisis que al final se resolvió sólo mediante el Compromiso de Luxemburgo. El compromiso mismo no tenía nada que ver con las propuestas financieras, que supuestamente habían causado la crisis. En vez de ello, el compromiso trataba exclusivamente el tema de la votación mayoritaria en el Consejo, que iba a entrar en vigor ese mismo año. El compromiso fue un "acuerdo de no estar de acuerdo" (Marjolin, 1980: 56-59). El texto del compromiso reafirmaba el deseo de los otros cinco miembros de la Comunidad Europea de avanzar con votación mayoritaria, aunque estaban dispuestos a retrasar las decisiones "cuando estuvieran en juego los temas muy importantes para uno o más países miembros". Sin embargo, los franceses declararon su opinión de "que, cuando hay de por medio temas muy importantes, se debe continuar con las decisiones hasta que se logre un acuerdo unánime" (Sesión Extraordinaria del Consejo, 18 de enero de 1966, Boletín de la CE 3/66, parte b, párrafos 1-3). Esta divergencia de opinión fue notada por los seis países miembros, y se llegó al acuerdo de que esta diferencia de opinión no debería obstaculizar, "que se reanudara el trabajo de la Comunidad de acuerdo con el procedimiento normal" (Boletín de la CE 3/66, parte b, párrafo 4).

Los efectos del compromiso fueron profundos y duraderos. Aunque inicialmente los otros cinco Estados miembros se opusieron al requerimiento de unanimidad, terminaron no sólo por aceptarlo sino también por respaldarlo y protegerlo de una serie de intentos de recuperar la votación mayoritaria. El Compromiso de Luxemburgo presagió "un cambio de carácter distintivo, que inicialmente los Cinco rechazaron, pero que más tarde, especialmente después de la primera ampliación, todos abrazaron de buen grado" (Dinan, 1994: 59).

2.2. El procedimiento de cooperación

El Compromiso de Luxemburgo gobernó el proceso legislativo en la Unión Europea hasta la ratificación del Acta Única Europea (AUE) en 1987. Esta acta introdujo el "procedimiento de cooperación" entre las tres instituciones legislativas, la Comisión, el Consejo y el Parlamento Europeo (elegido directamente desde 1979).

El procedimiento de cooperación no llegó a cubrir todas las áreas de la legislación de la Unión Europea. Se aplicó a unos diez artículos del Tratado de Roma y constituyó entre un tercio y la mitad de las decisiones tomadas por el parlamento (Jacobs y Corbett, 1990: 169). El procedimiento comprende dos lecturas de cada pieza de legislación (inicialmente introducida por la Comisión) en el Parlamento Europeo y el Consejo. El Consejo toma la decisión final ya sea por mayoría calificada o por unanimidad. En abstracto, el procedimiento se parece a un sistema de *navette* entre las dos cámaras de una legislatura bicameral donde la cámara alta (el Consejo) tiene la última palabra.[3]

El proceso legislativo se inicia cuando la Comisión presenta una propuesta al Parlamento Europeo. Al mismo tiempo, el Consejo puede empezar a deliberar, pero no puede llegar a una decisión hasta enterarse de la posición del Parlamento Europeo. El Parlamento Europeo en la primera lectura puede aceptar, enmendar o rechazar la propuesta; también puede guardarse su opinión, remitiendo la legislación de regreso a un comité, con lo cual hace abortar efectivamente la propuesta. Una vez que el Parlamento Europeo decide, la propuesta regresa a los miembros de la Comisión, quienes pueden revisar la propuesta inicial para adaptarla al Parlamento Euro-

[3] Véase capítulo VI. Para una discusión detallada del sistema de *navette* en diferentes países, véase Tsebelis y Money (1997).

peo. La Comisión presenta la propuesta enmendada al Consejo. Los miembros del Consejo adoptan una "posición común" por mayoría calificada (en el momento, con 12 miembros, 54 de 76 votos) si están de acuerdo con la propuesta de la Comisión, o por unanimidad si enmendaron efectivamente la propucsta. No hay límite de tiempo para las deliberaciones en esta primera lectura de la propuesta. Es obvio, por lo tanto, que cualquiera de las instituciones puede hacer abortar efectivamente la legislación en esta etapa del proceso.

Una vez que el Consejo adopta su posición común, se inicia la segunda lectura de la propuesta. El Consejo devuelve su posición común al Parlamento Europeo, junto con una justificación completa de las razones por las cuales adoptó esta posición. El artículo 149(2b) del Acta Única Europea requiere la justificación plena de la posición del Consejo y de la Comisión. Sin embargo, en la fase inicial de aplicación del procedimiento, el Consejo proporcionó razones extremadamente esquemáticas o incluso no dio ninguna razón en lo absoluto. En un caso, parece que no se enteró de que el Parlamento Europeo había postergado indefinidamente las enmiendas a la propuesta de la Comisión (Bieber, 1988: 720). El Parlamento Europeo protestó oficialmente, su presidente declaró el 28 de octubre de 1987 que "por lo menos, el Consejo debía dar reacciones específicas y explicadas a cada una de las enmiendas del Parlamento" (Jacobs y Corbett, 1990: 173). El 18 de noviembre de 1987 el Parlamento Europeo amenazó al Consejo con ejercer acción jurídica en lo tocante a dos resoluciones (Bieber, 1988: 720). Como resultado, el Consejo alteró su enfoque y proporcionó una explicación de su punto de vista sobre cada uno de los temas sustantivos planteados por el proyecto de legislación (Jacobs y Corbett, 1990: 173).

El Parlamento Europeo tiene entonces tres meses para seleccionar una de tres opciones: aprobar la posición común del Consejo (o, lo que es igual, no emprender ninguna acción), en cuyo caso el Consejo adopta la propuesta; rechazar la posición común por una mayoría absoluta de sus miembros (en el momento 260 votos); o enmendar la posición común, de nueva cuenta por una mayoría absoluta de sus miembros. En esta segunda vuelta, el tiempo es esencial. El reloj empieza a correr cuando el presidente del Parlamento Europeo anuncia que ha recibido todos los documentos pertinentes en los nueve idiomas oficiales.

La Comisión puede haber presentado o no al Consejo la legislación rechazada por el Parlamento Europeo; si tal legislación se introduce, el Consejo puede invalidar el rechazo por unanimidad. La legislación enmendada se presenta a la Comisión, la cual debe revisar la propuesta en el plazo de un mes. Las enmiendas parlamentarias que son aceptadas por la Comisión pueden ser adoptadas por el Consejo por mayoría calificada (54 de 76), mientras que cualquier otra versión requiere de unanimidad en el Consejo. Si el Consejo no logra actuar dentro de tres meses (cuatro, con el acuerdo del Parlamento Europeo), la propuesta prescribe.

Una vez que se inicie la discusión por una propuesta de la Comisión, no hay restricciones a las enmiendas que el Parlamento Europeo puede introducir en su primera lectura. En la segunda lectura, las reglas parlamentarias especifican que las enmiendas tienen que ser únicamente en aquellas partes del texto que el Consejo ha modificado, y que intenten adoptar un compromiso con el Consejo o restaurar la posición del Parlamento Europeo en la primera lectura (Bieber, 1988: 722).

Hay, sin embargo, una restricción muy importante a la capacidad de enmienda de la segunda lectura del Parlamento Europeo. Las enmiendas requieren mayorías absolutas para ser adoptadas. En la práctica, los 260 votos requeridos constituyen una mayoría de dos tercios de los miembros presentes. Por añadidura, dado que los miembros del Parlamento Europeo de los 12 países por entonces integrantes estaban organizados en más de 10 grupos parlamentarios (representación internacional) y que las alineaciones de votación ocurrían con mayor frecuencia por grupos políticos y menos a menudo por países, y dado también que la disciplina de los votantes es débil, 260 votos equivalen a un requerimiento de mayoría calificada, como se vio en el capítulo VI.

En resumen, de acuerdo con el procedimiento de cooperación, en su segunda lectura el Parlamento Europeo puede hacer una propuesta por mayoría absoluta de sus miembros, la cual, si es adoptada por la Comisión, puede ser aceptada por una mayoría calificada (54 de 76) del Consejo, pero requiere unanimidad del Consejo para ser modificada. Esta propuesta puede estar en cualquier parte entre la primera lectura del Parlamento Europeo y el Consejo de la legislación inicial, incluyendo una reiteración de la posición previa del Parlamento Europeo. Esto es lo que he denominado "poder condicional de establecimiento de agenda del Parlamento Europeo" (Tsebelis, 1994); analizo sus propiedades estratégicas en la siguiente sección.

2.3. El procedimiento de codecisión I

El Tratado de Maastricht introdujo un nuevo procedimiento en la toma de decisiones, que fue bautizado (en la bibliografía y en los debates cotidianos, no en el tratado mismo) como "codecisión". Este procedimiento esencialmente agrega algunas etapas nuevas al procedimiento de cooperación después de la segunda lectura de la legislación en el Parlamento Europeo. Si en su segunda lectura el Consejo está en desacuerdo con cualquiera de las enmiendas parlamentarias, el texto es remitido a un comité de conciliación, compuesto por un número igual de miembros del Consejo y de representantes parlamentarios. Si el comité llega a un acuerdo, éste tiene que ser aprobado por una mayoría en el Parlamento Europeo y una mayoría calificada en el Consejo para que se pueda convertir en ley. Si no hay acuerdo, la iniciativa regresa al Consejo, el cual puede reintroducir su posición previa, "posiblemente con enmiendas del Parlamento Europeo", por mayoría calificada o por unanimidad (dependiendo del tema). De no ser que una mayoría absoluta de los miembros del Parlamento Europeo discrepe, la ley es adoptada.

Una comparación de los dos procedimientos indica varias diferencias principales. Primero, el parlamento tiene capacidad de veto absoluta en el procedimiento de codecisión, pero necesita una alianza con la Comisión o al menos un miembro del Consejo para hacer que su veto se sostenga en el procedimiento de cooperación. Segundo, al final del procedimiento de codecisión, es el Consejo el que hace una propuesta de "tómenlo o déjenlo" al Parlamento Europeo. Tercero, en el procedimiento de codecisión, el desacuerdo aun por una sola enmienda parlamentaria activa el procedimiento de conciliación, mientras que en el procedimiento de cooperación el Consejo podría modificar únicamente aquellas enmiendas parlamentarias aceptadas por la Comisión que contaban con el acuerdo unánime del Consejo (dejando intactas a las otras). Cuarto, de acuerdo con el procedimiento de codecisión, en ciertas áreas (incluyendo programas de cultura y estructura en Investigación y Desarrollo) las decisiones del Consejo en el comité conjunto así como en la etapa final sólo se pueden tomar por unanimidad. Quinto, en la etapa de conciliación del procedimiento de codecisión la Comisión está presente, pero su acuerdo no es necesario: si el Parlamento Europeo y el Consejo llegan a un acuerdo, la posición de la Comisión es irrelevante.

2.4. El procedimiento de codecisión II

Al Parlamento Europeo le desagradaban intensamente los últimos pasos del procedimiento de cooperación I: el hecho de que un desacuerdo en el comité de conciliación no significara el rechazo de una propuesta de ley, sino que habilitara al Consejo para regresar a su "posición común" anterior, incluyendo posibles enmiendas del Parlamento Europeo. La idea del Parlamento Europeo fue adoptada en el Tratado de Ámsterdam, donde se reconoció que la incapacidad del comité de conciliación para llegar a un acuerdo implicaba el rechazo de una propuesta de ley. Es interesante estudiar cómo logró el Parlamento Europeo imponer su voluntad a los gobiernos que firmaron el siguiente Tratado.

Con el fin de dejar en claro sus preferencias, el Parlamento Europeo adoptó un conjunto de reglas nuevas después de Maastricht. Una de estas reglas (78) especificaba la reacción del Parlamento Europeo si no había ningún acuerdo en el comité de conciliación:

> *1)* Cuando no se llegue a un acuerdo sobre un texto conjunto dentro del Comité de Conciliación, el Presidente [del Parlamento Europeo] invitará a la Comisión a retirar su propuesta, e invitará al Consejo de Ministros a no adoptar en ninguna circunstancia una posición según el artículo 189b(6) del Tratado de la Comunidad Europea. Si no obstante el Consejo confirmara su posición común, el Presidente del Consejo de Ministros deberá ser invitado a justificar la decisión ante el parlamento en sesión plenaria. El asunto deberá ser colocado automáticamente en la agenda de la pasada sesión parcial para caer dentro de seis o, si se amplía, ocho semanas de la confirmación por el Consejo. [...] *3)* Ninguna enmienda al texto del Consejo puede ser postergada indefinidamente. *4)* El texto del Consejo en su conjunto deberá ser el tema de una sola votación. El parlamento deberá votar sobre una moción de rechazar el texto del Consejo. Si esta moción recibe los votos de una mayoría de los miembros componentes del Parlamento, el Presidente [del Parlamento Europeo] deberá declarar que no es adoptada la ley propuesta.

La Regla 78 se aplicó una sola vez, en el caso del proyecto de directiva sobre disposiciones para red abierta en telefonía de voz *(open network provision,* ONP). En otra ocasión cuando un texto conjunto no se pudo aceptar en conciliación (sobre el proyecto de directiva acerca de firmas de inversión e instituciones de crédito en 1998), el Consejo decidió no reafirmar su posición común.

Hix (próxima publicación) ha inferido que "este voto reveló que la Regla 78, respaldada por las preferencias institucionales del liderazgo del Parlamento Europeo, era de hecho una amenaza creíble. [...] Esta estrategia dio resultado, ya que estableció un compromiso en el comité de conciliación como el verdadero equilibrio del juego". Sobre la base de este análisis, Hix (próxima publicación) saca la conclusión de que el Tratado de Ámsterdam sencillamente reconoció una realidad *de facto*, que sólo había una manera para lograr que se aceptara cualquier legislación: hacer que el comité de conciliación la propusiera al Consejo y al Parlamento Europeo (véase también Corbett, 2001a). Sin embargo, la eliminación de la última etapa del procedimiento de codecisión I no era un asunto trivial, como lo demuestran Moravcsik y Nicolaïdis (1999). Hasta el último minuto, varios gobiernos estuvieron en contra de la eliminación del último paso de este procedimiento.

En la siguiente sección se examinará la diferencia entre las dos versiones de la codecisión, y en la última sección de este capítulo se considerarán algunas de las implicaciones empíricas de este análisis.

2.5. Codecisión II ampliada y el requerimiento de mayoría calificada

El Tratado de Niza amplió las áreas de aplicabilidad del procedimiento de codecisión II, pero al mismo tiempo aumentó el umbral de mayoría calificada. La mayoría calificada que se requirió en Ámsterdam (para una Unión Europea de 15 miembros) fue 62 de 87 votos en el Consejo (q = 0.7126). Niza (entre otras cosas) alteró el peso de diferentes países en el Consejo. Por ejemplo, los cinco países más grandes tuvieron 48 de los 87 votos (55%) hasta el Tratado de Ámsterdam.[4] En la actualidad reciben 143 de los 237 votos (60%).[5] Sin embargo, el cambio más interesante que ocurrirá en el futuro consiste en que junto con el agrandamiento de la Unión Europea a 27 miembros (por la expansión hacia Europa Oriental), el umbral requerido de mayoría calificada será 253 de 345 (q = 0.7333).

Sin embargo, este aumento oficial en el umbral subestima la situación. El requerimiento real especificado en el artículo 205(4) del Tratado de Niza

---

[4] Alemania, Francia, el Reino Unido e Italia tuvieron 10 votos cada uno, y España ocho votos.
[5] Alemania, Francia, el Reino Unido e Italia tienen 29 votos cada uno y España 27 votos.

es una mayoría triple: además del umbral de mayoría calificada, una decisión del Consejo tiene que ser respaldada por una mayoría de los estados miembros, y si un estado miembro lo requiere, tiene que ser respaldada por miembros que totalicen 62% de la población de la Unión Europea (Yataganas, 2001). Todas estas restricciones elevan significativamente el umbral de mayoría calificada para la toma de decisiones del Consejo, y como lo demostré en el capítulo II, acrecientan la estabilidad política. Analizo estas modificaciones con detalle en la sección 4.

3. Análisis de jugadores con veto
de los procedimientos legislativos

Estudiemos ahora las implicaciones de estas complicadas reglas de toma de decisiones tanto en lo tocante a la distribución del poder legislativo entre las tres diferentes instituciones como por las consecuencias de la discreción en la toma de decisiones de otros actores, como el Tribunal Europeo de Justicia. Por lo tanto, esta sección está dividida en dos partes: las consecuencias legislativas de los procedimientos de toma de decisiones y sus efectos sobre la burocracia y el poder judicial.

3.1. Consecuencias legislativas de los procedimientos
de toma de decisiones

En todos los procedimientos legislativos se busca llegar a un acuerdo entre las distintas instituciones. Lo que difiere es quién es el actor institucional encargado de formular el posible acuerdo (establecedor de la agenda) y qué sucede si no se puede lograr tal acuerdo (quién tiene poderes de veto).

Con el propósito de abordar estos temas, me concentraré en las últimas etapas de cada procedimiento. La razón por la cual me concentro en las últimas etapas es que cualquier actor racional cuando es llamado a decidir mirará el camino hacia las posibles consecuencias de sus acciones, y tomará las decisiones que habrán de dejarlo en mejores condiciones en ulteriores etapas del juego (y por supuesto en la etapa final).[6] Si todos los actores conocieran las preferencias y recompensas de los demás (el término que se

---

[6] Esto se denomina "inducción hacia atrás" en la bibliografía sobre la teoría de juegos.

usa en la teoría de juegos para tal situación es "información completa"), este modo de pensar conduciría a un final inmediato del juego legislativo: la Comisión propondría un proyecto de ley que será aceptado por todos los demás actores. De hecho, la Comisión nunca haría una propuesta que fuera rechazada en última instancia, y los otros jugadores no plantearían objeciones si supieran que no ganarían en un enfrentamiento. Sin embargo, dado que todos estos procedimientos se desarrollan con jugadas y contrajugadas de cada actor, que la cooperación llega a la segunda lectura, y que la codecisión va a conciliar las juntas de comités, la suposición más razonable que se puede hacer es que los diferentes jugadores no actúan en el mundo ideal de "información completa". Consideremos la última etapa de cada uno de los procedimientos.

La última etapa del procedimiento de cooperación es clara: el Parlamento Europeo propone una serie de enmiendas y la Comisión las incorpora todas, algunas o ninguna dentro del informe final que le presenta al Consejo. El Consejo acepta la propuesta de la Comisión por mayoría calificada, o la modifica por unanimidad. En otras palabras, es más difícil que el Consejo modifique una propuesta parlamentaria (siempre y cuando sea aceptada por la comisión) a que la acepte.

> Este procedimiento *puede* habilitar al Parlamento Europeo para que ofrezca una propuesta que deja en mejores condiciones a una mayoría calificada del Consejo que cualquier decisión unánime. *Si* tal propuesta existe, *si*[7] el Parlamento Europeo es capaz de hacerla, y *si* la comisión la adopta, entonces el Parlamento Europeo tiene poderes de establecimiento de agenda. Si, en cambio, estas condiciones no se dan, el Parlamento Europeo pierde su poder de establecimiento de agenda. Por ello llamo condicional al poder de agenda del Parlamento Europeo según el procedimiento de cooperación [Tsebelis, 1994: 131].

Daré un ejemplo de la forma como el Parlamento Europeo puede hacer uso de sus poderes condicionales de establecimiento de agenda. Empezaré con un espacio político unidimensional y entonces pasaré a un espacio bidimensional donde los resultados difieren.

El Consejo está representado por siete miembros (de tal suerte que se puede aproximar a la mayoría calificada requerida por cinco de los siete miembros). La dimensión implícita es integración, de modo que el Parla-

---

[7] Se le recuerda al lector que se requieren 260 votos para una propuesta.

mento Europeo y la Comisión están a la derecha de los países miembros, mientras que el *statu quo* está a la izquierda. Los cálculos estratégicos del Parlamento Europeo son los siguientes: tiene que ofrecer a cinco miembros del Consejo una propuesta que los dejará en mejores condiciones que cualquier cosa que el Consejo pueda decidir por unanimidad (véase Tsebelis, 1994, 1997).

Otros investigadores (Steunenberg, 1994; Crombez, 1996; Moser, 1996) argumentan que incluso si el Parlamento Europeo se comporta de la manera descrita por Tsebelis (1994) en la segunda vuelta, habría sucedido una de dos cosas en la vuelta anterior: a la Comisión le habrían gustado algunas de las enmiendas y las hará propias, o el Parlamento Europeo sabía que la Comisión rechazaría sus enmiendas y por lo tanto no las ofrecía. Así, el Parlamento Europeo no debería estar haciendo enmiendas, ya sea porque su opinión ya está incorporada en el texto, o bien porque cualesquier cambios serían rechazados. En la gráfica XI.1 la Comisión y el Parlamento Europeo tienen preferencias similares, de tal suerte que la Comisión debe iniciar el procedimiento haciendo la propuesta X. El Parlamento Europeo entenderá que ningún mejoramiento es posible o, si se le ofrece una propuesta diferente (por ejemplo, su propio punto ideal), la Comisión rechaza-

GRÁFICA XI.1. *Establecimiento condicional de agenda en una y dos dimensiones.*

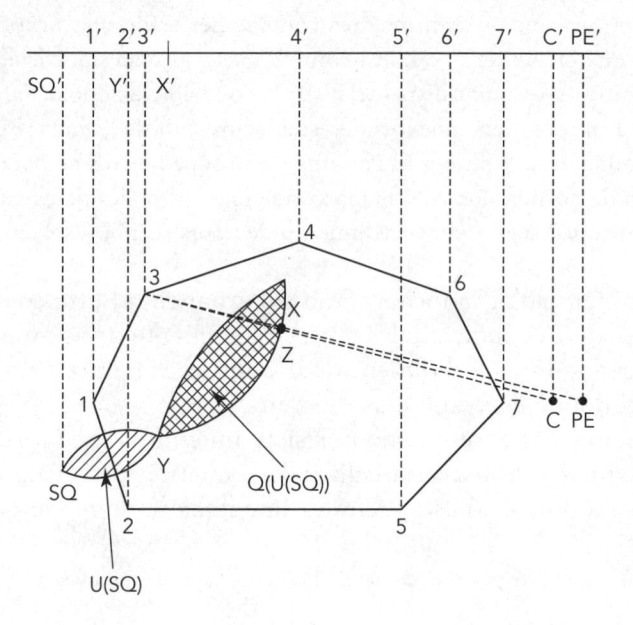

rá la enmienda. Crombez (1996: 218) lo expresa en pocas palabras: "Proposición 3: Según el procedimiento de cooperación, la oportunidad del Parlamento para enmendar la posición común del Consejo no afecta la política de equilibrio". Como resultado, esperan un Parlamento Europeo impotente y argumentan que el poder de establecimiento de agenda está en la Comisión. Ésta es una diferencia en la identidad del establecedor de agenda.

Sea como fuere, hay una segunda diferencia entre mi análisis y las expectativas de Crombez (1996), Steunenberg (1994) y Moser (1996). Ellos creen que el establecedor de agenda hará una propuesta que deje a una mayoría calificada en mejores condiciones que el *statu quo*, mientras que en mi análisis la propuesta dejará en mejores condiciones a una mayoría calificada que cualquier cosa que se pueda promover en el Consejo por unanimidad.

La gráfica XI.1 presenta las diferencias de los dos argumentos. Según mi argumento, el Consejo puede modificar unánimemente el *statu quo* y seleccionar cualquier cosa en el área SQ'Y'. Por lo tanto, si el Parlamento Europeo ofrece X', una propuesta que el miembro 3' apenas prefiere sobre Y', será aceptada por la Comisión y los miembros 3', 4', 5', 6' y 7' del Consejo. Según Crombez (1996), Steunenberg (1994) y Moser (1996) la propuesta ganadora estará ubicada cerca del punto 4' (es simétrica a SQ con respecto al miembro eje del Consejo: 3'). Además, la propuesta ganadora será hecha por la Comisión, y el Parlamento Europeo no hará ninguna enmienda puesto que no puede mejorar su situación (cualquier enmienda a la derecha de la Comisión será derrotada, y cualquier enmienda a la izquierda es menos preferida).

Una tercera dirección de investigación es la que adopta una posición intermedia. Bieber, Pantalis y Schoo (1986: 791) arguyeron: "En lo tocante al Parlamento Europeo, el Acta Única es un documento incongruente: cuando acrecienta los poderes de participación del Parlamento Europeo en la toma de decisiones, el efecto práctico es muy limitado o muy disminuido debido a que el ejercicio de los poderes depende de la *actitud* del Consejo y de la Comisión". De modo similar, Fitzmaurice (1988: 391) argumentó que "a pesar de las apariencias de un modelo de codecisión, el Consejo prácticamente retiene la última palabra". Jacobs (1997: 6) critica explícitamente el primer enfoque planteando dos argumentos: primero, que hay una tendencia a que el Consejo decida unánimemente y, segundo, que la Comisión tiende "ya sea a estar del lado de o al menos a no ir en contra del actor más poderoso, el Consejo, en las etapas finales del procedimiento […] incluso si han respaldado enmiendas del Parlamento en la primera lectura".[8] Corbett (2001a: 376) plantea un argumento similar: "Los poderes del Parlamento según el procedimiento de cooperación para formular una posición de 'tómenlo o déjenlo' hacia el Consejo depende de tantas condiciones que, en la práctica, habitualmente no se aplica". Por último, Lodge (1987: 23) afirma que el poder limitado del Parlamento Europeo proviene de la amenaza de bloquear decisiones, lo cual puede ocurrir "en una alianza con uno o más Estados miembros dispuestos a frustrar la consecución de las mayorías necesarias (calificadas o unánimes), de no ser que se acomoden a las opiniones y enmiendas del Parlamento Europeo".

Tsebelis (1997) abordó las críticas de los otros dos enfoques, argumentando que algunas de las teorías de no impacto o de impacto limitado se basan en suposiciones no realistas de información completa y unidimensionalidad del espacio de la cuestión. Una vez que estas suposiciones se relajan, es posible hacer enmiendas en el Parlamento Europeo. Tsebelis enumera varios de estos ejemplos. Por ejemplo, la Comisión puede estar deseosa de comprometerse con el Parlamento Europeo porque actúa como un "intermediario honrado" o para evitar fricciones. Pero, debido a información incompleta acerca de las preferencias del Parlamento Europeo, la Comisión puede esperar para observar antes el grado de la resolución del Parlamento Europeo (indicado, por ejemplo, mediante una mayoría fuerte o la asignación de un informador muy competente) y adoptar entonces estas enmiendas. Tsebelis arguye también que la Comisión puede adoptar enmiendas del Parlamento Europeo si estas últimas se introducen en una nueva dimensión. La mitad inferior de la gráfica XI.1 indica cómo la introducción de una nueva dimensión puede dejar a la Comisión en mejores condiciones que su propia propuesta inicial.

Supongamos que la Comisión comenzó con una representación unidimensional del problema y hace la propuesta X'. El Parlamento Europeo puede introducir ahora una enmienda sobre una dimensión diferente y generar un espacio político bidimensional. En este espacio, las preferencias del Consejo se presentan con los números 1 a 7, mientras que las posiciones

---

[8] En términos estrictos, el argumento de Jacobs no es una refutación de la tesis de Tsebelis (1994): el argumento de "establecimiento condicional de agenda" se basa en la aceptación de la Comisión, y la falta de unanimidad en el Consejo. No hace ningún pronóstico acerca de cómo se obtendrán estas condiciones. Sin embargo, si estas condiciones raras veces se cumplen, el establecimiento condicional de agenda va tomando menos importancia empírica. Por esta razón examinaremos empíricamente más adelante las afirmaciones de Jacob.

(punto C) del Parlamento Europeo y de la Comisión se indican a la derecha. De nueva cuenta, el Parlamento Europeo tiene que hacer los siguientes cálculos: encontrar qué puede hacer el Consejo unánimemente —cualquier cosa en el área U(SQ)—, y hacer una propuesta que deje a cinco miembros en mejores condiciones que cualquier cosa dentro del área U(SQ). Esto se indica en la gráfica mediante el área de sombreado cruzado Q(U(SQ)). Entre todos los puntos en Q(U(SQ)), el Parlamento Europeo selecciona el punto más cercano a su propia posición, mientras la Comisión tiene la alternativa de modificar ligeramente esta enmienda a Z o (si los costos de transacción son altos) aceptarla exactamente en la forma como el Parlamento Europeo la redactó. Las partes alta y baja de la gráfica XI.1 indican que la Comisión prefiere la propuesta en un espacio bidimensional (ya sea X o Z) más que su propia propuesta de espacio unidimensional.

Por lo tanto el Parlamento Europeo, al introducir una enmienda en una dimensión diferente, genera una situación estratégica distinta tanto para la Comisión como para el Consejo. Para el Consejo, la nueva situación es generada por la diferencia de opinión entre los miembros 2 y 3 a lo largo de la nueva dimensión. Dado que 2 y 3 tienen diferencias importantes en el cuadro bidimensional (pero no en la proyección unidimensional), el miembro 3 está dispuesto a hacer muchas más concesiones a la Comisión y al Parlamento Europeo que antes. La Comisión prefiere la enmienda del Parlamento Europeo porque deja a la Comisión en condiciones significativamente mejores en comparación con su propuesta inicial. Como resultado, el Parlamento Europeo sí hace una propuesta y su propuesta es aceptada (a diferencia de los resultados en modelos unidimensionales de información completa).

La gráfica XI.1 simplifica el proceso de la toma de decisiones de una manera importante. Presupone que el Parlamento Europeo es un jugador unificado, lo cual para un parlamento que presenta 15 nacionalidades y 12 ideologías es una simplificación verdaderamente heroica. Sin embargo, como lo ha demostrado el capítulo II, los resultados no cambian significativamente si sustituimos la suposición falsa del jugador unificado por la hipótesis más realista de "toma de decisiones cooperativa". Tsebelis (1995c) argumenta que debido a la organización del Parlamento Europeo, y en particular debido a los "ponentes" de las diferentes propuestas de ley, la toma de decisiones cooperativa es una suposición razonable.

Ésta es la segunda vez que encontramos casos concretos donde los modelos multidimensionales conducen a resultados diferentes de los unidimensionales, y por lo tanto se debe plantear el argumento de que la toma de decisiones está en una dimensión para que la sigan las conclusiones.[9] Estos ejemplos establecen un poderoso argumento en favor de la teoría de los jugadores con veto, con base en los espacios políticos multidimensionales. Veremos si la evidencia empírica corrobora estas expectativas en la siguiente sección.

El procedimiento de codecisión I tiene dos grandes diferencias. Primero, elimina a la Comisión de la última ronda de negociaciones, y como resultado reduce la influencia de la Comisión sobre la legislación. La influencia legislativa de la Comisión no es eliminada por completo, como han argumentado algunos investigadores (Crombez, 1997). La razón es que la Comisión puede hacer una propuesta al comienzo de los procesos, que será aceptada por los otros dos actores (se le recuerda al lector que el proceso legislativo empieza con una propuesta de la Comisión, de modo que la Comisión tiene un papel de establecimiento de agenda).

Segundo, hay dos posibles finales de la codecisión I, dependiendo del resultado de las negociaciones en el comité de conciliación: *1)* Si el comité de conciliación llega a un acuerdo, este acuerdo se presenta tanto al Consejo como al Parlamento Europeo; es adoptado si recibe una mayoría calificada en el Consejo y una mayoría en el Parlamento Europeo; de otro modo fracasa; *2)* si el comité de conciliación no logra llegar a un acuerdo, el Consejo puede hacer una propuesta al Parlamento Europeo; esta propuesta se considera aceptada a no ser que una mayoría absoluta del Parlamento Europeo vote en contra de ella, en cuyo caso fracasa. El contenido de la propuesta es la posición "con la cual se estuvo de acuerdo antes de que se iniciara el procedimiento de conciliación, posiblemente con enmiendas propuestas por el Parlamento Europeo" (artículo 189b(6) del Tratado de Maastricht). Dependiendo de cuál proceso sea seleccionado, difiere la identidad del establecedor de agenda. En el primer caso, es el mismo comité de conciliación (es decir, una combinación del Consejo y del Parlamento Europeo), mientras que en el segundo es el Consejo por sí solo.

El proceso de codecisión II elimina la segunda senda de codecisión I, y considera la incapacidad del comité de conciliación para poder alcanzar un acuerdo como equivalente a la terminación de un proyecto de ley. Hay dos diferentes interpretaciones de la codecisión I y la codecisión II. Según la primera, los poderes se apartaron del Consejo de la codecisión I hacia la code-

---

[9] El otro estaba en la discusión de políticas "eje" o "supermayoritarias" en el capítulo VI.

cisión II; de acuerdo con la segunda, esta diferencia se encuentra sólo en las reglas formales, pero no en la realidad.

En una serie de artículos (Garrett, 1995b; Tsebelis, 1997; Garrett y Tsebelis, 1996, 1997), Geoffrey Garrett y yo hemos planteado el argumento de que, como el Consejo esencialmente decide cuál de los dos posibles finales de la codecisión I será seleccionado (el Consejo puede conducir al comité de conciliación para que llegue a un acuerdo o no), en la codecisión I el Consejo puede en última instancia hacer una oferta de "tómenlo o déjenlo" al Parlamento Europeo. La transición de cooperación a codecisión implicaba que el Parlamento Europeo intercambiara su poder condicional de establecimiento de agenda por poder de veto incondicional. El impacto del intercambio del establecimiento de agenda condicional (cooperación) por veto incondicional (codecisión I) varía con la relación entre las preferencias del Parlamento Europeo y las de los miembros de la Comisión y del Consejo. Si el Parlamento Europeo y la Comisión tienen posiciones similares (y siempre y cuando los miembros del Consejo tengan diferentes preferencias ellos mismos), el trueque del establecimiento de agenda condicional en cooperación por el veto incondicional de la codecisión I fue un mal acuerdo para el Parlamento Europeo, así como para la agenda pro integración. Si por el otro lado la Comisión está en desacuerdo con el Parlamento Europeo, o si el Consejo es unánime, el Parlamento Europeo no tiene poderes condicionales de establecimiento de agenda, y por lo tanto está mejor con un veto.

Corbett (2001a) y Hix (2001) presentan un argumento distinto. Arguyen que debido a la adopción en el Parlamento Europeo de la Regla 78 (véase el análisis anterior) el Parlamento Europeo había modificado *de facto* las reglas de la interacción y eliminado la posibilidad de que el Consejo hiciera ofertas de "tómenlo o déjenlo" al Parlamento Europeo. En consecuencia, la codecisión II reconocía sencillamente lo que ya estaba en práctica desde la codecisión I.

Dejando de lado esta diferencia, hay un amplio consenso en que según la codecisión II el Parlamento Europeo es un colegislador igual con el Consejo. La razón es que el Consejo ya no puede decidir en contra del Parlamento Europeo (ni siquiera unánimemente, como en la cooperación) y ya no puede presentar propuestas de "tómenlo o déjenlo" al Parlamento Europeo (como fue el caso según el Tratado de Maastricht). En vez de ello, el Consejo y el Parlamento Europeo deben negociar en los mismos términos sobre el resultado legislativo final, sin ninguna ventaja negociadora *a priori* inherente a cualquiera de ambas instituciones.

Así, la única diferencia que queda en la bibliografía acerca de la codecisión I y la codecisión II es si hubo un importante cambio de poder en favor del Parlamento Europeo en Ámsterdam, o si este cambio ya se había logrado unilateralmente con la adopción de la Regla 78. Retornaremos a este punto en la última sección de este capítulo.

El Tratado de Niza modificó los requerimientos de mayoría del procedimiento de codecisión e introdujo una mayoría triple en el Consejo. Esta modificación equivale a aumentar el número de jugadores con veto en el sistema.[10] Como resultado, la toma de decisiones en la Unión Europea se vuelve más difícil, y aumenta la estabilidad política.

Lo interesante de estas discusiones es que diferentes análisis discrepan en lo tocante a los derechos "nominales" o "reales" de distintas instituciones, ya sea que las decisiones se tomen con información completa o incompleta, en una o en muchas dimensiones. Algunos lectores considerarán importantes estas preguntas y a otros les parecerán demasiado técnicas. A estos últimos, he de señalarles que las instituciones de la Unión Europea son complicadas y estos detalles tienen consecuencias importantes sobre la distribución del poder y sobre los resultados de las políticas. Sea como fuere, el cuadro más general es que las preguntas formuladas y las inferencias realizadas en todas estas obras de la bibliografía se basan, implícita o explícitamente, en preguntas que son motivo de estudio para la teoría de los jugadores con veto: quiénes son los jugadores con veto, cómo deciden, quién controla la agenda y cuánto.

3.2. Consecuencias del procedimiento legislativo sobre la burocracia y el poder judicial

La toma de decisiones legislativa en la Unión Europea ha cambiado en varias dimensiones: se inició por decisiones unánimes del Consejo, pasó después a una mayoría calificada dentro del Consejo junto con el consenso de los otros dos legisladores institucionales (la Comisión y el Parlamento Europeo), pasó entonces (y permanece hoy día) a una etapa de codecisión donde basta un acuerdo del Parlamento Europeo y de Consejo para adoptar las decisiones.

---

[10] Más exactamente, acrecentará las distancias entre los jugadores con veto existentes. Si los jugadores adicionales con veto tienen menores distancias que los existentes, serán absorbidos, y si están más alejados de los existentes, no serán absorbidos.

ANÁLISIS DE JUGADORES CON VETO EN INSTITUCIONES DE LA UE 339

Todos estos cambios tienen efectos sobre el número y las distancias ideológicas de los jugadores con veto, y como consecuencia y por las razones que hemos visto en el capítulo x, suelen afectar la discreción de burócratas y jueces. Dado que los procedimientos legislativos son muy complicados, tendremos que considerar más detenidamente las identidades y distancias de los jugadores con veto. Comenzaré con una representación más realista de la dinámica política en la Unión Europea que la versión simplista con la que empecé en la gráfica XI.1. Usaré una gráfica bidimensional (gráficas XI.2 y XI.3), al menos por dos razones: primera, como he argumentado, porque un enfoque unidimensional puede resultar engañoso, y segunda, porque muchas disputas políticas importantes en la Unión Europea contemporánea parecen ocurrir en un espacio al menos bidimensional. Una dimensión describe sus preferencias para la integración más regional; la otra es más afín a una división tradicional izquierda-derecha (muy especialmente sobre asuntos regulatorios) (Hix, 1999; Kreppel y Tsebelis, 1999). El análisis que sigue se basa en un artículo de Tsebelis y Garrett (2001).

GRÁFICA XI.2. *Instituciones de la Unión Europea en dos dimensiones.*

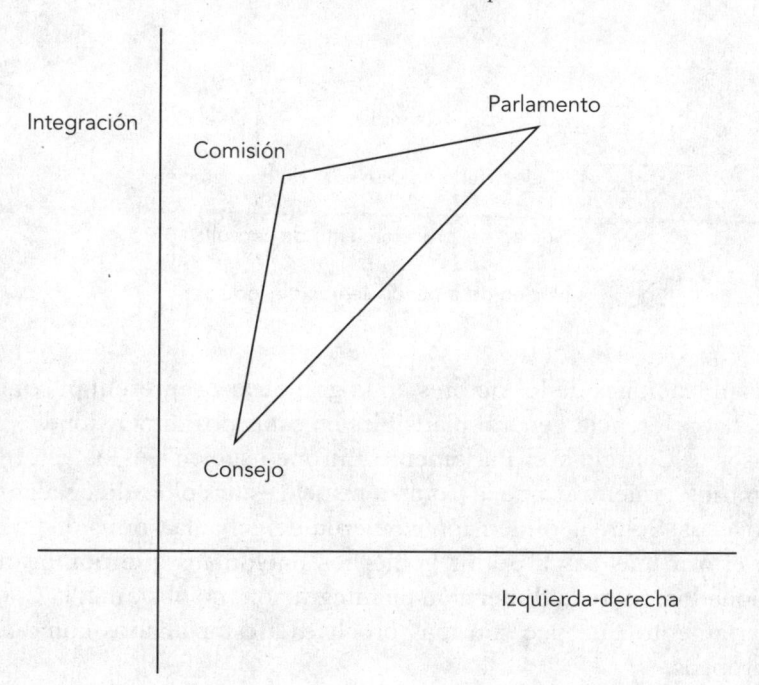

340   EFECTOS SISTÉMICOS DE LOS JUGADORES CON VETO

GRÁFICA XI.3. *El núcleo de los procedimientos legislativos de la Unión Europea.*

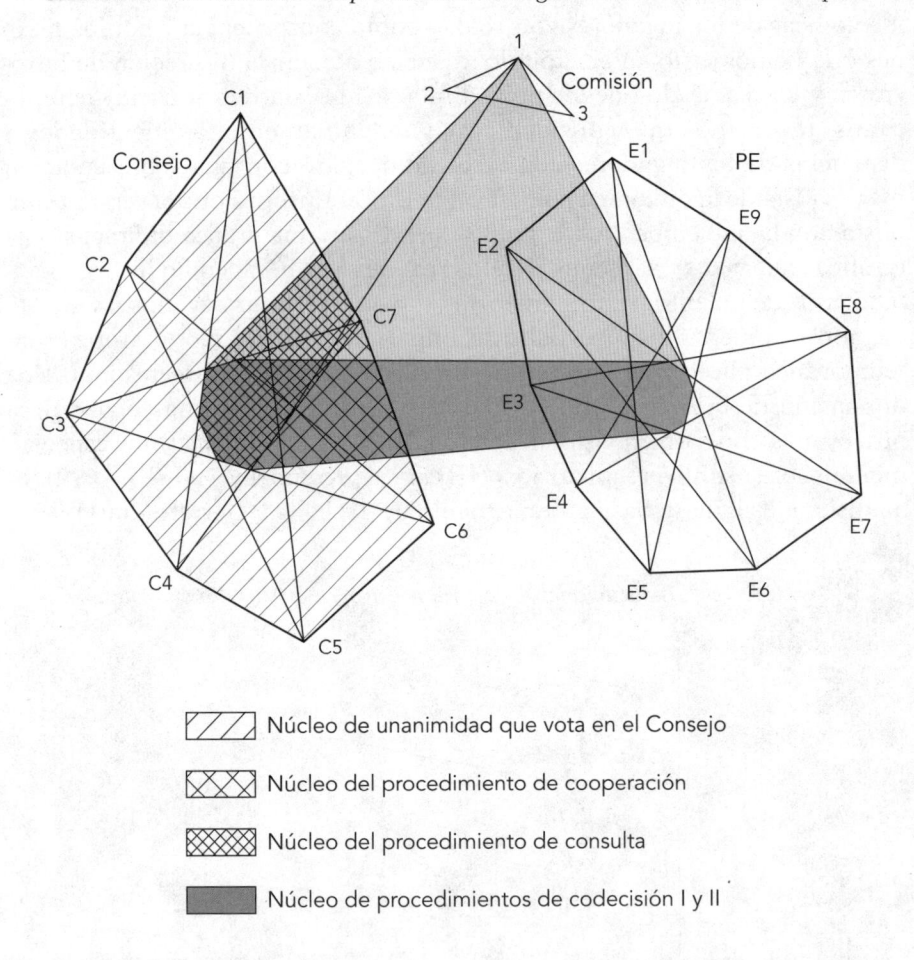

[////] Núcleo de unanimidad que vota en el Consejo

[XXXX] Núcleo del procedimiento de cooperación

[XXXX] Núcleo del procedimiento de consulta

[■] Núcleo de procedimientos de codecisión I y II

Las ubicaciones de los actores en la gráfica XI.2 representan configuraciones de preferencia general plausibles en estas dos dimensiones. En ambos casos el Consejo y el Parlamento Europeo suelen ser los actores más "extremosos", mientras que la Comisión suele estar colocada en algún punto entre ellos. Sobre la dimensión izquierda-derecha, la Comisión probablemente estará más cerca de los gobiernos nacionales que nombran a los comisionados; sobre la dimensión de integración, no obstante, la Comisión y el Parlamento Europeo son más proclives a estar aliados como actores pro europeos.

Lo que surge de estas suposiciones es que las ubicaciones de los tres actores representan los ángulos de un triángulo. Teóricamente, ésta es la representación más general de todos los casos en que los tres actores pueden tener cualquier posición en relación unos con otros, excepto cuando dos de ellos tienen posiciones idénticas,[11] o cuando uno de ellos está ubicado exactamente sobre una línea recta que conecta los puntos centrales de las otras dos. Convendría recalcar, por lo tanto, que la veracidad analítica de este análisis se mantiene, cualquiera que sea la posición relativa de los actores.

Hagamos girar ahora 45 grados la gráfica XI.2 (únicamente con propósitos de presentación) e incorporemos el hecho de que los tres actores institucionales son, de hecho, entidades con muchos miembros que deciden por mayorías simple, absoluta o calificada (gráfica XI.3). Presento las preferencias de un parlamento compuesto de nueve miembros para caracterizar lo que es, *de facto*, un umbral de supermayoría para votación en el Parlamento Europeo, de acuerdo con los requerimientos de mayoría absoluta para la aprobación en la segunda lectura de proyectos legislativos. Incorporo esta restricción dentro del modelo requiriendo una mayoría superior a cinco novenas partes para que un proyecto de ley se adopte. Así, en la gráfica XI.3 no hay mayoría a la izquierda de la línea E1E5, ninguna mayoría por encima de la línea E3E8, y así sucesivamente.[12] Como resultado de este requisito de supermayoría *de facto*, existen algunos puntos ubicados centralmente en el Parlamento Europeo que no pueden ser anulados por la mayoría calificada requerida. La Comisión tiene presencia con tres miembros, decide por una mayoría de sus miembros (dos de los tres), dado que ésta es la regla de decisión formal para el Colegio de Comisionados. Finalmente, analizo de nueva cuenta un Consejo de siete miembros, cinco de cuyos integrantes representan la mayoría calificada requerida para la toma de decisiones.

La característica central de la gráfica XI.3 es su descripción del "núcleo" de las instituciones legislativas de la Unión Europea según los diversos procedimientos legislativos. El núcleo de una regla legislativa es el conjunto de resultados que no pueden ser invalidados por la aplicación de esa regla. El

---

[11] Este fue el caso que presenté en la gráfica XI.1. Incluso en la gráfica bidimensional, la Comisión y el Parlamento Europeo tenían posiciones casi idénticas.

[12] Dado que hay únicamente cinco puntos en las direcciones especificadas y el requerimiento es de más de cinco novenas partes de los votos. El requerimiento de mayoría calificada aumenta el tamaño del núcleo, pero no es necesario para los argumentos que siguen (Tsebelis y Yataganas, 2002).

núcleo del diferente procedimiento legislativo de la Unión Europea describe el espacio discrecional asequible a la Comisión en la implantación de la legislación, y al Tribunal Europeo de Justicia en la interpretación estatutaria. Como lo he demostrado en el capítulo II, las proposiciones que siguen generalizan a más de dos dimensiones, incluso si el núcleo no existe.[13] Se presuponía también que el resultado de las interacciones legislativas (en el largo plazo) seleccionarán puntos dentro del núcleo. De hecho, sin importar cuál sea la regla de toma de decisiones, algún punto dentro del núcleo siempre puede invalidar cualquier otro fuera del núcleo. Así, en equilibrio, cabría esperar que el *statu quo* legislativo estuviera dentro del núcleo, incluso si en determinados momentos los actores no pudieran ponerse de acuerdo sobre tal movimiento.

Empecemos reinterpretando brevemente la dinámica política donde el Consejo decide por unanimidad. En tales casos, se requiere un Consejo unánime para un cambio del *statu quo* legislativo. Cualquier punto dentro del heptágono C1 ... C7 no puede ser modificado por unanimidad dado que al menos un miembro del Consejo objetaría cualquier cambio en el *statu quo*. El área plumeada en la gráfica XI.3 (independientemente de su sombreado) constituye por tanto el núcleo de los procedimientos legislativos basados en unanimidad (y para revisiones de tratados). En cuanto a la discreción, la Comisión y el Tribunal Europeo de Justicia podrían, por tanto, implantar o interpretar efectivamente una pieza dada de legislación (el *statu quo*) en cualquier forma que desearan, siempre y cuando el resultado político permaneciera dentro del núcleo. Esto sería verdad incluso si la implementación de la Comisión o la interpretación del Tribunal Europeo de Justicia no coincidieran con la intención del Consejo cuando aprobó la legislación.

La observación final se refiere a la ubicación espacial de los actores. Es obvio que la convergencia de preferencias (por ejemplo, si C1-C7 estuvieran más apiñadas bajo unanimidad, o si se acortaran las distancias entre el Consejo, el Parlamento Europeo y la Comisión) reduciría el núcleo y por ende también el alcance de la discreción en la implantación y adjudicación. Aumentar la heterogeneidad tendría el efecto contrario. En el contexto de la Unión Europea, cabría esperar que agregar nuevos miembros acrecentara la heterogeneidad en algunos casos (las accesiones del sur y, en el futu-

---

[13] El núcleo deja de existir formalmente si aumentamos lo suficiente la dimensionalidad del espacio político. Sin embargo, hemos visto en el capítulo X que podemos plantear argumentos similares sobre la base de los jugadores con veto incluso cuando el núcleo deja de existir.

ro, las de Europa Oriental),[14] pero la redujera en otros (Austria, Finlandia y Suecia, en muchos temas). Además, podría haber razones para esperar que se redujera la distancia entre las instituciones si, por ejemplo, los ciudadanos exigen mayor responsabilidad a los miembros del Parlamento Europeo (y entonces votan de la misma manera en elecciones nacionales y del Parlamento Europeo).

Aquí mantendré constantes las preferencias y analizaré las diferencias en los núcleos de la legislación de la Unión Europea (y, por lo tanto, el alcance para la discreción burocrática y judicial) en función de los procedimientos usados para agregar las preferencias de los actores legislativos. La legislación puede ser aprobada de dos maneras según los procedimientos de consulta y cooperación. Se puede tomar una decisión con un acuerdo de los actores correspondientes, o por unanimidad en el Consejo (actuando solo). Para consulta, los "actores correspondientes" son una mayoría calificada del Consejo y una mayoría de la Comisión. Para cooperación, se deberá incorporar en esta lista una mayoría absoluta del Parlamento Europeo. La gráfica XI.3 ya ha mostrado el núcleo de unanimidad del Consejo. ¿Qué restricciones impone la regla alternativa (acuerdo de la Comisión para consultas, o la Comisión y el parlamento para cooperación) a la discreción política?

Me concentro en el procedimiento de cooperación debido a las complejidades adicionales generadas por la participación del Parlamento Europeo en la legislación. Recuérdese que presuponemos que el requisito de mayoría absoluta en el Parlamento Europeo crea un umbral de supermayoría *de facto* de más de cinco novenos. En la gráfica XI.3 se puede identificar el núcleo de cinco novenas partes del Parlamento Europeo. Siguiendo el procedimiento que se describió en el capítulo VI, conecto a cada miembro del Parlamento Europeo con otro de modo que tres miembros están en un lado de la línea y los otros cuatro integrantes están en el otro lado. Tales líneas son los pares E1E5, E1E6, E2E6, E2E7, y así sucesivamente. Estas líneas definen un polígono dentro de E1 ... E9. Éste es el núcleo del Parlamento Europeo con mayoría absoluta. Denominemos este conjunto específico de resultados como el "núcleo de cinco novenas partes del Parlamento Europeo". Es evidente que el Parlamento Europeo no puede modificar nada ubicado en ese núcleo, incluso si pudiese actuar solo, sin el respaldo del Consejo o de la Comisión. La razón es que hay una mayoría de más de cinco novenas

[14] Bednar, Ferejohn y Garrett, 1996.

partes en contra de alejarse de cualquier punto particular de este polígono de nueve lados. De modo similar, hay un núcleo para el Consejo cuando decida por votación de mayoría calificada de cinco séptimas partes. Como lo muestra la gráfica XI.3 (y por razones similares como para el Parlamento Europeo), este "núcleo de votación de mayoría calificada" es un heptágono ubicado dentro de C1 ... C7.

El área ligeramente sombreada de la gráfica XI.3, que conecta lo que resulta ser el comisionado decisivo (1) con los puntos extremos del núcleo de cinco novenos del Parlamento Europeo y el núcleo de votación de mayoría calificada del Consejo, es por tanto el núcleo de legislación que requiere una mayoría calificada en el Consejo, una mayoría absoluta en el Parlamento Europeo, y una mayoría simple en la Comisión.

Pero éste no es el núcleo del procedimiento de cooperación, dado que un Consejo unánime también puede aprobar legislación. El núcleo de la cooperación se define entonces como la intersección del núcleo de unanimidad del Consejo (el área plumeada) y el núcleo interinstitucional (el área sombreada). En la gráfica, el área con rayas entrecruzadas denota este núcleo de cooperación. Obsérvese que esta área es siempre más pequeña que el núcleo de unanimidad del Consejo (que, como se recordará, define el espacio para la discreción política según el Compromiso de Luxemburgo, revisiones de tratado y legislación todavía sujeta a votación por unanimidad).

Es fácil calcular el núcleo de consulta, que es sencillamente un subconjunto del núcleo de cooperación, dado que la diferencia sobresaliente entre los dos procedimientos es que no se requiere el acuerdo del Parlamento Europeo. Este núcleo de consulta está representado en la gráfica XI.3 por el área de mayor sombreado (independientemente del tipo de rayado).

Si la Comisión o el Tribunal Europeo de Justicia quieren tomar una decisión que no sea rechazada según el procedimiento de cooperación, pueden implantar e interpretar la legislación en cualquier parte dentro del área con rayas entrecruzadas. Lo grande que sea esta área depende, por supuesto, de la posición relativa de la Comisión y el Parlamento Europeo con respecto al Consejo (y la cohesión de las preferencias de los actores individuales en estas instituciones). Si, por ejemplo, la Comisión estuviera ubicada cerca de E3, el núcleo se contraería. Cabría pensar que dado el mecanismo de selección para la Comisión (que requiere aprobación tanto del Consejo como del Parlamento Europeo), ésta es la posición más realista de los tres actores la mayor parte del tiempo. El núcleo se expandiría, no obstante, si el Consejo estuviera ubicado entre la Comisión y el Parlamento Europeo.

ANÁLISIS DE JUGADORES CON VETO EN INSTITUCIONES DE LA UE 345

Ambas versiones de la codecisión especifican que, al final del juego legislativo, un acuerdo mediante una mayoría calificada del Consejo y una mayoría absoluta del Parlamento Europeo puede invalidar a otros actores. En particular, pueden pasar de lado a la Comisión. En consecuencia, el área fuertemente sombreada de la gráfica XI.3 que conecta al núcleo de cinco novenas partes del Parlamento Europeo y el núcleo del Consejo de cinco séptimos representan el núcleo de codecisión (I y II). Cuanto mayores sean las diferencias políticas entre el Consejo y el Parlamento Europeo (y mayor la dispersión de preferencias dentro de estas instituciones), mayor será el tamaño del núcleo, y por ende mayor será la discreción disponible para la Comisión en la implantación de política y para el Tribunal Europeo de Justicia en la interpretación estatutaria.

La gráfica XI.4 se concentra en los efectos del Tratado de Niza. Como se ha presentado en la sección 2, el umbral de mayoría calificada aumentó ligeramente, y las preferencias en los países nuevos muestran una tendencia

GRÁFICA XI.4. *Después de Niza, el núcleo del Consejo y la Unión Europea se expande.*

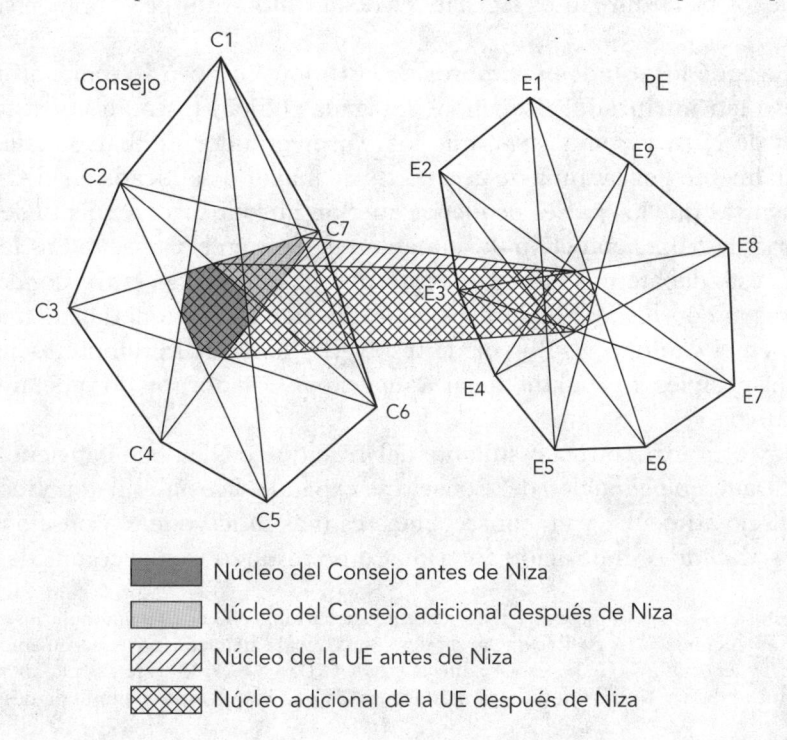

a ser menos homogéneas que las de los 15 miembros actuales. Estos dos cambios tienden a acrecentar el núcleo del Consejo. Sin embargo, aquí me concentraré en las otras dos modificaciones, el requisito de que la legislación sea respaldada por una mayoría de los países miembros y el requisito de que las propuestas ganadoras deben estar respaldadas por países que totalicen cuando menos 62% de la población de la Unión Europea. La gráfica XI.4 comienza a partir del núcleo del procedimiento de codecisión antes de Niza (como se presenta en la gráfica XI.3), y lo compara con el núcleo después.

Debido a la mayoría triple requerida en el Consejo, se sustituyen algunos de los divisores de mayoría calificada del Tratado de Ámsterdam. Por ejemplo, supongamos que C2C6 en la gráfica XI.4 no cumple con uno de los dos requisitos adicionales. Con el propósito de calcular el núcleo de mayoría calificada del Consejo, esta línea tiene que ser sustituida por los divisores reales de mayoría calificada. Consideremos que estas líneas son C2C7 y C1C6.[15] El volver a calcular el núcleo del Consejo según estas suposiciones indica que se expande, como lo señala la gráfica XI.4. Como resultado, el núcleo de los procedimientos legislativos de la Unión Europea también se expande.

¿Por qué los estados miembros de la Unión Europea seleccionaron un proceso tan intrincado? Tsebelis y Yataganas (2002) rastrean las negociaciones de Niza y demuestran que los países grandes estaban satisfechos esencialmente por la toma de decisiones de mayoría calificada en el Consejo, mientras que los países pequeños querían introducir el requisito de una mayoría de países con el fin de aumentar su peso en el Consejo. Los términos de este debate nos llevan de regreso a las diferencias entre Condorcet y Madison con respecto a la mayoría calificada y el bicameralismo, como se vio en el capítulo VI. En vez de resolver el tema, Niza adoptó todas las normas posibles, lo cual dio lugar a una expansión abrumadora del núcleo legislativo.

Hay otra expectativa resultante del Tratado de Niza que conviene subrayar. Dado que el núcleo del Consejo se expande, la estabilidad política en el Consejo aumenta, y en consecuencia es más difícil que el Consejo cambie el *statu quo* o su posición anterior. Como resultado, en el comité de con-

[15] Estas líneas deberían alejarse más del centro de la yema con el fin de cumplir los requerimientos adicionales. Es posible que ni siquiera estas líneas satisfagan los requerimientos adicionales, y tendríamos que pasar a las líneas C2C1, C1C7 y C6C7. En este caso la diferencia entre Ámsterdam y Niza sería todavía más acentuada que la que estoy a punto de describir.

ciliación de codecisión, será más difícil que el Parlamento Europeo haga que el Consejo altere sus posiciones previas, lo cual implica a nivel institucional un desplazamiento del poder hacia el Consejo (véase gráfica vi.3 y la discusión en torno de ésta).

En conclusión, el Tratado de Niza expande aún más el tamaño de los núcleos del Consejo y de la Unión Europea. El resultado de estas modificaciones es un desplazamiento del poder legislativo en favor del Consejo, y un aumento en la discreción de la Comisión y el Tribunal Europeo de Justicia resultante de la capacidad reducida de la Unión Europea para legislar. Es importante notar que en el análisis anterior, como en el capítulo x, "discreción" se refiere al comportamiento de la Comisión y el Tribunal Europeo de Justicia, no a las reglas institucionales que regulan sus actividades.

Sobre el tema de las reglas institucionales que rigen la conducta burocrática, Franchino (2000) ha argumentado que cuando la rama legislativa no puede invalidar el comportamiento burocrático (cuando el núcleo de la Unión Europea es grande), entonces será más restrictiva *ex ante:* redactará la legislación de modo que reduzca la discreción de la Comisión. He analizado este punto en el capítulo x.

4. La evidencia empírica

La bibliografía institucional que revisé comparte con este libro varias suposiciones importantes. Todos los autores consideran las instituciones como restricciones para el comportamiento de los diferentes actores. Como consecuencia, esperan que los resultados dependan de las instituciones en las cuales fueron producidos. Sin embargo, dada la complejidad de las instituciones que forman la Unión Europea, éstas frecuentemente llegan a diferentes pronósticos con respecto a procedimientos o resultados específicos. Permítaseme presentar algunas de estas diferencias como preguntas.

Pregunta 1: ¿Tiene el Parlamento Europeo poderes condicionales de establecimiento de agenda bajo cooperación? He argumentado que sí (Tsebelis, 1994), mientras otros investigadores (Crombez, 1996; Steunenberg, 1994; Moser, 1996) afirman que estos poderes corresponden a la Comisión.

Pregunta 2: Quienquiera que tenga poderes de establecimiento de agenda, ¿será (Q(SQ)) el resultado en el conjunto ganador de mayoría calificada del Consejo, como lo esperan Crombez (1996), Steunenberg (1994), y Moser (1996), o únicamente en los puntos que dictan una mayoría calificada sobre todo lo que el Consejo pueda hacer (Q(U(SQ))) unánimemente, como lo he argumentado (Tsebelis, 1994)?

Pregunta 3: ¿Hay una diferencia en la influencia que el Parlamento Europeo tiene entre cooperación y codecisión I? ¿Está la diferencia en favor del Parlamento Europeo cuando tiene a la Comisión de su lado y no está enfrentado a un Consejo unánime (es decir, cuando tiene poderes condicionales de establecimiento de agenda)? Garrett y Tsebelis (Garrett, 1995b; Tsebelis, 1997; Garrett y Tsebelis, 1996, 1997) han dado una respuesta afirmativa, mientras que la idea convencional es que el Parlamento Europeo ganó poder general con la codecisión I (véase Crombez, 1996; Corbett, 2001a, y Scully, 1997, entre otros).

Pregunta 4: ¿La Comisión ha perdido poder de establecimiento de agenda según la codecisión I (Crombez, 1997), o estos poderes sencillamente se han reducido en comparación con la cooperación (Tsebelis y Garrett, 2001)?

Pregunta 5: ¿Tienen poderes constantes la Comisión como burocracia y el Tribunal Europeo de Justicia como poder judicial, aumentan sus poderes con el tiempo (como argumentan las teorías neofuncionalistas) o varían en función de los procedimientos legislativos?

Estas preguntas acerca de la manera como operan las instituciones de la Unión Europea son mucho más precisas que las otras preguntas formuladas en este libro. Estas diferencias de resultados son un indicio acerca de lo lejos que puede llegar la empresa colectiva de investigación cuando hay un grupo de personas participando en el mismo programa de investigación. ¿Cómo podemos corroborar una de las respuestas en cada una de estas preguntas?

Se han hecho centenares de estudios empíricos sobre la Unión Europea. De hecho, hay al menos dos revistas dedicadas exclusivamente a ese tema,[16] pero estas publicaciones tienden a concentrarse en estudios de casos particulares. Tales estudios pueden darnos atisbos muy importantes, pero no está claro si sus conclusiones son generales o si se mantienen exclusivamente en el conjunto de los casos que estudiaron. Asimismo, las explicaciones propuestas pueden ser correctas, pero no está claro cómo se medirían las mismas variables en diferentes casos. En vez de tratar de extrapolar tales estudios, describiré los resultados de dos diferentes análisis estadísticos

---

[16] Por ejemplo, *The Journal of Common Market Studies* y *European Union Politics,* para no mencionar el *European Journal of Political Economy, European Journal of Political Research* y *West European Politics,* que también publican artículos sobre las políticas de diferentes países europeos.

y los relacionaré con las preguntas que he enumerado, uno de Thomas König (1997) y el otro de Tsebelis y colaboradores (2001).

König (1997) combinó dos distintas fuentes de datos relacionadas con un conjunto de siete proyectos de ley: por un lado, una lista de temas debatidos en el Consejo sobre la discusión de estos proyectos de ley; por el otro, evaluaciones expertas sobre las posiciones de los diferentes países, la Comisión y el Parlamento Europeo en todos los temas discutidos en el Consejo. Como resultado, localizó la posición de los actores, el *statu quo* y el resultado de varios proyectos de ley en un espacio dimensional elevado (identificó 78 temas o dimensiones). Usó entonces graduación multidimensional para reducir la dimensionalidad del espacio, y muestra los resultados en dos dimensiones. Presenta las dos gráficas siguientes (König, 1997: 187, 189).[17]

La gráfica XI.5 presenta el resultado legislativo promedio con decisiones que requieren unanimidad en el Consejo. La gráfica XI.6 presenta el resultado legislativo promedio obtenido con cooperación. He usado las gráficas de König y he introducido líneas rectas adicionales con el fin de calcular las predicciones de la bibliografía y compararlas con los resultados reales.

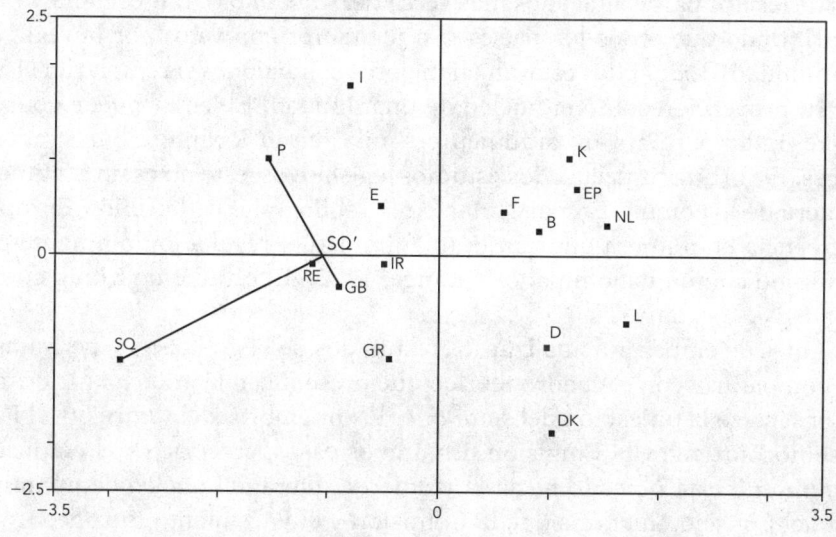

GRÁFICA XI.5. *Preferencias del Consejo y resultados de la votación bajo unanimidad.*

[17] Agradezco a Thomas König el haberme dado la versión electrónica de estas gráficas, que me permitieron elaborar gráficas subsecuentes. Debido a su origen, las gráficas tienen iniciales alemanas (D para Alemania, K para Comisión).

GRÁFICA XI.6. *Preferencias del Consejo y resultados según el procedimiento de cooperación.*

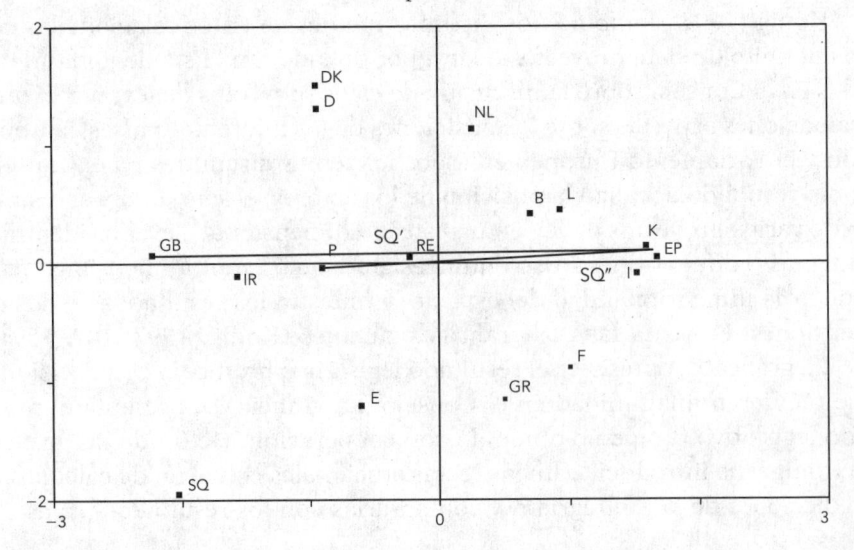

En la gráfica XI.5 he trazado una línea recta que conecta las preferencias de los dos países ubicados más cerca del *statu quo* (Gran Bretaña y Portugal). Dado que todos los países son jugadores con veto (por la regla de unanimidad), todos ellos estarán en mejores condiciones si remplazan el SQ por su proyección sobre el núcleo de unanimidad. El lector puede consultar la gráfica X.1 para un argumento similar en lo tocante a burócratas o jueces. En lo que respecta a los estudios legislativos, éste no es un argumento fuera de lo común. En particular, en la bibliografía de la Unión Europea la creencia común era que con la unanimidad el resultado dominante era "el último común denominador" (Lange, 1992). El estudio de König corrobora esta expectativa.

Antes de empezar a analizar los resultados de la gráfica XI.6, permítaseme compararla con el cuadro teórico que presenté en la gráfica XI.1. Primero, obsérvese la ubicación del *statu quo*, los miembros del Consejo y el Parlamento Europeo y la Comisión. En ambos casos, el teórico y el empírico, el *statu quo* está ubicado hacia la izquierda, fuera del núcleo de unanimidad del Consejo, mientras que la Comisión y el Parlamento Europeo están ubicados en el otro lado y cerca uno del otro. El cuadro empírico corrobora con mucha claridad una división entre estos actores, tal como se esperaba a lo largo de la dimensión de la integración.

En la gráfica XI.6 tracé dos líneas, una que conecta con el punto ideal de Gran Bretaña y otra que conecta con el punto ideal de Portugal con la Comisión (K) o el Parlamento Europeo (P) (dada su proximidad, no importa). La razón por la que tracé estas líneas fue identificar la ubicación de una propuesta ganadora del Parlamento Europeo y la Comisión al Consejo. Según Tsebelis (1994) y el argumento que presenté en la sección anterior, el Parlamento Europeo identifica todos los resultados que pueden anular al *statu quo* por unanimidad, e identifica el conjunto de puntos que dejarán a una mayoría calificada (q = cinco séptimos) en mejores condiciones que nada que el Consejo pueda hacer unánimemente (U(Q(SQ))). En la gráfica XI.6 no hay tales puntos, de tal suerte que el Parlamento Europeo seleccionará el punto que prefiera entre el conjunto de unanimidad del *statu quo* (U(SQ)).[18] ¿Cuál es el punto preferido en (U(SQ))?

En la línea que conecta a Gran Bretaña (en la extrema izquierda) con el Parlamento Europeo y la Comisión (dado que sus puntos ideales están muy cerca unos de otros, tracé una línea que pasa entre estos dos puntos) seleccioné un punto SQ', de modo que la distancia SQ'GB es la misma que la distancia SQGB. Éste es el punto ideal para el Parlamento Europeo y la Comisión entre todos los puntos de U(SQ). En realidad, el punto SQ1 pertenece a U(SQ) dado que GB es indiferente entre éste y SQ, y todos los demás países lo prefieren sobre el SQ; además, la Comisión y el Parlamento Europeo no pueden hacer nada ya que si seleccionan un punto más cercano a ellos, GB va a vetarlo.

Con el fin de identificar la propuesta de la Comisión siguiendo a Crombez (1996), Steunenberg (1994) y Moser (1996), tenemos que encontrar el punto que la Comisión prefiera más dentro del conjunto preferido de mayoría calificada (q = cinco séptimos) del *statu quo* Q(SQ). Este punto se puede identificar si la Comisión hace una propuesta a la mayoría calificada que tenga preferencias tan cercanas como sea posible a las suyas propias, es decir, si pasa por alto a Gran Bretaña (GB con 10 votos), Irlanda (IR con 3 votos) y España (ES con 8 votos) y se concentra en los otros 66 (= 87 − 21) votos del Consejo.[19] De hecho, la Comisión tiene que hacer indiferente a Portugal entre el *statu quo* y su propia propuesta, de modo que propone SQ".

---

[18] Acerca de ese punto, Tsebelis (1994) se equivocó al afirmar que en estas condiciones el Parlamento Europeo no tendrá una propuesta ganadora, ya que puede seleccionar el punto en U(SQ) que prefiera en vez de dejar que el Consejo decida por su cuenta.

[19] La Comisión no puede pasar por alto a Portugal, con cinco votos, ya que entonces perdería la mayoría calificada requerida de 62 votos.

Esto es lo mejor para el punto de la Comisión dentro de Q(SQ), dado que todos los países con excepción de Gran Bretaña, Irlanda y España lo prefieren sobre el *statu quo*, y cualquier punto más cercano a la Comisión sería vetado por Portugal.

Una comparación entre los dos pronósticos SQ′, SQ″ y el resultado real RE indica que SQ′ está más cerca de RE que SQ″. De este modo, mis pronósticos son corroborados por los datos de König (1997). Un problema del conjunto de datos de König es su tamaño: contiene pocos proyectos de ley con varios centenares de enmiendas. Preferiríamos contar con datos adicionales, pero creo que este problema lo abordarán en el futuro König y sus colaboradores. Otro problema es que las gráficas XI.5 y XI.6 agregan diferentes proyectos de ley. En un artículo posterior (König y Pöter, 2002), los autores abordan este problema: los datos son desagregados en un proyecto de ley, se agrega un nuevo proyecto de ley, junto con un método de comparación, dimensión por dimensión, de las diferentes teorías. La desagregación produce esencialmente los mismos resultados que los mencionados antes. El nuevo caso produce resultados muy alejados de mis vaticinios y se aproxima más a las expectativas de Crombez (1996), Steunenberg (1994) y Moser (1996). La comparación de dimensión por dimensión no discrimina entre los dos enfoques en su exactitud. Sin embargo, como lo he dicho varias veces en este libro y como lo he mostrado particularmente en la sección XI.3 y en la gráfica XI.1, reducir los problemas multidimensionales a problemas en una sola dimensión es un mal sustituto del análisis multidimensional.

Tsebelis y colaboradores (2001) adoptan un plan de acción empírico distinto. Usan únicamente datos de las enmiendas propuestas por el Parlamento Europeo a diversos proyectos de ley y estudian la tasa de adopción de estas enmiendas. Su método se concentra exclusivamente en los desacuerdos públicos entre los actores. Hay desacuerdos que se resuelven en privado antes de que la Comisión haga su propuesta inicial (que este análisis pasa por alto), y hay desacuerdos que pueden aparecer por otras razones estratégicas (adoptar una posición) en vez de seguir el propósito de resolverlos legislativamente. Tsebelis y colaboradores (2001) defienden su enfoque argumentando que no pueden incluir "políticas invisibles" en su análisis y que adoptar una posición no es muy frecuente en la legislación de la Unión Europea dado que el público no presta atención a la política legislativa, como lo indica gran parte de la bibliografía. Así, usan los resultados de la resolución de desacuerdos públicos como medición sustituta para la influencia de diferentes actores. El mismo enfoque ha sido adoptado por el Parlamento Europeo, el cual publica los porcentajes de sus enmiendas logradas, y por la mayor parte de la bibliografía que informa de estas mediciones como indicación de la influencia del Parlamento Europeo (Corbett, Jacobs y Shackleton, 1995; Westlake, 1994; Hix, 1999). Por ejemplo, en 1994 la Comisión informaba: "Dado que el Acta Única Europea entró en vigor el 1º de julio de 1987, más del 50% de las enmiendas del Parlamento han sido aceptadas por la Comisión y aprobadas por el Consejo. Ningún Parlamento nacional tiene una tasa de éxito comparable para someter al ejecutivo a su voluntad" (comunicado de prensa de la Comisión, 15 de diciembre de 1994, citado en Earnshaw y Judge, 1996: 96).

El conjunto de datos de Tsebelis y colaboradores (2001) produce los mismos resultados agregados que el Parlamento Europeo, es decir, que las enmiendas del Parlamento Europeo se incluyen con más frecuencia en el proyecto de ley final bajo la codecisión I que bajo la cooperación. La diferencia es de alrededor de 10 puntos porcentuales. Sin embargo, esta medición agregada acaso no sea apropiada para una comparación de la influencia del Parlamento Europeo bajo establecimiento condicional de agenda o veto. Por ejemplo, si la Comisión está en desacuerdo con el Parlamento Europeo, este último queda privado de poderes de establecimiento de agenda. De modo similar, no hay poderes condicionales de establecimiento de agenda si el Parlamento Europeo (o, para el caso, la Comisión) se enfrenta a un Consejo unánime. Por lo tanto, tenemos que introducir controles para estas posibilidades.

Tsebelis y colaboradores (2001) presentaron un requisito esencial para el establecimiento condicional de agenda: la aceptación por parte de la Comisión en su análisis de 230 piezas de legislación, que comprende 5 000 enmiendas. Empiezan controlando la aceptación de la Comisión según el procedimiento de cooperación (dado que es condición para el establecimiento condicional de agenda) pero no bajo la codecisión (ya que nadie ha afirmado que el Parlamento Europeo necesite el respaldo de la Comisión según este procedimiento). Encuentran que la tasa de rechazo del Consejo de las enmiendas del Parlamento Europeo que han sido aceptadas por la Comisión bajo cooperación es 20 puntos porcentuales más baja que para todas las enmiendas parlamentarias bajo codecisión.

Sin embargo, podemos argumentar que ésta es una prueba injusta, ya que las propuestas del Parlamento Europeo son tratadas en forma distinta en los dos procedimientos (como he dicho, sin ningún control los resultados apuntan en la dirección opuesta). Ésta es la ecuación pertinente de Tsebelis y colaboradores (2001) que estima el impacto del rechazo de la Comisión sobre el rechazo final del Consejo, según los procedimientos de cooperación y codecisión de Maastricht:

$$\text{Rechazo} = 0.2708 - 0.0938\text{SYN} + 0.3987\text{RCOM} + 0.3193\text{SYN} * \text{RCOM}$$
$$(6.46) \quad (-1.71) \quad (4.11) \quad (2.66)$$

Donde SYN es una variable falsa con el valor 1 para la cooperación y 0 para la codecisión I; RCOM es rechazo por la Comisión; y SYN * RCOM es la interacción entre las dos variables (estadísticas t entre paréntesis).

Esta ecuación implica lo siguiente: primero, el rechazo de la Comisión tiene consecuencias perniciosas para la supervivencia de una enmienda del Parlamento Europeo, y esto es verdad tanto para la cooperación como para la codecisión (el coeficiente es sustantivamente grande y de suma importancia). Segundo, la Comisión rechazó más enmiendas del Parlamento Europeo bajo cooperación que bajo la versión de Maastricht de la codecisión (el coeficiente del término de interacción es también positivo y casi igualmente grande y con significancia estadística). Tercero, controlando estos dos factores, el coeficiente para enmiendas hechas bajo el procedimiento de cooperación es *negativo* (esto quiere decir que el Consejo rechazó un número menor de las enmiendas del Parlamento Europeo bajo cooperación que bajo codecisión). Éste es un coeficiente más pequeño, y no tan importante como los otros (tiene significancia estadística al nivel 0.05 usando una prueba de una cola), así que no quiero abundar más en el tema. Sin embargo, va exactamente en la dirección que he esperado.

Sobre la base de los resultados estadísticos anteriores, Tsebelis y colaboradores (2001) calculan el porcentaje de veces que la posición de la Comisión sobre una enmienda del Parlamento Europeo es aceptada por el Consejo. Encuentran que, en promedio, el Consejo se somete al 85% de la Comisión bajo cooperación, y 70% bajo codecisión. Como resultado, el poder de la Comisión se ha reducido de manera importante bajo la codecisión, pero ciertamente no ha sido eliminado.

Corbett (2001a: 373-374) ha disputado los argumentos teóricos acerca del establecimiento condicional de agenda en comparación con el veto.[20] Su argumento principal ha sido que la codecisión I se ha alterado *de facto*

---

[20] Para el debate completo, véase Tsebelis y Garrett (2001), Corbett (2001a), Garrett y Tsebelis (2001) y Corbett (2001b).

por la Regla 78 (véase *supra*), y en consecuencia el Consejo no ha hecho ofertas de "tómenlo o déjenlo" al Parlamento Europeo desde el proyecto de directiva de 1994 sobre estipulaciones de red abierta en telefonía de voz (véase *supra*). Corbett interpreta la falta de tales propuestas por parte del Consejo como una victoria *de facto* del Parlamento Europeo y no ve ninguna diferencia entre la codecisión I y la II. En su opinión, el Tratado de Ámsterdam "no hizo más que afianzar la realidad dentro del tratado" (Corbett, 2001a: 374). Lo erróneo de este análisis es que una maniobra lograda del Parlamento Europeo no es equivalente al texto de un tratado, y la falta de ofertas de "tómenlo o déjenlo" por parte del Consejo puede deberse al temor del Consejo y/o al temor del Parlamento Europeo de un desacuerdo en el comité de conciliación. Corbett cree que fue el Consejo el que retrocedió, pero yo he encontrado evidencia que se puede interpretar de otra manera.

El cuadro XI.2 presenta una descomposición de las 4 904 enmiendas que cubren Tsebelis y colaboradores (2001) en enmiendas de cooperación y codecisión I. Además, divide estas enmiendas en cuatro grupos: introducidas por primera vez en la segunda vuelta, reintroducidas con modificaciones, reintroducidas al pie de la letra, y no reintroducidas. Si, a pesar de ello, son reintroducidas, el Parlamento Europeo adopta una actitud más agresiva bajo cooperación que bajo codecisión I. De hecho, reintroduciría enmiendas exactamente de la misma forma que en la primera vuelta: 50%

CUADRO XI.2. *Porcentajes de diferentes respuestas parlamentarias en la segunda vuelta de los procedimientos de cooperación y codecisión I.*

	Cooperación			Codecisión		
	Número	Porcentaje general	Porcentaje de la segunda vuelta	Número	Porcentaje general	Porcentaje de la segunda vuelta
Nueva enmienda	272	0.095	0.453	281	0.138	0.533
Enmienda de modificación	163	0.057	0.272	148	0.073	0.281
Enmienda reintroducida "como está"	165	0.058	0.275	98	0.048	0.186
Enmienda no reintroducida	2 266	0.791		1 511	0.741	
Total	2 866	1	1	2 038	1	1

de las veces (165 contra 163) y 40% de las veces (98 contra 148) bajo codecisión. Además, el Consejo introdujo modificaciones que provocaron la respuesta del Parlamento Europeo con mayor frecuencia bajo codecisión (281 de 2 038 = 0.138) que bajo cooperación (272 de 2 866 = 0.095). Probablemente una mejor manera de presentar estas cifras sea concentrándonos exclusivamente en el comportamiento de diferentes actores en la segunda vuelta. Bajo cooperación (véase cuarta columna del cuadro XI.2), 45% de las enmiendas de segunda vuelta son causadas por modificaciones introducidas por el Consejo y, del 55% restante de las enmiendas, la mitad son reintroducidas por el Parlamento Europeo como lo fueron en la primera vuelta, y la otra mitad en una forma enmendada de compromiso. Bajo codecisión (véase la última columna del cuadro XI.2), 53% de las enmiendas son causadas por modificaciones introducidas por el Consejo, y el Parlamento Europeo reintroduce enmiendas tal como estaban únicamente el 19% del tiempo. En otras palabras, de cooperación a codecisión vemos un aumento de ocho puntos de porcentaje de enmiendas causadas por el Consejo, y una disminución de ocho puntos del Parlamento Europeo adoptando una posición intransigente. Estas cifras indican una actitud más agresiva del Consejo, no el Parlamento Europeo bajo codecisión.

Sin embargo, hay un punto adicional interesante en este debate: los datos indican diferencias pequeñas en la identidad del establecedor de agenda. ¿Cómo podemos explicar esto? Me parece que la descripción de la Unión Europea que he presentado deja pocas dudas de que hay una considerable multiplicidad de jugadores con veto: mayorías calificadas en el Consejo, combinadas con las mayorías calificadas *de facto* en el Parlamento Europeo, y a veces el requisito de consenso por parte de la Comisión. Regresando al corolario I.5.2, la importancia del establecimiento de agenda declina con la introducción de jugadores adicionales con veto.

Finalmente, en cuanto a los poderes del Tribunal Europeo de Justicia para interpretar la ley y la Comisión como agente burocrático, los pronósticos anteriores indican que habrá fluctuaciones de sus poderes. Se ha realizado muy poco trabajo empírico acerca de estos puntos. Weiler (1991) sugiere que hubo una disminución en el papel del Tribunal Europeo de Justicia a mediados de la década de 1980; sin embargo, analiza casos donde el Tribunal Europeo de Justicia se refirió a tratados, mientras nuestro argumento trata de interpretaciones estatutarias. No se han hecho investigaciones en lo tocante a la independencia conductual de la Comisión, aunque Franchino (2000) ha escrito varios artículos en los que demuestra que la discreción institucional de la Comisión declina cuando las decisiones en el Consejo se toman unánimemente, ya que el Consejo prevé que la Comisión tendría más discreción *ex post*, de modo que la restringe *ex ante*. Aunque este investigador presenta sus resultados como prueba negativa "indirecta" de mis expectativas, me parece que acepta la lógica de mis argumentos, pero no somete a prueba las implicaciones.[21]

Para terminar, regresemos a las cinco preguntas que formulé antes:

Pregunta 1: ¿Tiene el Parlamento Europeo poderes discrecionales de establecimiento de agenda bajo cooperación? Sobre la base de la evidencia empírica, ocurre que el Parlamento Europeo ganó poderes condicionales de establecimiento de agenda con el Acta Única Europea y el procedimiento de cooperación: introdujo miles de enmiendas y, en general, 50% de ellas fueron aceptadas.

Pregunta 2: Quienquiera que tenga poderes de establecimiento de agenda, ¿será (Q(SQ)) el resultado en el conjunto ganador de mayoría calificada del Consejo, o únicamente en los puntos que dictan una mayoría calificada sobre todo lo que el Consejo pueda hacer (Q(U(SQ))) unánimemente? Los datos de König (1997) sólo contienen casos en que Q(U(SQ)) está vacío. En estos casos, los resultados están ubicados dentro de U(SQ), como espero, y no dentro de Q(SQ).

Pregunta 3: ¿Hay una diferencia en la influencia que el Parlamento Europeo tiene entre cooperación y codecisión I? ¿Está la diferencia en favor del Parlamento Europeo cuando tiene a la Comisión de su lado y no está enfrentado a un Consejo unánime? Las respuestas a estas dos preguntas son afirmativas, como demuestran los resultados empíricos de Tsebelis y colaboradores (2001).

Pregunta 4: ¿La Comisión ha perdido poder de establecimiento de agenda según la codecisión I, o estos poderes sencillamente se han reducido en comparación con la cooperación? Los datos de Tsebelis y colaboradores (2001) indican que cuando el comportamiento de la Comisión está controlado, la tasa de aceptación de las enmiendas del Parlamento Europeo es más alta bajo cooperación. La tasa incondicional de aceptación de las enmiendas del Parlamento Europeo es más alta bajo codecisión que bajo cooperación debido a que la Comisión era más negativa y más influyente bajo cooperación que bajo codecisión.

---

[21] Véanse los argumentos que presenté acerca de la independencia institucional y conductual de los bancos centrales en el capítulo x.

Pregunta 5: ¿Tienen poderes constantes la Comisión como burocracia y el Tribunal Europeo de Justicia como poder judicial, aumentan sus poderes con el tiempo o varían en función de los procedimientos legislativos? No hay evidencia empírica que corrobore o rechace mis expectativas en las burocracias y el poder judicial en la Unión Europea. Franchino (2000) presenta testimonios de que el poder institucional de la Comisión es reducido, pero no aborda el punto de la independencia conductual de la Comisión. Stone-Sweet (2000) argumenta en favor de una expansión del papel del Tribunal Europeo de Justicia, mientras que Dehousse (1998) está en favor de una reducción; sin embargo, sus argumentos se basan en decisiones constitucionales, no en estatutarias.

5. Conclusiones

La Unión Europea es una organización política complicada y que cambia con rapidez. De hecho, los analistas discrepan en cuanto a si se parece a un sistema presidencial o a uno parlamentario en cualquier punto de sus desarrollos recientes. En vez de utilizar las similitudes o diferencias de las instituciones de la Unión Europea con cualquier organización política particular como la base de mi análisis, describí las instituciones de la Unión Europea (sección 2) y entonces las modelé sobre la base de la teoría de los jugadores con veto, y llegué a una serie de conclusiones (sección 3) que son corroboradas por los datos (sección 4). Mis expectativas consideraron no sólo el sistema legislativo de la Unión Europea sino también el poder judicial y las burocracias.

En el nivel macro, mis conclusiones básicas son que la Unión Europea pasó de un sistema de seis, nueve, 10 o 12 jugadores con veto (dependiendo del número de países que participaron según el Compromiso de Luxemburgo) a un sistema legislativo de tres o dos jugadores con veto colectivos (de 1987 en adelante). Sin embargo, estos jugadores con veto colectivos decidían cada uno por mayorías calificadas: una mayoría explícitamente estipulada en los tratados en el Consejo; una mayoría calificada *de facto* en el Parlamento Europeo (debido a abstenciones). Como resultado, la estabilidad política es muy alta. Las reglas legislativas pueden acrecentarla o disminuirla según se ha demostrado en el análisis realizado en la segunda mitad de la tercera sección (gráfica XI.3), pero nos movemos en torno de un nivel muy alto de estabilidad política (núcleo grande). Todas las consecuencias de la estabilidad política están allí: quejas acerca del importante papel de

"Bruselas" (las oficinas centrales de la Comisión) en todos los países europeos, así como el importante papel del Tribunal Europeo de Justicia (desde una perspectiva comparativa).

Es probable que el Tratado de Niza exacerbe estas tendencias. La mayoría calificada en el Consejo va a aumentar, y está complementada por dos mayorías requeridas más: una mayoría de Estados miembros, y una mayoría calificada (62%) de los habitantes de la Unión Europea. Todas estas características acrecientan el núcleo del Consejo y, por lo tanto, de la Unión Europea. Por añadidura, más países entrarán a formar parte de la Unión Europea, lo cual muy probablemente producirá intereses más diversificados, y como resultado un núcleo legislativo aún más grande y conjuntos ganadores más pequeños de SQ. Las consecuencias de estos cambios serán un aumento de estabilidad política, y un papel acrecentado de la burocracia y el poder judicial.

No estoy haciendo un juicio normativo acerca de si tales cambios son provechosos o no. Ya he estipulado que esto depende de la posición del juez en relación al *statu quo*. Sin embargo, ya sea que hablemos acerca de la independencia conductual de los burócratas (como mis modelos lo vaticinan) o de las restricciones institucionales impuestas por la legislación más detallada que Franchino (2000) describe, parece que Niza ha colocado a la Unión Europea en una órbita de gran burocratización.

CONCLUSIÓN

En este libro se ha presentado un nuevo marco para el análisis de las instituciones políticas. Aunque cada una de las afirmaciones que se hacen en determinados capítulos tal vez ya existían antes (algunas de ellas, como lo mostré en la introducción, durante siglos o incluso milenios), la combinación proporciona un diferente punto de vista del análisis institucional. Las áreas de aplicación de la teoría de los jugadores con veto están tan diversificadas en los términos del análisis institucional tradicional (diferentes regímenes, partidos y sistemas de partido, países federales y unificados) y en sus áreas temáticas (legislación, burocracias, poder judicial, selección del gobierno y duración) que logré someter a prueba un conjunto de pronósticos intelectualmente congruentes en muchas situaciones distintas y proporcionar varias piezas de evidencia para corroborar la teoría.

La teoría de los jugadores con veto se concentra en las políticas legislativas, y en cómo se toman las decisiones legislativas, con el fin de explicar una serie de medidas políticas y otras características importantes de la política. Su ventaja es que rastrea de cerca el proceso de la legislación, de modo que sus expectativas tienden a ser más exactas que las tipologías existentes. Por ejemplo, en vez de formular las preguntas tradicionales acerca del tipo de régimen, sistema de partidos, tipos de partidos, etc., se concentra en la interacción entre las instituciones legislativas, es decir, los jugadores con veto. Las preguntas que he abordado son las siguientes:

1. ¿Quiénes son los jugadores con veto? Es decir, ¿quiénes son los actores cuyo consenso es necesario para lograr un cambio del *statu quo*? ¿Cuántos existen? ¿Cuáles son sus ubicaciones? ¿Está cualquiera de ellos ubicado en el núcleo de unanimidad de los otros, en cuyo caso se aplica la regla de la absorción (es decir, un jugador con veto no "cuenta" porque no afecta los resultados)?

2. ¿Cómo deciden estos jugadores con veto? ¿Son individuos aislados o colectivos? ¿Requieren mayoría simple, mayoría calificada o unanimidad? ¿Deciden mediante una combinación de lo anterior (como las instituciones de la Unión Europea)? En cada uno de estos casos, ¿cómo es afectado el conjunto de posibles resultados? ¿Tienen coaliciones internas estables o cambiantes? ¿Cómo afectan estas características el conjunto ganador del *statu quo*?

3. ¿Cómo interactúan los jugadores con veto? ¿Conocemos una secuencia específica de movimientos, en cuyo caso podemos restringir el conjunto de resultados; o sólo sabemos que un acuerdo entre ellos es necesario, y por ende no tenemos fundamentos para seleccionar un punto particular del conjunto ganador del *statu quo* en vez de otro?

4. Si podemos identificar un establecedor de agenda (primero en actuar), ¿cuáles son sus ventajas institucionales y posicionales? Es decir, ¿cuáles son las restricciones impuestas a otros jugadores con veto para no enmendar la propuesta inicial? ¿Cuán grande es el conjunto ganador del *statu quo* de los otros jugadores con veto (lo cual implica más poder de establecimiento de agenda)? ¿Está centralmente ubicado el establecedor de agenda entre los jugadores con veto (lo cual implica también más poder de establecimiento de agenda)?

Responder estas preguntas nos ofrece atisbos importantes acerca del proceso legislativo y sus resultados, así como otras características estructurales de diferentes sistemas políticos. Las trataré un poco más adelante, pero permítaseme abordar primero el modo en que las preguntas y clasificaciones comunes presentadas en la bibliografía se relacionan con estas preguntas.

Los tipos de regímenes difieren en su configuración de jugadores con veto: presidencialismo y parlamentarismo difieren en el número de jugadores con veto institucionales, así como en quién controla la agenda legislativa y por cuánto. Los países federales y unitarios también difieren según el número de jugadores con veto institucionales. Las coaliciones de varios partidos y los gobiernos de un solo partido difieren en el número de jugadores con veto partidarios. Los partidos fuertes y débiles difieren en su cohesión de partido. Todos los sistemas difieren en la distancia entre los jugadores con veto que afecta la estabilidad política.

Sin embargo, aunque cada una de las preguntas habituales en la bibliografía se traduce en alguna característica de los jugadores con veto, esta traducción no es directa y sencilla. Como lo expliqué en el capítulo VI, las mismas instituciones pueden tener resultados diferentes sobre la configuración de jugador con veto de un país: los referéndums pueden elevar (usualmente) o reducir (si tanto la activación como la formulación de la pregunta son prerrogativas del mismo jugador) el número de jugadores con veto. Los decretos ejecutivos pueden reducir (usualmente) o aumentar (como en Francia) el número de jugadores con veto, o pueden sencillamente alterar las distancias entre ellos. Sin embargo, la razón principal por la cual las instituciones no pueden traducirse directamente en declaraciones sobre los jugadores con veto es la "regla de la absorción", que se presentó en el capítulo I. Un jugador con veto ubicado en el núcleo de unanimidad (el conjunto de Pareto) de otros jugadores con veto existentes es absorbido, es decir, no altera la toma de decisiones políticas. Una segunda cámara, o un presidente con poderes de veto controlado por los mismos partidos que el gobierno, no va a establecer una diferencia si los partidos tienen cohesión, pero podría establecer una diferencia si no la tienen. Un partido ubicado entre otros partidos de una coalición en la dimensión izquierda-derecha no tendrá un impacto sobre la legislación en esta dimensión, pero podría tener un impacto si, por ejemplo, la legislación abarca muchas dimensiones diferentes. De hecho, el análisis de los jugadores con veto muestra por qué limitarse a contar instituciones sin considerar sus preferencias podría producir resultados erróneos o engañosos, o suponer que los espacios políticos son de una sola dimensión cuando son multidimensionales, o suponer que un país cabe en una categoría (por ejemplo, sistema multipartidista) cuando la composición del gobierno cambia de un gobierno de un solo partido a una coalición de muchos partidos.

Debido a su atención al proceso legislativo, la teoría de los jugadores con veto puede hacer pronósticos exactos acerca de los resultados políticos en función de quién controla la agenda, quiénes son los jugadores con veto, y las reglas según las cuales deciden. Además, ofrece explicaciones acerca de la relación entre el proceso legislativo y otras características estructurales de una organización política democrática, como el papel de jueces y burócratas, o la estabilidad gubernamental (en sistemas parlamentarios) y la estabilidad del régimen (en sistemas presidenciales).

En cuanto a pronósticos *específicos*, la teoría puede identificar los resultados esperados con gran exactitud cuando todos los actores identifican y conocen las posiciones de todos los jugadores con veto, el establecedor de agenda y el *statu quo* (información perfecta). De hecho, como vimos en el capítulo XI, el establecedor de agenda puede seleccionar entre los resultados factibles aquel que él prefiera, siempre y cuando haga que los actores correspondientes se muestren indiferentes entre el *statu quo* y su propia propuesta.

Sin embargo, con mucha frecuencia no se conocen la identidad o las preferencias del establecedor de agenda. La teoría de los jugadores con veto responde identificando el conjunto de todos los posibles resultados, el conjunto ganador del *statu quo*, y espera que los actores hagan inferencias a partir del tamaño de este conjunto. Por ejemplo, en los sistemas parlamentarios no está claro quién controla la agenda dentro del gobierno. Como resultado, los pronósticos de la teoría de los jugadores con veto sin esta información de establecimiento de agenda no son tan claros como en otras teorías (por ejemplo, teorías de negociación entre diferentes actores: Baron y Ferejohn, 1989; Baron, 1996; Tsebelis y Money, 1997; Huber y McCarty, 2001), o situaciones donde se supone que la mayor parte del poder de toma de decisiones reside en un actor particular como el primer ministro (Huber, 1996; Strom, 2000) o el ministro correspondiente (Laver y Shepsle, 1996); como resultado, los pronósticos de los jugadores con veto no son tan objetables o polémicos como lo anterior. De modo similar, en sistemas presidenciales, el Congreso hace una propuesta al presidente, pero la propuesta del Congreso usualmente depende del compromiso logrado en una legislatura bicameral.

A falta de tales conocimientos, la teoría de los jugadores con veto muestra los contornos de los posibles resultados sobre la base de suposiciones mínimas: que cada jugador con veto aceptará únicamente las soluciones que prefiera sobre el *statu quo*. Resulta que esta suposición de identidad o preferencias imprecisas del establecedor de agenda y los jugadores con veto que insisten en tener los resultados que ellos prefieran sobre el *statu quo* es una aproximación muy buena, de modo que las expectativas de estabilidad política de la teoría de los jugadores con veto resultó ser correcta. También resulta que otros actores en el sistema (gobiernos, burócratas o jueces) influyen sobre esta esperada estabilidad política.

Así, aunque la ventaja inicial de la teoría de los jugadores con veto era la planimetría precisa del proceso legislativo, resulta que tiene ventajas derivadas adicionales. La primera ventaja es que las suposiciones son mínimas y no son polémicas. De hecho, es muy difícil argumentar que los actores racionales aceptarán políticas que no prefieran sobre el *statu quo*, de no ser que incluyéramos en el análisis alguna forma de pagos adicionales. No quiero argumentar que tales pagos sean imposibles. No obstante, si se introducen como característica constante del análisis, la mayoría de los resultados (si no todos) se hacen factibles, y las teorías se vuelven tan generales que resulta imposible someterlas a prueba.

CONCLUSIÓN

Otra ventaja de la teoría de los jugadores con veto es que los modelos fundamentales son multidimensionales. Como resultado, no aplico suposiciones que generen resultados de votante medio cuando tales votantes medios tal vez no existan. De hecho, no genero equilibrios cuando tales equilibrios podrían no estar allí. Me limito a afirmar que cualquier resultado tiene que estar incluido en la intersección de los conjuntos ganadores de los diferentes jugadores con veto, y estudiar las propiedades de todos estos puntos.

En la parte teórica de este libro empecé con la suposición simplificadora de que los jugadores con veto son tomadores de decisiones individuales e identifiqué las condiciones en las cuales contarán o serán absorbidos (proposición I.2), e identifico los sistemas que producen mayor o menor estabilidad política (proposición I.4). Todas las proposiciones sobre estabilidad política se dieron en la forma de condiciones necesarias pero no suficientes. Aunque las proposiciones que identifican condiciones necesarias pero no suficientes se dan con frecuencia en las ciencias sociales, sus implicaciones metodológicas no han sido delineadas. En este libro demuestro que tales proposiciones conducen a expectativas no sólo acerca de la media de la variable dependiente (estabilidad política) sino también acerca de su varianza (heteroesquedasticidad). En los capítulos VII y VIII usé la técnica estadística apropiada para someter a prueba mis dos pronósticos.

Seguidamente expandí el análisis a los jugadores con veto colectivos y me concentré en sus reglas de toma de decisiones: mayoría, mayoría calificada o unanimidad. Demostré que la mayor parte del tiempo los resultados cualitativos no son alterados si enfocamos a un jugador con veto colectivo como si fuera un jugador individual, y que este resultado se mantiene incluso cuando consideramos que los jugadores con veto deciden secuencialmente (uno de ellos controla la agenda) en contraposición a la simultaneidad.

Apliqué estos principios sencillos a importantes preguntas teóricas de la bibliografía sobre política comparada: tipos de régimen, federalismo, bicameralismo, mayorías calificadas, partidos, sistemas de partido y referéndums. Veamos algunas de las conclusiones de este análisis.

Aunque la bibliografía existente establece una distinción entre los regímenes presidencial y parlamentario, los jugadores con veto encuentran un medio para unificarlos y hacer que la información acerca de un tipo de régimen nos informe de lo que podría suceder en el otro. Aunque la mayor parte de la bibliografía se concentra en la diferencia entre colaboración e independencia de las ramas ejecutiva y legislativa, señalo la importancia del establecimiento de agenda y la cohesión de los jugadores con veto. Estas dos variables pueden tener un efecto sobre la legislación, y en ambas variables hay una gran variación dentro de cada uno de los regímenes.

Sin embargo, no toda la bibliografía establece una distinción entre los regímenes presidencial y parlamentario. Arend Lijphart tuvo la buena idea de unificar el estudio de diferentes regímenes, introduciendo la variable "predominio ejecutivo" y ubicando la mayor parte de los sistemas parlamentarios por encima de los presidenciales en esta dimensión. Aunque considero que el enfoque de Lijphart tiene méritos importantes, la ecuación del predominio ejecutivo con la duración del gobierno es teóricamente insostenible y empíricamente débil. Demostré que el predominio ejecutivo depende de los poderes de establecimiento de agenda del gobierno, y sugerí un estudio exhaustivo sobre poderes de establecimiento de agenda en los regímenes presidencial y parlamentario. Tal estudio mejorará nuestra comprensión de las políticas en ambos regímenes.

Los referéndums han sido una institución muy discutida; parte de la bibliografía los considera la esencia misma de la democracia, mientras que otros autores critican la falta de información del pueblo, así como el hecho de que podrían ser un medio para empoderar a determinados actores. La teoría de los jugadores con veto, en vez de concentrarse en la distinción entre las democracias directa e indirecta, identifica al jugador adicional con veto que entra en el proceso de toma de decisiones en los países con referéndums (el "público" o alguna aproximación del votante medio, como demostré en el capítulo v), y se concentra en el proceso de establecimiento de agenda con el fin de comprender las propiedades de diferentes estructuras de referéndum. De hecho, he demostrado que los diferentes enfoques de los referéndums en la bibliografía se basan en extrapolaciones de distintas estructuras de establecimiento de agenda: los críticos de los referéndums extrapolan a partir de referéndums de jugador con veto, mientras sus defensores hablan de iniciativas populares. He identificado otros tipos intermedios de referéndums, donde el poder legislativo se divide entre gobierno y oposición, y donde se pide al pueblo que decida cuando existan tales desacuerdos (como en Dinamarca o en Italia).

El federalismo ha estado asociado con el bicameralismo desde la creación de la Constitución de los Estados Unidos. Sin embargo, antes de eso estaba asociado con mayorías calificadas. Ambas situaciones institucionales (mayorías calificadas y bicameralismo) aumentan el número de jugadores con veto, y producen mayor estabilidad política. Su diferencia es que el bicameralismo conduce a la aparición de una dimensión privilegiada de conflicto, mientras que las mayorías calificadas protegen a todas las políticas localizadas centralmente. El debate teórico acerca de las dos formas de gobierno se puede encontrar en los análisis de Montesquieu y de Madison. Hoy en día, el federalismo se asocia más frecuentemente con el bicameralismo que con mayorías calificadas (aunque organizaciones políticas como los Estados Unidos y la Unión Europea combinan ambas cosas). Las mayorías calificadas están asociadas oficialmente con ciertos procesos legislativos importantes: en particular cuando diferentes jugadores con veto están en desacuerdo o cuando un tema es de suma importancia. Sin embargo, como lo he demostrado, las mayorías calificadas son mucho más frecuentes y existen de hecho cuando algunos partidos son excluidos de la toma de decisiones o incluso cuando el abstencionismo en el parlamento convierte a las mayorías absolutas en mayorías calificadas.

Los capítulos empíricos de este libro demuestran que la estabilidad política está relacionada de hecho con los jugadores con veto no sólo cuando nos concentramos en la legislación (es decir, instrumentos legislativos), sino cuando estudiamos políticas macroeconómicas (es decir, resultados legislativos). En los capítulos VII y VIII se demostró también que puede ser necesario pasar de una a varias dimensiones, dependiendo del tema de estudio, y que los jugadores con veto permiten realizar investigaciones sobre cualquier número de dimensiones políticas (si los datos están disponibles). Ésta es una mejora importante en comparación con la mayoría de las teorías existentes, las cuales presuponen un solo espacio dimensional como un buen enfoque.

En la última parte de este libro nos concentramos en las diferencias estructurales generadas en diferentes países democráticos, debido a características de su configuración de jugadores con veto. En cuanto a la duración del gobierno así como la composición del gobierno, los jugadores con veto desplazan la atención de las características de los sistemas de partido a las características del gobierno. Como se vio, las distancias ideológicas entre los partidos determinan quién entra al gobierno, así como cuánto tiempo duran los gobiernos. Estas características de los sistemas parlamentarios se pueden explicar interpretando el *statu quo* como un resultado que depende no sólo de las políticas adoptadas sino también de una serie de otros sucesos que prevalecen en el ambiente político (crisis) y la teoría de los jugadores con veto.

Mi análisis indica que los gobiernos son formados por jugadores con veto ubicados cerca unos de otros, ya que los jugadores con veto tendrán más puntos que incluir en su programa de gobierno, pero también serán capaces de enfrentar crisis exógenas a la economía o el sistema político. Cuando existan tales grupos de jugadores, formarán un gobierno de coalición, mientras que cuando la dispersión de partidos sea elevada, los gobiernos minoritarios podrían ser la única solución. Estos gobiernos minoritarios usan las estipulaciones institucionales del establecimiento de agenda gubernamental con más frecuencia que otros tipos de gobiernos.

Estudiamos también, sobre la base de los jugadores con veto, el tema de la independencia del poder judicial y de las burocracias. Establezco una distinción entre independencia institucional y conductual, y me concentro en la segunda. Sobre la base de los jugadores con veto, la diferencia subyacente del papel del poder judicial en un país no es la tradición del derecho consuetudinario o derecho civil, sino el número (y las distancias) de los jugadores con veto. Los países con poca estabilidad política tendrán poca independencia judicial, y los países con gran estabilidad política tendrán jueces más independientes. Mostré testimonios empíricos que corroboran este pronóstico, junto con evidencia de que los sistemas federales tendrán un poder judicial más independiente, dado que estos poderes judiciales serán llamados a ejercer funciones de juez entre diferentes ramas del gobierno. Tengo una expectativa similar para los sistemas presidenciales, pero carezco de datos para investigarla. Demostré que el poder judicial debería ser un jugador adicional con veto únicamente en los casos donde haya revisión judicial, pero argumenté también que en la mayoría de estos casos resulta absorbido como un jugador adicional con veto debido a su modo de nombramiento.

En lo tocante a las burocracias, argumenté que es más fácil someter a prueba la independencia institucional que la independencia conductual, ya que las preferencias de la burocracia son un componente necesario del análisis. El único caso que encontré donde la bibliografía ha sido unánime al hacer tal suposición fue en el caso de los bancos centrales, y para estas burocracias particulares proporcioné evidencia existente de que mi expectativa de independencia conductual es corroborada.

Finalmente, una evaluación más global de los pronósticos de los jugadores con veto se podría realizar sobre instituciones de la Unión Europea, que con el tiempo cambian significativamente y con frecuencia. La teoría de los jugadores con veto no se basa en analogías "apropiadas" o "inapropiadas", sino que duplica la estructura institucional de una organización política y estudia las políticas que tiende a generar. Demostré que el poder legislativo se desplaza con el establecimiento de agenda y ofrecí las razones de los cambios con el tiempo de la significancia del poder judicial y de las burocracias. Demostré también que los modelos de una sola dimensión no son capaces de evaluar los poderes del parlamento, y por ende afirmé que algunos autores consideraban que un parlamento que hacía miles de enmiendas y que lograba la aprobación de una de cada dos enmiendas era un parlamento débil. Tanto las teorías como las pruebas presentadas en este capítulo eran considerablemente más avanzadas que en el resto del libro. En el caso de las teorías, esto se debió a que las instituciones eran más complicadas y exigían más desarrollos teóricos para abordar preguntas como el establecimiento condicional de la agenda. Las pruebas podrían ser más exactas debido a la existencia de pronósticos teóricos más claros en la bibliografía.

En conclusión, este libro contiene una serie de argumentos teóricos y de expectativas específicas. Estas expectativas suelen ser diferentes de las que aparecen en la mayor parte de la bibliografía: por ejemplo, acerca de si los tipos de régimen explican debidamente las diferencias entre países, si los sistemas de partido o características del gobierno son variables explicativas más importantes para el estudio de diferentes fenómenos, acerca del papel y la importancia de los referéndums, y sobre la importancia y las consecuencias del bicameralismo, el federalismo y las mayorías calificadas. Los pronósticos políticos fueron corroborados tanto en lo tocante a la legislación (instrumentos políticos) como a las políticas macroeconómicas (resultados de las políticas). Los pronósticos estructurales fueron corroborados, ya sea que se refirieran a burocracias, el poder judicial, la composición y duración del gobierno, o evaluaciones globales acerca de una estructura institucional variable, como la Unión Europea. Sobre la base de los argumentos presentados en este libro y la diversidad de la evidencia de apoyo, la teoría de los jugadores con veto puede convertirse en la base de un enfoque institucional a la política comparada.

BIBLIOGRAFÍA

Ackerman, Bruce (2000), "The New Separation of Powers", *Harvard Law Review*, 113 (3): 633-729.

Alesina, A. (1994), "Political Models of Macroeconomic Policy and Fiscal Reforms", en S. H. y S. B. Webb (eds.), *Voting for Reform*, Washington, D. C., Banco Mundial; Oxford, Oxford University Press.

Alesina, A., y A. Drazen (1991), "Why are stabilizations delayed?", *American Economic Review*, 81 (diciembre): 1170-1188.

Alesina, A., y R. Perotti (1995), "The Political Economy of Budget Deficits", *International Monetary Fund Staff Papers*, 42 (marzo): 1-31.

Alesina, Alberto, y Lawrence Summers (1993), "Central Bank Independence and Macroeconomic Performance: Some Comparative Evidence", *Journal of Money, Credit, and Banking*, 25 (2): 151-162.

Alivizatos, Nicos (1995), "Judges as Veto Players", en H. Doering (ed.), *Parliaments and Majority Rule in Western Europe*, Nueva York, St. Martin's Press.

Almond, Gabriel, y Sidney Verba (1963), *The Civic Culture: Political Attitudes and Democracy in Five Nations*, Princeton University Press.

Alt, James E., y Alec Crystal (1985), *Political Economics*, Berkeley, University of California Press.

Alt, James E., y Robert C. Lowry (1994), "Divided Government, Fiscal Institutions and Budget Deficits: Evidence from the States", *American Political Science Review*, 88: 811-828.

Ames, Barry (1995), "Electoral Rules, Constituency Pressures, and Pork Barrell: Bases of Voting in the Brazilian Congress", *Journal of Politics*, 57: 324-343.

—— (2001), *The Deadlock of Democracy in Brazil*, Ann Arbor, University of Michigan Press.

Arrow, Kenneth (1951), *Social Choice and Individual Values*, Nueva York, John Wiley and Sons.

Aspinwall, Mark D., y Gerald Schneider (2000), "Same Menu, Separate Tables: The Institutionalist Turn in Political Science and the Study of European Integration", *European Journal of Political Research*, 38: 1-36.

Axelrod, Robert (1981), "The Emergence of Cooperation among Egoists", *American Political Science Review,* 75: 306-318.
Baron, David P. (1995), "A Sequential Theory Perspective on Legislative Organization", en Kenneth Shepsle y Barry Weingast (eds.), *Positive Theories of Congressional Institutions,* Ann Arbor, University of Michigan Press.
—— (1996), "A Dynamic Theory of Collective Goods Programs", *American Political Science Review,* 90: 316-330.
Baron, David P., y John A. Ferejohn (1989), "Bargaining in Legislatures", *American Political Science Review,* 89: 1181-1206.
Baron, David P., y Michael Herron (1999), "A Dynamic Model of Multidimensional Collective Choice", manuscrito inédito, Universidad de Stanford.
Barro, R. (1996), "Democracy and Growth", *Journal of Economics Growth,* 1: 1-27
Bawn, Kathleen (1999a), "Constructing 'Us': Ideology, Coalitions and False Consciousness", *American Journal of Political Science,* 43 (2): 303-334.
—— (1999b), "Money and Majorities in the Federal Republic of Germany: Evidence for a Veto Players Model of Government Spending", *American Journal of Political Science,* 43 (3): 707-736.
Beck, N., y J. Katz (1995), "What To Do (and Not To Do) with Time-Series-Cross-Section Data", *American Political Science Review,* 89 (septiembre): 634-647.
—— (1996), "Nuisance vs. Substance: Specifying and Estimating Time-Series-Cross-Section Models", *Political Analysis,* 6 (1): 1-36.
Beck, Thorsten, George Clark, Alberto Groff, Philip Keefer, y Partick Walsh (1999), "Database on the Institutions of Government Decision Making", Washington, D. C., Banco Mundial.
Bednar, Jenna, William N. Eskridge, jr., y John Ferejohn (2001), "A Political Theory of Federalism", en John Ferejohn, John Riley y Jack N. Rakove (eds.), *Constitutional Culture and Democratic Rule,* Nueva York, Cambridge University Press.
Bednar, Jenna, John Ferejohn, y Geoffrey Garrett (1996), "The Politics of European Federalism", *International Review of Law and Economics,* 16: 279-294.
Beer, Samuel H. (1993), *To Make a Nation: The Rediscovery of American Federalism,* Cambridge, Harvard University Press.
Berger, Helge, Jakob de Haan, y Sylvester C. W. Eijffinger (2001), "Central Bank Independence: An Update of Theory and Evidence", *Journal of Economic Surveys,* 15 (1): 3-40.

Bernhard, William (1998), "A Political Explanation of Variations in Central Bank Independence", *American Political Science Review*, 92 (2): 311-327.

Bieber, Roland (1988), "Legislative Procedure for the Establishment of the Single Market", *Common Market Law Review*, 25: 711-712.

Bieber, R., J. Pantalis, y J. Schoo (1986), "Implications of the Single Act for the European Parliament", *Common Market Law Review*, 23: 767-792.

Binder, Sarah (1999), "The Dynamics of Legislative Gridlock, 1947-1996", *American Political Science Review*, 93 (3): 519-533.

Birchfield, Vicki, y Markus M. L. Crepaz (1998), "The Impact of Constitutional Structures and Collective and Competitive Veto Points on Income Inequality in Industrialized Democracies", *European Journal of Political Research*, 34: 175-200.

Blanpain, Roger (1977), *International Encyclopedia for Labour Law and Industrial Relations*, Ámsterdam, Kluwer.

Bogdanor, Vernon (1994), "Western Europe", en D. Butler y A. Ranney (eds.), *Referendums around the World: The Growing Use of Direct Democracy*, Washington, D. C., American Enterprise Institute Press.

Boix Charles (2001), "Democracy, Development, and the Public Sector", *American Journal of Political Science*, 45: 1-17.

Bowler, Shaum, y Todd Donovan (1998), *Demanding Choices*, Ann Arbor, University of Michigan Press.

Braeuninger, Thomas (2001), "When Weighted Voting Does Not Work: Multi-Chamber Systems For the Representation and Aggregation on Interests in International Organizations", artículo presentado en la reunión 29 del Consorcio Europeo de Investigación Política en Grenoble, Francia.

Braeuninger, Thomas, y Thomas König (1999), "The Checks and Balances of Party Federalism: German Federal Government in a Divided Legislature", *European Journal of Political Research*, 36: 207-234.

Browne, Eric, Dennis Gleiber, y Carolyn Mashoba (1984), "Evaluating Conflict of Interest Theory: Western European Cabinet Coalitions, 1945-1980", *British Journal of Political Science*, 14 (enero): 1-32.

Buchanan, James (1950), "Federalism and Fiscal Equity", *American Economic Review*, 40: 583-599.

Butler, D., y A. Ranney (1978), *Referendums: A Comparative Study of Practice and Theory*, Washington, D. C., American Enterprise Institute Press.

—— (eds.) (1994), *Referendums around the World: The Growing Use of Direct Democracy*, Washington, D. C., American Enterprise Institute Press.

Cameron, Charles M. (2000), *Veto Bargaining*, Nueva York, Cambridge University Press.
Cameron, David R. (1992), "The 1992 Initiative: Causes and Consequences", en A. Sbragia (ed.), *Euro-Politics*, Washington, D. C., Brookings Institution.
Carey, John M., y Matthew Soberg Shugart (1995), "Incentives to Cultivate a Personal Vote: A Rank Ordering of Electoral Formulas", *Electoral Studies*, 14: 417-439.
—— (eds.) (1998), *Executive Decree Authority*, Nueva York, Cambridge University Press.
Castles, Francis G., y Peter Mair (1984), "Left-Right Political Scales: Some 'Expert' Judgements", *European Journal of Political Research*, 12 (marzo): 73-88.
Chatfield, C. (1996), *The Analysis of Time Series: An Introduction*, Nueva York, Chapman & Hall.
Cheibub, José Antonio, y Fernando Limongi (2001), "Where Is the Difference? Parliamentary and Presidential Democracies Reconsidered", artículo presentado en el XVIII Congreso Mundial de Ciencias Políticas.
Christiansen, Thomas, Knud Erik Jorgensen, y Antje Wiener (1999), "The Social Construction of Europe", *Journal of European Public Policy*, 6: 528-544.
Clark, William R., y Mark Hallerberg (2000), "Mobile Capital, Domestic Institutions and Electorally-Induced Monetary and Fiscal Policy", *American Political Science Review*, 94: 323-346.
Cohen, Linda, y Roger Noll (1991), *The Technology Pork Barrel*, Washington, D. C., Brookings Institution.
Condorcet, Marie Jean Antoine Nicolas de Caritat, Marqués de (1968), *Oeuvres*, Stuttgard-Bad Cannstatt, Friedrich Frommann Verlag.
Cooter, Robert D., y Josef Drexl (1994), "The Logic of Power in the Emerging European Constitution", *International Review of Law and Economics*, 14: 307-326.
Cooter, Robert D., y Tom Ginsburg (1996), "Comparative Judicial Discretion", *International Review of Law and Economics*, 16: 295-313.
Corbett, Richard (2001a), "Academic Modelling of the Codecision Procedure: A Practitioner's Puzzled Reaction", *European Union Politics*, 1: 373-381.
—— (2000b), "Academic Modelling of the Codecision Procedure: A Practitioner's Puzzled Reaction", *European Union Politics*, 1: 373-381.

Corbett, Richard, Francis Jacobs, y Michael Shackleton (1995), *The European Parliament*, 3ª ed., Londres, Longman.

Cosetti, Giancarlo, y Nouriel Roubini (1993), "The Design of Optimal Fiscal Rules for Europe after 1992", en Francisco Torroes y Francesco Giavazzi (eds.), *Adjustment and Growth in the European Monetary Union*, Cambridge, Cambridge University Press.

Cowhey, Peter F. (1993), "Domestic Institutions and the Credibility of International Commitments: Japan and the United States", *International Organization*, 47 (2): 299-326.

Cox, Gary W. (1997), *Making Votes Count*, Nueva York, Cambridge University Press.

Crepaz, Markus M. L. (2002), "Global, Constitutional, and Partisan Determinants of Redistribution in Fifteen OECD Countries", *Comparative Politics*, 34 (2): 169-188.

Crombez, Christophe (1996), "Legislative Procedures in the European Community", *British Journal of Political Science*, 26: 199-228.

—— (1997), "The Co-Decision Procedure in the European Union", *Legislative Studies Quarterly*, 22: 97-119.

Cronin, Thomas (1989), *Direct Democracy: The Politics of Initiative, Referendum and Recall*, Cambridge, Harvard University Press.

Cukierman, Alex (1991), *Central Bank Strategy, Credibility and Independence: Theory and Evidence*, Cambridge, MIT Press.

Cukierman, Alex, Steven B. Webb, y Bilin Neyapti (1992), "Measuring the Independence of Central Banks and Its Effect on Policy Outcomes", *World Bank Economic Review*, 6 (3): 353-398.

Dahl, Robert A. (1971), *Polyarchy: Participation and Opposition*, New Haven, Yale University Press.

—— (1982), *Dilemmas of Pluralist Democracy*, New Haven, Yale University Press.

Davidson, Russell, y James G. MacKinnon (1981), "Several Tests for Model Specification in the Presence of Alternative Hypotheses", *Econometrica*, 49 (3): 781-793.

Davoodi, Hamid, y Heng-fu Zou (1998), "Fiscal Decentralization and Economic Growth: A Cross-Country Study", *Journal of Urban Economics*, 43: 244-257.

Dehouse, Renaud (1998), *The European Court of Justice*, Nueva York, St. Martin's Press.

De Swaan, Abraham (1973), *Coalition Theories and Cabinet Formation*, Ámsterdam, Elsevier.
Dicey, Albert Venn (1890), "Ought the Referendum to be Introduced in England?", *Contemporary Review*, 57: 506.
Diermeier, Daniel, y T. J. Feddersen (1998), "Cohesion in Legislatures and the Vote of Confidence Procedure", *American Political Science Review*, 92: 611-621.
Dinan, Desmond (1994), *Ever Closer Union?*, Boulder, Colo., L. Rienner.
Di Palma, Guiseppe (1977), *Surviving without Governing: The Italian Parties in Parliament*, Berkeley, University of California Press.
Dixit, Avinash, y John Londregan (1998), "Fiscal Federalism and Redistributive Politics", *Journal of Public Economics*, 68: 153-180.
Dodd, Lawrence C. (1976), *Coalitions in Parliamentary Government*, Princeton, Princeton University Press.
Doering, Herbert, http://www.uni-postdam.de/u/ls_vergleich/index.htm
—— (1995a), *Parliaments and Majority Rule in Western Europe*, Nueva York, St. Martin's Press.
—— (1995b), "Time as a Scarce Resource: Government Control of the Agenda", en H. Doering (ed.), *Parliaments and Majority Rule in Western Europe*, Nueva York, St. Martin's Press.
—— (1995c), "Is Government Control of the Agenda Likely to Keep Legislative Inflation at Bay?", en H. Doering (ed.), *Parliaments and Majority Rule in Western Europe*, Nueva York, St. Martin's Press.
——, próxima publicación, "Time Saving Government Prerogatives-A Case for Contentiousness?", en H. Doering (ed.), *Parliamentary Organizations and Legislative Outcomes in Western Europe*.
Dogan, Mattei (1989), "Irremovable Leaders and Ministerial Instability in European Democracies", en M. Dogan (ed.), *Pathways to Power: Selecting Rulers in Pluralist Democracies*, Boulder, Colo., Westview Press.
Downs, Anthony (1957), *An Economic Theory of Democracy*, Nueva York, Harper and Row.
Duverger, Maurice, 1954 (1969), *Political Parties: Their Organization and Activity in the Modern State*, Londres, Methuen.
Earnshaw, David, y David Judge (1996), "From Co-operation to Co-decision: The European Parliament's Path to Legislative Power", en J. J. Richardson (ed.) *European Union: Power and Policy-Making*, Londres, Routledge.
Eaton, Kent (2000), "Parliamentarism versus Presidentialism in the Policy Arena", *Comparative Politics*, 32 (3): 355-373.

Edin, P.-A., y H. Ohlsson (1991), "Political Determinants of Budget Deficits: Coalition Effects versus Minority Effects", *European Economic Review* 35 (diciembre): 1597-1603.

Eichengreen, B. (1992), *Golden Fetters: The Gold Standard and the Great Depression, 1919-1939*, Oxford, Oxford University Press.

Elgie, R. (1998), "The Classifications of Democratic Regime Types: Conceptual Ambiguity and Contestable Assumptions", *European Journal of Political Research*, 33 (2): 219-238.

Epstein, David, y Sharyn O'Halloran (1999), *Delegating Powers: A Transaction Cost Politics Approach to Policy Making Under Separate Powers*, Cambridge, Cambridge University Press.

Eskridge, W. (1991), "Overriding Supreme Court Statutory Interpretation Decisions", *Yale Law Journal*, 101: 331.

Feld, Lars P., y Marcel R. Savioz (1997), "Direct Democracy Matters for Economic Performance: An Empirical Investigation", *Kyklos*, 50 (4): 507-538.

Ferejohn, John (1974), *Pork Barrel Politics: Rivers and Harbors Legislation, 1947-1968*, Stanford, Stanford University Press.

Ferejohn, John A., Richard D. McKelvey, y Edward W. Packell (1984), "Limiting Distributions for Continuous State Markov Voting Models", *Social Choice and Welfare*, 1: 45-67.

Ferejohn, John, y Charles Shipan (1990), "Congressional Influence on Bureaucracy", *Journal of Law, Economics and Organization*, 6: 1-20.

Ferejohn, John, y Barry Weingast (1992a), "A Positive Theory of Statutory Interpretation", *International Review of Law and Economics*, 12: 263-279.

—— (1992b), "Limitation on Statutes: Strategic Statutory Interpretation", *Georgetown Law Journal*, 80: 565-582.

Finer, Samuel E. (1980), *The Changing British Party System, 1945-1979*, Washington, D. C., American Enterprise Institute Press.

Fiorina, Morris P. (1992), *Divided Government*, Nueva York, Macmillan.

Fitzmaurice, John (1988), "An Analysis of the European Community's Co-operation Procedure", *Journal of Common Market Studies*, 4: 389-400.

Franchino, Fabio (2000), "Delegating Powers in the European Union", manuscrito no inédito.

Franzese, Robert J., jr (2002), *Macroeconomic Policies of Developed Democracies*, Cambridge, Cambridge University Press.

Frey, Bruno S., y Goette Lorenz (1998), "Does the Popular Vote Destroy Civil Rights?", *American Journal of Political Science*, 42 (4): 1343-1348.

Gallagher, Michael, Michael Laver, y Peter Mair (1995), *Representative Government in Modern Europe*, Nueva York, McGraw-Hill.

Gamble, Barbara (1997), "Putting Civil Rights to a Popular Vote", *American Journal of Political Science*, 41 (1): 245-269.

Garrett, Geoffrey (1992), "International Cooperation and Institutional Choice: The European Community's Internal Market", *International Organization*, 46: 533-560.

—— (1995a), "The Politics of Legal Integration in the European Union", *International Organization*, 49: 171-181.

—— (1995b), "From the Luxembourg Compromise to Codecision: Decision Making in the European Union", *Electoral Studies*, 14: 289-308.

Garrett, Geoffrey, R. Daniel Kelemen, y Heiner Schultz (1998), "The European Court of Justice, National Governments and Legal Integration in the European Union", *International Organization*, 52: 149-176.

Garrett, Geoffrey, y George Tsebelis (1996), "An Institutional Critique of Intergovernmentalism", *International Organization*, 50: 269-300.

—— (1997), "More on the Codecision Endgame", *Journal of Legislative Studies*, 3 (4): 139-143.

—— (2001), "Understanding Better the EU Legislative Process", *European Union Politics*, 2 (3): 353-361.

Garrett, Geoffrey, y Barry Weingast (1993), "Ideas, Interests, and Institutions: Constructing the European Community's Internal Market", en Judith Goldstein y Robert Keohane (eds.), *Ideas and Foreign Policy*, Ithaca, Cornell University Press.

Gaulle, Charles de (1960), "Press Conference", *Major Addresses, Statements and Press Conferences, mayo 19, 1958-enero 31, 1964*, Nueva York, French Embassy, Press and Information Division.

—— (1971), *Memories of Hope: Renewal and Endeavor*, Nueva York, Simon and Schuster.

Gely, R., y P. T. Spiller (1990), "A Rational Choice Theory of Supreme Court Statutory Decisions with Applications to *State Farm* and *Grove City* Cases", *Journal of Law, Economics and Organization*, 6: 263-300.

Gerber, Elisabeth R. (1996), "Legislative Response to the Threat of Popular Initiatives", *American Journal of Political Science*, 40: 99-128.

—— (1999), *The Populist Paradox: Interest Group Influence and the Promise of Direct Legislation*, Princeton, Princeton University Press.

Gerber, Elisabeth R., y Simon Hug (1999), "Legislative Response to Direct Legislation", manuscrito inédito, Universidad de California, San Diego.

Gilligan, Thomas W., y Keith Krehbiel (1987), "Organization and Informative Committees by a Rational Legislation", *American Journal of Political Science*, 34: 531-564.

Golden, Miriam, Michael Wallerstein, y Peter Lange (1999), "Postwar Trade Union Organization and Industrial Relations in Twelve Countries", en H. Kitschelt, P. Lange, G. Marks, y J. Sthephens (eds.), *Continuity and Change in Contemporary Capitalism*, 194-230, Cambridge, Cambridge University Press.

Greenberg, Joseph (1979), "Consistent Majority Rule over Compact Sets of Alternatives", *Econometrica*, 47: 627-636.

Grilli, Vittorio, Donato Masciandaro, y Guido Tabellini (1991), "Political and Monetary Institutions and Public Finance Policies in the Industrialized Democracies", *Economic Policy*, 10: 342-392.

Haan, J. de, y J.-E. Sturm (1997), "Political and Economic Determinants of OECD Budget Deficits and Government Expenditures: A Reinvestigation", *European Journal of Political Economy*, 13 (diciembre): 739-750.

Haas, Ernst B. (1961), "International Integration: The European and the Universal Process", *International Organization*, 15: 366-392.

Hallerberg, Mark (2001a), *The Maastricht Treaty and Domestic Politics: The Effects of the European Union on the Making of Budgets*, manuscrito inédito, Universidad de Pittsburgh.

——, próxima publicación, "Veto Players and the Choice of Monetary Institutions", *International Organization*.

Hallerberg, Mark, y Scott Basinger (1998), "Internationalization and Changes in Tax Policy in OECD Countries: The Importance of Domestic Veto Players", *Comparative Political Studies*, 31 (3): 321-352.

Hallerberg, Mark, y Jürgen von Hagen (1999), "Electoral Institutions, Cabinet Negotiations, and Budget Deficits within the European Union", en James Poterba y Jürgen von Hagen (eds.), *Fiscal Institutions and Fiscal Performance*, 209-232, Chicago, University of Chicago Press.

Hallerberg, Mark, Rolf Strauch, y Jürgen von Hagen (2001), "The Use and Effectiveness of Budgetary Rules and Norms in EU Member States", informe preparado para al Ministerio de Finanzas de Holanda, Institute of European Integration Studies.

Hamilton, Alexander, James Madison, y John Jay (1961) (1787-1788), *The Federalist*, Papers, editado por Jacob E. Cooke, Middletown, Conn., Wesleyan University Press.

Hammond, Thomas H. (1996), "Formal Theory and the Institutions of Governance", *Governance*, 9: 2 (abril): 107-185.

Hammond, Thomas H., y Jack H. Knott (1996), "Who Controls the Bureaucracy? Presidential Power, Congressional Dominance, Legal Constraints, and Bureaucratic Autonomy in a Model of Multi-Institutional Policymaking", *Journal of Law, Economics & Organization*, 12 (1): 119-166.

—— (1999), "Political Institutions, Public Management, and Policy Choice", *Journal of Public Administration Research and Theory*, 9: 33-85.

Hammond, Thomas H., y Gary J. Miller (1987), "The Core of the Constitution", *American Political Science Review*, 81: 1155-1174.

Hayek, Friedrich von (1939), "The Economic Conditions of Interstate Federalism", reproducido en *Individualism and the Economic Order* (1948), Chicago, University of Chicago Press.

Heller, William, B. (1999), "Making Policy Stick: Why the Government Gets What It Wants in Multiparty Parliaments", artículo presentado en la junta de la Midwest Political Science Association, Chicago.

Henisz, Witold J. (2000a), "The Institutional Environment for Economic Growth", *Economic & Politics*, 12 (1): 1-31.

—— (2000b), "The Institutional Environment for Multinational Investment", *Journal of Law, Economics & Organization*, 16 (2): 334-364.

Hicks, Ursula K. (1978), *Federalism: Failure and Success, A Comparative Study*, Nueva York, Oxford University Press.

Hix, Simon (1994), "The Study of the European Community: The Challenge to Comparative Politics", *West European Politics*, 17: 1-30.

—— (1999), *The Political System of the EU*, Nueva York, St. Martin's Press.

——, próxima aparición, "Constitutional Agenda-Setting Through Discretion in Rule Interpretation: Why the European Parliament Won at Amsterdam", *British Journal of Political Science*.

Horowitz, Donald L. (1996), "Comparing Democratic Systems", en L. Diamond y M. F. Platter (eds.), *The Global Resurgence of Democracy*, 2.ª ed., Baltimore, Johns Hopkins University Press.

Huang, S. (2001), "MECH", *American Mechanical Review*, 1 (enero): 1-30.

Huber, John D. (1996), "The Vote of Confidence in Parlamentary Democracies", *American Political Science Review*, 90: 269-282.

Huber, John D., y Arthur Lupia (2000), "Cabinet Instability and Delegation in Parliamentary Democracies", *American Journal of Political Science*, 45 (1): 18-33.

Huber, John D., y Nolan McCarty (2001), "Cabinet Decision Rules and Political Uncertainty in Parliamentary Bargaining", *American Political Science Review*, 95 (2): 345-360.

Huber, John D., y G. Bingham Powell (1994), "Congruence Between Citizens and Policy-Makers in 2 Visions of Liberal Democracy", *World Politics*, 46 (3): 291-326.

Huber, John D., y Charles Shipan (2002), *Laws and Bureaucratic Autonomy in Moderns Democracies: Wise and Salutary Neglect?*, Cambridge, Cambridge University Press.

Hug, Simon (2001), "Policy Consequences of Direct Legislation in the States: Theory, Empirical Models and Evidence", manuscrito inédito, Universidad de Texas en Austin.

Hug, Simon, y George Tsebelis (2002), "Veto Players and Referendums around the World", *Journal of Theoretical Politics*, 14 (4).

Humphreys, Macartan (2000), "The Political Economy of Obstruction: A Model of Votes and Vetoes in Many Dimensions", manuscrito inédito, Harvard University.

—— (2001), "Core Existence in Multigroup Spatial Games", manuscrito inédito, Harvard University.

Inman, Robert P., y Daniel L. Rubinfeld (1997), "Rethinking Federalism", *Symposia: Fiscal Federalism. The Journal of Economic Perspectives*, 11 (4): 43-64.

International Labour Office, NATLEX, The Labour and Social Security Legislation Database (Permission to be obtained from International Labour Office. CH-1211 Ginebra 22 Suiza. ILO homepage: www.ilo.org).

Inter-Parlamentary Union (1986), *Parliaments of the World*, 2ª ed., Aldershot, Eng., Gower House.

Jacobs, Francis (1997), "Legislative Co-decision: A Real Step Forward?", artículo presentado en la Fifth Biennial European Communities Studies Association Conference, Seattle.

Jones, David (2001a), "Party Polarization and Legislative Gridlock", *Political Research Quarterly*, 53: 125-141.

—— (2001b), *Political Parties and Policy Gridlock in American Government*, Lewiston, Nueva York, The Edwin Mellen Press.

Kalandrakis, Anastassios (2000), "General Equilibrium Political Competition", disertación doctoral, UCLA.

Katzenstein, Peter J. (1985), *Small States in World Markets: Industrial Policy in Europe*, Ithaca, Cornell University Press.

Keefer, Philip, y David Stasavage (2000), "Bureaucratic Delegation and Political Institutions: When Are Independent Central Banks Irrelevant?", manuscrito inédito, Banco Mundial.
——, próxima publicación, "Checks and Balances, Private Information, and the Credibility of Monetary Commitments", *International Organizations*.
Kelly, Sean Q. (1993), "Divided We Govern? A Reassessment", *Polity*, 25: 473-484.
Kiewiet, D. R., y M. D. McCubbins (1991), *The Logic of Delegation*, Chicago, University of Chicago Press.
Kilroy, Bernadette (1999), *Integration through the Law: ECJ and Governments in the EU*, disertación doctoral, UCLA.
King, Gary, James Alt, Nancy Burns, y Michael Laver (1990), "A Unified Model of Cabinet Dissolution in Parliamentary Democracies", *American Journal of Political Science*, 32: 846-871.
Koehler, D. H. (1990), "The Size of the Yolk: Computations for Odd and Even-Numbered Committees", *Social Choice and Welfare*, 7: 231-245.
König, Thomas (1997), *Europa auf dem Weg zum Mehrheitssystem. Gründe und Konsequenzen nationaler und parlamentarischer Integration*, Opladen, Westdeutscher Verlag.
—— (2001), "Bicameralism and Party Politics in Germany: An Empirical Social Choice Analysis", *Political Studies*, 49: 411-437.
König, Thomas, y Vera Tröger (2001), "Haushaltspolitik und Vetospieler", artículo presentado en la Jahrestagung der Deutschen Vereinigung für Politikwissenschaft, Berlín.
König, Thomas, y Mirja Pöter (2002), "Examining the EU Legislative Process: The Relative Importance of Agenda and Veto Power", *European Union Politics*.
Krause, G. (2000), "Partisan and Ideological Sources of Fiscal Deficits in the United States", *American Journal of Political Science*, 44 (julio): 541-559.
Krehbiel, Keith (1988), "Spatial Models of Legislative Choice", *Legislative Studies Quarterly*, 3: 259-319.
—— (1991), *Information and Legislative Organization*, Ann Arbor, University of Michigan Press.
—— (1998), *Pivotal Politics: A Theory of U.S. Lawmaking*, Chicago, University of Chicago Press.
Kreppel, Amie (1997), "The Impact of Parties in Government on Legislative Output in Italy", *European Journal of Political Research*, 31: 327-350.

Kreppel, Amie, y George Tsebelis (1999), "Coalition Formation in the European Parliament", *Comparative Political Studies*, 32 (8): 933-966.
Kydland, Finn E., y Edward C. Prescott (1977), "Rules Rather than Discretion: The Inconsistency of Optimal Plans", *Journal of Political Economy*, 85: 473-491.
Lambertini, L., y C. Azariadis (1998), "The Fiscal Politics of Big Governments: Do Coalitions Matter?", manuscrito inédito, UCLA.
Lange, Peter (1992), "The Politics of Social Dimension", en A. Sbragia (ed.), *Euro-Politics*, Washington, D. C., Brooking Institution.
Lange, Peter, y Hudson Meadwell (1985), "Typologies of Democratic Systems: From Political Inputs to Political Economy", en Howard Wiarda (ed.), *New Directions in Comparative Politics*, Boulder, Colo., Westview Press.
Lascher, E., M. Hagen, y S. Rochliln (1996), "Gun Behind the Door: Ballot Initiatives, State Politics and Public Opinion", *Journal of Politics*, 58: 760-775.
Laver, Michael, y W. Ben Hunt (1992), *Policy and Party Competition*, Nueva York, Routledge, Champan & Hall.
Laver, Michael, y Norman Schofield (1990), *Multiparty Government: The Politics of Coalition in Europe*, Oxford, Oxford University Press.
Laver, Michael, y Kenneth A. Shepsle (1996), *Making and Breaking Governments: Cabinets and Legislatures in Parliamentary Democracies*, Nueva York, Cambridge University Press.
—— (1999), "Understanding Government Survival: Empirical Exploration or Analytical Models?", *British Journal of Political Science*, 29: 395-401.
Lijphart, Arend (1984), "Measures of Cabinet Durability: A Conceptual and Empirical Evaluation", *Comparative Political Studies*, 17: 265-279.
—— (1989), "Democratic Political Systems: Types, Cases, Causes, and Consequences", *Journal of Theoretical Politics*, 1: 33-48.
—— (1992), *Parliamentary versus Presidential Government*, Oxford, Oxford University Press.
—— (1994), *Electoral Systems and Party Systems: A Study of Twenty-Seven Democracies, 1945-1990*, Oxford, Oxford University Press.
—— (1999), *Patterns of Democracy: Government Forms and Performance in Thirty-Six Countries*, New Haven, Yale University Press.
Lindberg, Leon N. (1963), *The Political Dynamics of European Integration*, Stanford, Stanford University Press.
Linder, Wolf (1994), *Swiss Democracy*, Nueva York, St. Martin's Press.

Linz, Juan J. (1994), "Presidential or Parliamentary Democracy: Does it Make a Difference?", en J. Linz y A. Valenzuela (eds.), *The Failure of Presidential Democracy*, Baltimore, Johns Hopkins University Press.
—— (1996), "The Perils of Presidentialism", en L. Diamond y M. F. Platter (eds.), *The Global Resurgence of Democracy*, 2ª ed., Baltimore, Johns Hopkins University Press.
Lipset, Seymour M. (1996), "The Centrality of Political Culture", en L. Diamond y M. F. Platter (eds.), *The Global Resurgence of Democracy*, 2ª ed., Baltimore, Johns Hopkins University Press.
Lodge, Juliet (1983), "Integration Theory", en Juliet Lodge (ed.), *The European Community*, Londres, Frances Pinter.
—— (1987), "The Single European Act and the New Legislative Cooperation Procedure: A Critical Analysis", *Journal of European Integration*, 11: 5-28.
Lohmann, Susanne (1998), "Federalism and Central Bank Independence: The Politics of German Monetary Policy, 1957-1992", *World Politics*, 51: 401-446.
Londregan, John (2000), *Legislative Institutions and Ideology in Chile*, Nueva York, Cambridge University Press.
Lowell, A. Lawrence (1896), *Governments and Parties in Continental Europe*, Boston, Houghton Mifflin.
Lowenstein, Daniel H. (1982), "Campaign Spending and Ballot Propositions: Recent Experience, Public Choice Theory, and the first Amendment", UCLA *Law Review*, 29: 505-641.
Lupia, Arthur (1992), "Busy Voters, Agenda Control, and the Power of Information", *American Political Science Review*, 86: 390-404.
—— (1993), "Credibility and the Responsiveness of Direct Legislation", en William A. Barnett, Norman J. Schofield y Melvin J. Hinich (eds.), *Political Economy: Institutions, Competition, and Representation*, Cambridge, Cambridge University Press.
Lupia, Arthur, y Mathew D. McCubbins (2000), "Representation or Abdication? How Citizens Use Institutions to Help Delegation Succeed", *European Journal of Political Research*, 37: 291-307.
Lupia, Arthur, y Kaare Strom (1995), "Coalitions Termination and the Strategic Timing of Parliamentary Elections", *American Political Science Review*, 89: 648-665.
Macpherson, C. B. (1973), *Democratic Theory: Essays in Retrieval*, Oxford, Clarendon Press.

Manin, Bernard (2001), "Rousseau", en P. Perrineau y D. Reynié (eds.), *Dictionnaire du Vote*, 814-816, París, Presses Universitaires de France.

Maor, Moshe (1992), "Intra-Party Conflict and Coalitional Behavior in Denmark and Norway: The Case of 'Highly Institutionalized' Parties", *Scandinavian Political Studies*, 15:99-116.

Marjolin, Robert (1980), *Europe in Search of its Identity*, Nueva York, Council on Foreign Relations.

Marks, Gary, Liesbet Hooghe, y Kermit Blank (1996), "European Integration from the 1980s: State-Centric v. Multi-level Governance", *Journal of Common Market Studies*, 34: 341-378.

Marshall, T. H. (1965), *Class, Citizenship, and Social Development*, Nueva York, Anchor.

Martin, Lanny W., y Randolph T. Stevenson (2001), "Government Formation in Parliamentary Democracies", *American Journal of Political Science*, 45: 33-50.

Matsusaka, John G. (1992), Economics of Direct Legislation, *Quarterly Journal of Economics*, 107 (mayo): 541-571.

—— (1995), "Fiscal Effects of the Voter Initiative: Evidence from the Last 30 Years", *Journal of Political Economy*, 103 (3): 587- 623.

—— (2000), "Fiscal Effects of the Voter Initiative in the First Half of the Twentieth Century", *Journal of Law and Economics*, 43: 619-644.

Mattli, Walter, y Anne-Marie Slaughter (1998), "Revisiting the European Court of Justice", *International Organization*, 52: 177-210.

Mayhew, David R. (1991), *Divided We Govern*, New Haven, Yale University Press.

—— (1993), "Reply: Let's Stick With the Longer List", *Polity*, 25: 485-488.

McCarty, Nolan, Keith T. Poole, y Howard Rosenthal (2001), "The Hunt for Party Discipline in Congress", *American Political Science Review*, 95 (3): 673-688.

McCubbins, Mathew D. (1985), "Legislative Design of Regulatory Structure", *American Journal of Political Science*, 29: 721-748.

—— (1991), "Government on Lay-Away: Federal Spending and Deficits under Divided Party Control", en Gary W. Cox y Samuel Kernell (eds.), *The Politics of Divided Government*, Boulder, Colo., Westview Press.

McCubbins, Mathew D., Roger G. Noll, y Barry R. Weingast (1987), "Administrative Procedures as Instruments of Political Control", *Journal of Law Economics and Organization*, 3: 243-277.

—— (1989), "Structure and Process, Politics and Policy: Administrative Ar-

rangements and the Political Control of Agencies", *Virginia Law Review*, 75: 430-482.
McCubbins, Mathew D., y Thomas Schwartz (1984), "Congressional Oversight Overlooked: Police Patrols versus Fire Alarms", *American Journal of Political Science*, 28 (1): 165-179.
McKelvey, Richard D. (1976), "Intransitivities in Multidimensional Voting Models and Some Implications for Agenda Control", *Journal of Economic Theory*, 12: 472-482.
Meltzer, A. H., y S. F. Richard (1981), "A Rational Theory of the Size of Government", *Journal of Political Economy*, 89: 914-927.
Mikva, Abner, y Jeffrey Bleich (1991), "When Congress Overrules the Court", *California Law Review*, 79 (3): 729-750.
Miller, Nicholas R. (1980), "A New 'Solution Set' for Tournaments and Majority Voting", *American Journal of Political Science*, 24: 68-96.
Miller, Nicholas R., Bernard Grofman, y Scott L. Feld (1989), "The Geometry of Majority Rule", *Journal of Theoretical Politics*, 4: 379-406.
Moe, Terry M. (1990), "Political Institutions: The Neglected Side of the Story", *Journal of Law, Economics and Organization*, 6: 213-253.
Moe, Terry, y Michael Caldwell (1994), "The Institutional Foundations of Democratic Government", *Journal of Institutional and Theoretical Economics*, 150: 171-195.
Montesquieu, Charles-Louis de Secondat, barón de (1977), *The Spirit of Laws*, editado por David Wallace Carrithers, Berkeley, University of California Press.
Moore, Barrington, jr. (1966), *Social Origins of Dictatorship and Democracy*, Boston, Beacon Press.
Moravcsik, Andrew (1998), *The Choice for Europe*, Ithaca, Cornell University Press.
—— (1999), "Is Something Rotten in the State of Denmark? Constructivism and European Integration", *Journal of European Public Policy*, 6: 669-681.
Moravcsik, Andrew, y Kalypso Nicolaïdis (1999), "Explaining the Treaty of Amsterdam: Interests, Influence, Institutions", *Journal of Common Market Studies*, 37 (1): 59-85.
Moser, Peter (1996), "The European Parliament as a Conditional Agenda Setter: What are the Conditions?", *American Political Science Review*, 90: 834-838.
—— (1999), "Checks and Balances, and the Supply of Central Bank Independence", *European Economic Review*, 43: 1569-1593.

Mueller, Dennis C. (1996), *Constitutional Democracy*, Oxford, Oxford University Press.
Mueller, Wolfgang C. (2000), "Political Parties in Parliamentary Democracies: Making Delegation and Accountability Work", *European Journal of Political Research*, 37: 309-333.
Norton, Philip (ed.) (1990), *Legislatures*, Oxford, Oxford University Press.
Nugent, Neill (1994), *The Government and Politics of the European Union*, 3ª ed., Durham, N. C., Duke University Press.
Nurmi, Hannu (1998), "Voting Paradoxes and Referendums", *Social Science and Welfare*, 15: 333-350.
Oates, Wallace E. (1972), *Fiscal Federalism*, Nueva York, Harcourt Jovanovich.
Parrish, Scott (1998), "Presidential Decree Power in Russia: 1991-1995", en J. Carey y M. Shugart (eds.), *Executive Decree Authority*, Nueva York, Cambridge University Press.
Perotti, R., y Y. Kontopoulos (1998), "Fragmented Fiscal Policy", Manuscrito inédito, Columbia University.
Persson, Torsten, y Guido Tabellini (1999), "The Size and Scope of Government: Comparative Politics with Rational Politicians", *European Economic Review*, 43: 699-735.
—— (2000), *Political Economics: Explaining Economic Policy*, Cambridge, MIT Press.
Persson, Torsten, Gerard Roland, y Guido Tabellini (2000), "Comparative Politics and Public Finance", *Journal of Political Economy*, 108: 1121-1161.
Pindyck, Robert S., y Daniel L. Rubinfeld (1998), *Econometric Models and Economic Forecasts*, Nueva York, McGraw-Hill.
Plot, Charles R. (1967), "A Notion of Equilibrum and Its Possibility under Majority Rule", *American Economic Review*, 57: 787-806.
Pollack, Mark A. (1997), "Delegation, Agency and Agenda Settting in the EC", *International Organization*, 51: 99-134.
—— (2001), "International Relations Theory and European Integration", *Journal of Common Market Studies*, 39 (2): 197-220.
Pommerehne, Werner W. (1978), "Institutional Approaches to Public Expenditure: Empirical Evidence from Swiss Municipalities", *Journal of Public Economics*, 9: 255-280.
Poterba, J. (1994), "State Responses to Fiscal Crises: The Effects of Budgetary Institutions and Politics", *Journal of Political Economy*, 102 (agosto): 799-822.

Powell, G. Bingham (1982), *Contemporary Democracies: Participation, Stability and Violence*, Cambridge, Harvard University Press.
—— (2000), *Elections as Instruments of Democracy: Majoritarian and Proportional Visions*, New Haven, Yale University Press.
Prud'homme, Remy (1995), "On the Dangers of Decentralization", *World Bank Research Observer*, 10 (2): 201-220.
Przeworski, Adam (1991), *Democracy and the Market*, Nueva York, Cambridge University Press.
—— (1999), "Minimalist Conception of Democracy: A Defense", en Ian Shapiro y Casiano Hacker-Cordon (eds.), *Democracy's Value*, Nueva York, Cambridge University Press.
Przeworski, Adam, y Fernando Liming (1997), "Modernization: Theories and Facts", *World Politics*, 49: 155-183.
Przeworski, Adam, Michael E. Álvarez, José Antonio Cheibub, y Fernando Limongi (2000), *Democracy and Development*, Nueva York, Cambridge University Press.
Qian, Yingyi, y Gérard Roland (1998), "Federalism and the Soft Budget Constraint", *American Economic Review*, 5: 1143-1162.
Qvortrum, Mads (1999), "A. V. Dicey: The Referendum as the People's Veto", *History of Political Thought*, 20: 531-546.
Rae, Douglas (1967), *The Political Consequences of Electoral Laws*, New Haven, Yale University Press.
Rasch, Bjorn Eric (2000), "Parliamentary Floor Procedures and Agenda Setting in Europe", *Legislative Studies Quarterly*, 25: 3-23.
Remmer, Karen (1989), *Military Rule in Latin America*, Boston, Unwin Hyman.
Riker, William H. (1962), *The Theory of Political Coalitions*, New Haven, Yale University Press.
—— (1964), *Federalism: Origin, Operation, Significance*, Boston, Little Brown.
—— (1975), "Federalism", en Fred Greenstein y Nicholas Polsby (eds.), *Handbook of Political Science*, vol. 5., Reading, Mass., Addison-Wesley.
—— (1982a), "The Two-Party System and Duverger's Law: An Essay on the History of Political Science", *American Political Science Review*, 76: 753-766.
—— (1982b), *Liberalism Against Populism*, San Francisco, W. H. Freeman.
Robertson, John D. (1983), "The Political Economy and the Durability of European Coalition Governments: New Variations on a Game Theoretic Perspective", *Journal of Politics*, 45: 932-957.

Rogowski, Ronald (1987), "Trade and the Variety of Democratic Institutions", *International Organization*, 41: 203-223.

Rose-Ackerman, Susan (1981), "Does Federalism Matter? Political Choice in a Federal Republic", *Journal of Political Economy*, 89 (11): 152-165.

—— (1990), "Comment on Ferejohn and Shipan's 'Congressional Influence on Bureaucracy'", *Journal of Law Economics and Organization*, 6: 21-27.

Ross, George (1995), *Jacques Delors and European Integration*, Nueva York, Oxford University Press.

Roubini, N., y Jeffrey Sachs (1989a), Political and Economic Determinants of Budget Deficits in the Industrial Democracies", *European Economic Review*, 33 (mayo), 903-934.

—— (1989b), "Government Spending and Budget Deficits in the Industrialized Countries", *Economic Policy*, 8: 700-732.

Rousseau, Jean-Jacques, 1762 (1947), *The Social Contract*, traducción de Charles Frankel, Nueva York, Hafner.

Rueschemeyer, Dietrich, Evelyn Huber Stephens, y John Stephens (1992), *Capitalist Development and Democracy*, Chicago, University of Chicago Press.

Sanders, David, y Valentine Herman (1977), "The Stability and Survival of Governments in Western Democracies", *Acta Política*, 12: 346-377.

Sandholtz, Wayne (1992), *Hi-Tech Europe*, Berkeley, University of California Press.

Sandholtz, Wayne, y John Zysman (1989), "Recasting the European Bargain", *World Politics*, 42: 95-128.

Sani, Giacomo, y Giovanni Sartori (1983), "Polarization, Competition, and Fragmentation in Western Democracies", en Hans Daalder y Peter Mair (eds.), *Western European Party Systems: Continuity and Change*, Beverly Hills, Sage.

Sartori, Giovanni (1976), *Parties and Party Systems*, Nueva York, Cambridge University Press.

—— (1996), *Comparative Constitutional Engineering: An Inquiry into Structures, Incentives and Outcomes*, Nueva York, NYU Press.

Sbragia, Alberta M. (ed.) (1992), *Euro-Politics*, Washington, D. C., Brooking Institution.

Scharpf, Fritz W. (1970), *Die politischen Kosten des Rechtsstaats: Eine vergleichende Studie der deutschen und amerikanischen Verwaltungskontrollen*, Tübinga, J. C. B. Mohr.

—— (1988), "The Joint-Decision Trap: Lessons From German Federalism and European Integration", *Public Administration*, 66: 239-278.

Schofield, Norman (1977), "Transitivity of Preferences on a Smooth Manifold of Alternatives", *Journal of Economic Theory*, 14: 149-171.
—— (1978), "Instability of Simple Dynamic Games", *Review of Economic Studies*, 45: 575-594.
—— (1987), "Stability of Coalitions Governments in Western Europe", *European Journal of Political Economy*, 3: 555-591.
Scholtz, Evi, y Georgios Trantas (1995), "Legislation on Benefits and on Regulatory Matters: Social Security and Labor Matters", en H. Doering (ed.), *Parliaments and Majority Rule in Western Europe*, Nueva York, St. Martin's Press.
Schumpeter, Joseph R. (1950), *Capitalism, Socialism, and Democracy*, Nueva York, Harper & Row.
Schwartz, Thomas (1990), "Cyclic Tournaments and Cooperative Majority Voting: A Solution", *Social Choice and Welfare*, 7: 19-29.
Scully, Roger M. (1997), "The European Parliament and the Codecision Procedure: A Reassessment", *Journal of Legislative Studies*, 3 (3): 58-73.
Shapiro, Ian (2001), "The State of Democratic Theory", en Ira Katznelson y Helen Milner (eds.), *Political Science: The State of the Discipline*, Washington, D. C., American Political Science Association.
Shaw, Malcolm (1979), "Conclusions", en J. D. Lees y M. Shaw (eds.), *Committees in Legislatures*, Durham, N. C., Duke University Press.
Shepsle, Kenneth A. (1979), "Institutional Arrangements and Equilibrium In Multidimensional Voting Models", *American Journal of Political Science*, 23: 27-57.
—— (1986), "Institutional Equilibria and Equilibrium Institutions", en Herbert Weisberg (ed.), *Political Science: The Science of Politics*, Nueva York, Agathon.
Shepsle, Kenneth A., y Barry R. Weinsgast (1981), "Structure Induced Equilibrium and Legislative Choice", *Public Choice*, 37: 503-519.
—— (1984), "Uncovered Sets and Sophisticated Outcomes with Implications for Agenda Institutions", *American Journal of Political Science*, 29: 49-74.
—— (1987), "The Institutional Foundations of Committee Power", *American Political Science Review*, 81: 85-104.
Shugart, Matthew S., y John M. Carey (1992), *Presidents and Assemblies: Constitutional Design and Electoral Dynamics*, Cambridge, Cambridge University Press.
Siegfried, Andre (1956), "Stable Instability in France", *Foreign Affairs*, 34: 394-404.

Smith, Gordon (1975), "The Referendum and Political Change", *Government and Opposition*, 10: 294-305.
Smith, Steven S. (1988), "An Essay On Sequence, Position, Goals, and Committee Power", *Legislative Studies Quarterly*, 13: 151-176.
Snyder, James M., y Tim Groseclose (2001), "Estimating Party Influence on Roll Call Voting: Regression Coefficients versus Classifications Success", *American Political Science Review*, 95 (3): 689-698.
Spolaore, E. (1993), "Macroeconomic Policy, Institutions and Efficiency", disertación doctoral, Universidad de Harvard.
Stepan, Alfred, y Cindy Skach (1993), "Constitutional Frameworks and Democratic Consolidation: Parliamentarism versus Presidentialism", *World Politics*, 46: 1-22.
Steunenberg, Bernard (1992), "Referendum, Initiative, and Veto Power", *Kyklos*, 45: 501-529.
—— (1994), "Decision-Making under Different Institutional Arrangements: Legislation by the European Community", *Journal of Institutional and Theoretical Economics*, 16: 329-344.
Steunenberg, Bernard, Christian Koboldt, y Dieter Schmidtchen (1996), "Policy Making, Comitology and the Balance of Power in the European Union", *International Review of Law and Economics*, 16: 329-344.
Stone-Sweet, Alec (1992), *The Birth of Judicial Politics in France: The Constitutional Council in Comparative Perspective*, Oxford, Oxford University Press.
—— (2000), *Governing with Judges: Constitutional Politics in Europe*, Nueva York, Oxford University Press.
Stone-Sweet, Alec, y Wayne Sandholtz (1997), "European Integration and Supranational Governance", *Journal of European Public Policy*, 4: 297-317.
Strom, Kaare (1988), "Contending Models of Cabinet Stability", *American Political Science Review*, 79: 738-754.
—— (1990), *Minority Government and Majority Rule*, Nueva York, Cambridge University Press.
—— (2000), "Delegation and Accountability in Parliamentary Democracies", *European Journal of Political Research*, 37: 261-289.
Suksi, Markku (1993), *Bringing in the People: A Comparison of Constitutional Forms and Practices of the Referendum*, Dordrecht, Martinus Nijhoff.
Sundquist, James L. (1988), "Needed: A Political Theory for the New Era of Coalition Government in the United States", *Political Science Quarterly*, 103: 614-624.

Tanzi, Vito (1995), "Fiscal Federalism and Decentralization: A Review of Some Efficiency and Macroeconomic Aspects", *Annual World Bank Conference on Development Economics*, Washington, D. C., Banco Mundial.

Thies, Michael F. (2001), "Keeping Tabs on One's Partners: The Logic of Delegation in Coalition Governments", *American Journal of Political Science*, 45 (3): 580-598.

Tiebout, Charles (1956), "A Pure Theory of Local Expenditure", *Journal of Political Economy*, 64 (octubre): 416-424.

Treisman, Daniel (2000a), "The Causes of Corruption: A Cross-National Study", *Journal of Public Economics*, 76 (3): 399-458.

—— (2000b), "Decentralization and the Quality of Government", manuscrito inédito, UCLA.

—— (2000c), "Decentralization and Inflation: Commitment, Collective Action, or Continuity?", *American Political Science Review*, 94 (4): 837-858.

Tsebelis, George, http://www.polisci.ucla.edu/tsebelis

Tsebelis, George (1994), "The Power of European Parliament as a Conditional Agenda-Setter", *American Political Science Review*, 88: 128-142.

—— (1995a), "Decision Making in Political Systems: Veto Players in Presidentialism, Parliamentarism, Multicameralism, and Multipartyism", *British Journal of Political Science*, 25: 289-326.

—— (1995b), "Veto Players and Law Production in Parliamentary Democracies", en H. Doering (ed.), *Parliaments and Majority Rule in Western Europe*, Nueva York, St. Martin's Press.

—— (1995c), "Conditional Agenda-Setting and Decisionmaking *Inside* the European Parliament", *Journal of Legislative Studies*, 1: 65-93.

—— (1997), "Maastricht and the Democratic Deficit", *Aussenwirtschaft*, 52: 29-56.

—— (1999), "Veto Players and Law Production in Parliamentary Democracies: An Empirical Analysis", *American Political Science Review*, 93 (3): 591-608.

—— (2000), "Veto Players and Institutional Analysis", *Governance*, 13 (4): 441-474.

Tsebelis, George, y Eric Chang (2001), "Veto Players and the Structure of Budgets in Advanced Industrialized Countries", manuscrito inédito, UCLA.

Tsebelis, George, y Geoffrey Garrett (2000), "Legislative Politics in the European Union", *European Union Politics*, 1: 9-36.

—— (2001), "The Institutional Determinants of Supranationalism in the EU", *International Organization*, 55 (2): 357-390.

Tsebelis, George, Christian B. Jensen, Anastassios Kalandrakis, y Amie Kreppel (2001), "Legislative Procedures in the European Union: An Empirical Analysis", *British Journal of Political Science*, 31: 573-599.
Tsebelis, George, y Anastassios Kalandrakis (1999), "The European Parliament and Environmental Legislation: The Case of Chemicals", *European Journal of Political Research*, 36 (1): 119-154.
Tsebelis, George, y Amie Kreppel (1998), "The History of Conditional Agenda Setting in European Institutions", *European Journal of Political Research*, 33: 41-71.
Tsebelis, George, y Jeannette Money (1997), *Bicameralism*, Nueva York, Cambridge University Press.
Tsebelis, George, y Xenophon A. Yataganas, próxima publicación, "Veto Players and Decisionmaking in the EU after Nice: Legislative Gridlock and Bureaucratic/Judicial Discretion", *Journal of Common Market Studies*.
Uleri, Pier Vincenzo (1996), "Introduction", en Michael Gallagher y Pier Vincenzo Uleri (eds.), *The Referendum Experience in Europe*, Londres, Macmillan.
Ursprung, Tobias (1994), "The Use and Effect of Political Propaganda in Democracies", *Public Choice*, 78: 259-282.
Van Hees, Martin, y Bernard Steunenberg (2000), "The Choices Judges Make: Court Rulings, Personal Values, and Legal Constraints", *Journal of Theoretical Politics*, 12: 299-317.
Volcansek, M. L. (2001), "Constitutional Courts as Veto Players: Divorce and Decrees in Italy", *European Journal of Political Research*, 39 (3): 347-372.
Von Hagen, J., y I. J. Harden (1995), "Budget Processes and Commitment to Fiscal Discipline", *European Economic Review*, 39 (abril): 771-779.
Vreeland, James R. (2001), "Institutional Determinant of IMF Agreements", manuscrito inédito, Universidad de Yale.
Wallace, Helen, William Wallace, y Carol Webb (eds.) (1983), *Policy Making in the European Community*, 2ª ed., Nueva York, John Wiley and Sons.
Wallace, William (1982), "Europe as a Confederation: The Community and the Nation State", *Journal of Common Market Studies*, 21: 57-68.
—— (1983), "Less Than a Federation, More Than a Regime: The Community as a Political System", en Helen Wallace, William Wallace y Carol Webb (eds.), *Policy Making in the European Community*, 2ª ed., Nueva York, John Wiley and Sons.
Waltman, Jerold L., y Kenneth M. Holland (1988), *The Political Role of Law Courts in Modern Democracies*, Nueva York, Macmillan.

Warwick, Paul (1994), *Government Survival in Western European Parliamentary Democracies*, Nueva York, Cambridge University Press.
—— (1999), "Ministerial Autonomy or Ministerial Accommodation? Contested Bases of Government Survival in Parliamentary Democracies", *British Journal of Political Science*, 29: 369-394.
Weaver, R. Kent, y Bert A. Rockman (1993), *Do Institutions Matter?*, Washington, D. C., Brookings Institution.
Weiler, Joseph, J. (1991), "The Transformation of Europe", *Yale Law Journal*, 100: 2403-2483.
Weingast, Barry R. (1992), "Fighting Fire with Fire: Amending Activity and Institutional Change in the Postreform Congress", en Roger H. Davidson (ed.), *In the Postreform Congress*, Nueva York, St. Martin's Press.
—— (1995), "The Economic Role of Political Institutions: Market-Preserving Federalism and Economic Development", *Journal of Law, Economics, and Organization*, 11: 1-31.
—— (1997), "Political Foundations of Democracy and the Rule of Law", *American Political Science Review*, 91: 245-263.
Weingast, Barry, Kenneth Shepsle, y Christopher Johnsen (1981), "The Political Economy of Benefits and Costs: A Neoclassical Approach to Distributive Politics", *Journal of Political Economy*, 89 (4): 642-664.
Westlake, Martin (1994), *A Modern Guide to the European Parliament*, Londres, Pinter Publishers.
White, H. (1980), "A Heteroskedasticity-Consistent Covariance Matrix Estimator and a Direct Test for Heteroskedasticity", *Econometrica*, 48: 81-83.
Winter, Lieven de, próxima publicación, "Living up to One's Promises: Government Declarations and Law Production", en H. Doering (ed.), *Parliamentary Organization and Legislative Outcomes in Western Europe*.
Woldendorp, J., H. Keman, y cols. (1998), "Party Government in 20 Democracies: An Update", *European Journal of Political Research*, 33 (enero): 125-164.
Wornall, Robyn B. (2001), "Harmonic Dissidents? An Analysis of Party Cohesion in the German Bundestag", disertación doctoral, UCLA.
Wright, Vincent (1978), "France", en D. Butler y A. Ranney (eds.), *Referendums: A Comparative Study of Practice and Theory*, Washington, D. C., American Enterprise Institute Press.
Yataganas, Xenophon A. (2001), "The Treaty of Nice: The Sharing of Power and the Institutional Balance in the European Union-A Continental Perspective", *European Law Journal*, 7 (3): 239-288.

ÍNDICE DE GRÁFICAS

GRÁFICA 1. Efectos de muchos jugadores con veto 4
GRÁFICA 2. Diferencias en clasificaciones entre regímenes, sistemas de partido y jugadores con veto 6
GRÁFICA I.1. Curvas de indiferencia circular de un jugador con veto .. 28
GRÁFICA I.2. Conjunto ganador y núcleo de un sistema con tres jugadores con veto 30
GRÁFICA I.3. Conjunto ganador y núcleo de un sistema con cuatro jugadores con veto 32
GRÁFICA I.4. El conjunto ganador de jugadores con veto A y C está contenido en el conjunto ganador de jugadores con veto y B (B es absorbido) 36
GRÁFICA I.5. El conjunto ganador de jugadores con veto A, B y C está contenido en el conjunto ganador de D (D es absorbido) 38
GRÁFICA I.6. Los jugadores con veto A1-A3 producen más estabilidad política que B1-B5 (sin importar en dónde esté el *statu quo*) 41
GRÁFICA I.7. Distancia de la nueva política al *statu quo* en función del tamaño de W(SQ) 43
GRÁFICA I.8. Importancia del establecimiento de agenda 45
GRÁFICA I.9. La importancia del establecimiento de agenda disminuye con más jugadores con veto y aumenta con la ubicación central del establecedor de agenda 47
GRÁFICA II.1. Conjunto ganador y núcleo de unanimidad (7/7), mayoría calificada (6/7) y mayoría simple (4/7) 52
GRÁFICA II.2. SQ1 derrota a SQ por mayoría (de 1 y 3) 55
GRÁFICA II.3. SQ2 derrota a SQ1 por dominio de la mayoría 56
GRÁFICA II.4. Círculo (Y, d + 2r) contiene el conjunto ganador del *statu quo* de un jugador con veto colectivo (ABCDE) 60
GRÁFICA II.5. W(SQ) está contenido dentro del círculo ganador (Y, d+2r) 61
GRÁFICA II.6. Posibilidad de cambio incremental cuando dos jugadores con veto son colectivos (EUA) 64
GRÁFICA II.7. Comparación de círculo ganador de mayoría simple (4/7) con círculo ganador de mayoría calificada (5/7) 68

GRÁFICA II.8. (A) Y no cubre a X; (B) Y cubre a X 73
GRÁFICA II.9. Área propuesta por un jugador con veto colectivo 78
GRÁFICA III.1. Diferencia entre la presidencia de Gore y de Bush cuando el presidente controla o no la agenda 110
GRÁFICA IV.1. Un gobierno minoritario ubicado centralmente puede evitar derrotas graves (resultados en áreas X) 128
GRÁFICA V.1. Conjunto ganador de un grupo numeroso de votantes . . 154
GRÁFICA V.2. Diferencia entre democracia directa y mediada 156
GRÁFICA V.3. Preguntas que definen diferentes categorías de referéndums 162
GRÁFICA V.4. Resultados posibles cuando A controla la agenda del referéndum 165
GRÁFICA V.5. Resultados posibles cuando E controla la agenda del referéndum 166
GRÁFICA VI.1. Conjunto ganador de legislaturas bicamerales (por mayorías concurrentes) y unicamerales (por mayorías calificadas) 183
GRÁFICA VI.2. Núcleo bicameral y conjunto ganador bicameral de SQ 187
GRÁFICA VI.3. Resultados bicamerales según el sistema de *navette* (alternando ofertas) 189
GRÁFICA VI.4. Núcleo de mayoría 5/7 en dos dimensiones 192
GRÁFICA VI.5. Conjunto ganador por mayorías concurrentes y por unanimidad en la cámara alta 197
GRÁFICA VI.6. (A) Votantes ejes en una dimensión: dos obstruccionistas (F,F) y dos ejes con veto (V,V). (B) Casi cualquier votante puede ser pivotal en múltiples dimensiones 199
GRÁFICA VII.1. Número de leyes importantes por rango ideológico de la coalición 224
GRÁFICA VII.2. Residuos (valor absoluto) de leyes importantes por rango ideológico de la coalición 225
GRÁFICA IX.1. Diferentes efectos de choques sobre coaliciones de gobierno 279
GRÁFICA IX.2. Relaciones causales entre jugadores con veto, establecimiento de agenda gubernamental, duración del gobierno y "predominio ejecutivo" 283
GRÁFICA X.1. Selección de una política dentro del núcleo por parte del primero en actuar (burocracia o poder judicial) 286
GRÁFICA XI.1. Establecimiento condicional de agenda en una y dos dimensiones 332

ÍNDICE DE GRÁFICAS

GRÁFICA XI.2. Instituciones de la Unión Europea en dos dimensiones   339
GRÁFICA XI.3. El núcleo de los procedimientos legislativos de la Unión Europea   340
GRÁFICA XI.4. Después de Niza, el núcleo del Consejo y la Unión Europea se expande   345
GRÁFICA XI.5. Preferencias del Consejo y resultados de la votación bajo unanimidad   349
GRÁFICA XI.6. Preferencias del Consejo y resultados según el procedimiento de cooperación   350

ÍNDICE DE CUADROS

Cuadro IV.1. Control de agenda, duración y predominio ejecutivo del gobierno 137
Cuadro VII.1. Modelo de regresión heteroesquedástica multiplicativa de legislación importante 223
Cuadro VII.2. Modelos multivariables de legislación importante (lineal y binomio negativo) 227
Cuadro VII.3. Número de leyes, leyes importantes, jugadores con veto y control gubernamental de la agenda legislativa 233
Cuadro VII.4. Correlaciones entre jugadores con veto, establecimiento de agenda y legislación 234
Cuadro VIII.1. Resultados sencillos sobre estructura presupuestaria en 19 países de la OCDE, 1973-1995. (Modelo estimado por regresión heteroesquedástica multiplicativa.) 253
Cuadro VIII.2. Resultados multivariables sobre estructura presupuestaria en 19 países de la OCDE, 1973-1995. (Modelo estimado por modelo de series temporales de corte transversal de efecto fijo con errores estándar corregidos por panel.) 254
Cuadro VIII.3. Resultados estimados por cada categoría presupuestaria 256
Cuadro VIII.4. Comparación del poder explicativo de análisis unidimensional y bidimensional 257
Cuadro X.1. Independencia judicial 296
Cuadro X.2. Correlaciones entre variables independientes con y sin Australia, Canadá, Israel y Holanda 297
Cuadro X.3. Independencia judicial como función de los jugadores con veto 298
Cuadro X.4. Independencia del banco central 310
Cuadro X.5. Diferentes mediciones de la independencia del banco central (IBC) como función de los jugadores con veto y de la descentralización 311
Cuadro XI.1. Tres enfoques de la integración europea 319
Cuadro XI.2. Porcentajes de diferentes respuestas parlamentarias en la segunda vuelta de los procedimientos de cooperación y codecisión I 355

ÍNDICE ANALÍTICO

Ackerman, B.: 8, 175, 178, 288, 292, 303
Acta Única Europea: 155, 322, 324, 325, 353, 357
Alemania: banco central en: 313-314; coaliciones de ganancia mínima en: 124-125; cohesión de partido en: 97-98; democracia (directa/representativa) en: 157; derecho civil en: 289; discreción ministerial en: 142; duración del gobierno en: 273; establecimiento de agenda en: 46n, 131-136; federalismo de: 176, 180; jugadores con veto en: 106, 115, 118-119, 186; legislación laboral en: 216, 228, 233; poder judicial/jueces y: 288n, 291, 295; presupuestos en: 243, 246-247; referéndums en: 153n; reglas de toma de decisiones en: 194; restricciones políticas en: 261
Alesina, A.: 241-242, 245, 308, 310, 311
Alivizatos, N.: 294-300, 311n
Almond, G.: 5, 139
Alt, J. E.: 210n, 242, 250
alternación: 213, 220-221, 226-227, 229, 248, 251-257
Ames, B.: 99, 109, 148
Argentina: 102, 178, 194
Arrow, K.: 57, 90, 91
Australia: 153n, 177, 190, 250n, 289, 297, 308
Austria: bicameralismo en: 184-185; duración del gobierno en: 273; establecimiento de agenda en: 131-137; legislación laboral en: 216; poder judicial/jueces en: 295; tipo de régimen de: 146n; toma de decisiones en: 190
Axelrod, R.: 75

Banco Central Europeo: 321n
Baron, D.: 76, 364
Barro, R.: 261
Basinger, S.: 259, 260, 262
Bawn, K.: 7, 246, 247, 262
Bednar, J.: 180, 180n, 183, 285n, 299, 343n
Bélgica: derecho civil en: 289; duración del gobierno en: 273; establecimiento de agenda en: 132-137; legislación laboral en: 216, 228, 230; reglas de toma de decisiones en: 67, 194; restricciones políticas en: 261

Bernhard, W.: 307-309, 310
bicameralismo: conjunto ganador de: 182-183; diversidad y: 184-186; federalismo y: 16, 175-176, 180-181, 366-367; mayoría calificada y: 176, 196-201; número de jugadores con veto y: 202, 366-367; partidos políticos débiles y: 186-191
Bieber, R.: 325, 326, 333
Binder, S. 191
Birchfield, V.: 116, 117
Bogdanor, V.: 155, 163
Boix, C.: 100
Botswana: 145
Bowler, S.: 155, 158
Braeuninger, T.: 46n, 186n, 200
Brandt, W.: 124
Brasil: 98, 147-148, 149n, 178
Browne, E.: 216, 217n, 218, 273
Buchanan, J.: 175
burocracias y burócratas: de la Unión Europea: 338-347, 348, 358, 359; derecho administrativo y: 300-306; evidencia empírica acerca de: 306-315; federalismo y: 201; independencia de: 5, 18, 201, 266, 300-304, 305-306, 311, 368; independencia del banco central y: 307-314, 315; investigación sobre: 300-306; supervisión de las: 288; tipos de régimen y: 303-306
Bush, G. H. W.: 107
Bush, G. W.: 148
Butler, D.: 152, 153n, 159, 161, 172

Caldwell, M.: 96, 100, 288, 303-304
Canadá: 261, 297, 308-309
Carey, J. M.: 93, 95, 112n, 146-147, 148, 203
Castles, F. G.: 219, 220
círculo ganador: 69, 79-81, 105; bicameralismo y: 187-188; definición de: 62-63; en regímenes parlamentarios: 104-105; tamaño de: 69, 71, 75
Clinton, Bill: 107-108, 110-112, 148, 287
coaliciones de ganancia mínima: 124-125, 149, 212, 224-226, 228, 252, 269, 272
coaliciones de tamaño exagerado: 114-115, 122, 124, 125-127, 129, 145, 196, 212

coaliciones: decisiones fiscales y: 241-242; formación de: 138, 269, 271, 278, 283; ganancia mínima: 124-125, 149, 212, 224-226, 228, 252, 269, 272; tamaño exagerado: 114-115, 125-127, 129, 145, 196, 212, 224-226, 228n, 236, 252
Código Civil Alemán: 289
Código Napoleónico: 289
cohesión: 63-65, 69-71, 80-81, 89, 97, 101, 111-112, 118-119, 140, 186, 194, 344, 362-363, 366
cohesión-m: 62-63, 80n
cohesión-q: 69-70, 80n, 194
Comisión Europea: codecisión y: 327-329, 336-338, 345-348, 353-355, 357; cooperación y: 324-326, 331-335, 343-345, 353-354; delegación y: 307; establecimiento de agenda de la: 335, 348, 353, 357; independencia burocrática de: 338-347, 348, 356-357, 358; reglas de toma de decisiones y: 1, 322-359
comités: 76-77, 131-136, 190
competencia: 12, 90-92, 101-103, 138, 159, 202
Condorcet, M.-J.-A.-N. de Caritat, marqués de: 57, 180, 181, 191, 346
conjeturas: cohesión-m (II.1): 63, 70; cohesión-q (II.3): 70, 194; tamaño de los jugadores con veto colectivos (II.2): 63, 75. *Véase también* corolarios; proposiciones
conjunto Banks: 76
conjunto de Pareto: 29, 363
conjunto descubierto: 72-79, 188
conjunto ganador: 10, 81, 189-190, 281; bicameralismo y: 181-182, 187-189; de mayoría calificada: 182-183, 191-193; definición de: 3, 29-30, 153-154; en coaliciones de ganancia mínima: 124-125; en coaliciones de tamaño exagerado: 126; en Consejo de Ministros: 347-348, 356-357; en democracias representativas o directas: 154-155; estabilidad política y: 30-31, 42, 53-54; número de jugadores con veto y: 33-35, 141, 153, 182-183, 235, 237; referéndums y: 164, 170-171; tamaño del: 33, 40, 43, 46, 51, 53-54, 63-66, 71, 112, 287, 364
Consejo de Ministros (Unión Europea): codecisión y: 327-330, 336-338, 345-347; cooperación y: 324-326, 331-337, 343-344; delegación y: 307; establecimiento de agenda de: 336; reglas de toma de decisiones en: 1, 67, 192, 266, 322-359
consociacionalismo: 5, 16, 116, 144
Cooter, R. D.: 11, 285n, 294-296, 299, 300
Corbett, R.: 324, 325, 329, 334, 337, 348, 353, 354-355

corolarios: estabilidad política e importancia del establecimiento de agenda (I.5.2): 46, 48, 127, 141; jugadores con veto únicos (I.5.1): 46; ubicación del establecedor de agenda (I.5.3): 46, 48, 127, 129. *Véase también* conjeturas; proposiciones
corporativismo: 228-229
Cosetti, G.: 242
Costa Rica: 145, 146
costos de transacción: 31, 39, 280, 287, 335
Cowhey, P.: 98
crecimiento económico: 260-262
Crepaz, M. M. L.: 116, 117
crisis (choques): 9, 237, 239-240, 249-250, 280
crisis petroleras: 9, 239-240, 278
criterio numérico: 35, 38, 295
Crombez, C.: 332, 333, 336, 347, 348, 351, 352
Cukierman, A.: 308, 310, 311, 314
curvas de indiferencia circular: 28-29, 36-37, 54, 59, 62

Chang, E.: 247, 262
Cheibub, J. A.: 95, 98, 100, 148, 149n
Chile: 94, 147, 150, 194
China: 111, 178
Chirac, J.: 107

Dahl, R.: 91
Davoodi, H.: 175
de Gaulle, Charles: 163n, 168, 169, 322, 323
De Swaan, A.: 7, 272
decisiones de política exterior: 108
decisiones de políticas de defensa: 107
decretos ejecutivos: 107, 131, 148-149, 203-204, 291, 363
Dehousse, R.: 358
delegación: 113, 139, 303-306. *Véase también* discreción ministerial
democracia directa: 151-160, 168, 174
democracia mediada. *Véase* democracia representativa
democracia representativa: 151-160, 168
denegación legislativa. *Véase* vencer en la votación un veto presidencial
derecho administrativo: 300-301
derecho civil: 289, 299-300, 368
derecho consuetudinario: 289-290, 299-300, 368
descentralización: 175, 201, 299
Dicey, A. V.: 13
Diermeier, D.: 97, 140
dimensionalidad: 339, 352; de estructuras presupuestarias: 239, 245, 246-256; del espacio político: 65, 197-201, 363; en decisiones en la Unión Europea: 334, 335;

equilibrio y: 76; izquierda-derecha: 210, 213, 218-220, 338-341; *statu quo* y: 277; votante medio y: 66, 152-154, 170, 173, 365
Dinamarca: coaliciones de tamaño exagerado en: 126; democracia (directa/representativa) en: 155; derecho civil en: 289; establecimiento de agenda en: 132-136; legislación laboral en: 216; poder judicial/jueces en: 295; presupuestos en: 249; referéndums en: 153n, 163
directiva sobre estipulaciones de red abierta (ONP): 328, 355
discreción ministerial: 140-143. *Véase también* delegación
distancias ideológicas: 40-44, 58; estabilidad política y: 202, 203-204; independencia burocrática y: 303, 313-314; duración del gobierno y: 276, 277-280, 283; presupuestos y: 245, 246-248, 250-256. *Véase también* rango
divisores m (líneas medianas): 68-69
divisores q: 67-70, 80n
divisores: divisores m (líneas medianas): 68-69; divisores q: 68-69, 80n
divorcio, temas de: 171, 291
Dixit, A.: 175
Dodd, L. C.: 218, 269, 271
Doering, H.: 10n, 132, 134-137, 146-147, 213-216, 228, 231-233, 235, 236
Dogan, M.: 144
dominio de la mayoría: 51, 54-57, 80
Donovan, T.: 155, 158
Downs, A.: 90, 91, 101, 102, 128
Drazen, A.: 241
duración del gobierno: 137c, 265, 269-284; burocracias y: 269; coaliciones de ganancia mínima y: 272; discreción ministerial y: 122, 140-141; distancias ideológicas y: 275-276, 277-281, 284; en regímenes parlamentarios: 3, 17, 94-96, 121-122, 131, 137c, 138, 143-149, 265; en regímenes presidenciales: 3, 94-96, 146-147, 265; investigación sobre: 270-276; jugadores con veto y: 276-281, 283; legislación y: 226-228, 231, 236-237; partidos políticos y: 17, 271-272, 274-276, 280-281; poder judicial/jueces y: 295, 234-235; predominio ejecutivo y: 143-149, 269-270, 271, 281-283
Duverger, M.: 5, 16, 120, 137, 138, 139, 272

Eaton, K.: 100, 148
Edin, P.-A.: 242-244
Elgie, R.: 93
Encyclopedia of Labor Law (Blanpain): 215
enmiendas: 130-131, 136, 282, 326, 352-357

entidades legislativas. *Véase* países específicos en general
Epstein, D.: 288, 301, 306
equilibrio: 10, 75-76, 141-142, 319-320, 365
Eskridge, W. N.: 180, 183, 285n, 299
España: 132-136, 137c, 216, 220, 249n, 289, 291, 329, 351, 352
estabilidad gubernamental. *Véase* duración del gobierno
estabilidad política: 2-6; cambio y: 23, 50-51; cohesión y: 62-63, 69-70, 80-81, 194; definiciones de: 2-3, 49, 265; establecimiento de agendaestablecedores y: 3-4, 46-48, 141; federalismo y: 175; independencia judicial y: 11, 18, 293; interés metodológico en: 6-11; mayoría calificada y: 195-196, 330; núcleo de unanimidad y: 29-31, 209; número de jugadores con veto y: 33-40, 95-96, 151-52, 175, 200-201, 209, 243, 245-246, 338; regla de la absorción y: 202; *statu quo* y: 27-33; vencer en la votación un veto presidencial y: 203-204. *Véase también* conjunto ganador
establecimiento de agenda condicional: 326, 331, 332, 334n, 337, 353-354
establecimiento de agenda/establecedores: 3, 137c; competencia y: 12, 170, 173-174; condicional: 326, 331-334, 337; decretos ejecutivos y: 107, 131, 148-149, 203-204, 291; discreción ministerial y: 122, 140-143; en regímenes parlamentarios: 1, 44n, 89, 108-111, 123-150, 231-236, 281-282, 366; en regímenes presidenciales: 3, 89, 108-111, 145-149, 363-368; estabilidad política y: 2-3, 39-40, 46, 127, 142-143; legislación laboral y: 214-215, 229, 306; predominio ejecutivo y: 143-149, 281-283; referéndums y: 151, 164-169, 202-204; reglas de: 120-122, 130-137, 139, 203, 282; secuencia de movimientos y: 44-48, 72-79, 286-289, 362; ventajas posicionales en: 49, 120, 124-130, 139, 143, 362. *Véase también* países e instituciones específicas
Estados Unidos: bicameralismo en: 184-185; burocraciasburócratas en: 303; cohesión de partido en: 112; derecho consuetudinario en: 289; elección presidencial (2000): 109-111; establecimiento de agenda en: 109-111, 130, 148-150; federalismo de: 176, 178; gasto de campaña en: 173; jugadores con veto en: 27, 50, 63-65, 79-80, 103, 106-107, 184, 286-287; legislación sobre el uso de partidas del presupuesto para patronazgo político en: 98-100; longevidad de carrera en: 97; poder judi-

cial/jueces en: 292; política de defensa en: 107; predominio ejecutivo en: 145; presupuestos en: 242, 249; referéndums en: 123, 161-163; reglas de toma de decisiones en: 67, 71, 98, 182, 194-196; tipo de régimen de: 1, 4-5

Feddersen, T. J.: 97, 140
federalismo: 16-17, 175-184, 365-367; bicameralismo y: 16, 175-184, 366; competencia y: 177-179; conservando el mercado: 177-179; estabilidad política y: 175; independencia del banco central y: 308-311, 315; inflación y: 258; número de jugadores con veto y: 117-118, 200-203; poder judicial/jueces y: 118, 180, 183-184, 201, 299
federalismo de conservación del mercado: 8, 178-179
Feld, L. P.: 160, 180
Ferejohn, J.: 11, 59, 79n, 98, 153, 180, 183, 285n, 292, 299, 343n, 364
finanzas públicas, temas de: déficits: 9n, 17, 239-246; estructura del presupuesto: 246-257, 261; independencia del banco central: 307-315; inflación: 9n, 258-259, 313-314; legislación financiera: 99-100, 108, 132-133; legislación sobre el uso de partidas del presupuesto para patronazgo político: 98-99; legislación tributaria: 111-112, 259-260
Finlandia: derecho civil en: 289; duración del gobierno en: 273; establecimiento de agenda en: 132-136; legislación laboral en: 216, 220; presupuestos en: 249; tipo de régimen de: 146n, 309
Fitzmaurice, J.: 333
Fondo Monetario Internacional (FMI): 48, 98, 250
Franchino, F.: 302, 306, 347, 356, 358, 359
Francia: decretos ejecutivos en: 107, 203; derecho civil en: 289; discreción ministerial en: 140; establecimiento de agenda en: 130-131, 132-136, 150; jugadores con veto en: 107; legislación laboral en: 216, 218, 220; poder judicial/jueces en: 290, 291, 292, 295; predominio ejecutivo en: 145; referéndums en: 163, 168-169; reglas de toma de decisiones en: 67, 176, 190, 195; tipo de régimen de: 97n, 112n; Unión Europea y: 322-324
Franzese, R.: 243, 244, 245, 262
Frey, B. S.: 158

Gallagher, M.: 289
Gamble, B.: 158

Garrett, G.: 258n, 319, 337, 339, 343n, 348
Gerber, E.: 160
Ginsburg, T.: 11, 294-296, 299, 300
Gleiber, D.: 217n, 218, 273
gobiernos de un solo partido: 18, 46, 104, 117, 119, 120-121, 124, 127, 142, 230-231, 232, 236, 242, 260, 276, 303, 309, 314, 362-363
gobiernos minoritarios: 122, 124, 127-130, 149-150, 212, 224-226, 236, 252, 281
Goette, L.: 158
Grecia: derecho civil en: 289; establecimiento de agenda en: 132-136, 139; jugadores con veto en: 104; legislación laboral en: 216, 218, 220, 229; presupuestos: 249; tipo de régimen de: 4-6, 121, 309
Greenberg, J.: 192
Grilli, V.: 308, 310, 311

Haan, J. de: 243, 244
Hagen, J. von: 140, 241, 249, 305, 306
Hallerberg, M.: 140, 241, 249, 259, 260, 262, 305-309, 311
Hammond T. H.: 11, 65, 188n, 285n
Harden, I. J.: 241
Harris contra Forklift Systems: 287
Hayek, F. von: 177, 179
Heller, W. B.: 130, 131, 136
Helms, Jesse: 107
Henisz, W.: 8, 260, 261, 262
Herman, V.: 269, 272
Herron, M.: 76
heteroesquedasticidad: 43, 211, 222-226, 252, 365
Hicks, U. K.: 179
Hix, S.: 317, 329, 337, 339, 353
Holanda: democracia (directa/representativa) en: 156; derecho civil en: 289; duración del gobierno en: 273; establecimiento de agenda en: 132-136, 150; federalismo de: 180; legislación laboral en: 216; poder judicial/jueces en: 295, 297
Horowitz, D.: 5, 94, 95
Huber, J. D.: 11n, 91n, 102, 123, 131, 140, 141, 158n, 269, 302, 306, 364
Hug, S.: 160, 161, 163
Humphreys, M.: 38n, 62, 65, 66
Hunt, W. B.: 219, 220, 250

Immergut, E.: 159
independencia del banco central (IBC): 307-315
India: 178
inestabilidad, gobierno. *Véase* duración del gobierno

ÍNDICE ANALÍTICO

inflación: 9n, 258-259, 313-314
información, completa/incompleta (teoría del juego): 172-173, 320-321, 331-332
iniciativas populares: 163, 170-171, 203
intergubernamentalismo: 318-320
Irlanda: 132-136, 137c, 146n, 216, 220, 273, 289, 351, 352
Islandia: 132, 134-136, 137c, 146n, 215, 273, 289, 309
Israel: 127, 156, 273, 295, 297
Italia: bicameralismo en: 184, 185; coaliciones de ganancia mínima en: 124; decretos ejecutivos en: 203, 291; déficits presupuestarios en: 17, 243; derecho civil en: 289; discreción ministerial en: 140, 141; duración del gobierno en: 273; establecimiento de agenda en: 131-136, 149; jugadores con veto en: 27-29; legislación laboral en: 214-215, 220; poder judicial/jueces en: 289-290; referéndums en: 152, 163, 171; tipo de régimen de: 4-6

Jacobs, F.: 324, 325, 333, 334n, 353
Japón: 114, 142, 176, 186, 190
Johnson, Lyndon B.: 109

Kalandrakis, A.: 158n
Keefer, P.: 307, 313, 314, 315
King, G.: 269, 273, 275
König, T.: 46n, 186n, 247, 349, 350, 352, 357
Kontopoulos, Y.: 241
Krause, G.: 242
Krehbiel, K.: 198, 199, 200, 201, 278
Kreppel, A.: 131, 204, 323, 339
Kydland, F. E.: 8

Laver, M.: 121, 122, 125, 127, 128, 137, 140, 141, 142n, 219, 220, 250, 269, 271-274, 289, 304, 305, 364
legislación financiera: 99, 108, 131. *Véase también* asuntos de finanzas públicas
legislación laboral: 17, 210, 213-238; variable de control de agenda y: 228, 231-236; variable de corporativismo y: 226-231; variable de ideología de la izquierda y: 229; variable del rango y: 221-226, 230
legislación sobre condiciones laborales. *Véase* legislación laboral
legislación sobre desempleo: 209-211
legislación sobre el uso de partidas del presupuesto para patronazgo político: 98-100
legislación sobre horas de trabajo. *Véase* legislación laboral
legislación sobre violación: 185
legislación tributaria: 111-112, 259-260

legislación: calidad/cantidad de: 231-237; carácter restrictivo de: 288-289, 306; características de: 142; desempleo: 209-210; divorcio: 171, 291; duración máxima de vida de legislación pendiente: 136; enmiendas a la: 130, 136, 282; financiera: 99, 108, 133; horarios para: 134; impuestos: 111, 112, 259-260; laboral: 17, 210, 213-238; partida del presupuesto usada para patronazgo político: 98-99; por referéndum: 158, 170; violación: 185
Lijphart, A.: consociacionalismo y: 5, 16, 116-117, 144; duración del gobierno y: 270-271; independencia del banco central y: 308; independencia judicial y: 293-294, 295, 297, 300; metodología de: 143-144; partidos políticos y: 102; predominio ejecutivo y: 16, 120-121, 137-138, 143-147, 150, 269, 281, 366
Limongi, F.: 93, 95, 100, 148, 149n
Linder, W.: 173
Linz, J.: 5, 93-96, 99, 100
Lipset, S. M.: 109
Lodge, J.: 334
Lohmann, S.: 307, 312, 313
Londregan, J.: 147, 149, 175
Lowell, A. L.: 11, 284
Lowenstein, D. H.: 173
Lowry, R. C.: 242, 249, 250
Lupia, A.: 139, 155, 269, 280n
Luxemburgo, compromiso de: 322-324, 344, 358
Luxemburgo: 132, 134-136, 137c, 216, 220, 228, 249, 273, 289

Maastricht, Tratado de: 155, 320-322, 327-328, 336-337, 354
Madison, James: 11, 181, 346, 367
Mair, P.: 219, 220, 289
Malta: 289
Martin, L. W.: 281
Mashoba, C.: 217, 218, 273
Matsusaka, J. G.: 160
Mattson, I.: 232
Mayhew, D. R.: 190, 191, 198
mayoría calificada: 16-17, 86, 191-196; bicameralismo y: 175, 191-201, 346; capacidad de penetración de: 193-196; conjunto ganador de: 126, 183, 191-193; federalismo y: 180-182; núcleo de: 191-193; número de jugadores con veto y: 202, 366-367; referéndums y: 153n; teoría de: 51-54; umbrales de: 70, 193, 195, 280-281, 329-330, 345. *Véase también* naciones e instituciones específicas

ÍNDICE ANALÍTICO

mayoría monolítica: 50
mayoría simple: 53-54, 59-66
mayorías. *Véase* regla de toma de decisiones
McCarty, N.: 11, 64, 364
McCubbins, M.: 139, 285n, 288, 300, 302
McKelvey, R. D.: 10-11, 45, 57, 59, 74, 79n
Miller, G. J.: 11, 65, 188n
Mitterrand, François: 107, 162n, 218, 293
Moe, T. M.: 96, 100, 288, 301, 303, 304
Money, J.: 66, 77, 131n, 180, 184-185, 188, 190, 194, 324n, 364
Montesquieu, C.-L. de Secondant, barón de: 11, 180, 181, 367
Moravcsik, A.: 318, 329
Moser, P.: 307-309, 332-333, 347, 351, 352
Mueller, W. C.: 161, 305
multicameralismo: 182, 184-186
multipartidismo: 96, 102, 117, 138

NATLEX, base de datos: 214-216
Neidhart, L.: 159
neofuncionalismo: 318-320, 348
Neyapti, B.: 314
Nicolaïdis, K.: 329
Niza, Tratado de: 1, 322, 329, 338, 345-347, 359
Noll, R.: 11, 98, 285, 288, 300
Noruega: 125, 131-132, 134, 136, 215, 229, 273, 289, 296
núcleo bicameral: 66, 187-188, 192, 197, 200
núcleo de unanimidad: 29-31, 34-35, 36-38, 51-53, 191-193, 209, 340-343
núcleo multicameral: 18
núcleos: bicameral: 187-188, 192, 200; mayoría calificada: 191-193; multicameral: 18; unanimidad: 24, 29-31, 33-43, 46, 209, 211, 340, 343-344, 350, 361, 363
Nueva Zelanda: 153n, 177, 289
Nunn, Sam: 107

O'Halloran, S.: 288, 301, 306
Oates, W. E.: 175, 179
obstruccionista: 112, 185, 194, 201. *Véase también* reglas de limitación del debate
Ohlsson, H.: 242-244

Packell, E. W.: 59, 79n
Pantalis, J.: 333
paradoja del referéndum: 157
Parlamento Europeo (PE): codecisión y: 325-329, 335-338, 344-348, 353, 356-357; cooperación y: 324-326, 331-335, 343-345, 357-358; establecimiento de agenda condicional y: 326, 331-332, 337, 347, 353-354, 357; poder de veto de: 337; Regla 78

y: 328-329, 337-338, 359; reglas de toma de decisiones en: 1, 195, 324-359
partidos antisistema: 139, 195, 272
partidos comunistas: 42, 50, 195, 219
partidos extremistas: 91, 114, 274-275
partidos políticos: antisistema: 195, 272, 280-281; bicameralismo y: 186-191; burocracias/burócratas y: 305-306; cohesión en: 63-65, 97-99, 111-113, 118-119, 186; conjunto descubierto y: 76; cumplimiento de los acuerdos y: 75-76; duración del gobierno y: 18, 271-272, 274-276, 280-281; número de: 90, 95-96, 137-138, 240; regla de la absorción y: 202-203, 213; tipos de régimen y: 95-97, 101-104, 137-139. *Véase también* sistemas de partido
Perotti, R.: 241, 242, 245
Persson, T.: 97, 99, 140
plebiscitos. *Véase* jugadores con veto, referéndums de
Plot, C. R.: 10
pluralismo: 91, 138-139
poder judicial y jueces: 289-300; como jugadores con veto: 289-293, 314; derecho consuetudinario y: 289-290; duración del gobierno y: 295, 299; en el Tribunal Europeo de Justicia (TEJ): 318-321, 342, 344, 348, 356, 358; evidencia empírica acerca de: 293-300; federalismo y: 117, 180, 184, 202, 299; independencia de: 11, 18, 266, 293-300, 302, 368; regla de la absorción y: 291; supervisión del: 288; tribunales constitucionales y: 152, 286-288, 290-292, 315
políticas supermayoritarias: 194, 197-200, 303, 336n, 341
Polonia: 50
Pommerehne, W. W.: 159
Pompidou, George: 163, 169
Portugal: 132-136, 137c, 146n, 216, 218, 220, 221, 228n, 289, 309, 350-351, 352
Poterba, J.: 242, 249
Powell, G. B.: 102, 139, 158n
predominio ejecutivo: 137c; duración del gobierno y: 143-149, 269-270, 281-283; establecimiento de agenda/establecedores y: 143-149, 281-283, 366; independencia del banco central y: 308; tipos de régimen y: 121
Prescott, E. C.: 8
presupuestos: déficits en: 9n, 17, 240-246, 262; estructura de: 246-257, 262. *Véase también* temas de finanzas públicas
problema del fondo común: 240
procedimiento de codecisión: 327-330, 336-338, 340, 345-347, 353-356

procedimiento de consultas (UE): 322, 343
procedimiento de cooperación: 67n, 324-328, 331, 333-334, 343-344, 350n, 353-354, 357
proposiciones: distancias ideológicas de los jugadores con veto (I.4): 41-44, 49, 62, 204, 209, 248, 251, 280, 281-284, 313, 365; número de jugadores con veto (I.1): 34-35, 38, 43, 44, 62, 209; regla de absorción (I.2): 38-39, 62-63, 114, 213, 365; regla de la cuasiequivalencia (I.3): 30, 39-41, 62, 291; similitud de jugador con veto colectivo/individual (II.5): 78; umbrales de mayoría calificada (II.4): 70-71, 193, 195; ventaja de establecimiento de agenda (I.5): 45, 49, 108-109, 111. *Véase también* conjeturas; corolarios
Protocolo Barber: 320
proyectos de ley sobre finanzas. *Véase* legislación financiera
Prud'homme, R.: 175
Przeworski, A.: 91, 92n, 93, 96, 101, 177

rango: 213, 220-226, 229-230, 245, 251. *Véase también* distancias ideológicas
Ranney, A.: 152, 153n, 159, 161, 172
Rasch, B. E.: 10n
referéndums: 16, 152-174, 362, 365-367; como iniciativas populares: 163, 170-171, 203; como vetos populares: 163, 171-173; como votos de jugador con veto: 163-169, 202-203; en democracias directas o representativas: 152-160, 168, 175; número de jugadores con veto y: 11-12, 151, 153, 155-158, 173-174, 202; regulación institucional de: 161-163; votante medio en: 12-13, 153-154, 158-160, 170-172
regímenes autoritarios: 90-92, 101-103
regímenes democráticos: 89-93, 100-103, 119, 151-160, 170
regímenes parlamentarios: burocracias/burócratas en: 287-289, 303-306; delegación en: 113, 139, 238-239; duración del gobierno en: 3-4, 16-17, 94-96, 121-122, 131, 137c, 138, 143-149, 265-266; establecimiento de agenda en: 3, 44n, 89, 108-111, 118-119, 123-150, 180-236, 282, 363-364; investigación sobre: 89, 93-100; jugadores con veto en: 15-16, 85, 103-105, 362-363; longevidad de carrera en: 96; partidos políticos en: 49-50, 96-99, 111-113; referéndums y: 137-138
regímenes presidenciales: burocracias/burócratas en: 303-306; delegación en: 113, 304-305; duración del gobierno en: 3-4, 94-96, 146-147; establecimiento de agenda en: 3-4, 89-90, 108-111, 118-119, 146-149, 363-364; investigación sobre: 89, 93-99; jugadores con veto en: 15-16, 85-86, 107-108, 362-363; multipartidismo en: 265; partidos políticos en: 95-98, 111-113; referéndums y: 163-168; supervisión de la burocracia en: 287-288
Regla 78 (PE): 328-329, 337-338, 355
regla de la absorción: 14-15, 17, 35-40; crítica a: 114-115,118; en diferentes regímenes: 103-104, 106; estabilidad política y: 202; partidos políticos y: 213; poder judicial/jueces y: 290-293
regla de la cuasiequivalencia: 36-40, 62-63, 291
regla de la toma de decisiones: mayoría calificada como: 16-17, 51-53, 67-71, 78-79, 80, 86, 126, 153n, 175-176, 180-183, 191-201, 281, 329-330, 346, 366-367; mayoría simple como: 53-54, 59-66; unanimidad como: 50, 53-54, 79, 180-181
reglas de la toma de decisiones: "ejes" en: 197-200; déficits presupuestarios y: 240-241; en democracias directas o representativas: 151-160, 168; política de defensa y: 107; política exterior y: 108; transparencia de: 98, 102. *Véase también* naciones e instituciones específicas
reglas de limitación del tiempo de debate en el parlamento: 71, 106, 135. *Véase también* obstruccionistas
Reino Unido: bicameralismo en: 184; derecho consuetudinario en: 289; establecimiento de agenda en: 132-136, 149-150; jugadores con veto en: 104; legislación laboral en: 216, 230; partidos políticos en: 138; poder judicial/jueces en: 295; predominio ejecutivo en: 145; presupuestos en: 249; referéndums en: 167; tipo de régimen de: 5; toma de decisiones en: 190
Remmer, K.: 102
restricciones políticas: 260-262
Riker, W. H.: 66, 90n, 158, 175, 177-179, 269, 272
Rockman, B. A.: 8
Roe vs. Wade: 288
Rogowski, R.: 127
Roosevelt, Franklin D.: 104
Rose-Ackerman, S.: 175, 292
Roubini, N.: 241-243, 245
Rousseau, Jean-Jacques: 90, 152, 158, 168, 174
Rusia: 148

Sachs, J.: 241-243, 245
Sanders, D.: 269, 272

Sani, G.: 220
Sartori, G.: 5, 16, 91, 120, 137-139, 158, 220
Savioz, M. R.: 160
Sbragia, A.: 266, 316
Scharpf, F.: 176, 288n, 289, 316
Schofield, N.: 10, 57, 125, 127, 128, 220, 269, 271-274
Schoo, J.: 333
Schumpeter, J.: 90-92, 101, 158
Schwartz, T.: 76, 302
secuencia de movimientos: 44-48, 72-79
Shepsle, K. A.: 98n, 121, 122, 137, 140-142, 198n, 304, 305, 320, 364
Shipan, C.: 141, 302, 306
Shugart, M. S.: 93, 95, 112n, 146, 147, 148, 203
Siegfried, A.: 141, 144
sistemas de *navette*: 131n, 189-190, 324
sistemas de partido: fragmentación de: 180, 183-184, 274, 280-281; multipartidismo y: 96, 102, 117, 138, 363; pluralismo y: 91, 138. *Véase también* partidos políticos
sistemas electorales: 138, 156-157
Skach, C.: 93, 95-96, 109
Smith, G.: 161, 198
Spolaore, E.: 241
Stasavage, S.: 307, 313-315
Stepan, A.: 93, 95-96, 109
Steunenberg, B.: 292, 332, 333, 347, 351, 352
Stevenson, R. T.: 281
Stone-Sweet, A.: 290-292, 358
Strauch, R.: 249
Strom, K.: 93, 96, 113, 118, 126-128, 139, 196, 225, 252, 269, 280n, 288, 303, 306, 364
Sturm, J.-E.: 243-244
Suecia: democracias (directa/representativa) en: 157; derecho civil en: 289; duración del gobierno en: 273; establecimiento de agenda en: 132-136; jugadores con veto en: 233; legislación laboral en: 216, 220, 229, 230, 232
Suiza: bicameralismo en: 184; déficits presupuestarios en: 17, 243; establecimiento de agenda en: 132-136; federalismo de: 180; gasto de campaña en: 173; legislación laboral en: 216, 219, 228; predominio ejecutivo en: 145; referéndums en: 153n, 159, 162-163; toma de decisiones en: 190
Suksi, M.: 161
Summers, L.: 308, 310, 311

Tabellini, G.: 97, 99, 140
Tanzi, V.: 175
teorema de imposibilidad: 90
teoría de juegos: 75, 270, 330-331

teoría de los jugadores con veto: colectivos: 24, 50-82; crecimiento económico y: 260-262; curvas de indiferencia circular y: 28-29, 59, 62; descripción de: 2-3, 27-29, 49, 361; distancias ideológicas y: 40-44, 58, 202-204, 213, 220-226, 237, 245, 247-248, 250-257, 303; duración del gobierno y: 276-281, 283; individuales: 24-25, 27-49, 54-55, 79-80; institucionales: 2, 27, 104-105, 113-114, 118; número de: 14, 33-40, 46, 95, 104-105, 106-108, 118-119, 126, 141, 146n, 151, 153, 156-158, 175, 182, 201-202, 235-236, 238, 245, 258, 280, 288, 307, 313-314, 338, 362-363, 366-367; partidaria: 2, 27, 104, 113, 119; referéndums de: 161-169, 203; secuencia de movimientos por: 33-48, 72-79, 285-289, 300; selección de: 100-103. *Véase también* establecimiento de agenda/establecedores; conjeturas; corolarios; proposiciones
teoría del caos: 251
teorías de acción colectiva: 240-241, 245, 258
Thies, M.: 142, 305
Tiebout, C.: 175-177, 179
Tito Livio: 12, 45n
Tocqueville, Alexis de: 158
Tournament Equilibrium Set (Schwartz): 76
transitividad de preferencias: 54-58
Trantas, G.: 216n
Tratado de Ámsterdam: 322, 328-329, 346, 355
Tratado de Libre Comercio de América del Norte (TLCAN): 111, 112
Tratado de Roma: 322-324
tratados: Acta Única Europea: 155, 322, 324, 325, 353, 357; Ámsterdam: 322, 328, 329, 346, 355; Compromiso de Luxemburgo: 322-324, 344, 358; Maastricht: 155, 320-322, 327-328, 336-337, 354; Niza: 322, 329, 338, 345-347, 359; Roma: 322-324
Treisman, D.: 118n, 175, 179, 258, 259, 262
Tribunal Europeo de Justicia (TEJ): 318-321, 342, 344-345, 348, 358
Tribunal Supremo, Estados Unidos: 286-288, 292, 297
tribunales constitucionales: 143, 152, 290-293, 311n, 315
Tröger, V.: 247
Tsebelis, G.: sobre bicameralismo: 66, 185, 188-190; sobre codecisión: 348-349, 352-354, 357; sobre conjunto descubierto: 77; sobre el Tratado de Niza: 346-347; sobre estructura en la Unión Europea: 319; sobre estructuras presupuestarias: 247-257, 262; sobre procedimientos legislativos en

la Unión Europea: 332, 334-335, 339, 351-353; sobre referéndums: 163
Tucídides: 12, 102

Uleri, P. V.: 161
unanimidad: 50, 53-54, 79, 180
Unión Europea (UE): 18, 266; consultación y: 322, 342; federalismo de: 176; investigación sobre: 317-321; jugadores con veto en: 185-186, 318, 252-253, 356; núcleo legislativo de: 341-342; presupuestos en: 248-249; referéndums sobre: 153-154, 167; reglas de toma de decisiones en: 1, 181, 196, 266, 321-347. *Véase también* instituciones específicas
Uruguay: 147

Van Hees, M.: 292
vencer en la votación un veto: 66, 103, 203, 285-288, 289-292, 300-301
Verba, S.: 5, 139
vetos populares: 163, 171-173
Volcansek, M. L.: 291
Volokh, E.: 287
Von Hagen, J.: 140, 241, 249, 305-306
votante medio: "como si", en espacio multidimensional: 154, 171, 173, 203; competencia por: 90, 102, 172-174; en espacio dimensional sencillo: 66, 152-153; equilibrio y: 76; modelo de información incompleta y: 172; referéndums y: 12-13, 16, 153-154, 159-160, 172-173;
voto de confianza: 94, 131, 138, 140, 180n
Vreeland, J. R.: 98

Warwick, P.: 18, 141-144, 214, 216, 217n, 218, 220, 266, 269, 274-276, 281, 284
Weaver, R. K.: 8
Webb, S. B.: 314
Weiler, J. J.: 316, 356
Weingast, B.: 8, 11, 98, 130, 136, 175, 177, 178, 198n, 285n, 288, 292, 300
Willoch, K.: 125
Winter, L. de: 115, 142, 143
Wornall, R. B.: 97

Yataganas, X.: 12n, 330, 341n, 346
Yeltsin, Boris: 148
yema: 59-64, 67, 69-70, 74, 77-78, 153-154, 156, 171, 188-189, 198, 200, 202, 346n

Zou, Heng-fu: 175

Este libro se terminó de imprimir y encuadernar en el mes de diciembre de 2006 en Impresora y Encuadernadora Progreso, S. A. de C. V. (IEPSA), Calz. de San Lorenzo, 244; 09830 México, D. F. En su composición, parada en *Imagen Editorial,* se utilizaron tipos New Aster y Avenir de 10:13, 9:13 y 8:9 puntos. La edición, que consta de 3 000 ejemplares, estuvo al cuidado de *Víctor Hugo Romero.*